War and Peace

On the Principle and Constitution
of the Rights of Peoples

Pierre-Joseph Proudhon

(1861)

Edited and introduced by Alex Prichard

Translated by Paul Sharkey

Praise for *War and Peace*:

When it comes to just war theory, Proudhon is the missing link between Kant and Comte on the one hand and Tolstoy and Foucault on the other. Yet, overlooked by the Left and selectively appropriated by the Right, his *War and Peace* (1861) has largely eluded capture within conventional political categories. This fresh translation, with a substantial introduction, makes Proudhon's ethical masterwork accessible to a wider readership and should help to place it accurately on the map of modern international thought.

David Armitage, Lloyd C. Blankfein Professor of History, Harvard University, author of *Foundations of Modern International Thought* (Cambridge University Press, 2004)

War and Peace is one of Proudhon's most fascinating books. While the phenomenon of war is analysed through the lens of the right of force, the book is no justification for violence. Proudhon's obsession with law leads to a challenging opposition of war's horrors with war's ideals, where the clash or balance of antagonistic forces produces justice. After *Justice, Order and Anarchy* (Routledge, 2013), Alex Prichard explores Proudhon's opus with his knowledge of modern debates and the latest work in International Relations. Thanks to this translation, English readers will rediscover one of Europe's leading socialist thinker in his lifetime, someone Faguet once said was "impossible not to take into account and ridiculous to disdain".

Anne-Sophie Chambost, Professeure d'histoire du droit, Sciences-Po, Lyon, and author of *Proudhon et la Norme: Pensée juridique d'un anarchiste* (Presses Universitaires de Rennes, 2004)

A fascinating study for scholars of the just war tradition, Proudhon's writings straddle both classical and contemporary articulations of the right to war. On the one hand, Proudhon's thinking illuminates otherwise obscure historical debates about the right of conquest that we could learn much from today. On the other, it offers a critique of just war as a thinly mannered variant of the "might is right" doctrine that speaks powerfully to present-day controversies. This, then, is quite the find— one that is likely to lead scholars to view the just war tradition with new old eyes.

Cian O'Driscoll, Associate Professor of International Relations, Australian National University, and author of *Victory: The Triumph and Tragedy of Just War Theory* (Oxford University Press, 2020)

This fascinating text broadens and deepens the history of international thought and just war theory and adds to recent recoveries and reassessments of the international thought of Hobbes, Grotius, Kant, and others. Prichard's introduction offers the novice and expert reader a new way into the text and will help bring this work into existing debates on the relationship of war and justice.

Jonathan Havercroft, Associate Professor of International Political Thought, University of Southampton, and author of *Captives of Sovereignty* (Cambridge University Press, 2011)

This new translation of Proudhon's *War and Peace* is going to be of great interest for Political Thought and International Relations. Proudhon's sociological study complements the more common legal and political approaches to questions of war and peace. Moreover, as Alex Prichard's wide ranging introduction shows, re-introducing Proudhon into the canon of modern European thought rectifies some of its political and intellectual biases and limitations and recovers important influences on authors from Michel Foucault through Raymond Aron to Stanley Hoffman.

Beate Jahn, Professor of International Relations, University of Sussex, and editor of *Classical Theory in International Relations* (Cambridge University Press, 2006)

War and Peace is an eye opener, crammed with quotable lines, provocative historical insights – about America and the state of European politics – and Proudhon's characteristically incisive critiques of his rivals: Kant, Grotius, and Hobbes. Alex Prichard's informative, warm introduction is the perfect guide to the core concepts – the right of peoples, right of force, collectivity and war – and their interrelation and resonance for contemporary international relations. Paul Sharkey's translation transforms the whole into a highly readable page-turner.

Ruth Kinna, Professor of Political Theory, Loughborough University, and author of *The Government of No One* (Penguin, 2019)

War and Peace: On the Priciple and Constitution of the Rights of Peoples, Pierre-Joseph Proudhon
Translation © 2022 Paul Sharkey
Introduction [CC.By.4.0] 2022 Alex Prichard
This edition © 2022 AK Press (Chico / Edinburgh)

ISBN: 9781849354684
E-ISBN: 9781849354691
Library of Congress Control Number: 2021944660

AK Press
370 Ryan Avenue #100
Chico, CA 95973
www.akpress.org
akpress@akpress.org

AK Press
33 Tower St.
Edinburgh EH6 7BN
Scotland
www.akuk.com
akuk@akpress.org

Please contact us to request the latest AK Press distribution catalog, which features books, pamphlets, zines, and stylish apparel published and/or distributed by AK Press. Alternatively, visit our websites for the complete catalog, latest news, and secure ordering.

Cover design by John Yates | stealworks.com
Cover photograph is Roger Fenton's 'The Valley of the Shadow of Death' (1855), see page 27, note 88 for more information
Printed in the United States of America on acid-free paper

CONTENTS

War and Peace

Introduction

On the second of September 1861, just five months after publication in Brussels and then Paris, *War and Peace* was reviewed very favourably in the *New York Times*. "M. PROUDHON", the reviewer wrote, "has just published a new work, marked by that extraordinary mingling of profundity and paradox which characterizes all the productions of his mind". It is a work from an "incomparable logician, one of the most vigorous thinkers of the age", marked by a "deep love of humanity" and shaped by "bold truths and equally bold fictions, paradoxes, vagaries and extravagances that seethe as in a cauldron through his pages".[1]

But it was not so well received in France. "*On ne me comprends pas*" Proudhon lamented.[2] "My friends don't understand me [...] while my enemies celebrate".[3] His republican critics satirised him: here was the man who championed death to private property and the state, now also proclaiming the historic significance and virtues of the martial impulse, the centrality of the right of force to politics and society, and the enduring virtues of the Austro-Hungarian Empire and the 1815 Vienna Treaties to the revolutionary cause. His friend, Jérôme-Amédée Langlois, told him he had to read the book twice before he understood it – no mean feat in less than a month.[4]

Part of the misunderstanding is surely down to Proudhon's attempt to reach two very different audiences at once, and the relative absence of popular reflections on the rights of war and peace in literary circles at the time. On the

---

1. *New York Times,* 2nd of September 1861.

2. Letter to Rolland, 7th of July, 1861. Hervé Trinquier has collated and reprinted the correspondence surrounding the troubles Proudhon had in publishing this book, and the reception it received, as an appendix to his edition of *War and Peace*. See, Pierre-Joseph Proudhon, *La Guerre et la Paix. Recherches sur le Principe et la Constitution du Droits des Gens*, edited and introduced by Hervé Trinquer (Paris: Editions Tops, 1998), 191–291. All letters are from this collection, unless otherwise indicated.

3. Letter to Altmeyer, 5th June, 1861.

4. Letter to Rolland, 3rd June, 1861.

one hand, his aim was make this a "classic", a reflection on war and the philosophy of right that he hoped would be "destined to send everything published on
the topic since Grotius and Vattel up to the attic".[5] But he also wanted it to have
popular appeal, both educational and political. Unfortunately, in making concessions to both sides, Proudhon lost both audiences, and so, notwithstanding
Leo Tolstoy's appreciation for the book, it made no significant mark on public
or academic debate for at least the next forty years.

With a century and a half of hindsight, a deeper, critical appreciation of *War
and Peace* is now possible. In the meantime, we have seen the flourishing of academic reflections on international relations, just war theory (*jus ad bellum* and *jus
in bello*), and the rights of peoples, or *jus gentium*, while the writings of those who
eventually turned to the book for inspiration provide us with new insights on the
text.[6] In addition, Proudhon's reflections on the course of modern warfare take on
much deeper significance in the shadows of two World Wars and the genocidal
xenophobia that has animated the age of nation states. The aim of this introduction, and the new annotations of the book, is to bring a new level of contextual
analysis to our understanding of the work. With hindsight and the critical appreciation of the work, it is possible to understand Proudhon's influence and his
foresight much more clearly and develop a new appreciation for the text in turn.

In what follows, I begin by offering a brief summary of Proudhon's argument,[7] and make the case that *War and Peace* as one of the first socialist

5. Letter to Hetzel, 9th January, 1861. The philosophy of right should be distinguished
from a theory of justice. In contemporary writings on this topic, the latter established the
conditions of justice: when or under what conditions could such and such an event or action
be considered just? Whereas the former, historically, aimed to establish where justice came
from in the first place: does justice derive from reason or from God, or are we so materially
determined that to talk of justice is nonsensical?

6. For book-length engagements with *War and Peace*, see, for example, Nicolas Bourgeois, *Les Théories Du Droit International Chez Proudhon: Le Fédéralisme et la Paix* (Paris:
Marcel Rivière, 1927); Madeleine Amoudruz, *Proudhon et l'Europe. Les Idées de Proudhon en
Politique Étrangère* (Paris: Éditions Domat Montchrestien, 1945); Edouard Jourdain, *Proudhon, Dieu et la Guerre: Une Philosophie du Combat* (Paris: L'Harmattan, 2006). The most
recent French engagement, by the Bergson scholar Alain Panero, focuses on its phenomeno-
logical theory. See, Alain Panero, "Avant-propos: D'une phénoménologie inédite de la guerre
à une nouvelle éthique du regard", in Pierre-Joseph Proudhon, *La Guerre et la Paix*, édition
critique de Alain Panero (Paris: Nuvis, 2012), 1–66. The most recent English reading is Edward Castleton, "Pierre-Joseph Proudhon's *War and Peace*. The right of force revisited", in B.
Kapossy, I. Nakhimovsky, and R. Whatmore, eds., *Commerce and Peace in the Enlightenment*
(Cambridge: Cambridge University Press, 2017), 272–299. See also, A. Noland, "Proudhon's
Sociology of War", *The American Journal of Economics and Sociology*, 29 no. 3 (1970): 289–
304, and the posthumously published article by Georges Sorel, "*La Guerre et la Paix*: Essai
d'Exégèse Proudhonienne", *Mil Neuf Cent. Revue d'histoire intellectualle* (19), 2001 [1917]):
159–207.

7. For a fuller account see Alex Prichard, *Justice, Order and Anarchy: The International*

expositions of the philosophy of war, history and right. It is this aspect of the text that I then trace through its subsequent intellectual history in the third part, tracing *War and Peace* through the works of Tolstoy, Georges Sorel and the twentieth century French sociology, including the work of Michel Foucault.

However, the bulk of my introduction situates *War and Peace* in eighteenth and nineteenth century debates about the place of war in human (albeit largely European) history, in particular the writings of Immanuel Kant and Auguste Comte. I show how Proudhon charts a course between their writings, seeking a new balance between the individualist, transcendental idealism of Kant, and the collectivist, materialist, philosophical realism of Comte; between Kant's account of the republican freedom, and Comte's subsumption of the individual into the macro forces of history.

This broad philosophical context allows us to see what was unique in Proudhon's approach to war. He developed an "ideo-realist" philosophy, one which took ideas as seriously as material forces, placing the individual on an equal ontological footing to the collective, and seeing freedom as the emergent property of the confluence of each of these forces.

But most strikingly, Proudhon refutes what I call below the secular theodicy at the heart of Kant and Comte's philosophies of history: the idea that good will always emerge out of evil, and that history has a transcendent telos, leading eventually to some sort of "perpetual peace", or in Comte's case, the transcendent unity of the human sciences and society in the age of positivism. Proudhon calls this hopeful account of history a philosophy of "providence". For Kant and Comte the republican tradition, political constitutions would break the historic link between force and law, grounding right on reason. Proudhon disagreed.

In brief, Proudhon argued that the history of war and violence are the domain of chance and brute force, and contrary to his interlocutors he also denied that force could be removed from politics. The right of force, a key concept in this work, is central to collective agency and it therefore underpinned the struggle for justice. Forces are ubiquitous in nature, and manifest in human society as social power (*puissance*) – the collective coordination of groups. The rights and force of individuals, groups and peoples are fired in the kiln of history, and war is the macro expression of this. Relations of (military, industrial or intellectual) force, latent in times of peace, sustain the rights of peoples, while in times of war

Political Theory of Pierre-Joseph Proudhon (Abingdon: Routledge, 2013). The shorter version can be found here: Alex Prichard, "Justice, Order and Anarchy: The International Political theory of Pierre-Joseph Proudhon (1809–1865)", in *Millennium. Journal of International Studies*, 35: 3 (2007): 623–645.

they create new societies. Peace treaties, for example, are the constitutional shell which enable national systems of justice to develop. In this respect, Proudhon rejects the standard republican argument that force and law can be separated. Our systems of law and justice are founded on, sustained by, and dependent upon pacification, the latent relations of force and the threat of violence within society. In turn, the development of different societies can be attributed to war and its consequences, but that process has no inevitable outcome. This philosophy of history is one of "immanence", rather than transcendence or theodicy.

Proudhon's quasi-pacifism, which will be unpacked further below, derives from his concern with the philosophical foundations of the standard "providentialist" accounts of war in the context of the industrialisation of warfare, the emergence of "governmentalism", "militarism", and "pauperism", each exacerbating an endemic "social war". War, Proudhon argued, was caused by a "rupture in the economic equilibrium", not by human nature or the will of gods. His political economy of the causes of war led him to the view that the possibility of social peace lay in the transformation of the inclination to war for plunder and conquest, into the use of social power for industrial production, and the recalibration of society on a new balance of economic powers. Proudhon argued that in providing a fuller understanding of war, the latent right of force in society could be "transformed" into more productive modes. But the unifying and militarising European nation states were determined to use conquest to resolve the problems of "pauperism", a "rupture in the economic equilibrium" that pitched elites against one another and forced workers into penury. From the point of view of this socialist political economy, Proudhon was worried that Europe was approaching the nadir, not the apex of its history. The future of society depended on the reconstitution of society, through recognising the right of force immanent to the emerging labouring classes. But, as Nicolas Bourgeois put it, while the problem is "courageously posed" in *War and Peace*, "the true Proudhonian solution"[8] emerges in his subsequent works, in particular, *The Federative Principle* (1863).

This recovery of *War and Peace* is not uncontentious. As with much scholarship on the centrality of war and violence to human history, it has more often been situated on the right of political thought than the left. In addition, like many of his contemporaries, Proudhon's analysis and solutions are sometimes racist and sexist, underpinned by long-discredited scientific claims. A selective, decontextualised and partisan reading of *War and Peace* has routinely been used to present Proudhon as a proto-fascist. Objections to universal suffrage, his anti-feminism and racism, his defence of the patriarchal family and the virtues of war, are certainly now associated with the far right, not the far left. Proudhon's feminist

---

8. Bourgeois, *Les Théories du Droit International Chez Proudhon*, 26.

critics at the time drew attention to these contradictions in his thinking, and tried to rescue the liberatory anarchism in his thought from these provincial prejudices. I give them voice once more below, but more remains to be said on this topic.

SUMMARY

Proudhon seeks to answer a two-part question: what is war, and how are war and justice related? Previous answers conflated war with the will of god(s), or a manifestation of original sin. But none, he says, have studied how it is depicted in the historical oratory of the poets and the philosophers, *and* on the battle fields. We need to understand war in this dual aspect, its idealisation and its brute materiality, if we are to understand it at all, he argues. So what are Proudhon's general arguments? In a letter to his friend Auguste Rolland, he summarised them:

1. War is a psychological fact, much more than a material one. If we want to understand anything about it, we must study how it manifests in human consciousness.

2. It is because the moral aspect of war has seemed in such contradistinction to the bloodletting, that the latter is conflated with its empirical aspect, and its true meaning remains a mystery.

3. This moral element, forgotten, misunderstood, and denied despite the evidence, is the RIGHT OF FORCE.

4. The laws of war are deduced from the competent and intelligent pursuit of the right of force. The *Rights of Peoples* rests upon these laws of war and form a juridical institution.

5. Unfortunately, these laws are routinely violated in practice, either due to the ignorance of the jurists or the passions of the Warrior, or due to the influence of the PRIMARY CAUSE of war, which is nothing other than pauperism and cupidity.

6. Can the violations of the laws of war be avoided? No, war cannot be reformed.

7. So, war must have some end other than its reform, and that is what I have tried to explain.

If the nineteenth century is to avoid permanent moral decline, its mission must be *the end of militarism*.[9]

---

9. Letter to Rolland, 3rd June, 1861.

Proudhon argues that, contrary to the republican, natural law and humanist tradition, associated with Thomas Hobbes, Hugo Grotius and Kant, amongst others, the laws of war are not derived from reason, or from the authority of states, but from the exercise of the right of force in practice: that is, they are immanent in the practice of war, there being no transcendent arbiter of these rules. However, might does not make right, it merely sustains contingent conceptions of it, conceptions that await some counter force to change them.

For Proudhon, this force and right stand in "antinomic" relation to one another. In other words, right without force to sustain it would be ineffective, but force without a conception of right to justify it would be brutish. Following Kant, Proudhon argues that the "antinomy", translated in this work into "antagonism" is the motor of thought and society. Consequently, *jus gentium*, or the rights of peoples, are immanent in the practice and outcomes of the exercise of what Proudhon calls "collective force" in general, and war in particular, and the social systems of morality and "collective reason" that justify it.

The contrary claim, that force has nothing to do with right, leads to an impossible paradox:

> If it were true, as the unanimity of the jurisconsults contends, that any such jurisdiction [of war] was merely a legacy of barbarism, an aberration of the moral sense, it would follow that all our institutions, our traditions and our laws are blighted by violence and tainted at the root; terrifying though it may be to think, it would follow that all power is tyranny, all ownership usurpation and that society is in need of being rebuilt from top to bottom. There is no unspoken acquiescence, prescription or subsequent conventions capable of redeeming such an anomaly. One does not lay down prescriptions for the truth; one does not compromise on behalf of injustice; in short, one does not build right upon its very negation.[10]

Where the natural law and republican tradition argued that law begins where force ends, Proudhon argues that war and law are intricately connected and cannot be sundered without razing modern civilization. But Proudhon also rejected the pervasive nineteenth century call to violent revolution, fearing the cure would be worse than the malady. Rather, his aim here is the more modest one of asking us to see the moral and historical contingency at the heart of all our political institutions. All our institutions of law and justice rest on the outcome of war or the looming threat of violence. In the presence of endemic "pauperism" the absence of violence is due to the prevalence of modes

---

10. See below, p. 169.

of "pacification".[11] Only federation, and an aescetic philosophy, he argues, can resolve this.

Pauperism is a concept Proudhon borrows from Malthus and the Malthusians and adapts to his own ends.[12] Pauperism is a social condition endemic to those societies wherein consumption outstrips production, leading to economic crisis. In a twist on the Malthusian argument, Proudhon argues that when cities swell in size, and demand for food and luxury products outstrips the capacity to produce them; where landlordism or rent, monopoly, wage-labour and bourgeois gluttony and epicureanism, drains society, pauperism prevails. Pauperism is not directly related to population growth, but to the inability of society to properly organise to mitigate it. This imbalance between production and consumption in the context of population growth causes a "rupture in the economic equilibrium".[13] Communities can cope with relative poverty, but pauperism is a structural crisis that prompts societies to turn on themselves, precipitating what Proudhon calls the "social war". Then, they turn outwards, first, towards plundering, and then, from the reign of Alexander the Great, to conquering peoples and territory for economic gain. In short, for all its appeal to glory, war is at root no more than the grubby attempt to mitigate pauperism and pacify the social war, caused by inequality and over-consumption, by robbing one's neighbours.

Modern "social science", however, promises to reveal how to substitute hard work for war. Proudhon argued that labour, the nuclear family, mutual dependence in the context of the complex division of labour, "miscegenation" (the mingling of races), and polytechnical education to master this new social organisation, would breed temperance and civic virtue in the short term, and population stabilisation and decline in the long term, all tending towards social equality and peace.[14]

The evidence for these empirical claims about the psychological aspect of war, the right of force, pauperism and plunder, is ubiquitous, Proudhon argues. He finds it in the epics of ancient Greece, the legal scripture of the Roman Digest, the poems of Virgil, the myths of Titus Livy, and the injunctions of Cicero; the allegories and narratives of the Old and New Testament,

---

11. See below, p. 502.

12. See Book four, chapter two, below. Proudhon's engagement with Malthus was a central aspect of his theory of political economy, and his positions changed over time. For more, see Pierre-Joseph Proudhon "The Malthusians" (1848), translated by Benjamin Tucker, in McKay (ed.), *Property is Theft!* (Oakland: AK Press, 2011), 353–358. For a fuller discussion of Proudhon's account of demography, which differs somewhat from my interpretation, see Yves Charbit, *Economic, Social and Demographic Thought in the XIXth Century. The Population Debate from Malthus to Marx* (Amsterdam: Springer, 2009), 93–120.

13. See below, p. 340.

14. See below, p. 454.

the providentialist histories of European state formation, and the natural law tradition of the philosophy of right, that has both animated and followed these transformations in the use of force in modern European history.

War saturates our conceptions of right, he argues. From the warring gods of the scriptures and epics, through to the writings of Hobbes, Vattel, Wolff, Pufendorf, and Kant (a group he labels *les auteures*, which we have translated as "the authors" or "the jurists"), the philosophy of right has co-evolved with the changing character of warfare. The novel doctrines of "utility" and "reason" pervades nineteenth century studies of the Napoleonic campaigns, for example in the writings of the Prussian diplomat and historian Friedrich Ancillon, the military strategist Baron Antoine-Henry Jomini, and Adolphe Thiers's multi-volume *History of the Consulate and the Empire of France under Napoleon (1799–1815)*, all of whom feature extensively in Proudhon's analysis. By historicising these debates, Proudhon shows us how the philosophy of right emerges in particular contexts and shapes both the conduct of war and its justification – and is shaped by war in turn.[15]

War and Peace unfurls across five books, broadly aligning with the summary above. The first develops a sociological or moral phenomenology of war, setting out what war is, how it manifests and wherein war's moral and material reality and causal powers lie. The second explores the theory of the right of force, its near universal acceptance in practice and its denial in theory. The third book looks at the "how" of war: how it is the exercise of the right of force, how that has changed over time, and how the practice of war routinely undermines and contravenes the moral ideals and philosophies which animate it. Book four sets out the theory of the causes of war. Here he develops the first sustained socialist theory of the economic causes of war. Proudhon's claim is that war has always been caused by a "rupture in the economic equilibrium"; not poverty per se, but an imbalance between production and consumption leading to economic crisis and the need for wars of plunder and then conquest to rectify it. In book five, Proudhon argues that only through the "transformation" of social economy, from militarism to the socialist organisation of production and exchange, can a positive social peace be created. Two years later in *The Federative Principle* (1863) he calls this new economic arrangement "agro-industrial federalism", which he juxtaposed with the developing "industrial feudalism" of the modern age, and he argued that, "[t]he twentieth century will open the era of federations, or else humanity will resume a thousand years of purgatory".[16] Few were listening, fewer still heeded the warning.

---

15. For a late-modern statement of this problematique see Hew Strachan and Sibylle Scheipers, eds., *The Changing Character of War* (Oxford: Oxford University Press, 2011).

16. Pierre-Joseph Proudhon, *Du Principe Fédératif et de la Nécessité de Reconstituer le Parti de la Révolution* (inc) *Si Les Traités De 1815 ont Cessé d'éxister*. (Paris: Ernest Flammarion,

The Italian anarchist Bartolomeo Vanzetti and the German anarcho-syndicalist, Rudolf Rocker were two notable exceptions. Vanzetti and his compatriot Nicola Sacco were convicted of murder in one of the most famous (mis) trials in American legal history. While awaiting the electric chair, Vanzetti produced the first unpublished translation of Proudhon's *War and Peace*, which he undertook to practice his English. Proudhon's meditation on the right of force resonated deeply with him.[17] In a letter to Abbott Laurence Howell, President of Harvard University, eighteen months into the translation, he remarked: "Proudhon was right, abused, ridiculed. I dare say that even the anarchist [*sic*] have scorned at his stern truth. But the historical events, from his time to this miserable Thanksgiving Day, have proven his assertions – revindicated his genius".[18] Rudolf Rocker remarked much the same in *Nationalism and Culture*, published in 1937: "Proudhon foresaw all the consequences of the great development of the state and called men's attention to the threatening danger, at the same time showing them a way to halt the evils. That his word was regarded by but few and finally faded out like a voice in the wilderness was not his fault. To call him from this 'utopian' is a cheap and senseless trick".[19] So what was the inspiration for the book and why did cause such controversy?

THE SOCIAL AND POLITICAL CONTEXT OF *WAR AND PEACE*

At the end of book one, Proudhon praises "the exile that brought me the inspiration for this book".[20] What did he mean by this? Napoleon III's *coup d'état* in December 1851 had forced many of Proudhon's socialist contemporaries to flee France for England. There they were confronted with the dark unfurling of modern industrial capitalism. Proudhon was in prison at the time and was only released in 1852, but a brush with the censors on publication of *De la Justice* in

---

1863), 109.

17. Vanzetti's case had immense influence on academic debate at Harvard at the time. Harold Laski and Justice Oliver Wendell Holmes, both deeply moved by Proudhon's writings too, would fight in his corner, and Sacco and Vanzetti's correspondence and papers were archived by Felix Frankfurter, Professor at Harvard Law School in 1933, and later a Supreme Court Justice. I am grateful to Theresa Warburton for taking the time to copy this manuscript and selected unpublished correspondence for me.

18. Bartolomeo Vanzetti, letter to Abbot, December 11th, 1926. In Nicola Sacco and Bartolomeu Vanzetti, *The Letters of Sacco and Vanzetti*, edited with a foreword by Bruce Watson (London: Penguin, 2007), 436–37.

19. Rudolf Rocker, *Nationalism and Culture* (St. Paul: Michael E. Coughlin, 1978), 231–32.

20. See below, p. 110.

1858, forced him into his first extended exile. Lacking any grasp of the English language, other than the term "self-government", which he used regularly in his writings, he chose Brussels instead. Belgium's key strategic place in European Great Power politics, and the heated debates around Italian and Polish unification that shaped public discourse at that time, turned Proudhon's attention to European international relations. *War and Peace* is only one of seven books on international relations that he wrote during these last five years of his life.[21]

But war was an ever-present part of Proudhon's life. He was born in Besançon, the capital of the Franche Comté region of France, on January the 15th, 1809. These were formative times for France and Europe. The Napoleonic wars were turning in favour of the Holy Alliance, and it was the beginning of the end of the First Empire. In 1814, a year before the fall of Napoleon, the Austrians sucessfully laid siege to Besançon, and following the end of the war, the city was struck by successive waves of famine, compounding the family's poverty – no doubt a hugely formative experience for this young boy.

France's subsequent place in the European concert system was secured through the restoration of the Bourbon Dynasty in 1814. But this Catholic monarchy could not solve the fraught social and political problems laid bare by the revolution and the Napoleonic wars. Proudhon felt these personally. Pierre-Joseph's father was a cooper and taverner, who infamously refused, and failed to profit from his customers, and his mother was a cook and cleaner from a peasant family. These deprivations forced him to work for the family and made a timely, formal education impossible. Nevertheless, his intellect stood out, and his father urged him to take an apprenticeship as a proofreader and typesetter for a local press, which was highly skilled intellectual work at the time. Printing endless bibles, alongside the revolutionary works of his fellow *Bisontin*, Charles Fourier, was life-changing employment.

In 1832, at the age of twenty three, Proudhon's brother, Jean-Etienne, died in mysterious circumstances while serving in the French army. The event made Proudhon an "implacable enemy of the established order".[22]

21. The others are *La Fédération et l'Unité en Italie* (Paris: Dentu, 1862), *Si les Traités de 1815 ont cessé d'exister? Actes du futur Congrés* (Paris: Dentu, 1863), *Du Principe Fédératif* (1863), *Nouvelles Observations sur l'Unité Italienne* (Paris: Dentu, 1865), all published during his lifetime and two posthumous volumes: *France Et Rhin.* (Paris: Lacroix, 1868); *Contradictions Politiques: Théorie du Mouvement Constitutionnel au IX Siècle.* (Paris: Lacroix, 1870), and one which still remains to be fully published: *La Pologne. Étude d'histoire et de politique,* (1862). Chapter three of this work was published in 2016 by Federico Ferretti and Edward Castleton in "Fédéralisme, identités nationales et critique des frontières naturelles: Pierre-Joseph Proudhon (1809–1865) géographe des 'États-Unis d'Europe'", *Cybergeo: European Journal of Geography* (2016), https://journals.openedition.org/cybergeo/27639?lang=en (online only).

22. Cited in K. Steven Vincent, *Pierre-Joseph Proudhon and the Rise of French Republican*

Five years later, Proudhon won a scholarship to study in Paris and turned his attention to the "social question", a general European debate on the best way to organise society to the ends of equality and social justice. The standard French responses were framed in terms of the 'utopian socialism' of Saint-Simonian and republican thought, which was scientific, communalist and exceptionally technocratic, with institutonal architectures that were recognisably nationalist and statist. Proudhon's first significant contribution to these debates was *What is Property? An inquiry into the principle of right and of government* (1840). In it, Proudhon famously argued that "property is theft!" and that government was a general "usurpation". Against bourgeois natural law theories of property, he argued that private property was sustained by state force, and, by denying any democratic right for the workers to control the instruments of their own social reproduction (land, tools and education and labour), wage slavery was merely a "transformation" of chattel slavery. He announced himself an "anarchist" and spent the rest of his life working out what this meant. However, contrary to the myth of Proudhon's incoherence, the subtitles of *What is Property?* and *War and Peace*, and the discussion on pages 361 and 490 below, point towards a remarkable consistency between these two seminal works.

However, in the intervening years, Proudhon's pen ranged far and wide. He extended his anarchist political philosophy into areas as mundane as the prize-winning *Theory of Taxation* (1861), as politically confrontational as *General Idea of the Revolution in the Nineteenth Century* (1851), and his seminal four-volume work *De La Justice dans la Révolution et dans l'église* (hereafter *On Justice*, 1858). But apart from a very general article on foreign affairs, published in *Le Représentant du Peuple,* on the 14th of May 1848,[23] there is no direct discussion of international relations in his writings before 1861, and where it does arise it is fairly superficial. For example, in the final chapter of *General Idea of the Revolution*, Proudhon remarked that war was always likely for as long as the economic problems of the day remain unresolved and kings and politicians are unencumbered by the will of the people. This thesis – that international relations were epiphenomenal, emerging out of (and so solvable) by better domestic constitutions – was a standard republican trope well into the twentieth century.[24]

Socialism (Oxford: Oxford University Press, 1984), 48. For a discussion of the iniquity of military hierarchies and the democratization of the army, see p. 311 below.

23. See "Foreign Affairs", translated by Paul Sharkey, in McKay (ed.) *Property is Theft!,* 329–33.

24. In *Si les Traites* (1863) Proudhon ultimately came to answer the opposite, that all domestic constitutions are forged in the wars of international relations and are dependent on the structural solidity of international treaty law. In other words, domestic politics are emergent from international relations, this latter argument being the one he develops here.

The revolutions of 1848 offered Proudhon a unique opportunity to try and put his anarchism into practice , and his failures shaped his theory of war and peace. He stood successfully as a Deputy in the 1848 Revolutionary assembly, but quickly realised that not even revolutionary states could affect the social reforms necessary to realising the sorts of freedoms he advocated. As he remarked in his election manifesto, "governmentality" socialises revolutionaries in the trappings of the state and bourgeoise politics and diverts them from the revolutionary cause. Seeing the corruption of the revolution everywhere, he quickly fell out with his fellow assembly members.

One dispute was particularly portentous during this time in public office, and no doubt had a direct bearing on his understanding of war and peace: he was challenged to a duel. Felix Pyat, an Assembly member and future Communard, accosted Proudhon in the corridors of parliament for an apparent slight, calling him an "abominable pig". Proudhon retaliated by punching him in the face. Pyat promptly challenged Proudhon to a duel. A few days later, they met at dawn. Two shots were fired. Both missed. They retreated with dignity, but Proudhon was challenged again by Louis Charles Delescluze (minister of military and foreign affairs during the Paris Commune from 1870–1871). He declined, suspecting a plot to get rid of him, and, lo and behold, a few months later his immunity was revoked and he was jailed for insulting the President – soon to be Emperor Napoleon III, for calling him an "usurper" (with considerable foresight as it transpired).[25]

While he subsequently and here below denounced duelling as a practice, he did not denounce it in theory. In fact, this first-hand experience of the duel is developed into a philosophy of history in *War and Peace*.[26] Proudhon argues that the history of war has travelled in the opposite direction to that of the duel. Where duels have progressed from horseback jousting and proxies, to pistols at dawn, war has moved from the valour and virtue of hand-to-hand combat, to instrumental rationality and indiscriminate killing through the use of long-distance artillery. Military revolutions have denuded war of its moral element, while the invention of pistols heightened the moral integrity of the duel, Proudhon argues.

Proudhon's writings on war and peace should be read against the backdrop of the rise of positivist science and the dawn of the military-industrial age, what we today call the changing character of warfare.[27] New ways of warfare were be-

---

25. For a full discussion of this, see Vincent, *Pierre-Joseph Proudhon*, 187–89.

26. See, book one, chapter six, and book two, chapter eight.

27. See, for example, Hew Strachan and Sibylle Scheipers (eds.) *The Changing Character of War* (Oxford: Oxford University Press, 2011). See also Barry Buzan and George Lawson, *The Global Transformation: History, Modernity and the Making of International Relations*

ing developed, from iron hulled ships to advances in logistics and communications, and, of course standing national armies. The development of long-range
artillery, defensive trenches and rapid fire, rifled machine guns, most notably in
the Crimean War (1853–1856), precipitated the end of hand-to-hand combat
and cavalry charges. These innovations also generated epochal arms races that
continue to this day with international relations constituted as much by the nuclear balance of power as by the United Nations.

Militarisme, as Proudhon defined it, also emerged at this time. The concept captures the conjoining of industry and the military by the state, the transformation of citizens into soldiers, and the administration of society through
increasingly military means. Both at home and abroad, militarised colonial
and class hierarchies were imposed on subject populations, making nationalities through the development of military techniques of cultural and political
re-education.[28]

These military and social innovations were first tested in the colonies and
then rolled out across the metropolitan centres. The world's wealth, in particular slaves, was expropriated and shipped between the colonies and the European
imperial metropoles, while subject populations were managed with ever more
technocratic ferocity by states and private bodies, like the British and Dutch
East India Companies. Industrial capitalism and enclosures began to generate
an impoverished and landless proletariat in northern Europe, forcing peasants
into fetid cities to work in factories or mines, or to rent a piece of land from the
parasitic local lord, and pay him a share of the annual product.

This expropriation was unsustainable. The aristocratic rulers of the
European empires were beginning to crumble under the weight of these economic contradictions, with few able to keep pace with or harness for themselves
the technological changes enriching the industrial bourgeoisie, who in turn
financed the republican nationalists. The age-old marriage of state and church
began to crumble as the old regime was unable to articulate an ideology that
could counter the emerging doctrines of science and reason. But, the end of
the old order and the rise of the techno-industrial age worried Proudhon that
Europe was heading toward a redoubling of "the horrors of the iron age".[29]

(Cambridge: Cambridge University Press, 2015); William H. McNeill, *The Pursuit of Power:
Technology, Armed Forces, and Society since A.D. 1000* (Oxford: Basil Blackwell, 1983); and
Paul W. Schroeder, *The Transformation of European Politics 1763–1848* (Oxford: Oxford Uni-
versity Press, 1994).

28. For more on this, see Tarak Barkawi, *Soldiers of Empire* (Cambridge University Press,
2017).

29. See below, p. 99.

WAR AND THE PHILOSOPHY OF HISTORY

With this summary in mind, I now want to change gears and ask, why is *War and Peace* so self-evidently, and primarily, a philosophy of history, rather than just a history of war, and what sort of moral philosophy does a theory of the right of force promote?[30]

The contextual starting point is Proudhon's four volume *magnum opus*, *De la justice dans la révolution et dans l'église*, published, in 1858. These four volumes, which won him his exile, are divided between twelve, *études*, or studies, ranging from "Work" to "Education", "The State" to "Love and Marriage". The scope of the work led Metternich to dub him the "illegitimate child of the Encyclopaedia".[31] What is most striking for our purposes is that eleven of the twelve books were extended by up to 100 pages each for the second edition, and only the ninth book, "Progress and Decline", was left relatively untouched. This book was "one of the most difficult [to revise] because of the very nature of the question", he remarked.[32] Rather than tinker with it, he wrote *War and Peace* instead. In other words, *War and Peace* was intended as an extended case study of the philosophy of history and morality that was begun in *De la Justice*. A few more words about the philosophical structure of *De la Justice* are therefore in order.

The central purpose of *De la Justice* was to replace a mainstream philosophy of "providence" with an anarchistic theory of "immanence". Much modern philosophy was "providential", Proudhon argued, with the telos of reason or of material history taking us to a transcendent utopia.[33] The first task was to

---

30. The philosophy of war is divided between just war theory, or of perpetual peace, but few if any of these studies are drawn from the study of war itself. The empirical study of war and violence has been left to sociologist and military psychologists. See, for example, Siniša Malešević, *The Sociology of War and Violence* (Cambridge University Press, 2010); Lt. Col. Dave Grossman, *On Killing: The Psychological Cost of Learning to Kill in War and Society* (Boston: Black Bay, 1995); and Randall Collins, *Violence: A Micro-Sociological Theory* (Princeton, NJ: Princeton University Press, 2008). *War and Peace* combines these two literatures.

31. Cited in George Woodcock, *Pierre-Joseph Proudhon: A Biography* (London: Routledge and Keegan Paul, 1956), 204.

32. Letter to Chaudey, 23rd of July, 1861.

33. For an excellent discussion of Proudhon's anthropology of modern states, which draws heavily from *War and Peace* and Proudhon's unpublished writings on Poland, see Edward Castleton, "Une anthropologie téléologique: fins et origines des peuples et des hommes selon Pierre-Joseph Proudhon", Vincent Boudeau and Arnaud Macé, *La nature du socialisme, pensée sociale et conceptions de la nature au XIXe siècle* (Besancon: Presses Universitaires de Franche Comté, 2018), 197–242.

fathom this telos and all great thinkers thought they'd found the key in "reason". The problem was how to convince anyone that a positive outcome could emerge from the demonstrable irrationalism of the times? How could anyone be convinced that a negative or "fallen" initial state (either capitalism, feudalism, religion, ignorance, etc) could issue anything better? How could a positive future be forged in the fires of iniquity?

The answers to these sorts of questions were a type of secularised theodicy. Theodicy is that branch of theology that seeks to explain evil in relation to God's omniscient plan: can good come out of evil and catastrophe?[34] Writers from Adam Smith, to David Hume, Thomas Hobbes and Immanuel Kant, all argued that a "hidden hand" and its synonyms would guide society: if only men could reason and act according to transcendent or natural, rational first principles (happiness, self-preservation, and so on), the future was bright, they argued. "Providence", then, was derived from the structures of reason itself, rather than from scripture, and once "right reason", to use Hobbes's term, had been divined, it would constitute the basis for a rational, practical politics, in harmony with this providential and pre-determined end point.[35] As Proudhon recognised in a letter to Langlois, this was an epistemic exercise, with little or no relation to history or the real, phenomenal world around us.[36]

Proudhon's theory of "immanence", by contrast, was less theodicy than science and history, he argued. If we want to understand humans, we should study how ideas about good and evil are socially constituted, in and over time. There is no transcendent reason in history, Proudhon argued, only ideas that shape and guide people and actions in specific times and places. In this sense, the future is not determined or providential, it is "immanent".

34. See below, page 88.

35. In "Perpetual Peace" Kant argued that nature is "mechanical" and "providential". "Perpetual peace is *guaranteed* by no less an authority than the great artist *Nature* herself (*natura daedala rerum*). The mechanical process of nature visibly exhibits the purposive plan of producing concord among men, even against their will and indeed by means of their very discord. This design, if we regard it as a compelling cause whose laws of operation are unknown to us, is called *fate*. But if we consider its purposive function within the world's development, whereby it appears as the underlying wisdom of a higher cause, showing the way towards the objective goal of the human race and predetermining the world's evolution, we call it *providence*". Immanuel Kant, "Perpetual Peace: A Philosophical Sketch", in *Kant: Political Writings*, Hans Reiss, ed. (Cambridge: Cambridge University Press, 1991), 108. In "The Idea of a Universal History", where he develops these ideas, he asserts a "teleological theory of nature", which is not only explanatory but normative. If we abandoned the teleological theory of nature, it would imply that "we are faced not with a law-governed nature, but with an aimless, random process, and the dismal reign of chance replaces the guiding principle of reason". Immanuel Kant, "Idea of a Universal History with a Cosmopolitan Intent", in *Kant: Political Writings*, 42.

36. "Kant has taught us to stop asking, what is God?, for example, and ask *how do we believe in God*? Descartes never got that far". Letter to Langlois, 30th of May, 1861.

History, Proudhon argued, is the story "of IMMANENCE, or of the in-
nateness of Justice in the conscience".[37] What is rational is the emergent product of what feels right combined with what makes sense in any given situation.
While we may all share basic moral impulses, context matters. What is right in
one context may or may not be right in another: there is no *a priori* right. All
of human history is a history of the unfurling of different conceptions of justice
and right over time, fought for and established, acquiesced to and accepted, until some other conception emerges. He who speaks "as a partisan of immanence
[is] a true anarchist", he said.[38]

Despite this break from Kant's transcendental idealism, Proudhon's philosophy of history is deeply indebted to him. Proudhon read his friend Joseph
Tissot's translation of Kant's *Critique of Pure Reason* in his early twenties, and
his communications with Tissot on these matters continued throughout his
life.[39] Proudhon's first extended engagement with Kant was his attempt to
craft an "ideo-realist" ontology in *De la Création de L'Ordre dans l'Humanité*,
published in 1843, which, he noted to Tissot, would likely "bring all the
Kantians down on me".[40] But it was not until Tissot published a translation of
Kant's *Metaphysical Elements of Right* (1797) in 1853, that Proudhon became
familiar with Kant's political philosophy and his philosophy of history.[41] This
translation included the essays "What is Enlightenment?", "Perpetual Peace",
"Theory and Practice" and the "Contest of the Faculties", which amounts
to a near complete collection of Kant's political writings. Almost immediately Proudhon set about framing his own response to them, which began as
Philosophy du Progress (1853) and culminated in *De la Justice dans la revolution
et dans l'Église* (1858).

In a move echoed in Foucault's injunction that modern philosophy still
had to "cut off the sovereign's head" (to which I will return below), Proudhon
argued that modern philosophy had yet to "demonarchize the Universe":

Every social theory necessarily begins with a theory of reason and a solution of the cosmotheological problem. No philosophy has lacked that requirement. This is what explains why the partisans of political and social

37. Pierre-Joseph Proudhon, *De La Justice Dans la Révolution et Dans L'église. Études de
philosophie pratique,* Rose Marie Ferenczi, ed., IV vols. (Paris: Fayard, 1988–1990), 177. See
also, page 496, below.

38. Proudhon, *De la Justice,* 637.

39. Vincent, *Pierre-Joseph Proudhon,* 62.

40. Cited in Henri De Lubac, *Un-Marxian Socialist: A Study of Proudhon,* trans. R. E.
Scantlebury (London: Sheed and Ward, 1948), 140.

41. Immanuel Kant, *Principes Métaphysiques Du Droit, Suivis Du Project Du Paix Pérpetu-
elle,* trans. Joseph Tissot, 2nd ed (Paris: Librairie Philosophique de Ladrange, 1853).

hierarchy all begin from a theosophic idea, while the democrats generally incline towards an absolute emancipation of reason and conscience. In order to democratize the human race, insists Charles Lemaire, it is necessary to demonarchize the Universe.[42]

As far as Proudhon was concerned, the democratisation of reason could only be pursued through positive science in the Comtean mould. But the problem was that Comte's positivist science was a toxic mix for an anarchist. Its materialism, determinism, and the denial of free will, reason and justice, all in favour of a highly technocratic political philosophy, was the antithesis of Proudhon's philosophy.

However, as Bouglé and Cuvillier note in their introduction, *De la Création de l'Ordre dans l'Humanité* (1843) was not only a critique of Kantian metaphysics, it was also fundamentally an engagement with Comtean sociology in which he adopts a version of Comte's three stage view of history.[43] Proudhon's debt to Comte, is as little known as Marx's. Ten years later, in a rather surprising twist, Comte sent Proudhon complimentary copies of *Système de Politique Positive* (1854), with an odd invitation to join him in proselytising the positivist "Religion of Humanity".[44] Proudhon did not reply, but the impact of Comte's relational, realist ontology is striking in *War and Peace*.[45]

Proudhon follows Comte in arguing that "Philosophy is all in the observation, internal and external: there is no exception to that rule".[46] Our ideas are real, relational and causal, and shaped by history and society. This was a fundamental departure from Kantian and neo-Hegelian rationalism, and an endorsement of Comtean sociology.[47] Alongside a Comtian staged philosophy

---

42. Pierre Joseph Proudhon, *The Philosophy of Progress*, trans, Shaun Wilbur, with the Assistance of Jesse Cohn, revised by Shaun Wilbur in 2012 (Corvus Editions, 2012), 26, n. 11.

43. Celestin Bouglé and A. Cuviller, "Introduction", in P-J. Proudhon, *De la Création d l'Ordre dans l'humanité, Ou principes d'organisation politique*, Celestin Bouglé and A. Cuviller, eds. (Paris: Marcel Rivière, 1927), 17.

44. For more on this interesting episode, see Mary Pickering, *August Comte: An Intellectual Biography* (Cambridge: Cambridge University Press, 2009), Vol III., 85–95.

45. Comte, "made the relation the basis of his positivism, and has excluded metaphysics and theology in its name", in Proudhon, *De la Justice*, 1140.

46. Pierre-Joseph Proudhon, "Justice in the Revolution and in the Church", [extracts] translated by Shaun Wilbur and Jesse Cohn, in McKay (ed.) *Property is Theft!*, 621–623.

47. Kant was a key intellectual inspiration for Comte too. As Comte stated in a letter to Gustave d'Eichatel, who had recently translated Kant's "Idea of a Universal History" and fragments of the *Critique of Pure Reason* for him, that, "[a]fter reading this, I hardly find ... any value [in my own *Opuscule Fondamental*] other than that of having systematised and fixed the conception sketched out by Kant without my knowledge", cited in Pickering, *Auguste Comte*, 291.

of history, Proudhon transforms Comte's theory of "social facts" into his own theory of "collective consciousness".[48] Like Comte, Proudhon subscribes to the idea that society moves through three historical epochs, which Proudhon calls the religious, the metaphysical or philosophical stage, and the scientific. But unlike Comte, Proudhon argues that there is no transcendent telos to this progression, with one stage leaving the other behind. Indeed, the "divine", or the hitherto unfathomable, lives on in and animates the scientific era. As *War and Peace* makes clear, for Proudhon, there is as much to learn about war and peace in the Bible as there is in Adolphe Thiers's history of the French revolution, or Jomini's geometric rules of military strategy. Each is a contingent reflection of the morality of its time, but no less illuminating about the human condition for that. Likewise, as the discussion of theodicy indicated, religious themes are secularised routinely, so understanding them helps us better grasp our own secularised ideals.

In *War and Peace*, the writings of "the ancients" and "the moderns" are all treated as examples of what Proudhon calls "universal testimony". These ideas are real, phenomenal, contingent and social, expressed in books and through practices, and they have causal effects that predispose us to psychological and social states of mind.

However, Comte was of the view that it was transformations in the material workings of society that precipitated changes to our collective conscience, not vice versa. It is only possible to understand how gasses work in enclosed spaces after the production of boilers, not before. Science, he argued, follows technological advances, which is why the industrial bourgeoisie and the scientific cadre of society, were at the forefront of history, with him it's High Priest.

Our cognitive capacities are emergent from fixed biological traits, Comte thought. We are therefore the manifestations or products of biological forces we cannot shape, and social forces we had no hand in creating. Free will is a dangerous fiction, Comte thought, leading to an individualist "anarchy" that would divert people from the true path of "order and progress" – the Comtean motto still inscribed on the Brazilian flag.

---

48. Comte argued that: "we shall see that the same course followed by the new system had been necessitated by the situation of its elements at their origin". See, Auguste Comte, "Summary Appraisal of the General Character of Modern History", in *Comte: Early Political Writings*, H. S. Jones, ed. (Cambridge: Cambridge University Press, 1998), 24. "By the very nature of the human mind, each branch of our knowledge is necessarily liable in its course to pass in its turn through three different theoretical states: the theological or fictional state; the metaphysical or abstract state; the scientific or positive state". But the theological age was "indispensable if we are allowed to go further". "Plan of the Scientific Work Necessary for the Reorganisation of Society", in *Comte: Early Political Writings*, 81.

Understood in this way, it is little wonder Proudhon refused to associate with Comte. Nevertheless, Proudhon's twin concepts of "collective reason" and "collective force" are as indebted to Comte as they are to Kant. Proudhon agreed that we are shaped by the past, and that this is both an intellectual and material structuring of our ideas and our society. *War and Peace* is a case study of this process. But he diverges from Comte in defending the sovereign autonomy of individuals. Like Comte, he argues that "collective beings are just as real as individuals",[49] but unlike for Comte, while groups are real, and are "very different from, often even quite opposite to the conclusions of the individual "I" [...T]his conversion does not [...] condemn individuality; it presupposes it".[50] Constance Hall has argued that Proudhon was "one of the first social thinkers to attempt the primitive synthesis of these levels of social reality".[51]

The collective intentionality of these groups, just like our own individual intentionality, depends on how we organise (ourselves).[52] Individuals/groups are an emergent property of multiple forces, from without, and within, both biological and intellectual. We and our society are never one, we are always already plural and emergent.

The strength of personality and of groups lies in their power, or ability to direct their intentions. Proudhon divides power into two types: *puissance*, and *pouvoir*. The former is an unthinking force, including "inertia"[53] but also, for example, a riot. *Pouvoir*, is a purposive, directed social power, what he calls "*pouvoir sociale*".[54] The quantity of social power is proportional to the internal "relational law" of a given collective force or rationality. In other words, how well organised the group/individual is, is not reducible to the virtues (or vices) of the individuals that compose it, but how they relate to one another.

Despite this innovative social theory, like Comte, Proudhon was convinced that while there was a wide variety of men and women, men and women had fixed natures that distinguished them from one another, and this underpinned his anti-feminism. Miscegenation may equalise the races, but it could not, he thought, equalise the relations between men and women.

---

49. Proudhon, *De la Justice*, 1261.

50. Proudhon, *De la Justice*, 1261. Emphasis added.

51. Constance Margaret Hall, *The Sociology of Pierre-Joseph Proudhon 1809–1865* (New York: Philosophical Library, 1971), 32. For more, see Cayce Jamil, "Resurrecting Proudhon's Idea of Justice", *Journal of Classical Sociology* (forthcoming), and Dana Williams, "A Society in Revolt or under Analysis? Investigating the Dialogue between 19th-Century Anarchists and Sociologists", *Critical Sociology*, 40: 3 (2014): 469–92.

52. For an application of Proudhon's theory of collective intentionality, see Alex Prichard, "Collective Intentionality, Complex Pluralism and the Problem of Anarchy", *Journal of International Political Theory* 13: 3 (2017): 360–77.

53. Proudhon, *De la Justice*, 693.

54. See below, p. 166.

Proudhon understood the purpose of his mutualist social science as an attempt to develop better ways of organising society to enable the fullest possible human flourishing, or "justice" within the parameters of this sexist social
ontology.[55]

Proudhon's differences with Kant and Comte can also be seen in their
respective readings of the history of the European revolutionary wars. Both
Comte and Kant believed war's providential purpose lay in its production of
positivist or republican states respectively.[56] While there may be practical or
prudent reasons for going to war, these pale into insignificance in comparison
with the historical and providential causes of, and reasons for war, reasons beyond the comprehension of the average mind. For Kant, war compels the creation of the "civil commonwealth". It is a *"pathologically* enforced social union
transformed into a *moral* whole".[57] For Kant this providential outcome is vital
for realizing perpetual peace, but for Comte, necessary for the evolution of
positivism and the state: "The only means by which human association can be
carried to its fullest extent is [through] Labour. But the first steps in the development of labour suppose the pre-existence of large societies; and these can be
founded only by War. Now the formation of large societies came to pass naturally from the spontaneous tendency of military activity to establish the *universal dominion*".[58] This developmentalist thesis, which Proudhon objected to
so strongly, were at the heart of modern sociology and political science for a
century.

While he may have objected to their conclusions, Proudhon's starting
point and method are strikingly similar. Like Kant, Proudhon begins with antagonism. As he puts it: "Something widely acknowledged, in that it is a matter
of experience, is that civilization has antagonism as its starting point, and that
society, or in other words, rights, international law, public law and civil law have
evolved under the inspiration and influence of war, which is to say, under the

55. For more, see Alex Prichard, "Proudhon's Mutualist Social Science" in *The Cambridge
Companion to Socialism* Vol. 1, Marcel Van der Linden, ed. (Cambridge: Cambridge University Press), 286–308.

56. "All wars are accordingly so many attempts (not indeed by the intention of men, but
by the intention of nature) to bring about new relations between states, and, by the destruction or at least the dismemberment of old entities, to create new ones. But these new bodies,
either of themselves or alongside one another, will in turn be unable to survive, and will thus
necessarily undergo further revolutions of a similar sort, till finally, partly by common external agreement and legislation, a state of affairs is created which, like a civil commonwealth,
can maintain itself *automatically*". Immanuel Kant, "Idea of a Universal History", in *Kant:
Political Writings*, ed., Hans Reiss, 48.

57. Kant, "Idea of a Universal History", 45.

58. Auguste Comte, *System of Positive Polity*, vol. III (New York: Burt Franklin, 1968), 49.

jurisdiction of force".[59] War, then is, the expression of moral, social, economic and political antagonisms. It is also an ajudicator.

> Go through all the histories and you will find not a single thing to contradict this theory. It carries its certainty with it. War is the verdict delivered by force; it is the assertion of right and the prerogatives of force by force of arms; it turns into a nonsense as soon as some contrivance is used to score a victory over force. Which is why the waging of war does not end on the battle-field. Conquest, which is its ultimate purpose, only becomes final with the assimilation of the conquered. Unless that condition is fulfilled, victories are just odious dragonnades and conquerors merely despicable charlatans chastised sooner or later by the force they misuse.[60]

All of our institutions are thus temporary truces, not the pinnacle of civilization, and our laws are the codification of the existing and historic relations of force in society. Right is the endlessly emergent property of relations of force. As he puts it: "force on its own proves nothing; it has to be authorized and commanded by a higher power, which is itself the organ and representative of justice. Since no such authority exists, the right of peoples has no guarantor other than the reason and morality of governments, which is to say, that, in reality, the right of peoples rests on thin air".[61] This rhetorical flourish obscures the deeper point he makes here and above: historically speaking, it is not reason alone, or any authority derived from it, which grounds order and right, but crucially force.

Revolutionary France was the expression of the breakdown of a temporary truce in the social war between the labouring and the propertied classes. The interests of the rich could only be satisfied through the expropriation of the poor or the conquest of foreign lands. Book four of *War and Peace* turns to political economy to illustrate this argument. The basic per capita daily income needed in 1861, Proudhon argued, was around "3.50 francs".[62] This baseline level of subsistence is what Proudhon called "poverty" and Proudhon lauds it. Like Tolstoy who follows him here, Proudhon argued that temperance, frugality and work are our lot, and simple tastes are more easily met through a sustainable balance of production and consumption.[63] The gastronomes and epicureans,

---

59. See below, p. 129. These words could have been taken directly from Kant. In the "Idea", Kant writes, "By antagonism I mean in this context the *unsocial sociability* of men, that is, their tendency to come together in society, coupled, however, with a continual resistance which constantly threatens to break this society up". Kant, "Idea of a Universal History", 44.
60. See below, p. 238.
61. See below, p. 316.
62. See below, p. 352.
63. See below, p. 351.

the materialists, and encourage others to do so too. This causes "ruptures in the economic equilibrium", because luxuries become "a levy on essentials".[64] When there is nothing left in the coffers to pay off the people, the ruling class will go to war to address the "rupture" or contradiction this causes. War begets war, and, Proudhon argues, the people pay. "We are the offspring of heroes, they used to say, with their heads full of Homer. In fact, the topic most frequently mentioned in *The Iliad* and *The Odyssey* is loot".[65]

The epics relate how pirates were transformed not just into kings, but into Gods, who later associated their estate with the state and then both with themselves. Today, Proudhon argues, liberal tropes of liberty, fraternity and equality enable the army to "feed on its own people",[66] "turning citizenry into fodder for their soldiers".[67] In the presence of this imbalance, this pauperism, "society is always in a state of war"[68] and "politics is warfare".[69]

The resolution of the "social war" demands universal engagement with the positive science of political economy, which at this time was deeply historical and normative. Looking around him, Proudhon saw in the emergence of an industrial working class one of two possible paths. The first pointed to the rise of the industrial labourer, and portended a new constellation of social forces, one akin to the rise of the citizen soldier, and in whom society can invest great moral worth. If we are to address the problem of pauperism, the labourer, not the soldier, should become the epitome of civic virtue, he argued "In labour, production follows upon destruction; forces used up are resurrected again out of their dissolution, with renewed vigour".[70] Elsewhere Proudhon says "just as the hero proves himself in the fray, so the worker can be judged by his handiwork".[71]

The worry was the emerging prevalence of "*militarisme*", a term he coins here.[72] Rather than labour shape the future, the more likely outcome was the further centralisation of states, the militarisation of state and society, and the turning of workers into cannon fodder. Only "federation" could lead us away from the travesties he foresaw. Society must be organised, he argued, not from the top down, but from the bottom up. "I will concede that we can only come

---

64. See below, p. 357.
65. See below, p. 392.
66. See below, p. 441.
67. See below, p. 441.
68. See below, p. 482.
69. See below, p. 449.
70. See below, p. 488.
71. See below, p. 501.
72. Volker R. Berghahn, *Militarism: The History of an Intellectual Debate 1861–1971* (Leamington Spa: Berg Publishers, 1981), 1.

up with an as yet indefinite notion of the economic arrangement which, I contend, should take over from the reign of politics or war",[73] he says but: "The establishment of right in humanity is the very abolition of warfare; it is the organisation of peace".[74]

THE MIXED LEGACY OF *WAR AND PEACE*

War and Peace historicises war. It explores the transformaiton in war's practice and idealisation from an historical point of view, and does so without lapsing into the providentialist narratives of his contemporaries. By linking war to justice, Proudhon also historicises systems of right and the rights of peoples. This, in turn, deflates the grandiose claims about the providential character of the state in human history, and shows how political right emerges from the bottom up.

This illumination of the relationship between violence and justice made a significant and lasting impression on writers as diverse as Leo Tolstoy and Michel Foucault, Raymond Aron and Georges Sorel. Tolstoy would reject all law except conscience on the basis of Proudhon's association of positive law with state violence. Foucault would historicise the state in much the same way as Proudhon, refusing the grand teleologies of modernity in favour of a discontinuous, positive history of the state. Aron, Foucault's contemporary deployed Proudhon's historicised ethics in the service of a pluralist international morality in a thermonuclear age, and Sorel used Proudhon's moral phenomenology of violence to explain the virtues of the syndicalist general strike.

But if so much was made of this text by such significant twentieth century writers, why is the book not better known in Anglo-American circles? The reason for this is at least partly due to the association of Proudhon's theory of war and peace with conservative and reactionary political thought. A brief survey of this association will help set up the value of the more plausible readings.

For all its insight, for all the moral value of defending individual and collective sovereignty and the mutual dignity of all, Proudhon's philosophy of history is racist and sexist. He was neither the first nor the last to espouse such views, but a highly selective reading of his arguments about martial valour, the family and the historic virtues of religion and personal property as a bulwark against the state, led to Proudhon becoming a key intellectual marker on the

---

73. See below, p. 490.
74. See below, p. 491.

French right, and for those on the left who sought to discredit him by associating him with fascism.[75]

Proudhon's anti-feminism and his racism are both based on the same error: ignorance and prejudice. As mentioned above, Proudhon believed that men, women had fixed natures: women were two thirds weaker than men, physically and intellectually. While races had characteristics that changed as they intermingled and mixed, the capacities of women were fixed by nature. A woman's social role was to enable her husband as a housewife. For example, below he argues that, "The people are of a mind with women. The man of war is noble everywhere; he represents a caste. The slave has no entitlement to lay a finger on weapons; he would be dishonouring combat. If his master would but allow him to arm himself, that very act alone would make him a free man; what is more, it would bestow nobility upon him".[76] However, where slaves might rightly take up arms, women cannot be combatants: "War conjures up a colossal and irretrievable inequality between man and woman. For anyone who has once and for all grasped this great law of our nature, war, the fact of woman's unsuitability in warfare speaks volumes. Woman only truly exists in the family context. Outside of it, all her worth is borrowed; she cannot be anything and has no entitlement to amount to anything, for the crucial reason that she is not suited to combat".[77] This is of course untrue.

But what is going on here? There is no doubt that this is set of first order contradictions in Proudhon's thought, so how does he reconcile them with his anarchism and egalitarianism – his theory of justice? To begin with, Proudhon dabbled with phrenology, a branch of nascent race science in the nineteenth century that posited that the size and shape of the skull was a direct indication of the character and moral worth of a person. For example, he argues below that "The Caucasian stands out from all the others and not merely on account of fairness of face and elegance of figure; there is a superiority of physical, intellectual and moral strength".[78] A similar scientific consensus underpinned his sexism. Proudhon also defended the common idea that women played no active

---

75. See for example, Édouard Berth. "Proudhon en Sorbonne", *L'Indipéndence*, no. 27 (1912): 122–40; E. H. Carr, "Proudhon: The Robinson Crusoe of Socialism", in *Studies in Revolution*, E. H. Carr, ed., (London: Macmillan, 1950), 38–55; J. Salwyn Schapiro, "Pierre-Joseph Proudhon, Harbinger of Fascism", *The American Historical Review* 50, no. 4 (1945): 714–37. On Proudhon's uptake by the far right, in particular Action Française (established in 1899) and the Cercle Proudhon (established in 1911), see, for example, Géraud Poumarède, "Le Cercle Proudhon ou l'impossible synthèse", *Mil neuf cent: Revue d'histoire intellectuelle*, 12 (1994): 51–86.

76. See below, p. 96.

77. See below, p. 95 n59.

78. See below, p. 207.

role in procreation – they were a receptacle for "the seed" (a not uncommon belief at the time), making them naturally passive, while men were naturally active.[79] This translated into masculine virility and strength and feminine beauty. These were characteristics that attracted men and women to one another and constituted a natural balance between them – an incarnation of justice.

The problem is the social state in which women and men find themselves. To continue the quote from above, Proudhon argues that the "superiority of [Caucasian] nature is increased tenfold by the social state, so that no race can stand in our way. A few English regiments contain and govern one hundred and twenty million Indians, and we have just seen that it took only a tiny army of Europeans to conquer China. What comparison can there be between the Anglo-Saxon and the Redskin who would rather death than civilization, or the negro imported from the Sudan?"[80] Like all racism, these claims are the product of ignorance, and were/are shared by many on the left and right. Like Marx, Proudhon argued that it is because society is unequal that we need a division of labour, and given the iniquities of capitalism, only a transformation of social conditions could progressively equalise natural inequalities. Capitalism transformed slaves into wage slaves; only socialism could free workers. But Proudhon's anti-feminism went shamefully further.[81]

Proudhon believed French society was in decline due to the emasculation of men and the widespread attacks on the institution of the family and marriage. Proudhon thought that left to fend for themselves, outside the family, in society, women would be exploited sexually and socially. He blamed the Saint Simonians for this social malaise, in particular their campaign against the bourgeois marriage contract (which effectively made women chattel) and their concomitant defence of free love. Bourgeoise male dalliance and endemic

---

79. A good discussion of Proudhon's gender politics can be found in Anthony Copley, "Pierre-Joseph Proudhon: A reassessment of his role as a moralist", *French History* 3:2 (1989): 194–221.

80. Below p. 207. In *The Federative Principle*, published two years later, Proudhon reiterates his argument that emancipation in the context of wage slavery is no emancipation at all, but mollifies his argument about natural racial inequality. He says: "Notice, with regard to *black workers*, that physiologists and ethnographers recognise them as being of the same species as whites; – that religion declares them, along with whites, children of God and of the Church, redeemed by the blood of the same Christ and consequently their spiritual brethren; – that psychology sees no difference between the constitution of the negro conscience and that of the white, no more than between the comprehension of one and the other; – finally, [and] this is proven by daily experience, that with education and, if needed, interbreeding, that the black race can yield offspring as remarkable in talent, morality and industry as the white one can and that more than once already it has been an invaluable help in reinforcing and rejuvenating it", Proudhon, *The Federative Principle*, § 3, IX.

81. See below, p. 208.

concubinage was rife at this time: "modern life is killing our women", he wrote to Langlois.[82]

The solutions to natural "infirmity" included marriage for women, "miscegenation" (the intermingling of "races"), and education and work for the previously enslaved. While women would never reach the heights of men, men, whatever colour, had the same natural capacity for hard work and learning. But the biological difference between the sexes (but not "races") was insurmountable: men and women could never be full equals. It was for these reasons that women had to be confined to the home, he thought: the family unit protected women, and equalised this physical inequality, giving women a social function suitable to their relative biological capacity.

A bottom-up, federal society that harnessed the division of labour for socialist ends, would equalise men, he thought, while the division of labour in the family equalised men and women. Proudhon defended marriage not only because he saw it as the basis of the family, but also because he thought that it equalised sexual differences in an androgynous unit. By balancing what he thought were insurmountable differences, marriage and the family was the epitome and the foundation of social justice. However, the family was not a model for society as a whole, because the public domain was the preserve of men.

Proudhon's sexism had been the subject of sustained critique from women on the French left since at least the publication of *On Justice* in 1858. These criticisms were principled and analytical, and deeply political. Feminists defended his anti-statism and supported his scepticism of universal suffrage within the pre-existing structures of an imperial nation state. But there was disbelief that he would dismiss the possibility of equality of the sexes on the basis of plain predjudice. Jenny D'Hérricourt, also born in Besançon in the same year as Proudhon, wrote that "you have mistaken your imagination for the scalpel of science".[83]

Whatever we might say to bring Proudhon's theory up to date, or to make the case for its more progressive aspects, there is no doubt that Proudhon's anti-feminism and racism, not to mention what others saw as his "panegyric to war",[84] and his argument that modern civilization was in a death spiral, led him to be influential on the political right. For example, the 1927 editor of Proudhon's *War and Peace*, Henri Moysset, took a Ministerial role in Marshall Pétain's collaborationist government in 1941. In the aftermath of the Second World War and the Holocaust, Proudhon was not the only socialist

---

82. Letter to Langlois, 30th May, 1861.

83. For a fuller discussion, see Copley, "Pierre-Joseph Proudhon: A reassessment of his role as a moralist".

84. Carr, "Proudhon: The Robinson Crusoe of Socialism".

labelled "a harbinger of fascism", but it seems to have stuck to him more so than others.[85]

Proudhon's sexism and racism was ignored (rather than exposed and criticised) by those who sought to develop his thiking in more progressive directions. Four notable examples also help us understand the text and its historical significance: Leo Tolstoy, George Sorel and the Sociology department at the Sorbonne, including two of its most notable luminaries, Rayomnd Aron and Michel Foucault.

In 1861, Tolstoy received a written introduction from Alexander Herzen, a mutual friend, correspondent and comrade, and paid Proudhon a visit as he was putting the finishing touches to *War and Peace* and still searching for a publisher. In a letter to his lawyer Gustave Chaudey, on the 7th of April, 1861, Proudhon recalls spending a few days with Tolstoy, who he described as a "hugely knowledgeable" man.[86] While their discussion, he recounts, was of the place of the Catholic Church in Russia, the discussions over those few days may well have shaped both their writings significantly.[87]

For example, in *War and Peace* Proudhon recounts a curious anecdote from the Crimean War: "During lulls in the bitterest of fighting of the Crimean war, the French and Russians mingled as friends, as hosts, swapping a pipeful of tobacco, a swallow of brandy. This furnishes the most beautiful commentary I could offer on my thinking and on how the right of force should find expression".[88] Could Tolstoy, who served at Sebastopol, have recounted this anecdote to Proudhon? Tolstoy's memoirs of the front line, *Sevastopol*, were unavailable in French until 1902, but recount a similar

85. Schapiro, "Pierre-Joseph Proudhon, Harbinger of Fascism".

86. For a full discussion of Tolstoy's relationship with Proudhon, see Boris Ëïkhenbaum, *Tolstoi in the Sixties*, translated by Duffield White (Ann Arbor: Ardis, 1982), 175–94. On Tolstoy's anarchism, see Alexandre Christoyannopoulos, *Tolstoy's Political Thought: Christian Anarcho-Pacifist Iconoclasm Then and Now* (Abingdon: Routledge, 2019).

87. Pierre-Joseph Proudhon, *Correspondence: Vol X, 1860–1861*, J.-A. Langlois (ed.), (Paris: Lacroix, 1875), 341.

88. Roger Fenton's iconic 1855 photograph, "The Valley of the Shadow of Death" was chosen as the cover image of this book for several reasons. The image is contemporaneous with the writing of this book, and its subject was well known at this time. It depicts the aftermath of continuous shelling of "The Valley of Death" so-named by the soldiers who fought there, with obvious reference to Psalm 23, and subsequently deployed by Tennison in his 1854 poem "The Charge of the Light Brigade". The constant bombardment left the land desolate and barren. The photograph is also significant because of its contentious staging. Errol Morris, the director of the outstanding *The Fog of War*, has argued that the photograph was staged for dramatic effect. The original photo had only cannonballs in the gullies beside the road, while the one that graces the cover of this book has them strewn across the road. If the latter is staged, not only is this one of the first examples of war photography in history, it was also, crucially, one of the first examples of pacifist war photography.

anecdote: "White flags had been hung out from our bastion, and from the trenches of the French, and in the blooming valley between them lay disfigured corpses, shoeless, in garments of gray or blue, which laborers were engaged in carrying off and heaping upon carts. The odor of the dead bodies filled the air". During this brief surrender, Tolstoy recalls how French and Russian officers came together, shared tobacco and would "shake with laughter" at their mutually poor language skills, only for the commanding officer to yell: "Don't leave your lines; back to your places, *sacré nom*! [...] and the soldiers disperse with evident reluctance".[89]

Tolstoy's pacifism was no doubt derived from these and no doubt other more horrific experiences of the front line. In addition, Tolstoy's asceticism is strikingly reminiscent of Proudhon's arguments for temperance, frugality and toil in Book Four below. But his philosophy of history and of war was almost certainly shaped by his reading of Proudhon's *War and Peace*. When Proudhon died, in January 1865, Tolstoy was in the midst of penning his own magnum opus, *The Year 1805*, which was released in serialised form in *The Russian Messenger* between 1865 and 1867. Two months after Proudhon's death, on April 13th 1865, Tolstoy remarked in his diary that Proudhon's dictum, "property is theft is [...] is an absolute truth".[90] When Tolstoy decided to republish the serialised novel in two volumes in 1867, he renamed it *War and Peace*.

Beyond this, what textual evidence is there of the influence of Proudhon on Tolstoy? Interestingly, the first mention of Pierre, the central character of Tolstoy's *magnum opus*, presents a striking resemblance to his anarchist namesake. Pierre is a "stout", "burly", "bespectacled" and "foreign educated" man, "observant" but always seemingly caught up in his own thoughts. To break the ice of an awkward first encounter, Anna Pavlovna asks Pierre:

> "Do you know the Abbé Morio? He is a most interesting man...".
> "Yes, I have heard of his scheme for permanent peace, and it is very interesting but hardly practical ...". "You think not?" said Anna Pavlovna for the sake of saying something in order to get back to her duties as hostess. But Pierre now committed a blunder in the reverse direction. First he had left a lady before she had finished speaking, and now he detained another who was wishing to get away from him. With head bent and long legs planted wide apart, he proceeded

89. See Lyo Tolstoï, *Sevastopol*, trans. from the Russian by Isabel F. Hapgood (New York: Thomas Y. Crowell & Co, 1888), 115–19.

90. Tolstoy, diary entry, 13th April, 1865, cited in Pierre Haubtmann, *Proudhon: Sa vie et son oeuvre*, vol II (Paris: Beauchesne, 1982), 220.

to explain to Anna Pavlona why he considered the *Abbé's* plan an idle dream.[91]

While Pierre might be read as a teasing caricature of Proudhon, Proudhon's influence can also be read in the idiosyncratic epilogue to *War and Peace*. Here Tolstoy sets out his philosophy of history in ways that parallel Proudhon's account almost to the letter, but in reverse order. Section ten frames the debate about free will and history as a contest between philosophical idealists and materialists. Section nine, reflects on the "antinomies" of freedom and necessity, and how we ought to derive conceptions of necessity or free will from a "causal nexus" of "phenomena", not solely from an "idea" of it. Tolstoy derives these conclusions from an account of "power" understood as a relational "force", "a combination of [...] the activity of *all* the people who participate in the event". For these reasons, Tolstoy, like Proudhon, cannot countenance the idea that great men such as Napoleon are the primary cause of history. Like Proudhon, who also made this point, Tolstoy argues that writers like Thiers have mistaken Napoleon's "will" for the force of society that gave issue to him. Like the wake at the prow of a moving ship, he analogises, we spot its movement but do see the forces that gave rise to it. In another telling (perhaps Proudhonist) analogy, Tolstoy compares historians like Thiers to a man, "who, watching the movement of a herd of cattle, and paying no attention to the varying quality of the pasturage in different parts of the field, or the drover's sick, [...] attributes the direction of the herd to what animal happens to be at its head".[92]

Tolstoy politics later developed in pacifist, ascetic and anti-militarist directions, and this anarchistic politics also had world changing consequences. In a particularly telling exchange of letters with Mahatma Gandhi, one of his most famous followers, Tolstoy seemingly paraphrases Proudhon in order to impress on Gandhi the iniquity of the structures of imperial society and the value of conscience. "The question now is, that we must choose one of two things—either to admit that we recognize no religious ethics at all but let our conduct of life be decided by the right of might; or to demand that all compulsory levying of taxes be discontinued, and all our legal and police institutions, and above all, military institutions, be abolished".[93] Tolstoy finds and develops a pacifist reading of Proudhon's *War and Peace* and this had a significant influence on Gandhi. Indeed, Tolstoy's appeal to the divine echoes Proudhon's appeal to

91. Leo Tolstoy, *War and Peace*, translated with an introduction by Rosemary Edmonds (London: Penguin, 1957), 10. I am grateful to Ruth Kinna for pointing out this connection.

92. Tolstoy, *War and Peace* (vol II.), 1417.

93. Letter to Gandhi, 7th September 1910. Available at: https://en.wikisource.org/wiki/Correspondence_between_Tolstoy_and_Gandhi.

justice and collective reason, but the conclusion is the same: modern society is founded on violence and must be radically reformed if justice is to be realised. Gandhi's non-violent *satyagraha* movement was first established at Tolstoy Farm, in the Transvaal in 1910.

Over in France at this time, Proudhon had become a key intellectual marker for the emerging anarchist and anarcho-syndicalist movement, but also a staple of French professional sociology and epistemology at the Sorbonne. In terms of the former, Georges Sorel was among the most influential French commentators on revolutionary syndicalism. On the face of it, his *Reflections on Violence* could not be more starkly contrasted with Tolstoy and Gandhi's pacifist non-violence, but there are similarities too and can be accounted for in terms of Sorel's reading of *War and Peace*.[94]

Sorel's *Reflections on Violence* combines a Proudhonist theory of violence, and a Marxist theory of class conflict. In terms of the former, Sorel follows Proudhon in considering "violence only from the point of view of its ideological consequences".[95] Direct violence, killing and maiming, is a *"relic of barbarism"*.[96] From the ideological point of view, however, violence is as myth that evokes and plays on "intuitions", generated through the "intensity" of "powerful memories of conflicts", which are experienced as a psychic "whole, perceived instantaneously".[97] These myths of violence are "the feelings which move the masses to form into groups",[98] with new constellations of social forces generating new groups with new understandings of violence and of themselves.

Sorel argues that society is constituted by the ideological phenomenology of violence (including non-violence). The latent or explicit myths of (non) violence are partly constitutive of how social groups understand their relations to one another: violence is experienced in, through and as social hierarchy, domination and inequality. Where Tolstoy and Gandhi pursued pacifist non-violence, Sorel advocates the general strike. The general strike need not be physically violent to be understood as violence, since what the general strike achieves, even in the absence of violence, is the articulation or enactment of class consciousness and resistance: a new idelogy of violence would bring about radical social change by collapsing the

---

94. See Sorel, *"La Guerre et la Paix*: Essai d'Exégèse Proudhonienne", 2001. The secondary literature on this topic is overabundant and impossible to condense in a few paragraphs. See, Patrice Rolland, "La référence proudhonienne chez Georges Sorel", *Mil neuf cent*, 7, (1989): 127–61, and Jeremy Jennings, *Syndicalism in France: A Study of Ideas* (London: Palgrave, 1990).

95. George Sorel, *Reflections on Violence*, ed., Jeremy Jennings (Cambridge: Cambridge University Press, 1999 [1908]), 178.

96. Sorel, *Reflections on Violence*, 65.

97. Sorel, *Reflections on Violence*, 118.

98. Sorel, *Reflections on Violence*, 40.

bourgeois order.[99] Through the syndicate and the general strike, the working class comes to understand itself as a social group, and through the institutionalization of this counter-power, in education, social insurance, health provision and so on, the working class "builds the new in the shell of the old", to borrow the words of the Industrial Workers of the World.

Where Proudhon hoped that the emergence of the industrial working class would bring about a general pacification of society, for Sorel, writing forty years later, it had rather hardened battle lines. In Proudhonist prose with a Marxist inflection, Sorel wrote that class war and the general strike are the new motor of history.

> Proletarian acts of violence [...for example, sabotage] are purely and sim-
> ply acts of war; they have the value of military manoeuvres and serve to
> mark the separation of classes. Everything in war is carried out without
> hatred and without the spirit of revenge; in war the vanquished are not
> killed; noncombatants are not made to bear the consequences of the dis-
> appointments which the armies may have experienced on the field of bat-
> tle; force is then displayed according to its own nature, without ever pro-
> fessing to borrow anything from the judicial proceedings which society
> sets up against criminals.[100]

Sorel argues that proletarian violence seeks to transform society, not to destroy it. By contrast, the republican state, in outlawing the general strike or revolutionary acts of violence in the name of peace, monopolizes the right to violence, pacifying society in the interest of the ruling classes. Republicanism does not remove violence from politics but relocates it. It is for these reasons that Sorel rejected the parliamentary path to social change: "if, by chance, our parliamentary socialists come to power they will prove themselves worthy successors of the Inquisition, of the ancient *régime* and of Robespierre".[101] In this he was right, but whether the general strike, the embodiment of new modern industrial consciousness, can set society upon a stable footing, is another matter.

Proudhon's proselytisers in the Sorbonne at this time were less militant but the influence of *War and Peace* was no less significant. Celestin Bouglé, a holder of Emile Durkheim's chair of Sociology, placed Proudhon alongside Comte and Durkheim, as a progenitor of French sociology.[102] Following Proudhon,

---

99. Sorel, *Reflections on Violence*, 74–75.
100. Sorel, *Reflections on Violence*, 105–106.
101. Sorel, *Reflections on Violence*.
102. Celestin Bouglé, *La Sociologie de Proudhon* (1911); Celestin Bouglé, ed., *Proudhon et Notre Temps* (Paris: Editions & Librairie, 1920); Joshua M Humphreys, "Durkheimian

Bouglé sought to establish "collective conscience" as an independent object of analysis for modern sociology. Perhaps unsurprising in itself, the significance is twofold: first, this established a clear separation between French sociology and Marxist materialist reductionism, and secondly, it enabled a political critique of state centralisation and a defence of decentralised federalism. The recovery of Proudhon was central to both these moves.

Proudhon resurfaced in the Sorbonne after World War II. First, Raymond Aron, who graduated in the same class as his friends Jean Paul Sartre and Georges Canguilhem (Michel Foucault's future doctoral advisor), used Proudhon to think through the ethics of war in his monumental *Paix et guerre entre les nations* (1962). In this text he invites his readers to take seriously the role of force and war in the establishment of international law, and uses Proudhon's *War and Peace* to this end.[103] Stanley Hoffman, who wrote about Proudhon's political geography, was Professor of Political Science at Harvard, and a key proselytiser of Aron's ideas in the United States.[104] Hoffmann distanced himself from Aron's more conservative politics, as did many, particularly around the time of the May 1968 uprising in Paris, but Hoffman was a central character in the development of American International Relations scholarship in the 1970s.

One of Aron's colleagues, Georges Gurvitch, who also held the Durkheim chair of Sociology, used Proudhon's writings to theorise the sociology of knowledge and law, and popularised Proudhon's philosophy in turn.[105]

Sociology and 20th-Century Politics: The Case of Célestin Bouglé", *History of the Human Sciences* 12: 3 (1999): 117–38; Pierre Ansart, "La Présence du Proudhonisme dans les Sociologies Contemporaines", *Mil Neuf Cent: Revue d'Histoire Intellectuelle* 10 (1992): 94–110. Georges Gurvitch, *Proudhon: Sa vie, Son Oeuvre Avec un Exposé de sa Philosophie* (Paris: Presses Universitaires de France, 1965).

103. Raymond Aron, *Peace and War: A Theory of International Relations*, trans. Richard Howard and ed. Annette Baker Fox (New York: Doubleday, 1966), 600–606.

104. See Stanley Hoffmann, "The Areal Division of Powers in the Writings of French Political Thinkers" in A. Maas and Paul Ylvisaker (eds.) *Area and Power: a theory of local government* (Glencoe: University of Illinois Press, 1959), 133–35. Hoffman would also go on to champion Hedley Bull's "Grotian" theory of international relations, which saw both law and order as possible in anarchy. This "English School" account of international relations has many parallels with Proudhon's theory and deserves further thematic comparison and contextualisation. For example, see the discussion of war and sovereignty below, Book III, Chapter IX. See Stanley Hoffmann "Foreword to the Second Edition" in Hedley Bull, *The Anarchical Society: A Study of Order in World Politics*, (Houndmills: Palgrave, 1995), vii–xii.

105. Georges Gurvitch, *Proudhon: Sa Vie, Son Œuvre, Avec Un Exposé De Sa Philosophie* (Paris: Presses Universitaires de France, 1965); See also, Georges Gurvitch, "Proudhon et Marx" in Arthur Doucy (ed.) *L'Actualité De Proudhon: Colloque De Novembre 1965*, (Brussels: Editions de l'Instutut de Sociologie de l'Université Libre de Bruxelles, 1967), 89–97; Georges Gurvitch, *Sociology of Law* (New Brunswick, NJ: Transaction Publishers, 2001).

Gurvitch was critical of Proudhon's views on colonialism, and his anti-colonial views of Algerian independence made him a target of far right terror-ism.[106] But in locating collective conscience and individual reason at the heart of sociology, Gurvitch was also a central figure in the development of French epistemology.

But it was arguably one of Bouglé, Aron and Gurvitch's most famous students, Michel Foucault, who would develop Proudhon's ideas with most dramatic impact. Much as Comte and Kant are spectres in Proudhon's work, Proudhon is one of the "great absences" in Foucault's.[107] As Foucault's reading notes show, he drew upon Proudhon's theory of the "dialectic", his theory of federalism, and much more, but direct reference to Proudhon is hard to find.[108] What seems to have interested Foucault most, if we take his notes as a starting point, was the anti-transcendental aspects of Proudhon's philosophy of order, and in particular the place of struggle and antagonism in history. But recent studies have shown that the connections run far deeper.[109]

One hundred years after Proudhon's call to "demonarchise the universe", Foucault famously lamented that "In thought and political analysis we have still not cut off the head of the king". For Foucault, historicising reason would enable political thought to end the fetishization of sovereignty in political thought, and close off the eschatological approach to politics. Following Canguilhem and Comte's positivist unification of the human sciences, Foucault also sought to broaden the understanding of politics, from adminstration to a sociology of power. Like Proudhon, Foucault saw governance as techniques of social con-trol, the management of bodies and of populations. Central to this was force.

It is in *Society Must be Defended* that we see this Proudhonist account of war and force most clearly. But Foucault has to begin by releasing left politics from the hold of Marxist reductionism in the analysis of power. Power can-not be reduced to repression caused by the economic means of production, he argues. Power is a much more plural "implementation and deployment of a relationship of force" which we can theorise as "war". "At this point, we can

106. For more on this, see Abdallah Zouache, "Proudhon et la question coloniale algéri-enne", *Revue économique*, 67: 6, (2016): 1231–44.

107. See, Judith Revel, "Les grands absents. Une bibliographie par le vide", in *Michel Fou-cault* (Paris: Cahier de l'Herne, 2011), 130–135.

108. See Michel Foucault, *La dialectique chez Proudhon*, éditeur: équipe FFL (projet ANR Fiches de lecture de Michel Foucault), plate-forme EMAN: https://eman-archives.org/Foucault-fiches/items/show/3490.

109. See Derek C. Barnett "The Primacy of Resistance: Anarchism, Foucault, and the Art of Not Being Governed". Unpublished PhD thesis, The University of Western Ontario (2016); Teresa X. Fernandes, "The Postanarchist, an Activist in a 'Heterotopia': Building an Ideal Type", unpublished PhD thesis, Loughborough University (2019).

invert Clausewitz's proposition and say that politics is the continuation of war by other means. This would imply [...] that power relations, as they function in a society like ours, are essentially anchored in a certain relationship of force that was established in and through war at a given historical moment that can be historically specified".[110] The echoes of Proudhon are striking.

With this Proudhonist conception of force and war in hand, Foucault offers an alternative historical method. In "Nietzsche, Genealogy, History", he argues that genealogy is not a search for origins, nor a linear history, but an account of history that is "always produced through a particular stage of forces", with "insurmountable conflict" as its basic point of inquiry.[111] Genealogy is a history of the present, one which takes discontinuities and ruptures as a primary feature of the development of society. Like Proudhon, Foucault is happy to tell an empirical story about the emergence of the present, but refuses to argue that there is a transcendent telos to that historical process.

Like Proudhon, Foucault also recognises the evolution of moral orders and their role in rationalising, or "disciplining" society. Both Foucault and Proudhon use the term "*governementalisme*" to describe this and, notwithstanding certain key differences, both understand it as a certain mentality of rule adopted first by statesmen, who are shaped by it in turn, and then internalised by the rest of society.[112] Also, both understand government as much more than the writing and enacting of laws, and more as "governance". Let me turn to each of these claims in turn.

The concept of *governementalisme* is first developed in Proudhon's "Election Manifesto" of 1848, where he rebukes a form of thinking, typical of republican politicians, that reduces the problem of the realisation of freedom to technical and instrumental policy problems. A year later, in *Confessions of a Revolutionary* (1849), Proudhon here equates communism with governmentalism and technocracy, and argues that through the conscious centralisation of government, the ability of the people to self-govern is removed. What we are left with is government "[f]or the people, but all by the State".[113] Proudhon then

---

110. Michel Foucault, *Society Must be Defended. Lectures at the Collège de France, 1975–76*, trans. Arnold Davidson, ed. Mauro Bertani and Alessandro Fontana (New York: Picador: 2003), 14–16.

111. Foucault, cited in Bennet, *The Primacy of Resistance*, 318 n. 870.

112. The standard translation of Foucault's *governementalisme* is as governmentality, which we have not adopted in this text in order to maintain some distance between the two writers.

113. For more see Michel Foucault, *The Birth of Biopolitics: Lectures at the Collège De France, 1978–79*, translated by Graham Burchell, edited by Michel Senellart (Basingstoke: Palgrave Macmillan, 2008), chapters 1 and 2; Michel Foucault, *Security, Territory, Population: Lectures at the Collège De France, 1977–78*, trans. Graham Burchell and ed. Michel Senellart (Houndmills: Palgrave, 2009), chapter eleven.

uses the term *"governmentalisme"* three times in *General Idea of the Revolution* (1851), to refer to a logic of rule, a mentality that politicians adopt in power. What is unique in this latter work is that by now his conception of political power has also widened from the instruments of the state to a more encompassing mode of *governance*:

> To be GOVERNED is to be kept in sight, inspected, spied upon, directed, law-driven, numbered, enrolled, indoctrinated, preached at, controlled, estimated, valued, censured, commanded, by creatures who have neither the right, nor the wisdom, nor the virtue to do so. . . To be GOVERNED is to be at every operation, at every transaction, noted, registered, enrolled, taxed, stamped, measured, numbered, assessed, licensed, authorized, admonished, forbidden, reformed, corrected, punished [...].[114]

This is arguably one of the most ubiquitous citations from Proudhon's works. But here, ten years later in *War and Peace*, he develops this position considerably. Now, governance is a process: "as governmentalism grows, it deepens",[115] "the Old Continent's monarchical, communist and governmentalist instincts [...] wields a powerful influence over civilization generally, even now".[116] Here we see Proudhon hinting at one of the most striking developments in political theory in the twentieth century: Foucault's governmentality.

Foucault's understanding of neoliberal governmentality is a unique contemporary articulation of this Proudhonist problematique. For Foucault, governmentality is a process of self-rule, internalised by neoliberal subjects and consumers. This insidious form of self-government reproduces and embeds structures of domination through our habitual daily actions, leading us to self-pacify as part of what it means to be an upstanding member of a peaceful, liberal community.[117] Society has been pacified not by the rebalancing of social forces in the name of justice, or through practicing the virtues of frugality, temperance and thrift, as Proudhon hoped, but by liberal subjects having come to identify with, and administer their own material subjugation.

---

114. Proudhon, "General Idea of the Revolution", in McKay (ed.) *Property is Theft!*, 598.

115. See below, p. 440.

116. See below, p. 81 n. 40.

117. For more on this, see Baron, Ilan Zvi, Jonathan Havercroft, Isaac Kamola, Jonneke Koomen, Justin Murphy, and Alex Prichard, "Liberal Pacification and the Phenomenology of Violence", *International Studies Quarterly* 63, no. 1 (2019): 199–212.

CONCLUSION

War and Peace is a rich, profound, and captivating text, full of shattering insights, but it is an uncomfortable read too. It has sustained multiple readings, been praised and subject to numerous distortions, and it has inspired generations of scholars, students, statesmen and revolutionaries, few of whom were pulling in the same direction. How this book acted as a node in the history of European thought is not yet fully understood, and its full significance for contemporary thinkers, as well as for students of Proudhon's thought, is only slowly coming into view. Like light from a distant star, this book gives sight on the past, and illuminates the present. Engaging with its arguments, failings, legacy and potential, destabilises contemporary regimes of thought, and invites us to reassess the contemporary constitution of social order, thereby reconstituting the normative foundations of collective force once more.

Note on the Translation

La Guerre et la Paix was first published by Hetzel in Brussels on the 7th of April 1861. The first Paris edition was published six weeks later, on the 21st of May. The Paris edition was reproduced for the definitive Marcel Rivière (1927) collection of Proudhon's complete works, and extensively annotated by Henri Moysset. Moysset's edition, including the annotations, was reproduced by Trinquier for his 1998 edition, with further annotations added to the text. A further edition was published by Alain Panéro in 2012, which also reproduces the Paris edition.

We have carefully compared and cross-referenced the Belgian original with the Paris 1861 and 1927 editions and note only two significant differences between them. First, the preface was rewritten for the Paris edition, cutting extraneous sentences, and focusing the argument. Secondly, Proudhon removed the more egregious orientalist racism of the Belgian edition as we point out on p. 297 n68. We assume this reflects a certain enlightenment on Proudhon's part and so take this second edition to be the definitive text.

We have used the 1998 Trinquier edition as our source text for translation. We have included two paragraphs missing from this 1998 edition, and corrected minor errors. All corrections, and any issues of interpretation, have been verified with both 1861 editions. However, we have not verified the extensive referencing added by Moysset and Trinquer. Using this 1998 edition has allowed us to preserve both sets of annotations and show something of the editorial history of the text. The authors of each of the footnote annotations are indicated in square brackets at the end of the footnote text: P-J.P Proudhon [P-J.P], Hervé Trinquier [H.T.], Henri Moysset [H.M]. Paul Sharkey [P.S.], Alex Prichard [A.P.], Mitch McBain [M.MB.] Gerry Hughes [G.H.] and Iain McKay [I.M.].

English translations have been provided for the Latin, missing from both the 1927 and 1998 editions, except where Proudhon provides the translation immediately preceeding its use. All biblical references have been verified and corrected. The Latin Vulgate was generally Proudhon's original source, but we have used the King James version, unless otherwise noted. All citations from the Latin have been verified, translated and corrected where necessary, with reference, in all but one instance, to the Loeb Classics collection from Harvard University Press. For Hobbes, we have referred to Deborah Baumgold's 2017 edition of *De Cive* published by Cambridge University Press.

Proudhon's style was sometimes difficult to translate faithfully. He seemingly refused to use parentheses, and paragraphs are often a single sentence, and a page long, with umpteen clauses, compounded by double negatives, making the line of argument very difficult to follow in its English transliteration. While Proudhon's conversational and polemical style has been retained, we have removed or anglicised the more eccentric punctuation in the text and have tried to make it more readable where absolutely necessary.

We have retained Proudhon's gendered language when the modern English translation would not call for it. Also, key terms are translated in keeping with those used in other English translations of Proudhon's works. Some are trickier and will be noticed immediately by scholars of international law and international politics. In particular, the rendering of *droit* in English has a long and complex history. On the whole, we have translated *droit* as right, and *droit des peoples* as the rights of peoples. On occasion, *droit* is translated as righteousness, to indicate a more biblical, epic rendering of Proudhon's meaning. Because Proudhon goes to considerable lengths to distinguish nations, nationality and nationalism, from *peoples* and does not mention human rights [*droit des gens*] until the final pages of the book, we have translated *droit des peoples* as the rights of *peoples*, not of *nations*. Proudhon's use of the term generally corresponds with the Latin *jus gentium*. However, Grotius's use of *jus gentium*, for example, is normally translated in English as *the rights of nations*, a common convention in English, but arguably anachronistic. Proudhon had a far more modern meaning of nations at his disposal than Grotius, and still declined to use it. A *people*, as Proudhon used the term, is *any* community held together by the force of their collective enterprises. *War and Peace* is a study of the violent interactions between these groups, the moral and legal norms developed to regulate their interaction, and the ways in which this violence and law has evolved from the ancient to the modern era.

Acknowledgments

This book has taken five years to bring to fruition, and it has been an exceptional collective effort. It would have been impossible without Paul Sharkey engaging so enthusiastically with the monumental task of translating Proudhon's words, and without the University of Exeter and AK Press supporting the costs of that translation. Mitch McBain provided diligent additional editorial support by cross-checking the translation with the Paris and Belgian 1861 editions. Iain McKay went above and beyond in providing a thorough read-through of the final text. His experience of working with translations of Proudhon's work has been invaluable. I am also grateful to Henri Trinquer for his permission to use translations of his extensive annotations to the 1998 edition.

Gerry Hughes has been a constant source of support over the past twenty years, and his help with the footnotes deserves an honourable mention. Additional thanks to Ivan Gololobov, for scouring Tolstoy's untranslated Russian correspondence for references to Proudhon for me. I am also very grateful to Edward Castleton, Iain Hampsher-Monk, Ana Juncos, Iain McKay, Ruth Kinna, and Steven Vincent, for helpful and thought-provoking comments on an earlier draft of the introductory materials. A note of thanks is due to David Armitage, Anne-Sophie Chambost, Cian O'Driscoll, Jonathan Havercroft, Beate Jahn and Ruth Kinna, for generously endorsing the project. Finally, thanks to Zach at AK Press for supporting the project and shepherding the text to print.

War and Peace

On the Principle and Constitution of the Rights of Peoples

Pierre-Joseph Proudhon

(1861)

Guess, or I devour you.
—The Sphinx

Preface

I beg the French public's pardon for daring to stand before it and, worse, with a book printed outside the country.[1] I beseech my compatriots, before damning the author and his work, to lend an ear to a few words of explanation regarding both. It is a matter of concern not just to myself but to all who, though mistreated by events over the past thirteen years, cling invincibly to certain ideas and certain things.

First, on the personality of the author.

For the past ten years or so, France has embarked upon a new life; there was no need for me to come to Belgium to discover that. The ideas to which she had seemed attached up until around the end of the Second Republic, she now appears to only half-understand and cares about them in just about the same measure. The men who served as her guides and who, by the ingenuity and very diversity of their opinions, embodied the stirrings within her, she has repudiated; their message bothers her. Above all the ones that, in the wake of the February revolution, looked as if they had won the nation over, the most recent ones, these have become obnoxious to her. She has told them: "Stay back!"

I have a notion of this about-turn and, speaking for myself, I am resigned to it. Similar developments are not rare in the life of peoples. The vanquished may well rail against the determinations of Providence; even so, they have no choice but to bow before the sovereignty of the masses. Time marches on, the world has turned, France has done as she pleased: what can we republicans and socialists of 1848 have left to say to her that is of any interest? Are we simply to follow in her tracks? Our hearts have remained unbending; our aspirations fly in the face of the times; the progeny of parents who were witnesses to '89 and '93, our sensibilities are not the same as the generation of 1830; in spite of the most illustrious examples, in spite of the amnesties from which we have benefitted, we

---

1. Prosecuted for *On Justice in the Revolution and in the Church* and sentenced in absentia on the 28th of July 1858, to three years in prison plus a 4,000-franc fine, Proudhon fled to Belgium. He published *War and Peace* there in April 1861 and did not return to France until September 1862. [H.M.]

have changed neither our minds nor our maxims. As Sieyès[2] used to say, *we are today what we were yesterday*. That constancy is the very thing that damns us. After so many and such terrible defeats, there is a judgment against us.

With cruel bluntness we have been told, and, as usual, the least merciful have been those whom we looked upon, up until that moment, as political friends and co-religionists: "The men of 1848 are finished, laid to rest, forgotten. The *émigrés* should know this (following the coup d'état, certain republicans within have taken to calling those outside by the name *émigrés*): even inside the party, every favour is stripped from them. They are not *up to the mark*; they are out of step with the *trend*; they are outside of the *movement*. They have lost even the *feeling of Frenchness*. *Great things* have been done, and all they can do is *speak ill* of them. In exile, they have borrowed the language and ideas of the *foreigner* and can no longer articulate an idea that is not an *insult* to the nation. Let them *keep quiet*, if, in the absence of common sense, they have a glimmer of patriotism left. Abstention is their right and, more than ever, their duty".

As for me, despite the murmurs of my heart, I make no appeal against this condemnation. I consent to playing dead, such is the extent to which I feel myself genuinely mortified. God willing, let me imitate the elderly Buonarotti,[3] making a comeback after thirty-six years, mingling with the bourgeoisie in July, to plead the case for Babeuf and consign the corruption of the Directory to the fading memories of a sceptical posterity! Society evicts us; well then, I acknowledge that eviction order.

But this is what has prompted me, after so many misadventures, to speak out again and what I would beg my fellow citizens to receive it in good faith.

---

2. EMMANUEL-JOSEPH SIEYÈS (1748–1836). Abbot and politician, he was to make his name in 1789 through his famous pamphlet "What is the Third Estate? Everything. What has it been in political terms thus far? Nothing. What is it asking for? That it should become something". Elected by the Parisian third estate to the Estates-General in 1789, he drafted the Tennis Court Oath. On 23 June 1798 Louis XVI instructed the Marquis de Dreux-Brézé to break up the assembly. "Go tell the King that we are here at the people's behest and will only be leaving at bayonet-point", was Mirabeau's response. Sieyès then encouraged his colleagues to continue their deliberations in spite of the absence of the other two estates: "We are today", he stated, "what we were yesterday: let us deliberate". He was to be one of the founders of the Breton Club which was to evolve into the Jacobin Club and he would vote for the king's execution but was to stand aside during the Terror. Won over to the 18th Brumaire coup d'état, Sieyès became one of the three consuls before being made a senator and count of the Empire. Outlawed by the Restoration as a regicide, he would only return to France after the July Revolution. [H.T.]

3. FILIPPO-MICHELE BUONARROTI (1761–1837). A native of Pisa, he arrived in France in 1792 and played a very active part in the Babeuf conspiracy in 1797. After several years as a prisoner on the island of Oléron, he fled to Belgium, returning to France in 1830. His *History of the Babeuf Conspiracy* was highly influential in shaping the communist movement under the July Monarchy. [H.M.]

It is a matter of some interest to them, a topic that is neither republican nor socialist, and could not cause the slightest offence to Church, Emperor, nor even property. On the contrary.

In 1859, war broke out between Piedmont and Austria,[4] France sided with the Piedmontese. We know how that lightning-fast campaign turned out: the deeds were done before opinion had even had time to form regarding the venture itself. Even today, two years on, the majority of minds are still entirely undecided as to the moral, political and historical value of the occurrence. Many people find that war is no longer fitted to our times: the glory of arms and conquest have little impact on a society given over to commerce, that knows what battles cost and does not believe them profitable. As to matters of nationality, unity, borders and so on, it is not a criticism of anyone to say that contradiction is everywhere. Nationality might appear respectable, if it did not keep company with as many interests denying it as there are prejudices that affirm it; the unity acclaimed by some is scolded by others; in short, in this labyrinth of international politics, about which everyone argues with such high competency, the only positive thing that a man of good sense can discern is that there is no path nor exit to be found.

Like everybody else, at the sight of cannon replacing discussion, I wanted to embrace this extra-dialectical means of settling international difficulties and to learn what prompts peoples and governments into action when, instead of using persuasion, they put their efforts into mutual destruction and, since events were having their say, work out what the meaning of these events was.

So, like so many others, I argued endlessly about Italy, Austria, their relations and their history; about France and her legitimate influence; about the treaties of 1815, about the principle of nationality and that of natural borders, and then I noticed, not without some embarrassment, that my conclusions were wholly conjectural, arbitrary, the product of my secret sympathies and antipathies, and did not rest upon any principle.

I looked around me, I read, I listened, I informed myself. We are dealing here with the stuff of history, I said to myself; what principles govern this

4. At this time, the numerous states of Italy, many under foreign rule, were in the process of being united by the King of Piedmont (inc. Sardinia and Turin), and his prime minister Benito Cavour, a process known as the *Risorgimento*. In 1859, the northern and eastern part of the peninsula was under Austrian rule. Napoleon III was to help Victor-Emmanuel II, King of Piedmont, fight the Austrians and liberate Lombardy. He became King of Italy on 17th of March, 1861. For Proudhon's views on Italian unification, see Pierre-Joseph Proudhon, *The Principle of Federation or the need to reconstitute the party of the revolution*, trans. and ed. Richard Vernon (Toronto: University of Toronto Press, 1973 [1863]), *Fédération et l'Unité en Italie* (Paris: Dentu, 1862), and *Nouvelles Observations sur l'Unité Italienne.* (Paris: Dentu, 1865). [A.P.]

construction? ... My memories flew back to 1849, to the time of the Roman ven-ture[5] and the war in Hungary[6] and I was eager to see again what we had to say at the times of those events. I ask my erstwhile collaborators and confederates to forgive me; back then, they were speaking, as they have done since, in accor-dance with their democratic leanings, but without ever adducing the slightest morsel of philosophy, without any serious reasoning, in short, without princi-ples. And what I spotted in the republican press I found also in the conservative press; interests, prejudices, throughout; but rights-based arguments? Nowhere to be seen.

The revolution, I reckoned, must have left us a few clues ... But here again my research was in vain. Our fathers of 1792, like those who came after them during the imperial period, acted, but they did not philosophize. There was the occasional word, here and there: *War on the castles, peace to the cottages,*[7] or maybe *Peoples are brothers to us*, etc. But science or jurisprudence? Not a trace.

I looked to the specialist writers who, since Grotius[8] and Hobbes,[9] have dealt with the doctrine of peace and war, conquest, the revolutions of States, the rights of peoples, and who as a profession had to reduce everything to con-siderations of metaphysics and right. What a disappointment! That the authors sought principles is certain; but it is equally obvious to anyone who can read that they have not found them. As to their alleged science of the rights of peo-ples, what can I say? The entire corpus of right, such as they have devised and

5. POPE PIUS IX (1792–1878) had been driven out of Rome, and a republic established in February 1849. In June 1849, Louis-Napoleon Bonaparte sent in General Oudinot, at the head of fourteen thousand men, to attack the Roman republicans and reinstall the Pope. [H.T.]

6. In 1849, LAJOS KOSSUTH (1802–1894) had proclaimed Hungarian independence. The independent Hungarian state was crushed by Austria with the aid of Russia. On this, see István Deák, *Lawful Revolution: Louis Kossuth and the Hungarians 1848–1849* (London: Phoenix, 2001). [A.P.]

7. ANARCHARSIS CLOOTS (1755–1794). Philosopher and supporter of the French revolution. His report on the bill authorizing the Republic's generals to levy taxes upon en-tering enemy territory was presented to the Convention on 20 October 1792. [A.P./H.M.]

8. HUGO GROTIUS (1583–1645). One of the founders of the *rights of peoples*. Re-nowned primarily for his writing on the freedom of the seas, *Mare Liberum* (1608), to which the Englishman John Selden replied with *Mare Clausum* (1635). His seminal text is *De Jure Belli ac Pacis* (1625), in which he attempts to lay down a genuine code of public interna-tional law, opposes slavery and delves into the means of forestalling and regulating wars. The standard English text is Hugo Grotius, *On the Law of War and Peace*, ed. and annotated by Stephen C. Neff (Cambridge: Cambridge University Press, 2012). [A.P./H.T.]

9. THOMAS HOBBES (1588–1679). English philosopher of absolute sovereign power. Proudhon engages the Latin original of *De Cive* (1642) extensively in Book Two, Chapter VI, below. *Leviathan* (1654) was published in English only, and so not available to him. See Deb-orah Baumgold, ed., *The Three-Text Edition of Thomas Hobbes's Political Theory: The Elements of Law, De Cive and Leviathan* (Cambridge: Cambridge University Press, 2017). [A.P.]

framed it, is a flimsy construction made of figments in which even they themselves place no credence.

Yet, I still told myself, the principles do exist. Principles are the soul of
history. It is an axiom of modern philosophy that everything has its idea, from
which its principle and its law derive; that every deed is sufficient for an idea;
that nothing in the universe comes to pass that is not the expression of some
idea.[10] The rolling stone has its idea, as do the flower and the butterfly. It is ideas
that stir up chaos and render it fertile; ideas lead humanity through revolutions
and catastrophes. How could war not have its higher reason, its idea, its principle, the same as labour and liberty? There is a law of storms and there is also one
of combat. By themselves, principles shape the lives of peoples and the morality
of constitutions, they govern the movements of States and the death and resurrection of societies. I have searched for those principles and cannot find them.
Nobody can supply me with an answer, neither in France nor abroad.

How terrifying! We boast of our discoveries and our advancements. And,
to be sure, we have reason to boast of them. But it is no less true that as of yet we
know nothing about the physiology of societies and the functioning of States,
we do not even know the basics. We operate on the basis of hypotheses; in the
most civilized century ever seen, nations live alongside one another without
guarantees, without principles, without faith, without rights. And, because we
have no certainty about anything, no faith in anything, it follows that in politics as in business, that trust, for which we have fought so hard since 1848, has
become a utopia.

To be sure, such considerations relate to our own time; and they cannot be
chided for being more revolutionary than conservative, more republican than
dynastic. They embrace all opinions, all interests.

The Lombardy campaign was over; the Treaty of Villafranca was replaced
by the Treaty of Zurich,[11] and I was no further on than I had been on day one,
and in my doubt, and despite all provocations I refrained from passing judgment. As a Frenchman, as a democrat, I could celebrate, up to a point; as a
friend of truth and righteousness, I was only half satisfied.

Finally, determined to solve the enigma, I believed that through the thicket
of jurists, in the jumble of histories, in the darkest recesses of the popular consciousness, I could make out a fleeting glimmer of light. I seized upon that ray,

---

10. Proudhon is likely being ironic here. He described himself as an "ideo-realist". By this
he meant that ideas were real, not noumenal, as Kant argued, and that as such they were causal
phenomena. This "revolutionary ontology" also assumed that ideas were historical, emergent,
or immanent in humanity. See Pierre-Joseph Proudhon, "Little Political Catechism", in *Property is Theft! A Pierre Joseph Proudhon Anthology*, ed. Iain McKay (Oakland: AK Press, 2011),
654–83. [A.P.]

11. In 1859 these treaties brought the Franco-Austrian war over Italy to a conclusion. [H.T.]

multiplied it, concentrated it; in short, I built out of it this essay, which I present to the kind reader and in which I hope my fellow-citizens will detect no socialist flavour beyond the taste of Belgian soil.

But on to the book.

Here I can gauge how dismal the position of a man who, committed to the service of a defeated cause, has brought some tussle with the authorities down on his own head for that very reason. No one believes a word he says; no one trusts his judgment; his intentions are suspected; conspiracy detected even in his soundest reservations. Assuming that he has written something harmless, the claim is that that text, out of character for a writer with those aspirations, could not be of the slightest interest to the public.

I would blush to regale the public with my tribulations as a writer with suspect notions, grappling with the terror of the booksellers, were it not that this should be seen as a feature of our age, an odd one, to be sure, but one that weighs singularly upon one's heart and mind. At first, I was given to understand, and with all conceivable consideration, that they would not be taking on the publication of my manuscript other than on the advice of some counsel selected from among the Paris bar's most distinguished barristers. However irksome to my self-regard this condition of prior censorship may have been, I submitted to it nevertheless, even undertaking to rectify, correct, amend, re-jig, add to and remove anything that my censor might bring to my attention.

But it was not a matter of my being dependent upon correction, something that the Inquisition never denied a heretic: it was absolute condemnation, against which there was no appeal. The honourable barrister came down emphatically on the side of rejection, on grounds the substance of which I could only guess.

We can only suppose, and the reader will be the judge of this, that on certain minds the appearance of a new idea has the impact of a ghost. What ogres the publisher and his counsel were able to discern in my manuscript, I know not; the fact is that, by common accord and unanimous in their opinion, my book was rejected on the grounds that it was both dangerous and insipid. "This fellow just keeps on digging", said my Aristarchus;[12] "raising matters that compete with one another in crudity: one sets the head spinning, another takes your breath away, still another leaves you stunned. After having waged war for twenty years on property, government, Church, Stock Exchange and economists, here we have him, in relation to war and peace, targeting jurisprudence and falling upon the lawyers. This is an all-out attack upon the Emperor's policies! ..." We

---

12. ARISTARCHUS (c. 250 BC.). A renowned grammarian and critic from Alexandria. His name has become a by-word for severe criticism. [H.T.]

shall let the reference to lawyers pass; as to the Emperor's policies, the very opposite is the truth. I explained earlier that in part I had embarked upon my book
as a means of demonstrating to myself the perfect regularity of the recent war,
in terms of principles. But fear, as well as *esprit de corps*, make for a topsy-turvy
outlook.

I suppose that the prudent counsellor, working on the bookseller's sentiments, then added: "It would not be appropriate for a respectable company to
collude with such diatribes. This is no longer 1848; thanks be to heaven; those
days are long gone. Let us drop these eccentric spirits, bound for deserved obliv-
ion, whose names, worn-out scarecrows, now elicit only disdain and impatience".

In the wake of this expert report, it would have been most undignified of
me to press the matter further. I went away greatly perplexed and then I bumped
into M. Hetzel,[13] an exile, no less, a man to whom the condition of being suspect
was no black mark against a writer and he, knowing that I had been condemned
in the first instance, was willing to handle my appeal before the public.

I wanted to bring this up and point the accusing finger at myself in order
to warn the imperial government that, whilst there are times in the history of
nations when the public mind breaches the law that encompasses it, as if it were
some fragile web, there are other times when it is the law that strangles the public mind, and that we are living in one of the latter moments. Some through
fear, others due to zeal, all out of idiocy, betray freedom, even when it is offered
to them. The imperial government may brag of having carried the cult of order
aloft in minds; but if it is not careful it will never be congratulated upon having
allowed the intellect to spread its wings.

But I am forgetting that it is not for me to accuse others, since I am the one,
I and my like, who stand accused of having corrupted the public mind in France
and squandered freedom. The only thing I am allowed to do is to protest that
my thinking is loyal and my message moderation.

What, then, is there within this book that is so exorbitant, so inimical to
the common spirit of our age, that a clever, sceptical, liberal barrister felt himself duty-bound to act, pre-emptively, as the executor of the verdicts of opinion?
Allow me to tell you, reader.

I set myself the task of rehabilitating a right shamefully misunderstood
by all the jurists, one without which neither the rights of peoples, nor political
right, nor civil right have any real, sound foundation: that right is the right of

---

13. JULES HETZEL (1814–1886). Writer and publisher who had played an active part in
the republican opposition under Louis-Philippe and the February Days. He was *chef de cabi-
net* and then general secretary of the executive in 1848, was outlawed after the 1851 coup d'état
and stayed in Belgium until the amnesty in 1859. Hetzel agreed to the publication of *War and
Peace* after Garnier and Michel Lévy had declined it. [H.M.]

force. I have argued and proven that this righteousness in force, or of the greater force, cited, day in and day out, as an irony of justice, is an authentic right, as deserving of respect and as sacred as any other right and that this right of force that the human conscience, no matter the meanderings of its various schools, has been believed throughout history and is that upon which the social edifice ultimately rests. But I did not say therefore that force makes right, that it was the be-all and end-all of right, nor that it was to be preferred over the intellect in all things. On the contrary, I voiced objection to such errors.

I have paid tribute to the warrior spirit, vilified by the industrial spirit; but I have nevertheless acknowledged that henceforth heroism must yield to industry.

I have given war back its former prestige; I have, in defiance of the opinions of the legal profession, pointed out that it is essentially a dispenser of justice, whilst not arguing that there is any need for our courts to become councils of war; far from it, I have demonstrated that, in all likelihood, we are moving toward an age of indefinite pacification.

This is what I have said and which I reckoned I had made intelligible enough for a specialist. It seems that I was wrong in my reckoning.

In addition, dear friend, read this little narration, lifted from *Appendix de Diis et Heroibus poeticis*, offered in the schools to year six children, and you will discover the basis and underpinnings of this terrifying treatise. You will even be able to spare yourselves from delving any deeper into it. When the doctors of law have lost the capacity to understand the law through argument, the time has come to speak to them in parables, as Jesus Christ used to do.

Hercules

The younger Hercules, a young man already famed for his many feats, but whose education had, in those unhappy times, been sorely neglected, received the instruction from his father, Amphitryon that he was to abide by the Theban school. Besides music, as it was then called, religion and laws, it taught the writing that a foreigner from the Orient had brought to Greece. At the time, Orpheus was filling the mountains with his songs; somebody else invented the lyre; others had come up with the art of forging iron and turning it into all sorts of instruments. It was an age of renaissance, when princes and peoples competed against one another in wisdom and advancement.

The young hero was delighted to comply, having no doubt that he would conquer all learning, divine and human, just as he had bandits and monsters. He took up a stylus and some tablets and set about dutifully learning letters, numbers, the range of sounds, geometrical shapes and taking down dictation from his teacher the better to commit to memory the poets' anthems and the apophthegms of the sages.

But Amphitryon's son applied the full force of his determination and understanding to these subtle studies in vain. He made no progress and was forever getting the lowest marks in the school. The slightest mental challenge left him dizzy. When he sat in the study hall, head lowered over his seat, he would strain to trace written characters or numerals in the sand, mouthing their names, the blood rushing to his face; he could feel his arteries throbbing in his temples; his eyes protruded from their sockets; bloody droplets trickled all down his face. His intellect, all intuition, could not quite grasp anything analytically. The art of assembling letters, shaping them into words, the contrivance whereby young children today are entertained, was a real brain-teaser as far as he was concerned. In the middle of every lesson, he had to be sent out into the orchard for a breath of air and for refreshment. He did manage to sign his own name, ΗΡΑΚΛΗΣ; but in order to do it he had recourse to a strip of leather, on which the seven letters making up his name were gouged by a punch and through the gaps in which he threaded his reed pen.[14] But that was all; he never learned the sixteen letters in the Cadmean alphabet. As to numbers and geometrical shapes, he never mastered them either. Although his speech, which was extremely naïve, may not have been incorrect, the rules of grammar passed right over his head, leaving not the slightest trace in his memory. The oh so simple suite of numbers, genders and cases bearing on substantives and of tenses and persons relative to verbs were, to him, akin to a labyrinth in which his reason struggled to find its bearings. Nature has endowed each of us with one special gift: in one, a quick mind and the gift of the gab, in another, courage and bodily strength. The scholar should not be contemptuous of the strong man, nor the strong man of the scholar each of them is going to feel the need for the other equally.

Nor did Hercules manage to practise his scales: his prodigious boom of a copper baritone drowned out and broke choirs. On the feasts of Bacchus, he would blow into a huge trumpet, deafening the entire town. Flute and lyre set his nerves on edge. Finally, he was never able to march in step nor dance the sacred dances. His inability to learn caused laughter among his co-disciples who used to call him *bull-headed*. He was the first to poke fun at his slow wits; he was otherwise the best companion in the world.

---

14. *Calamus*: A sharpened reed used much like a goose quill. [H.T.]

At the end of a year, Hercules knew absolutely nothing. By contrast, his physique, already exceeding that of the greatest and strongest athletes, had grown by half a head. His strength was super-human; his bravery, his application to every exercise, matched his strength. Stopping a cart drawn by a pair of horses whipped into a gallop was child's play for him; or seizing a bull by the horns and felling it with a twist of its neck. His hands were talons; his long, mighty thighs, tireless. He could cover forty-five leagues in eighteen hours and maintain that pace for seven straight days. Which is how he came to run down a deer supposed to have hooves of bronze. Having captured it, Hercules then tamed it. He had only to break animals for them to become attached to him and they would have died rather than be parted from him. There is no love like the love that strong men inspire.

He had made himself a bow, reinforced with strips of steel, one that a man of ordinary strength had difficulty lifting and his arrows were like lances. It was with that bow that he killed the Stumphalids, a breed of antediluvian vulture, capable of carrying a two-year-old pig or heifer back to its eyries. In the forest of Nemea, there lived a lion, the terror of the land, who, year on year, claimed a toll of at least a hundred oxen from the herds, not to mention cows, calves, hens and other lesser game. Advice had been sought about this on lots of occasions and no one had any idea of how to get rid of it. Hercules said that he would fight it at close quarter, with no weapon but his club. This was the fire-hardened trunk of a holm oak, fitted with a thick, wide grip and sturdy iron studs. Hercules entered the thicket where the lion was, provoked it, pelted it with stones and just as the carnivore pounced on Hercules, he struck it in mid-flight and felled it with a single blow. The beast's head, a cubit wide, had been crushed by the terrifying club, as if it had been crushed under a boulder fallen from the top of a mountain.

Of all Hercules's battles, the most glorious was the one he fought in the swamps of Lerna against a huge serpent. Time and again, the ghastly reptile had been seen to seize a bull or a mighty horse, smother it in its coils and then drag it back to its lair where it devoured it. It looked as if there were no power alive that could deliver the land from this monster. At first, it occurred to Hercules to sneak up on it while it was digesting its meal; but, aside from the fact that an ox was no more of a burden upon the fearful boa than a frog to a grass snake, the wicked words of a certain Lachis, who was jealous of Hercules – there were those envious of Hercules – prompted him to abandon the plan. Since, in the undertaking of such an expedition, he could not rely upon his club, it being too lightweight for his liking and too short and not hard enough, he picked out an iron rod, long, thick, flexible and weighing as much as two men and he saw to the forging of it himself, wielding it two-handed the way a thresher of corn wields his flail. So armed, naked except for his girdle, Hercules set off to do battle with the serpent in its lair. Even as the latter lunged at its enemy like an arrow, with a blood-curdling hiss, Hercules, who had gambolled with the Nemean lion, never flinched. Jumping aside, he struck the boa crosswise with so much dexterity and force as to shatter its spine and those who were watching the engagement from some distance watched as the snake collapsed as if it had been cut in two. Lachis hurried up to sneer: "Couldn't you have tried", he said to Hercules, "to smother him in your arms the way you smothered poor Antaeus, the son of the Earth?" With the back of his hand, Hercules smashed Lachis into a rock; his brains were spilt and the denigrator was swallowed like the hydra by the mud of Lerna.

Like all heroes, once face to face with the enemy, Hercules was overwhelmed by a sort of inspiration. There and then he could see what needed doing; his quick wits then outstripped even the cleverest. The wild cat seizes its prey by the throat; the bull drives his horn into the adversary's belly; the goat turns tail, and delivers a double back-kick; the snake wraps itself around its victim and smothers him. Thus, the fighting man, in whom courage, skill and strength meet, knows instantly and for sure which tactics he needs to employ, in any circumstance. The only use he has for reflection comes when he needs to explain his intentions to others; but the genius of war, what the military describe simply as "the eye", is not taught in schools, and one is born a hero and captain the same way as one is born a poet.

As we might imagine, bandits, giants, pirates, no matter how strong, well-entrenched and numerous they were, made no headway against Hercules. One particular barbarian chief from the line of the ancient Pelageans, a man of extraordinary stature, had ensconced himself in a pass where he was robbing and scalping travellers. Hercules, having been fooled by him, challenged him to a fight, crushing him between his arms until his heart burst and he made his hair into a fly-swat for his stableboys. One tyrant fed his horses on human flesh: Hercules fed him to them, alive.

And so, he was soon policing the whole of Greece. Whilst he lived, the roads were safe. He was in demand everywhere: off he would go, alone, with his club, his bow and his arrows. His expedition over, he would bid his hosts farewell, seeking no reward beyond the booty wrested from the enemy. His reputation spread far and wide and was rivalled only by his good-natured ways.

Despite his outstanding services and even though undoubtedly none of Greece's princesses would have held it against him, Hercules lived the life of an adventurer; he never conquered a throne. Not one of the towns that he had rescued offered to take him on as its prince. Invincible in war, he had no understanding of politics. If only I knew how to read! he used to tell himself with touching modesty. If only I knew how to ride on horseback! the ambitious lawyer, Robespierre, was wont to say.

Come the end of the school year, the schoolmaster informed his pupils that there would be a prize-giving. There was a magnificent programme: after a sacrifice to the gods, there was to be dancing, singing and oration. A tragedy composed by the teacher would be performed by the pupils. The whole thing would conclude with the award of laurels.

On the appointed day, the entire town turned out for the ceremony. The magistrates were positioned on a dais surrounded by green garlands and topped by a triumphal arch, the orchestra to their left and the pupils to their right. There were badges displaying the names of the winners; a stack of wreaths rested upon a marble tripod; in front of the dais, an altar had been positioned, with perfumes burning upon it. The master had overseen their studies with some skill, varying the exercises and bringing out the different aptitudes in the subjects in which every one of these lovely young people had, without exception, earned at least one reward. The parents, the children, everyone was happy.

Hercules alone received no prize. For all his prowess, for all his freely delivered services, the master had not awarded him so much as an honourable mention. He showed up with his ballista-like[15] bow, his club resting in his hand, the pelt of the Nemean lion covering his broad shoulders, his bronze-footed doe following on behind like a young pup. A male slave carried the head of the Arcadian boar which he had slain, its tusks two palms long. Another waved the tresses of the giant that he had scalped; four more dragged the skin of the boa, seven times Hercules's own length.

The instant he appeared, the people began to cry out "Bravo, Hercules. Hail the son of Jupiter!" Nobody could credit that the noble Amphitryon, one of the bravest, sturdiest horsemen, had managed to sire such a son. The young girls tossed posies at him that contained more than one flirtatious message that the tamer of monsters was unable to read.

There he stood, with his heroic stature, his mighty limbs, his mane as curly as that of the bull of Marathon, a festive band around his forehead.

---

15. *Ballista*: a catapult hurling hundred-kilo weights over a distance of a hundred metres. [H.T.]

He asked the master, "How come you have awarded me no laurels and humiliate me with the town looking on?"

"You know nothing", the pedagogue answered him: "You refuse to be taught, you do not even attend classes. In three days, the youngest of these children learns more that you will in your entire life-time. Your place is by your father's plough which you would do well to rejoin with your slaves. Apollo and the Muses shun you".[16]

At which the onlookers laughed.

Incensed, Hercules kicked through the dais, toppling the triumphal arch, knocking over the benches, the chairs, the perfumed altar, shattering the tripod, scattering the wreaths, reducing them all to a heap and called for a torch. Then he seized the schoolmaster, forced him into the boa skin, the fellow's head poking out of the snake's jaws, capping him with the boar's head and dangled him, in that condition, from one of the poplars under which the prize distribution was to have been held. The womenfolk were terrified; the students cowered; the people reeled back: no one dared face the wrath of Hercules.

The din reached the palace where Hercules's mother, the worthy Alkmene was. She had been a ravishing beauty; now, even in her more mature years, she might have been mistaken for the goddess of strength. She showed up, spoke a word to her son, whose wrath, in the presence of his mother, fell away, only for him to burst into sobs. Then she asked the half-dead master what was the meaning of this scene. The latter did his best to excuse himself and protested his respect for the princess but could not disguise from her the fact that her son, the mighty, the proud, the magnanimous Hercules, was, when all was said and done, merely a dunce. Barely able to avoid bursting into laughter, so funny did she find the master's face, she told him: "You half-wit, could you not have had a gymnastic prize too in your school? Do you think that the town needs nothing but musicians and lawyers? Let us away, my son, forget about this pedant: your studies are over". And, surveying the posies tossed to the hero, she added "You have won first prize ... in the opinion of the young ladies of Thebes".

It was in the wake of that adventure that Hercules devised the Olympic games, later aped by the Nemean games, the Pythian games, and the Isthmian games, which were held throughout Greece for centuries. Historians and poets went to those games to parade their talents, and the athletes their vigour. Herodotus read out his history there; Pindar made his name there with his odes.

---

16. Apollo, god of the arts. [H.T.]

Two men, *ex aequo*, created the Greek ideal, Hercules and Homer. The former, a figure of fun because of his strength, proved that, on occasion, strength can be more spirited that spirit itself and that, if it has its reason, it has, consequently, its right too. The other one devoted his genius to celebrating heroes, strong men, and posterity has been applauding his songs for upwards of twenty-five centuries.

The book you are about to read, a book that has scandalized one of the celebrities from the Paris bar, is merely a commentary upon that old myth. The State as the collective identity; the people, the ignorant, well-meaning but indomitable multitude, being Hercules. Between one State and another, the only right acknowledged is the right of force; in the masses, all freedom and all rights derive from that very same source. Is there anything in that to justify a hue-and-cry? And, given that it is a revolutionary who is saying it, must he be denied any public forum? Ah but of course, we being pure in spirit, it is pointless our letting ourselves be governed by the laws of thought only. But since nature, in moulding us of flesh and bone had simultaneously made us subject to force, let us unabashedly acknowledge that and, if we may, embrace it. We will not be any the less deserving of it if, rather than grovelling like Pygmies, we occasionally manage to act with generosity, like Hercules.

Let there be no mistake, however. Heroism was a beautiful thing; but heroism has had its day. Hercules and his ilk are mythology. I have a high regard for force; here on earth it has gloriously introduced the reign of right; but I do not want it for a king. I no more welcome the plebeian Hercules than I do the governmental Hercules, nor the councils of war any more that those of the Holy Vehm.[17]

Here is my book. Let them refute it if they can; but let them not try to smother it under quibbles about the name of the author or government convenience. Which would be equally odious and ridiculous.

Ixelles-sur-Bruxelles, 1st of March, 1861.

---

17. *Holy Vehm*: A secret tribunal set up in medieval Germany to deal with those beyond the reach of the ordinary courts, particularly lordlings and knights who had turned to banditry. [H.T.]

BOOK ONE

THE PHENOMENOLOGY OF WAR

The Eternal One is a Man of War[1]
—Moses

SUMMARY

In humanity, war, like religion and justice, is more of an internal than an external phenomenon, a feature of moral life rather than of the life of the body
and the emotions. Which is why war, forever judged by the common man and
the philosophers by its appearances, has never been understood, except perhaps in the times of the heroes. Yet everything in our nature supposes it and
its presence, as well as the notion, is implicit in everything. War is godly, which
is to say, primordial, essential to life, to the very production of man and society. It has its home in the depths of consciousness and the idea encompasses
the universality of human relationships. Through it are revealed and expressed,
from earliest times, our highest faculties: religion, justice, poetry, the fine arts,
social economics, politics, government, nobility, bourgeoisie, royalty, ownership. Through it, down through the succeeding ages, mores drew refreshment,
nations regeneration, States balanced, progress pursued, justice established its
empire, freedom found its guarantees. Let us suppose that the notion of war
is done away with: nothing is left standing of the human race's past or present.
What society might have become in its absence is unthinkable; there is no telling what it may yet become. Civilisation tumbles into the void; its previous

---

1. *Bible*, Book of Exodus, 15: 3. [H.M.]

movement is a myth unmatched by any reality; its subsequent development an unknown, fathomable by no philosophy. Peace itself, ultimately, in the absence of war, defies understanding; it has nothing positive or true about it, it is bereft of value and import; it is NOTHINGNESS. Yet mankind wages war and strives with all its might for peace. Basic facts and society's authentic aspirations are at loggerheads. The problem thus posed is the object of these enquiries.

FIRST CHAPTER

On the Phenomenality of War

I do not think that any of my readers needs me to tell them what war is, physically or empirically speaking. Everybody has some sort of a notion of it; some from having been witnesses to it, others from having read many accounts of it, and a good number from having waged it. We shall take that as our starting point.

What is not known quite so well to many, and here I venture to say that military men, historians, jurists and publicists partake in the common ignorance, is the essentially juridical nature of warfare; its moral phenomenology, its idea; and, consequently, the equally positive and legitimate role it plays in the constitution of humanity, in its religious displays, in the development of civilizing thought, in the virtue and even in the happiness of nations.[2] What we know of war pretty much boils down to the outward deeds and displays, to the staging, to the din of battles, to the crushing of the victims. The more diligent apply themselves to the study of strategy and tactics; others concern themselves with the formalities: all things which are to war what procedure, police, penalties are to justice, ritual to religion, but which are no more warfare than legal formulas are law, or the ceremonies of worship are religion. No one, thus far, has tried to grasp war in its essential idea, in its rationale, in its consciousness – but, more to the point – in its lofty morality. Yet it is there, in that realm of pure reason and consciousness, that war needs to be studied and its vagaries observed, if we want to learn the first thing about it.

Writers witter on about right and the laws of war. But anyone who has read them knows that the expressions *right of war*, *laws of war* refer only to certain

---

2. *Phenomenology* (a disquisition upon phenomena, upon what is accessible to our senses) and *phenomenality* (the status of phenomenon) are terms borrowed from Hegelian terminology. [H.T.] Not able to read German, Proudhon's understanding of Hegel was derived entirely from that recounted to him by Marx and Bakunin in the early 1840s, and as such was thin. Kant's writings, however, were made available to Proudhon via his friend Joseph Tissot, who had translated many of his writings into French by the 1860s. Proudhon refers to Kant's *Metaphysical Principles of Right*, translated by Joseph Tissot (1853) in Book One, Chapter V, below. [A.P.]

curtailments imposed upon its ravages, certain conventional reservations on the part of humanity, rather than any positive right inherent in force or emanating from it; a right which, having been made manifest and enshrined in victory, would impose itself upon the consciousness of the vanquished the way the determination of a civil court overrides the consciousness of the unsuccessful litigant. According to the jurists, the right of war, in the literal sense of the word, is a contradiction in terms, a fiction, a euphemism that it would be puerile, laughable, nonsensical to take seriously. Actually, according to the testimony of all who have written on the subject, there is no righteousness in war, no thought, no morality in acts of force; which is plainly to reduce warfare to its material manifestations and thus to deny it any moral phenomenality, all spirituality. We brag of our progress, and rightly so: where war is concerned, we are a hundred times cruder than the barbarians ever were; for them at least, warfare was the loftiest manifestation of justice and of the will of the gods.

What would someone who had seen of religion only the ceremonies of worship, the baptism, communion, confirmation, mass, vespers, processions, holy water, know about religion? Not a thing at all. Religion is a wholly internal affair; its actions are immaterial and discernible only to the mind, albeit that, due to the inexplicable ties that bind the moral world to the physical, they are manifested by means of sensory signs such as water, bread, oil, chants, genuflexion, priestly garments, etc. These *signs*, although they form part of worship, do not add up to religious phenomenality; they offer no clue to an understanding of religion; quite the reverse, it is the prior understanding of religion that renders these signs intelligible. Now, if we are to understand religion, we must study the human soul: meaning that religious phenomenality belongs, not to physical observation, but to psychological observation. And it is because our age, better than any preceding age, has delved into this religious mind-set, because it has sought out its roots within the consciousness, that it has also attained a better understanding of it and gauged its importance and high import appropriately, and might even, despite the spread of rationalism and incredulity, be said to be the most religious age of all.

Likewise, what would anyone who might have seen only the external apparatus, the hearing, the magistrate's gown and cap, the armed force, the prison, the scaffold, etc., know about justice? Like religion, justice is an internal thing. Its actions take place within the consciousness; therefore, internal reflection alone can reach them. As to the judicial machinery, far from that spectacle being the gateway to an understanding of justice, it can only be understood with the aid of justice: meaning that, where the latter is concerned, one must, as in the case of religion, search one's consciousness, rather than refer to the solemnities of the courts. Never more so than in our own day has justice been stripped of the symbolic accoutrements with which the formalist, or rather, artistic, mentality of the ancients was pleased to surround it. You may ask: does it follow from that that we have a better understanding of right, that we used to show it more respect? There are grounds for believing so. Our present decadence is in relation only to ourselves; in the final analysis, we are the betters of our parents.

To these two examples, we might add that of speech and writing. It is not the noises of the larynx, the articulations of tongue and lips, any more than the letters of the alphabet that, by themselves, hold the secret of language, of human speech. Quite the contrary; it is thought that introduces reason to the procedures of speech and writing: the upshot being that grammar, the art of speaking and writing, has its laws within the concepts and operations of communication, its home within the consciousness and it is not in schools that great writers are moulded.

It is the same with war. As long as one stops at the materialism of battles and sieges, one is unfamiliar with it; and tracing the movements of armies across the map, counting the men, horses, cannons, powder flasks and haversacks, or detailing the messages and counter-messages traded between the belligerents prior to its declaration, is not the same as having seen it. Strategy and tactics, diplomacy and chicanery, have their places in warfare, just like the water, bread, wine and oil do in worship; just like the gendarme and the bailiff, the dungeon and the chains do in justice; just as the laryngeal sounds and letters of the alphabet do in the manifestations of the mind. But, by itself, none of these reveals a single idea. At the sight of two armies cutting each other's throats, one might wonder, even after sight of their manifestos, what these good folk are doing and what they want; whether what they call battle is a joust, an exercise, a sacrifice to the gods, a judicial execution, a physics experiment, an act of sleep-walking or dementia, performed under the influence of opium or alcohol.

In fact, not only do the material acts of strife have nothing to say for themselves, but the explanations of them devised by the jurists, and, after them, by the historians, statesmen, poets and warriors, to wit, that war is waged due to a clash of interests, is no explanation at all: it would simply mean that men, like dogs, spurred by jealousy and greed, bicker and graduate from insults to fighting; that they fight over a mate, over a bone; in short, that war is an act of pure bestiality. Now, this is refuted by universal sentiment and the facts, and is repugnant to a moral, free, intelligent being. No matter how misanthropic one might be, man cannot be equated with beast entirely in this regard: it is, as I say, impossible to attribute war purely and simply to some baser passion, as if humanity was quite capable of splitting itself in two and showing itself by turns to be angel or savage beast, depending on whether prompted entirely by conscience or the irascibility of its appetites.

Therefore, neither the materialism of the military nor the verbiage of the jurists and diplomats have anything to teach us here and we are left with but one option: to look upon war, as we do upon worship and legal proceedings, as the manifestation of an event in our inner life; and consequently, to look for its forms and its laws, not just to external experience, the historian's narrative, the poets' enthusiastic descriptions, the *factums* of the plenipotentiary, the schemes of the strategist, but also and above all, to the revelations of consciousness, to psychological observation.

At first glance, war rouses only thoughts of misfortune and bloodshed. Let the reader banish those gloomy images from his mind for a few moments: he will be quite startled to see that we do and think nothing of the sort and that our understanding does not form a wider, more indispensable category. War, like time and space, like the beautiful, the just and the useful, is a form of our reasoning, a law of our soul, a condition of our existence. This is the universal, speculative, aesthetic and practical character of warfare that it falls to us to highlight before we delve more deeply into its nature, causation and laws.

CHAPTER II

War is a Divine Fact

Initially, in all peoples, war appears as a divine fact.[3]

By *divine,* I mean everything in nature that is directly derived from creative power, or, in man, from spontaneity of mind or conscience. In other words, I mean by divine everything which, breaking the mould or serving as the initiation of a brand-new mould, admits neither question or doubt on the part of the philosopher. The divine imposes itself by sheer force, it does not respond to questions posed to it, and is indifferent to proof.

The appearance of man upon this earth is a divine fact. Where, indeed, does man come from? How did he get here? We do not know. The spontaneous generation to which speculation inevitably clings, is anything but an experiential fact and even if we were able to cite examples of it, it would still be unfathomable to us. If science ever gets to the heart of this mystery, the divinity of our origins will be pushed into the background and the fact of our earthly existence will cease to be divine; it will be a scientific fact. But that will not add to knowledge of the creation of our world and that of the universe; that, as far as we are concerned, is still going to be a miracle. Miracle, whatever we make of it, is the inevitable *involucrum*[4] of our science. Whatever is accessible to analysis, or can be defined, classified or catalogued, is, by that very fact, no longer a mystery. It belongs with those facts that, by dint of differentiation and development, form

---

3. Proudhon is here introducing the first example of his historical sociology of war. Influenced by Auguste Comte's *positivism*, Proudhon's social science was explicitly directed at uncovering the historical causes and consequences of what he termed "collective force" and "collective reason". Like Comte, Proudhon's three stage view of history began with the religious age, proceeds through to the metaphysical and on to the scientific. Unlike Comte, however, Proudhon's philosophy of history was one of increasing free will and the ever increasing pluralisation of global order. In this normative respect he was closer to Kant's philosophy of history than Comte, but derived his conclusions from Comte's sociological starting point, rather than Kant's idealism. For a fuller discussion, see Alex Prichard, *Justice Order and Anarchy: The International Political Theory of Pierre-Joseph Proudhon* (Abingdon: Routledge, 2013), chapters 3 and 4. [A.P.]

4. *Involucrum*: Sheath which peels back exposing petals or spines once certain flowers have bloomed. [H.T.]

genera and species, and thereby furnish a thousand access routes to understanding, and they come under the heading of knowledge and are thus amenable to reason and free will.

I am saying, therefore that war is, or at any rate thus far remains a divine thing, as far as we are concerned; in turn, celebrated and cursed, an inexhaustible subject of accusations or eulogies; in essence, thus far, beyond the reach of our will and with a theophany-like[5] unfathomability as far as our reason is concerned.

But of what does the divinity of war consist?

If war were, as I have just been saying, merely the clash of forces, passions, interests, there would be nothing to distinguish it from the battles animals wage; it would fall under the heading of animal phenomena; it would be, like anger, hatred or lust, an aspect of the life force and that would be that. There are even grounds for thinking that it should have been banished ages ago by the combined operation of reason and conscience. Out of self-respect, man would have ceased waging war against his fellow man, just as he has ceased eating him, enslaving him, living a promiscuous life, or worshipping crocodiles and snakes.

But there is something else within war; a moral element that makes it our species' most splendid and, simultaneously, ghastliest manifestation. What is that element? Unequipped to uncover it, the jurisprudence of the past three centuries has made it its business to deny it. This otherwise meritorious jurisprudence, so deserving of recognition, posits as an axiom that war, in at least one of the belligerent parties, is necessarily unjust, given that black and white cannot both be right at the same time. Then, in order to support that axiom, it treats acts of war, some as equivalent to acts of banditry, others as equivalent to the methods of constraint that the civil law permits for use against the malefactor and malicious debtor, so that, depending on whether the cause he serves is just or unjust, the warrior must, as a matter of logic, be deemed as a hero or a villain. Now I maintain and will demonstrate that such a theory is gratuitous, starkly refuted by the facts and we shall show it to be dangerously and deeply immoral. As we shall see, war, real war, is, by its very nature and concept, motives and avowed purpose, and the eminently juridical tendency of its forms, not only no more unjust on the one side than on the other, but is, on both sides, of necessity just, virtuous, moral and holy, making it a phenomenon of divine order, I might even say miraculous in character, and this elevates it to the stature of a religion.

---

5. *Theophany*: An apparition or manifestation of a divinity. [H.T.]

"War is divine in itself", says de Maistre,[6] "because it is a rule of the world.

"War is divine in terms of the mysterious glory that surrounds it and in the no-less unfathomable attraction that it holds for us.

"War is divine in terms of the protection that it provides for the great captains, even the rashest of them, who are seldom struck down in the fighting, and only once their renown is beyond further increase and their mission complete.

"War is divine in terms of the way in which it is declared. How many of those viewed as the authors of war are carried away by circumstances!

"War is divine in terms of its outcomes, which are far beyond men's speculation".

Thus spoke de Maistre,[7] the great theosophist, his theosophy a thousand times more profound than the so-called rationalists scandalized by his message. De Maistre was a pioneer, making war a sort of manifestation of the will of Heaven, and precisely because he admits to finding it unfathomable, showed that he had some grasp of it.

The same conscience that produces religion and justice also brings forth war; the very same fervour, the very same spontaneous enthusiasm drives the prophets and avengers, sweeping the heroes along: that is what constitutes the divine character of war.

And now, how are we to account for the genuinely singular mystery when conscience or righteousness, mercy and murder come together in brotherly embrace? Yes, if war ceases to be divine and, what is more, loses its divinity, it draws to an end. If, on the other hand, that ghastly myth in action is unfathomable, then war, I have no compunction in stating, is eternal.

Hail war! It is through war that man, barely risen from the mud that served him as a womb, poses in his majesty and valour; it is over the body of a slain enemy that he dreams his first dream of glory and immortality. The blood-letting, the fratricidal carnage leave our philanthropy aghast. I fear lest this softheartedness may herald a cooling of our virtue. What is so terrible about standing by a great cause in a heroic battle in which the honour of the combatants and the presumption of right, just like the danger of dispensing or suffering death, is equal on both sides? Moreover, where does the immorality lie? Death is the

6. *Saint Petersburg Evenings*, 7th conversation. [H.M.]

7. JOSEPH DE MAISTRE (1753–1821). One of the most ardent opponents of the French Revolution, which he argued was the fulfilment of God's will, not of reason, which suggested the legitimate restoration of God, Pope and King. His thesis was that society was an organic whole, bound by shared religious morals which shaped society. These ideas were developed by Auguste Comte and Proudhon too. [H.T./A.P.]

culmination of life: for what other more noble end could man, that intelligent, moral, free creature, ask?

Wolves and lions do not wage war on one another, any more than sheep and beavers do; acknowledgment of that has long been held up as a rebuke to our species. Why can we not see, instead, that it is a token of our greatness; that if, by some freak act, nature had made man an exclusively industrious and sociable beast and not a warrior, he would have fallen, on day one, to the level of the animals whose gregariousness is the sum total of their destiny; that he would have lost, along with the pride in his heroism, his revolutionary aspect, the most wonderful and most fertile of them all? If we lived in unadulterated community, our civilization would be a stable. Would we know the value of peoples and races? Would we be any further forward? Or would we just have this notion of *merit*, transposed from the warrior world to the shopkeeper's? ... There is not a single people in the world that has earned any renown, that does not pride itself primarily upon its military credentials; in the eyes of posterity, those are the highest accolades. Are you about to turn them into a record of infamy? You speak, Philanthropist, of abolishing war; beware of degrading the human race ...

But, you say, by what despicable sophistry has the most generous of creatures managed to turn the murder of his fellow into an act of virtue? ... Ah! You are the one indulging in sophistry here, for you are misreading and vilifying the human conscience which you fail to understand. That conscience takes exception to the equivalence you draw between war and murder. And it is that very exception that constitutes the mystery and which makes war a divine phenomenon. How is it, and I put this question to you, that humanity had its eyes opened to virtue, to society, to civilization precisely by war? What makes blood the first function of royalty? How does the State, organized for peace, have its foundations in carnage? That, Philanthropist, is what you need to explain, without succumbing to impatience or insult, by dint of substituting your wavering reason for the spontaneity of the human race and creating mayhem for the very civilization you purport to serve. Science and morality are not built on irony, and your sarcasm, replicated from the Greeks, is more impertinent and insipid than ever. Listen to what is coming, and then slander, if you dare, what you do not understand.

CHAPTER III

War as Religious Revelation

War, I have stated, is one of the categories of our reason. We shall see it grow in that respect and leave its mark on all manner of thinking. Let us start with religion.

War, having given rise to conscience, conjured up religion from a representation of the eternal mysteries of the sub-lunar world. It is to this that war is indebted for its most glittering myths, its profoundest dogmas. So, we can coin this aphorism: Warrior peoples are religious and theological peoples. In the nobler races, war and religion work hand in glove.

According to Bergmann, among the ancient Scythians, the notion of Divinity scarcely existed, and faced with the powers of nature, God promptly lays claim to the status and attributes of the warrior. Tivus, the sky god, the oldest and greatest of the gods, is simultaneously the god of battles. His successors, Odin, Thor, Apollo, Hercules, Mars, Pallas, Diana, etc., receive that honour from him and share it with him.[8]

The descendants of Shem are of the same mind here as the descendants of Japhet: "Jehovah is a man of war", the Bible says; "Who is like him?"[9] Elsewhere, it refers to him as the *God of hosts, whose glory fills heaven and earth.*

War, in this life and the next, is the entire religion of the ancient Nordic peoples. They had no other aspiration, no other happiness in mind. What! Has the poetic depiction of Valhalla,[10] where the heroes indulged in endless battles

8. FRÉDÉRIC-GUILLAUME BERGMANN (1812–1887), *Les Gètes, ou la filiation généalogique des Scythes aux Gètes, et des Gètes aux Germains et aux Scandinaves* (Paris: Treuttel, 1859). A lecturer in Foreign Languages and Literature at the Faculty of Letters in Strasbourg, BERGMANN was the author of a study of the *Origins of Romances of the Holy Grail* and of numerous works of philology. [P-J.P]

9. *Bible*, Book of Isaiah, 6:4. [H.M.]. According to Biblical tradition, Ham, Shem and Japheth were the sons of Noah and the ancestors of part of humanity (See Genesis, 10). [H.T.]

10. In Scandinavian mythology, Valhalla was the warrior paradise. Its walls were draped with shields and bloodstained swords. The heroes would engage in violent battles there. Their wounds miraculously healed, they would gather around Odin, drinking the mead served by the Valkyries. [H.T.]

as a reward for their having fought well on earth, has this paradise of battles nothing to say to your imagination, nothing to your conscience, nothing to your heart! Or are your dreams of lions and tigers only!

Older than Moses, Zoroaster[11] taught that Ormuzd and Ahriman, the principles of Good and Evil, are locked in an eternal battle; out of this divine contest comes creation, or the perpetual replication of existence. Thus, according to this theology, which can be found among the Indians, the world was not created, but the Eternal Victor humbled Satan and his angels, his victory ensuring man's victory over sin, shaping Providence's plan and the economy of the universe.

Christianity merely teased out the notion of the magi. Who is Christ? The vanquisher of demons, founder of the chosen monarchy, come to bring *not peace but a sword.*

Of course, the Christian paradise is the very opposite of the Scandinavian paradise; there, all is adoration and hymns. Virgil had heralded that revelation by depicting the heroes on the Elysian Fields, no longer in the thick of battle, but engaged in physical exercise and jousts – images of warfare. The messianic idea entered the world under the aegis of Augustus, that peaceful emperor. But who could not foresee that Christianity would spawn chivalry, that the Pope, Jesus Christ's vicar, would go on to enter into alliance with the prince of Paladins, with Charlemagne? Such was the inseparability of the notion of war and conquest from this divine revolution!

Long before Christ, long before the likes of Caesar, Alexander, Cyrus, Nebuchadnezzar, Semiramis, Sesostris, way before all the State annals, Bacchus and Osiris had roamed the earth as conquerors. Allah was to follow the same example.

If we banish the notion of war then theology becomes impossible, the gods lose all meaning; furthermore, they have nothing to do. But for war, the earth would have no notion of heaven. Shem and Japhet, Noah's two valiant sons, have no religion. Now, if religious thinking is brought to a halt, what do you make of Asia and Europe? What becomes of civilization?

Reiterating an old and quite mediocre joke, the objection will be voiced: *God made man in His own image; man reflected it back at Him.* What do religion and society care for such imagery from barbarians bent on mutual destruction and making their heavens the imitation of their hordes? Does the ferocity of the fathers compromise the gentleness of the progeny, and might the latter not resort to reason just because the former were idolaters?

11. ZOROASTER (ZARATHUSTRA) regarded as the man who reformed the ancient religion of Persia. Proudhon mistakenly considers Zoroaster older than Moses. The former was supposedly born around 660 AD; Moses sometime between 1400 and 1200 BC. Proudhon was no doubt thinking of the origins of Persian religion. [H.T./P.S.]

To put it another way: we bluntly repudiate the theology of the ancients, which is serious, since discovering the idea of war there, we regard it as tainted, the mischievous product of mischievous thinking. Leading where? Does that render the theology of the moderns more reasonable and their morality purer? But who will fail see that whilst war has served theology as a primitive mould, it was not through the impact of runaway superstition, but rather because war has always been deemed the law of the Universe, a law played out, in the eyes of the earliest humans, in the heavens, in the form of thunder and lightning, and on earth through the antagonism between tribes and races? The life of man is a struggle, says Job: *Militia est vita hominis super terram.*[12] And the reason for the strife? Here, once again, we find mystery, the divine act. Everything that traditions, popular symbolism, the speculations of the metaphysicians and the epic fables of the poets have taught us about this terrifying subject is that humanity is divided between itself; within humanity and within nature, Good and Evil, akin to two inimical forces, are in conflict; in short, war is the condition of every creature until the end of time.

Hence, religion; hence, theology.

Even if we set to one side the dogma of the Fall, war is the basis of religion. It obtains between peoples just as it obtains throughout the whole of nature and in the hearts of men. It is the orgasm of the life universal which stirs and renders the chaos fertile, prefaces all creation and, like Christ the redeemer, triumphs over death through death itself.

Take away the religious thinking, banish from the human heart this notion of strife, not only do you not halt the scourge of destruction, but you destroy the whole system of religions; without explanation, without criticism, without compensation, you do away with the framework of ideas within which the human race has been living for more than forty centuries and but for which you could not say how it might otherwise have lived. You are denying, I say, civilization, in its two chief aspects: religion and politics. You are destroying the very possibility of history. Come on! War carries so many things within itself, it is the answer to so many things, yet you would regard it as a fit of bestial savagery sustained by superstition and barbarism! That cannot be countenanced.

Another thing. Not only has war inspired dogma; it has also determined the form of worship. Looked at in terms of its toll, war, according to de Maistre, is a variety of human sacrifice, the only one that matches the scale of the offence given and the only one that might have served us as expiation, but for the dispensation from it that we have obtained through Jesus Christ's willing

---

12. *Bible*, Book of Job, 7:1. [H.M.]

sacrifice. The priesthood has been built upon that principle. Initially, the priest was the squire of the warrior, patriarch or clan chief; he is their minister, *cohen*,[13] charged with the immolation of victims for him and in his name; and which victims? Captives.

The immolation of the enemy, and in earliest times, his ingestion: at first, there was the propitiatory sacrifice made in advance of battle, then the granting of pardons in the wake of victory. In that sense the Druid and the Cohen are brothers; their religions are identical. In the depths of the Arabian wastes as in the oak forests of Celtic climes, the hymn to the deity is nothing but a war chant. But the notion of redemption spread early; sacrifice was replaced by Abraham with animal sacrifice and by Melchizidek with bread and wine.[14] From which derives the eucharist. At the risk of representing the Almighty of the Gospels as an eater of human flesh, like the Phoenicians' Moloch, the Greeks' Bacchus Omestes, the Gauls' Teutates, de Maistre, like Feuerbach,[15] acknowledges Christianity's anthropophuistic origins. Are you now going to abolish worship and dogma alike? Are you going to do away with priesthood? ... Then do away also with crime and punishment, the penal code, prison, the scaffold, executioners and judges. For your penitential arrangements and all their paraphernalia are merely a segmentation of the priestly function, a reworking of the warrior cult.

Of course, and this is yet another argument raised by the incompetent devotees of peace, religion is not necessarily a religion of terror; it is also a religion of love. Not only is there a vengeful God, there is also a God of benevolence, a *kindly God*. Worship, with its concomitant expiations, also has its offerings of praise, *hostiam laudis*, which, it seems, exclude any notion of war and human sacrifice.

But which of us still cannot see that all these notions are inter-related and automatically self-suggesting? The granting of pardons is the same thing as the victory chant; it is warfare. Pardon, or help dispensed from on high, is

---

13. Cohen is the term for a member of the Jewish priesthood. [A.P.]

14. *Bible*, Book of Genesis, 14:18–20. [H.T.]

15. LOUIS-ANDREAS FEUERBACH (1804–1872), German philosopher from the Hegelian left. Proudhon is referring here to *Das Wesen des Christentums* (1841) as well as to *Das Wesen der Religion* (1845), in the translations by Ewerbeck in 1850 and by Roy in 1864. He argued that man is the object of religion and that the deity is merely the ideal of a people. Karl Grün briefed Proudhon on Feuerbach's doctrine, and German philosophy, more broadly, between 1844–1846. For Proudhon's annotations of Feuerbach and the influence of Ewerbeck and Karl Grün on his writings, see Pierre Haubtmann, *Pierre-Joseph Proudhon. Sa vie et sa pensé 1809–1849* (Paris: Beauchesne, 1982), 440–87, 508–545. For a shorter, English discussion of Proudhon's views on Feuerbach, see K. Steven Vincent, *Pierre-Joseph Proudhon and the Rise of French Republican Socialism* (Cambridge: Cambridge University Press, 1984), 94–108. [H.T./A.P.]

suggestive of natural and social wretchedness, discord between the elements and divided consciences; war again. So it is that the Mass, the sacrifice of the man-God, which opens with an act of contrition, *Asperges me*, closes with an act of thanksgiving, *Deo gratias*. Step outside of that circle and you tumble into the void; there is no religion, no civilization, no humanity.

And so, the idea of war envelops, dominates and, by means of religion, governs the whole gamut of social relations. Everything in the history of humanity implies it. Nothing can be explained without it; nothing can exist other than through it; whoever knows war knows all there is to know about the human race. An innocent philanthropy querying the means by which society will triumph over this parricidal rage is within its rights so to do. War is a sphinx that our unfettered reason is called upon to transform, if not destroy.

What is certain is that, in order to be done with war, one must first have understood it; one may challenge philosophy to dispense with it, not just when it comes to explaining preceding ages and the understanding of the present day, but even when it comes to sheer prognostication of the future; eventually, once peace is achieved and secured for good, humanity will nonetheless follow the path opened up for it by war, by its principle and by its very notion.

Of which the following chapter will furnish you with fresh proof.

CHAPTER IV

War as Justice Revealed

War is divine right in its artistic expression: *God and my sword.*

Now, if religion with its dogmas, its worship, its priesthood is nothing other than the mystical representation of our warrior nature and its concomitant external phenomena, divine right is only the face of human right; better yet, it is its introduction, its instigator. So, we can lump them together, particularly because divine right, which we imagine we have done away with, is pretty much still the only one that governs us.

Some liberal braggarts reckon that they are beyond the reach of jurisdiction from above because, since the 1789 revolution guaranteed miscreants impunity, they consider themselves having outstanding courage by not doffing their cap to a passing emperor or a crucifix erected at a crossroads. Which is how the world came to see the people in 1793, having enacted the 21st of January, bestowing its repetitive applause upon, 31st May, 13th Vendémiaire, 18th Fructidor, 18th Brumaire, and, stumbling from *coup d'état* to *coup d'état*, finishing joyously in 1804 by saddling itself with a master more absolute than Louis XIV had ever been.[16] So, let us learn to appreciate our elders, they being our models to this very day.

What is the right of conquest, still so dear to all modern nations? Divine right. The people bows its head respectfully before battle orders. Such worship of strength is, deep down, less unreasonable and less inhuman than one might imagine; but we have to ask how and why? Our critique demands as much:

---

16. Louis XVI is executed on 21st of January 1793; on the 31st of May 1793 the armed sections overrun the Assembly and demand the arrest of the Girondin (moderate) deputies. The Mountain had the whip hand; on 13 Vendémiaire, Year IV (5 October 1795), the sections led by the bourgeois and the royalists rose up against the Convention, only to be seen off by Bonaparte who was in command of the artillery; on 18 Fructidor, Year V (4 September 1797) a coup d'état annulled the May elections won by the royalists in forty-nine departments and united military commissions to arrest and execute royalists and priests plotting against the Republic; on 18th Brumaire, Year VII (9th November 1799) Bonaparte mounted his own coup d'état and by appointing himself as First Consul made himself sole master of France. The Empire was proclaimed in May 1804. [H.T.]

without that, all the gains made in the name of revolution would be lost, liberty and nationality, and all the most sacred principles such as those over which the god Sabaoth[17] presided, will be incidents of war and myths, and yet we claim no longer to be governed by myths.

As it establishes and shapes the State, conquest conjures up the sovereign. Right now, we have before our eyes a striking instance of this in the person of Victor-Emmanuel.[18] Our idealist formalism is proven; conquerors are the only princes for whom the masses have any respect; peace-loving, weak ones are sneered at and held up to ridicule and dispatched to the scaffold or monastery. What does it signify if they were carried shoulder-high, as was done in the 1804 and 1852 elections?[19] War carries its entitlement, which is to say, its divine right. Clovis, founder of the Frankish monarchy, was war. His posterity has been written off as ne'er-do-wells; so much for peace. When Pepin[20] sounded Pope Zachary about the validity of his act of usurpation, what was the pontiff's response? Very straightforward, which it amazes me to find held up as a rebuke to the Pope: that, according to the laws of nature, royalty is the preserve of the strongest, given that royalty is power and divinity par excellence, the essential underpinning of divine right. The Merovingians, their courage grown flabby, had forfeited their dominion, authority, command and wealth. Everything had shifted to the major-domo; therefore the major-domo was king. In such instances, right followed upon fact: the Pope's pronouncement has nothing more to add to that. If force counts at all in human affairs, we have to acknowledge that that pronouncement was accurate.

Henri IV was legitimate: but what good would his birth-right have done him, what good would it have done him to attend Mass, had he not also had strength? Henri IV, the gentlest and most legitimate of princes, ruled by right of conquest; at that point he was fulsomely recognized by the people. No offence,

---

17. *Sabaoth* meaning the *host of heavenly spirits*. As applied to God, it is generally associated with the name Jehovah; *Jehovah Eloe Tsebaoth*, Eternal God of Hosts. [H.T.]

18. VICTOR EMMANUEL II (1820–1878), king of Piedmont. With the encouragement of his prime minister, CAMILLIO BENSO, COUNT DE CAVOUR (1810–1861), he made himself the hope of Italian liberals aspiring to the unification of the country. He annexed its hereditary states in Lombardy in 1859, following a war fought jointly with France against Austria; then central Italy in 1860, in the wake of popular unrest; in 1866 he conquered Venetia, by means of a further war on Austria driven by an alliance with Prussia; in 1870, the city of Rome and its territory were evacuated by French troops. Victor Emmanuel II, who had proclaimed himself king of Italy in 1861, successively moved his capital to Florence in 1864, and then Rome in 1871. His military panache earned him huge popularity. [H.T./A.P.]

19. The First Empire, 1804; the Second Empire, 1852. [H.T.]

20. PEPIN *LE BREF*, or the Short, was King of the Franks from 751–768 and father of Emperor Charlemagne. [A.P.]

but the people subscribes to the religion of force. It may well be in error; but let me just ask, how come it has erred over such a long time and with such obstinacy? Oddly enough, in 1814, the man with the divine entitlement was Napoleon, the conqueror; the man with human entitlement, the revolutionary, was Louis XVIII, author of the Charter. In the minds of the masses, which of these was accepted as legitimate?

Just as it has served as royalty's underpinning, so war serves as democracy's foundation. The Champ de Mai[21] was where the warriors mustered together; what was true of the Franks holds still truer for the French. By proclaiming every citizen a National Guard, the 1830 Charter[22] had implicitly determined that every citizen would be an elector; what you describe as political right is, in terms of its principle, nothing but the right of arms. And there is further evidence of this: military service aside, the entire merit of universal suffrage, rests upon this maxim, blithely rehearsed by our tribunes and which is unadulterated divine right: *Vox populi, vox Dei*.[23] Which, as we shall see, ought to be translated as: the right of peoples is the right of force.

The parliamentary principle of majority rule is a deduction from popular suffrage, be it universal or restricted, direct or indirect; does it not remain and is it not always the right of force? To be sure, force is something considerable in nature and which must be acknowledged: but what is the right of force? You jurists and philosophers do not believe in such a right. Tell me, then, how comes it that universal opinion subscribes to it so strongly?

The political constitution, in essence warmongering or founded on divine right, leads on to the civil law, the fulcrum of which is *property*. What is property, according to tradition and to the code? A working out of the right of conquest, *jus utendi et abutendi*.[24] For there is no point in our quibbling; in

---

21. The Champ de Mai (Mayfield) has two meanings. Traditionally, it occurred when the king of the Franks assembled his warriors as a means of marshalling his armies and as a gathering for the promulgation of new laws. Champ de Mai also refers to the public assembly held on 1 June 1815 by Napoleon I on the Champ de Mars, Paris, a large open area near the *École militaire* during the "Hundred Days". [H.T./G.H.]

22. Come the restoration of the monarchy in 1814, Louis XVIII bestowed upon the French people a Charter introducing a constitutional monarchy. In 1824, Charles X attempted to reintroduce a form of absolute monarchy. In 1830, Louis-Philippe, hoisted into power by the July Revolution, issued another charter approximating that of Louis XVIII. [H.T.]

23. "The voice of the people is the voice of god". [A.P.]

24. "The right to use and abuse". Proudhon is repeating the definition of property he had developed in 1840. See Pierre-Joseph Proudhon *What is Property? Or an Inquiry into the principle of Right and of Government*, trans. Donald R. Kelly and Bonnie G. Smith (Cambridge: Cambridge University Press, 1994/1840), Chapter II, §1. [A.P.]

the final analysis, we have to fall back upon Romulus's[25] definition. The ancient demarcations between patricians and plebeians, nobles and commoners, bourgeois and journeymen, has given way to the division into property-owners and wage-earners. The inequality of fortunes, that is to say of powers or faculties, neutralizing political inequality, can in turn be traced back to the honorific distinctions and titles of the nobility. Society revolves around the feudal principle, which is nothing more than the warrior idea, the religion of force. Well then, are we going to abolish property on the grounds that it, like monarchy, has warlike, divine origins?[26]

In rehearsing these facts, far be it from me to succumb to any critical intention. I take society just the way it is, neither approving nor disapproving of its institutions; and I ask whether, in the light of such general, such persistent, such perfectly connected facts as these, it is reasonable to label as chimerical, superstitious and fanatical an idea that has been a guide to the world for the past sixty or eighty centuries; which floods society the way the light of the sun floods the surface of the planet; which introduces order and security in peoples as well as planting dissension and revolutions; an idea that is all-encompassing, all-governing: GOD, FORCE and WAR; for it is becoming plain, as we make our way through this review, that, deep down, those three words are synonymous in the minds of the masses.

Let me move on.

It is by means of the ideas of sovereignty, authority, government, prince, hierarchy, classes, etc., that the notion of righteousness is embedded in the masses of humanity. Now, all of that is derived from the idea of an army and, consequently, forever implicit is the idea of warfare. Equality comes later: what is the meaning of equality? That every citizen is as entitled to wage war as any of his neighbours, or, to phrase that differently, that he is equally entitled to freedom of competition, guaranteed by the abolition of warranty marks and masterships.[27] Thus, *de facto* and *de jure*, the social state is always a state of war. In that, I am not advancing an argument of my own, I am merely spelling it

25. Romulus killed his twin brother Remus to become Rome's first king in 750 BC. So one legend has it, Romulus and his twin were sons of a virgin conception, between Rhea Silvia and Mars, the God of War. Fearing for their safety, their mother abandoned her children and they were nursed by a she-wolf. [A.P.]

26. In Book Four and Five, Proudhon argues that the origin of the state and private property is in plundering, conquest and war, and calls for the "transformation" of war in terms that echoed his call for the "transformation" of property in *What is Property?* (1840) [A.P.]

27. Would-be goods sellers had to obtain a *mastership* by making a masterpiece for submission to masters and jurors from the guilds. The oathsmen (*jurandes*) was a panel of jurors elected by the masters for the purpose of exercising a higher authority, chairing assemblies and seeing to it that the quality of manufactured goods lived up to the king's regulations. They were finally abolished in 1791. [H.T.]

out; and one would have to be willingly blind to query the accuracy of my exposition.

Yes, war dispenses justice, in spite of its witless detractors. It has its forms, its laws, its rituals which have made it the prime and most solemn of jurisdictions and from which the whole system of entitlement has derived: *The Right of war and peace; the Rights of peoples; public Rights; civil Rights; economic Rights; legal Rights.*[28] What is judicial debate? The word gives it away, it is an imitation of warfare, an un-bloody warfare, a *contest.* Why judges? Well, because in authentic armed conflict, victory attests to right; whereas in verbal sparring, one must have arbiters, of equal merit with the litigants, and who attest to and swear that righteousness, insofar as reason can determine, is on this side and not on that.

This affinity between justice and warfare is evident even in matters of an economic order, even though these may appear to be the very negation of it. Is slavery, upon which almost the whole of production among the ancients was based, not warfare?[29] And serfdom, which replaced slavery; and wage labour, which replaced serfdom; are these not still warfare? Are customs levies not warfare? The tension between capital and labour, between supply and demand, between lender and borrower, the entitlements of authors, inventors, improvers, and the penalties imposed on counterfeiters, forgers and plagiarists, do these not all point to warfare?

Behold a nation, deemed, once upon a time, one of the boldest and to-day the most industrious and powerful of all in terms of its capital, calling for wholesale disarmament and speaking out against war at every opportunity.

---

28. See below, Book Two, Chapter XI, "The Range of Rights." [H.M.]

29. Slavery is a persistent theme in Books One, Two and Four, and Proudhon's reading of the issue is classically republican in so far as it associates slavery with domination, warfare, plunder and state formation. In Book Two, Chapter X, he juxtaposes this "unadulterated right of force" with freedom through association and labour. Proudhon's abolitionism is nevertheless deeply racist, paternalist and Eurocentric. This is not uncommon, but where he differs from the republican norm is in his rejection of the need for a nation state to resolve the issue of slavery and domination in modern society. For Proudhon, legal emancipation is a truncated freedom. Positive freedoms require the resolution of the "social question", in particular "pauperism", caused by problems of association, production and exchange (Books Four and Five). Without republican responses to these problems, the proletarianization of slaves is inevitable, he argues. However, Proudhon displayed no understanding of the lived experiences of slaves, nor did he see slaves as agents of their own history. More research is needed in this area. See, Elisée Reclus, *Histoire de la guerre de sécession aux États-Unis (1861–1865)*, ed. Federico Ferretti (Paris: Pocket, 2016); Lewis Perry, *Radical Abolitionism: Anarchy and the Government of God in Antislavery Thought* (Ithaca: Cornell University Press, 1973); Ruth Kinna and Alex Prichard, "Anarchism and non-domination", *Journal of Political Ideologies* 24 no. 3 (2019): 221–40; Ruth Kinna, "What is Anarchist Internationalism?" *Nations and Nationalism* (forthcoming). [A.P.]

But is it actually doing anything other than changing its armour and challenging its rivals to a fresh contest, in which it believes itself assured of victory?[30] How on earth, I ask myself, did Portugal ever agree to peace with the English?[31]

The Emperor Napoleon I had a profound grasp of this, to us, paradoxical truth, that war, by which I mean war as conceived and affirmed by the conscience of the human race, and justice are one and the same. One of the aspects of his character was that, in equal measure with his fondness for displaying his force, he was jealous when it came to the assertion of his rights:

> Napoleon waged war in order to win kings and peoples over to his way of thinking; he was out to win them over; that was his innermost vow, his dearest wish. Embarking upon a campaign, he spelled out his intended purpose, the change that he meant to effect in the European economy, to the power he was attacking. He would beseech it to see reason; but was obliged to join battle; and, having won it, what did he want? To sign a peace in the foreign capital, content, delighted, and believing that he had convinced those whom he had defeated.[32]

The certain fact is that in Napoleon the urge to lay down the law was at least equal to the urge to fight; he had that much in common with all conquerors. Furthermore: the most warlike nations, which we have already identified as the most theological ones, are at the same time the most justice-dispensing ones. What would have become of civilization but for the Roman conquerors, by which I mean, Roman law? What would have become of Christianity, but for Charlemagne's pact? What has been European society's greatest achievement since that celebrated alliance between sword and mitre? Why, the Treaty of Westphalia,[33] which built the foundations of universal balance atop the con-

---

30. Proudhon is referring here to Richard Cobden's campaign on behalf of disarmament and the introduction of the principle of arbitration in international relations. At the Peace Congresses held in Paris (1849), in Frankfurt (1850), and in London (1851), Cobden suggested a universal peace based upon the expansion of trading relations and free trade. That campaign culminated in the commercial treaty between France and England that was signed in 1860. See below, Book Four, Chapter VIII. On Cobden, see Nicholas C. Edsall, *Richard Cobden, Independent Radical* (Cambridge, MA: Harvard University Press, 2014). [H.M./R.B.H.]

31. Portugal had secured England's backing against Spain in return for ceding Bombay and Tangiers. In 1703, that alliance was sealed by a trading treaty known by the name of its negotiator, Lord Methuen, and it reduced Portugal to a position of economic and political vassalage. [H.M.]

32. LERMINIER, *Philosophie du Droit*, 3rd edition, 1853, 58. [H.T.]

33. The 1648 Peace of Westphalia is the collective name for two peace treaties (Osnabrück and Münster) that brought the Thirty Years' War to an end and formally recognised

tending forces, and under the aegis of the god of hosts. Damn the publicists who cannot fathom these things! Damn the nations that misconstrue them! By stripping right of this ancient basis in force, there is reason to believe that that would be tantamount to turning force into the merely arbitrary; instead of peace, wealth and happiness, we would have been grappling with lifelessness, atrophy and dissolution.

---

the Protestant faith, leading to increased religious tolerance, and making "religious liberty a matter of international responsibility". Derek Croxton, "The Peace of Westphalia of 1648 and the Origins of Sovereignty", *The International History Review*, 21 no. 3 (1999): 569–82, quote at 575. [G.H.]

CHAPTER V

War as Revelation of the Ideal

There is no people that does not have its Bible or its *Iliad*. The epic is the popular ideal, outside of which a people has neither inspiration, nor national anthem, nor drama, nor eloquence, nor art. Now that epic is entirely founded upon warfare! ... What? Are you peace-loving sages going to let your zeal get the better of you and reduce poetry to the levels of Theocritus and Florian?[34] But you could not even manage that. Sweet pastorals need the contrast of scenes of warfare. Now do you have some sense of how essential war is to our nature, mindful that, but for it, not only might man never have conceived of religion and justice, but he would still be bereft of his aesthetic faculties and would not have been capable of producing and savouring the sublime and the beautiful?

But I must return to an objection that deserves to be answered once and for all.

I am told: "This is the same old sophistry: *Post hoc, ergo propter hoc*. Because man's primitive condition was savagery and warfare, you want to make warfare the principle, or, at the very least, the coefficient of everything that man has since dredged up from the treasury of his conscience and his reason. Because warfare was the first topic upon which religious, juridical, poetic thought was brought to bear, and because that topic has rubbed off on institutions and ideas, you would turn warfare from a mere accident of historical development into the formative principle behind civilization, the essence of humanity! That is too crude a sophistry to seduce anyone.

"That warfare has provided the subject matter for poetry is very plausible, given the precept":

> *No serpent nor odious monster is there*
> *That cannot be made a pleasant sight by an artist's impression*

---

34. THEOCRITUS (c. 300 BC). Greek poet regarded as the creator of the bucolic or pastoral genre. FLORIAN (1755–1794). Fabulist, songwriter and novelist whose works evinced a tender and naively idyllic sensibility. [H.T.]

"Does it follow that warfare has to be taken as the principle behind all poetry, if not of poetry per se? No, of course not: poetry has a life of its own; it is a prerogative of our natures, like reason, religion, work; a faculty to which war is offered, like everything else, as an aid to the composition of its pictures and its songs, but which is independent of warfare and which is perfectly understandable detached from any warlike accoutrements.

"Likewise, are we to conclude from what war has made available to the theology of symbols, the jurisprudence of formulas, the political economy of analogies and metaphors that it, war, conjured them into existence? Likewise, no. Religion and justice, like poetry, have existences of their own, predating any conflict; rather, it is to the primordial existence of religion and justice within us that war owes its reserved character, one that does not acknowledge the beasts and which, up to a point, mitigates the atrociousness of combat. If, in their jargon, theology and entitlement have borrowed anything from the practices of warfare, it is the mode of expression, a comparative terminology which they could very well have done without. Have you ever heard it said of two items being compared that one of them should have been deemed, by virtue of their being compared, the copy, or indeed the product of the other?...".

Those of my readers who raise this objection with me seriously cannot yet have understood me.

I realize that in everything one needs to consider the *substance* and the *form*, the *material* and the *work*; the objection raised with me boils down to precisely that. But I know too that, despite the distinction necessarily drawn between them, these terms are implied or imagined in such a way that form, in the absence of substance, or substance in the absence of form, substance in the absence of form or form in the absence of substance, is utterly meaningless. So, there is no religion in the absence of dogma, no justice without formula; likewise, no poetry in the absence of an idea and subject, and no art in the absence of mouldable substance.

Insofar as it affects RELIGION, JUSTICE and *War*, the first two of them deemed as the basis, and the last as the expression, symbol or formula, the question is, the issue, I say, is not how to distinguish between basis and form, but of first finding out if the substance could have existed in the absence of form; secondly, whether, having no existence in the absence of form, it could have assumed one other than has been bestowed upon it, which I emphatically deny. Likewise, as far as POETRY goes, it being deemed a faculty of the ideal, and *War* deemed a target for epic or artistic exploitation, the issue is no longer about making a broad distinction between the form and the substance, but of finding out whether poetry, the faculty for conjuring up the ideal, such idealization being in need of a material, living reality, could have fully manifested itself in the absence of war themes; which, again, I deny with all the strength of my conviction.

No, there is no religion, and more emphatically no theology, no worship, no priesthood and no Church, in the absence of this deep-seated tension that governs man and nature and which brings forth or, if one prefers, occasions suffering and sin, and which assumes the form of warfare where we mortals are concerned.

No, there is no justice, no jurisdiction, no authority, no legislation, no politics, no State outside of that very same tension which, in the absence of any other spur, we would merely have to seek the destruction of in order to cut it adrift in an instant. Where did it emanate from, that horrific communism that came about in 1848 and that plunged European society into a retrogression that of which we barely see the end? Analyse, summarize everything that has been spouted upon this matter and, at root, what do you find? This prodigious idea, of which no one, to be sure, was aware, namely: that in order to remain worthwhile, moral, pure, generous and, indeed, hard-working, society had, above all else, to cling to its tensions, to the state of war...

Well, the same holds for poetry and literature. War which is said to drive out the peaceful Muses is, instead, food and drink to them, the topic of their eternal conversation. The rivers of blood spilt by Bellona[35] are, as far as Apollo and those chaste sisters are concerned, the real Hippocrene.[36] Of all the subjects from which the poets, historians, orators, novelists draw their inspiration, the most inexhaustible, the most varied, the most affecting, the one that the multitude prefers and is forever clamouring for, and without which poetry loses its flavour and colour, is this one. Do away with the secret relationship that makes war an indispensable condition, in any way, of creations of the ideal and you will promptly discover the human soul diminished everywhere, individual and social life itself stricken with an unbearable pedestrianism. If war did not exist, poetry would invent it. Of course, the warrior's courage and the poetic flame should not be confounded; the statue is not the marble from which it has been carved. But if the artist came up with the idea for the statue, is that not partly because nature has provided the marble? Then go and make a Venus out of schist. Likewise, if the poet came up with the idea of his songs, is that not also because he had inside him something of the enthusiasm of which heroes are made, and in admiration of which war has been described as divine? I am, therefore, entitled to state, and I say again, that the most potent revelation of the ideal, as well as of religion and righteousness, is war.

---

35. BELLONA: The Roman goddess of war. [H.T.]

36. Renowned fountain in Attica around which, according to mythology, the Muses (the *Sisters*) liked to dance. To Greek and Roman poets, it came to symbolize inspiration. [H.T.]

In the estimation of all peoples, there is no more beautiful, no more magnificent sight than an army. The Bible could come up with no fitter comparison when it sought to depict the beauty of Shulamite woman: "Thou art beautiful, O my love", cried the husband in the *Song of Songs*,[37] "terrible as an army with banners". Which is why, in every land, the army holds pride of place in national festivities, in the pomp and circumstance of worship and the funerals of illustrious figures. Napoleon, who had been through so many battles, could not get enough of reviews and the people are the same. It is a positive thing that sensibility to beauty and art should develop within nations with the warrior spirit; it is no less true that where the latter dies out, poetry and the arts peter out. The centuries of masterpieces are centuries of victories. There is no poetry, no art for the defeated, any more than for the shopkeeper and the slave.

The modern world has before its eyes the spectacle of a society which, having sprung from vigorous stock, a bright and strong breed, placed in exceptional circumstances, has spent the past eighty years growing through the endeavours of peace alone. To be sure, the American is an indefatigable pioneer, a peerless *producer*. But apart from the produce of its farming and its industry, what has that youthful nation had to offer? Neither poets, nor philosophers, nor artists, nor politicians, nor legislators, nor captains, nor theologians: not one great achievement, not a single figure to represent humanity in the pantheon of history.

The American is wonderfully well versed in the production of wheat, maize, cotton, sugar, tobacco, steers and pigs. He makes money; he accrues wealth; he shapes the earth, and already depletes it, he builds cities, breeding and multiplying in such a way as to terrify the Malthusian school of thought.[38] But where is his idea? Where his poetry, or his religion or his social destiny, his purpose? Has he, on his free soil, learnt how to resolve the problem of labour, equality, social balance, harmony between man and nature? ... There is, to be sure, a need for man to house, clothe, feed, and afford himself some comfort: he takes care to save, to fill his barns and maintain his warehouses. But, my God, what to become, where to make towards? Would the already so-troubled American be able to tell us that? All of this is the wherewithal, the instrument of life; neither its purpose nor its import. Wealth! There is nothing easier to achieve where the land is plentiful, where man, blessed by virgin nature, looks to his fellow-man

---

37. *Bible*, The Song of Songs, 6:4. [H.T.]

38. THOMAS MALTHUS (1766–1834). English cleric and economist. He proposed the influential theory that the scarcity of food and its distribution was relative to the size of a population in a given, finite territory. This scarcity thesis became a central problem of liberal economics in the eighteenth and nineteenth century. Proudhon will refer to these economists as the Malthusians throughout this text. See also, Pierre-Joseph Proudhon "The Malthusians" (1848) in *Property is Theft!*, ed. Iain McKay, 353–58. [A.P.]

only to come to his aid. But there is nothing so susceptible to corruption, nothing less robust. Of itself, wealth counts for little; its value is bestowed by the mind that uses it, the heroism which it serves, the poetry that lights its way. It could be said of a nation that can only produce wealth that it has created and brought into the world to manufacture manure. From Washington to Franklin, America has a fine tradition of political and domestic probity; but Washington, an army general, is from the old world; as to Franklin, I do not envy the republic of the United States, that sort of utilitarian virtue. Even now, for all its immeasurable wealth, the vices of the civilization that American society has emerged from are jealously resurfacing; the proletariat is expanding; pauperism is starting to bite; slavery cannot be transformed there any more than it can be abolished; the coloured man, no matter how hard he may try to "pass" for white, is as much outcast by the North's hypocrisy as by the South's avarice. On the other hand, America had given us the séance table and the Mormons: *Risum teneatis.*[39] ... No, don't laugh, America feels her affliction and is stirring. Insolent, sneering and insatiable, she asks nothing better than to go to war; and if the foreigner lets her down, she will wage war on herself. God grant that the war may then rescue her, if she is still in time to equip herself through war with a faith, a law, a constitution, an ideal, a character.[40]

---

39. "Can you help but laugh?" [A.P.]

40. For some time now, it has been the fashion to make extravagant boasts about American civilization. In France this was an opposition stratagem, and unanswerable retort in favour of universal suffrage. As the proverb has it, *Everything new is beautiful.* Since then, it has been used as a way of denigrating European democracy – irreligious, materialistic, incapable of self-governance and unworthy of a free constitution. And so, every faction adds grist to the mill and tinkers with the truth.

Stunned by the apparent fruitfulness of marriages there as well the fertility of her countryside, the very first visitors from the old continent to the United States made much, upon their homecoming, of their admiration and the hospitality they had received. To hear them, and in actual fact they were not lying, never, in civilized memory, had anyone set eyes upon such expanses of still virgin soil; and, upon that soil, such vast, game-stocked forests, such verdant prairies, such abundant harvests secured with such little effort, such affordable arable land, such low-priced livestock, such a well-nourished population, children so happy to be alive, mothers so happy to carry them and, finally, settlers housed within a few leagues of one another and perfectly free in a land of which they could literally have called themselves the kings and boasted of having reaped its first fruits. Everything about the American that was exceptional was credited to his virtue. The greatest things were expected of him; except that it did not occur to anyone that that democratic virtue would flag as the population density grew and the day was not far off when these paragons of democracy would sink back into the vulgarity of their ancestors. Today, that enthusiasm is beginning to cool again, and one need not have gone strolling in Ohio or Niagara to get a better gauge of society in the United States and recognize the good points and the bad.

The people of the United States are not, in the historical and physiological sense of the word, a young people, any more than the one that has supplanted the native peoples of

Mexico, Bolivia and Brazil; it is an agglomeration drawn from every corner of Christendom and mainly from England and Germany. As a rule, these immigrants were not, of course, drawn from the elites of their respective nations; instead, most belonged to the ranks of the plebs. On arrival in America, what did they find? Land free for the taking all around them. With the exception of the two kingdoms of Mexico and Peru, destroyed by the Spaniards at the time of the discovery, no State had had the time to ensconce itself upon the new continent. The natives survived by hunting and fishing; the entire area occupied by the United States today was, so to speak, brand new. These were the circumstances in which the invader population settled in; one can readily appreciate the arrangements it was initially able to devise for itself in terms of intelligence and mores.

These immigrants having for the most part quit their homelands in order to escape from hunger and to seek their fortunes, it was only natural that their minds were applied mainly to everything that might afford them well-being and wealth. In every other area, they showed no initiative; they must have been all the more scornful of the ideas that had inspired so much agitation, so many revolutions in old Europe that they could, with some semblance of reason, have accused such ideas of futility. They had enough in the way of ideas; it was time to get down to the serious business of living and, consequently, producing. This is readily seen if we take a bird's eye view of America and its institutions. There is nothing over there that is native, not to mention not imported from Europe; religion, politics, government, prejudices and languages, and trifles such as tastes and fashions. Whether the stock transplanted from Europe to the United States will ever boast a character, a genius or faculties of its own – the sort of things found in all Old World natives and as can still be found in the three quarters-gone peoples of the New – I could not say. Man is to the country where he lives and which has produced him as the soul is to the body; they are made for one another, each being the expression of the other. What does appear to be beyond doubt is that it will take centuries before the American has matched his nature to that of his soil and his climate; before he has grown himself a soul, a thought, a genius attuned to his continent; before he has achieved that nativeness without which man, an outsider in his own surroundings, is like the soul of a Plato ordered by God, after its separation from the body that served as its vehicle, to inhabit the body of a tyrant from Sudan or Dahomey. Until such time as the American has achieved such naturalization, he is going to be nothing more than a branch broken off from the Indo-Germanic trunk and, so to speak, exiled from high civilization. Without the influence of nativeness operating on his being, the living spirit of traditions petering out or diminishing to vague and distant recollections, there has to be an ensuing degeneration in everything to do with social living. To cite but one example of this, the American people which started out with the most absolute freedom (albeit a negative freedom) has not at all abided by the trend from which it emerged. Similarly, its religion, rather than leading toward practical philosophy, has lapsed into superstition and gloom, just as his supposed democratism has ground to a halt in the most abject individualism. Finally, the idea of economic Right, the idea of humanity's social constitution, of equality and fraternity for all men has not surfaced in the United States. The proud Yankee has not the slightest suspicion of the transformation which is looming in old Christendom, the benefits of which his offspring shall some day enjoy without having had any inkling of their approach.

The impoverishment we have just identified in the American in terms of spirit is palpable in terms of mores. Ultimately, what is American society? A pleb suddenly enriched. Now, far from rendering the common man more urbane, wealth most often merely throws his uncouthness into relief. Talleyrand's canard about the Americas is well known: I shall not repeat it, but there is undeniably some truth to it. The American people further exaggerate

What have I said! I would snap my pen in two before I would breathe any discord into peaceful populations. I warn my readers, I too shall conclude by opposing the war-mongering *status quo*, opposing the institutions of militarism,[41] opposing its poetry, opposing its mores. But the fact is that I believe, not in the abolition but rather in the transformation of war and by that alone to a complete renovation of humanity's circumstances in everything relating to religion, ideas, rights, politics, arts, work, family and urban relations. But for my heartfelt belief in the Revolution, I would refrain, as I would from blasphemy, from uttering a word against war: I would regard the devotees of perpetual

---

the utilitarian mind of the English people, from which most of them come; in it, British pride has turned into insolence; lack of refinement into brutality. Freedom, for the American, is definable as: *the ability to do anything that is disagreeable to others*. – LOOK TO YOUR OWN DEFENCES, is its maxim. I will openly admit that in order to get the better of an uncouth individual, my preference is for the help of the gendarme and, if need be, the gaoler; that is all uncouthness deserves. You can be killed, robbed, murdered: look to you own defences! In certain instances, we have Lynch law, I believe they call it. At the insistence of the public, the culprit is arrested, tried and strung up; all in a matter of a few minutes. This was the people's justice during the February incidents; it is the justice of councils of war too. I would rather trial by jury.

The American sees no disgrace in bankruptcy, even fraudulent bankruptcy, no matter the scale of the fraud (*Revue britannique*). European businessmen know what American *crises* are all about.

On arrival in Europe and stepping into a hotel lounge, the American makes to remove his boots in front of the fire; he puts his feet up on the fireplace, stinking out his neighbours, hogs to himself whichever dishes take his fancy at table and arranges them in front of himself, as if they were shop goods and indulges himself in all manner of such vile behaviour. Is he not a free man? And is the *table d'hôte* not a marketplace? Is he not paying for all his purchases? Follow his example: look to your defences. One respectable English lady of letters so captivated them that they began, so it is said, to spruce themselves up a little. A number of these adventurers then reverted to savages, throwing themselves with gusto into forest living. They are heroic murderers: I should like to know if they would hold the line if faced by our civilized soldiery.

The real merit of American society is the family life developed to the highest degree and surrounded by all sorts of assurances and which could easily be made into a substitute for religion, once education has spread the philosophical spirit further through the masses. Add to this an excessive freedom, the ridiculousness of which is easily corrected, but which seems to me destined to serve as a counterweight to the Old Continent's monarchical, communist and governmentalist instincts which, in this regard, wields a powerful influence over civilization generally even now. It is through these two great forces, family and freedom, rather than through her political energy and fabulous wealth that North America can expect to balance Europe this century. The future will decide upon the rest. [P-J.P]

41. Proudhon is here coining the neologism militarism. By this he means the conjoining of social, political with military values, and their deployment in public policy. The concept is more fully fleshed out, and linked to "governmentalism" and "social economy", at the end of Chapter X, Book Four below. See, Volker Berghahn, *Militarism: The History of an International Debate 1861–1979* (Cambridge: Cambridge University Press, 1981), 7. [A.P.]

peace as the most despicable of hypocrites, the scourge of civilization and a blight upon societies.

CHAPTER VI

War, the Discipline of Humanity

No longer is it the people's instinct, no more the legend: it is for philosophy incarnate, Hegel,[42] to now have his say:

> "War" – he tells us – "is indispensable for the moral advancement of humanity. It throws our virtue into relief and sets a seal upon it; it re-tempers nations made soft by peace, consolidates States, bolsters dynasties, puts races to the test, awards dominion to the most deserving and spreads movement, life and flame to everything within society".[43]

There would need to be a lot of truth in this bellicose philosophy for a

---

42. FRIEDRICH HEGEL (1770–1831) identifies the real with the rational, and being with thinking, all amalgamating into a single, universal principle: the idea. There are three aspects to the latter. It is posited (*thesis*), runs into opposition (*antithesis*) and then resolves itself by reconciling thesis and antithesis (*synthesis*). The notion that all that is real is rational leads him towards this conclusion: *History is the expansion of the universal mind over time.* The State stands for the idea; it represents the substance to which its citizens are merely incidental. Strife between peoples represents different paths leading to the realization of the idea. Force, therefore, betokens right. This view of the history of right leads to the negation of freedom of the individual. Conservatives, Catholics, and Orthodoxes on the one hand, plus socialists and Marxists on the other, will be heavily influenced by this thinking. [H.T.]

Proudhon's method was antinomic, not dialectic, borrowing more from Kant than he did Hegel. In Proudhon's system, the terms of the antinomy are real, not only ideal, and they perpetually re-balance as our scientific understanding of the nature of phenomena evolves. While there has been considerable discussion of Marx's use of the dialectic, less has been written on Proudhon's method. An exception is the work of the Jesuit, Henri de Lubac. See, *Un-Marxian Socialist: A Study of Proudhon* (Octagon Books, 1978). [A.P.]

43. Hegel, *Philosophie des Rechts, 3er;* THEIL, 3e Absch. II, § 324; WERKE, vol. VIII, 409–413; *Phénoménologie des Geistes,* II, §§ 546–48. Also see Victor COUSIN, *Cours de philosophie,* 1828. General von Clausewitz's major work, *Vom Kriege,* had been translated into French by a Belgian officer, Major Neuens (1849–1851). [H.M.]

It is not clear if Proudhon had read Clausewitz's *On War,* though its themes of strategy, virtue and the transformation of war echo in this work. [A.P.]

peace-lover like, Ancillon,[44] a minister of the Holy Gospel, inimical to war by calling and profession, to have associated himself with it:

> "Peace" – he states – "leads on to opulence; opulence multiplies the pleasures of the senses and indulgence of those pleasures leads to softness and selfishness. Acquisition and enjoyment become everyone's motto; souls become irritable and characters go into decline. Warfare and the misfortunes it brings in its wake exercise the manly, sturdier virtues; but for it, courage, patience, steadfastness, devotion, contempt for death would perish from the earth. Even those recruits not participating in the fighting learn to brave privations and to make sacrifices ... In a people civilized to the point of corruption, it is occasionally necessary for the entire State to collapse, so that public spirit can experience a revival; and there are grounds for saying what Themistocles used to tell the Athenians: *We were perishing, if not perished!*"[45]

M. le Comte de Portalis, in a memorandum addressed to the Toulouse Academy,[46] expressed himself in much the same terms as Ancillon. His opinion deserves notice, precisely because the author's purpose in putting pen to paper was to challenge de Maistre's theory regarding the providential nature and divinity of war:

> The inescapable outcome of the play of the human passions in the dealings between nations, war, is, in the schemes of Providence, a mighty agent employed sometimes to inflict harm and sometimes as a reparative tool. War successively builds and overthrows (like the Jehovah of Deuteronomy), in turn, destroying and rebuilding States. At once prolific in calamities and in improvements, slowing down, interrupting or accelerating progress or decline, it imprints upon an incipient civilization, is eclipsed and reborn, only to be eclipsed yet again, that fateful movement that sets in motion all of the potential and faculties of human nature in turn, by means of which

---

44. JEAN-PIERRE ANCILLON (1767–1837), the Berlin-born son of French refugees, was a pastor with the Reformed Church and minister of Foreign Affairs in Prussia (1831). The work cited by Proudhon was published in Berlin in 1803, earning him Europe-wide celebrity and opened the doors of academia to him. [H.T.]

45. Ancillon, *Tableau des révolutions du système politique en Europe*, Vol. I, 35 (Berlin 1803) et seq., 5 volumes in 8°, Vol. I, foreword, LIV–LV (and not p. 35). [P-J.P]

46. PORTALIS, *Mémoire sur la guerre considérée dans ses rapports avec les destinées du genre humain*. (Séances et Travaux de l'Académie des Sciences morales et politiques, vol. XXXVIII, 45). Proudhon is quoting from the Martens edition [translated by Vergé], vol. II, 200. [H.M.]

the lifespans of empires and the prosperity of nations follow one upon the other and are measured.

Thus, the Protestant doctrinarian Ancillon, the mystical constitutionalist Portalis, and the idealist Hegel join hands with the Catholic feudalist de Maistre: something that we are all the more entitled to be surprised at when the first of them, with his system of counter-forces, the second with his attachment to representative forms, the third by his *a priori* theory of right, likewise tend to create a system for the curtailment of war among civilized nations. Warfare, these authors cry in unison, is by its very nature a bad thing; but is providentially, or, to put it a better way, prophylactically necessary for humanity, which it preserves against corruption the way discipline protects the religious from laxity, the way the cane cures the schoolboy of his bad inclinations, the way a bitter medicine purges the ailing. Warfare remakes us through combat, *castigat pugnando mores*; it is the counterpart of comedy, which chastizes us by means of ridicule.

But I doubt the reader will be content with these rather mystical, superficial and even declamatory considerations, in spite of the gravitas of the authors furnishing them to me. Citing the lofty virtues of which war is the occasion, the regret it generates and the rehabilitation to which it may lead,[47] just to conclude that it is morally and politically effective; would that not amount to using the same sort of logic as the theologian who, after having made his deduction from what he calls the established fact of our original sin, that we are in need of redemption, and goes on to deduce, equally logically, that original sin is necessary for Jesus Christ's mission here on earth and the sublimeness of his sacrifice, to which the Gospels bear witness? Happy the sin, he would cry out, that earned us the Redeemer's coming and victory![48] If we want to stay away from that vicious circle, we must establish warfare's proper virtue in terms of the conservation and betterment of mores, after which we will be entitled to say that the greatness and shortcomings of States depend upon what Providence ordains, which sometimes delivers them up to the delights of peace and sometimes imposes the manly tests of war upon them.

In any organized being, the primary condition of life, health and strength is action. It is through action that it develops its faculties, boosts its energy and achieves the full measure of its fate.

The same goes for the intelligent, moral, free being. The essential condition of life for him too is action, intelligent, and of course, moral action, since what is at stake here is primarily of an intellectual and moral order.

47. Rehabilitation: Acceptance of repentance; deigning to forgive a failing. [H.T.]
48. This is a paraphrase of a Church prayer: *o felix culpa quae talem tantum meruit habere redemptorem* (Office for Holy Saturday). [H.M.]

What, then, does it mean to act?

Before there can be any action, physical, intellectual or moral activity, there must be a context relative to the actor, an "other" that stretches out before the ego as a locus and wherewithal for action, one that resists and stands in contradiction to him. So action is going to be a contest: to act is to fight.

As an organized, intelligent, moral and free being, man is therefore caught up in a contest, which to say an action-and-reaction relationship, first of all with nature. Even there, he will find more than one occasion to display his courage, his patience, his contempt for death, his commitment to his own glory and the happiness of his neighbours, in short, his virtue.

But man's dealings are not with nature alone; along the way he also meets his fellow man, who contests his ownership of the world and the approval of other men, who engage him in competition, who contradict him and, as a sovereign, independent power, they use their *veto* against him. This is inescapable and it is a good thing.

On the one hand, I say it is inescapable. In fact, there is no chance of two creatures, in whom science and awareness are on the increase but which do not march in step, who, subscribe to differing views on every issue, who have opposing interests and who strive after infinite growth, ever seeing entirely eye to eye. Divergent ideas, contradictory principles, controversy, the clash of opinions are the certain outcome of their coming into contact.

I added, besides, that this is a good thing. It is by means of diversity in opinions and feelings and through the tension which it generates that a new world, the world of social interactions, the world of right and liberty, the political world, the moral world comes into being, atop the organic, speculative and affective world. But, before the interaction, there must, of necessity, be a contest; before the peace treaty, the duelling, warfare and, this is always the case, at every instant of life.

Genuine human virtue is not entirely negative. It does not consist solely of abstaining from all the things that are condemned by law and morality; it consists also, and to a much greater extent, of the deployment of energy, talent, determination and character against the over-reach of all those persons who, by their very existence, have a tendency to overshadow us. *Sustine*, the Stoic says, *et abstine*: uphold, which is to say, fight, resist, use force and conquer, which is the first and most essential aspect of life, *hoc est primum et animum mandatum*: abstain, being the second. How far will this duelling go? In certain cases, to the very death of one of the parties; such is the answer of nations. And all of this without injustice, without treachery, without outrage and, by the mere effect of this law of nature which makes us struggle, even armed struggle, even, in certain cases, to the bitter end, a condition of life and virtue. The warrior who insults his foe, who uses unlawful weapons against him, or devices that honour forbids, is dubbed a war criminal: he is a murderer.

Thus, war is inherent in humanity and must live as long as it does; it is a part of morality, independently even of the manner of its manifestation, of the rules governing combat, of the determination of the *rights* of the victor and the *obligations* of the vanquished. Not only does it not fade, albeit that, like everything having to do with humanity, its aspect and character change over time; but, like fire, it stops only when it has run out of fuel; like life, which peters out only for want of sustenance, war proliferates and is aggravated between peoples in keeping with their religious, philosophical, political and industrial development; it seems as if only extinction of the moral life itself can extinguish it. The very same organic and animal causes that create contradiction and antagonism between us wish this antagonism to be eternal, wish it to spread through the acquisition of knowledge and talents, of the interests and self-esteem at stake, and the contending passions.

Moreover, it must be understood that throughout all this, virtue and honour have to be kept safe. Warfare has nothing in common with acts that ordinary morality reproaches; nothing that might fall under the remit of the criminal courts belongs in its armoury. There is no warfare, no duelling between the scoundrel and the honest man; above all else, *God's judgment*, as it used to be called, stipulates honesty, fealty and a clear conscience. This is the virtuous, chivalrous side of warfare that has gone unnoticed by Hobbes who, after having astutely acknowledged that war is immanent within humanity, and, so to speak, the latter's natural state, promptly contradicts himself by contending that that state of nature is a brutish condition, that war is evil and mischievous and, in a new contradiction, claims that the State has been devised for the sole purpose of preventing it.[49] As if the study of politics, of the rights of peoples, as if the necessary dealings of nations, as if their annals did not bear witness, instead, that the State was created as much for the purposes of external warfare as for internal order!

But, the objection goes, if warfare between the subjects of the same State has ceased, why might it not be ended between the States themselves? Which is what Hobbes was trying to say, and his thinking has been espoused by all the publicists.

If warfare, still extant between nations, rarely erupts in the form of bloodshed between private individuals, this can be put down to, on the one hand, the growth of civil law, which has no use for combat in interactions and the settling of disputes; and, on the other, to the conditions of the political order, which

---

49. *De Cive,* chap. I, §§ VI–XV; chap. V, §§ VI–XII. See below, Book Two, Chapter VI. [H.M.]

can only survive and weather attacks from without, if the citizenry abjures all private warfare and, where nations are concerned, makes the privilege of seeking justice with weapons in hand the preserve of the State. Now, it is far from being the case, as we shall demonstrate later, that all matters of contention between States can be amicably settled through straightforward arbitration; much less that said States can defer to a common authority that sits in judgment of the differences between them. It was long the case, the duration of which period we today would still not dare to pronounce is over, that nations had to settle their differences by resorting to force; that sort of resolution was, as far as they were concerned, the only judge, the only rationale, the only honourable course. From which it follows that war, which, between one citizen and another, underwent and had to undergo a complete metamorphosis, neither had nor was able to undergo the same transformation between nations. And which of us would dare guess the date appointed by fate for that great overhaul? Who could guarantee us that on the day that peace might, through some arbitrary force and contrived combination, be concluded and consolidated between the powers; might war not flare up again between individuals and in a fiercer, more bitter and no doubt less chivalrous manner?

Let us therefore conclude with the mystics Ancillon, de Maistre, Portalis and the materialist Hobbes, but in the name of a higher reason to which neither mysticism nor materialism could possibly attain, that war, in one form or another, is essential to our humanity; that it represents a vital, moral aspect thereof. But for amendments made to it in terms of substance and form and advances in science and morals, it is as much a property of civilization as of barbarism, and, in all these aspects, the most grandiose manifestation of our individual and social existence. Strength, bravery, virtue, heroism, the sacrifice of assets, liberty and life and, more precious than life itself, the joys of love and family, labour's well-deserved rest, the honours of genius and the city; these are what warfare conjures up in us and the sublimeness of virtue to which it summons us.

CHAPTER VII

The Warrior, Greater than Nature

It is primarily through the exaltation of a manly figure that war manifests its prestige. Man, armed, seems larger than nature; he feels worthier, prouder, more alive to his honour, more capable of virtue and commitment. Without as much as his uttering a word, without his making a move, an aura of glory seems already to surround him. "Strap your sword on your hip, O most mighty; with thy glory and thy majesty". These were the terms in which the Hebrew bard addressed the young king: *Accinge gladio tuo super femur tuum, potentissime; specie tua et pulchritudine tua intende!*[50]

Among the ancients, the warrior was the friend, the *protégé* of the heavenly powers. His courage came to him from on high; a god covered him with his shield, rendering him invincible and invulnerable. "Touch not mine anointed", said Jehovah,[51] the god of hosts. His anointed! Hear that? The anointing or consecration of the warrior, the tattoo, still in vogue among our soldiers and sailors, is the sign of divine protection. The anointing of the warrior sets the pattern for that of the priest; and as Volney has very shrewdly observed,[52] the anointing of kings is a further imitation. The warrior is hallowed for his defence of righteousness, his punishment of crime and his protection of the weak: that was the earliest form of justice in society. Prior to the organization of the State, there was chivalry, one might even say errant justice. Which is why the warrior marches with head held high, his cap topped with a plume, his breastplate sparkling. He does not hide within the crowd, does not use his mercenary's cassock as a disguise. His entire craving is to be recognized from afar, to measure himself against an adversary beloved of the gods, δηιον

---

50. *Bible,* Psalm 45:3. [P.S.]

51. *Bible,* Book of Chronicles, 16:22. [H. M.]

52. CONSTANTIN FRANÇOIS DE CHASSEBŒUF, COMTE DE VOLNEY (1757–1820). An erudite traveller, in 1789 he became Anjou's third estate's representative to the Estates-General. Clerk of the Assembly in 1790, he turned down the position of Interior minister offered to him by Bonaparte under the Consulate. Under Louis XVIII, he openly retained his attachment to notions of freedom. Proudhon's reference is to Chapter XIII of *The History of Samuel, Inventor of the Consecration of Kings* (1819). [H.T.]

ανδρα, and to be worthy of him, standing in the sunlight between the two armies.

Glory be the war-maker and him alone: the word and the thing were invented for him. When the sacred author tells of the glory of God, he is making a comparison between Him and the warrior. The people look to that predestined one for their salvation and have faith in him alone. Philosophy piques the people's interest, provided it can make itself understood; the poet touches and delights it, but only the warrior can get it to follow him, because, in the people's eyes, he alone seems superhuman in stature. Was it Mazzini, a missionary,[53] or was it Monsieur Cavour, a diplomat, that swept the Italians along last year? No, it was a hero, Garibaldi.[54] The people always magnifies and idealizes its men; above all, it remembers to dress them in helmet, sword and buckler. It makes them handsome, valiant and victorious. Ah! If only Robespierre had known how to ride on horseback! If only Girolamo Savonarola[55] had donned the breastplate of a Trivulce, a Gonzalo and a Bayard rather than his Dominican's cloak! ... Ah! If only the Papacy had, like the Caliphate, carried the sword that spills blood and the sword of excommunication in the same hand! ... Ah, had the Nazarene, whose words enthralled the multitudes, but managed to bestow the sanction of arms upon his religion! ... Greatness on that scale is not bestowed upon mere mortals: the qualities of hero and saint, of emperor and of pontiff cannot coexist within the same person. Also, how crestfallen the masses are when the action that erupts does not conform as closely as they might prefer to the message. What a furore there was at first, when, instead of the warrior foretold by the sibyls, the missionaries of the Gospel held up their crucified master for mortals to worship! Jesus, the Christ of the slaves, long-suffering, weaponless and nailed to a gallows, Jesus was dismissed as Anti-Christ. As far as the masses are concerned, Alexander, Caesar, Charlemagne and Napoleon, these are the true Christs.

---

53. Proudhon's opinion of GUISEPPE MAZZINI (1807–1872) and the other leaders of the *Risorgimento* were first formed during his time imprisoned in Saint Pélagie (1849–1852). During this incarceration he struck up a close friendship with the noted Italian federalist GIUSEPPE (JOSEPH) FERRARI (1812–1876), who would convince him to combine federalism with his anarchism; he also wrote three books, was married and conceived his first child. [A.P.]

54. The reference here is to the Expedition of the Thousand by means of which Garibaldi liberated Sicily from the Spanish and made himself master of Sicily and the kingdom of Naples in 1860. [H.M.]

55. GIROLAMO SAVONAROLA (1452–1498). Dominican preacher who endowed Florence with a new semi-democratic, semi-theocratic constitution (1495). He sought to foist a sort of quasi-monkish lifestyle on the Florentines and this split the people into two factions. He was excommunicated and arrested under the lordship of Florence, then burnt alive. [H.T.]

The word *hero*, which we have borrowed from the Greek, is an augmentative meaning strong man, committed man, fearless and irreproachable. He had a god on his side, a god oversees his every action. He himself is the son of gods and he partakes of both natures. The dogma of the incarnation sprang from this notion of heroism.

Cara Deûm soboles, magnum Jovis incrementum.[56]

The natural judge of man is woman. Now what does woman prize above all else in her partner? The worker? No; the warrior. A woman may like a hard-working, industrious fellow for a servant, a poet or an artist as an adornment, a sage as a rarity; she respects the just man, the rich man will win her favour, but her heart belongs to the soldier. In a woman's eyes, the warrior is the very ideal of manly dignity. It is when she glimpses him armed for combat that she calls him her lord, her baron, her knight, her conqueror. And since love shows itself through imitation, she too wants to be a warrior, a heroine; she turns into an amazon. For every single god of war, like Ares or Mars, there are four goddesses like Bellona, Pallas, Diana the Huntress and Venus, yes, Venus herself, the *Bellatrix*.

"Mars was ever the friend of Cytherea",[57] said Voltaire. That frivolous poet did not think that he was giving expression to so serious a thought. What a story it is, the tale of Abigail, wife of Nabal the wealthy man, and of David, the vagabond warrior, the penniless king, the homeless conqueror.[58] The whole of the bourgeoisie is mad about uniforms. When it comes to following her hero, woman acknowledges neither danger nor vow. O Jupiter! You alone were to blame for the misfortunes of Vulcan. What were you, the *paterfamilias*, thinking of when you gave Venus over to a blacksmith?[59]

---

56. VIRGILE, Eclogues IV. [H.M.] At source: "cara deum soboles, magnum Iovis incrementum!" Trans: "dear offspring of the gods, mighty seed of a Jupiter to be!". From *Virgil. Volume I: Eclogues. Georgics. Aeneid: Books 1–6*, trans. H. Rushton Fairclough, revised G. P. Goold (Cambridge, MA.: Harvard University Press, 1999), 52–53. [A.P.]

57. CYTHEREA: Aphrodite, goddess of beauty and love. [H.T.]

58. *Bible*, Book of Samuel, 25. [H.T.]

59. War conjures up a colossal and irretrievable inequality between man and woman. For anyone who has once and for all grasped this great law of our nature, war, the fact of woman's unsuitability in warfare speaks volumes. Woman only truly exists in the family context. Outside of it, all her worth is borrowed; she cannot be anything and has no entitlement to amount to anything, for the crucial reason that she is not suited to combat. Among the supporters of equality of the sexes, some, basing themselves on ingenious fictions, have claimed that woman could, equally as man, serve as a national Guard, horse- or infantry-soldier and have not hesitated to issue her with cape and sword. But military uniform will, as far as woman is concerned, never amount to anything other than a lover's disguise, a genuine act

The people are of a mind with women. The man of war is noble everywhere; he represents a caste. The slave has no entitlement to lay a finger on
weapons; he would be dishonouring combat. If his master would but allow him
to arm himself, that very act alone would make him a free man; what is more, it
would bestow nobility upon him.

The Revolution had done away with the nobility: in their zeal, the men
of 1789 flattered themselves that they were closing down the temple of Janus
and bringing the warrior age to an end. Napoleon revived the nobles: a warrior himself, he was abiding by his principle, just as the Revolution had had to
abide by its. What was left of the nobility following the Tennis Court Oath,
following the night of 4th August, by which time the Third Estate, the worker
and the bourgeois were everything? Nothing, anymore. But by 1805, amid the
fire of battles, the situation had altered. Therefore, the people assented to the
restoration of nobility and the establishment of the Legion of Honour as acts of
lofty justice. Whoever says army, says nobility: except that whereas hitherto nobility and warfare had meant caste privileges, these had, thanks to conscription,
become accessible to all Frenchmen by 1805. What a triumph for the multitude
it was to hail its own flesh and bone in a Duc de la Moskowa, a Prince d'Essling,
a King of Naples![60]

Little wonder, after everything that I have just been saying, that the head
of State must always be, in the estimation of the people, a warrior, the prince
of heroes, the strongest of the strong men, the noblest of the noble ones? The
1814 Charter, the 1830 one, just like the Constitutions of 1791, 1799 and 1804
enshrined this principle: "The king or the emperor has command of the armies".

Napoleon said, shortly after his arrival on Saint Helena: "We shall see
now what Wellington is going to do".[61] His understanding was that Lord

---

of worship offered by the weaker sex to the stronger. History has its Joan of Arcs; for every
heroine, there are heroes by the millions. Others have sought to circumvent this difficulty
by purely and simply denying war and making the abolition of it into the emblem of wom-
en's accession to civil and political equality; which amounts to postdating the timing of that
accession to the Greek kalends. Let them do better: instead of stripping man of his warrior
attributes, let them strip him here and now of the seal of his manliness. But then women will
have no further grudge against him; indeed, what would they love if they no longer loved
anyone stronger than themselves? [P-J.P.]

60. Ney, the Duke of Elchingen and Prince of La Moskowa, was the son of a cooper from
Sarrelouis. Masséna, Duke of Rivoli, Prince of Essling, had started out as a cabin boy before
becoming an NCO in the Royal Italian Navy for fourteen years. He was the son of a vintner
from the Nice area. Murat, the king of Naples, was the son of an innkeeper in a village in the
Quercy region. [H.M.]

61. Cf. P.-J. Proudhon, *Parallèle entre Napoléon et Wellington,* published by Cl. Rochel, in
Commentaires sur les mémoires de Fouché, 1 vol. in-8°, 1900. For Napoleon's views regarding the
government of England and its commercial policy, see *Mémorial:* 7th September 1816. [H.M.]

Wellington, as England's leading general, having won the victory for her, ought to have lorded it over the government. This epic figure had no understanding of shopkeeper England's *bourgeois character*, which the 1848 Republic tried, albeit in vain, to import into this country. Pity would have moved him to laughter at the sight of a French assembly appointed by means of universal suffrage, gravely determining by way of an article in its Constitution, that the president of the Republic could not exercise *personal* command of the army.[62] In the belief that they had arrived at liberty's golden age, the republicans had sought to make the head of State merely a civil magistrate. Which led to a huge furore when Louis-Napoleon turned out for the reviews in Satory in general's uniform. But the real authors of the furore were the authors of that Constitution which, by dint of that curious reservation, flew directly in the face of popular sentiment and, I dare say, reason itself. At a time bristling with war-mongering notions, a head of State who was not a general was a nonsense. That was the people's view. Within that view, an underlying reason behind Louis-Napoleon's transition from dark-suited president to grand-epauletted emperor has passed unnoticed.

The Latin *imperator*, emperor, is the grammatical equivalent of the Greek *tyrannos* or *kyranos*, master, boss, commander, from which we get *tyrant*. How is it the Latin term sits so well with us when the Greek one is looked at askance? Does the blame lie exclusively with Plato who, as he was writing in favour of government by aristocrats, and bent on discrediting plebeian tyranny, depicted the tyrant as a sort of a monster?[63] There is a possibility that Plato may have had a point there; but there is a consideration which Plato did not mention; that the emperor is an army general, whereas the other is a chief of administration and police, a burgomaster. Weapons are suggestive of despotism; between equals, command is odious and out of place. Which is why the French people has no respect for its representatives and likewise for its constitutional kings. Did we not hear Louis-Philippe dismissed as a tyrant? He was nothing more than the king of civilians... *Glory to God, Honour to arms!* Once upon a time that motto was on display in every fencing room. The people's wit went further; it blended scales and sword into a single emblem. Do not go telling it that the warrior's sword must be lowered when faced with magistrate's toga, *cedant arma togae.*[64] It might well retort that you have no Latin: that in Rome, justice and warfare were not, as they are among us, two powers and that the poet was merely trying to use those words to indicate the ranking within the same men,

---

62. On the basis of Armand Marrast's report, the Constituent Assembly passed this amendment to the 1848 constitution. [H.M.]

63. Plato, *Republic*, Book IX. [H.M.]

64. "Yield, ye arms, to the toga; to civic praises, a ye laurels". Cicero, *On Duties*, Translated by Walter Miller, (Cambridge MA.: Harvard University Press, 1913), 78–79. [A.P.]

inside every citizen, of the peaceful and warrior callings. Judge, general and, if need be, like a dictator, that is what the people reckons its leader is. Happy, therefore, thrice happy is the nation whose leader is at once the bravest and the most just! Which has only been witnessed twice in modern times, in the shape of Gustavus Adolphus[65] and George Washington.

---

65. Gustav of Sweden (1594–1632), known in English as Gustav II Adolf [or Adolph], was King of Sweden from 1611 to 1632. He is also known as Gustav the Great. [H.T.]

CHAPTER VIII

War and Peace, Correlative Terms

How could men not wage war when their heads are full of it; when their understanding, their imagination, their dialectic, their industry, their religion, their arts are drawn to it; when within them and surrounding them, all is opposition, contradiction and antagonism?

But there is, opposed to warfare, a no less mysterious divinity, no less venerated by mortal men: PEACE.

The idea of universal, everlasting peace is as old and as categorical in the consciousness of nations as that of warfare. Out of that conception sprang, first, the fable of Astraea,[66] the heavenly virgin who returned to Heaven at the end of Saturn's reign, but who is someday due to reappear. Whence she will reign over an endless, serene peace, as pure as the light playing over the Elysian Fields. That is the fateful time towards which our aspirations carry us and where the trend of events is steering us, according to some forecasters of progress. As time slips by, and as warfare becomes more furious and the horrors of the iron age are redoubled, then *armorumque ingruit horror*,[67] as the poet has it. Peace becomes the favoured goddess, just as we begin to despise war, that hellish ogre. This turning of minds in the direction of peace, this ancient aspiration to a dampening-down of discord, may in part have been due to the messianic movement, in which Augustus was the main actor, Virgil the eulogist, the Gospels the code and Jesus Christ the God.

How much truth is there in this inkling which the prognosticators flatter themselves they are seeing realized every time humanity is faced with a huge crisis?

War and peace, which the common man views as two mutually exclusive states of affairs, are alternating conditions in the life of peoples. They cry out

---

66. Astraea, goddess of justice, who dwelled among men during the Golden Age. [H.T.]

67. "Clarescunt sonitus armorumque ingruit horror". Virgil, *Aeneid*, Book II, §300: Trans: "clearer grow the sounds and war's dread din sweeps on". *Virgil Volume I: Eclogues. Georgics. Aeneid: Books 1–6*, trans. H. Rushton Fairclough, revised G. P. Goold. (Cambridge MA.: Harvard University Press, 1999), 336–37. [A.P.]

for each other and define each other and complement and support each other, like the inverse, though adequate and inseparable terms of the same antinomy. Peace demonstrates and confirms war, and war, in turn, is a cry for peace. The messianic legend even states as much: the Peacemaker is a conqueror, his reign established by means of triumph. But there is to be no final victory, no definitive peace, until the Anti-Messiah appears; his defeat, in the end-time, will be a sign both that wars are at an end, and of the end of the world.

Which is why, throughout history, we have seen warfare unfailingly reborn of the very idea that had brought peace. After the battle of Actium, a single, worldwide empire was proclaimed, in the belief that war could be ended. Augustus closed Janus's temple: it stood for the revolts, the civil wars and the barbarian invasions afflicting the empire, and which had been undermining and degrading it for upwards of three hundred years.

Diocletian, with a high-mindedness worthy of the ancients, once again sought peace through partition: and in his own lifetime, the twin emperors waged war on each other in order to resurrect unity.

Constantine strove to resurrect that unity by embracing Christianity: but then wars erupted between the old and the new religion, between orthodoxy and heresy. And this endured and the war grew worse until that empire, the admitted enemy of the human race, might be done away with and unity dismantled.

Whereupon the long-suppressed nationalities were resuscitated and rejuvenated by the Christian faith and by barbarian blood lines, but only to begin the carnage anew and strive towards their mutual extermination.

War weariness had led to a reversion to the idea of a Christian empire: a compact was signed between the Pope and Charlemagne. And for five centuries, the squabble was over how that compact was to be interpreted.[68] A frightful business! It was after the sovereign had been proclaimed as the prince of peace that we witnessed bishops, abbots and the religious, gripped by a warrior fury, donning breastplates and strapping on swords, as if peace, taken unduly seriously, had amounted to an attack upon religion, a blasphemy against Christ.

And what did the wisdom of the nation then devise in order to rescue the faith which was enmired in universal hostilities and to reopen a doorway to peace? The separation of the powers so unhappily conjoined. But the tragedy

---

68. The battle of Actium took place in 31 BC – Diocletian partitioned the Empire in 286 AD and replaced the dyarchy that had lasted for seven years with a tetrarchy, or government by the four emperors, in 293 AD. Constantine restored the unity of the Empire following an eighteen-year battle (306–324 AD). The compact between the Pope and Charlemagne, sealed in 800 AD, was followed by the Investiture dispute, which lingered until 1268 and the death of King Conrad the Younger. [H.M.]

merely took a ghastlier turn. Christianity was divided against itself more than ever: Pius II, Aeneas Silvius, the most prudent, most saintly and most venerated of pontiffs, could not quite rally the Christian princes against the Ottomans. And then died of sorrow.[69]

The cry goes up on all sides: It was not the Turks who sowed division between the peoples; that was the Church. No salvation, no peace for the world without a reformation! And, with reform as their pretext, the wars of religion flared up again, with political wars hot on their heels. The sixteenth, seventeenth and eighteen centuries echoed to the din of battle. Amid this upheaval, Grotius wrote his treatise *De Jure Belli ac Pacis*.[70] But even the events were overwhelming: along came the Revolution and the ghastly concerto was raised to hitherto unprecedented levels.

Let us pause here for a moment. What was the Revolution, or what should it have been?

Like Christianity, like Charlemagne's compact, like the Reformation, the Revolution should have spelled the end of war, the brotherhood between peoples, the groundwork for this having been laid by three centuries' worth of philosophy, literature and art. The Revolution was what one might have called the revolt of reason against force, of righteousness against conquest, of the workings of peace against the brutalities of warfare. But the Revolution had barely been named before war was on the rise again. The world had never beheld such funerals. In under twenty-five years, ten million human sacrificial victims were burnt offerings in these contests between giants.

In the end, the world drew a breath. A solemn peace was pledged, a mutually reassuring treaty signed between the sovereigns. The genie of war was nailed to a rock by the Holy Alliance. This was the age of representative, parliamentary institutions: by means of an artful coalition, the burnt-out torch of warfare was surrendered into the custody of interests which abhorred it. The wonders of industry, the growth of trade, the study of a brand-new science, a peaceful science if ever there were one, political economy, all of these conspired to direct minds towards the ways of peace, to inspire an abhorrence of carnage, to attack the very ideal of warfare. Societies calling for disarmament took shape simultaneously in England and in America. Propaganda won the Old World round: there were meetings, congresses gathered, addresses to all governments published.

69. AENEAS SILVIUS PICCOLOMINI (1405–1464), became Pope as Pius II, having appealed in vain to all the princes of Europe, placed himself at the head of an expedition against the Turks and met his end in Ancona. [H.M.]

70. This treatise, translated into French by Jean de Barbeyrac in 1724, was drawn up during the disturbances in the Dutch Republic, which prompted Grotius, sentenced to imprisonment for life, to seek refuge in Paris. [H.M.]

Catholics, Protestants, Quakers, Deists, materialists, fell over one another as they competed in pronouncing warfare ungodly and immoral:

> War is murder; war is thievery.
>
> It is murder and it is thievery, taught to and commanded of peoples by their governments.
>
> It is murder, it is thievery acclaimed, feted, dignified and crowned.
>
> It is murder, it is thievery, minus the punishment and the disgrace but with the addition of impunity and glory.
>
> It is murder, it is thievery, spared the scaffold thanks to the triumphal arch.
>
> It is the absence of legal consequences, for it is society ordering that which it forbids and forbidding what it orders; rewarding that which it punishes and punishing what it rewards; glorifying that which it stigmatizes and stigmatizing that which it glorifies; the deed being the same, just the name being different.[71]

Just as in the days of Christ's birth, a warm breeze blows over humanity, *pax hominibus*. At the Peace Congress held in Paris in 1849, the Abbot Deguerry and Pastor A. Coquerel, representing the Catholic church and the Reformed church, shook hands with each other, achieving reconciliation over a joint anathema targeting war.[72] It looked as if an endless life of riches and happiness was in prospect; what was the deadly influence turning it into an era of trouble and discord?

What compromised the peace of Vienna was peace itself, by which I mean the ideas that it articulated, ideas that could all be traced back to just one thing: the establishment of constitutional monarchies.[73] As elements and symptoms of a future conflict, note that in the forty-five years since the Treaties of Vienna,

---

71. EMILE DE GIRARDIN, *Le Désarmement européen* (1859). [H.T.]

72. The ABBOT GASPARD DEGUERRY (1797–1871), curate in Saint-Eustache in 1849, was curate at the Madeleine at the time of his shooting in 1871. PASTOR ATHANASE COQUEREL (1795–1868) was a representative of the people in 1848. See *Discours,* (1850). On the 1849 peace congress, see *Congrès des amis de la paix* (1850) [H.M./A.P.]

73. Despite ushering in an unprecedented forty-year peace, the Vienna Treaties were considered by the republican left to be a travesty of international law, suppressing the nationalist ambitions of peoples across Europe. Proudhon diverged from the mainstream on this, as on so much else. In *Si les Traités de 1815 ont Cessé d'Exister* (Paris: Dentu, 1863), Proudhon argues that the Vienna Treaties are both the beginning of the secularisation of European international order and the end of the centralising tendencies of empires. He also argued that to destroy the 1815 treaties would be a disaster for European revolutionary movements because of their relative weakness. For a fuller discussion of this, see Alex Prichard "Deepening Anarchism: International Relations and the Anarchist Ideal", *Anarchist Studies* 18 no. 2 (2010): 29–57. See also Book Two, Chapter VII, § 4 and Book Three, Chapter X, §13 below. [A.P.]

Italian carbonarism, the fifteen years of liberalism,[74] doctrinairism,[75] the socialism that emerged from the July Revolution; the war in Spain, the war in Greece, the uprising in Poland, the separation of Belgium, the occupation of Ancona, the troubles of 1840 on the occasion of the Eastern Question, the Sonderbund, the massacres in Galicia, the 1848 revolution, the striving after unity in Austria and Germany, thwarted by the Hungarian uprising and the resistance from Denmark; the war in Novara, the Roman expedition, the two campaigns in Crimea and Lombardy, the failure of the Papacy, the unity of Italy, the emancipation of the serfs in Russia, not to mention the minor wars in Algeria, Kabylia, Morocco, the Caucasus, China and India.

For the past fourteen years, the whole of Europe has been at arms. Far from the appetite for warfare having cooled, gallantry within the armies has grown; the populace's zeal has peaked. Yet never before was there such a softening in mores, a greater disdain for glory and less of a thirst for conquest; never have the soldiery shown themselves more humane and driven by more chivalrous sentiments. By what unfathomable frenzy have nations which respected and honoured one another been induced to fight one another?

Maybe it will be said that, had their interests been taken into consideration, peaceful resolutions might have carried the day. Experience gives the lie to that supposition. The theoreticians of constitutional rule had lulled themselves into thinking that the way to cast warfare aside was to make it subject to the ruminations of representatives. Well, what do we find, right after the February Revolution? Even as the Stock Exchange was panicking, an increasingly conservative and peaceful Parliament unanimously voted through subsidies, making pledges to peace all the while. One of the reasons the last monarchy lost was that it had been too firm in its resistance to the country's bellicose instinct. Louis-Philippe has still not been forgiven for his *peace-at-any-price* policy. What had swung the country over to war in the interim? Nothing, except, maybe, the desire to assuage the martial ardour of an over-excitable generation; nothing, I say, as we have seen from the outcomes of both the Crimean and Lombardy wars, *nothing, not a thing*.

So, war and peace, interconnected with each other, affirming both their reality and their necessity, are the two main functions of the human race. In history, they alternate, like the waking state and sleep in the life of the individual; like the expenditure of energy and its recuperation; like production and consumption in political economy. Peace is therefore warfare and warfare is peace; to imagine them mutually exclusive is childish.

---

74. Under the Restoration, (1815 to 1830). [H.T.]

75. The *Parti de juste-milieu*, led during the Restoration by PIERRE-PAUL ROYER-COLLARD (1763–1845) and FRANÇOIS GUIZOT (1787–1874). [H.T./A.P.]

Monsieur de Ficquelmont says:

There are some people who seem to think of the workings of the world in terms of a play divided into acts. They reckon that, during the intervals, they can, without fear of being disturbed, indulge in their pleasures and private affairs. They fail to see that those intervals, during which events seem to have been interrupted, are the interesting point in the play. It is during this apparent calm that the causes of the brouhaha to follow later are being prepared. It is ideas that form the chain of time. Those who can see only the big events, who hear only the detonations, have no understanding of history.[76]

By way of our conclusion regarding peace, let us therefore state here, again, what we stated at the outset of this book when we spoke about war:

Peace is a divine act; for it has remained for us a myth. We have seen nothing of it save its shadow and are familiar neither with its substance nor its laws. No one knows when, how and why it begins: when, why or how it ends. Like war, it has its place in our thoughts; along with the latter, it makes up the first and largest category of our understanding.

Peace, to be sure, ought to be a positive reality since we hold it to be the greatest of blessings. How is it that our notion of it is purely negative, as if it conveyed only the absence of struggle, strike and destruction? Peace ought to have an action of its own, its own expression, life and movement, its own particular creations; how does it come to pass that in our modern societies it is still what it once was in ancient societies and even in the philosophers' utopias: the sleep of warfare?

For the past forty-five years, Europe has been permanently ruled by armies; and the economists rail against that enormous and pointless expenditure.[77] Which is what the ancients used to do: in times of peace they were preparing for war. Such was the recommendation down through the ages, from Plato to

---

76. *Pensées et réflexions morales et politiques* by De Ficquelmont, published by de Barante, in 8°, 1859, 120. THE COMTE DE FICQUELMONT (1777–1857), an Austrian diplomat and statesman, was the author of a number of political works, notably on the Eastern Question and on England. [H.T.]

77. The rants of the economists and reformers of 1848 add up to a formidable arsenal of books and pamphlets, whether dealing with ways of reducing military expenditure or schemes for using the army for productive purposes. Following in Fourier's footsteps, they opposed *"the armies of destruction which from time to time ravage the earth,* the *industrial armies* which, *rather than having devastated thirty provinces on campaign, might throw up thirty bridges across the rivers",* etc. (*Theory of the Four Movements* [1808]). Hence the schemes for army reforms and colonization plans. [H.M.]

Fénelon, from those who dabbled in offering instruction to peoples and kings. While the peace lasted, there was practice in the handling of weapons and we engaged in petty skirmishes. For the last forty centuries during which Europe has been dabbling in theology, metaphysics, poetry, comedy, novels, science, politics and agriculture, it never imagined any other diversion, any more agreeable recreation, no nobler exercise when it came to its moments of ease. Peacemonger, when you preach free trade and concord to us, do you even realize that what you would have our reason believe in and our wills practice is a mystery?

CHAPTER IX

The Problem of War and Peace

War, as now we can scarcely doubt, is primarily a phenomenon of our moral life. It has its part to play in the psychology of humanity, just as religion, justice, poetry, art, industry, politics and liberty have theirs; it is one of the forms of our virtue. We must examine it against the backdrop of the universal conscience, and not that of the battle-fields, sieges and clashes of armies, the procedures of strategy, tactics and armaments. All this materialism, with which the historians' accounts are full and which makes up the background to the poets' images, is pretty well useless; it has nothing to teach us about the philosophy of warfare. War is one of the powers within our souls; it has its phenomenality within our souls. Everything that is part of our intellectual and moral make-up, everything that constitutes our civilization and our glory, is conjured up, item by item, and developed through the dazzling activity of warfare and under peace's humble incubation. The former might say to the latter: "I plant; you, Sister, water; in turn, God brings growth to all".

Minds with a penchant for mysticism, such as the Comte de Maistre and Monsieur de Ficquelmont himself, happy to have discerned these great things, like to loiter in the half-light. The divine holds them enthralled; unadulterated truth, sought by the philosopher, has no charm for them, a dismal reality that we cease to admire as soon as we possess it. According to them, there is a grave danger in depriving man of his sense of wonder and banishing all the mysteries from his gaze, one by one.

Such considerations might easily have been applicable in the days of Bossuet.[78] In the wake of eighteenth-century philosophy and the German critics, following the French Revolution and the establishment of an Academy of the *Moral and Political Sciences*,[79] following the explosion of socialism, they have had their day. These days, such reservations are forbidden us; they would

---

78. JACQUES-BÉNIGNE BOSSUET (1627–1704) Bishop and orator who advocated, *inter alia*, the relative independence of the French Church from the Papacy. [A.P.]

79. The Academy of Moral and Political Sciences was launched in 1795 as a sort of an Institute, only to be abolished in 1803 and resurrected in 1832. [H.M.]

amount to our failing in our destiny, our duty. So, since it is our nature always to eat the fruit of science, let us eat, even should we die thrice.

What is war? Something incidental, ephemeral, or a necessary mode of our existence? Is war, peace's thesis or antithesis, one of those component antinomies that is easily criticized from a position sometimes at one extreme or sometimes at the other, but which nothing can destroy because they are part of the essence of humanity and one of the conditions of his life? Is there, by any constitution of States, some improved implementation of the rights of peoples, a chance that we might end war once and for all, or is it merely susceptible to amelioration and honing? In which case, where war is concerned, what do we mean by amelioration, honing or progress? Does it mean that warfare must become increasingly atrocious, or rather that, keeping pace with civilization, it should boost our courage and virtue, together with our contempt for death? In either instance, rather than delving into the philosophy of warfare, we would merely be delving deeper and deeper into mysticism and harking back to the ideal of the Cimbri and the Teutons. In short, are we to see war as a scourge upon humanity, or as the exercise of its sovereignty? Is it a phenomenon of the physiology or the pathology of nations? Does it fall within or outside the definition of right, within or outside religion? Is it commanded, tolerated or condemned by morality? In the first case, what can we do to make it better, more effective, more edifying, more heroic? In the second, how can we set about stamping it out?

In my own view, it is plain that war has deep roots, scarcely discernible, in the religious, juridical, aesthetic and moral sentiments of peoples. It might even be argued that it has its abstract formula in dialectics. War is our history, our life, our very soul; it is legislation, politics, State, homeland, social hierarchy, the rights of people, poetry, theology; it is, once again, everything. We hear talk of doing away with war, as if it were some sort of toll or tariff. And there is no appreciation that if we discount war and its associated ideas, nothing, absolutely nothing remains of humanity's past and not a single atom upon which to build its future. Oh, I may well say to these clumsy peace-mongers, as I myself was once told in respect of property: How do you envision society, with war abolished? What ideas, what beliefs are you offering? What literature, what poetry, what art? What would you make of man, that intelligent, religious, justice-dispensing, free, individual and, for all of those very reasons, a warring creature? What would you make of the nation, that independent, outgoing, autonomous collective? What becomes of the human race in its eternal repose?

All in vain, a pointless philanthropy bewails the hecatombs offered up to the God of battles; in vain does a grasping commercialism parade, besides its countless products, its railways, its shipping, its banks, its free trade and the appalling consumption that war brings in its wake, the burning-down of towns, the ruination of the countryside, the mothers', wives' and young girls' despair, the depopulation, the degeneration of races, the hobbling of societies in terms of the production of wealth and the exploitation of the globe. For as long as imaginations and consciences have no other interest in denying it, and have nothing against it other than the waste of human lives and money, stagnating business, or a drop in savings and bankruptcy, war is not about to go away. In quarters high and low within society, there will even be a degree of animosity towards those who combat (I almost said calumniate) it.

See to it, if you can, that this supernatural fanaticism, this cult of force of which philosophy has thus far grasped nothing, is assailed in its morality and in its ideas; strip warfare of the prestige that makes it the pivot of all poetry, the basis for all political organization and all justice; then you will be in a position to hope for its abolition and, on the basis of the affinities which we have detected within it, to jettison what traces of prejudice and servitude still remain upon this earth.

"We are" – Monsieur de Lamartine[80] has said somewhere – "in the first of the mighty eras through which the human race may have to pass as it strides towards the aim of divine destiny; an age of renovation and transformation akin, perhaps to Gospel times ... We are on our way to one of the most sublime staging-posts, to a complete organization of the social order. For our children's children, we foresee a series of free, religious, moral, rational centuries, an age of truth, reason and virtue in the midst of the ages ... Taking God as our starting point and our goal, and the general welfare of humanity as our purpose, and with morality as our torch, conscience as our judge and liberty as our path, you will not be running any risk of going astray ...

"The men of the National Assembly were not Frenchmen; they were men of the world. They were misunderstood and belittled when not looked upon as just priests, aristocrats, plebeians and loyal subjects, seditionists and rabble-rousers. They were and felt themselves to be better than that: God's WORKMEN, called by him to *restore* humanity's *social reason* and to re-establish right and justice in the world.

"The declaration of rights is the Ten Commandments of the human race in any language".

---

80. *Histoire des Girondins,* 8 vol. in-8°, vol. I, 435. [H.M.]

These are magnificent and prophetic words such as ooze effortlessly from Monsieur de Lamartine every time a beam of the *social reason* that he invokes sheds its light upon his soul.

Yes, we are in one of those heady times that determine the fate of nations; one of those times of renewal and worldwide transformation; a time without analogy in the past except that of the Gospels, a time of which the French Revolution was the Mount Tabor,[81] and the men of the Constituent Assembly the first, immortal missionaries. Now, if Monsieur de Lamartine is to be believed, what is the identifying feature of this *divine* and oh so wonderfully regenerative era going to be? He is going to tell us: as in Gospel times, it is going to be a promise, the promise of peace, an olive branch heralding an end to strife and catastrophe. After the storm comes the lull: every period of warfare ends that way.

> The modern revolution summoned Gentile and Jew alike to share enlightenment and brotherhood. And not one of its apostles failed to proclaim peace between the peoples. Mirabeau, Lafayette and Robespierre himself erased war from the symbols they put before the nation. It was the seditionists and the ambitious who later insisted upon it; not the great revolutionaries. By the time the war broke out, the revolution had degenerated.[82]

To say poet is to say interpreter to the gods. I accept those recent words from Monsieur de Lamartine as oracular. But when will they be fulfilled? That is what we should like to know. Meanwhile, I cannot help having reservations in favour of the revolutionaries who, in spite of the Court and in spite of Robespierre, seized the initiative in the struggle and had war declared on the counter-revolution, represented at the time by the foreigner. No, it was neither the ambitious nor the seditionists who issued the call to arms: yet they had more of a genuine feel for the Revolution than Robespierre and his friends. What, then, might have befallen that Revolution but for the endorsement of blood and victory? War is divine; war delivers justice; war brings a regeneration of mores; how could Monsieur de Lamartine, with all his familiarity with matters *divine*, have forgotten that? Give the Revolutionary Wars their due, if you please!

War is the most ancient of all the religions, and will be the last of them.

---

81. The mountain in Palestine where, legend has it, Christ supposedly revealed his divinity to his disciples. [H.T.]

82. Extracted from Émile De Girardin, in his pamphlet on *Le Désarmement européen*, 52 (LAMARTINE, op. cit. Vol. I, 435–36). [H.T.]

I give an undertaking today to explain what philosophy has to date left un-explained due to an oversight. I will also identify the cause: the warrior myth. I shall strip warfare of its divine character; and will deliver it, unveiled, to the free judgment of peoples and kings. May this work of mine, like the hymn to peace sung by the angels over Christ's manger, serve to herald a better future to the world! I would bless the exile that brought me the inspiration for this book, and, though I may yet appear somewhat suspect in terms of my teachings, I would die in communion with the human race.

BOOK TWO

ON THE NATURE OF WAR
AND RIGHT OF FORCE

Dulce et decorum est pro patria mori.[1]
—Horace

SUMMARY

Universal opinion affirms the existence of a positive RIGHT of WAR, analogous with, related and equivalent to the rights of peoples, *political rights* and *civil rights*, in short, rights of any description. By contrast, the unanimous opinion among the jurists holds that there is no substance to the right of war; that to designate the semblance of rules abided by in war as such is not proper; that force, of itself, is as incapable of creating a right as of delivering a judgment; in short, that the expression *rights of war* ought to be deemed a euphemism, a fiction. This pronouncement by the jurists has caused a turmoil in ideas. With the right of warfare denied, the rights of peoples is left bereft of its principle, its sanction; public rights and civil rights in turn collapse along with it; the spirit of revolt invades the universal conscience and society shifts from the state of war to the state of banditry. The theories of Grotius, Wolff, Vattel, Kant, Hegel and Hobbes. Who is mistaken as to the spontaneity of the human race in affirming war's juridical status, or who is going to deny the wisdom of the jurisconsults?

---

1. "It is sweet and fitting to die for one's country". Horace, *Odes and Epodes,* Book II, Chap. 2, verse 10, ed. and trans. Niall Rudd (Cambridge: Harvard University Press, 2004), 145. [A.P.]

The theory of the right of force. The reality, straightforwardness and primordial character of this right: its application to international relations. Examples borrowed from times ancient and modern. How, historically, the following have been deduced from the right of force: 1. The right of war; 2. The rights of peoples; 3. Public right, or the constitutional right of States; 4. Civil rights and economic rights. Warfare defined. An instrument of justice, it is legitimate in terms of its holy, sacred essence.

FIRST CHAPTER

On the Disagreement Between the Testimony of the Human Race and the Jurisconsults' Doctrine Regarding the Act and Right of War

It is one of humanity's misfortunes that its teachers rarely have any understanding of it and, because it does not operate as they would like, they denigrate it.

When it comes to warfare and international law, as practised by nations, three fundamental propositions govern:

1. There is such a thing as a right of war;
2. War is of itself a judgment;
3. That judgment is delivered in the name of and by virtue of force.

True or false, this is the belief, held more or less explicitly by the common man; what the academy ought to rebut or justify; in the absence of which civilization is left tainted or at least suspect, and the science of rights falters on its foundation.

Let us begin by drawing a comparison between the general belief and the teaching of the academy regarding the first of those propositions: *There is such a thing as a right of war.*

All peoples affirm a right of war, which is to say, a right emanating from superior force, a right that victory proclaims and sanctions, and which, by virtue of that sanction and proclamation, becomes legitimate through practice and as legitimate and respectable in its outcomes as any other right, such as, say, liberty and property claim to be. As a result, all peoples affirm the legitimacy of conquest, achieved in the desired circumstances and in accordance with the prescribed forms; as I say, they assert it as vigorously as the working man asserts his rights over what he produces.

When the universality of the human race says one thing, it is always worth philosophy taking an interest in it; this has unfailingly proved the case, when it comes to religion, family or government. When it comes to the moral order of things, universal acceptance, should the propositions not always be clear cut, has always been achieved by means of the citation of some higher reason, if not through the very articulation of that reason.

No, what I find immediately striking when one comes to read the authors who have dealt with warfare, say, Grotius and Vattel,[2] is the stark contradiction between the opinion of those jurisconsults and the unanimous sentiment among peoples. Grotius, initially, plus his translator Barbeyrac;[3] Wolff,[4] and then Vattel, Wolff's abridger; Pinheiro-Ferreira,[5] who annotated Vattel; Burlamaqui[6] and his successor, de Felice;[7] Kant[8] and his school; Martens and his publisher, Monsieur Vergé;[9] as well as Pufendorf;[10] Hobbes, and the multitude of Catholic, Protestant, philosophical jurists, all deny the reality of any

---

2. EMER (EMMERICH) DE VATTEL (1714–1767). Minister of August III and disciple of Leibniz, author of *Défense du système leibnizien* (1741) and *The Law of Nations: Or, Principles of the Law of Nature Applied to the Conduct and Affairs of Nations and Sovereigns* (1758). [H.T.]

3. JEAN BARBEYRAC (1674–1744). French Calvinist who fled to Berlin following the repeal of the Edict of Nantes. Jurisconsult, law professor, translator and annotator of Grotius and Pufendorf. [H.T.]

4. JEAN-CHRÉTIEN WOLFF (1679–1754). German mathematician, philosopher and publicist, a disciple of Leibniz. Banished by Friedrich Wilhelm in 1723, only to be recalled by Friedrich II, after having lectured in Marburg. Author of *Jure naturae* (1740–48) and of *Jure gentium methodo scientifica pertractatum* (1750). [H.T.]

5. SILVESTRE PINHEIRO-FERREIRA (1769–1846). Portuguese jurisconsult, diplomat and statesman, forced to step down from his chair at the University of Coimbra for having lectured on socialist teachings (1797). Minister of War (1821–1824), he then tendered his resignation once absolutism had prevailed and he left for exile in Paris up until 1843. Author of *Essai sur la psychologie* (1825) and *Principes du droit public, constitutionnele, droit adminstratif et des gens* (1834). [H.T.]

6. JEAN-JACQUES BURLAMAQUI (1694–1748). Swiss publicist and jurisconsult, a member of the Genevan Council of State and author of *Principes du droit de la nature et des gens* (1766–1820). [H.T.]

7. FORTUNATO BARTOLOMEO DE FELICE (1723–1789). Publisher and commentator upon Burlamaqui's complete works, *Principes du droit de la nature et des gens* (1766). [H.M.]

8. IMMANUEL KANT (1727–1804). Built up a following in the subject with his *Metaphysical Principles of Morals* (1797) and *Perpetual Peace* (1795), translated [into French] by Tissot in 1853. [H.M.]

9. GEORG FRIEDRICH VON MARTENS (1756–1821), German diplomat and publicist, lecturer in law, councillor of State (1803–1813), Hanover's representative to the Frankfurt Diet (1816). Author of *Precis du droit des gens modernes de l'Europe* which first appeared in 1789. A revised edition by Charles Vergé, complete with notes by Pinheiro-Ferreira, with an introduction and complementary exposition of the teachings of contemporary publicists, and an added *"Bibliographie raisonée du droits des gens"*, appeared in 1858. [H.T.]

10. SAMUEL PUFENDORF (1632–1694). Author of *De jure naturae et gentium* (1672), French translation and annotation by Barbeyrac as *Le droit de la nature et des gens* (1720 and 1734). [H.T.]

right of war. What they understand by that term is not what the natural meaning of the words suggests, and which popular common sense universally proclaims: the RIGHT OF WAR, the way one would speak of *the right of labour, the right of intelligence, the right of love*. To them, the right of war is merely a sort of legal figment suggested by the wretchedness of the times, designed to put paid to the contention between passions and interests and to forestall, by means of moderation on the part of the victor and resignation on the part of the vanquished, the utter destruction of the latter and sometimes of both. In itself, these learned men say, warfare is incompatible with the notion of rights; it contains nothing resembling such. Even though it may give rise to rights of various sorts, even though it may pose as the assertion or exercise of a right, it is, by its very nature, a stranger to rights; being the violent and insulting suspension of them.

It is in the light of that explanation that we are to understand these authors whenever they speak about *just* war and *unjust* war. By just war, we are not to understand that they are referring to an armed struggle conducted in accordance with certain rules in pursuit of a dispute which needs resolving in that manner; which would suggest that in a just war, rights being unsure or equal, both belligerents stand equally upon their claims and honour, and that the matter at issue hinges upon the competency of their arms. In the jurists' view, and according to all their definitions, justice in warfare is essentially one-sided; for A to be able to wage a just war, it is vitally necessary that there is injustice in B, his antagonist; in which case, all means are fair when it comes to ensuring that that right is enforced, except for whatever is due to respect for humanity. As for the idea of warfare serving as right's actual manifestation, that, these jurists state, just goes to show the barbarism of the nations in contention; it is the very opposite of justice.

So, according to these authors, one has to take great care not to see the provisions of what are commonly referred to as the *laws of war*, drawn up in chapter and verse, as a sort of right *sui generis*, of which war is the expression. *Right* and *war*, they tell us, are mutually exclusive terms. By the laws of war, we mean certain humane exclusions which common practice among peoples has introduced into the gory play of battles and which opinion imposes upon the belligerents, solely in order to put a stop to the abuses and confine the carnage, so to speak, to what is strictly necessary. As Hobbes says, war is not, in fact, to be regarded as an essential feature of the life of nations, a phenomenon which, bearing its laws in itself, would then give rise to a positive right. Instead, it is diametrically inimical to the happiness of peoples and to the preservation of the human race. Being, like famine, pestilence or madness, a manageable scourge. Which is why, Grotius adds, even in the heat of battle, man must never forget that he is a man and that he is dealing with fellow-men. The laws of war have no meaning beyond that.

With regard to morality, we could not cite another example of such dissonance between the belief of the masses and the sentiments of learned men. Philosophical reasoning and intuitive belief have never seemed in such blatant contradiction to one another. And stranger still, even though philosophical reasoning prevails in schools, in books, in courts of justice and the councils of princes, and appears that it is possessed of everything that it needs in order to enforce its edicts and impose its definitions, it is the ideas of the common man that continue to rule the world and govern the affairs of nations.

Here, the objections fairly gush from the pen. If the right of war is a chimera, how might such a spontaneous, universal and persistent belief have come about? How has religion sanctified it everywhere? How come this ghastly superstition has not yet retreated in the face of the progress in ideas and mores?

We can imagine childish brawls, a fracas between youngsters, strife between herdsmen, workmates, sailors, occurring under the spur of sheer animalistic passions. We can even imagine banditry, piracy and, to some extent, criminal gangs. None of that is anything other than the more or less violent and spectacular effect of animality, erupting into vice and crime. But war, a conflict between two sides, each of them made up of the elite of a country, swathed in honours and lawful formalities and religious ceremonials like some holy, sacred act, this warfare is unfathomable if, from one vantage point or both, it must, as a matter of principle, be held to be unjust.

Unjust warfare, as the jurists inevitably posit, whether coming from one side or from both, is the greatest of crimes. Now, if justice can be placed in jeopardy as far as an individual is concerned, by the maelstrom of passions, it finds it harder to yield in the context of a group. The weightier the group, the city, the State, becomes, the more justice gains the upper hand within it, thanks to the impact of the law governing that body; the upshot being that we can say that justice, in the context of the human race as a whole, is incorruptible. So, once again, if war is a crime – and by its very nature it cannot be anything else according to the jurists – then how, I ask, is it deemed honourable at all? Why has universal reprobation failed to fend off such a monstrous iniquity? Why has war become more frequent throughout history, become more intense as civilization has increased? Why is half of the human race still made up of villains. Finally, how is it, if war is bereft of any juridical element, if there is nothing to be said for it, if it amounts to murder and thievery, as the advocates at the Peace Congress denounced it, why is it met with so little opposition in nations made up of twenty, thirty, sixty million souls? Likewise, why has it sometimes embraced the whole world – become widespread? It is unheard of for individuals with criminal records, living off the proceeds of crime, to form themselves into regular societies; the brigand's first enemy is his accomplice. To speak of association is to speak of justice: now, justice and crime, the former being the means and the latter the end, are incompatible. It is even more repugnant that a people as a whole should wax so enthusiastic about war if it is convinced of the iniquitousness of its cause; and, moreover, it defies explanation that, in any war, a cry of disapproval, targeting one or other of the belligerents, should not ring out to stop it in its tracks.

The issue of the right of war must therefore be posed in a quite different fashion to the one understood by the academy. Throughout the ranks of the warring parties and the neutrals, minds must be persuaded that the feelings aroused by war, in terms of its morality, are the diametrical opposite of those which might be inspired by the spectacle of a caravan of pilgrims under attack from a band of robbers.

Let us question the army commanders. The courage of the soldier is underpinned by, above all else, his conscience. The soldier not only counts on the good faith of his commanders, which is that of his nation, which is that of the human race, but also on the good faith of his innermost senses. True, war is the most terrifying, yet most grandiose manifestation of justice, that is, for that very reason, surrounded, like some great feudal assize, with solemnities and rules; but, notwithstanding the blood-letting, humanity still has its place there, and the executions of war are determined by a higher law that states that, as a rule, such executions are just, because carried out in the name of force.

The soldier also tells himself that in a war carried out according to the rules, everything becomes selfless and sublime; that if there, as anywhere else, murder, rape, depredation and debauchery get their chance to disport themselves, such misdeeds are no more evidence to be used against war than the ditherings of a judge are against the institutions of the courts. Further, that the army is the genuine representative of a country in its dealings with the foreigner, and, that army being the people's force, it becomes, in the event of war, its conscience; that, even in the prospect of defeat, war is, as far as the citizen is concerned, the most sacred and glorious of duties, because what is at stake is the salvation of the homeland and that renders it honourable, come what may. Further, what brings victory is moral energy, as much as and more so than material force; that within victory there is, therefore, not merely pride, but also a just appreciation of the righteousness which, where nations are concerned, is not established by procedures, but by the selflessness of the sacrifice, the scorn of death, probity, temperance and leniency wedded to courage.

Which is why the real soldier neither hates nor feels contempt for his foe. Instead, he honours him and, outside of the battle, offers him his hand;

he knows that this foe fights, as he does himself, for his prince, for his home-land; that, like him, he represents a nation's conscience and champions a great cause. What more sublime sight can there be than that of two armies suddenly suspending their hostilities in order to pay honourable tribute to the brave, as happened at General Meusnier's funeral during the siege of Mainz![11]

Finally, the soldier tells himself that war is much less to be feared than the faint hearted might imagine; that it is good, useful and fertile; that its effect upon nations is akin to a health crisis as it puts an end to an ambiguous situ-ation and from individuals draws a sort of a reaction that reveals in them the virtues of discipline, the treasures of sensitivity and the greatness of soul which they might never have displayed in any other circumstance.

This is what the soldier says to himself in his heart of hearts, in accordance with the common sense of the human race; that which elderly jurists, strangers to action and indifferent to rights, may misconstrue; the comic side of which may well provoke a smile in peace-time, but which becomes a much more se-rious affair at the first sign of difficulty arising between States. It has been said that in 1793, France's honour had taken refuge under her colours. We quiver lest the same be true of Europe today. The soldier's courage is in contrast with the corruption of all sorts that devours civil society and would bode ill for civilization.

The point, therefore, is to delve deeply into this religion of warfare handed down from age to age and still so ardent. Until such time as that scrutiny has been carried out, until such time as the puzzle has been explained, humanity will not only remain mired in a state of war, but will be swept along by war. The destinies of States being exclusively dependent on the courage of their armies, nations are going to bob along on the ocean of history, sometimes riding high, sometimes swamped by the wave; and since, when all is said and done, war is not the whole and all of humanity, even though it seeps into everything, it is also not the final word; since there is more to this world than force alone, it will come to pass that if force retains the upper hand, right, mores, civilization, ideas and liberty will all be in jeopardy.

Warfare, everything assures us, is therefore more than a fact, more than a circumstance, more than a habit. It is not the insult from one triggering the self-defence of the other; it is a principle, an institution, a belief, and we are one step away from saying a doctrine. Let us set the teary-eyed declamations and sentimental invectives to one side. Speaking through the mouths of nations, war

---

11. On learning of the wounding of the French general J-B MEUSNIER (1751–1793), the Prussian general Schönfeld had him sent oranges and gave the order for a ceasefire during his funeral. The King of Prussia was credited with this unlikely saying: "Meusnier did me great damage but the world has lost a great man". [H.M.]

affirms its reason, its righteousness, its jurisdiction and its function; it is this that we have to penetrate.

CHAPTER II

War is Brought Forth as a Judgment Delivered in the Name and by Virtue of Force. Universal Conscience Declares this Judgment the Norm; the Jurisprudence of the Authors Rejects It

The second proposition on which there is a manifest parting of the ways between universal sentiment and scholarly opinion is this: *War is a judgment.*

In accordance with the commonly held view, Cicero defines war as a way of settling differences through the use of force. He adds, with sadness, that one is obliged to do so when every other means of resolution has become unfeasible. Discussion befits man; violence the beasts. *Nam, cum sint duo genera decertandi, unum per disceptationem, alterum per vim; cumque illud proprium sit hominis, hoc beluarum, confugiendum est ad posterius, si uti non licet superiore.*[12]

It is evident from that quotation that the great orator accepted the traditional definition of war conditionally, as a way of passing judgment. Back in his day, the very notion of the right of war had been eclipsed: such was the number of injustices the war-mongering Roman permitted! Before Cicero, Aristotle[13] had written that the most natural warfare was the sort waged against ferocious beasts and the men who resembled them. Following the example set by the Greek philosopher and classifying recourse to arms as a beastly thing, Cicero positively denied that warfare was of any juridical validity and cast such a slur upon that primitive means of resolving differences between nations as to render it beyond redemption in the estimation of the scholars. His words did,

---

12. CICERO, *De Officiis,* Book I, ch. XI. [H.M.] "For since there are two ways of settling a dispute: first, by discussion; second, by physical force; and since the former is characteristic of man, the latter of the brute, we must resort to force only in case we may not avail ourselves of discussion". From, *Cicero. De Officiis.* Book 1, section 34, trans. Walter Miller (Cambridge MA.: Harvard University Press, 1913), 37. [A.P.]

13. Aristotle, *Politics*, Book IV, ch. II, § 9. [H.M.]

though, provoke objections from the old *Quirites*,[14] those devotees of the lance, or *quir*, religiously observant of the right of warfare in order to invest their opinions with greater authenticity. On their expeditions they refrained from using the element of surprise and guile against their foes, trusting to courage alone and looking upon every victory scored by means of underhanded combat as sinful.

Thus, at every step, a discrepancy breaks out between the testimony of the human race and scholarly thinking. According to the former, there is a righteousness in warfare; according to the latter, such righteousness is simply fiction. War is a judgment is the consensus among nations; war has nothing in common with the courts, the scholars retort; it is a dismal and baneful extreme. Jurisprudence hasn't changed since Cicero.

Grotius sides with Cicero's view. The idea of a verdict delivered by force of arms reminds him of the trial by combat employed during the Middle Ages, and he dismisses that as superstition. Far from regarding war as a judgment, he detects within it, instead, the result of a complete absence of justice, the very negation of all judicial authority. It was with that thought in mind that he composed his book. He says: if the nations will but do as citizens do and learn to discern their mutual rights; let them but set themselves up as a court of arbitration and there will be no more war.[15] In short, Grotius, like Cicero before him, deems war a painful extreme, bereft of any juridical value, with the responsibility falling upon whoever embarks upon it or provokes it unfairly.

Pufendorf is of much the same mind: "Peace is what sets man apart from the beasts".[16]

Vattel expresses the same view: "War, he says, is *that state wherein one's rights are pursued through force*".[17] So, it is no judgment. How does one assert one's rights under the civil law? In front of the courts; and it is after securing the judgment of the judge that one resorts, if need be, to forceful means, distraint, forcible dispossession, house raids, selling off at auction, garnishment,[18] arrest warrant, etc. On the other hand, war, according to Vattel's definition, being confined solely to forceful means absent any prior judgment, could not stand in a starker contrast to justice. As we have just been saying, a consequence of the absence of justice and international authority. Moreover, Vattel, like Grotius,

---

14. Citizens of Rome. [H.T.]

15. GROTIUS, op. cit., Book II, chap. I, § 15; II, 23, §§ 8 et 10; III, 20, §§ 43–46 and 53. [H.M.]

16. PUFENDORF, Barbeyrac translation, op. cit., Book VIII, ch. VI. [H.M.]

17. VATTEL, *Le droit des gens*, trans. Royer-Collard (1837), vol. II, Book III, ch. I, 75. [H.M.]

18. The boarding of someone with a slow-paying debtor to live at his expense until such time as the debt was cleared. This practice was done away with in 1877. [H.T.]

embraces the principle that, if a war is just on one side, it must of necessity be unjust on the other, from which he concludes that the responsibility for the injury done lies with the aggressor or unjust defender, quite independently of how the recourse to arms may turn out.

Vattel's commentator, Pinheiro-Ferreira, essentially embracing the sentiments of his leader, but more heedful of the nature of the *prosecution of it*, defines war as the art of paralysing the enemy's forces. Others before him had argued that war is "the art of DESTROYING the enemy's forces".[19] Now, whether it is about the *destruction* of the enemy's forces or the simple *paralysis* of them, which would be less inhumane, it is plain that we are still speaking of an extra-judicial circumstance. For Pinheiro, as for Vattel and Grotius, war is still but a matter of constraining, in the absence of any prior judgment, an act of bad faith, or of defending oneself against an unjust attack. In both cases, the idea of a war tribunal, judgment by trial of arms, or of a legality inherent in combat, in short, of a right of war, evaporates entirely.

There is no point in my carrying on with these quotations: the authors all imitate one another.

So, the deeper we delve in our examination, the more we see the difference being drawn between scholarly jurisprudence and universal belief.

According to the former, the right of war is an empty word, at best a legal fiction. There is no righteousness in battle; victory proves nothing; the conquest that results from it is only made legitimate through the formal or unspoken, but freely given, consent of the vanquished, through the passage of time, the merging of races, the absorption of States; all of which are subsequent to war and they have the effect of banishing the remnants of the former strife, mitigating its cause and preventing its resurgence. Ranking warfare as a form of judicature would be an affront to justice.

By contrast, in the minds of the masses, warfare assumes a different character. Given the uncertainty of international law, or, what amounts to the same thing, given the impossibility of its formulas being enforceable against litigants such as States, the belligerents, out of necessity or unspoken convention, fall back upon the decision of arms. War is a sort of an ordeal,[20] or, as they used to say during the Middle Ages, a judgment of God. This explains how two nations in conflict, before coming to grips over an issue, each look to the assistance of Heaven for its own case. It is as if human Justice, conceding its powerlessness, were beseeching divine Justice to demonstrate through

---

19. VATTEL, *Le droit des gens*, Vol III, Notes et table Générale analytique de l'ouvrage par M. S. Pinheiro-Ferreira, 1838, vol. III, 358. [H.M.]

20. *Ordeal*: Torture believed to prove the guilt of a criminal, failing divine intervention. [H.T.]

battle which side is or will be the righteous one; in slightly more philosophical language, as if the two peoples, equally persuaded that the right of superior force is here the best, wanted by some prior religious act to whip up their
moral strength, essential to the success of their physical force. The prayers for
victory uttered by each side, prayers that scandalize our society, which is as
ignorant of its origins as it is ignoble in its incredulity, prayers as rational as the
opposing pleas delivered by barristers by way of grounding the verdicts of the
courts. But, whereas here the verdict is merely *indicative of righteousness*, it may
be argued, again from the point of view of the masses, that victory CONFERS
RIGHT, the outcome of the war being precisely to ensure that the winner gets
what he wanted and not just because, prior to the fighting, he had, by reason of
his presumed force, an entitlement to it, but rather because victory proved that
he actually was deserving of it. Take away this idea of judgment, which opinion
inevitably attaches to war, and it is whittled down, in accordance with Cicero's
expression, to a squabble between animals; a notion which our species' morality, a morality nowhere unleashed the way it is when war is concerned, does
not allow us to entertain.

   In fact, the deeds which in every nation are the overtures, companions and
sequels to hostilities, demonstrate that there is something here other than what
the jurists saw in it. For a start, what would the meaning be of this expression
RIGHT of war, as old as the human race itself, and found in every language
and reiterated by all the authors who have been tormented by it? Have the people that create languages given a name to anything but realities? Does the people not speak of the abundance of its sentiments as well as its sensations? Is it
the one that devises legal fictions? Does it dream up constitutional monarchs,
answering through their ministers? Does it worship nominal or metaphysical
divinities?

   And then how should we account for the multitude of honourable formalities with which nations surround themselves in their dalliance with warfare?
For example, the giving of notice, the making of declarations, the suggestion
of arbiters, mediations, interventions, ultimatums, the invocation of the gods,
the withdrawal of ambassadors, the untouchability of parliamentarians, the
trading of hostages and prisoners, the rights of neutrals, the rights of refugees,
of supplicants, of the wounded; the respect due to the dead; the rights of the
victor, the rights of the vanquished; the postliminary rights;[21] the limits upon
conquest, etc.: Is this whole code not a fully-fledged jurisprudence? Can it possibly be argued that all of these juridical accoutrements are wrapped around
sheer nothingness? That idea alone, that there is a formality to warfare; that

   21. Postliminary rights: The lifting of any measure derived from the de facto power
wielded by an enemy during an occupation. [H.T.]

fact alone, accepted by the policy of the nations, that men with respect for one another do not wage war after the manner of bandits and wild animals is proof that, in the general opinion, war is an act of solemn jurisdiction, in short, a judgment.

But behold something very different.

In the name of what authority, by virtue of which principle is such judgment of warfare delivered? The answer might appear blasphemous, were it not the cry coming from humanity: *In the name and by virtue of FORCE.*

Which brings us to our third proposition. Here we have to concede the most absolute contradiction between the judgment of the masses and the viewpoint of the scholars.

At this point, our authors fail to stand their ground any longer: they are flummoxed. Cicero cries out, and I quote:

Force is the reason of brutes, *hoc bellarum.*

Grotius takes up the refrain:

Force does not confer right, albeit that it helps with the upholding and wielding of it.[22]

To which Vattel adds:

One claims one's rights on the basis of qualifications, or testimonials or evidence: but one pursues them through force.

Ancillon says:

Force and right are mutually repugnant ideas: the one can never provide the basis for the other.[23]

That incomparable metaphysician Kant, who was able to tease out the laws of thought, and who was the first to come up with the idea of a phenomenology of mind, knows nothing about war. He falls into line behind Grotius, Wolff and Vattel:

---

22. This is Proudhon's encapsulation of a dictum that makes up § XIX of the Prolegomena of Grotius's *Treatise.* [H.M.]

23. ANCILLON, *Tableau des révolutions du système politique en Europe,* Introductory discourse. [H.M.]

The elements of the rights of peoples are: 1. that States, in terms of their mutual external relations (like lawless savages) are by nature in a non-juridical condition; 2. that said condition is a state of war (force is right) although in actual fact there may not always be warfare and always be hostilities. That particular condition is unjust in itself and it is the whole purpose of rights to leave it behind.

Elsewhere he states: "Nations are entitled to wage war, as the legitimate means of *asserting their rights through force*, should they have been slighted and since that claim cannot be asserted through a *trial*".[24]

Martens and his French publisher, Monsieur Vergé, espoused precisely the same argument. The first is absolute in his condemnation of warfare: "War is a permanent state of gratuitous acts of violence between men".[25]

Monsieur Vergé makes a few exceptions for the State that finds itself compelled by an *unjust* assailant to fall back on defending itself:

"Naturally", he states, "war is not to be regarded as the Comte de Maistre regards it as some grand law of the world of spirit, nor, as Spinoza does, as the normal state of the creation.[26] – It is an infuriating last resort, the only means of compelling a collective, sovereign entity to honour its commitments and abide by international mores". (SCHUTZENBERGER)[27] – "War is always *unjust per se*, in the sense that force determines right, or, to be more precise, that there is no right other than force". (BARNI, translation from Kant.)[28]

In turn, Monsieur Hautefeuille, the most recent person in France to have written on this scabrous subject, has this to say, echoing Hobbes: "It is part of the natural order that the rule of force *precedes* that of right".[29]

And the ranks of commentators, translators, publishers, annotators repeat, in unison: No, force can never confer right. Whereas, on occasion, it may intervene in the workings of justice, it is as a means of torture or constraint, like the gendarme's handcuffs and the executioner's axe. It would be monstrous to see that as the basis or expression of a right.

---

24. Kant, *Metaphysical Principles of Right,* Tissot translation (1853). [H.M.]

25. Martens, Precis du droit des gens modernes de l'Europe, vol II. [H.M.]

26. Martens, Precis du droit des gens modernes de l'Europe, vol II., 230, n. [H.M.]

27. SCHUTZENBERGER, *Studies in Public Law* (1841). [H.M.]

28. See JULES BARNI, *History of Moral and Political Ideas in the XVIIIth Century, vol.* I, 87 et seq.; vol. II, 217 et seq. [H.M.]

29. L. B. HAUTEFEUILLE, *Rights and Duties of Neutral Nations in Time of Maritime War,* 2nd ed., 1858. [H.M.]

We have heard from the scholars; let us now examine the universal evidence and see how a quite opposite sentiment has embedded itself in the conscience of the peoples.

Initially, during that phase of humanity wrongly or rightly referred to as the age of savagery, prior to its having discovered how to use its intellectual faculties, physical force was all that was known and respected. At that point, force, reason, righteousness were held synonymous. The degree of force was indicative of the degree of merit, insofar as there are grounds for talking about rights and duties obtaining between creatures so recently hatched and bound together by such rare and weak relations.

Society took shape and the regard for force grew alongside it; likewise, the notion of force and the notion of right separated from the other, little by little. Force is glorified, consecrated and deified through such human names and examples as Hercules, Thor, Samson. The population is split into two types: the *aristoï* or *optimates*, literally the mightiest and, by extension, the bravest, the most virtuous and the best; and the plebs, made up of weaklings, slaves and anybody lacking in force, the *ignavi*. The former make up the *pays légal*, the men of law, which is to say, the ones that have entitlements: the others are outside of the law, *exleges*; they have no entitlements; they are individuals with human faces, *anthrôpoï*, and are not men, *andres*.

That society of strong men and aristocrats makes up a *sovereignty*, a *power*, two terms which, taken as synonymous with each other, serve as reminders of the identity of those two notions: entitlement and force.

Up to that point, arising from the prerogatives of strength, disputes were regulated and slights made good by means of the *duel* or *trial by combat*, the putting of force to the test. But it was not long before such combat was replaced by the prince as representative of collective sovereignty or force that no one was strong enough to defy and who, not wishing to see his men fighting one another, took it upon himself to dictate who had right on his side and to deliver justice. But where did that substitution of the judgment of the prince for combat between the parties come from? Quite simply from this principle, that whoever commands force commands right and that no one has the right to dissent from the verdict delivered by the prince. Is the worm about to rise up against the lion, or the hyssop[30] against the cedar? That would be equally nonsensical.

But who is to be the repository for this public force or power, one of the main attributes of which being the ability to determine what is right? – The strongest.

---

30. Hyssop: small plant. In an echo of Biblical language, it is cited, in contrast to the cedar, as something tiny and unimportant. [H.T.]

Let us be clear here; none of that means, as the jurists seem to be arguing, that force is the whole and all of right, that there is no right but force; it merely means that force represents the first and most non-negotiable of rights; that if, at a later date, other rights are created, they will still, in the last analysis, defer to that; that, consequently, whereas trial by combat between persons from the same city is replaced by the verdict of the prince, between independent cities the only acknowledged right, the only valid right, will still be the right of force.

Which is why, in the view of all peoples, conquest, seizure by means of strength and courage, is deemed legitimate, the most legitimate of possessions, based as it is upon a right that is superior to all civil conventions, *usucaption*, hereditary succession, sale, etc.: upon the right of force. Hence the peoples' admiration for conquerors and the untouchability of those who take things into their own hands, the deference upon which they insist, the hush that descends in their presence: *siluit terra in conspectu ejus.*[31]

Respect for force, belief in its juridical authority, if I may say so, is suggestive of the expression of a just and holy war, *justa et pia bella*; this, as I see it, has less to do with the homeland that needs defending than with the very conditions of war, which, as the ancient Romans used to think, shuns all trickery, industry and stratagem, as if a sort of sacrilege, an adulteration of combat, a corruption of justice, and countenance no means other than brute strength.

It was for that reason also that in times of revolution, when there is a cooling-off of civic, religious and moral sentiments, war, which, by some mysterious contrivance, continues to marry force and right, serves as a principle for those who no longer have any; which is why a nation, no matter how corrupted, will not perish and will not even experience decline, as long as it can keep that justice-delivering, regenerative fire of the right of war burning in its heart. War, which the bankocracy and businesses pretend to regard as piracy, is the same thing as right and force indissolubly united. Strip that away from a nation that had invested all its beliefs in their being synonymous and it is done for.

I offer these facts, or rather opinions, only for what they are worth, which is to say, as testimonies; meaning, as far as the nature and morality of war and the juridical merits of force go, that the feeling of the human race is the polar opposite of that of the gentleman lawyers. We shall soon have to discover on which side the truth lies; for the time being, let us make do with registering our preliminary conclusions:

War, according to universal testimony, is a judgement delivered by force. The right of war and the right of force are, thus, one and the same right. And

---

31. *Bible*, Book of Maccabees, 1: 3: "He advanced to the ends of the earth, and plundered many nations. When the earth became quiet before him, he was exalted, and his heart was lifted up". This book retells the legend of Alexander the Great. [A.P.]

that right is not the vain fiction of the law-maker; it is, according to the multitude which asserts it, an authentic, positive, primitive, historic right that is
therefore capable of serving as a principle, motivation and basis for a judicial
decision; all things that scholarly jurisprudence formally denies.

None of which would amount to anything if the misunderstanding concerned only a word. If that initial hurdle were overcome, in relation both to
right and history, the men of learning and the ignorant would see eye to eye on
everything else. But the discrepancy does not stop there; it encompasses the full
range of rights; people's rights, public rights, civil rights, economic rights. So
that, depending on whether universal opinion is declared mistaken or scholarly
jurisprudence incorrect, society will rest upon crumbling foundations, or the
teaching of rights will have to be completely revised. This is something that we
need to be absolutely clear about.

CHAPTER III

Consequences of the Doctrine Professed by the Authors Regarding the Right of Force

I know of no spectacle more intriguing than that of philosophical reasoning pitted against popular reasoning; the former defining, analysing, extrapolating, reasoning and, with masterly dignity, coming to a conclusion that contradicts what it terms prejudice; the latter, not knowing how to present a plea or defend itself, incapable of hammering home an argument, framing an objection and never knowing any better than to reply to all the difficulties placed in its way with these naïve words: *Est, est: Non, non*; What is, is: What is not, is not; and, that being said, toying with the erudition of men of learning as if it were a cobweb and dragging civilization and the world into its practice.

Something widely acknowledged, in that it is a matter of experience, is that civilization has antagonism as its starting point, and that society, or in other words, rights, international law, public law and civil law have evolved under the inspiration and influence of war, which is to say, under the jurisdiction of force.

If it were true, as the unanimity of the jurisconsults contends, that any such jurisdiction was merely a legacy of barbarism, an aberration of the moral sense, it would follow that all our institutions, our traditions and our laws are blighted by violence and tainted at the root; terrifying though it may be to think, it would follow that all power is tyranny, all ownership usurpation and that society is in need of being rebuilt from top to bottom. There is no unspoken acquiescence, prescription or subsequent conventions capable of redeeming such an anomaly. One does not lay down prescriptions for the truth; one does not compromise on behalf of injustice; in short, one does not build right upon its very negation. If, instead, it is the jurists themselves whose superficial philosophy has misconstrued reality and the legitimacy of the right of force, then the harm done would be greatly reduced; but the teaching of rights would need to be thoroughly overhauled, lest legislation, courts, the State, public morals and the morale of the army be exposed to the most lamentable upsets.

Let us pose the question in all seriousness.

Warfare exists and is as old as man himself. It was through it that humanity began its education, inaugurated justice. Why that blood-stained debut? It does not matter. We shall be looking into the motives and cause of that later, but we must first accept it as a fact at least. There is, they say, nothing as absolute, nothing as unsparing as fact.

Now, science and classical learning reject the morality of this fact and, consequently, its juridical value. Hobbes reduces everything to the compulsions of matter, denying the immanence of justice within us and its social impact, and sees the fact of warfare as just a manifestation of blind, immoral force. Universal conscience, however, sees that as just one factor, unhesitatingly affirming the reality of a right of war, consequently the jurisdiction of force.

In men's battles, there is something more than passion; something which Hobbes's harrowing theory does not take into account. There is this singular pretention, exclusive to our species, that not only do we see force as force, but also as something more, something that enshrines a right and, in certain instances, it makes right. As we have observed, animals fight with one another, but they do not wage war; regulating their contests is never going to occur to them. The lion has an instinct of his strength, which is where his courage comes from; he has no inkling of a right deriving from that strength and those who have credited this carnivore with who knows what brand of chivalrous generosity have not painted him from nature. Ask Gérard, the lion-killer: they have unwittingly drawn him in their own image. Man, on the other hand, better or worse than the lion, let the critics decide, man aspires with all the energy of his moral sense, to turn his physical superiority into a sort of an obligation upon others; he wants them to embrace his victory like a religion, a rationale, in short, a duty, corresponding with what he terms his right. This is the nub of the idea of war; what sets it apart from the contests between wild animals; this, with the passage of time, has gradually introduced those singular conventions between people that are known as the *laws of war*. Neither Hobbes nor the others ever managed to discern this in phenomena, but the human race has never hesitated to affirm its universality.

It is due to this deep-seated feeling that there is a right conferred by victory, that we hold to this view, innate within us, that all legislation is, at source and in its essence, warfare. Let us not be afraid to say it, as it need not make us blush, but it is to this cult of force that we must trace all of the acknowledged juridical relations among men. For a start, consider the earliest inklings of a right of war and the rights of peoples, followed by the establishment of collective sovereignties, the formation of States, their expansion through conquest, the establishment of magistracies, etc. The right of force may be queried; it may be deemed contradictory, a nonsense, but then have the decency to query its handiwork too, and call for the break-up of those immense human agglomerations, France, England, Germany, Russia. Let the attack be directed at these powers, which assuredly did not spring fully armed from the energies of nature, and that no sophism can make fall under any another principle than that of force.

Plainly, it is this formula of the *right of war, the right of force*, so little understood, that underpins the constitution of society and civilization in their entirety. What can the scholars take exception to in these considerations of such enormous gravity?

Going by their words, the scholars say the same as everyone else; they recognize the right of war. But deep down in their hearts, they deny it, and all their reservations, all their theorizing show that they have no belief in it. *The right of force is no right at all*; among the men of learning, that is invariably the unanimous sentiment. As to the hypothesis, slipped in during the Middle Ages, that seeks to present warfare like a trial by ordeal, or judicial contest as a manifestation of the will of Heaven, well, it goes without saying that Grotius and his successors repudiate it. In which they are correct: this is not the sense in which peoples understand the right of war.

But, if the right of force is not a right, what do the scholars mean by *the right of war*? How do they account for, justify, the formation of States, the establishment of jurisdictions or the validity of legislation, all things which ordinary mortals trace back to the right of force? Evidently, this is not a case of plain dealing. Their teaching is a shield for hypocrisy. After having pronounced, loud enough for all to hear, that they do not believe in a right of war, much less that force is righteous, they proceed to talk like everybody else does, compromising their consciences and striving, with much equivocation and mental reservations, to bring their esoteric teachings into line with the commonly held belief.

I have already spelled out what the scholars mean, *in petto*, by this term, *right of war*. Let us state it again and try to embarrass our learned jurisconsults a little.

There was one thing of which Grotius was profoundly aware and which is a credit to his memory: that we feel better about ourselves the more civilized we are, that no matter the lengths to which two nations may be driven by anger, interest, fanaticism or hatred, mankind must never entirely lose its rights; so, as a result, even in the midst of the blood-letting, charity and justice still have their place; that, there being no positive prescription, this restraint is commanded of us all, the strong and the weak alike, for the sake of our dignity and our moral survival. It is through this sentiment that, from ancient times to our own day, century after century, war has been diminishing in its atrociousness; and, among other things, it is in order to curtail the killings and the devastation even further that these laws have been introduced which, taken together, make up the *laws of war* and bear high witness to the perfectibility of our species.

In short, the *right of war* is the showing of respect to humanity in warfare; so says Grotius and all the publicists who have come after him.

It is certainly something to have grasped and then expanded eloquently upon this truth. Regrettably, it fails to address the issue. The point is not the manner in which military executions are to be carried out; it is the RIGHT which prompts them and motivates them, and which is the product of them. Penal legislation has also felt the influence of humanity: torture and the infliction of unusual suffering have been done away with; there is talk of abolishing the death penalty. But, in whatever form, punishment remains, in everyone's estimation, a juridical fact; hence the rigorously proper expression, *penal law*. By analogy, one wonders in what sense and why warfare is a juridical fact; from where the notion of a *right in warfare* would logically follow. Now, it is obvious that Grotius's ruminations do not even touch upon the problem. They have nothing to say to us about how war might be, by its very nature, a manifestation of right, an act of jurisdiction. Instead, they encapsulate the formal reproach in every respect. Take note; the only thing that follows from those ruminations is that acts of humanity performed in time of war are exceptions from warfare; that, if men were just, there would not even be any warfare; which clearly leads to this, that war is a departure from justice, provoked by a violation of right.

In fact, according to Grotius, *the right of war* is respect for humanity. In theory, this is nothing other than what the grammarian term an antiphrasis.[32] It would be laughable to infer from such terminology that, implicit in war *per se*, as in marriage, labour, association, property, government and every other individual or collective manifestation of the human being, there is a series of mandatory conditions, or, to put it another way, that warfare is the subject of juridical decision-making and legal prescriptions.

But, judging by history, that is exactly what it should be. It is this essential analogy between war, labour, State, family, government and religion, that Grotius was obliged to adopt, lest he build castles in the air and indulge in fantasy. For, if war may be looked upon as a lawful, legitimate contest, summoned up by justice and prompted on both sides by the grandest and holiest of interests, and if there is no right of war in the strict sense of the term, then the whole of history becomes inexplicable and nonsensical. The arrangement of societies is built upon a rhetorical flourish. If there is no right of war, if all that one can argue with certainty is that any such right may be a positive and *sui generis* manifestation of justice, then there is no other meaning in history: chance rules the

32. Antiphrasis: Employing a word or phrase in a sense opposite to that of its true meaning, almost always in an ironic way. [H.T.]

earth; States are founded upon iniquity; the rights of peoples become a mirage; international treaties are fundamentally worthless; civilization turns into tragi-comedy; the realm of man, as Fourier used to call it,[33] is simply the animal realm raised to the higher power. For there is nothing either in the rights of peoples or in public law or in civil law, nothing in institutions and in mores, nothing in religion and in economics that is not dependent in its origins upon war. War has made us all that we are, and it functioned without right! Have you thought this through, master?

I know that neither tradition nor antiquity confers right; that humanity was all the more likely to err insofar as its youthfulness left it wide open to igno-rance, and that our progress consists of scarcely anything other than the adjust-ments which we are relentlessly making to our initial hypotheses. But that does not make it any the less extraordinary that justice has taken as its starting point what the jurists deem its negation, to wit, war; that, thereafter, the historical development of humanity has taken place against the backdrop of a right of war, so much so that, if that right is done away with, absolutely nothing is left of humanity past, present and, I dare say, even future, since it could neither shrug off its tradition nor regenerate itself outside of that same tradition and consti-tute itself in accordance with some other arrangement. Therein lies the gaping hole in Grotius's work. Not only did that great man fail to understand the right of war; not only was his view of that right based upon a misapprehension, but he saw that right was at odds with the faith, the tradition and the consistent practice of the human race; he never even suspected that in denying the right of force, he was building castles in the air and raising a monument, not to justice, but to the arbitrary.

---

33. For the relationship between Proudhon's thinking and Fourier's, see Pierre-Joseph Proudhon *De la création de l'ordre dans l'humanité* (Paris: Prévot, 1843), Ch. III: La Métaphy-sique. [H.M.]

CHAPTER IV

More on the Same Subject.
The Theory of Wolff and Vattel

Grotius's successors, especially Wolff and Vattel, seem to have spotted the danger: all their effort was poured into warding it off.

According to Wolff, nations ought to be regarded as moral agents, to which *natural* law is as applicable as it is to individuals, but with the adjustments implicit in the differentiation between the particular and the general.

As far as nations go, natural law, becoming the rights *of peoples*, therefore breaks down into the *necessary* rights of peoples, and the *voluntary* rights of peoples.

The necessary rights of peoples, which Grotius called *internal* right, consists of the fact that natural right commands nations, in their heart of hearts, just the same as it commands individuals: it is immutable.

The voluntary rights of peoples, or *external* right, is, according to Wolff, the result of the fiction of some sort of higher power, upon which every other would be dependent and which would foist upon each and every one, depending on the circumstances, certain prescriptions unjust in terms of natural law but which have, in the practice of nations, become indispensable. According to Vattel, that same right is a product of those nations being independent and sovereign, and, incapable of alleging fault in one another, or of persuading one another or compelling one another, they are mutually obliged to put up with certain more or less irregular things, granting more or less deplorable concessions to one another with an eye to forestalling greater misfortunes.

It is important to stress here, as Vattel has, the sovereignty and respective independence of States. Apart from this, his theory of the voluntary rights of peoples is the same as Wolff's. Indeed, whatever the international concessions that may be made (the sum of which would therefore constitute the rights of peoples), they spring from the fiction of there being some higher power foisting these upon them, or enduring them with resignation, provided that, both writers contend, there are, hovering over the nations, in addition to the direct and positive prescriptions of conscience, unhappy circumstances resulting from their being antagonists, but which their interests, properly construed, require them to endure and which, as far as they are concerned, become the principle, occasion or substance of a sort of right. That right is described as *voluntary*, not because it derives from the free will of nations, but because it is an effect of their antagonistic subjectivity, which plainly is no less than free, but which, making a virtue of necessity, accepts the law of its affliction as an emanation of its will.[34]

An example will make this clearer.

Two townships, two cities, are founded simultaneously, a few kilometres from each other. Within the boundaries of their respective territories, those two townships are independent and sovereign. Each of them constitutes a collective entity, a moral agent governed, *a priori*, by natural law. In their dealings with each other, and insofar as those dealings have no effect upon their sovereignty and survival, those two townships are therefore governed by the necessary rights of peoples, which is to say, by a law that is an inner compulsion within them, as if they were individuals. They should neither harm, offend, nor invade each other; all trespass against these rules is an affront to the necessary rights of peoples.

But, as time goes by, the populace on both sides proliferates and the two townships expand; soon they become contiguous, so that the inhabitants and their homes more resemble a single mass. The sovereignty of the one or other of them is placed in jeopardy, at least for their mutual individuality (nationality). The antagonism then erupts with formidable consequences. Suppose these two authorities are beholden to a higher power, kingdom or empire; the issue will then be susceptible to settlement, to the cost of one or other of them, by that royal or imperial power which imposes the law and ensures that it is, like it or not, accepted. If it were otherwise, that is, in the case where both townships might be two absolutely independent sovereign States, how is the matter going to be settled? Wolff starts from the hypothesis of there being a higher power and Vattel from the necessity of things, in order to effect, gently or through the use of force, a revolution (plainly, non-juridical, but inevitably a revolution) in

---

34. Proudhon is attributing what is today known as a "structural" theory of "international anarchy" to Vattel and Wolff. As he understands them, both argue that states' mutual negative freedoms, consecrated by their mutual right of war, determine their interests, and that natural law is deducible *a priori*, independently of observation. To extend this contemporary reference, Proudhon is here engaging with what is known as the "English School", or "Grotian tradition" of International Relations. Hedley Bull, the pioneer of this line of thinking, argues that war is one of the five primary institutions of international relations, or the anarchical society, which safeguards the autonomy of states. See Hedley Bull, *The Anarchical Society: A study of Order in World Politics*, 2nd ed. with an introduction by Stanley Hoffman (New York: Columbia University Press, 1995). [A.P.]

the make-up of the two States, the circumstances in which they exist and in their dealings. Such is the voluntary rights of peoples.

Out of this voluntary *right of peoples* will then sprout the *customary* rights of peoples and the *conventional* rights of peoples; and, to a lesser extent, *public* right and *civil* right, etc. Add, if you will, the distinctions between *perfect* rights and *imperfect* rights, *historical* right and *philosophical* right. Bundle up this whole theory, which is convinced of its own profundity, and which is, instead, sheer nonsense, according to which right is born of duty, which in turn is going to have to derive from right, and, as Vattel states, we have only received rights in order to assist the performance of our duties ... and you will have some notion of the complicated mechanism whereby jurisprudence strives to take on board that which, in the minds of the masses, flows directly from the right of war and the right of force.

But let us leave the verbiage to the authors. We know what the voluntary rights of peoples consists of and we have seen, from example, in what instances it becomes applicable. Now, what does that right say? In relation to war, what are its maxims, its formulas? Vattel boils them down to two fundamental rules:

The first is, *that in terms of its effects, war, in the proper sense, ought to be regarded as just on both sides.*

Second, *that whatever is permitted for one is permissible for the other.*[35]

Conquest is legitimized by virtue of the first rule: "In principle", Vattel says, "the victor, in the wake of a just war, is allowed to seize only that which is his due by natural right, or whatever is vital for his safety and to compensate for his expenditure; as for the winner in an unjust war, the conquest in which he indulges is yet another crime. But, given that the nations have no courts and that the two belligerent powers must be presumed to be equally in the right, it is accepted, under the voluntary rights of peoples, that in formal warfare any acquisition is valid, regardless of the justice of the cause; which is why conquest is a legitimate entitlement between nations".[36]

From the second rule can be deduced the following: that a State defeated following an unjust aggression is liable only for reparations proportionate with the losses caused by that war. But when we come to moral harm, looting, devastation, etc., which are, in the case of an unjust war, according to natural law, just so many crimes, impunity is granted. The war being held just on both sides, what is permitted for one side is permitted for the other: as a result, evil wrought by the warrior is excusable.

The reader knows now where to stand vis à vis the theory of Wolff and Vattel. On the very threshold of science, just when it is vital that right be

35. Vattel, *Le Droit des Gens*, Vol II, 221 and 222. [H.M.]
36. Vattel, *Le Droit Des Gens*, Vol II, 225. [H.M.]

founded on facts, that its positive expression be apprehended and, if possible, its material expression too, just before moving to make deductions from and settle on their applications, those two publicists throw themselves, so to speak, headlong into fiction. Society, the testimony of the human race states, is founded upon antagonism; Wolff and Vattel deny that. Within that antagonism, continues the voice of nations, right, the sovereign arbiter, finds its primary expression in the superiority of force. This appears equally inconceivable to our two authors and they deny it. After those two negations, the rest goes without saying: which is to say that the rights of peoples is dismantled, piece by piece, and becomes sheer illusion.

So, imagine that two nations join in battle, each with the same positive and equal right and without affront on one part or the other: in practice, we are compelled to countenance it but in principle it is denied. That, they say, is just some hypothesis dreamt up as an explanation for an abusive transaction. That conquest, a just, sacred, inviolable conquest should be the natural price of victory; the legitimate product of legitimate warfare strikes them as an even greater monstrosity. But, deferring to an invincible fatality which, having first turned men and independent, sovereign nations into fighters, casts them all into an antagonism from which there is no escape, our learned men hasten to conclude, in order to put an end to the arson and slaughter and step away from chaos, albeit by lying to their consciences, that it is a good thing to grant the winner what he demands and the decent thing to impose the confusion of defeat upon the vanquished, at the risk of legitimizing thievery and glorifying murder. No doubt Monsieur de Girardin's outraged cry *War is murder; war is theft*, is to be credited to this queer jurisprudence.

Monsieur de Girardin was able to brave the thunderbolts from the prosecuting authorities; he had the master-teachers and their teachings on his side.

But the conscience of the human race takes exception to these theories as well as to such insult. Not only does it assert the reality of the right of war, but, even then, it is very well aware that it can, if need be, reject the application of, and protest against, what it then described as *abuse of force*, the very same way that, in front of the ordinary courts, the litigant can reject the jurisprudence under which he has been summoned, without thereby rejecting justice; falsely challenging testimony, without denying the usefulness of testimony-based proof; protesting the misuse of property without thereby denying property as such.

Universal conscience, I say, upholds the reality of the right of war and the competency, in respect of certain quarrels, of the jurisdiction of force. International relations and, furthermore, the entire system of civil and political rights, are built upon that right and upon that competency as if they were solid foundations. And it is by virtue of that right of war, by virtue of the competency of a jurisdiction of force, that Vattel's two rules, sheer fictions within his system of voluntary right and destructive of all morality, are again rendered strictly truthful:

1. *In terms of its effects, war, in the proper sense, ought to be regarded as equally just on both sides.*
2. *In war proper, what is permitted for one is permitted for the other.*

Let me inform Vattel: not only ought war to be deemed as equally just on both sides, but it IS just, and CANNOT BUT BE just on both sides, since, if it were unjust on one side, or on both, it would no longer be war; since, in that case, society would be founded upon injustice and civilization's progress dictated by the randomness of violence and treachery; since, but for that equal justice, there would be no difference between banditry and warfare, and any gang of malefactors would simply need to inform society that it is prosecuting a war in order to arrange an amnesty for itself in the eventuality of defeat.

CHAPTER V

That the Negation of the Right of Force Renders the Philosophy of Right Impossible

Not a single theory of the right of war and of peoples has been forthcoming since Wolff and his abbreviator Vattel. None have tried to bridge this enormous gap which, leaving international law as bereft of sanction as of principle, ruins public right and civil right, compromising the power of the prince, State sovereignty, the legitimacy of the magistrates, the authority of the courts, the security of property-owners; it places armies on a par with hellish gangs, breathes contempt and revolt into the populace and threatens to bring civilization to ruin.

According to the authors, there is no right of war and no rights of peoples; those are two hypotheses conjured up to meet the needs of civilization and the human race's sense of honour, but they are two utterly gratuitous hypotheses. The upshot is that the whole body of law is a rag-bag of fictions. At the time of writing, this is what the entirety of juridical science boils down to.

It is in vain that Kant, the immortal author of the *Critique of Pure Reason*, has tried to accommodate the problem that concerns us within his mighty categories. Misled, right from the outset, by the negation of the right of force, all he could do was fall into line behind Wolff, and has, pitifully, wound up mired in utopia.[37] That horrific phenomenon, warfare, is troubling in the highest degree to the methodical, peaceful reasoning of the philosopher from Königsberg; it is his system's stumbling-block. In fact, for want of a precise theory of war and its rights, the system of practical reason collapses, and the Kantian edifice is left relying on just one wing. We have to look at the ferocity with which the philosopher takes issue with this sphinx derailing his logic. He casts around

---

37. While Proudhon may have distanced himself from the idealist foundations of Kant's philosophy of right, he retained much more than he admits here, in particular his teleological view of history as a secular theodicy. In *Perpetual Peace* (1795), and *Idea of a Universal History With Cosmopolitan Intent* (1784), Kant derives a progressive account of history from the brutality of war and the "crooked" nature of man. For more, see Prichard, *Justice, Order and Anarchy*, chapter 3. [A.P.]

for rebuttals of it, counter-arguments against it, and any negations there may be, anywhere. Where can such fury in men be coming from? In respect of that question, Kant is left bewildered and he concludes, not by solving the puzzle, but by slicing through it, by using the resources of general policy-making to blank out this ghastly warfare, which shatters his philosophy of right:

"War", Kant says, "has no need of any particular motive. It seems to be rooted in human nature, passing for an act of nobility to which love of glory must lead, in the absence of any vested interest. Thus, among the savages in the Americas, as in Europe, in the age of chivalry, military valour secures great honours, not only if there is war, as would be only fair, but also *in order that* there may be war and as a means of testifying to it. So that a sort of a dignity is conferred upon warfare and even philosophers have been found singing its praises as a noble prerogative of humanity, forgetful of the dictum of one Greek: *War is an evil, in that it generates more evildoers than it sweeps away*".[38]

So, Kant contends that *there should be no war*, be it between individuals or between peoples; that it is an *extra-legal* state and that the authentic rights of peoples will end such *execrable* contests, by striving to create and consolidate PERPETUAL PEACE.

We have fallen from those learned doctors Grotius, Wolff and Pufendorf to the skirts of the philanthropic and utopian Abbé de Saint Pierre![39] But we have not yet hit rock bottom. Is the project of perpetual peace feasible? Kant takes the view that one indication of the possibility of containing the passions lies in pitting them against one another:

"The problem of the constitution", he says, "even *were it for a people of demons,* is not impossible to solve, as long as that people has the gift of understanding. The advantage would be that, we would not need to expect world peace through some sort of *moral reform* of humans, which is impossible to obtain".[40]

This is nothing short of Ch. Fourier's[41] theory of the passions married with Ancillon's system of balancing or *counter-force*. These days, Fourier's theory has been banished to the ranks of the utopias that no one even bothers to try out anymore: but why? Precisely because impassioned men, who are in that

---

38. Kant, *Principes Métaphysiques du Droit et Paix Perpetuelle*, trans. Tissot [1853], 286. [P-J.P.]

39. Abbé DE SAINT-PIERRE (1658–1743), author of a *Projet pour rendre la paix perpétuelle* (1713) was scathing in his criticism of the handiwork of Louis XI, for which he was expelled from the Academy. [H.T.]

40. KANT, *Principes Métaphysiques du Droit et Paix Perpetuelle*, 288. This passage is a paraphrase rather than a verbatim citation from the translation of Kant. [H.M.]

41. See Proudhon, *De la création de l'ordre dans l'humanité*, Chapter IV: L'Économie politique. [H.M.]

sense comparable with demons, are also endowed with understanding and that understanding, far from helping to reconcile or balance out their ambitions, is the very thing that makes their attack all the more ferocious. As for Ancillon's system, that is nothing other than the principle of *European stability* by virtue of which nations, in order not to go to war against one another, are obliged to ensure that they are constantly under arms.

However, as if this philosophical instinct were sounding a warning to Kant about the puerile nature of his thinking, after having identified the basis for a general pacification, he ends on this thought which the gentlemen from the Peace Congress would be well advised to mull over:

> Perpetual peace is IMPRACTICABLE: but it is *indefinitely approachable*.[42]

Hegel feels none of the same embarrassment that Kant does. But Kant believed in man's *practical reason*, distinguishable in principle from *pure* or *speculative reason*, and giving rise to an order of facts, ideas and sentiments, that understanding, on its own, cannot quite account for. Kant even made such *practical reason* a sort of endorsement of *pure reason*, by demonstrating how certain ideas, such as those about God, the immortality of the soul, the certainty of external objects and consequently of our knowledge, ideas that *pure reason*, according to him, left undetermined, were guaranteed to us as essential postulates of *practical reason*; meaning that in the final analysis, intelligence in man has no certainty other than that which it draws from conscience. Hegel rejects that dualism; and traces everything back to a single principle, the evolving of logic through noumena and phenomena.[43] In light of that evolution, then, what happens is what has to happen. Hegel announces that this is right, no matter what it may be, and is never bothered by the subjective protestations of conscience. In his eyes, right is a word: just like truth and just like justice. There being no difference between science and conscience. Hegel has cast his eagle eye over war and he approves of it, announces that its overall outcomes are good, in which he is not wrong. But he has no other

---

42. Kant, *Principes Métaphysiques du Droit et Paix Perpetuelle*, 321. This phrase is Proudhon's own. Neither paraphrase nor translation. The original states: "If there be a duty, if it is even conceivable that there is any hope of accomplishing the rule of public law, even should it only be by means of endless advances, the perpetual peace that is to follow the truces hitherto known as peace treaties, is therefore no chimera but rather a matter for which time, most likely shortened by the onward march of the human mind, offers us the promise of a resolution". [H.M.]

43. *Noumena*: Things as they essentially are in themselves, as opposed to *phenomena* which are things as they appear to us. [H.T.]

explanation for such goodness in the overall outcomes of war, other than that they exist, and he cares not whether the principle behind them be moral or immoral; he contends that war, being inevitable, is, by that very fact, infallible and that it cannot be mistaken. And look at the consequences. Whereas Fichte preached a crusade against Napoleon,[44] Hegel phlegmatically admired the dialectical march of the conqueror.[45] Had the Germany of 1813 been a little less Kantian, and somewhat more Hegelian, Napoleon I would have been victorious in his Saxon campaign and the invasion of France in 1814 would not have taken place; on the contrary, the disastrous Russian campaign having been made good, and the coalition crushed once and for all, the empire of the tsars would have been conquered; Napoleon would have died on his throne and his son, the Duke of Reichstadt, restored to health by his father's victory, might well have been crowned with the crowns of France and of Austria. As a matter of patriotism, we in France can accept this Hegelian ending to the age of the Empire; but it has to be said that, on grounds of the very same patriotism, the Germans would not be so comfortable with it. Hence, contrary to Hegel's system, it follows that the rationale of war is not the same as the rationale of necessity and, whilst force must incontrovertibly count for something, it is still not the whole story.

Building on the right of war, conceived in pretty much those terms, Hegel concluded at the same place as Hobbes, at governmental absolutism, State omnipotence and the subordination of the individual. Whether Hegel still has a single supporter in Germany for that strand of his philosophy, I do not know; but I can state that talking about war and the rights of force in such terms and blending the good with the bad, the true with the false, brings philosophy into disrepute. Hegel would have deserved this emphatic condemnation from Mager, one of his own disciples:

> A philosophy whereby fatalism and the right of the strongest are hoisted
> on to the throne; whereby the individual is stripped of his personhood,
> his responsibility, and degraded until he is a mere droplet in the torrent
> of the universal mind, and which explicitly states that virtue and justice,

---

44. *Die Reden an die deutsche Nation* (1807–1808). Cf. French translation by Philippe as *Discours à la nation allemande*. See also: *Ueber den Begriff des Wahrhaften Krieges in Bezug auf den Krieg im Iahre* (1813), the depiction of Napoleon that Fichte offered his audience in Berlin. That pamphlet was translated into French by Lorter as *De l'idée d'une guerre légitime* (1831). [H.M.]

45. In a letter sent from Jena, and dated 13 October, 1806, Hegel wrote to his friend Niethammer: "I saw the Emperor, that world soul – *diese Weltseele* – riding through town. The sight of such an individual concentrated at one point there, encompassing the world at a glance and lording over it, was actually a wonderful feeling". [H.M.]

iniquity and violence, vices and talents, personal deeds, passions grand
and petty, crime and innocence, greatness in public or individual life, independence and the fates of nations, are viewpoints with which universal
history need not concern itself.[46]

Let us complete that sentence ourselves: Such a philosophy is an affront to common sense and a mockery of what it purports to glorify: fate, warfare, force.

What other quotation might I cite right now? And to what end? The
right of war being denied, the rights of peoples, about which the gawkers still
prattle, adds up to nothing. Let us hear from the latest census-taker of science,
Monsieur Oudot:

> In terms of international law, is there any sanction other than that of con-
> science and the evil that it brings down, sooner or later, upon the head of
> the party guilty of perpetrating injustice?
>
> For that to be answered in the affirmative, one would have to em-
> brace semi-fatalistic beliefs which, whilst acknowledging freedom where
> individuals are concerned, denies it to peoples. One would have to argue,
> along with Domat: *that trials between nations have force and God as their
> judges, the incidents that God adds to wars*; in short, one would have to
> contend, with the modern philosophers, that war has never erred; that
> God guides its steps so as to ensure the birthing of a few advances de-
> manded by force in the name of justice.

To which our author responds:

> Human liberty can be as ill-served between nations as in private debates;
> the canon, *ratio ultima regum*, is not infallible when it comes to award-
> ing victory to the right side. So we have no option but to acknowledge
> that a sanctioning international law is unclear in respect of the means of
> external sanction. The *preventive*, *probative*, *reparatory* or *penal* means at
> its disposal amount to force alone; its procedure is the skill of some gen-
> eral; its courtroom the battlefield. Montesquieu acknowledges these dis-
> mal truths. And from them draws this consequence, that *princes, who do
> not live alongside one another in accordance with the civil laws, are not free.
> For the chief characteristic of freedom is that one cannot be forced into doing
> something not ordained by the law; and one is in that state only because one
> is governed by civil laws.* D'Aguesseau adds, in the same vein: *Whereas in*

---

46. WILLM, *Histoire de la philosophie allemande*, vol. IV, 330. [P-J.P]

ordinary jurisprudence the law sits in judgment of the deed, here, it is nearly always the deed that serves to ensure observation of the law.

The absence of such a considerable part of sanction amounts to a profound mutilation of the idea of right. And Burlamaqui, Pufendorf and other writers admit that sanctioning international law scarcely deserves the description of law in the precise meaning of the terms: *a precise understanding of the notion of right always encapsulates the idea of a supreme power, capable of compelling men to submit to it.*[47]

In short, the rights of peoples, the faith in accordance with which nations have lived, that sovereign right, is a fairy-tale; classical jurisprudence, the established, formal science tells us so. Everything in existence, in terms of kingdoms, empires, republics, the whole system of States more or less independent of one another, mutually acknowledged, though not guaranteed, sovereignties, is the product of chance, violence and perfidy, the unfathomable outworking of fate and arbitrariness, and liable to be destroyed by whim and fate tomorrow.

Behold consequences coming to pass and juridical chaos gradually ushering in social chaos.

Since, as the venerable professor whom I have just quoted says, *a precise understanding of the notion of right always encapsulates the idea of a supreme power, capable of compelling men to submit to it;* and, as Ancillon has it, *authority is the sole source from which flows right;* and since the absence of international law is because humanity is divided into independent sovereignties which acknowledge no supreme arbiter, it follows that the first thing to do is to draw all States back into unity and overcome those old prejudices of nationality and fatherland that stand in the way of the achievement of right. As the learned Monsieur Oudot has it:

> This fragmentation of men into diverse *nations* or *societies* is a matter of regret. One might aspire to some day see the peoples reunited in unity. Happy day, when the dismal name of *foreigner* is stricken from human languages, and with it that contention between interests and principles that narrow patriotism translates into wars![48]

That is also the opinion of Monsieur Vergé, Martens's publisher and commentator. According to him, the notion of fatherland is a negation of the rights of people. Under that principle, he writes:

---

47. OUDOT, *Conscience et science du droit*, vol. II, passim. [H.T.]
48. OUDOT, *Conscience et science du droit*, vol. II, 362. [H.M.]

Are the crusades not the negation of the rights of people? Instead of the Greek fatherland and the Roman fatherland, there was Christendom.[49]

So, fatherland no longer counts for anything, nationality counts for nothing, the autonomy of races, the differentiation between peoples, the determinations of States, nothing.

Thus, the Alexanders, the Caesars, the Charlemagnes, the Charles Vs, the Philip IIs, the Louis XIVs, the Napoleons, all these would-be universal monarchs, these fatherland-destroyers, destroyers of national and individual freedoms, were benefactors of the human race, the true representatives of righteousness; the heroes who fought against them, the likes of Memnon, Vercingetorix, Witikind, William the Silent, Gustavus Adolphus, William III, Kosciuzko, Wellington, rebels against Providence, foes of the rights of peoples, deserving of all the bitter fruits of defeat and history's blemishes. For right derives from authority alone; and since the supreme State has not deigned to establish its throne among nations, there is nothing better for us to do than to make up for that absence of a God of order by conjuring up an omniarchy of the earth by centralizing the five parts of the world!

True, over the past twelve years, we have seen the hounding of much less dangerous utopians than these; men who, though they may have strayed from their aspirations for the future, at least did not abuse the public's trust and did not strive to discredit the State that paid them in the minds of their audience. In the long run, why would patriotic virtue not weaken in a nation taught such beautiful things by its doctors? Above all, how would the army hold on to the slightest respect for righteousness and morality, when all it ever hears is that it is not, nor could ever be anything other than an instrument of brutal violence?

The Epicurean poet, Horace, who came along after the civil wars and who, as he himself has told us, was not exactly a glittering example of martial virtue, emphatically denies that war and right have anything in common. "Your Achilles", he said to his young poet, "recognizes no law nor right outside of arms": *Jura neget sibi nata, nihil non arroget armis.*[50]

It is in accordance with that fantastic model and on the strength of the word of ignoramus jurists, that you will hear more than one military man, albeit a brave one bestowed with honour, but forgetting that the first magistrate was

---

49. VERGÉ, Introduction to Martens, *Précis du droit des gens*, vol. I, foreword, XI. [H.M.]

50. "Let him be impatient, passionate, ruthless, fierce; let him claim that laws are not for him, let him ever make appeal to the sword". Horace: *Satires. Epistles. The Art of Poetry*, trans. H. Rushton Fairclough (Cambridge: Harvard University Press, 1926), 460–61. [A.P.]

an army commander, naively agreeing that justice is not the handiwork of the warrior, that the only law the soldier knows is his sword and that if, in battle and in victory, it suits him to be moderate in the use of it, then that is sheer generosity on his part and because it adds to his glory. Warfare and righteousness, the military readily admit, are, like virtue and vice, contraries, unrelated to each other and irreconcilable. Here, Grotius cites a host of famous dicta, preserved by the authors but proving just one thing, namely: that whilst the notion of the right of war has corrupted armies, this is primarily thanks to the mistaken ideas spread by the jurists, thanks to the pernicious practice, adopted by modern nations as a State maxim, of separating justice and warfare one from the other, as if they were two incompatible elements, and allowing only the man who fights, at the risk his life, for right's sake to be familiar with righteousness and bear it in mind.

That the Right of Force Was not Known to Hobbes. A Critical Examination of that Author's System

The writer who sets about rehabilitating either an idea or an epoch or a man, could not surround himself with too many precautions and seek too many guarantees against slanderous backlash. True, these days there is no shortage of people who, no matter how little pretext I afford them, would be happy to say that the theory of the right of force, as I have just now laid it out, is borrowed from the renowned Englishman Hobbes, known to the average man of letters for having been the publisher and panegyrist of the most immoral and most atrocious propositions that have ever appeared regarding the rights of peoples. I imagine that few of my contemporaries and compatriots, have taken the care to read the writings of that publicist, whom I venture to call a genius, albeit that I regard his teaching as containing only half of the truth, and that he had the glory of being one of the first to look to *pure and right reason* for the principles of social order, and beyond faith or religious revelation.

It is one of the inevitable effects of progress that as our reason dawns and then melts away the fog from the chaos of our ideas, the old authors, the ground-breaking pioneers of thought, are gradually forgotten about and their books consigned to the attic. But it behoves those aspiring to carry on their work to remind posterity of them from time to time and pay their efforts the proper tribute of gratitude which they have earned.[51]

Here is what I read about Hobbes in the *Biographie portative universelle,* published by Garnier frères in Paris in 1852:

---

51. On 30 May 1861 Proudhon wrote to Langlois: "You are correct in saying, to be sure, that the *science* of right is only in its infancy. Hobbes was the first (I am excluding the religious movement). Since that Englishman, the juridical world has been stuck in the status quo. Now some slight progress has been recently achieved and, pointless modesty aside, I think I may profit from it. There is a huge amount still to be done". [H.M.]

HOBBES (Thomas), celebrated English philosopher, political writer, English and Latin poet: Malmesbury 1588–1680. During the civil wars he showed himself to be a zealous supporter of the royalist cause and was forced to flee to France (1640). On his return to his homeland (1653), he earned himself many enemies on account of his opinions and the intolerance of his character. Hobbes was a friend to Bacon, Gassendi and Galileo. A bold and sometimes profound thinker: a strict logician but, at the same time, a narrow-minded and paradoxical genius, he deployed remarkable power to no great effect. *His system is a blatant and rounded materialism, with God left out. In morals and in politics, he starts from this hypothesis: that man is by nature selfish, mischievous, hostile to his fellow-man. He contends that rights only came about by means of contracts and have no other basis, and he concludes from this that the best government is that of force, the most absolute form of monarchical despotism.* It was in his book *De Cive* (1642) that he expounded this still notorious doctrine.

That little entry is a summary of everything that, even today, is commonly believed about Hobbes. *Materialist, atheist,* advocator of absolute power ... could one ask for anything darker or more horrific? He was also a maverick thinker, geometer, poet, Hellenist, friend of Bacon, Galileo and Gassendi, three names as good as hundreds of others; he even knew persecution and exile on account of his views; this is remembered but not taken into account. The man is judged. The seventeenth century's clericals framed the indictment; the so-called critics of the nineteenth adopted their conclusions, and that is that. This is how hucksterish literature executes authors. And there you have your justice, o Posterity!

The purpose behind Hobbes's writings, his lifetime's thought, throughout his ninety-two years, was to employ the force of reason, or, as he liked to call it, "right reason" alone to seek out the principles of morality and right.

Is a mind tormented for ninety-two years by such a notion an immoral mind? Because, ultimately, the labels *atheism, materialism* and *absolutism* tossed around wrongly and coming from some who certainly were no more knowledgeable than Hobbes about what God, matter and the absolute are, suggests nothing less.

Thomas Hobbes was part of that mighty generation that came along in the wake of the Reformation, but which was unsatisfied with the Reformation itself, a generation for which the entitlement to interpret the Bible freely, soon turning into an entitlement to think freely about everything, meant that the entire edifice of knowledge, hitherto faith-based, had, finally, to be founded upon reason. Within that generous phalanx of thinkers and standing out on varying counts and in differing directions were Bacon, Gassendi, Galileo, Hobbes's friends, and Descartes, Grotius and Spinoza. Hobbes walked in step with these great men and, though his teaching may be somewhat in error, he deserves to retain his place, especially since his impact upon his own century and the centuries thereafter has been greater than generally supposed.

Where does society come from? Hobbes asks himself. What is the State? What are the foundations of political order? What is the extent of the prince's power? What is its principle? What is meant by *democracy, aristocracy, monarchy*? What value has the oath? What do these words mean: *contracts, obligations*, etc.? Religion offers us enlightenment on these issues: its answers we know. It has its own solution to these formidable problems: and our lives are lived according to its precepts and we cling to its tradition. But, setting faith and God's express order aside, what are we to think of all these things?

There we have the thesis. True, it was a mighty mind that, back in the first half of the seventeenth century, was grappling with such issues; and there is no denying that the man who attempted to resolve them was a man of genius.[52]

Now that the labels materialist and atheist have come to mean someone questing after truth and the governance of mores by the power of reason, in the light of experience, then Thomas Hobbes must certainly be deemed an atheist and materialist. But Descartes is also an atheist and the same goes for Bacon and all the rest. Taken as a whole, our modern society can ultimately, perhaps, be described as atheist and materialist, in that it is distinct and determined to distinguish itself ever more from the philosophy of theology, the way the temporal is distinct from the spiritual. Even those who have clung to religious beliefs are the first to acknowledge the need to separate religion from reason. That said, we next need to know if Hobbes himself, a speculative atheist in the way that Descartes was a Pyrrhonian, was also one at heart; whether he proclaimed in his soul and conscience, like the disbelieving psalmist: *No, there is no God.* I confess that I am not in the least inclined to clarify that. What interests me is Hobbes's teaching; his salvation bothers me not.

So, setting to one side the idea of God and religion in respect of social science and geometry alike, Hobbes wonders what social or juridical truth there is, as far as man is concerned, in this state which he imagines is open to the inspiration of his understanding alone and which he describes as the *state of nature*, rather than the religious state. And our philosopher, despite his desire to

---

52. A "man of genius" was a popular Saint-Simonian term which signified a rarity of human excellence, a category of person, including, for example, Napoleon, who were entitled to govern society absolutely, as part of a phalanx of leaders and "Priest Scientists". Napoleon was the archetype Man of Genius for the Saint Simonians. Proudhon is no doubt using the term with some degree of irony here. [A.P.]

be guided solely by reason and to break free of the undergrowth of revelation, nevertheless failed to separate moral conscience from religious conscience successfully, just like the theologians and moralists of his day and our own; as these two ideas, religion and morality are still, as far as he is concerned, indissolubly wedded, not to say identical, his response, along with all the theologians of his day and all the believers of our own day, is that, in a state of nature, which is to say, outside of the idea of God and the influence of religion, man (Adam the sinner) is prey to the governance of antagonism and selfishness; that, consequently, answering only to the promptings of his appetite and knowing no law beyond his own will, he is, by nature, an enemy to his fellow-man, a savage beast, *homo homini lupus*, unless, by some heaven-sent miracle he becomes his benefactor, his god, *vel deus*.

Hobbes's conclusion could not have been other than it was. The notion of immanent justice, the distinction between two sorts of moralities, religious morality and rational morality, between two sorts of rights, God-given rights and human rights, deeper and more delicate than the division between the spiritual and the temporal or indeed between religion and reason, was not clearly thought out in Hobbes's time, and everything inclines me to think that it never will be.

Following this first proposition from Hobbes, that, in a state of nature, man is the foe of his fellow-man, it seems that the debate ought to have stopped there. In the absence of doctors of theology, the first peasant to come along could have said to Hobbes: "Good sir, if it be true that in the state of nature we are only savage beasts, ever ready to devour one another, then plainly there is no morality other than in God and religion, no justice other than in religion, no authority other than in religion, no real, decent policy other than in religion: and that your right reason is, consequently, a nonsense and you would be well advised to return to the catechism; and instead of philosophizing, you would have nothing better to do, like us poor peasants, than ponder Holy Scripture, work during the week, and sing psalms on Sundays".

That line of argument might have gone unanswered. But Hobbes could not succumb to it because, whilst it is true that once one accepts that moral principle and religious principle are identical, one need no longer quest after the rational foundations of society, and the distinction between religion and reason, between sacred science and profane science still stands, regardless; and Hobbes was still within his rights to wonder, maybe not whether what we term justice and morality still applied outside of religion, but how, absent religion, with or without justice, with or without morality, man and his neighbour might struggle free of their antagonistic condition and come to an accommodation.

Thus, defeated by his own weapons, which are those of dialectics, but loyal to the indestructible principle of the distinction between faith and reason, Hobbes presses onwards. Faltering with every step. And here is where he finally arrived.

That the German philosopher Hegel starts from nothingness in order to arrive at BEING, we know; Hobbes follows a similar procedure. He starts from the state of war in order to arrive at the state of society, from unrighteousness to arrive at righteousness; therein lies the originality of his system.

In the state of nature, he says, such as we can only imagine it outside of the institution of religion; in that condition, where there is no law-giver, since God had yet to put in an appearance; with no laws, no authority; where there is a war of each against all; where the dividing-line between good and evil is non-existent, what is then to regulate the actions of man? In other words, what are we to imagine as being the sovereign driver of his will, and, consequently, the law governing his existence? Plainly, that he should DO EVERYTHING *to avoid death and suffering.* Common sense tells him: *the preservation of his body and his limbs, by all possible means*; that, as far as man in a state of nature is concerned, is the only authentic rule, the *dictamen*[53] of pure, right reason.

From there Hobbes derives his definition of right, the definition that he will employ as the scaffold for his system; Everything that man in a state of nature can do rationally, or, to put that a better way, logically, vis à vis and in defiance of all, with a view to preserving his body and his limbs, that, I say, is done justly and righteously, *id juste et jure factum dicam.* So that the underpinning of right, according to Hobbes, is that every person, insofar as he can, looks to the preservation of his body and his limb, *ut quisque vitam et membra sua, quaetenus postest, tueatur.*[54]

Manifestly, such a right, entailing, as Hobbes most explicitly states, the ability to kill and steal, is not right; it is a non-right. The idea of right implies mutual respect and reciprocal decency: if the affinity is on one side only, if it is unilateral, it amounts to sheer selfishness. Which is why I said that Hobbes started from non-right in order to arrive at right, just as Hegel, in his metaphysics, begins with nothingness and arrives at being. We shall see how the English publicist made that transition.

Having set out that definition of right, Hobbes is dauntless in his exploration of it.

---

53. *Dictamen*: inspiration. [H.T.]

54. *De Cive* (1642), ch. I, § 7. "That every man as much as in him lies endeavour to protect his life and members". Deborah Baumgold (ed.), *Three-Text Edition of Thomas Hobbes's Political Theory*, 136. [A.P.]

Who wishes the end wishes the means, our author states. Whoever has right on his side, or, to put that another way, whomever right reason commands to protect his body and limbs at all costs, is also commanded by the very same right reason to deploy all possible means to achieve this.

This term *right reason*, employed by Hobbes in accounting for thievery and murder in the state of nature, has something about it that we find revolting. But we have to grasp the thought and, above all, bear in mind the writer's aim, which is to remove us, as soon as he can, from that state of nature where right reason commands us to rob and murder; and then, by dint of that very same reasoning, to raise us to a higher state in which we will be instantly commanded to keep the peace and honour our pledges. In Hobbes, *right reason* is the equivalent of the geometers' *straight line*; it is the shortest course whereby man, prompted solely by the law of self-preservation, can encompass his purpose.

Thus, we say that right reason commands us to resort to all possible means to keep ourselves safe. Now, knowing which of all the means that may be on offer are the ones we ought to be using is, Hobbes contends, left to each of us to judge for himself, insofar as it affects him, by virtue of his natural right.

> For, if it were contrary to right reason that I should be my own judge of my danger, someone else would doubtless judge it. If someone else is judging a matter which concerns me, I in turn can judge what concerns him, which amounts to my setting myself up as the sole judge of my interest, the sole judge in my own case.[55]

So, we are still in a state of non-right: which Hobbes himself implicitly recognizes, when, following his line of argument, he goes on to say:

> Nature has gifted each of us with a right over all things. But in practice, that right over all things accorded to us all, is equivalent to each of us having nothing, universal competition allowing no one to claim anything at all with any assurance and guarantee. Hence the war of which the state of nature consists.[56]

From those words, which I have quoted verbatim, we can see that as far as

55. *De Cive*, ch. I, § IX. (Proudhon''s, translation) "For if it be contrary to right reason that I should judge of mine own peril, say, that another man is judge. Why now, because he judgeth of what concerns me, by the same reason, because we are equal by nature, will I judge also of things which do belong to him". Baumgold, *Three-Text Edition*, 136. [A.P.]

56. Only the first line of this citation appears in *De Cive*. The remainder appears to be Proudhon's interpretation, rather than a paraphrase, of the remainder of the section. See *De Cive*, ch. I, § X. Baumgold, *Three-Text Edition*, 137. [A.P.]

Hobbes was concerned, absolute entitlement was synonymous with absolute nullity of rights. Can we not see in this also Hegel's logic where it makes absolute being synonymous with nothingness?

The point is to know how we are going to get away from this absolute right of all to all things, in which it is plain that humanity cannot survive. To that end, Hobbes brings in a brand-new factor with the aid of which he effects within that juridical absolute, this un-right, a series of determinations giving rise to special, positive rights, in short, to authentic rights.

Not everything I am entitled to do is equally advantageous to me. I am in a state of war with all my fellows; I do have the right to take whatever pleases me, to kill the first person to happen along, and to everything I need in order to sustain my body and hold on to my limbs; an immense faculty and one which leaves me with a good many options, it would seem. However, I would readily consent to forego a morsel of this absolute entitlement, in return for some guarantee and safety, for I may be killed myself; which proves, if we extrapolate from the hypothesis, that war is a poor preserver of the human race. Viewed from this new angle, my entitlement to do anything in order to preserve my body and my limbs will change by itself; it will take my interest as its boundary and rule: *In statu naturali mensuram juris esse UTILITATEM.*[57]

Utility, that is Hobbes's great principle. Which is where Bentham and all the utilitarians got it from. The case can be made that it makes up the foundation of the English conscience and is embodied in English blood. It is the theory of *interest rightly construed*. Those who profess it fall far short of having clung to the master's rigorous deduction; Hobbes has been buried under the weight of the curse placed on materialists and atheists. Bentham and his acolytes, with their hypocrisy, are greeted as honest fellows and outstanding Christians. Far from its being associated with the real inventor and theoretician of the idea, it is Bentham who is conventionally deemed the HEAD of the *utilitarian* school.

We shall now return to the remainder of the patriarch's propositions:

Prior to the formation of societies and outside of the religious institution, men's natural state is war, the war, as I say, of each against all. Indeed, what is war other than a time during which man serves notice upon his fellow men, orally or by deeds, of his urge to fight and resort to violence? Outside of that time, there is peace: *Status hominum naturais, antequam in societatem coiretur, bellum est; neque hoc simpliciter, sed bellum omnium in omnes. Bellum enim quid est, praeter tempus illud, in quo voluntas certandi per vim verbis factis vel satis declaratur? Tempus reliquum pax vocatur.*[58]

---

57. *De Cive* ch. I, § X. "in the state of nature, Profit is the measure of *Right*". Baumgold, *Three-Text Edition*, 137. [A.P.]

58. Hobbes, *De Cive*. I, § XII. "the natural state of men, before they entered into society,

Thus war, although it may be man's natural state (we already know what Hobbes meant by the natural state or state of nature), and such warfare is an evil; and the very same right reason that authorizes us to have recourse to it, vis à vis and against all odds, as a means of self-preservation, prompts us to prefer peace over it.

It requires only the most cursory attention to understand the philosopher's dialectic and do justice to his views. Hobbes is not at all an advocate for warfare and violence; quite the contrary, he desires peace and seeks right. Resolved to ask nothing of theology, but rather to abide exclusively by common sense, strict logic and sheer selfishness, he voluntarily stands by the least favourable hypothesis, the way that Descartes commits to his methodical doubt. And it is in the name of that same selfishness, by virtue of that unbending logic that he credits to it and which he dubs *recta ratio*, that he reaches his abrupt conclusion, without the slightest detour, without any surprise, without sophistry, regarding the superiority of peace over war and the need for man, on pain of contradiction, to wish it.

Man's primordial state, Hobbes says, is the state of war. In that state, man is entitled to do anything to his fellow men for the sake of self-preservation. But humanity cannot wish for its own destruction: so it obeys the law of leaving its state of nature behind in order to arrive at peace. There we have Hobbes's line of argument.

How then are we to leave behind our state of nature in order to enter the social state? How is peace to be established in the middle of this warfare? – By means of contract, Hobbes replies. – And what is contract? – "The actions of two or more people who transfer their rights to one another": *Duorum vel plurium jura sua mutuo transferentium actio vocatur contractus.*[59] At which point Hobbes builds his State: he shows how all of man's positive rights and obligations within society may flow from the very same principle of selfishness which had initially served only to orchestrate warfare: and this, let us take note, always in the name of what Hobbes terms *right reason, state of nature* or *natural law*.

So now we can see what Hobbes's theory consists of. To be truthful, it is, at bottom, merely a demonstration of the need for justice, through the *reductio ad absurdum* of the hypothesis of the non-existence of justice. A law lecturer who, prior to tackling direct evidence of the existence of a positive principle of justice in man's reason and conscience, might want, by way of prolegomena, to

---

was a mere war, and that not simply, but a war of all men against all men. For what is war, but that same time in which the will of contesting by force is fully declared, either by words or deeds? The time remaining is termed peace". Baumgold, *Three-Text Edition*, 138. [A.P.]

59. *De Cive*, ch. II, § IX. "But the act of two, or more, mutually conveying their rights, is called a contract". Baumgold, *Three-Text Edition*, 149. [A.P.]

demonstrate to his students the impossibility of any contrary system: he could not go about it better than Hobbes has done.

He would tell them: "The reality of the principle known as justice is denied; the claim is that justice, right, morality are hollow words, mere conventions. Well then, gentlemen, before having you put your finger on what those words cover, let us, for a moment, stand upon our adversaries' ground. There is no right; so be it. Human society is the product of an arbitrary convention, a legal fiction; I am willing to accept that. So, it needs saying that, outside of that convention, Hobbes used to say outside of religious institutions, man exists in a natural state of antagonism wherein everything is permitted him, where his only law is to seek satisfaction of his appetites, *per fas et nefas.*[60] But, after having fought over a relatively long period of time and indulged his savage instincts, it becomes apparent that, for the sake of the preservation of his belief that nothing is forbidden him, for the sake of and by virtue of his selfishness, he will seek, initially by means of an armistice and later through some sort of treaty to leave behind the state that results in nothing less than the utter destruction of the species. If he but takes one step down that road, he will be able to take a thousand more; he will abjure his right to kill and rob and he will form a city-state. In short, with the help of the reason which at the outset had him looking to war and all manner of crime for his happiness, he will make for himself, little by little, a law of peace and of all its concomitant virtues. Justice is not, therefore, a hollow word, since it is necessary and from that necessity alone we can rigorously deduce an entire system of legislation and morality..."

That is what the lecturer would say. Now let me say again that Hobbes, the materialist, the atheist, the apologist for tyranny, has done nothing else. In which regard his system can and should be preserved in almost its entirety.

So wherein does the weakness in Hobbes's theory reside? I identified that right in the very first lines in this chapter and I have just explained it: that it contains only one half of the truth. Yes, justice, the social condition are necessary things, since the opposite leads to nothingness; since the very same man, whose absolute right over all persons and things we acknowledge, is prompted by his own interests and his own selfishness, to step back from such absolutism and go in search of peace, security, wealth, well-being, in short, his own self-preservation through a voluntary curtailment of his rights. But the science of right does not stop at this conclusion of necessity; in the most positive fashion, on behalf of inner sensibility and psychological experience, it affirms that there is a principle of justice which all the religions have presented as revelation and a God-given order, and which a more attentive philosophy looks upon as

---

60. "For right or wrong". [A.P.]

the *dictate* of reason and conscience. Justice, we tell ourselves today, being at once idea and sentiment, a rule of the mind and a potentiality of the soul, is immanent in our nature,[61] and as real and readily recognized as love, sympathy, motherliness and all the affections of the heart. From which it follows that man is not only drawn into the social and juridical condition by a mere calculation of interests or by necessity, as Hobbes says: the prompting of interest might, on its own, have been powerless to sustain the social state. Since everyone craves peace as long as it serves his purpose, but rejects it and rips up the pact the moment he reckons it works counter to his selfish interests, the mass of humanity would have been living in a state of perpetual dissolution. Treachery would have been added to warfare and this sham peace, this sham social condition might have been worse for our species than the primitive state of open war. A cohesive force is crucial here; that force we find in the principle of justice, which, being in the long run a mightier influence upon our hearts than interest and necessity, pushes man in the direction of association, making and sustaining States.

Now, what is this principle of justice or power, the most universal and consistent of our instincts, if not always the most vigorous? Respect for our own dignity, respect for our soul, a respect that takes possession of us not merely the moment we see something that tarnishes and offends us, but at the sight of anything that offends and tarnishes our fellows...

So, Hobbes was wrong, in the first place, about religion, in which he saw either an institution from on high, or an invention of the priests and which we today regard as the symbolic or primitive form of society and of justice. He was wrong about the nature of society, which he deemed the outcome of mere necessity and calculated interest, whereas it is also the product of a specific faculty of our soul, which pushes us towards it, even as our irascible appetite pushes us to war. He was wrong about the character and essence of peace, which he defined negatively *as all the time not given over to warfare*. He was wrong about war itself, which he regards as a state of calamity, the antithesis of genuine right. Finally, he was wrong in his definition of right, which he describes, in absolute terms, as the faculty which man possesses to DO EVERYTHING, making no distinction between good or bad, for the purpose of preserving his body and his limbs, what we look upon as respect for the dignity of men, in our own person and in the person of each of our fellows; a respect that is, deep down, nothing more than the respect religion inculcates in us in the name of heavenly powers and the effect of which upon our will is to render us subject to society and force us to abide by its laws.

---

61. Proudhon first developed the idea that justice was immanent to man and society in *De la Justice* (1858). *War and Peace* is arguably an extended case study of that sociological and biological claim. [A.P.]

These reservations, the importance of which will be appreciated by the reader, are articulated with a marvellous and forceful logic that Hobbes displays as he presses on with deductions from his principle and assembles this social edifice, which critical nitwits and brazen plagiarists accuse him of overturning. Hobbes has made reason take the first and maybe the hardest step in the science of right; it falls to our century to take the second.

And naturally the reader will be asking me, what has Hobbes to say of the right of force? Nothing. If he chances to bring it up, which I have not noticed, it can only be in an ironic way, by way of antiphrasis, as do all the jurists who speak of it: meaning that he acknowledges it not at all. Indeed, Hobbes's theory starts from the hypothesis of humanity's passing through two successive states, the state of war, bad, which he shuns, and the contractual state or state of peace, the only one he endorses. In the first state absolute entitlement prevails and this, as I have stated already, is nothing but non-right, with *utility* as its sole maxim. In the second state, that absolute, uniform entitlement narrows and is restricted in a thousand ways by means of contracts, but again under the aegis of *utility*. In both these states, force features only as a method of action *vis-à-vis* the enemy or infringers of the compact; far from Hobbes recognizing it as an element or form of right, and the establishment of a contract-based society as a counter to the barbarous, anarchic, immoral exercise of it. Representing Hobbes as the theoretician of or apologist for the right of force, of the right of the strongest, is quite simply an inversion of his thinking and unadulterated calumny.

You will ask, however: does Hobbes not teach that the *best government is the government of force*: isn't he the supporter of *absolute power*? We need to understand one another here. Here we have, indeed, exposed the flaw in Hobbes's system; but at the same time, it is here too that this philosopher has demonstrated the power [*puissance*] of his genius.

Let us remind ourselves of what we so recently stated. Relying solely upon the conclusions of necessity and interest, justice is but a fiction of the understanding, society an unstable state. Which is why there is something more in justice than some law of necessity and calculated interest; there is a potentiality in our soul that prompts us to assert the just quite independently of any egoism; which has us craving public order above all else and which is a stronger bond within the city-state than we have with our family, our loves and everything traceable exclusively to our selfishness.

Like us, Hobbes was aware of the importance of the social mortar that was supplied by religion and which, in our view is nothing other than justice per se.[62] Unable to demand it of conscience, which he discounted on account of

62. Proudhon understands religion as the first manifestation of justice, the second historical stage of justice being metaphysics or philosophy, the third science. [A.P.]

the way it muddled moral sentiment and religious sentiment, he was obliged to seek it in the very organization of the State. This novel factor, this sanctioning principle, which, according to him, ought to have completed the task so well begun by necessity and developed by means of contract, is force, still, of course, invoking the argument of *utility*, of the widest common interest. Are our philosophical jurisconsults, I mean the most spiritualist, most liberal of them, doing anything today other than Hobbes did? Does he not identify *public force* as the entire sanction of right? Is he the only one among them ever to have grasped that, if justice per se is a thing rather than a word or a mere idea; if it represents a principle to live by, a force of nature or humanity, an affection, if I may make so bold as to say, and at the same time a law of our very soul, is it not self-sanctioning rather than endorsed by some outside power or authority?[63]

We who believe in the reality and immanence of justice can state that it offers compensation and vengeance, that it carries its consecration within itself, and that while, in certain cases it is permissible to deploy against scoundrels rendered less-than-brutes by crime, the rigorous means deployed against brutes, such corporal punishments are, in themselves, negligible; that the authentic correction of crime has its roots in the conscience of the culprit; and that the authentic sanction of right, in short, is the joy that accompanies virtue and the remorse that follows upon crime.[64]

Hobbes did not get to that point. He no more believed in the efficaciousness of conscience than he likely had in that of religion and he fell back on force. Not that he acknowledged any sort of right of force; to him force was a guarantor, an agent or organ of reassurance. Do our jurists and our statesmen do anything else? And he concluded, as our jurists and statesmen do, that the best government is the one best established in authority or in force; that one feature of that force and authority is that the prince, the organ of power, be

---

63. One character entirely missing from this roster of philosophers is Rousseau, and yet he looms large in nearly all Proudhon's other writings. Proudhon's silence here is conspicuous, and the proximity of Proudhon to Rousseau ought not to be overlooked. For a brief statement on Rousseau, see note 124 on p. 216, below. For a fuller discussion of Proudhon's reading of Rousseau see Aaron Noland, "Proudhon and Rousseau," *Journal of the History of Ideas*, 28 no. 1 (1967): 33–54. Cf., Karma Nabulsi, *Traditions of War: Occupation, Resistance and the Law* (Oxford: Oxford University Press, 1999), and on the intellectual genealogy from Grotius to Kant, via Rousseau and Hobbes, see Richard Tuck, *The Rights of War and Peace: Political Thought and the International Order from Grotius to Kant* (Oxford: Oxford University Press, 2001). [A.P.]

64. This is as strong a statement of Proudhon's anarchism as we will find in this book. As noted in the introduction, to talk in terms of "immanence" is to be a "true anarchist" in Proudhon's terms, and to find justice not in penal law or incarceration, but in conscience was a radical abolitionist position then and now. This is a line of argument developed considerably by Tolstoy.

declared untouchable, unaccountable and even, no matter what he does, unpunishable, the prince's crime appearing to him to represent a lesser danger than the undermining of the supreme authority. He went on to say that the prince or council invested with sovereign power had to have the entitlement to censure and forbid all sorts of writings; that the distinction between monarchy and tyranny is a nonsense, etc., etc. Apropos of which let me say again that all of the governments for the last two centuries which purported, as the English philosopher did, to be guided by the rules of *right reason*, independently of religious law, have merely been following Hobbes's maxims at every step. Moreover, there is still the quiet understanding that, in everything that this *absolute power* does and undertakes, it has to act with a view to the widest common interest, which is none other than peace, since it was established in the name of that interest. Here again I imagine that our self-styled democrats, devotees of strong government, are prompted by the most utilitarian sentiments.

That, in summary, is Hobbes's system: it is nothing short of the theory of temporal power, regarded as distinct from all religious, spiritual and moral factors. A host of curious observations could be made regarding this theory, as vigorously framed by Hobbes; I shall make do with a single remark from the lips of the strongest and most absolute man of modern times, Napoleon: *Force is not the foundation of anything*, he stated, meaning that a society in which the moral conscience has collapsed, and which has no other guarantor of order, no sanction for right other than force, is a society in jeopardy; it has to regenerate or perish.

As for the *right of force*, taken, as we have in the chapters above, in the literal sense of the term, that would have drawn a smile from Hobbes and Napoleon alike and, in all truth, it can be argued that *De Cive* represents a most thoroughgoing demolition of it. So the issue remains: posed by the wailing of the masses, it has not been raised by anyone and no writer has skimmed the surface.

It is high time that we brought this part of the discussion to a close, because it is not our primary concern, the summation of which was not a matter for me.

Is there a solid foundation to the ancient, traditional opinion of war, in other words, the belief in the actual right of force, or does it, as the scholars contend, carry an implicit contradiction within it? That is the question it falls to us to resolve.

For it is plain that if the religion of warfare – here I call religion any belief not rationally demonstrated – has no foundation other than an illusion of conscience, if it is nothing but a crude fetishism, it will be enough to have established, once and for all, that force has not and cannot have any bearing upon right, that, far from creating it, destroys it, the establishment of that proposition will, as I say, suffice to bring war into disrepute and the debate, barely launched, is instantly over. War survives only on its good reputation: demolish that reputation and you have perpetual peace.

The issue is all the more interesting in that we do not really know which side has the greater chances of error. Could it be that so many and so wise men have been so grossly and so stubbornly wrong? Moreover, can the reason of peoples be capable of such a durable and deep-seated aberration? Given that so many superstitions have disappeared, been swallowed up by one another, or been dispelled by philosophical analysis, can it be that we, all unsuspecting and unable to prevent it, have fallen victim over so many centuries to the stupidest and most contemptible of them all? On this occasion, who will ultimately carry the day, the instinctive reasoning of the masses, or the ponderous reasoning of our jurisconsults?

CHAPTER VII

The Theory of the Right of Force

Universal evidence holds that the right of war is a positive right, *sui generis*, a vital component in the establishment of the rights of peoples.

The rights of peoples being, in turn, the root from which, historically, first, public right and then civil right, etc., emerged, it follows that right of any sort has its historical starting-point in warfare.

Now, what is war? We have already said. A judgment, true or false, delivered by force. So the issue boils down to knowing:

1. If a right of force or of the strongest genuinely does exist; in other words, if there are instances in which force may truly constitute right and operate as an arbiter;
2. What the boundaries of that right are; in what circumstances, to which ends, and in what manner should such arbitration operate.

In primitive nations, that question would have been well-nigh an impertinence, so uncomplicated and natural did the matter appear. A small number of ideas, wrapped in facts, or represented by symbols standing in for facts, carried their justification within themselves; no one felt any need to reason otherwise.

This is no longer the case where we moderns are concerned. Our civilization is all analysis. We survive on reason, accepting only that which has been demonstrated to us and rejecting any principle, any fact, any tradition and any law that flies in the face of received wisdom, or which can only be accommodated within our encyclopaedia through translation into a series of reliable propositions. Pending such clarification, reason takes exception to a law that fetters it and the fatalism by which it is obsessed; and does itself as much harm by its negation as it sustains from the act itself, or from the prejudice which it denies, because of its failure to grasp this.

As regards warfare, the disadvantage would be mediocre if it had lessened along with the firm belief in the right of force, of which it purports to be the enforcement or exercise. Unfortunately, almost the precise opposite has been

the case: belief in the right of war scarcely exists any longer, and the scourge has
never been harder to master, nor seemed more terrifying. So that, through, on
the one hand, a brand-new variety of contradiction, jurisprudence looks upon
the right of warfare as a fairy-tale; philosophy, horrified by this right which it
cannot comprehend, bridles at the facts and dives into utopia; commerce, literature and science join forces and enter into a coalition in order to foist general
disarmament upon heads of State. On the other hand, governments are always
at odds, people dream of battles and band together, the better to be crushed;
armies proliferate; nations' entire savings are squandered on war munitions; finally, right and left vie with each other in asserting, without knowing what they
are saying, like Caiaphas[65] prophesying redemption, that force is the only hope
of a solution to the economic, political, national and social problems that arise
everywhere.

The world has, perhaps, never been prey to such pressing worries. And why
should that surprise us? The world seeks a principle to govern relations between
nations; now, the only one they can come up with is force, and they no more
have faith in force than they do in God Himself. How to exit this maze?

Let us go back to first principles.

Justice is not an imperative suggested by a higher authority to some inferior being, as most of the authors who have written about the rights of peoples
teach; justice is immanent in the human soul; it is its foundation, representing
its highest power and its supreme dignity.

It consists of each member of the family, or of the city, or of the species,
even as he asserts his freedom and dignity, acknowledging these things within
others and showing them as much honour, consideration, power and enjoyment as he seeks for himself. That respect for humanity in our selves and in our
fellows is the most basic and most consistent of our affections.

By virtue of this innate disposition to treat one another in a RIGHTFULL
manner, we are all entitled to call ourselves simultaneously dispensers of and
subject to justice. It is because the *right of justice*, as they used to say back in
feudal times, is present within every one of us, that the determinations of the
courts are legitimate, the judge, as the people's representative, as is the prince
himself, being merely a mandatory.

Now man, being an organized being, is a composite of powers. He wishes
to be acknowledged in all his faculties; as a result, he has to acknowledge those
of others; but for that, all our dignities would be trampled under-foot and right
would be flawed.

Again, it is in accordance with this principle that justice frames its

---

65. According to biblical tradition, Caiaphas was the Jewish high priest who accused
Christ of blasphemy. [H.T.]

judgments. It has only one means of judging, namely, by comparing, depending on the matter under consideration, the merits and demerits of the parties, the worthiness of their handiwork, the excellence or shortcomings of their faculties.

After that, there are as many varieties of the application of justice, or, to put it more simply, as many sorts of rights as there are faculties and, in the realm of actions, items with the capacity to furnish justice with bases for comparison. Psychological analysis breaks down the soul into its potentialities, right splits into as many categories, and it can be said of each of them that right has its place within the potentiality that sires it, just the way that justice, considered as a whole, has its place in the conscience.

Thus, there is a *right of labour*, by virtue of which every product of human industry, no matter what it may be, belongs to its producer, as do his talent, his genius and his virtue.[66] That right is inherent within labour, which is to say, to man made manifest in the guise of the hypostasis[67] of labour; it is an emanation from labour, it belongs to him, not as some concession from the State, but as an expression of the worker, as his inviolable prerogative.[68]

There is a *right of intelligence* which demands that every man is able to think and be educated, to believe in what strikes him as true, to reject what strikes him as false, to debate plausible opinions, to make his thinking public, to secure, on the basis of his learning, certain positions within society ahead of the ignorant, even should the latter be more hardworking, wealthier or even more moral in their conduct. The right of intelligence is inherent within intelligence just the same as the right of labour is inherent within labour, just the same as right and duty are, broadly speaking, inherent within man himself.

There is a *right of love* which consists not merely of every person being entitled to love and, if he may, be loved in return; but, by its very nature, love commits the lovers to certain reciprocal obligations, the infringement of which

---

66. As Robert Hoffman argues, "Proudhon believes that there is a 'right of labor' by virtue of which the product of human industry belongs to the producer. [...] The right of labor also serves to define the relationship between workers in collective endeavor and as the basis for rejecting any system whereby workers are simply wage-earners with no interest in the disposal of the product. All men working together ought to be equal associates who share in the rewards, both material and immaterial, which result from creation of a product and its sale". See Robert L. Hoffman, *Revolutionary Justice: The Social and Political Theory of P.J. Proudhon* (Urbana, University of Illinois Press, 1972), 298. [I.M.]

67. Hypostasis: In theology, this term indicates the distinct person of the Father, the Son and the Holy Spirit, found together in a single substantial divinity. According to Proudhon, in man there might be several different hypostases (labour, force, intelligence ...). [H.T.]

68. Here Proudhon is paraphrasing ideas he spelled out in *De la justice dans la Révolution et dans l'Église* (1858). See Étude VI: Le travail: Étude V – L'éducation: X and XI: Amour et mariage. [H.M.]

implies the negation of love per se. This right of love is one that every people has tried to endow with formulas, in the guise of *marriage*.[69]

There is a *right of seniority* which insists that, where merits are equal, lengthier service secures a higher ranking. This law is no more a concession by the prince, nor a figment of the jurist, than the preceding ones, but is directly traceable, like all the rest, to human dignity and the respect which due to it, in every one of its manifestations or hypostases.

This is not to say, it will be universally understood, that right and work, right and intelligence, right and love, right and seniority are one and the same thing. The result would be that the worker, because he labours, arrogate to himself all manner of privileges, just as the noble once did on the basis that he was a noble. The same would hold true for the scholar, the lover, the veteran. In its broadest sense, let me say again, right is the respect which every man can claim from his neighbour, as much by virtue of his person as of his family and his property, by reason of their shared nature and of the fellowship of their interests. But right, when it comes to its application, diversifies and is regulated: here, by virtue of the sum and quality of the labour; there, by virtue of the intellect; elsewhere, in terms of the earnings paid or promised, etc.

Likewise, there is an understandable difference between the right OF work and the right TO work. The latter derives from man's higher, absolute right, his very existence requiring daily action and the exercise of all his faculties; the former, being narrower, derives from labour itself and is measured by its product. In the right TO work, there is work to be sought and to be done; in the right OF work, it is more a matter of work done and for which payment or privilege is being sought. The very same distinction exists between the right of love and the right to love, the right of ownership and the right to ownership, etc.[70]

Let me say now that there is a *right of force*, by virtue of which the strongest is, in certain circumstances, entitled to preference over the weakest and to be paid at a higher rate, even should the latter be more industrious, wiser, more loving or older. And as we have seen, the right of work, intelligence and love are emanations from the faculty which serves to define them and of which they are the crown and sanction; likewise, the right of force also has its principle in force, which is to say, always in the human person, manifested under the guise of strength. The right of force exists, no more than the rest, as a tacit convention; it

---

69. The subject of love and marriage is the topic of the final book of *De la Justice* (1858). His treatment of the subject rightly incensed his compatriot from Besançon, Jenny De Herricourt. See, Jenny De Héricourt, *A Woman's Philosophy of Woman or, Woman Affranchised: An Answer to Michelet, Proudhon, Girardin, Legouvé, Comte, and Other Modern Innovators* (Westport, CT: Hyperion Pres, 1981). [A.P.]

70. For more on this topic, see also Pierre-Joseph Proudhon, *Le droit au travail et le droit de propriété* (Paris: L. Vasbenter, 1848). [A.P.]

is neither a concession nor a fiction; any more than it is purloined; it is, in a very real way and in the full sense of the term, a right.

And what I have said elsewhere with regard to labour, the intellect, love and seniority, I say again of force. Right and force are not the same thing; of all our faculties, conscience alone helps us to know, feel, assert and defend righteousness and is alone in being acknowledged by justice as identical with it. Force has no place in matters of the intellect and of love; it has nothing to do with age and time; even in the case of labour, its contribution is merely as an instrument, so it is no substitute for, nor can it usurp, prerogatives. But force is part of what it is to be human, and makes its contribution to our dignity; consequently, it too has its right, which is not right, all of right, but which we may not misconstrue, lest we fall into folly.

Were the right of force to be denied, we should have to deny, on similar grounds, the right of labour, the right of intelligence and all the other rights, even the least contested ones; one would have to conclude by denying the right of man, the dignity of the human person, in short, justice. We would have to say, with the utilitarian materialists, that justice is a fiction of the State; or, with the mystics, that it stands outside of humanity, which is in line with the absolutist theory of divine right, long since convicted of immorality and abandoned.

So, force is not zero in the face of right, as some would have it. Force per se is good, useful, productive, necessary, to be venerated for its handiwork and therefore worthy of consideration. All peoples honour it and offer it recompense; woe betide those who would neglect it! Along with the potential to identify, produce and love it, they would soon lose even the moral feeling for it.

Thus, force is, like all our potentialities, the subject and object, the principle and substance of right. Part and parcel of the human person, it is one of the thousand faces of justice; as such it may, in the right circumstances, deliver justice itself through its mere manifestation. That will be the lowest measure of justice, if one will; but justice it will be: the whole point will be to bring it to bear appropriately.

Here again I cannot help but highlight a contradiction in the authors. According to them, force is the very opposite of right: albeit that they accept it as its necessary sanction:

"Force" – says Ancillon – "is right's necessary guarantor; but for it, it remains a hollow word, a veritable ghost. Such force exists only within the social order and for the social order, or, rather, it constitutes it. The morality of men does not have the capability to offer assurances against the misuse they might make of their resources; it is not morality that ensures

that right and justice prevail; it is the existence of public force that makes
for that splendid effect".[71]

The Protestant Ancillon argues just like the atheist Hobbes; he curses humanity, denies justice and bases his authority upon force alone. It never occurs to
him that justice has no sanction other than its self; that, consequently, force
serves merely as a sanction for the right of force; and that it plays such a huge
role in men's affairs; it is because, seemingly, this right of force, which we do
not even possess the good sense to acknowledge, is itself the starting point and
underpinning of all rights. If it can be said, by a sort of interversion familiar to
poets, that public force is the sanction for public order, it is because force is implicit as a special, primordial right in public justice, without which public order
itself would be nothing better than public tyranny. This is what Hobbes, who
devised the theory of brute force, otherwise known as absolute power, failed to
grasp: without it, he would have moved from respect for force to respect for the
human person, and he would have affirmed the reality of justice and remade his
system from top to bottom.

Force is even more central to the theory of the origin and development of
rights than in modern metaphysics, which traces everything to forces. Matter
is a force, every bit as much as mind, science, genius, virtue, the passions, just
as capital and machines are forces too. We call a politically organized nation a
power [*puissance*]; potentiality [*pouvoir*] is the concept we use to describe the
collective political force of that nation. The greatest of all strengths, in the spiritual and moral sphere, as well as in material terms, is association, which can be
defined as the embodiment of justice.[72]

Here there looms before us, as plain as day, what we so recently merely suspected, to wit, that the right of force, so despised, is not only the earliest and the
most anciently acknowledged, but also the bedrock and foundation of all manner of rights. Truth be told, other rights are merely its ramifications or transformations. So that, far from force being repugnant to justice, it might be more
accurate to say that justice itself is merely the respect for the dignity of force.

The ascendancy of husband over wife, of father over child boils down to the
right of the stronger party. Why deny it? Why should we men blush at this? Why
would you womenfolk draw up a list of grievances? *Papa is master*, one little girl

---

71. *Histoire du droit des gens* by F. LAURENT, Volume II, 205; ANCILLON, *Tableau
des révolutions du système politique en Europe*, Volume I, 6. [P-J.P.]

72. Proudhon first developed a full account of how disparate powers are institutionalized
and thereby transformed into intentional consciousness and collective force in the "Little
Political Catechism", an appendix to book four of *De la Justice*. It is available in translation in
Iain McKay's anthology, *Property is Theft*, 654–684.

told her brother who dared to query a fatherly instruction. In the estimation of that child, the father was right because he wielded power and that, in struck her as sublime and in essence true, but only becomes false when one gets embroiled in distinguishing between faculties and rights. Primitive peoples follow the very same line of reasoning. They know little of what we call talent, science or genius; among them, knowledge is communal and intelligence; they do not work, in the economic sense of the word and trace everything back to force. So, as far as they are concerned whoever is the strongest is the most deserving; they have but one word, *aristos*, to cover those two ideas. In our colleges, are the top students in every year not also the *strongest [les forts]*? To the strong go the honours and the commandment. With every bit as much reason as the metaphysician, the savage may state that justice is nothing more than considered force.

What is it that has society in permanent upheaval, splitting it up menacingly into aristocracy and democracy, bourgeoisie and proletariat, other than the right of force never having been acknowledged, as it should be, as residing within the masses? Prior to the revolution, nobility, clergy, royalty and bourgeoisie had ended up established in pretty regular fashion by means of a mutual acknowledgment of their strengths. The revolution upset that system: but the bourgeoisie resuscitated the economic state in which '89 and '93 had left society; and the people's strength, considered separately, went unacknowledged. The people is always the monster to be fought against, muzzled and clapped in chains, *in camo et freno maxillas eorum constringe*;[73] whether skilfully led, like the rhinoceros and the elephant; or broken by hunger, bled by colonization and warfare, but, as much as possible, steered away from rights and politics. The rulers of nations acknowledge one another; the upper classes also acknowledge one another; in truth, the people never receives anything other than formal acknowledgment, and this because it carries nothing within, except force.

What caused the jurists to go astray with regard to the right of force is that that righteousness was, so to speak, hidden beneath the dense foliage of rights that had sprouted from that ancient trunk; it was their failure to grasp anything about force other than violence and misuse; finally, it was the fact that they had failed to discern in the onward march of justice a sort of expansion and differentiation of the right of the strongest and, likewise, in times of decline and dissolution, they also failed to see that loss of freedoms and rights amounted to falling back on the plain right of force.

In a society that has attained a high degree of civilization, abusive force diminishes of itself and has a tendency to fade away. By trespassing against rights

---

73. *Bible*, Psalm 31:9, Latin Vulgate. "Do not become like the horse and the mule, who have no understanding. *With bit and bridle bind fast their jaws, who come not near unto thee*". [A.P.]

born on its stem, it renders its own right odious and places its own existence in jeopardy. Therein lies the ghastliness of tyranny, it being simultaneously suicide and infanticide.

If each faculty, potentiality [*puissance*], force, carries its own right within itself, then the forces within man and society ought to balance one another out rather than annihilate themselves. The right of one cannot prejudice the right of the other, since they are not of the same nature and could not run up against one another in the same action. Quite the opposite: they can only develop through the reciprocal assistance that they render to one another. What generates rivalries and conflicts is the fact that on occasion heterogeneous forces come together and are indissolubly bound together in a single person, such as we might see occur in man as a result of the union of passions and faculties, or in government as a result of the union of different powers, or in society through the agglomeration of classes. Sometimes, on the other hand, a similar potential is shared between different individuals, and we find that sort of thing in business, industry and proprietorship, where hosts of individuals perform precisely the same functions, aspire to the very same advantages and exercise the very same rights and privileges. Thus it can come to pass that either the forces wedded together clash, rather than maintaining a fair balance among themselves, and that just one of them overrules the rest; or that those separate forces cancel one another out by dint of competition and anarchy. Such outcomes are inevitable when, under the sway of impetuous passions, dignity within the individual, justice within the State, and the feeling of fellowship in the guild is weakened.

In a soul that is its own master, in a well-ordered society, forces clash momentarily until they take cognizance of one another, get the measure of one another, confirm one another and weigh one another up. Just as, within the family, fatherly power is counterbalanced by love, which often tilts the scales in favour of the weakest member; so, within the city, trade forces balance one another out and bring about a general happiness through a fair balance. So, the end point of contending forces is harmony between one another. In which regard, the fate of States around the world is none other than that of the citizens within a single town, or the provinces within a single State. Any antagonism wherein the forces, rather than balancing out one another, destroy one another, is not a war any more, but a subversion, an anomaly.

All of which is so simple and so self-evidently true that I find it rather hard to spell it out and am eager to be done with it. Force, the first of the human faculties in terms of age, but the last in terms of rank, and rightly so, commands its right like any other, and, like any other, may be called upon to lay down the law. On the understanding that the rule of force is applicable solely to the affairs of force, just as the law of love governs love, or the law of labour the affairs of labour.

It is for reason to see, in every dispute, which law should be applied in the delivery of a verdict, and how the judge identifies the article in the code, in accordance with which he delivers his determination. There is nothing in all this that falls outside ordinary common sense conditions, or should I say of common law. How is it, then, that the authors do not have a word to say about this, and that which lies at the root of all legislation, that which history indicates as the first moment in judicial evolution, i.e., that the right of force, is universally misconstrued, sacrificed, trampled underfoot or, worse still, odiously distorted and travestied?

The truth is that humanity, in its imperturbable onward march, refuses to be led astray by the hallucinations of its supposed learned men. The overall outcomes of the political movement have been what the principle of antagonism that presides over it wanted them to be, pretty much. But how much bloodshed and tears might the world have been spared had we but had a more wholesome understanding of war! What services might the Church have rendered if, whilst celebrating the God of Hosts, she had been able to address peoples and kings in precise terms about the right of war! In which case the Church's teaching, ascending to the level of revelation, might perhaps have secured temporal dominion through the legislation of force and never again have lost it.

CHAPTER VIII

Application of the Right of Force.

1. THE DEFINITION AND OBJECT OF THE RIGHT OF WAR

One thing is now certain: that right made its debut in the world as force; that the long-vilified right of the strongest is the oldest, the most elementary and most indestructible of all rights. We shall now follow this through some of its applications.

Right is specific to our species. But it assumes different names depending on the objects to which it is applied: right of force, right of labour, right of intelligence, right of ownership, right of love, family law, criminal law, civic right, etc.

What was long known as the *right of nature* should henceforth be stricken from the vocabulary of rights. If we take the term to signify righteousness in its earliest form and in its most concrete manifestation, it is nothing but the right of force. If we use it as the antithesis of *divine or revealed right*, we should stop doing so, given that divine right, supposedly predating and superior to man, is, deep down, absolutely the same as ordinary right, as posited by the conscience and set out by practice and reason. Even from a supernatural vantage point, the distinction has become pointless.

Canon law is divine right drafted by the Church: therefore, there is even less reason for us to concern ourselves with it.

So, the right of force being, in the order of historical development, the source from which all of the others flow, the right of war naturally followed from it and constituted its very first branch, in the wake of which, one after another, there followed the rights of peoples, or international law, political law, civil law, etc.

This genealogy, consistent with history, is the opposite of what is generally embraced. Following the by-ways of psychology or metaphysics, the authors have, after some preliminary considerations regarding right, first broached personal rights which, promptly made into actual right, give rise to civil law. After which come, one after the other, political rights, the application of civil law; people's rights, the appliance of political rights; and, lastly, the right of war as a specific segment of the rights of peoples. We would have nothing against this approach, as it essentially matters little where one starts the teaching of rights from, were it not that it culminates in the denial of the right of war and, with it, the right of force, before going on to turn the rights of peoples into a right bereft of foundation and sanction, resulting in the ruination of every other right.

Therefore, we shall adopt a different approach and, after having posited the right of force, we shall, in accordance with history and logic, proceed to deduce the right of war from it.

It is a law of nature that weakness seeks the protection of strength: this is the principle behind the pre-eminence accorded to the paterfamilias, the tribal chief, the warrior. Where common welfare is at stake, having the weakest command and the bravest obey is repugnant; in this respect, it has never occurred to anyone to seriously query the right of force.

That principle conceded, everything else flows from it. The family grows through procreation, especially where polygamy is countenanced. If the chief is strong, the family grows through the amalgamation of several other families who willingly seek amalgamation and pledge loyalty and obedience to the patriarch, which is how the tribe comes into being. In the event of war, it is bolstered by captives of both sexes whose labours add to its wealth and boost its capacity for war. Wealth being a form of strength.

But how does war come about?

Two tribes encounter each other. Lest they irk each other or run the risk of coming to blows, the first thing they do is to keep their distance. However, there is a chance that one of them, weakened by poverty or disease, or for some other reason, asks to be taken over. In which case the weaker surrenders itself into the care of the stronger, the person of the chief of the latter embodying both sovereignties. Which is why, in a business setting, the entrepreneur with access to capital seldom looks for a partner. He will accept auxiliaries, employees, clerks, workers, foremen, but no equal. Suggest to him that he should amalgamate, he will make it his business, after weighing up the options, to reserve the general managership for himself, making that the *sine qua non* of his consent. I will not, for the moment, go into whether the coming-together of workers does not generate a collective force that outweighs that of the boss;[74] the

---

74. Proudhon consistently argued that, "By virtue of the principle of collective force, workers are the equals and associates of their leaders". *Système des contradictions économiques ou Philosophie de la misère* (Paris: Guillaumin, 1846), 377. For more on this see Iain McKay,

right of force would be undiminished by that. I shall confine myself to noting that, in terms of the mores current within industry, the stronger party wields the upper hand, which is fair, and nobody raises any objection to that.

Now, note this: the right of force is, by its very nature, like every other right, peaceful. It does not necessarily have the implication of warfare; it does not go looking for it. Far from it: it protests against that extremity from which the most valiant themselves always shy away.

Let us discount minor incidents and focus solely upon the logical course of events. Previously isolated tribes soon come into contact as they expand. Straightforward neighbourly relations, though not yet rights nor conventions, are established; they trade with one other; then, driven by the very same rationale that ensured that they provided services for one another, it turns out that there is a problem, and they notice that their initial independence is daily becoming more and more difficult to maintain until in the end it becomes impossible. Amalgamation or elimination is inevitable.

What happens next? Man clings to freedom at least as much as he is disposed to association. This feeling of independence is much stronger in the masses, tribes, cities and nations. They find all neighbourliness suspect; everything that commits them and binds them, they instinctively repudiate. What happens in the event of an absorption that threatens to swallow their individuality, their autonomy, in short, their whole being? Belonging to a nation means independence and sovereignty. However, the causes nudging the two tribes closer to each other are unstoppable; the position is becoming urgent; the two rivers draw nearer and a point is reached where their waters are about to meet.

There is no possible way to state that there is wrong on either side here. Plainly, each is equally in the right. The amalgamation could be amiable; but that is a rare occurrence, given that the encounter entails, for at least one of the cities about to amalgamate, and sometimes for both of them, a loss of originality. The towns of Attica, gathering together under the shared protection of Minerva, adopted a plural, collective title, *Athenæ*. Those were merely hamlets peopled by a population who were of the same blood, spoke the same language, shared the same interests and were separated by, at most, the ambitions of their aldermen. Even so, it was no easy undertaking to bring them together: the distinctions lingered on and bled into the government. The Athenians used to appoint generals on a rotational basis, each commanding the same army for a day; Athenian democracy was always a competition between neighbourhoods.

But what was the amalgamation of Minerva's twelve walled towns into a single city when compared with the centralization of Italy? In Romulus's day,

"Proudhon's Constituted Value and the Myth of Labour Notes", *Anarchist Studies* 25 no. 1 (2017). [A.P.]

Italy was home to a hundred small peoples, all of them independent and their simultaneous development was soon going to compel them to unite. Rome was the centre of this absorption which lasted for nigh on six centuries. Now, just take a moment to gauge the difficulties in such an amalgamation, of which more modern times can show us not a single instance, and you will appreciate what war is.

The first war the Romans had to fight was against the Sabines. The abduction of women, depicted by Titus Livy as the cause or pretext of that war, plainly suggests that the distinction between the two cities had become impossible. Therefore, the conditions of amalgamation needed resolving and the constitution to be determined; had the two States been monarchies at the point of amalgamation, which dynasty was to end? In the event that only one of them was a monarchy and the other republican, the issue was either to set up a mixed government, or to modify the traditions and political mores of one of the two peoples. Then there was work to be done reconciling the different laws, reconciling customs and generating tolerance, etc. Even in her earliest wars, Rome offered her neighbours *isonomy*, which is to say, access to the civil and political rights of her own citizenry; and, rightly, such adroit moderation on the part of the government of old Rome was marvelled at. But what did isonomy mean for a sovereign city, for kings, princes and patricians used to exercising sovereign rule at home? Sheer suicide. It is clear, in fact, that even by affording equality of rights and honours to the incorporated towns, Rome, as the capital, retained the upper hand; the towns could only hope that, through their electoral rights, they might wield a morsel of influence within the government; and it takes a long time to even get that far. To be used by parties and intrigues, in order to be able to use them in turn: what a share in a republic! What a compensation for sovereignty!

And very rarely did Rome have grounds to congratulate herself upon a willing surrender. Titus Livy, Book VII, cites the case of Capua and the peoples of Campania "*Itaque populum Cympanum, urbemque Capuam, agros, delubra Deûm, divina humanaque omnia, in vestram, patres conscripti, populique Romani ditionem dedimus*".[75] Yet that was merely a case of submission pure and simple. Vattel, who quotes that passage, does not even seem to appreciate its importance and meaning. The meaning is that no people can think itself obliged

75. LIVY, Book VII, ch. 31 §4. "Since you decline to use a righteous violence to protect from violence and injustice what belongs to us, you will at least defend your own; to your sovereignty, therefore, Conscript Fathers, and to the sovereignty of the Roman People, we surrender the people of Campania and the city of Capua, with our lands, the shrines of our gods, and all things else, whether sacred or profane; whatever we endure henceforth, we shall endure as your surrendered subjects". Livy, *History of Rome*. Volume III, trans. B. O. Foster (Cambridge MA.: Harvard University Press, 1924), 462–63 [A.P.]

to dissolve itself, to abdicate its sovereignty and independence; and yet it is a certainty that necessity, the overwhelming logic of things, nudges peoples together and the very progress of civilization requires it.

In the Middle Ages, nations such as Hungary and Bohemia, attracted by imperial prestige, superior civilization, and religious influence, and, naturally, impelled by a sense of their own infirmity, discarded their dynasties[76] and surrendered to the emperor willingly and without constraint. But the political mores of the time provided an excuse: with every medieval principality subordinate to the emperor, the inhabitants believed that they were more honoured and better than if they were under the immediate protection of that suzerain than under the rule of their own princes; furthermore, we know that in surrendering themselves, these nations took care to hold on to their nationality, their customs and their privileges. They were joining the empire more as federated partners than as subjects; and the Magyars' eternal argument against the encroachments of Austrian despotism is to say that they have never been vanquished or conquered, but had voluntarily amalgamated on conditions that rule out their being conflated with the emperor's serfs. They were no part of his patrimonial domain; in their eyes, he is merely the successor to their kings.

Let us grapple with the facts. Such issues can only be resolved in two ways; through voluntary action, after the fashion of the Capuans, or through the decision of arms. The former being most often shameful: which leaves the latter.

A question arises here: is the decision of arms right? Can it confer right? – I answer in the affirmative, except in respect of the manner of the warfare and the use made of the victory, and that is something we shall have to explore further.

In principle, every war is indicative of a revolution. In primitive times, it represents the act whereby two peoples, driven into amalgamation by proximity and interests, have a tendency to seek mutual absorption, each to its own particular advantage. Suppose that, at the point where battle is joined, Right were suddenly able to appear, like a god, and address the two armies. What would Right say? It is inescapable that revolution is fated to work changes in the circumstances of both peoples, changes that are legitimate, providential, sacred. As a result there are grounds to proceed, whilst preserving each nation's rights and prerogatives and sharing the sovereignty of the new State between them,

---

76. Dynasty being one of the "givens" of the sociology of force outlined in *War and Peace*; it affords an understanding of Proudhon's stance on the nationalities trend in 1860 and accounts for his notion of Europe's political physics. See below, Book Two, Chapter X and Chapter XI: Book Three, Chapter II. [H.M.]

IN PROPORTION WITH THEIR STRENGTH. The divine verdict here would merely be the application of the right of force.

But, with the gods fallen silent, men will not accept revolutions that run counter to their interests; they even conclude that revolutions are an affront to Divinity. With the gods silent, they deny that proportional sovereignty is an adequate recompense for undiluted sovereignty, and they repudiate any such contrivance. With the gods silent, finally, they refuse to acknowledge the superiority of the enemy; they would feel it an affront to their honour to surrender to a lesser force without a fight. They all opt instead for recourse to arms, each of them hopeful and flattering himself that a clash of arms will be resolved in his favour.

Therefore, the duel is inevitable. There is legitimacy in it since it is the agent of a necessary revolution; its outcome will be fair, since victory serves no purpose other than to indicate which side has the greater force and to consecrate its right. For let us not forget the right of force, which ultimately determines the timeliness of the revolution and the position of the two peoples within the new State, antedates the war; and it is because it antedates the war that it can then assert itself in the name of victory.

Such is the origin, theoretical and historical alike, of the *right of war*, setting to one side specific incidents and unwarranted acts of violence. That right derives from and implies the right of force, but it is not the same thing as the right of force. It is to the right of force what the code of civil procedure is to the civil code, or the code of criminal indictment to the penal code. The right of war is force's procedural protocol; and it is why we are going to define war as *the vindication and demonstration of the right of force through force of arms.*

The souls of the ancients were filled with this principle; it hovers over their entire history, mingled, it is true to say, with fearful abuses, prey to wrongheaded interpretations and made odious by the barbarism attendant upon its application. But since when has smoke been an acceptable argument against light, and superstition been called as a witness against ideas? It is incumbent upon every even-handed history to sift the true from the false, the just from the unjust, in the thinking of nations as well as in their deeds.

In the year 416 BC, during the Peloponnesian War, the Athenians laid siege to the island of Mela. The talks which were held at the time between the Athenians and the Melians, as recorded for us by Thucydides, is one of the most remarkable landmarks in the rights of peoples from that time, as well as one of the most misconstrued by the critics.

"We must" – the Athenians argued – "start from a universally accepted principle, that, among men, matters are governed by the laws of justice,

when equal necessity compels it; but those with the greatest force do all in
their power, and it is for the weak to give way".

The Melians acknowledged that they found it hard to withstand the power
of the Athenians; but they were hopeful that in resisting the unjust, the gods
would watch over them.

In their response, the Athenians made the gods complicit in their policy:

> "What we are asking for" – they said – "what we do is in tune with the
> opinion men have of the Divinity. As a matter of natural necessity, the
> gods prevail because they are the strongest; the same applies to men. We
> are not the ones who have laid down this law: we are not the ones who
> first enforced it; it came to us ready-made and we shall pass it on forever
> through the times to come. We shall also act now in accordance with that
> law, in the knowledge that you yourselves, and every other people, had
> you possessed the same force as us, would behave in the same way".[77]

I have followed the translation by Monsieur Laurent,[78] because that writer, one
of Belgium's most learned men, is also one of the most strenuous opponents of
the principle I am championing, the right of force. But Thucydides's Greek is
explicit: he indicates that the right of force is at once a prompting of the conscience, on the basis of the understanding that all men have of Divinity, and a
law of nature which intends that wherever force lies, there too command resides. So much for this profession of the right of force which has revulsed most
historians and which Denys of Halikarnassos, who was writing four centuries
later, no more grasped than did Cicero, finding it suitable for a brigand or a pirate. Monsieur Laurent points out, however, that Denys himself was subscribing
to that right when he asserted the right of the Romans to rule over nations, on
the grounds that they wielded greater force.

Following the battle of Aegos-Potamos, in which the Athenians' force was
wiped out, Lysander gathered together his allies to ponder the fate of the prisoners. He summoned one of the Athenian generals, Philocles, and asked him
what punishment he reckoned he was due for having issued an order for the
Greek captives to be put to death. Philocles replied: "Level no accusation at
men who are not judges; as victor, deal with the vanquished as you would have
yourself dealt with if you were in our place".

Monsieur Laurent, who also mentions this fact, has overlooked the lofty

---

77. F. LAURENT, *Histoire du droit des gens*, Vol. II, 205. [P-J.P.]
78. FRANÇOIS LAURENT (1810–1887), professor of civil law at the university of
Ghent; ardent supporter of the Belgian liberal party. [H.T.]

morality in it. It is not Philocles's ferocity that we should be admiring here but his sense of justice. Lysander and his allies sought to incriminate the Athenians for indulging in the executions of prisoners of war; as a result, they were inviting Philocles to say what punishment he was due. This was the stigma to which the Athenian general took exception: "We have no judges", he cried, "all we did was enforce the right of war, rigorously I grant you, but legitimately. See to what you, in turn, must do". Of course, the real jurisprudence of force forbids the slaughter of captives; but we should note that where the ancients erred was in respect only of the interpretation of the law, whereas in our modern authors the error relates to the principle itself.[79]

But of course, the right of force is terrifying in its performance, where what is at issue is breaking a recalcitrant population all the more deserving of our esteem because of the strenuousness of its refusal. But the excesses attendant upon warfare ought not to blind us to the principle of right implicit within it; any more than judicial error, venal magistrates, the obscurity of the law, the wiles of litigants can blind us to the justice that presided over the organization of the courts; any more than an adulterer is an argument against marriage, or fraud and the broken word an argument against the usefulness and morality of contracts.

It is this invincible sense of a righteousness implicit in war that at first swathed it in robes of formality, which conditioned it and governed its consequences, as if it were a sort of court proceedings. For instance, it is universally the case that the conditions imposed upon the vanquished are less generous than those which he might have obtained by means of voluntary submission, and this again is entirely fair. Here, the defeated party, like the losing litigant, pays the costs; his lot is made worse due to the compensation he must pay for the damage done because of his resistance to the victor.

Be it understood, and I would do well to reiterate this, so as to ward off any pretext for calumny, that there can be no question here of justifying any sort of warfare, any more than there is of excusing or endorsing every deed done in war. The same applies to that right as to all the rest, the acknowledgment of which in no way legitimizes abuses. Man's heart is filled with passions; his handiwork is tainted; but the right is wholesome, whether it relates to warfare, labour or property.

The circumstances in which the right of force becomes applicable and, consequently, war legitimate as an action asserting that right and the

---

79. Monsieur Laurent's five-volume work in 8°, is just one long protest, in the form of an historical repertory, against the right of force. It is irritating that the writer has failed to notice that the very right that he impugns makes up the entire substance and soul of history and that, in denying it, he has denied himself the idea and thus the glory of a magnificent opus. (Laurent's book, since completed, comprises 18 volumes in 8°, 1859 et seq.) [P-J.P.]

resolution of an international quarrel, are of various sorts; let us note the four main ones.

1. *Incorporation of one nation into another, of one State into another State: absorption or amalgamation of two political societies.* – This being the instance which we used as our example, it was the first to arise and the most important, if not the most commonplace of all. All modern States, once their populations reach one or two million souls, are the more or less legitimate products of warfare, of the right of force. The erstwhile kingdom of France took shape little by little that way, initially through Roman conquest, which brought all of the nationalities making up primitive Gaul under the same yoke; then by means of the Frankish conquest which, at the time of the break-up of the empire, and with the aid of the bishops, preserved the union; finally, through the gathering into the royal domain of all the provinces that had broken away from the heart of the feudal regime. A simple glance at the map makes it plain that, on the basis of the needs of neighbourliness, much more than any more or less pronounced kinship in terms of language, religion, usages and customs, the host of statelets sitting between the two seas, the Pyrenees, the Rhine and the Alps, were nudged into amalgamating into a single State, which naturally had to assume the name, title and law of the one whose central location and superior force foredoomed it to be the centre of attraction. Under the Roman external conquerors, the centre was pretty much everywhere; but under the Frankish kings it was established as Paris; and to anyone studying the disposition of the various basins into which French soil is broken up, it is plain that the choice of that capital was not at all men's doing; it was the handiwork of nature itself.

Here, for the very first time, we find, at the root of war and conquest, in the very origins of societies, a principle that we shall find here after perpetually at odds with the right of force: the right of nationality. Ever since Hobbes it has been stated and restated a host of times: A nation, a State, is a collective entity, endowed, like any other individual, with a life of its own; having its freedom, its character, its genius, its consciousness and, consequently, its rights, the first and most essential of which is the retention of its originality, its independence and its autonomy. But, as we have observed, all of those rights must defer to the necessity which, through the proliferation of men and the growth in populations and States, compels them to join together, mingle and amalgamate; hence war and hence the prerogatives of force. What happens, therefore, is merely what happens in any policed society, when two different rights clash; it is the lesser interest that has to defer to the greater and its right is consequently swallowed up by the latter's right. Thus, if public usefulness so requires, a mere particular interest may find itself dispossessed, but without any prior compensation. Expropriation here is merely the exercise of the right of force; the compensation attendant upon it represents the private right which the general right absorbs.

Warfare between one nation and another, the exercise of the right of force, and the conquest that follows upon it is therefore the sacrificing of one or of several of these moral entities that are known as nations or States, to a higher need which in this instance outweighs the respect owed to that moral entity and its right to exist.

2. *Reconstitution of nationalities.* – This theme is the preceding one turned on its head. It comes into play following the break-up of some large State, where its component parts had hitherto been amalgamated within a shared State, and have a tendency to go their own way, no longer responsive to the attractions of the centre, more to their own particular attractions and revulsions. Thus, following the death of Alexander, out of the erstwhile Persian empire formed by Cyrus, all those minor kingdoms that were the apanages of Macedonian generals took shape, and they endured up until the Romans arrived. Thus, out of the break-up of Rome, encouraged by the barbarian invasions, all of the nationalities that Rome had swallowed up re-emerged; Italy herself was part of this backlash and all of her towns were found detaching themselves from the metropolis with youthful fervour and there is no denying that as far as Italy was concerned this was the starting point for a life of splendour, universal influence and glory. In a day, the handiwork of six centuries was destroyed and what Italy had been in the world in terms of her unity, she became again thanks to federation.

This is the explanation for the agitation that is racking the Austrian empire before our very eyes. That at once monarchical and federative agglomeration of nations, united half by war and half by treaties. Just when the imperial government was on the brink of completing its centralizing endeavours, we see the long-subdued nationalities, protesting against their being amalgamated with one another, asserting their privileges, their former charters, their autonomy: which, if the centrifugal force were to outweigh the centripetal one, would entail the break-up of the empire.

Given the extent of the condensation at which they have arrived, grouping into large masses remains the law of peoples in Europe, pending some new re-ordering. Their shared security, the interests of their commerce, their industry, their intellectual and moral development, the higher interest of universal civilization make such large associations a necessity. These were the background conditions to the formation of Austria's empire, the largest fragment of that apostolic empire founded by Charlemagne and illuminated by Otto the Great, Barbarossa and Charles the Fifth. Now fresh ideas, fresh needs agitate the populace. Whereas the Vienna government, under pressure from incursions from outside, looks to a concentration of the forces of the empire for its salvation, its constituent peoples are fearful that greater cohesion may, as far as they are concerned, prove to be an aggravation of their servitude and, at the most critical point, they invoke the benefits of their nationality. Whereupon war becomes an issue, unless some compromise, which in this instance would bring no disgrace upon anyone, forestalls conflict. Maybe, in order to restore some cohesion to this difference of opinion, all that will be required is the sacrifice of a dynasty: the sacrificing of dynasties, like the sacrificing of nationalities, is also a law of history. *Videbit Deus.* Are morality, conscience, force, to be found in Vienna, Pest, Prague or Zagreb? That is the whole point.

3. *Religious incompatibility*. – War sometimes meddles in matters of religion, but not as a judge in respect of doctrine; clearly, theology has nothing to do with the exercise of force. Also, war does not purport to decide which of two beliefs is the true one; or, in the case of two theological opinions, which is orthodoxy and which heresy. As far as war is concerned, it is merely a matter of deciding, between two fractions of the same people divided over matters of religion and which find tolerance impossible, which of the two fractions is going to have to embrace the religion of the other, the way a child abides by the religion of its father, lest it find itself out of communion with the father. *Thy people shall be my people and thy God my God*, said the grieving widow Ruth to her mother-in-law Naomi, who had suggested to her that she go back to her homeland in Moab.[80] In terms of religion, this is the very same maxim that war foists upon the weak.

In the earliest societies, where religion merges with legislation, priesthood with authority, worship with justice and morality, tolerance, based wholly on the separation of Church and State, is not feasible: the unity of religion is necessary. Religion, identified with justice, politics and mores, is the very life of society. It is to the soul what food is to the body. The truly religious man can no longer suffer the dissenter or the ungodly, mortal man can no longer endure a mischievous neighbour polluting the very air that he breathes, the water he drinks, the bread he eats, poisoning his livestock, killing his trees, destroying his crops and threatening his household. It is possible that neither of the competing

---

80. *Bible*, Book of Ruth, 1:16. [H.T.]

religions is the right one, that both are of equal value; it is possible that the religion of the weaker is better than that of the stronger. But this is no concern of
war; as I have stated, it acknowledges no dogma. The only thing that falls under
its remit is to determine in a trial of strength which side must make the sacrifice, since the two sects cannot bear each other and one must be sacrificed, and
neither one can argue that war is unfair. It is not war that excommunicates: far
from it, the decision which it falls to it to make implies that, in its eyes, all religions are valid insofar as they are a presentation of pure justice; in which respect
it can be said that war's reasoning is consonant with that of the philosopher. In
matters of religion, war is the very essence of tolerance.

History is full of bloody executions, from which no Church, no synagogue
and no priest has ever shied away. The Albigensian war is a case in point. Point
an accusing finger, if you will, at human folly, superstition, prejudice, fanaticism
and hypocrisy. That is easy for those of us who live without religion, most of us
having lost all sense of religion and even sense of morality. But if it is a fine thing
to die for one's country, it is equally fine to die for one's faith; after all, there
is no difference between one and the other. As for war, it is beyond reproach
here. On the day when sectarian fury compelled it to step in, it did the only
thing that needed doing: sacrificing, as bloodlessly as possible (I am arguing the
hypothesis of formal warfare), the weaker to the stronger. Of course, it is a sad
affair for a believer to lose his religion and his God in a swordfight. But such immense griefs are only to be found at the Opera these days. In the end, what did
civilization lose by switching from Osiris to Baal to Mithra to Jehovah, from
the latter to Jupiter, from Jupiter to Christ, from the Pope to Luther? It was
through those switches and apostasies[81] that we have learned how to separate
faith from reason, worship from justice, Church from State.[82] I would venture
to say that never has the judgment delivered by force been better grounded, nor
more fruitfully or legitimately enforced.

4. *International balance [équilibre]: its limitations upon States.* – This contentious principle, fixing a term to the territory and maximum extent of a State,
which it would be easy to show was a factor in most wars ancient and modern, has, since the Congress of Vienna in 1814–1815, been the very purpose of
the European law of peoples. Applications of the law of balance are frequent in
history, as Ancillon has demonstrated in his *Tableau des révolutions du système*

---

81. *Apostasy*: Public renunciation of a belief at the prompting of personal interest. [H.T.]
82. Writing in *Voix de Peuple*, on the 22 December 1849, Proudhon warned about the
creation of an oppressive Trinity of capital, the state and the church. See, Roger Price, *The
Church and the State in France, 1789–1870: "Fear of God is the Basis of Social Order"* (Basingstoke: Palgrave Macmillan, 2018), 111. [G.H.]

politique en Europe. It was a law that spurred eighteenth century Prussia to suddenly turn into a great power, becoming simultaneously a counter-weight to Russia, Austria, France and the Scandinavian States.[83] As posited in the treaties of 1814 and 1815, the principle of international balance cannot but be considered the latest formulation of the rights of peoples, as we shall show in the next volume. Equally, we cannot fail to see this as paving the way for a higher order of things, and as the cornerstone of a definitive peace.[84]

> "Political balance" – Eugène Ortolan[85] says – "consists of orchestrating among the nations belonging to the same system such a distribution and counter-positioning of forces that no State is in a position, on its own or in association with others, to impose its will, nor to curtail the independence of any other State. And if it is correct to say that the balance of different forces is ensured through the marriage of those two facts, intensity and direction, it will be acknowledged that between nations intensity is composed of all the sundry material or immaterial factors which by nature have constituted power [*puissance*], or the effective means of acting. As for direction, that is determined by interest. Therefore, we have to marry the distribution of various power resources and the kindred or opposing interests in order to create within a group of nations, at a given moment, a state of balance, whilst not losing sight of the extreme mobility of the elements of power and, above all, of interests. They are liable to change on a daily basis and the balance will run the risk of being upset by what some will increase or reduce and what others may venture to unite or divide".[86]

Implicit in those considerations of Monsieur Ortolan's is a whole theory of the right of force, a whole philosophy of war, terms, it seems, which howl at being yoked together, but which nevertheless, when juxtaposed, express a rigorous truth. They led to this consequence which I take the liberty of offering to the learned jurisconsult for him to ponder; that, for the past century, thanks to the principle of balance or, as Ancillon put it, of counter-balance, the rights of peoples has made some headway, and that headway it owes, not to the negation of the right of force, but to its affirmation and I might even argue its restoration in the literal and material sense with which the ancients vested it.

---

83. Between 1640 and 1786, Prussia was to become one of the great European powers. [H.T.]

84. See below, Book Five, Chapters III and IV. [H.M.]

85. EUGÈNE ORTOLAN (1824–1891), jurisconsult and composer. [H.T.]

86. *Ways to acquire the international domain.* Not having Monsieur Ortolan's book to hand, I have borrowed this quotation from Monsieur Vergé, Martens's publisher (Vol. II [1851], 317). [P-J.P.]

Such, broadly speaking, were the powerful drivers, the hallowed, enforce-able interests that once upon a time filled the warrior soul with enthusiasm. Much more than the subject within our great States, lost like a droplet in the Ocean; much more than the peasant in our county districts, the bourgeois and the working man in our towns; the ancient city dweller had an inner feeling for homeland and sovereignty. Only there was he a man; anywhere else and he lost everything, his wealth, his dignity, his liberty. This is what invests Tertius's great dictum, translated by Horace as *Dulce et decorum est pro patria mori* – It is sweet to die for one's country – with such meaning; this was a dictum that the Roman plebians by Augustus's time were starting to misunderstand and which modern nations have no great grasp of either. What difference does it make to a peasant in Lombardy, say, whether he lives under the protection of Piedmont or Austria, if the rent he must pay to the bourgeois is still the same and if, like the ancient *colonus*, he is doomed to remain a poor wretch forever?

In this struggle of strength, everything is splendid, selfless, sublime. Here honour in life is boosted in proportion with that citizens' sacrifices: dare I say that it is by means of this magnanimity of warfare that the vanquished reduced to servitude is more to be honoured than he who, without putting up a fight, agrees to the absorption of his country and the abrogation of their sovereignty.

If justice is our prerogative, and its daily cultivation the price of our happi-ness, days of battle, I mean legitimate battles, should be times of blessed joy for the combatants. The time set aside by fate is upon us. Two nations are standing by: the point is to know which must hand over its name to the other and, by absorbing it, double its own sovereignty. Who pushes them into this contest? The force of events, the order of Providence, says the Christian: the law of the spheres, as Machiavelli would have it.[87] Well then! They all cry in unison, let us perish, or let us salvage the honour of our forefathers and the immortality of our race!

Warfare, hate- and insult-free, between two unselfish nations over some in-evitable and otherwise insoluble affair of State; war, as an assertion of the right of force and of the sovereignty that goes along with force: that, I make no bones about it, strikes me as the ideal of human virtue and the ultimate rapture. Who dares to speak here of *thieves* and *murderers*?

---

87. Machiavelli (1469–1527) subscribed to a sort of an astrology, the first principle of which was the movement of the spheres; seasonal rotation, the organizing of societies and States, the shift from monarchy to aristocracy and from aristocracy to democracy and then a reversion to monarchy, plagues, famines and human lives and deaths being determined by the circular movement of the universe. According to a second principle, all great events were heralded by prophets or prodigies. [H.M.]

Would you like startling testimony as to the reality of the right of war and its necessary impact upon society? Look at what is happening right now to the head of the Christian Church. With the collapse of the empire, under the repeated onslaught of the barbarians, Italy falls apart. Her towns, surrendering to their natural attractions, strive, each on its own behalf, to recover their independence. Christianity was the universal law: the Church, centred on the Papacy, the only power. It would have been easy for Christian Rome to rebuild a compact Italy armed against any outside influence, had the head of the Church been, like the consul of old, like the pagan emperor, simultaneously pontiff, magistrate and general. But Christ had declared that his kingdom is not of this world and he himself had been careful to separate the spiritual from the temporal; there are formal passages in the law that prohibit the priest from taking up the sword. In order to reassemble the Italian State, all the Pope had was that thunderbolt from the sanctuary, excommunication. His opinion carried enormous weight: everybody prostrated themselves whenever he issued a blessing or enunciated the anathema; but once he wants to govern, conquer or fight, everybody stood tall and resisted him. Thanks to this powerlessness on the part of the pontiff of peace, Italy stayed deeply divided. Alone, the Pope is incapable of carving himself out a domain; from the lance of the Frankish king,[88] or the munificence of a countess,[89] he will await the dowry that he will almost never savour. Unable to turn conqueror, he will serve to stymie any other conquest; sometimes curbing the emperor's momentum, sometimes undermining the king or breaking up republics. And medieval Italy, after having spent a thousand years re-enacting the heroic scenes and all the splendours of ancient Greece, after having initiated Europe into politics, the sciences and the arts, then slumped, exhausted, and fell prey to the foreigner. Italy's downfall came about because the Pope, in whom the greatest authority in Italy was vested, was sovereign in moral terms only; because as the vicar of Jesus Christ he is barred, according to the testament of his divine creator, from ever becoming a conqueror, king or emperor; because, in short, the make-up of his Church forbids him from wielding the prime and most quintessential of the rights of the State, the right of force.

To no avail. Ever since Charles V and the Reformation, the temporal princes have gradually joined forces to acknowledge and guarantee the spiritual leader

88. Pepin the Short gifted the Roman Republic (meaning the exarchate of Ravenna) to Pope Stephen II in 754, thereby endowing the Papacy with a territorial domain that he confirmed following his second Italian expedition in 756. [H.M.]

89. The Countess Matilda, the daughter and sole heir of Bonifacio, the marchese of Tuscany, Count of Modena Mantua and Reggio. It was to her castle in Canossa that the Germanic emperor Henry IV (1056–1156) came to repent before Gregory VII. On her death in 1113, she bequeathed all her lands to the Holy See. [H.M.]

a State of his own. The 1815 treaties gave their blessing to that arrangement and ensured that the Roman pontiff enjoyed the support of allied armies, Catholic, Greek and Protestant alike, in vain: the paradox of a non-warring power kept falling apart. To be sure, the nineteenth century was a century of diplomacy, if ever there was one. More than at any other time, affairs of public reason have a tendency to be sorted out by means of compromises and Congresses. What a boost for a government that purports to owe everything to religion, to the piety of the peoples, to the most venerable traditions, to the fellowship of altar and throne! Is it not the case that, had peace been the principle, condition and purpose of States, that greatest of all States, the Church, should supposedly have been the one with the greatest capacity for absorbency!

But whenever it has the floor, diplomacy is merely war's official mouthpiece; deep down, politicking between nations boils down to the logic of armies, to the right of force. Which is why, when powers assemble in Congress, the sovereign pontiff has no voice,[90] other than when it comes to chanting the *Te Deum* and invoking the Holy Ghost. Which is why, counting for nothing on the battle-fields, or at the conferences of the sovereigns, his own policy, his priestly policy is to dismantle whichever forces he can dominate. Unable to conquer Italy, all of the Pope's efforts are designed to paralyse her, sometimes on the basis of her own divisions, sometimes by force of foreign arms. This was apparent back in 1848 when Pius IX refused to follow the people into war against Austria. He stated: "I am the father of all the faithful; I am not allowed to wage war on one portion of my flock" – "What, Holy Father? Not even in pursuit of the liberation of the Italian homeland?" "No, not even for the sake of the liberation of the Italian homeland. The homeland is a matter for the State and the kingdom of Christ is not of this world". "In which case do not serve as Italy's head of State, *noli ergo imperare*: for with you in charge, Italy's life would be suicide. Italy cannot stay pontifical and live".

It looks as if Italy today is waking up. She has driven out the foreigner, or nearly so; and the Pope's subjects are deserting him. Henceforth, the Church has been pushed out of politics, outside of temporal affairs, in Italy and in the so-called Church States, as well as in France, Austria and the Catholic States. Can you imagine an idea banished from universal life and from the reality of things? One dictum, one single dictum, has determined this huge calamity: *The kingdom of Christ is not of this world*. His vicar carries a crook and not a sword. How could this *shepherd* rule over men, if he cannot lead them into battle? Think about that: if there is anything irredeemably damning of the Popes' temporal sovereignty, look no further, for there you have it. The Pope is not a

90. Most publicists do not see the Pope as a figure in international law, his relations with the various States being governed by the domestic public law of each State. [H.M.]

Caliph: he is forbidden to command his armies. And take care, if you give him a
general, he will sooner or later be supplanted by him.

In the next Book, we shall be looking into the rules governing recourse to
force, what is conventionally described as *the forms of war*. But first let us finish
what we have to say of the short-term and longer-term applications of the right
of force.

CHAPTER IX

Application of the Right of Force.

2. THE DEFINITION AND OBJECT OF THE RIGHTS OF PEOPLES

That the right of war follows directly from the right of force, or, rather, that the former is merely the formula for claiming and establishing the latter, is what the reader must now consider to be beyond all challenge, even though the authors have never seemed to understand it, even though they have never seen war as anything but a modality of the use of force employed among civilized peoples against one another with as little savagery as possible.

The rights of peoples is a derivative of the right of war, just the same as the later derives from the right of force. As a result, the rights of peoples are, if I may say so, a third generation of the right of force. This is something that the jurisconsults cannot countenance and something that turns all of their theses on their heads. Indeed, not only do they not acknowledge the right of force, but the right of war, the purpose and specialness of which we have so clearly set out, and the rules of which we shall shortly make known, is, in their eyes, a mere fiction, constituting a specific, exceptional, abnormal article of the rights of peoples, which supposedly then would represent the first rank of right.

So, according to our learned publicists, where do the rights of peoples come from and in what do they consist?

The rights of peoples, they answer, flow from natural law. – And what is natural law?

Vattel quotes Hobbes who divides natural law into the natural law of man and the natural law of States. The latter being what is ordinarily referred to as the rights of peoples. The maxims of both of these laws are the same. – Vattel endorses Hobbes's deduction: merely commenting that natural law, as it applies to States, is liable to certain alterations: we spoke of these earlier.

Pufendorf and Barbeyrac, like Vattel, endorse the view of the English publicist.

Montesquieu says, roughly, natural law is what people *do*: he does not know the first thing about what it is.

> The rights of peoples are, by nature, based upon the principle that the various nations should live in peace with one another as best they can and, in war-time, do one another as little harm as possible, without injury to their authentic interests.
>
> The object of warfare is victory; that of victory being conquest; that of conquest, retention. All of the laws making up the rights of peoples should derive from that principle and precedent.
>
> All nations possess people's rights; even the Iroquois, who eat their captives, possess one. They send out and receive ambassadors; they are familiar with the rights of war and peace; the evil is that these people *are not based upon real principles.*[91]

But why are nations at war and why do they have recourse to force? Of that, Montesquieu knows nothing. And how could he? He does not acknowledge the right of force. He sardonically cites the Iroquois, whose international law is not, he argues, built on authentic principles. But the Iroquois who ate their captives and precisely because they used to eat them, knew more about the rights of peoples than Montesquieu does. The eating of the enemy was the enforcement against individuals of the verdict that victory had delivered only against the State, to wit: that the State of the vanquished is about to be swallowed up by the State of the victor.

If the jurists know nothing of the origin and principles of the rights of people, are they any more knowledgeable about what they consist of? According to Mackintosh:[92]

> The rights of peoples covers the principles of the independence of nations, their peace-time relations, the privileges of ambassadors and junior ministers, relations between mere subjects, the just causes of war, the mutual obligations of belligerent powers and neutral powers, the limitations upon legitimate hostilities, the rights of conquest, the faith to be observed between enemies, the rights conferred by armistices, safe-conducts and

91. *The Spirit of the Laws*, Book I (Chapter 3). See also Book X, Chapter 1: "*The rights of peoples...* is the political law of nations considered in terms of the relations they have with one another". [P-J.P.]

92. Sir JAMES MACKINTOSH (1765–1832) Scottish orator, publicist and philosopher. *His Vindiciae Gallicae* earned him the title of French citizen, awarded by the National Assembly (1792). A professor of civil law and people's law in India, he returned to Europe in 1813 and drafted six plans which helped the economy recover from the English penal laws. [H.T.]

passports, the nature of alliances and the obligations born of them, negotiating procedures, the authority and interpretation of peace treaties.[93]

Open the very first writer you come to on the table and you will see that
Mackintosh is merely summing them all up here.

Now there are plenty of serious reproaches that might be directed at this
catalogue. For a start, that the right of war is deemed part and parcel of the
rights of peoples, which cannot be countenanced; secondly, that the relations
between nations and the obligations deriving from these are, in terms of purpose, in no way different from the relations and obligations that exist between
individuals, which destroys the distinction some would draw between civil law
and the rights of peoples; thirdly, that none of the special relations between one
nation and another, none of the serious issues raised by those relations, are even
mentioned; fourthly, that the primordial right from which, first, the right of
war and later the rights of peoples, the right of force arose, is, as ever, wholly
misconstrued. At which point we shall call a halt.

Authors who have dealt with the rights of peoples appear to have ignored
even the rules of classification. As they had observed, say, that the right of war
is exclusive to heads of State, to the exclusion of private individuals, they concluded from that that the right of war was part of the rights of peoples. And so
on. But, for one thing, everybody knows that the right of war has not always
been the privilege of the prince; that, for centuries, it applied to every free man
and, to this day, in time of war, governments accord it to common individuals
by means of *lettres de marque*.[94] Then again, that right is not differentiated according to the importance of individuals but according to the natures, faculties
or actions to which they give rise. Therefore, it is not that there is a rich man's
right and a poor man's right, a noble's right and a commoner's right, a wholesal-
er's right and a retailer's right, a right for States of fifty thousand souls and one
for those of fifty million. Such distinctions are what is called in law *personhood*:
it is an affront to justice and the revolution eradicated it root and branch. There
is a right of force, a right of intelligence, a right of work, a right of exchange, a
right of family, a right of ownership, a right of criminal law, a right of civil and
criminal proceedings, a right of war. These rights are differentiated one from
another by the faculties or functions that produce them and are utterly identical
for every subject, big and small, individual and collective.

---

93. *Discours sur l'Étude du droit de la nature et des gens,* translation by Royer-Collard,
published as a preface to Vol. I of the cited edition of Vattel's *Droit des gens.* [H.M.]

94. A common example in the discussions to follow, a letter of marque was a state sanctioned larceny. It was awarded to a ship's captain, turning a *corsair* into a lawful belligerent, as
opposed to a *pirate.* They were abolished in France in 1856. [A.P.]

So, if there is to be an authentic right of peoples, there has to exist within the moral being, let us call it the nation, an order of relations that does not obtain in the ordinary citizen. Do such relations exist? This is the whole issue. On what score is the nation, which jurisprudence likens, in several respects, to the individual, different in such a way as to prompt the discernment of a brand-new right? For it must be plain that, in the absence of some such difference in the nature and function of the subject, the rights of peoples is empty verbiage or at best a stepping-stone, an empty framework.

We have an answer to that question, one we stated in the preceding chapter, about the right of war and the circumstances determining its operation.

From the point of view of rights, what sets the collective entity known as the nation or State apart from the private individual; what draws an unbreachable demarcation line between social personhood and individual personhood, is that the sacrifice of the former may be required for the sake of some higher interest, whereas the sacrificing of the latter can never be, other than in the case of some crime meriting capital punishment. Therefore, the republic cannot, by invoking the general good, command the sacrifice of the innocent, send Aristides into exile, order the death of Curtius or the suicide of Thraseas.[95] It cannot, on the pretext of self-protection or excessive population, expel the useless mouths, nor order the slaughter of innocents and the elderly. Every head is sacred: society only exists in order to preserve them. In no circumstances, I say, can man lay claim to any right to kill his fellow man, nor the majority to secure itself more room by eliminating the minority.

But it is different with States. In a number of circumstances it will be necessary for that collective entity, which has its soul, its genius, its dignity and its force as well; and to which every individual defers as he would to his sovereign; it will be necessary, as I say, for it to vanish when absorbed into some superior entity. Such is the price of the onward movement of civilization and the improvement of States.

Countless facts from modern as well as ancient history, prove that in any war it is this collective entity, the State, or, as we would say these days, nationality, which is in jeopardy; the destruction of cults (Cambyses in Egypt;

---

95. ARISTIDES (c. 540–468 BC), Athenian distinguished in terms of his integrity, which earned him the nickname of "The Just". He was a rival of Themistocle; the people decided between the pair and determined that Aristides should be ostracised (484 BC). Titus Livy tells us that around 393 BC, a chasm supposedly opened up in the forum. According to the oracle, it would only close over if what constituted Rome's power were tossed into it. MARCUS CURTIUS, armed and on horseback, leapt into it. The chasm closed over. THRASEUS (Publius Clodius Thrasea Paetus), a senator, had publicly condemned the actions of Nero. The Senate sentenced him to death. He cut his wrists to avoid execution in 66 AD. [H.T.]

Antiochus, king of Syria, in Palestine; the Muslims); the destruction of the aristocrats (Tarquin the Proud's advice to his son; Nebuchadnezzar's deportation of noble Jewish families from Judaea; the Galician massacres);[96] the destruction of the priests (Darius's persecution of the Magi; that of the Druids by the Romans); the massacre of all the males and sometimes of entire populations (see the *Pentateuch*); the eradication of languages; the destruction of books and monuments; alterations to constitutions; the relocation or destruction of capitals, etc., etc. Such things patently demonstrate that considered thought, knowing what it wants and where it is headed, presided over all these exterminations. Such thought, let me reiterate, is nothing but the sacrificing, by virtue of the right of conquest, of the collective entity that goes by the name of the State, and which the victor hunts down wherever he thinks he can see it alive in worship, in language, institutions, dynasty, nobility, etc.

The purpose of the rights of peoples is therefore to determine in broad terms and barring a later decision of war, when, how and on which conditions there are grounds for proceeding with the amalgamation or incorporation of one or several smaller States into a larger State. Plainly, as far as the former and occasionally the latter are concerned, such amalgamation is tantamount to suicide. Likewise, when, how and under what conditions are there grounds for carrying out the reverse operation, which is to say, a dismemberment?

There are some very serious issues arising from this principle and, to date, these have been poorly studied, only cropping up in treatises dealing with the rights of peoples, but which are nonetheless all unrelated to civil law. Volumes have been penned about ambassadors, which, when all is said and done, are merely devolved authorities established in accordance with the principles of civil law; but one will find not a single line of wholesome jurisprudence bearing upon the following questions:

"What might the normal extent of a State be?
"To what degree are the boundaries of a State set by geography, race, language, religion, tradition, the measure of civilization, etc.?
"Can and should States be equal to one another, or are they doomed, by the logic of things, to inequality?
"Can and should the amalgamation of nationalities extend as far as the absorption of the human race, until a universal monarchy is formed?
"Would it not be more accurate to imagine that the political unity of the human race consists either of a hierarchy of States, or of a

96. For the destruction of the aristocracy, see below, Book Four, Chapter IX. Proudhon refers to the uprising by the Polish nobles in Galicia in 1846, against whom the Austrian government incited the Ruthenian peasants to revolt. [H.M.]

confederation? In the first case, what is going to be the hierarchical relationship between States? In the second, does the principle of federation not lead, by way of analogy, to the resolution of large States into federated provinces?

"Or is balance ultimately contingent upon universal independence, an *anarchy* of city-states?

"Can this balance be replaced by a court of arbitration? If need be, does the political group most advanced in terms of civilization, the strongest one or the wealthiest one, have a right to some sort of privilege over the lesser? What is the nature of this privilege?

"When and how can a nation that has amalgamated with another reclaim its autonomy?

"How are newly discovered territories peopled by supposed savages to be shared out? What sort of protectorate over those peoples are the civilized to exercise? What are their reciprocal rights and obligations?

"What was the role of slavery in ancient times? What might it be today?

"Is a nation entitled to close itself off and refuse to trade with the foreigner?

"*What about* private political alliances? Do these not pose a threat to the liberty of other States, on the basis that they breach the rights of peoples? ..."[97]

There is enough there to make our least intelligent readers appreciate what the rights of peoples consists of, which all the publicists confuse, sometimes with political right, sometimes with natural or civil law, sometimes with political right, sometimes with the right of war, and reduce, other than in relation to

---

97. This program of study in public international law, outlined in 1861, has since become the subject of countless writings in the light of developments: the war in Europe [between 1914 to 1918] raised or re-raised all of the issues posed by Proudhon to the top of political concern and the League of Nations was designed to resolve a number of them. [H.M.]

Writing in 1927, Moysset was no doubt here referring to works such as Norman Angell's *The Great Illusion* (1910, reissued in 1933), which sold over two million copies in over twenty-five languages. Angell's liberal anti-militarism won him the Nobel Peace Prize in 1933. Like Proudhon, he was not a professional academic. Indeed, the academic discipline of International Relations is conventionally dated from around 1919, with the establishment of the Woodrow Wilson Chair of International Politics at the University of Wales, Aberystwyth. While revisionist histories date its commencement as far back as the 1880s, and the study of colonial administration, what is striking is that in 1861 Proudhon here (and at the end of the next chapter) sets out a programme of study that would only come to characterize the field of IR in the 1940s and 1950s, nearly a century after his death, and following two world wars. For more on this relative absence of anarchism from the canon of IR, see Alex Prichard, "What can the absence of anarchism tell us about the history and purpose of IR?" in *Review of International Studies*, 37, no. 4 (2011): 1647–1669. [A.P.]

civil, political and war-making rights, to childish minutiae about the apparel of ambassadors.

A few practical observations about the rights of peoples, in respect of its relationship with the right of war and the right of force, will bring what we have to say to a conclusion.

As we have seen above,[98] what sets the right of war apart from the right of force is that the latter is the right by which an individual, a corporation, a State lays claim to something as being properly his by reason of the superiority of his force, whereas the right of war is designed to govern the manner in which he will, in the event that his denier refuses, proceed with a demonstration of his force, which will at the same time deliver a verdict.

In turn, the rights of peoples differ from the right of war in that it is designed, not to regulate the forms of warfare, and the concomitant parleying, armistices, peace treaties, embassies, etc., but to determine instances of war and decide the outcomes, by anticipating the conclusions of victory regarding all matters that might trigger opposition between the powers and, possibly, conflict between them. In short, since war arises from the negation of the right of force and aims to ensure its enforcement, the object of the rights of peoples is either to avert war, or to reduce it to what is strictly necessary, or, ultimately, to determine its effects by making a theoretical determination, in accordance with the right of force, of the obligations of some peoples towards the rest and the consequences of the strife between them.

All the issues involving the rights of peoples are matters of pre-eminence, liable to be sorted out by combat and which, indeed, recognize no other court, no other arbitration than that of force; these are, therefore, issues the resolution of which can always be prejudged, in accordance with the balance of forces, and without the alterations that battle will make to that, if the parties concerned see fit to come to blows. We can imagine how important a repertoire of such solutions might have been for the handling of international frictions, the shortening of wars and the consolidation of peace treaties. If the rights of peoples, about which so many pointless books have been published, was as advanced as it pleases the vanity of the authors to claim it is, none of the wars that have blighted the world since the Revolution would have been feasible; they would have deferred to the jurisprudence of States. How is it that we are not living, definitively, in peace? It's because the rights of peoples has not been defined; because the jurist and statesmen, for all their haughtiness, are equally careless of issues it is their job to concern themselves with, that it has been left to the bayonet to resolve them.

---

98. Book Two, Chapter VIII. [P-J.P.]

Where international relations are concerned, I will go so far as to say that there is no acknowledged principle. There are *practices* reduced more or less speciously by the professors into theories, and subject to as many exceptions as it suits the diplomats to devise. Policy, once upon a time directed from on high by the Church, by virtue of the bond connecting the two powers, spiritual and temporal, has, since the end of the feudal regime, remained an art: it has not become doctrine again. The diplomat writes, swaps notes and scandalizes the world with his impotence, without as much as suspecting that his impotence springs from the fact that there are no dealings tougher than those designed to regulate life-and-death issues, in which war is the sole arbiter. Each State stands by its tradition, each people its instinct, at the risk of its greed being exposed and that is that. In politics, the Italian is Machiavellian; the Englishman, utilitarian and Malthusian; the Frenchman glorious and artistic; the Russian, as Napoleon I stated, is a Greek of the late-Empire; the German quests after but cannot find his historic right, which explains why there is still no Germany. Everything awaits its creation: the French Revolution itself sired only aspirations; it talked of universal brotherhood and perpetual peace, as did the poets of the Golden Age. But the first word remains to be said and that very simple word which I would have ring out loud enough for the dead to hear, is that WAR IS NOT GOING TO END, NOR JUSTICE AND LIBERTY BE ESTABLISHED BETWEEN MEN, WITHOUT ACKNOWLEDGMENT AND DEFINITION OF THE RIGHT OF FORCE.

The right of force, the right of war and the rights of peoples, defined and circumscribed as we have just done, being supportive of, implicit within and generative of one another, govern history. They are the secret providence that steers nations, making and unmaking States, and, in reconciling force and right, leads civilization down the surest and widest path. They account for a host of things that are not susceptible to detection by ordinary law, nor by any historical system nor even by the capricious vagaries of chance. Let us list a few examples of the better known of these.

Our sense of democracy is outraged at the sight of princely marriages determining the amalgamation of numerous peoples, as if those peoples were the property of the kings and could be passed as endowments over to their sons or given to their daughters by way of dowry. Aragon and Castile were united through the marriage of Ferdinand and Isabella; in England, the two Roses were reconciled through the marriage of Henry VII with the last remaining heiress of the House of York; Brittany was wedded once and for all to France by the marriage of Charles VIII and, after his death, Louis XII's marriage to Anne of Brittany.[99]

---

99. The marriage of Ferdinand and Isabella occurred in 1469: that of Henry VII in 1486: Charles VIII's in 1491 and that of Louis XII in 1499. It will be noted that these events, which

The protests, the fury that such actions would provoke today! Up until 1766, we witnessed Lorraine returned to Louis XV following the death of Stanislas I, the king of Poland, whose daughter he had married. The spirit behind the 1815 treaties put paid to that system of inheritance, borrowed from civil law and applied to international relations, it has to be said, with happy results, thanks to the common sense of the princes. Now, there is quite another principle governing the annexation or dismemberment of States, the principle of the balance of power. It was also the right of force that, in the guise of a marriage, effected what was a long-anticipated, continually sought and in the end became necessary. Look to history, indeed: the marriage arrangements of princes amount to nothing nowadays when they run counter to the right of force, which is nothing other than the rights of peoples. It will do Louis XII no good to invoke the claim on the duchy of Milan that he has inherited through his grand-mother Valentine;[100] there will be no annexation. France and Italy being separated by the Alps and by differences in nationality, there is no longer any case for asserting the right of force, no pretext at all for annexation or incorporation and the finest armies have nothing to commend them here. Like birth, genius or liberty, force per se is powerless in the absence of right; and the most spectacular gallantry is wasting its time fighting.

Who, on reading the story of Louis XIV, has not been shocked by the poverty of the grounds cited by that prince as justification for his invasion of the Low Countries? The right of devolution which he traces through his wife's line,[101] was not at all applicable in the circumstances, and we are embarrassed for France and for her sovereign at the sight of a cause, once upon a time so plausible, backed up with such pig-headed bad faith and such hateful arguments. No one could speak the real rationale: there was no gainsaying it. Faced with the justice of nations, as evident from the requirements of political amalgamation, Spain had no more claim over the Low Countries and Franche-Comté than France herself had over Milan, or England over Guyenne. On the other hand, the very same law of incorporation which, under Ferdinand and Isabella, had decided that Aragon and Castile should be united; which, under Charles VIII and Louis XII, decided that France and Brittany be united; which later, under Louis XV, had Lorraine, that erstwhile imperial fief, returned once and for all to its rival kingdom; that law had it that France should complete her expansion

---

had a telling impact on the formation of three major states, all occurred within the space of 30 years. [H.M.]

100. VALENTINE VISCONTI (1370–1408), wife of the Duc d'Orléans, brother of king Charles VI. [H.T.]

101. This is set out in *Traité des droits de la Reyne très chrétienne sur divers États de la monarchie espagnole* (1667). France's claims triggered a huge number of rebuttals and pamphlets listed in the catalogue of *Histoire de France,* vol. II, 233 et seq. at the Bibliothèque Nationale. [H.M.]

by annexing a number of provinces bordering it to the east and north. And is this effort to fix the boundaries of the French empire now over? Is there not the odd addition yet to be made, some adjustment to be made? That is a burning issue which I am unwilling to go into here. I shall stop short of saying that French patriotism is feeding exaggerated hopes here; France's right may find itself being determined by such events as might trigger further annexations on its part. What I will say is that, in my opinion, since the French Revolution and the ensuing wars, faced with the representative institutions emerging everywhere, and the economic issues that have been posed, the right of peoples has undergone such a modification in its essence that it cries out for quite different solutions...[102]

Why was the Hundred Years' War between France and England an unjust war on the part of the latter? The Salic Law disposition, which barred women from succeeding to the crown, was a prosecutorial invention which Edward III was perfectly right to hold up to ridicule. But, between France and England, nature erected barriers that render any unification impossible. Here, as in the case of Lombardy and Milan, it can be argued that the law of incorporation did not apply and, consequently, that there were no grounds for the king of England to have recourse to war. Far from there having been an obligation upon the king of France to acknowledge the claim which his rival was asserting as the grandson of Philip the Handsome,[103] he could easily have told him, had he not been precluded from so doing by his regard for feudal rights:

> The law governing the formation of States holds that no incorporation takes place unless it is required by absolute necessity. Only in that case is there any basis for uniting two States by making the weaker submit to the political case of the stronger. So, if there is reluctance on the part of the former, there are grounds for recourse to arms. But you as the king of England, a foreign prince, separated from my country by the Ocean, what is it that you are asking for? What do my people and yours have in common? Were you the older son of the king of France, my own father, you could only assert your first-born rights on condition that you renounce your title as king of England, or turn England into a French province. Therefore, not only do I, my barons and my loyal commoners refuse to recognize you

102. Proudhon is referring here to Napoleon III's designs on Belgium, Luxembourg and the left bank of the Rhine, which Proudhon thought was a ridiculous idea. A satirical article he wrote on the matter in 1863 was misconstrued by Belgian nationalists and prompted two riots outside his house in the Ixelles suburb of Brussels. Proudhon then took advantage of an amnesty and returned to Paris. [A.P].

103. KING PHILIP I OF CASTILLE (1478–1506). Known as Philip the Handsome or Philip the Fair. [A.P.]

as our sovereign lord; but we in turn have drawn up against England, and you, a claim on this province of Guyenne[104] that you retain illegitimately and by a false interpretation of the rights of peoples. Guyenne, for which you owe me feudal homage, cannot belong to an anti-French prince; as a matter of natural law, it belongs to France and is part of her union. It was with this thought in mind that, almost two hundred years ago, one of my predecessors, Louis the Younger entered into a marriage with Eleanor who was subsequently driven out for her adultery and harboured by one of your forefathers. The right of feudal succession, which you invoke, cannot take priority over the eternal law of nations, which I represent. Prepare yourself, therefore, to return to my hands this province which does not belong to you, or to defend it by force of arms. God and victory will decide who has right on his side.

In the fourteenth century, as in the twelfth and the nineteenth, the incorporation of one of two powers, or of a fraction of one of those powers, England and France, into the other, went beyond the bounds of the right of conquest. Besides, England did not have the force to incorporate France, any more than France could England. No matter how one looks at the issue, from the viewpoint of the right of force or the rights of peoples, the claims of the English monarch flew in the face of common sense. Wise policy required that he turn a blind eye to the perhaps somewhat irregular succession, in terms of strict feudal law, (i.e., Philip de Valois's succession). France and Great Britain cannot lay a glove on each other; they are fated to coexist with each other without ever being able to absorb the other; which is the firmest foundation for an alliance between them. Today, more than ever, and no matter what their grievances with each other, anything which one of those powers, momentarily victorious, might undertake against the other, would collapse after a short while under the pressure of events, which are mightier than the force of armies.

---

104. Guyenne was a French province encompassing the Gironde, Les Landes, the Dordogne, Lot, Aveyron, Lot-et-Garonne and Tarn-et-Garonne. Having passed to Henry II of England through his marriage to Eleanor of Aquitaine, who was divorced by Louis VII, known as Louis the Younger (1154), it remained in English hands up until the end of the Hundred Years' War (1453). [H.T.]

CHAPTER X

The Same Subject Continued:
Contemporary Issues

My intention on starting this work was to give a wide berth to current affairs. I thought I owed that duty of discretion to the public, as well as to the government. I said to myself that a book of doctrine being above any national or partisan interest, there was a duty on the author to steer clear of polemic.

It occurred to me later that this scruple might instead look all the more ill-advised since I cannot remain indifferent in such agitated times; that I have not hesitated in other writings to make my opinions plain and, ultimately, the reader is entitled to insist that I put my principles to the test, *hic et nunc*,[105] by offering solutions, or at any rate, elements of solutions to international issues that are so rightly of concern to the whole of Europe.

I intend, therefore, to frankly beseech the reader to bear in mind that what I am putting forward is not so much my own opinion as much as forecasts regarding disputes that may possibly be settled by force of arms.

Above all, this is a principle of which the reader needs to be strongly persuaded, if he wishes to understand anything about politics and history:

In the exercise of their sovereignty, nations are absolute; in terms of that same sovereignty, they are not inviolable. They are not answerable to any court; but they can lawfully be stripped of their political life by warfare. In the event of a dispute between two powers, the issue is settled by means of conflict, which entails, if need be, the political extinction of the defeated side, never its subjugation. Where the right of war and the right of the people are present, respect for nationhood is non-existent.

The Eastern Question. – No one in Europe is in any doubt that the Turkish empire is approaching the conclusion of its decline and that there may be cause for all powers to worry about what will succeed it. So, what we have to address is a case of political demise.

In civil law, the maxim is that *the dead seize the living*, meaning that the son

---

105. "Here and now". [A.P.]

or closest relative takes over the management of the deceased's assets and affairs. The laws of State formation and the evidence of history prove that the same holds true for political entities. The western Roman Empire, which perished, like Turkey, from disintegration from within, was succeeded by the nationalities which were its component parts, and which can be deemed its natural heirs. The barbarians who gave their names to several of the brand-new States, like the Franks in Gaul, the Ostrogoths in Italy, the Visigoths in Spain, figure in all this, so to speak, merely as executors, at once agents of destruction and of rebirth, preserving everything they could of the empire, converting to its law and faith and they were swiftly absorbed by the native population.

Can whatever States that emerge from the break-up of the Turkish Empire be looked upon, in accordance with the rights of peoples as we have finally defined it, as its natural heirs? In short, how and for whose benefit should the dismemberment proceed?

Two hypotheses suggest themselves:

Either the nationalities hitherto conquered by the Turks and since reduced to serfdom are about to see their rulers replaced and themselves resurrected as political entities, the way that the peninsular Greeks and some of those from the Archipelago were thirty-five years ago, under the protection of the European powers; just as Moldavia and Wallachia have just done; and which could easily apply to Serbia, Bulgaria, Roumelia[106] and Montenegro; though a more difficult prospect perhaps in the Asian provinces where there are larger numbers of Turks closer to the heartland of Islam.

Or those States neighbouring Turkey – Russia, Austria, the Danubian provinces, Greece, Egypt, France and England [in the Suez and Crimea] – will step in as heirs by virtue of the right of superior force, according to which any State whose political life becomes bankrupt is absorbed by its powerful neighbour. The partition of Poland last century is one instance of this. As Poland's political dissolution was deemed beyond all remedy, given that the power of the State was wholly vested in the aristocracy, and, once that aristocracy is abolished, there was no class below it by which a State could be reformed. What followed was the partitioning of Poland between those three neighbour States, Russia, Austria and Prussia.

At first glance, the current focus on the principle of nationality would appear to ensure that the first of these solutions is to be preferred; that would simply be the restoration of the native races after four or five centuries of subjugation by the Turks. But if we think that those races on their own cannot do anything against the Ottoman corpse, any more than the Greeks in 1825 were

---

106. Formerly part of Turkey prior to the Treaty of Berlin (1878), Roumelia was effectively annexed by Bulgaria in 1885. [H.T.]

able to achieve liberation without the assistance of Europe's Christian States; if
we ponder the fact that the Turks are very numerous and still very strong in the
provinces of their empire and starkly distinct from the Christians by religion,
language and blood and still hostile, we have no option but to acknowledge
that, since the native element has need of outside force, this is the force that
will in fact supplant the strength of the Ottomans, and that, as a result, in the
absence of outright selflessness from the great powers, which is in the mores of
the age, the true heir to the Turkish empire, is the confederation of the great
States of Europe, what has been known since 1815 as the Holy Alliance. Greece
and Egypt themselves could only be accepted as heirs thanks to the munificence
of the aforementioned States, without whose contribution they would still be
marooned, powerless.

Indeed, where can we point to anything in the native populations capable
of replacing Turkish government in Candia, Rhodes, Cyprus, Syria, Anatolia,
Armenia, if the Turks refuse to convert to Christianity, inter-marry with the
natives or to return to their steppes?

I shall not labour the point: the truth here is glaringly obvious.

So, I would regard a partition of Turkey by the aforesaid powers as being
consistent with the law of people, precisely because they alone possess the political force that is indispensable in the life of societies, a force that Turkey has lost
and which her subject peoples are a long way from having recovered. If that partition does not come to pass, as the Polish one did so smoothly in the eighteenth
century, that is because the problems it raises, and the principle of balance and
international jealousies, have placed hurdles in its way. Perhaps the powers, unable to come to an agreement on partition, will end up occupying and governing
jointly; that would allow the natives to gradually build up strength and, perhaps,
for the Turks to soften. In any event, no matter what comes to pass, the principle
stands: that the right of the powers, overriding any consideration of nationality,
is, when we strip away all the philanthropic cant, rooted in force.[107]

The Polish Question.[108] – In my view, Poland perished due to disintegration

107. Proudhon's two hypotheses have been borne out by the wars between 1912 and 1918.
The Balkan Wars brought the former subject peoples of Greece, Serbia and Bulgaria the
bulk of the Turkish territories in Europe. The treaties of Sèvres (1920) and Lausanne (1923)
detached the nationalities from Asia and placed them under the mandate of the major European powers. [H.M.]

108. Proudhon's extensive reflections on Poland were the subject of a dedicated manuscript, *La Pologne. Étude d'histoire et de politique*, which remains unpublished. Proudhon
withdrew publication at the eleventh hour on account of the 1863 Polish uprising and his
critical commentary of Polish independence in the book. However, Chapter III has been tran-
scribed and published. See, Federico Ferretti and Edward Castleton, "Fédéralisme, identités
nationales et critique des frontières naturelles: Pierre-Joseph Proudhon (1809–1865) géographe des 'États-Unis d'Europe'", *Cybergeo: European Journal of Geography (Epistemology,*

from within. The 1772 partition was merely the inevitable consequence of that. This is easily seen if we trace the Polish movement from the founder of the first Piast dynasty,[109] through to Stanislas Poniatowski who mutely bore witness to the three partitions of Poland in 1772, 1793 and 1795.[110] Poland's history is one long agitation, the sole purpose of which is to establish whether PanSlavism's[111] main heartland is to be in Warsaw or in Moscow. The law of force, after having operated for a time in the Poles' favour, has finally come out in favour of the Russians. Added to which nonsense we have the Polish constitution and the political ineptitude of the venal and undisciplined nobility, forever in search of foreign sovereigns.

Therefore, let me declare on my behalf, that having scrutinized as best I could the elements of the process, the 1772 partition and the ones since, painful and even regrettable though these might appear to non-participants, these strike me, in terms of the rights of peoples, as being quite beyond reproach and I cannot fathom the ranting and the whingeing that has surrounded that partition for the past forty years. Whilst Louis XV and his ministers let that partition go through unopposed and without demanding compensation for France, that was a fault on their part and a misfortune for France. As to the deletion of Poland from the list of States, I will confess that whilst touched by that deplorable tragedy, whilst regarding Kosciuszko as the greatest citizen of his age, I have no quarrel with an act that had become a necessity, and which was performed in accordance with the rules. I am above all outraged by those of our democrats who, since 1830, have been using the restoration of Poland as a platform of opposition to the government.[112] It does a nationality no honour

History, Teaching), http://journals.openedition.org/cybergeo/27639. [A.P.]

109. The dynasty whose first representative was Mieszko the First (tenth century) and which petered out with Casimir the Great (died 1370). [H.T.]

110. STANISLAS II (1732–1798), the last king of Poland, placed on the throne by the Tsarina Catherine II whose lover he had been. In 1768, a civil war erupted. For four years the *confederates* battled Stanislas's troops before they succumbed. In 1772, Prussia, Russia and Austria carried out the first partition of the country. Stanislas found his powers reduced to a token authority. The Polish people tried to shrug off the yoke weighing it down and promulgated the 2 May 1791 Constitution. Stanislas pledged to uphold that Constitution but reneged on his oath and sided with the nobles close to Russia. In 1793, a second partition was signed. The patriots appointed Tadeusz Kosciuszko dictator (1794). For seven months the insurgents resisted the Russian troops. In 1795, the latter finally extinguished the Polish-Lithuanian state and Stanislas signed his own abdication order. Kosciuszko remains Poland's greatest national hero. [H.T./R.B.H.]

111. Pan-Slavism was a nineteenth century movement recognising a common ethnic background among the Slav peoples of eastern and east central Europe, and the struggle for the political unity of the Slav peoples. [R.B.H.]

112. In 1831 the Chamber of Deputies expressed "confidence that Poland shall not perish". A few days later, the Polish uprising was crushed and the news that Warsaw had fallen

and does it no service to turn it into a tactical weapon against the government of one's own country; it merely worsens its position by marshalling against it the ill-will of the indifferent and the hatred of the incumbents.

But we also know from the theory of the right of force that nations do occasionally spring back to life; and we may wonder if this might not one day be the case with Poland. Among the prevailing thinking, there are in fact three ideas regarding the impact that might be expected of such a re-establishment: the idea of nationality, the idea of parliamentary government, the idea of European stability. To which I reply: 1. That any such move towards the idea of nationality, boiling down, as far as the Poles are concerned, to the idea of Pan-Slavism, which is at least as dear to them as it is to the Russians, would merely result on their part in a displacement of the central power, but, again, heedless of national differences. – 2. That as regards the establishment of constitutional freedoms, since the Russians agree with the Poles on this, any notion of opposition and thus of schism finds itself discarded yet again. – 3. As for the principle of stability, it is plain that Poland's restoration being of much greater concern to the Latin and Germanic races than to the Slav races, the issue of a dismemberment of the empire of the czars would only need to be raised for the Russians and Poles, already in agreement on the question of race, in agreement on the system of government, to immediately unite against foreign interference and assert the ascendancy of the Slav race over Europe in the name of nationality, liberty and the right of force.

As I see it, not enough thought has been given to the fact that the nationality issue is trumped by the issue of political freedoms; that it is not as if it is in the light of the latter that the former is being brought up everywhere today; that, having secured political liberty, the Poles and Russians would be very close to agreeing, especially in the face of the dual trend driving the Germanic and Latin races in the direction of unity.

I cannot see anything other than economic revolution, its principle laid down by 1848, being likely to cause that revolution within the Russian empire, the dearest wish of the Western States, and simultaneously driving their own decentralization and recreating across the whole of Europe as many nationalities and as many States as there were provinces, duchies, counties and towns, etc., as there were in the Middle Ages.

The Austrian Question. – The revolution convulsing Austria at present

---

triggered rioting against the government that was taken to task by the democrats for having failed to intervene militarily. The opposition then mounted annual demonstrations in support of Poland each time the issue came up for debate. On 15 May 1848, the National Assembly was invaded in a move timed to coincide with a demonstration calling for Poland's liberation. See PROUDHON, *Confessions d'un révolutionnaire*, Ch. IX. [H.M.]

strikes me as being due much less to the nationality principle so fervently championed in Italy, but of which, I imagine, is very little felt by the peoples who were voluntarily subsumed into the empire centuries ago, than to the craving for political freedoms that has been discernible in the peoples of Europe since 1815.

In this regard, the Viennese bourgeoisie is every bit as impatient as Hungary's; loyal Tyrol is as restless as her neighbour, Croatia, Protestants and Catholics marching in step; least hostile to the views of the court in Vienna, perhaps, are the Magyar nobles. What is in jeopardy in Austria may well be the dynasty itself, not the empire.

The characteristic feature of the Austrian story is that, unlike the ancient peoples of Italy brought under Rome's yoke by means of the law of warfare, one after another, the nations that make up the Austrian empire were spontaneously drawn to it by the sheer allure of a superior civilization, but whilst clinging solely to their own particular constitutions and national privileges. The outcome of this is that, rather than a unitary empire like the ancient Roman empire or the current French empire, one has a sort of a federal empire, the principle and I dare say the touchstone of which is precisely that spontaneity of adherence. The ambition of the emperors and the Vienna government's tendency towards despotism produced the terrible idea of turning that federal arrangement, the only one the peoples are willing to acknowledge, into a unitary centralization. That initial grievance is today joined by another one: the Aulic Council's refusal to introduce reforms. In which regard, it is important that the national movement led by the Magyars in Hungary not be muddled up with the liberal movement around which the bourgeoisie and people everywhere are rallying.

The upshot of all this is that the real antagonist of imperial power, the infringer of the rights of peoples, destroyer of public strength, is not Hungary, nor is it Bohemia, but the Emperor. Let the emperor but try to concentrate and take unto himself the force of his empire and Hungary instantly breaks away, Bohemia following suit and the Germans themselves applauding; leaving the emperor isolated. With only his own person to embody the lives of thirty-seven million souls scattered through ten or twelve distinct nationalities and split into nobility, bourgeoisie and plebs. Is that not madness? And if it failed in the past, when the Germanic empire was at the peak of its prestige, how could it succeed today when it has become the empire of Austria and when the thinking of the nations has been boosted by three additional centuries of experience and the principles of the Revolution?

In short, whereas France's public right is founded upon conquest, which is to say the preponderance of a central power, which then went on to draw in all surrounding powers by means of the right of war, Austrian public right

is rooted on the mutual recognition of diverse forces which, anticipating conquest, federated with one another in order to form the empire and preserve as
much of their autonomy as they could. Added to that wish to cling on to such
ancient privileges, there was also, throughout the empire, the no less lively craving for a liberal regime. Now, it is equally evident that, on the first count, the
opposition to the Vienna government is conservative, and, likewise, on the second, it is revolutionary.[113]

The German Question. – This is absolutely the same as the Austrian question. In Germany as in Austria, the people are clamouring equally for, on the
one hand, through mutual acknowledgment of their strengths, and without
having to undergo the trials of war and conquest, their right to band together
into a big, federative State enjoying the advantages of unity, without any of the
perils of centralization; and, on the other, enjoyment of all the political freedoms promised to them at the time of the grand coalition against Napoleon in
1813. And, as in Austria, it is the princes, the king of Prussia, who are digging in
their heels against the wishes of the populace, who are repudiating the benef-
icent juridical principle of the collectivity of free forces, in order to replace it
with that of the amalgamation of said forces into a single power, which would
be wielded by the prince, just the same as the thunderbolt clutched in Jupiter's
hand.

This tendency on the part of the States of Germany, as well as those of
Austria, to federate with one another outside of the force of arms and remit of
warfare, and without being resolved into a contrived unity, seems to me, insofar
as it relates to the right of war and the rights of peoples, to be the most substantial development in history; at the time of writing, it marks the most advanced

---

113. These pages were on their way to the printer's when news reached me of the imperial statute endowing Austria with a constitution. Insofar as I can judge from a newspaper
extract, the Austrian government could claim today to be the most liberal country on the
continent. It offers the double advantage of a parliamentary system plus the provincial, or,
rather national freedoms so vigorously demanded by the Hungarians. And I would not be
surprised if one effect of this constitution was to afford the empire with the unifying strength
the former government craved. What an Aulic Council, an organ of absolute power, could
not do, the Chambers will accomplish without difficulty. But the important point to note
here is that Austria's new constitution is portrayed as a product of the rights of people, a pact
between nations in voluntary association, which, in my opinion, places it above all existing
constitutions. [P-J.P.]

By the decree of the 20th of October, 1869, the Austrian Emperor conceded to the
Reichsrat the power to legislate on all royal matters, and all the provincial Diets which
pertained to local affairs. This concession did not appease the Hungarians who wanted their
independence and to take advantage of the disaster of Sadowa [Battle of Königgrätz, 1866.
A.P.] in order to achieve it. The compromise (*Ausgleich*) of 1867 installed a dual monarchy.
[H.M.]

point of progress. This loyal and energetic tendency on the part of the populace is what the kings and nobles contend against. United at all times against the third estate, as soon as they no longer have to fear it they are continuously divided among themselves.[114]

The Italian Question. – Is Italy, re-enacting the course of her earlier revolutions, and having done away with her pontifical government, and expelled her Germanic emperor, to become a unitary kingdom like France, or is she to stick with federalism? Plainly, that is a matter that falls within the remit of the rights of peoples, since Italy was but recently made up of several independent States. As a result, this is a matter directly affecting the right of force.

For the past two years, Italy's different populations have been called upon to determine their own fate, but there has been little progress towards a solution. Universal suffrage and war have both been invoked at the same time. The outcome has been the same: war and the ballot-box have delivered the same verdict. Unfortunately, given the way in which the question has been framed, that verdict might appear dubious; consequently, it cannot be said that it is unappealable. The question of unity has been confused with the question of nationality and freedom; there are grounds for believing that it will, sooner or later, again be back on the agenda. Therefore, there is going to be civil war. If king Victor Emmanuel emerges as the victor, it will be a case of northern Italy taking over southern Italy, and we will have a centralized monarchy like there is in France; if the spirit of localism triumphs, as it has in Austria and Germany, we will have a federal State which, relying upon political liberty, may make Italy into one of the freest States in Europe. Those two very different outcomes can be traced back to the same principle, the right of force, amended, in the first instance, by the right of war and in the second by the principle of collectivity, which is part of the rights of peoples and comes closer to constitutional forms. Messrs Cavour, Mazzini and Garibaldi do not appear to have drawn this distinction, the consequences of which may have grave consequences as far as Italy is concerned. Instead, all three are in agreement on applying force to drive their country into a system of concentration and militarism which may very well some day be rued by the peasants, if not the bourgeois, the emperor and the Pope.

The Venetian question is connected to the Italian question. I have stated somewhere that on no account could the Austrian empire lose the eastern Adriatic coast. Even had Hungary and Austria as a whole carried through their

---

114. For Proudhon's thinking with regard to the unity of Germany, and the dilemmas of Germany or Prussia, federation or union, issues that Bismarck was to resolve, see *The Federative Principle.* [H.M.]

revolution by means of an alliance between Klapka[115] and Garibaldi, it would not have been within the gift of those two leaders to dispose of that portion of Austrian territory to which Italy has staked her claim. A great State has need of an outlet to the sea.[116] Here the right of the masses trumps considerations of nationality and language and, if need be, war would again resolve the issue in force's favour.

The American Question. – The Northern States and the Southern States, long since split over the issue of slavery, have now separated.[117] In a robustly constituted State, surrounded by powers ready to profit from its weakening, such a separation would be highly perilous and would not be tolerated: there would be war. In America, thanks to the security surrounding the territory, there is a chance that things will work out differently. This is Israel bidding Judah farewell: the Eternal One would make it clear which people he holds in his heart.[118] But there is also a chance that they will fight: in which case, there are two issues that need settling. On the one hand, there is the question of whether the southerners are entitled to secede, whether the North has the right to force them back and to use force to settle the issue of slavery; and, on the other, what we should think of slavery per se, setting aside the political issue.

For a start, are there grounds for war here? Let me answer that initial query the way I have already done regarding the wars of religion: Combat, no matter what form it may take, will prove absolutely nothing for or against the phenomenon of slavery per se. The right of war knows nothing of civil law or the rights of peoples. War wills what war wills. We could answer, on the one hand, that a puritan majority is not entitled to abolish, within the nation it stands for, a practice injurious to its religious and humanitarian principles; on the other hand, the minority, taking a quite different approach to things and given that furthermore no compensation is on offer and no workers offered as replacements for its slaves, is likewise entitled to fight against emancipation and defend its own interests. Let me say right now what that minority can

---

115. GEORGE KLAPKA (1820–1892) was one of the leaders of the 1849 Hungarian uprising. For the Italian question, see below, Book Three, Chapter II and *The Principle of Federation.* [H.M.]

116. Here Proudhon is clearly registering the rights of peoples to access to the sea, which was to become one of the major principles of the 1919–1923 treaties and which characterized the problems of the peace. In his treatise, cited earlier, MARTENS had stated that the major oversight in the rights of the peoples at the congresses in Munster, Utrecht and Vienna, was the absence of maritime balance. [H.M.]

117. The American Civil War broke out in April 1861 and lasted until 1865. [H.M.]

118. Following the death of Solomon (930 BC), Jeroboam led ten tribes into schism and established the royal house of Israel. Rehoboam was left with just two tribes, those of Judah and Benjamin, under his authority. The name of the first of those tribes was used to designate the new kingdom. (*Bible*, The Book of Kings, 1:12.) [H.T.]

argue by way of defence. War, fomented by the incompatibility of principles, and rendered inevitable by the danger or threat of secession, is legitimate and legal on both sides; and, insofar as it might have been intended to enforce the thinking of the greater part of the country, that would be a fair decision. It remains, therefore, for us to examine this issue of slavery per se, for it will have to be resolved sooner or later, either through the right of force or by means other than force.

On this score, and even though I, as a man of the world, repudiate slavery in principle, far be it from me also to hold the exploiters of the Southern States as entirely to blame, as they are wont to be held in Europe. Such a matter of practical morality, humanitarian economics and overall civilization cannot be judged on the basis of quotations from the Bible and sentimental novels. Humanity is due respect in all its races, that I know; in my view, justice has no basis other than such respect. Which is why, according to the Gospels, all nations have been called to *salvation*; we positive philosophers say to civilization and liberty. I embrace this universal calling of peoples and races to liberty as the first article of the rights of peoples. But who wishes the end wishes the means; to everything there is a season, *tempus laborandi et tempus liberandi*, as Ecclesiastes has it. Now, if the American Southerners can justifiably be suspected of avarice, might the Northerners be immune to the reproach lacking foresight and even of Phariseeism?

We think about blacks as if they were our peers, just as the Roman or the Greek might have thought about the Gaul or the Jew, their equal as a man, but one who has become their slave due to the fortunes of war. But what ought to strike all minds and is impossible for any serious friend of humanity not to take into account, is the inequality that obtains between human races and which makes the problem of social and political balance so problematical. The Caucasian stands out from all the others and not merely on account of fairness of face and elegance of figure; there is a superiority of physical, intellectual and moral strength. And that superiority of nature is increased tenfold by the social state, so that no race can stand in our way. A few English regiments contain and govern one hundred and twenty million Indians, and we have just seen that it took only a tiny army of Europeans to conquer China.[119] What compari-

---

119. The expeditionary corps sent to China in 1860 consisted of 7,500 French and 12,600 British. In the crucial battle of Palikao, 800 Frenchmen routed a 40,000-strong army. [H.M.] For a postcolonial retelling of this history, see J. C. Sharman, *Empires of the Weak: The real Story of European Expansion and the Creation of the New World Order*. (Princeton: Princeton University Press, 2019). Sharman shows that racist histories, like Proudhon's, are a myth. European rule was short lived, secured through alliance with and acquiescence to superior Asian and African empires, and had little if anything to do with European military technology. [A.P.]

son can there be between the Anglo-Saxon and the Redskin who would rather death than civilization, or the negro imported from the Sudan? The New World races retreat before the advance of the Whites; the massacres by the Spanish have been less murderous of them than contact with civilized folk. Finally, have we forgotten that, since the feudal system was done away with, freedom in this industrialist society of ours has meant to the weak-bodied, weak-minded individual, whose family connections have not been able to guarantee an income, something worse than slavery: proletarianism? This is dictated by force, insofar as it is still the overriding law in society; and I say that the right that rules over us to this day, is not the right of labour, which has yet to secure recognition, nor the right of intelligence, that source of so many disappointments, it is still, whatever we say, the unadulterated right of force.

To be sure, I need to be careful here not to refute my own argument and combat the very thing that I have set myself the aim of rehabilitating, when I stand up on behalf of the Blacks against the hypocritical notion which, under the pretext of emancipating them, tends to do nothing less than to cast them back into the pure domain of force and turn them into a proletarian sludge a hundred times more hideous than that of our capital cities. It is, rather, because I want to restore the honour of the long-misconstrued right of force that I speak out against the unintelligent, odious application that would be made of it in respect of slavery. What! The working man of the English race, the strong race *par excellence*, is dying of hunger on the streets of London, so what fate awaits the black man on the streets of Washington and Baltimore?

The abolition of slavery is a matter that falls under the remit of the rights of peoples, or rather, the right of races, since here we need to draw the distinction signalled by those two terms; essentially it boils down to the right of force, from which derive, as we have seen, all international relations, all State formation, incorporations, centralizations and federations.

But in this case, is the right of force, strictly enforceable where States alone are concerned, no longer to be followed, and why if so? Because it has a tendency towards the extermination of individuals and, as was explained in our definition of the rights of peoples, whereas the sacrifice of a State may be required for the sake of the right of force and in the interest of civilization, the human person remains sacred and, as a superior race, all that we can do with regard to the inferior one, is to raise them up to our level and try to improve them, strengthen them, instruct them and ennoble them.

Who are the real enemies of the blacks? Those who, knowingly or not, it does not matter, are contemplating making them perish in the desolation of the proletariat. Who, on the contrary, are the real negrophiles? Those who, whilst holding them in slavery, and, to be sure, exploiting them, guarantee them subsistence, improving them imperceptibly through labour and increase their numbers through marriage.[120]

What needs doing, therefore, is not a pure-and-simple emancipation of the slave; that would be tantamount to displaying him at the Gemonian Stairs.[121] Rather the state must intervene adroitly and impose a serious responsibility upon the master, to make him an educator, a tutor, a *patron* for the slave, not the consumer of the slave, the property which the right of force made him.

Every race is called to labour. If there were one which could not or would not work, that very fact alone would leave it doomed and it would soon disappear. Sooner or later, Europeans will settle in the heart of the Sudan just as they have settled in the heart of the two Americas; then there will be a sore need for the blacks to labour. They must work now; it is our right to force them to do so. In this respect, I confess, I would prefer it if, rather than the slave trade being abolished, it were placed under the supervision of governments.

Every race had a duty to better itself, improve itself morally and educate itself. So, let the law that protects the weak and the strong alike, watch over the inferior race employed in agriculture and industry, as it does over its own proletarians. Therein lies the real solution to the issue of slavery...

Those few examples will, I hope, suffice to convey to the reader what I mean by the rights of peoples and the application of the right of force to international relations.

Let me now add, at the end of this chapter, to the broad questions set out above, questions that make up the overall object and corpus of the rights of peoples, all of them of current relevance.

According to the duly re-established law of people and demonstrated by the evidence of history, what are France's natural boundaries?

Quid the union of Ireland and England?

Quid the issue of the separation of Holland and Belgium, the unification of the Flemish and Walloons, the relations between France and the Low Countries?

Quid the re-establishment of Poland?

Quid Hungary's opposition to the Viennese court's centralization plans?

---

120. Since the rift between the American North and the South over slavery, there have been unrelenting incitements to revolt and to murder the masters coming from the Northern states and from England herself. The British minister backs these: certain French liberals repeat them. Such provocations run counter to the rights of people. It is not love of the negro that prompts them: they are, rather, the effect of a conspiracy which, not daring to resort, as the sixteen century Spaniards did, to massacres, is out to exterminate inferior races through dispossession, disease and misery. [P-J.P.]

121. Many of those executed in Rome in the first century would be tossed down the Gemonian Stairs in shame, left to be scavenged by dogs. [A.P.]

Quid Germanic federalism?

Quid Italian unity?

Quid Pan-Slavism and Scandinavianism?

Quid the partitioning of the Turkish empire?

Quid the restoration of the Greek empire?

Quid stability in Europe and the re-drawing of the political map of Europe?

Quid a Holy Alliance of States, represented by a congress at which all international issues would be decided?

Quid so-called wars of principle?

Quid extradition?

Quid the 1815 treaties as compared with the 1648 ones? Have these treaties been, as some argue, torn up or do they still apply?[122]

---

122. In a work on the rights of peoples, printed in Turin in 1859, under the title *D'un nuovo diritto europeo*, a work published on behalf of the Italian cause and reviewed in the French press, the author, Monsieur MAMIANI, one of king Victor Emannuel II's ministers, summarizes into a short series of propositions what he terms ancient public law (the right of people) and modern public law. By ancient public law Monsieur Mamiani means those maxims professed, according to him, or understood at the Congress of Vienna, maxims naturally unfavourable towards the freedom of peoples; by new public law, he means diametrically opposed maxims such as those suggested by patriotism or, rather, Italian Jacobinism. This simple observation alerts the reader to the fact that he need not expect no more truth from the one side than from the other, given that, if the absolutist powers have never failed to vilify the Revolution, the self-styled liberals have had even less trouble denouncing the Congress of Vienna. I thought this quotation useful, in light of the positive data just supplied to us by the analysis. It may serve to convey some idea of the average state of thinking in Italy.

I. *Ancient public law*, according to M. MAMIANI

"1. The power of the monarchs is absolute. The people has no rights higher, nor even equivalent to theirs; in no circumstances may it dethrone them and transfer the crown from one head to another.

"2. The entirety of the State is embodied in the monarch. To courts and congresses, he despatches ambassadors which represent him alone. Everything he deals in, everything he concludes, in person or through his ministers, is concluded on behalf of the State, whether his subjects like it or not.

"3. Every prince is legitimately entitled to appeal to and deploy the assistance of foreign arms against his own subjects.

"4. Any freedom the people might enjoy is an act of generosity on the part of the prince, which revolt can always cause to be revoked and annulled.

"5. Provinces are traded and partitioned between kings, either through the right of war and conquest, or by means of agreements and pacts reached between them, with no requirement that the inhabitants be consulted about nor supportive of the partitioning.

"6. The principle of spontaneity or nationality being behind the formation or alteration of States is a hollow one.

"7. Several crowns may be worn on a single head: a range of different nations can depend on one another, in accordance with a range of modes of subordination and subjection.

"8. The legality of a treaty must prevail over the citation even of a principle of right that might contradict it.

"9. European affairs are governed by a pentarchy. One after another, the minor powers abide by this arrangement: and it matters little if they do not.

"10. People without official representation in the courts are in no position to seek redress against their oppressors by means of diplomacy; instead, diplomacy should deem them trouble-makers and rebels.

"11. Protestant princes govern the reformed Churches as they see fit. Catholic princes reach concordats with Rome, so fashioned as to subject Church to State, insofar as possible, unless they no longer agree with Rome, the better to hamper and repress the freedom of their peoples".

II. *New public law*, according to the same writer.

"1. The absolute sovereignty is the sovereignty of justice. It is vested neither in princes nor in peoples. Only the most learned and virtuous of men have the right to exercise it in some measure.

"2. If it is to be legitimate, government requires the consent of the governed and should abide by the purpose of societies, which is progress. Any government that fails to live up to one or other of these conditions becomes illegitimate and, from that point, ought to be changed.

"3. The State is not embodied by the person of the monarch nor of any man; and those representing the State at courts or congresses, represent the nation itself, the interests, ideas and sentiments of the people.

"4. The freedom or domestic autonomy of a people has no boundary other than that which it discovers in reason and the principle of non-intervention is absolute.

"5. Civil relations are formed and broaden, or else shrink, depending upon the dictates of spontaneity and nationality.

"6. Never-ending conquests have no basis in righteousness; but many ancient conquests have attained legitimacy through the unification of vanquished and victors into a single homeland. Any alteration to or cession of a territory requires the assent of those who live there.

"7. A single head may not wear several crowns; one people cannot be dependent upon another; such dependency, no matter how fashioned and regardless of its extent, is always illegitimate.

"8. Faith in treaties is whole-hearted and irrevocable, as long as they are not at odds with the eternal principles of justice.

"9. General treaties are subscribed to by all States that embrace and abide by them; special, wholly righteous treaties by all interested States. The votes of each of them are free, equal and absolute.

"10. Unrecognized peoples are likewise possessed of an unchallengeable right to have their just demands heard.

"11. In terms of their authority and charges, Church and State are separate, but they are united in terms of a shared sentiment and enthusiasm. Concordats must one day outlive their usefulness. Ecclesiastical rights cannot impinge upon private rights".

I need scarcely say that the understanding is that these articles, some of which have deliberately made themselves odious and others refreshed by the commonplaces of the *Social Contract*, are especially targeted at Austria and the Pope. We have here a sample of Italian genius, with its consummate gift for disguising ideas and killing through slander and ridicule. Besides, I should have been wasting my time had I asked Monsieur Mamiani under which right, the *ancient* or the *new* dispensation, the government of which he was a member placed the crowns of Piedmont, Lombardy, Tuscany and Naples upon the head of Victor-Emannuel;

---

by what right under the *ancient* or *new* dispensations that very same government transferred Savoy and Nice to the emperor of the French; by what right under the *ancient* or *new* dispensations, it countered Garibaldi's challenges to that cession with reasons of State. I might even press Monsieur Mamiani for a rather clearer explanation of the wrong-headed propositions he so slickly misuses: That *the absolute sovereignty is the sovereignty of justice. It is vested neither in princes nor in peoples. Only the most learned and virtuous of men have the right to exercise it in some measure*; that *civil relations are struck up and broaden, or else shrink, depending upon the dictates of nationality*; that *treaties can always be appealed to the eternal principles of justice*, etc. I shall bypass these petty thoughts: we are too used to Jacobinic declamations, reticence and recantations for anything of this sort to surprise us.

What I do have to highlight in Monsieur Mamiani's side-by-side summation is that the right of war and thus history in its entirety are wholly misconstrued there: that, as spelled out by him, the rights of peoples, no longer reliant upon respect for and the rights of force and being built upon nothing real, boils down to sheer whimsy; finally, that, thanks to that doctrinal vacuum, he fails to see that he is putting all the powers in Europe on trial, by relating their formation to a hollow cause, and that he is compromising his own argument.

Italy, which in the Middle Ages led the European choir, has lost all sense of movement; she is hanging from Robespierre's tail. She does not suspect that, should Victor-Emmanuel have grounds for the annexations in which he has been indulging one after another, it is only and can only be by virtue of the old European right that Monsieur Mamiani denounces, meaning under the eternal laws of war, the principles of constitutional government, the era of which was ushered in by the treaties of Vienna, and of stability in Europe, which it has become so fashionable to hold up to ridicule. [P-J.P.]

CHAPTER XI

More on the Same Subject:
3. Political Right, Civil Right, Economic Right.
The Range of Rights

Let us collect ourselves for a few moments.

RIGHT, broadly speaking, is the dignity of man acknowledged in all his faculties, attributes and prerogatives. There are, therefore, as many special rights as man has different claims to stake, because of the diversity of his faculties and the exercise thereof. As a result, the family tree of rights will shadow that of men's faculties and their manifestations.

The *right of force* is the bluntest and most elementary of them all; it is the tribute rendered to man by reason of his force. Like every other right, it is contingent upon reciprocity. Just as the acknowledgment of greater force in no way implies the negation of the inferior, the entitlement enjoyed by the former does not demolish that of the latter. Whilst the earth may be attracted by the sun, the sun in turn is drawn to the earth and the other planets; by virtue of this dual attraction, the centre of the vortex lies not at the core of the sun, but at a remove proportional with the reciprocal power of attraction of sun and planets.

So, no matter what the fabulist may have to say, the right of the stronger is a positive right and its rationale a genuine rationale; in all of this, error comes either from overstatement of the right of force or from wrong-headedness in its enforcement. *The lion's share*, per se, is legitimate. The moral in [La Fontaine's] fable of the *Lion* and his three associates, the *Cow*, the *Nanny-Goat* and the *Doe*, and what amounts to the mischief-making of the first, is not that he stakes a claim to a larger share on the basis of his strength and courage, but that he resorts to a prosecutor's trick to confound his lion-ness with his strength and then his courage, as if these were three identical terms, each entitling him to a share of the spoils and employs his claws to threaten any associate who might venture to claim more than the others, thereby claiming fully four times the due of a single partner.

The *right of war* follows immediately upon the right of force. It aims to regulate fighting and determine its effects whenever, might having been denied or its rights misconstrued, it becomes necessary to proceed with conflict in order to settle the dispute. Which is why we have stated that war is a form of proceedings which, of itself, conjures up no rights, not even the right of force, but merely registers it, indicates it and sanctions it by means of victory and delivers its conclusions by deploying the ultimate argument of force to bring the antagonism to an end.

It is equally the case, however, that antagonism is the law of social life and, we might even venture, of universal life, so much so that it could be argued that bloody war offends man's social instinct. No matter how belligerent a nation may be, its first act, in the event of difficulty, is at all times to avoid war, if it can. Hence the notion of the *rights of peoples*.

The rights of peoples draws its principle from this consideration that, between one State and another, and in certain circumstances, force constituting a positive right, it is possible, in the event of a quarrel between two States, to determine *a priori*, through the weighing up of forces, which of the two sides ought to have preponderance; and, consequently, to forestall the decision of war by means of some sort of amicable settlement, or at the very least, prescribe the effects of victory and make the peace treaty more equitable.

If the quarrel is of such a nature and seriousness that a resolution requires the sacrifice of one of the warring sovereignties, the rights of peoples teaches us, and it is this that makes it one of the most settled categories of the science, that such sacrifice can be insisted upon by whichever of the two powers reckons it is the stronger and effected by force of arms. Anything in international relations that can be boiled down to a life-or-death issue for the State to decide through force, falls under the remit of the rights of peoples.

We come now to *public right* or *political right*.

The purpose of political right is to thwart any sort of aggression by the individual upon the community or against other individuals, by defining as far as possible the rights and obligations of the citizens towards one another and towards the State, and placing them all under the protection and authority of a public force, to wit, the government.

But between international law and political right there is this difference, that the former essentially implies the eventuality of States' absorbing each other and, consequently, in the event of conflict, the legitimacy of their being sacrificed, whereas under political right neither State sovereignty nor civic liberty is a perishable; far from it, the master-stroke of the constitution is that it ensures that they consistently grow side by side and through one another. In international law, if a balance of power cannot be struck amiably, there will be suppression through warfare of one or of several of the antagonistic States; in political law, by contrast, order is imperiously required without the price being the sacrifice of a single freedom or a single life: here, proscription[123] which is, so to speak, the very soul of the rights of peoples, turns out to be a contradiction.

Thus, the notion of the right of force is always present in the mind of the eternal law-giver. It follows him through all his creations, be it the founding of a State, or the coordination of independent States; and, except where the applications vary, it is always to be found in every one of the metamorphoses of the law.

But we need to delve deeper into the spirit of constitutions and demonstrate this ubiquity of the right of force in a factual manner. To be sure, not everything in public law is traceable to force; but everything assumes it, not just as a modus operandi and organ of authority, *instrumentum regni*, but also as the principle and source of right, which is very different.

In Chapter VII above, we saw patriarchy or patrician status take shape spontaneously through the just acknowledgment of the right of force. One consequence of that principle was the formation of the aristocracy or of castes. The notion that force spawns force, that the mighty are born mighty, bringing forth the institution of the hereditary nobility, is, as I have just been saying, right asserting itself within and in the name of the most striking quality, force. Therefore, at bottom, it is – unless a new factor, kinship, is introduced – always force that determines what is just.

But the nobility misuses its privileges; on the one hand, it is corrupted by power and wealth, and on the other, it exploits the plebs far beyond what is warranted by the right of force. Soon, even the superiority of force, which had been at the root of the aristocracy, switches over to the people's side, and one finds the nobles, bereft of any understanding of their privilege, staking a claim to the benefits of force when in actuality they already possess none; talking about their seigneurial entitlements when they no longer have any inkling of lordship, neither as individuals nor as a caste.

Whereupon along comes revolution, a revolution in force's name.

Sieyès's pamphlet *What is the Third Estate?* means nothing else. Likewise, every despotism boils down to aristocracy by virtue of the force and the right at its command, just the same as every aristocracy results in bourgeoisie and commoners. This is inevitable, and just.

Here we have a fresh amendment to the right of force. Through the nobility as an institution, the right of force had been rolled into kinship rights and had become a birth-right; through the advent of democracy, it turns into the right of numbers or of the majority. Collective force being the starting-point and basis of the *social contract*.

---

123. *Proscription*: A sentence of death or outlawry. [H.T.]

By virtue of that contract which, by the way is a sheer, unspoken fiction, every citizen is called upon to make a voluntary surrender of some of his force, liberty and property, in order to create a public force capable of overcoming all private resistance and guaranteeing justice and protection for all.[124]

Now, this public force, in whom is it to be vested? A magistrate, an elected person representative of the collective, or the bulk of the collective, which is to say, yet again, force. No matter how you look at it, universal suffrage is just a peaceful acknowledgment of force and the system of representation, with its majority rule, a reasoned application of the rights of the stronger. The Polish nobility was never able to fathom this transformation of the right of force, acceptable to every people. Every time it came to electing the prince, the Diet would vote for two candidates; the minority would use its *veto*, there would be a fight and the most numerous faction obliged to assert the validity of the election by means of a defeat inflicted upon the dissidents.

No doubt about it, within majority rule there is something more than mere

---

124. This way of interpreting the social contract is a far cry from Rousseau's.

According to the Genevan philosopher, the people's sovereignty derives from the communion of freely expressed individuals' wishes; from whence it follows that the rights of man, the root of the rights of the nation, is rooted in man's will.

But it should be obvious that a gathering of 100,000 electors cannot, juridically speaking, invalidate the wishes of a single person, nor, as a result, lay the groundwork for a proper sovereignty, in spite of his protests. My right, the expression of my will, is beyond destruction and alienation; and if I refuse, there is actually nothing in the chorus from my 100,000 gainsayers to outweigh my refusal. Thus, a single person, by countering the will of the majority with his veto, could prevent the passage of a law, stymie the actions of the government and make the sovereign impossible. The example of the Poles, as cited below, demonstrates this. The nonsensicality of the outcome proves the falseness of Rousseau's purely metaphysical theory.

I am well aware that, in order to have done with it, it will be claimed that the majority's rights are greater than that of the minority, which simply means that there is to be an appeal to force. But, unless force commands some sort of entitlement of its own, one will merely have used violence; that will be a usurpation and not an act of justice. Therefore, it is the right of force and the respectability inherent within force, as a human faculty, that represents the first seat of righteousness, the first echelon of the legal and political order.

The objection will be raised that the possessor of force, the people, may very well not be right at the same time: in which case do we still have to argue that it is sovereign?

To which my answer is, invoking the very same principle, that force only has rights insofar as it is humane; that a force bereft of intelligence is nothing more than brutishness, a tool in the hands of an intelligent power that will know how to use it and with which the latter will curb and enslave the people. This we have seen down through the ages and it is what happened in 1848 when the people, summoned to electoral meetings, appointed reactionary assemblies and it was manifest more palpably still following the coup d'état. Force, let me say again, only has rights if it is humane, which is to say, intelligent, moral and free. The moment it is reduced to a brutish condition, it falls to thought to seize control of it and deploy it to its advantage. [P-J.P.]

strength of numbers. There is this principle of vulgar prudence which, in questionable matters, takes the view that the opinion of the greater number is more likely to be the conscience of the nation than the view of a handful or the view of a sect. But the majority view, we have to concede, would be due very little respect if it also spoke for the majority of interests. Now, interests are forces and, supposing that the majority view and the minority view are of equal worth, the former would still have going for it the fact that, where there is doubt, the weightiest interest is to be given preference.[125]

So, in a republic or representative monarchy, what can trigger insurrection? Certainly not the argument, in itself very persuasive, that in matters of right or science, numbers are meaningless and that twenty-five may as likely be right as five hundred. I do not think that insurrection has ever relied on any such grievance. As far as I know, no government with the multitude on its side has ever been criticized in the people's name, because it has the right derived from that multitude, the right of force on its side. Insurrection comes when the government, like Charles X's, having lost its majority, seeks to act in defiance of the majority and to overrule force; or, the majority, having trampled over the law, gives the lie to the constitution and demands more, therefore, than it is granted by the right of force.

One observation that needs making here relates to the choosing of the prince, and above all to the additional fact that he rarely fails to take up his power, in spite of resistance from the friends of liberty. Down through the ages, it has always been the dream of the sages to put a sage in charge of things, and to so well regulate his powers that, though sufficiently armed to uphold order, he would not be in any position to ride roughshod over the rights and liberties of the citizenry. And we know how rarely this hope has been fulfilled. If authority is elective and the election is in the hands of the multitude, it is going to be a military man, a general with a record of feats of arms, who will most often top the poll. Let us imagine the prince, waging war through his generals, emerging victorious from a few campaigns, so that he is credited with that victory as if he

---

125. This discussion of the relationship between forces and the institutional and constitutional means of articulating the democratic voice, is self-evidently underdeveloped by modern standards. The innovative checks and balances, universal suffrage, modes of proportional representation, majoritarianism or consensus, presidencies or parliamentary systems, were all designed to deal with the clash of forces and the innumerable intersecting oppressions we experience. They evolved out of the failure of the constitutional and imperial monarchies of his time. Proudhon therefore anticipates many of the problems the study of modern comparative politics aims to resolve. What is striking, however, is that Proudhon never makes a categorical or conceptual distinction between "domestic" and "international" relations. Both are governed by force and manifest through the varying constitutional forms of collective agency. [A.P.]

had achieved it personally. Then, in that instance as well as the previous one, the victorious leader never fails to stake his claim to the widest powers and the highest prerogatives, which it would not occur to anyone to dispute with him, and any querying of which would be in vain.

Such is the prestige of force that, wheresoever it may be present, the common man is inclined to concede that authority and, consequently, right obtain.

Now we can grasp how war, which wields such huge sway over thinking, wields a no less mighty sway over public liberties and the constitution of the State. A nation at war is a nation fallen back upon itself, formed up in battalions and now exclusively obedient to a military commander and leading an exclusively centralized, governmental existence. The man directing the war is such a highly placed being that everyone is, against their will, obedient to him; he becomes the judge of others, the representative of right and force alike, and simultaneously law-giver, judge and general. If he should thrash the enemy, everybody adores him; the power he was afforded for the purposes of the fight stay with him; lo and behold, he is master.

What a range of precautions were taken in Rome to prevent the rise of the dictator, sovereign for fifteen days, a year at most! And despite Marius, Sulla managed to achieve mastery; Caesar followed suit; there were enough of them to fill six hundred years. In our own day, hereditary, constitutional monarchy has been our way out of military despotism; but only on the further condition that the exercise of political rights is set aside for the bourgeoisie. The moment the plebs steps into the arena, it equips itself with a leader of its own devising, which is to say in accordance with its force. After a republican interregnum, Cromwell took over from Charles I through the good offices of puritan democracy; and Bonaparte from Louis XIV thanks to the Jacobin plebs.

Under the Roman emperors, heredity, no matter how favourably disposed the soldiery and the people were to it, never managed to embed itself. The reason for this is that in Rome it was not his condition as heir that secured recognition for the emperor; it was, instead the imperial title, deserved or already secured, which consecrated his succession. Titus and Marcus Aurelius slickly succeeded, in one case, his father Vespasian, and in the other, his father-in-law Antoninus the Pious. But Titus and Marcus Aurelius, prior to their achieving the imperium, had distinguished themselves by services rendered; succession was just a further gilding of their military credentials. Every victorious general among the Romans was de facto and de jure *imperator*; as Augustus had only his birth on his side, it was unusual that he did not sooner or later succumb to a more authentic *imperator*. Which is what happened to Caligula, Nero, Commodus, Heliogabalus, Alexander Severus, the younger Gordius and others.

In actual fact, a country has only two ways of protecting public freedoms from the trespasses of force and warding off despotism: by organizing, as England did, a hereditary monarchy operating through ministers answerable to a Parliament and reserving electoral privilege for the bourgeoisie; or, if the country's constitution is founded upon universal suffrage, by conferring the enjoyment of political rights and economic rights, meaning equality of education and fortunes, upon the multitude.

Were I allowed to use past analogies to conjecture about the future, I dare say that Napoleon III, having been made emperor, not on the basis of military success but on the basis of heredity, and with the French nation repudiating praetorianism,[126] it strikes me as, on both these grounds, inevitable that the current empire will revert to being a parliamentary monarchy. But then again, since the very same head of State traces his entitlement back to universal suffrage and his government having thus far had no chief purpose other than the fending off of economic revolution, the restoration of a parliamentary monarchy seems equally unfeasible, for those same two reasons; and it is this that makes the situation so novel. *Fata viam invenient.*[127]

Just as the political constitution is, in the final analysis, built upon force, so it is also sanctioned by force; on which basis, public force is conflated with international law. In fact, any nation incapable of organizing itself politically, and in which power is unstable, is a nation doomed to be consumed by its neighbours. Like a nation that could not or would not wage war, or which might be too weak to defend itself, it is not entitled to occupy a space on the map of States; it is irksome and must be brought under a suzerain. Neither religion, language nor race count for anything here; the preponderance of interests overrules everything else and lays down the law. Whereupon the right of force, the right of war, the rights of peoples and political rights become synonymous: Where force is absent, a government cannot stand, much less than where nationality is absent. A frightful right, you may say, a regicidal right in which one would be reluctant to discern any form of justice. Well, no; away with pointless sensibilities. Bear in mind that the demise of a State does not entail that of its citizens and that there is nothing worse for the circumstances of the latter than a decrepit State ripped asunder by factionalism. When the mother country is

---

126. Praetorianism: A state in which the military wields over-arching influence. Derived from the power of the Praetorian Guard who, during the Roman Empire, installed and removed a number of emperors. After the war in Italy and under the decree of November 1860, Napoleon III authorized the printing at length of parliament's proceedings; after the war in Mexico, the Chamber was afforded the right to question ministers about domestic and foreign policy; in 1869, an English-style parliamentary regime known as the Liberal Empire was introduced, with ministers answerable to the Emperor alone. All these were phases in the organization of the opposition. [H.M./R.B.H.]

127. "Fates will find the way". Virgil *Aeneid*, Book III, §395, 398–99. [A.P.]

resistant to freedom, when public sovereignty is at loggerheads with the sovereignty of the citizen, nationality turns into disgrace and regeneration by an outside force, a necessity.

Just a few words about civil law and economic rights.

Civil law is made up of the range of the rights of man and the citizen; family rights, property rights, rights of succession, work, exchange, housing, etc. all of which are placed under the care of the public authorities and subordinated to the public interest, and their sanction resides in the right of force.

Even though it tends increasingly to justify itself in terms of work and the fair relationship between real estate income, interest on capital and wages, property is no less obviously tied into the right of force, based, originally as it is upon the right of first occupancy or of conquest and subject to the condition that it is incumbent upon the property-owner to exploit it as a good paterfamilias, in the best interests of his family and of the State. As Napoleon I put it, if an owner could not work his land or have it worked, if he allowed it to lie fallow and derelict, I would assert my authority and confiscate it from him and hand it over to the more capable and deserving. Whoever cannot use, the conqueror reckoned, is not worthy of the possession; in other words, no force, no right. When it comes to landed property, that is the principle. So, it is only by a subsequent convention, a sort of a legal fiction supported by the State, that the property-owner is able to have possessory title and work it through the intermediary of a farmer. The nature of entitlement, like that of things, does not countenance such abstract ownership; society is marshalled against it; and on a daily basis we see the land slip from the hands of the rentier into those of the farmer.

And so, the right of force is transformed by the mutuality of guarantees between citizen and citizen, family and family, association and association, company and company. It has somehow to be stripped down only to be built up again. We are aware of it only now and again, in an indirect way, in the rental agreement, the limited company, etc., where the superiority of force, labour, capital or industry leads to the superiority of wages. As if force, being an animalistic thing, brought shame on intelligent, free humanity, the law-giver disguises it as best he can. You might say that, having achieved such heights, he reckons the right of force as unworthy of a well-reared fellow as wrestling and fisticuffs. This is the *fleur de lis* denying the bulb from which it sprouts. What seems improper in the citizen is glorious in the prince. The right of force is the preserve of sovereignty, the emblem of justice. In which case, far be it from anyone to lay claim to and insist upon it: *Woe betide any who might lay a hand on it!*[128]

128. This warning had been uttered by the Lombard kings in the act of donning the iron crown. Napoleon I adopted this tradition. [H.M.]

Under the feudal regime, the right of force had been only partly curtailed, some of it having remained vested in the baron who, by virtue of the right of force, also enjoyed the right of war and the right to administer justice. The Revolution completed the task begun by the kings by imposing eternal silence upon feudal squabbles by reducing the great feudal lords to the same level as their serfs when it came to the right of force.

Furthermore, even in the civil order, the right of force is a long way from having the final say. It alone can end the debate between the so-called bourgeois class and the working or wage-earning class, that has been raging over the past thirty years. Whether by means of battle or some consensual constitution, it does not matter much; but the rule of labour, credit and commerce is undergoing change; wages and value, the freest things in the world, are coming around to being policed [*se policier*]. To be sure, there will be no denying that brawn is better and worthier to justice than the metal which mediates exchange; labour being more honourable than trading, lending and investment; surviving on hard work and frugality, the labouring masses are more moral than the parasitism that exploits them. Force, and with it, Right, are on the side of brawn, labour and the masses; but neither brawn, nor labour nor the masses are receiving their due.

It is when the citizenry, taking stock of their interests as toilers and comparing them alongside their interests as privileged persons, entrepreneurs and capitalists, come to a recognition of the superiority of the former over the latter; once the petty bourgeois, the small property-owner, the small industrialist, as well as the peasant, the shopkeeper and the working man come to the conclusion that they have more to gain from toil than from rent and speculation; it is at that point that the people, the industrial democracy, will break, and in the name of the right of force, being a synonym for the right of labour, a synonym for the right of the intelligence, the suzerainty of money, will weigh up rent and taxation, rein in property to its just limit, change the relationship between labour and capital, and enshrine economic right as the capstone of the whole edifice. And that will be justice, force will yet again have enforced right.

If now, from the vantage-point of force, so new to jurisprudence, we look upon the development of right in its main categories, we will discern a series or range of rights that would have gladdened Fourier's heart:

1. The right of force;
2. The right of war;
3. The rights of peoples;
4. Political right;
5. Civil or domestic right;

6.   Economic rights: this breaks down into two branches, just like its
     component factors, labour and exchange.
7.   Philosophical rights, or the freedom of thought;
8.   The RIGHT OF FREEDOM, whereby humanity, moulded by war,
     by politics, by its institutions, by labour and commerce, by the sciences
     and the arts, is no longer governed by anything other than sheer free-
     dom, obedient to the logic of reason alone.

Within this spectrum of rights, force sings bass and freedom an octave
higher. The keynote varies depending on the character of the race and the degree of civilization: family or patriarchal right among the nomads; property
right, or land-based patricians, among the ancient Romans; the right of labour
in the industrious medieval cities in Italy and Flanders; mercantile right in Tyre,
Carthage, Athens, Corinth, Marseilles and in modern England.

The trend is towards undiluted freedom becoming synonymous with the
pure Right; that is civilization's ideal, the highest expression of Force.

Conclusion

In our first Book we have stated:

Warfare is the driver of society. Its thinking, its influence are omnipresent. It is the driving force that shapes all our powers, religion, justice, philosophy, the liberal arts and the useful arts. Warfare has made society what it is, so much so that, were warfare, the thought of warfare and its handiwork discounted, we could not conceive of what civilization might look like, what the human race might be.

Those propositions, spelled out at length, albeit in a few short pages have, in Book Two, *taken on* a very different yet serious meaning. By discovering that there is a moral content to warfare; that, in its very idea, themes and in its purpose, there is, implicit within it, an idea of right, it therefore boils down to an out-and-out bench warrant. We can now see that this is the view of every people, the belief at the heart of hearts of the human race. We have therefore come to realize that we held the key to this mysterious and massive phenomenon, and the more that formidable apparition had previously seemed to represent a degradation of our species, the more suddenly sensible we became of its having buoyed us up.

All our effort has therefore been poured into the precise determination of this moral factor. To that end, we have had to overcome the universal reproach from the authors, in whose eyes war is purely and simply an evil, not to say Evil itself, and the right of force the negation of all righteousness and justice. We have found that, with regard to the supposition, inherent in the very idea of warfare, that there is a reality to right and legitimacy in the jurisdiction of force, all the authors, jurists and publicists, philosophers and poets radically and unanimously part company from the belief held among the nations. Those who have recourse to force by way of a necessary sanction of right, only do so with a heavy heart, by invoking a principle alien to right, the principle of utility. Alternatively, on the understanding that there is no sanction for justice in terms of principle, other than God, and humanity having fallen, the sanction of force is the badge of our mischief-making and the rod that punishes us. The right of force, they all say, is not a right; it is the very negation of right. From which it follows, if these authors have things right, that war in turn has no juridical powers, on which they have been quick to agree. Furthermore, albeit that they have overlooked this, the rights of peoples is meaningless cant, political right a fiction, civil law and economic right bereft of guarantees or principles.

Such a clear-cut contrast between universal sentiment and scholarly authority, and the disastrous consequences that the jurists' theory would entail in terms both of certainty of principles as well as the running of societies, made it imperative that we embark again upon a thoroughgoing examination of the issue.

Now, the outcome of that examination is contrary to what the scholars argue, but in accordance with the belief of the nations. It is in accordance with the hopes raised within us by this grandiose phenomenology of war: it is as certain that justice is a real faculty and positive notion of man's, as it is true that there is an actual, positive right of force. That said right is subject to the same conditions of reciprocation as the rest; like every other right, it has its speciality, and therefore its boundaries, its competency and its incompetency; that the most ordinary assertion of it, since the earliest societies were formed, has taken place between States, whether apropos of their formation or aggrandizement, or indeed, their divisions and their stability. Finally, it has been shown that war is the modus operandi of the right of force, given that its sole purpose, in specific instances, is to pursue claimed prerogatives by means of force by making such force manifest through battle. Like property rights and labour rights, like the right of intelligence and the right of love, the right of force is one of the rights of man and of the citizen, the premier right of all in terms of order of manifestation. The only thing is that, as a result of the impact of the social contract, the citizen surrenders the right of force into the care of the prince who, alone, is invested with the right of war and the right of justice, for the benefit of all.

The right of force and therefore that of war, once accepted as authentic rights, re-established within legislation and within science, pose not the slightest problem to the deduction of other rights. The rights of peoples is designed to legalize warfare, so to speak; to anticipate and regularize its effects and, if need be, to pre-empt them by laying down, in advance, the relations between their powers and prerogatives. Political right grows out of the substitution of public force, acting on everybody's behalf, for the scattered force of individuals. Civil law and economic rights can be traced back to people being equal before the law, and universal mutual acknowledgment of all the rights that may result from their respective attributes and from the unfettered exercise of their faculties, insofar as these attributes and faculties serve the deployment of their force.

So, from here on, everything is coordinated to perfection; everything follows, stands, is connected and knits together. We have a principle, a *modus operandi*, a perspective, a purpose, a method. No more split within man or within society; force and right, mind and matter, war and peace all blended into one homogeneous, indissoluble thought.

We now know what makes nations enthusiastic about battle. We can tell by what mystery religion and warfare are two expressions, one in the real world and one in the ideal world, of the same nature and the same law; why the notion of warfare permeates all poetry and all love, just as it does all politics and all justice; how it comes to pass that in every people the manly ideal is a composite of magistrate, priest and warrior; and, finally, how it comes to pass that when societies are corrupted by protracted delights, war can put them back on course. The fact is that, as we foretold right at the start of Book One, there is a moral aspect to warfare; because war delivers justice and that justice is by any account of the sublimest, most incorruptible, and most solemn sort.

It now remains to be seen in what way war, which to us appears so normal, so glorious, so fruitful, lives up to its mandate; how it conducts itself with regard to its requisitions, its executions and, let us be blunt about it, its proceedings; the extent of its attributions and its remit; the value of its judgments; what assurances of justice it offers nations; the abuses into which it might fall through the immoderate use of force, and what the consequences its prevarications might entail for the world order. Because, as yet, we possess only half of the truth; having unearthed the principle of the sublimity of warfare, it remains for us to discover the reason behind its horrors.

This we propose to explore in the next Book.

BOOK THREE

WAR IN ITS FORMS

Furor impius ... saeva arma.[1]
—Virgil

SUMMARY

Warfare is a form of judicial action between States, designed to amalgamate, separate or strike a balance between them. Such action is *just*; it relies upon a positive entitlement which we have demonstrated in the preceding Book. Furthermore, it is *efficacious*; the whole of history provides proof of that. As a result, the verdicts of war, just in terms of principle and format, efficacious in their action, can be deemed as judicially *sound*; so that in the determinations of force, effectiveness and validity are synonymous. We explore factors that, in certain instances, render victory uncertain, ineffective and therefore the judgment of war null and void; examples.

From these further considerations added to those set out in Book Two, it transpires that the act of war, like the duel, and, much more forcefully than the duel, must be held to certain strict rules and said rules are indicated *a priori* by the definition of warfare and its purpose. On this count, universal acquiescence, the conscience of military men and the arguments of the jurists are pretty much

---

1. Virgil, *Aeneid,* Book I, 282–83: "*Furor impius intus saeva sedens super arma et centum vinctus aënispost tergum nodis fremet horridus ore cruento*". Trans: "within, impious Rage, sitting on savage arms, his hands fast bound behind with a hundred brazen knots, shall roar in the ghastliness of blood-stained lips". [A.P.]

in agreement. But what are those rules? Does the practice abide by them? That is the question we must now discuss.

So, in the present state of affairs, and since the origins of societies, what have the laws governing warfare been? What are its usages and customs? What should they be? Does warfare respond through its acts to that which its principle and purpose would suggest should be expected of it? This is something it is important to scrutinize, painstakingly. We turn to the critique of military operations: the constant contradiction between the theory of the right of force and its application. Sublime and holy in conception, war is ghastly in its handiwork; as much as the theory ennobles man, the practice of it is a stain upon his honour.

CHAPTER 1

On Warfare and Its Validity

In Chapters VII and IX of the preceding Book, we saw how warlike activity develops between two nations. Let us briefly review that argument.

Considered in terms of its constitutional unity, the nation is sovereign and independent. Its autonomy defers to no authority, no court. Between one people and another, terms such as Authority, Sovereignty, Suzerainty, Government, Supreme Council, Diet, Prince, Majesty, Command, Law, etc. are out of place. These are a whole order of ideas and facts that no longer obtains. Just try to slip anything of that sort into some treaty or congress and there will be a hue and cry and, unless the expression is withdrawn, a falling-out.

It is the very essence of a State and of its dignity that it repudiates anything that might, directly or remotely, represent a trespass against its independence: close alliance, amalgamation of interests, the importation of mores, laws, language, ideas and even, in certain instances, of goods; in short, anything that might generate between it and the foreigner the merest semblance of community and fellowship. No doubt, these days nations are too dense and have too many points of intersection, too many necessary dealings, for them to be in a position to make a reality of this ideal of political independence, even though they might want to. But the principle stands, and governments depart from it as little as they can. Neither England, nor Germany, despite their countless connections to France, has adopted her system of weights and measures. Russia, whose vastness and remoteness are protection enough against her being assimilated, clings to the Julian calendar which these days is running twelve days behind the sun.

But, no matter what the heads of State may do to preserve their independence from one another, a point is reached where that independence is in jeopardy. There is no one to blame for this. Swelling populations, their proximity to one another, their points of resemblance, the intercourse between them, neighbourly relations, their bonds of hospitality, marriage, association, the irksomeness of barriers are all factors which, here and there, endanger the diversity, autonomy and nationality of governments. Once the intermingling begins to gradually make itself felt, and the situation becomes ever more urgent, the escape route initially suggests itself to every mind: it is to bring all nations under the same authority and to share and standardize government, dynasty, worship, legislation, in short, bring them all together into a single State.

Now, as we have pointed out, when States are at loggerheads such an amalgamation is a matter of overwhelming seriousness. It implies abdication by the greater part of them, if not a transfiguration of them all. But, for a nation to abdicate means abjuring everything that has hitherto constituted its glory, its life, its happiness and the pride of its citizens; it represents a moral death, a suicide. A nation cannot tell its neighbour, as Ruth told her mother-in-law: Let me stay with you: *your people shall be my people, your God shall be my God.*[2] A nation does not offer itself up as a sacrifice; it cries out against amalgamation; at the very least it demands compensation, privileges, guarantees that are dangerous and often impossible to offer.

Whereupon war becomes obligatory: what does it mean?

Let us attempt for a moment to rise above our parochial instincts, which are, deep down, as lacking in virtue as they are in patriotism. Modern man, lost in immense States, and with no ties to the government other than through taxation, knowing nothing of his homeland than the name or rather the myth, is quick to reason like the ass in the fable: *What does it matter who the master is, as long as I wear a pack-saddle?* A full manger, freedom from beatings, doing the master as little service as possible, pilfering from him should the opportunity arise: for many folk civil rights and civic duties pretty much boil down to that. We have a hundred ways of expressing those fine sentiments: *The true Amphitryon is the Amphitryon where one sits down to dine; He who will be my priest, I will be his parishioner.* Or indeed: *That government is legitimate which adds to our earnings and asks least of us.* I forget who said it in Latin: *Ubi bene, ibi patria.* Wheresoever I fare well, that is my homeland. But I do not recognize the ancient mind there. Such scepticism regarding where the homeland lies is the mark of our age.

Man in the ancient city thought along quite different lines. Naturally, the risking of his assets, the loss of his honour, were a factor in his horror of foreign domination. But spiritual matters had to be acknowledged too: the religion of the gods, the remembrance of the ancestors, the country's institutions, the honour of the race were close to his heart. Such an eclipse of the laws, mores, and everything making up the originality, character and life of a people, the effect of

---

2. *Bible,* The Book of Ruth, 1:16. On the death of her Jewish husband, the pagan Ruth is supposed to have refused to be parted from her mother-in-law Naomi, been converted through love of her, and, following a second marriage, to have become an ancestor of King David. [H.T.]

incorporation, struck ancient man as worse than death. We have gone past that now; together with living in the provinces, we have lost the true sense of the country, nationality, homeland. There is no point casting around for the causes of this. And warfare these days is more governmental than national, which helped in no small way to blind us to its spirituality and lofty morality. With its blood-stained weaponry and its piles of corpses, does war strike us as any less ghastly from any particular point of view? Is it evidence of our progress? Come what may, it is no evidence of our intelligence, much less of our *virtue*.

For early man, therefore, war had this meaning which it retains from government to government:

That, in the inevitable course of events – thanks to a decision of fate – one of the existing States is doomed to perish;

That, by virtue of the right of force, a sentence is pronounced against the weakest one.

That, as a result, because killing is inescapable, the best course for the citizens of that State is to courageously embrace the last desperate hope by taking up arms to affirm the inviolability of their homeland. War is the delivery of the verdict of force; expressed by the myth of Jupiter weighing the fates of Achilles and Hector, the two champions of Greece and Troy, in the balance.

Our moralists call such justice cannibal justice. It seems they would rather that the belligerent powers appoint commissioners charged with compiling statistics about the two countries; that done, we might get on with the constitution of a brand-new State where the interests of each people could be so handled and balanced as to satisfy everyone's self-esteem. These outstanding pacifists overlook just one thing, that religion, homeland, liberty, institutions are not things to bargain over; the very notion of compromise over these things is of itself apostasy, a badge of failure, on which no one wants to take the initiative. Hence the reason for the powerlessness and pointlessness of diplomacy. If it were merely a matter of giving force its due, compromise would be easy, honourable and mandatory. I would venture to say that, reduced to that expression, war would never be waged. But there is something in our moral existence, the honour of the city, the collective personality that goes by the name of homeland, and which is mirrored in every one of us, and in the absence of which we lapse back into a state of nature, and for the sake of which we are called upon to make sacrifices. Now the sacrificing of the homeland by its citizens cannot be countenanced. Fate should have condemned it at the right time! We shall defer to fate's verdict. But it behoves the beneficiary to carry out the will of the gods at his own risk and peril. – *Hand over your arms*, Xerxes told Leonidas. – *Come and take them*, the Spartan retorted. And over the past twenty-four centuries the applause of the human race has drowned Leonidas's words.

Come on, *barristers* – I cannot help here applying to my authors the label that the Republic's soldiers hung upon the representatives of the Nation, – brace yourselves. The spilling of blood is nothing; the attention should be on the cause that has shed it. Can you remember the Roman woman who, while attempting suicide, told her husband, under threat from the tyrant: *Poete, no dolet*. Poetus, this does not hurt.[3]

What matter life where right is at stake? Is not righteousness the whole and all of man and isn't justice by itself no more than life, love, wealth and liberty?

Two litigants, by virtue of the very fact that they bring a suit against each other, commit more than their fortune and their life; they commit their rights, their word, their oath, in short, their honour, since right and dignity or honour are synonymous, and the dishonest litigant is held beneath contempt. Now, if righteousness can be decided through combat, through the testimony of force, courage and inspiration; if it is the case, in short, that the stronger, the braver, the more industrious party, the side more disposed to virtue and sacrifice, must at the same time have and be held to have right on its side, how keen will it be to join battle? In which case, are their weapons not going to be holy and blessed?

This is the very thing that happens in warfare, with this difference: that we are not dealing here with two private individuals but with two peoples; that the crux of the dispute is not some pointless interest, but rather their sovereignty, and that neither party can be assumed to be acting in bad faith. What is the meaning of futile debates before such a court, where some long-winded barrister, aided by some clever attorney, stands before a weary judge to argue with tongue and quill that right is on the side of his client; where there are quibbles over texts; where panache, talent and hard work count for nothing; where the most honest man is bamboozled every day, deceived by the greater scoundrel? Is this not making a mockery of justice? You speak of the spilling of blood. But can you not see that justice, like love and liberty, is found in death; that only those who know how to face death are worthy of living and commanding; that everything else is slavishness, *ad servitutem nati*?...

With force the instrument of justice, devised as a settler of the differences between powers, war is inescapable; all that remains is to regulate its conditions. Which takes us to the very heart of right, or, to put that better, to the procedures of war.

However, before getting to grips with that, one final scruple gives us pause. This judgment of force, so well grounded in theory and which destiny foists upon nations at the cost of disgrace, can we at least be certain that it is not going

---

3. Arria, the wife of Poetus Cecina, who had tried to get Illyria to rise up against the Emperor Claudius, plunged a dagger into her breast, thereby encouraging her husband to take his own life. [H.M.]

to have been a purely pointless exercise? Can we place our trust in it, embrace and affirm it as good, effective, sound and authentic? Dying for a great cause is all well and good; but the sacrifice of so many selfless lives would be monstrous if civilization, if humanity were not to reap the fruits of it. And what does experience tell us, in this regard?

The philosophical study of history shows that human agitations, insofar as they relate to the formation, amalgamation, decline, decomposition and re-composition of States, are responses to an overall trend, the purpose of which is to gradually introduce harmony and liberty across the globe. And the agent or minister of that lofty intent is war.

The verdicts of warfare are consistent with the schemes of providence, they become definitive, and no power can void them. On the other hand, if those verdicts are tainted by fraud, chance, ambush, incompetence or abuse, they cannot stand; they are set aside by historical reason. There is no sound victory outside of the plan drawn up by that loftier reason and the fighting conditions that it prescribes.

Which is why warrior justice, like civil justice and criminal justice, is surrounded by norms that stand as a guarantee for its competency, integrity and validity. In war, it is not enough merely to be the stronger, if that war is waged without grounds; any more than it is enough, supposing that the conflict is legitimate, to have fought the enemy, unless one genuinely is possessed of superior force. Should the right of war be tainted, victory is rendered sterile and nullified; for, just as war has its remit and its norms, and just as it has its prevarications and errors, it also has its sanction, an incorruptible and I might even say godly sanction, in which it has the edge over all courts.

Since earliest antiquity, we have seen huge political groups formed at the expense of smaller groups, without any sign of resistance or heroics placed in the way of their incorporation. Then after a more or less lengthy existence, those groups fell apart, with no force capable of arresting the break-up. What does this two-pronged phenomenon mean? For a start, that in terms of civilization, the State, as the expression of a collective entity and an agency of right, has to occupy a certain area below which it remains inadequate and beyond which it becomes a burden upon the peoples, incapable in both instances of properly fulfilling its mandate. And then, once the conquest is over, the assimilation of the vanquished peoples into the same State should proceed according to certain conditions which, if they are overlooked, swiftly re-endow the incorporated elements with their respective attractions, generating antagonism within the body of the State and leading to disintegration. Victory is not everything; one has to know how to put that victory to use. Post-conquest assimilation is the first duty of the conqueror and I will even say the entitlement of the conquered people.

In the absence of such assimilation, warfare is abusive since it serves no purpose and the verdict delivered by force becomes fraudulent and tyrannical; nature and Providence are deceived: there are grounds for annulment.

At other times, abruptly formed States have been seen to fade away with no less swiftness. What can that mean? That the growth of States, like that of animals and plants, takes time; that if multiple annexations follow one another too hurriedly, they overwhelm the State's powers of assimilation; that, as a result, the victories that pave the way to them are not worthy victories produced by genuinely superior force; which divests war of its efficacy and repeals its determinations.

Why, then, did the Greek republics, so jealous of their independence and so inimical to unity, wage war on one another? In order to endow the State with boundaries that accorded with the rules of political existence, the overall scheme of civilization and with Greece's historic mission. It fell to Greece in the fifteenth century before Christ to assume the leadership of mankind. But what happened? The narrow-mindedness of those tiny republics, the rampant selfishness by which they were prompted, did not allow them to achieve their own amalgamation, and left them incapable of laying the foundations of the universal State, the expression of the universality of right. Greece only ever attained any such semblance of unity in the person of Alexander of Macedonia. But, unified in that form, and even with the Ionian coast included, Greece was not equal to absorption by the Persian empire, much less foisting her laws upon the world. With the conqueror dead, his generals carved up the empire between them; some middling-sized States were re-formed and with their aid, Asia, whilst remaining true to herself, gradually absorbed the Greek spirit. Pending the advent of the Romans, there followed the completion of the war with the Medes, the Peloponnesian wars, the Macedonian conquest and, finally, the wars between Alexander's successors.

The real patricians of the right of war were the Romans. It took them five centuries to combine the Italian peninsula, a far cry from the stunning swiftness of the conquests of Semiramis, Nebuchadnezzar, Cyrus, Cambyses and Alexander. And its outcome was to be that much more fruitful and long-lasting. Italy conquered, a movement of a new type began to surface, in which war would have its part to play too; this was the conversion from Greek, Latin, Gallic, Spanish, Egyptian, Asian polytheism, to a monotheism common to all the civilized races. Religious unity, anticipated by the philosophers, was therefore established by taking political unity as its expression, in accordance with the ancient mind; this was what we term the Roman Empire. But the movement that pushed for the unity of worship only temporarily involved the unity of the State; no sooner did the monotheistic propaganda cease than the dismemberment of the empire took effect; the emperors were the first to take a hand in this. The Latin conquest was self-defeating, as if, setting the establishment of Christianity to one side, Roman triumphs from Appius Claudius's arrival in Sicily, through to the battle of Actium, had been merely the consequences of tactics rather than proper feats of force.

The very same laws of annexation and boundary-setting governed the formation and general march of modern States. It would be hard to tell where the current agitation will end up; but there is no gainsaying that for the past fifteen centuries, Europe has had a consistent and insurmountable tendency to break down into a given number of groups. Indeed, contesting their boundaries seems to be the sole focus of contemporary international law. Among those groups, some appear to have reached their point of maximum expansion, whereas others are in the throes of getting there. The measure of civilization being pretty much the same everywhere, there is also the same forceful revulsion everywhere to amalgamation; meaning that the hypothesis of a European monarchy is anti-European. Now, mark this well, it is through seemingly unstoppable war, by dint of unrelentingly refreshed and, so to speak, rewarded strife, that the formation of diverse States has taken place.

The barbarian invasions were the instrument employed by providential justice to break up the Roman Empire and to shape brand-new States out of its fragments. Once achieved, the first thing we saw was barbarism evaporate everywhere. Strong enough to smash the imperial armies, the conquerors nevertheless lacked the strength to assimilate the conquered peoples who swallowed *them* up instead. Such was the fate of the Ostrogoths, Visigoths, Franks, Lombards and so on, all of them swamped, one by one, by the natives. Thus spoke the law of force.

The same principle presides over the formation of new States. The argument of force, the conditions of their equilibrium, determine the importance of the kingdoms, republics, principalities and indeed towns. Every policy undertaken by the Princes that was consistent with the laws of force and the right of the strongest has brought them success. Whereas, every time the warring States, drunk on success, sought to step over the boundaries set for them by the logic of things, despite their prestigious victories they have remained powerless and the upshot has been only needless slaughter.

What was the point of the Hundred Years' War between France and England? Where were the fruits of the victories the English achieved at l'Écluse, Crécy, Poitiers, Agincourt? What was achieved by the treachery of the Dukes of Burgundy in throwing in their lot with the kings of England in order to finish France off? All that glory and all that criminality added up to nothing. It was just as everything seemed lost that everything was saved. The voice of a young girl,[4] genuinely representative of the people, injected fresh courage; a political display, the coronation of Charles VII, provided the signal for the final expulsion of the foreigner. A cautious, by no means warrior king added the finishing touch by demolishing Burgundy, after having consigned its last prince to a death from shame and fury.

What was the point of the Italian campaigns of French kings Charles VIII, Louis XII and Francis I? What did the victories at Fornovo, Ravenna or Marignan bring us? Only a proverb: *Italy is the burial ground of the French*.

And what was the point of the victory scored by Charles V over Schmalkalden's confederates at Mühlberg, and all the butchery by Tilly and Wallenstein? At a time when the Reformation had been crushed and was on its death-bed, a fresh actor, a real hero, Gustav Adolphus, swooped down from the North with a handful of Swedes and all the exploits of those phoney victors were reduced to nothing, like deeds tainted with fraud.

In the previous Book, I quoted the example of Louis XIV. I stated that no war ever looked more unjust and treacherous than the one he waged against Spain over the claim to Franche-Comté and the Low Countries, from 1666 to 1672. No conqueror has ever had to face such strident criticism for what they did. But I went on to add that while the king of France's motives, as expounded by his diplomats, were supremely iniquitous, in the eyes of the higher justice of States, and according to the right of force, that should have been enforced, Louis XIV's conquest had legitimacy. Which is why the annexation of French Flanders, Franche-Comté, Alsace, the Three Cathedral Cities, never faced a serious challenge and why, during the monarchy's darkest days, in 1713 and 1815, the unity of France was never even called into question. The repeated onslaughts of Marlborough and Eugène made no headway. Just as the wars of unadulterated ambition undertaken by Louis XIV had proved fruitless, the one pursued against his properly constituted monarchy was also doomed to prove futile. At one point, in Denain, the allies lost their advantage. The day Villars saved France, just as Masséna had saved Zurich in 1799, was just another demonstration of the futility of a war waged against a country pronounced indivisible by the nature of things, the laws of history, and even the reasoning of its rivals.

What was the result of the coalitions formed against the Revolution?

---

4. This is no doubt a reference to Joan of Arc (1412–1431) and is significant because it contradicts one of the central tenets of Proudhon's anti-feminism. Proudhon claimed that patriarchy derives from women's inability to be soldiers. While Joan of Arc may have been the exception that proved the rule, this is no longer the case, demonstrating the spuriousness of Proudhon's claim. For more see the posthumously published, Proudhon, *La Pornocratie* (1875). [A.P.]

Nothing. Likewise, what was the outcome of Napoleon's campaigns and all his endless victories? Nothing. On the one hand, France had to carry out her revolution within the boundaries set down for her by her kings, and no power had any right or capacity to prevent this. Yet, on the other, revolutionary France also was to serve as pioneer for the continent, becoming the embodiment of freedoms that precluded conquest on her part. *Twenty successes to every setback*, our military historians proudly proclaim. No doubt: but that setback, bringing up the rear, undid everything that went before it and determined the outcome. The Empire's wars dealt telling blows insofar as they served the cause of the Revolution and carried the spirit of freedom beyond France's borders. In that regard, at least, Napoleon's victories were not pointless. His sword was the rod employed by humanitarian justice to get governments and kings to shift; *Reges eos in virga ferrea.*[5] But as a means of conquest, the empire's battles were worthless.

Which is why France was ultimately defeated in Leipzig; why all her annexations backfired against her; why not one of her conquests has been left to her; why the peoples that, she flattered herself, she had won over began defecting by way of protest against French domination and took up arms defend their as yet untouched nationality. That's why, since 1815, France has only waged war on behalf of others; she gained nothing, or next to nothing, from her campaigns in Spain, Greece, Belgium, Crimea, Rome and Lombardy. The annexation of Nice and Savoy has been portrayed by the imperial government as a *border adjustment*, prompted by Piedmont's sudden expansion; the silence from the powers-that-be is evidence enough they don't know either way. Algeria is our sole conquered territory; but thirty years later, indeed, from day one, that conquest has been reduced to a military occupation. The civilized find nothing so hard to absorb as barbarism and the desert. In an average year, France spends fifty million and twenty-five thousand men on retaining this prize. The imperial government complains about this just as the government of Louis-Philippe used to do; we have made barely any inroads into the territory and no inroads at all into the minds of the natives.

Go through all the histories and you will find not a single thing to contradict this theory. It carries its certainty with it. War is the verdict delivered by force; it is the assertion of right and the prerogatives of force by force of arms; it turns into a nonsense as soon as some contrivance is used to score a victory over force. Which is why the waging of war does not end on the battle-field. Conquest, which is its ultimate purpose, only becomes final with the assimilation of the conquered. Unless that condition is fulfilled, victories are just odious

---

5. *Bible*, Psalm 2:9. [H.M.] "Thou shalt break them with a rod of iron". [P.S.]

dragonnades[6] and conquerors merely despicable charlatans chastised sooner or later by the force they misuse.

The average person, who understands nothing of such reactions by outraged force, plumps for the most laughable explanations. He tells himself that Chance has swapped sides and, being fickle, has deserted her favourites; that one cannot be a winner in war all the time, any more than one can in a lottery; that malicious fortune delights in unmaking the plans of genius, etc., etc. Add to all that a dash of fatalism or belief in providence and you get the full picture. And those who write the tales of war now have no other philosophy. If we are to believe them, wisdom would consist of halting time, like the clever gambler who, making do with his winnings, bows out at the first sign of luck turning against him. We have read lengthy, massive, shabby histories. Will it require such great effort of common sense to understand, with the facts staring us in the face, that what determines the downfall of the conquerors is quite simply that, with battles won, they imagine they have reached the peak of their power, when they have in actual fact plunged to the lowest ebb of weakness? For a country like France, it took several generations to annex and assimilate the provinces falling between her borders of 1790 and the waters of the Rhine. And Napoleon did not go so slowly. Given the course upon which he had embarked in the wake of Marengo and Hohenlinden, he was doomed to conquer, conquer and conquer, which is to say, to fight ever more numerous foes, amassing ever more insubordinate subjects, just to be deeply undermined by all the territory he was gaining and to run ever greater risks. No matter his own skills and the clumsiness of his enemies, the day had to come when, all the odds being against him, his empire would collapse like a house of cards and he would be bamboozled by his own fancy.

When I come to deal later with tactics, I will revisit the causes of the formation and swift downfall of the First Empire. My concern here has been merely to quote the fact in support of the law.

---

6. Louis XIV's policy of terrorising French Huguenots (protestant), by quartering, or housing the French military with families that refused to convert to Catholicism. [A.P.]

CHAPTER II

More on the Same Subject.
The Legality of the Italian Revolution
Demonstrated By the Right of Force

Since I've begun discussing contemporary affairs, I cannot help saying a little more about them, and show, by means of a spectacular example how force, invoked by the discord between States, can deliver its verdict with clarity and sure-footed judgment in matters that even the cleverest diplomats could not resolve. The reader will be all the quicker to forgive me this digression because no sovereign and no nationality will be able to take umbrage at what I have to say.

For the past fifteen centuries, Italy, that strange country, has been living under starkly contrasting principles and influences which it has not managed, thus far, to eliminate or reconcile. As Joseph [Guiseppe] Ferrari[7] has explained, up until the nineteenth century, Italy remained at once imperial, pontifical, federal and municipal. She has been exposed to and been deeply marked by the consecutive influence of the barbarians, Constantinople, the Germans, the French, the Spanish and the Arabs. She has been targeted by a host of adventurers who have left a strong impression. After a revolutionary effort of nearly a thousand years, the grandest ever witnessed; after the corruption of the fifteenth, sixteenth, seventeenth and eighteenth centuries; Italy was spent, and plunged into the lethargy that has made her the fable of nations and turned her, as Monsieur Metternich had it, into a *geographical expression* at the disposal of the most powerful.[8] Occupied by the French from 1797 to 1814, the treaties of 1814–1815 divided her between the rule of Austria on one side, and that of the princes on the other, who followed Austria's policy and gloried in their power.

---

7. *Histoire des révolutions d'Italie* (Paris: Didier, 1858), 4 vols., in 8°. [P-J.P.]

Joseph (Giuseppe) Ferrari (1811–1876) made Proudhon's acquaintance while he was incarcerated in Saint Pélagie between 1848–1851. They became close friends, and Ferrari is credited with converting Proudhon to federalism. [A.P.]

8. KLEMENS VON METTERNICHT (1773–1859). The Austrian Prince was arguably one of the most significant and skilful diplomats of the Revolutionary period. [A.P.]

Given the density, intermingling and fellowship in which the nations of Europe live, it was inevitable that Italy should find herself in this situation; it was fair even. By virtue of its very weakness, a people that cannot manage to constitute itself politically and which cannot bear the aggression of the rest, creates a right of supremacy for them. It cannot claim independence; it would pose a danger to the rest, a source of disintegration, by virtue of its disobedience.

Italy was therefore plunged into the circumstances reserved for inert, ambiguous or contradictory societies. Devoid of political principles, precisely because it followed divergent principles, she was bereft of political existence. What befell her was logical and, let me say it again, in terms of the rights of peoples, it was fair.

But then, from 1814 and 1815 onwards, under the sway of the ideas that had made the French Revolution, a new spirit began to evolve in Italy. The brightest minds set about delving into the causes of their country's decline and ways of regenerating her. They countered the ancient divine law with the rights of man; Roman faith with philosophical reason; the idea of Empire with the constitutional system; the hostility of her towns, blamed on the foreigner, was countered with ideas of homeland and Italian nationality. The times were eminently favourable for this renaissance. In spite of everything that has been said about the celebrated treaties, the dates 1814–1815 were nevertheless, as I have shown somewhere, the era of constitutional governments and the balance of powers; on both grounds, Italy was able to stake a claim to her political liberty and to her autonomy.[9]

In short, new ideas were spreading in Italy. They spread, let us note, legitimately by virtue of the imprescriptible right of intelligence, or, to put that another way, the right of unfettered scrutiny or freedom of thought, which is independent of the right of force and falls entirely outside of its remit. Due to the impact of these ideas, a day would have to come when Italy, like the France of 1789, would raise up her head, shake off the dust of her past and clamour: "I have the right to live, as I both think and live; I have the right to live because I can feel my strength. Therefore, I want to live, to resume my place in the sun among the States and to ensure that I too become a great power". After 1848, Piedmont became the engine-room of this movement.[10]

As we might imagine, this unsolicited and legitimate desire, was not, at the

---

9. In the wake of the Napoleonic wars, the Italian states either became feudatory states or French departments, which paved the way to unification. [H.T.]

10. Piedmont encompassed Sardinia and Savoy. The latter included lands from the borders of France, down through Turin to Genoa. Its king, Victor Emmanuel I, and his right-hand man, Count Camillo de Cavour, would, with some skill and skulduggery, annex the whole of the Italian peninsula by 1861. [A.P.]

very outset, shared by the majority of Italians. At a stretch, it may enjoy majority support now. But that desire was most certainly not shared by the governments whose very existence it threatened.

The young Italy was at loggerheads with the following powers: The Pope,
whose temporal power is, today, denied; the Emperor, which is to say Austria,
substituted for the rights of the *Holy Roman Empire*, his possession guaranteed
by the 1814–1815 treaties; the king of Naples, the dukes of Tuscany, Parma and
Modena rallying around the papal idea and Austrian policy.

Now, note that whilst young Italy had its rights, these sovereigns, unques-
tionably, had theirs as well. Before the rights of peoples, the only one applicable
here, and the court of war, the only one competent to make this enforcement,
both parties ought to be regarded as equally honourable, in equal good faith,
and equally well-founded in their demands. Indeed, if one is entitled to be
a freethinker and to seek its development through free thought, the other is
equally entitled to remain Catholic and to look to Catholic institutions for
its salvation. Likewise, whilst the former is free to express a preference for the
representative system, that most recent creation of political genius, the latter
cannot be precluded from clinging to absolutist rule, which dates back to time
immemorial. But those two trends, tolerable in private persons subject to the
same government, cannot be reconciled within one government. The State cannot be both liberal and absolutist, believer and philosopher; it has to make a
choice. Who is to retain power? That is the question.

Therefore, I say, and this is the theory which I am striving to assert here,
that when we step down from the heights of intellectual speculation, emerge
from the secret recesses of conscience and leave the philosophical arena behind,
in order to stand on the terrain of *raison d'état*, this question can only be resolved by force. And I have on my side the support of the freethinkers themselves, those supporters of universal suffrage and of the parliamentary principle
of majority rule. Indeed, what is the law of numbers other than a transfiguration
of the right of force, as I pointed out in the previous Book? The only difference
being that, in the realm of public right, decision-making is based upon strength
of numbers, and in the realm of the rights of peoples, it rests on the effective
superiority of not just intellectual, but also moral and material forces. And this
difference, on account of the realities in Italy, does not favour public right.

So, this is how the various cases for war break down in this oh-so-
complicated revolution in contemporary Italy.

1. *Between Piedmont, the heartland of the revolution on the one hand, and, on the
other, Austria, a conservative, absolutist power.* – If the Italian State of Piedmont
were dealing only with a purely Italian Austria, the outcome of the war would

not seem to be in doubt. The imperial power would be deserted by part of the population it rules over and, by virtue of that desertion, the superiority of force would shift across to king Victor Emmanuel and the matter would be settled. All that would be missing would be endorsement, someday inevitable, of victory.

But Austria is not merely an Italian power; she is simultaneously a Germanic and Slav power. So, with regard to Piedmont, which she is capable of crushing, she has the upper hand; and the verdict of force, delivered in these circumstances, would manifestly run counter to Italy's cause. What to do, then? To balance the outside force drafted in by Austria in support of her Italian possession with some other outside force; which is what happened when the French stepped in. How are we to account for that intervention? The fact is that the same conflicting principles and ideas that have split Italy since 1815 have also divided Europe; that, as a result, all powers have an interest in the contest, some as absolutist powers, others as liberal powers; and a second battle of Novara, lost by the king of Piedmont, even though it may, on this occasion, have served Austrian interests, would have posed a danger to revolutionary Europe and, primarily, France. Now, with France siding with Italy and against Austria, the latter, being left to her own devices and condemned by the mere fact of Europe's impassive stance, a judgement had been delivered once and for all and pronounced in the name of force. The victories at Montebello, Palestro, Magenta and Solferino spoke with sovereign reason;[11] they were legitimate and sound. The Emperor Franz Joseph was left at liberty to appeal against his defeat; and the emperor Napoleon III to go back on his word and drop his ally, Victor Emmanuel. Nothing that diplomatic intrigue could produce in this context would raise a query over the decision delivered in the recent campaign. The fact is that Italy, in the incorruptible minds of France and Europe, must be free and any contrary solution would be an abandonment of the right of force.

2. *Between Piedmont, that hotbed of philosophical propaganda, and the Papacy, the stubborn religious power.* – The Church does not wield the sword: as far as it is concerned, that is an article of faith. By virtue of that exclusively Catholic principle, deciding between king Victor Emmanuel and the Holy Father by feat of arms becomes impossible, not to mention that the Pope's subjects would not fight against Victor Emmanuel's Italians. But the Pope's temporal power

11. Montebello, 20 May: Palestro, 31 May: Magenta, 4 June: Solferino, 24 June 1859. [H.M.] Napoleon III committed to support Victor Emmanuel II until Italy was free as far as the Adriatic. Within two months, the House of Austria's hegemony over northern Italy was ended. Officially reeling from the sight of the battlefield of Solferino, Napoleon III suggested an armistice to Austria and left his ally Victor Emmanuel II to conquer the remainder of Italy: especially Venetia. He had already sensed the rising threat from Prussia along the Rhine and wanted to muster his troops there. [H.T.]

concerns the whole of Catholicism; in addition, the Pope had his States restored to him under the Treaty of Vienna. It remains to be seen whether those Catholic nations that have more or less gone over to the new principles, will interpret the Vienna Treaty in the same way as the Pope does, and whether they will close ranks in order to defend the Papacy against Italy's formal wish. Well, that decision went against the Pope in the battle of Castelfidardo,[12] in which General Lamoricière was the loser. The mind of the populace today is not quite the same as it was in the days of Hildebrand.[13] Back then, the people sided with their spiritual leader against their temporal leaders. Today, one will not find enough devoutness, enough faith, enough men in the entire Catholic world, to champion the Pope's temporal sovereignty against the Piedmontese army. No matter what Roman Catholic dogma may make of it, the war placed it on record that a crowned pontiff is no longer viable; it has, if I may be so bold, passed God's judgment upon it.

3. *Between Piedmont, representing Italian emancipation, and the dukes of Tuscany, Parma and Modena, the emperor's allies or feudatories.* – To pose the issue in those terms is to resolve it. If, where the emperor is concerned, young Italy's ambition is just, is it also just where the dukes are concerned. Then why were they not the first to endorse it? And if the verdict of the war against the former is sound in all its ramifications, it extends also to his allies and feudatories, unless these are in a position to join battle with it in their turn. Why did they not line up in person and with their armies in tow, either on Victor Emmanuel's side or against him? In the first instance, they might have held on to their States; in the second, they might not have lost them. But these Highnesses made a stand against the movement and have found themselves on their own; their subjects have abandoned them. Such sovereigns are unworthy of life; they did not have the strength for it.

4. *Between the king of Piedmont, crowned king of Italy by popular acclaim, and the king of the Two Sicilies, friend to Pope and Emperor and secessionist to boot.* – The public initially welcomed the Italian people's enthusiasm for its regeneration with such pronounced sympathy. But it was somewhat irked by king Victor Emmanuel's readiness to exploit that gusto in order to seize the States of the

12. The Papal army commanded by General de Lamoricière was beaten by the Piedmontese on 18 September 1860. [H.M.]

13. As Gregory VII, this Pope had the backing of the German princes against the Emperor Henry IV in the conflict that ended in Canossa in 1077 AD. [H.M.] "To go to Canossa" is now a part of speech that means to become or make oneself humble, do penance or seek absolution for some wrongdoing. The phrase was famously used by Otto von Bismarck in a dispute with the Vatican in 1872. [G.H.]

Dukes, the Pope and the king of Naples, one after the other. His performance was viewed as ambitious more than patriotic. The young king of Naples, Francis II,[14] was given credit for his somewhat belated concession to his subjects' desire for a constitution; he was also given credit for his proposal for an alliance with the new king of Italy. Finally, the splendid defence he put up earned him universal sympathy. But the people were not convinced that it was yet Italy's calling to set up a great unitary power, especially since Italy's intellectual leaders were divided on this score. Finally, there was a weariness with all these seeming trespasses against customary rights and the written law in Europe. What has the right of force to say now?

Force is equally insusceptible to error and to going back on its verdict. It may be misused; one can even, to some extent, avoid it; but it is, nevertheless, infallible.

Note, for a start, that in Europe's current circumstances, there is a universal trend towards unity and the centralization of government. Since the end of the great wars, Great Britain, despite her individualist genius, has provided plenty of evidence of her centralizing tendency and that trend will only grow under the impact of social democracy, presently getting itself organized. Belgium, no less liberal than England, is committed to the same course. Germany, bourgeois and plebeian alike, is clamouring for unity. Austria might not have failed in her drive for unification had she previously engaged in political reform in the spirit of the age, by which I mean of the 1815 treaties themselves. A day will come, and it may well not be far off, when this trend towards concentration may go into reverse; once the experience of bourgeois parliamentary arrangements has become widespread and the great economic issues have been added to the agenda. The social revolution that failed in February 1848 will then be carried out right across Europe.

For the time being, however, there is no question that on every score opinion is mostly for unity. So, it is only natural that it should be so in Italy as well, but in spite of the federalist antecedents of that country, a country which is, more than any other perhaps, inimical to unity. It is also easy to see that if Italy were left to her own devices, and if no outside influence was brought to bear there, and if the question of unity went hand in hand with the question of emancipation, the battle between Piedmont's king and the king of Naples would have to work out to the advantage of the former.

Is that solution, which may not be the last word, to be looked upon as an injustice of war?

---

14. Francis II who ascended the throne in May 1859, lost Sicily in 1860. The constitution he bestowed upon his subjects failed to stop developments in their tracks. Garibaldi entered Naples on 7 September. [H.M.]

No. Italian unity currently strikes most people as a precondition of independence, and because, whilst it is legitimate to have one's suspicions about the efficacy of that grand amalgamation, it is equally legitimate to query the king of Naples's conversion. Until such time as a new order is installed, the overwhelming sentiment in Italy, and therefore right, is on the side of unity.

But Italy does not exist alone in Europe; she belongs to a vast system of States more or less independent of one another and governed by certain principles. Just as in her struggle against Austria, she was the beneficiary of French intervention and of the passivity of other States, so she must also take account of the opposition that those same States may put up against her unification. Now, those States are not merely Austria, defeated but yesterday, but guaranteed half of her Italian possessions under a brand-new treaty. We also have France, rueful perhaps of seeing the force that has served her so well turn against her; there are the Catholic enemies of revolution; and soon there will be the socialist democrats, increasingly vocal against political centralization and bourgeois constitutionalism; we see all the sovereigns outraged at the sight of one of their own being treated in such an off-hand fashion and appealing to public propriety regarding princes and States, pending recourse to force.

To be brief, for the idea of Italian unity to succeed once and for all, king Victor Emmanuel must make his peace with force. Not just in Italy but throughout Europe. In the absence of that, it will fall short and every victory and conquest might prove a sorry disappointment to him. The French are still in Rome, the Austrians in Verona; England, Russia, Germany have withdrawn their sympathies from him. Let him make a move and he is done for, and poor Italy joins him in his downfall. In the event that Piedmont succeeds in the assimilation of the Two Sicilies, the only thing the government in Turin has to do, is, first, marshal the Italian forces in order to forestall any return by the foreigner and then win general endorsement for the unification arrangements for the Peninsula and the adjacent islands. This is Monsieur Cavour's task, and it is a much thornier undertaking than Garibaldi's.[15]

---

15. There has been a disgraceful silence in France's self-styled democratic or patriotic press on the matter of the war between the kings of Piedmont and Naples. The mania for unity has been taken to such lengths and the hatred of the house of Bourbon been so blinkered, that the champions of Francis II have been designated *Bourbonians*. There has been a refusal to see that these *Bourbonians* were the only patriots who remained in the kingdom of Naples; that all the rest, betraying Francis II, had sold out their country to the foreigner. What would they say in Paris about a faction which, under cover of establishing a European homeland, and not content with abandoning Napoleon, would hand France over to the Tsar? What is going on in Naples is, on a smaller scale, the very same thing. True, let me say it again, Victor-Emmanuel's cause may very well be able to defend itself against Francis II's, but it will be thanks to the Piedmontese, maybe the Tuscans, indeed some of the Romagnols but not the Neapolitans. It may well be that the sacrifice of the Neapolitan State and Neapolitan

Let us re-state our case in summary. Force, per se, is a stranger to doctrine. But since doctrine, more or less plausible and embraced by a number of minds, sustained by certain blocs of interests, is inclined to proceed from theory to application, and consequently to supplant other doctrines and different interests, the issue is naturally referred, where States are concerned, to the court of force. The jurisdiction of which is not open to challenge. Ideas that do not know how to fight, and which shun warfare or scuttle away from the bayonet's glint, are not equipped to rule over societies; men who cannot die for their ideas are not made for government; a nation that would refuse to arm itself and which could only scowl at its rulers, would be unworthy of autonomy. The right of nationalities exists only in this regard; force creates it and victory provides its endorsement. The fortunes of the king of Naples have been boosted by a half since his act of war; he has sanctified himself through his courage. No matter what comes to pass, Italy will have no need to blush at her kings. The pope alone is impossible.

Let us sum up our first two chapters.

In principle, the moulding of humanity into independent, sovereign States seems to be a law of civilization and a law of history. That being the case, we have to believe it.

States are of varying sizes; as a rule, they far exceed the boundaries of the tribe and city; however, it does not look as if they can encompass a sizable portion of the globe, much less the actual entirety of the globe.

Warfare is the *deed* that animates the political agglomeration of *States*, in accordance with certain circumstances bearing upon force, time, area and assimilation.

As an action that shapes States, there is, therefore, a legitimacy to war; it has its remit as the arbiter in their squabbles; its verdict, serving no purpose other than as an indicator of where force lies and as a dispenser of prerogatives, is authentic. Finally, that verdict is effective. As a result, war can and should be held as judicially sound. As any annexation must abide by the law of greater force, in the circumstances and under the conditions prescribed, the dispute is settled, justice done. The efficacy of the operation and soundness of judgment are synonymous here. The first of those expressions serves to signal the material effect of warfare and the latter its moral impact.

The conventions of war are the conditions and practices that guarantee the

---

nationhood is required for the wellbeing and advancement of the entire Italian nation: but, since the sovereign was making an effort, it was up to the citizen to back him, to die for the homeland or face eternal disgrace. Such is the law of war and such its morality. That morality is certainly worth more than the frightful shamelessness, with which certain newspapers entertain the French people. [P-J.P.]

fairness of the fight, which the belligerent powers are required to fulfil towards each other. The efficacy of the victory and thereby the legitimacy and irrevocability of the annexation, depend on them.

Trespasses against the forms or laws of war does not always imply the invalidation of conquest. In regular courts a verdict may be unjustified, prompted by passion, delivered following scandalous proceedings, without its necessarily being unjust per se, and open to appeal. The tasks that bring it into disrepute fall to the litigants, their lawyers, the judges, but do not preclude it having its full and unadulterated effect.

But it is often the case that contempt for the laws of war generates mediocrity, which are later translated into defeats that overturn initial victories and restore things to their initial status. We have cited some examples of that. Moreover, as the reader will appreciate this is of the utmost gravity. The costs of civil justice are infinitesimal compared with those of war; and if one might succeed, by stricter observance of the principles, in only limiting the incalculable disasters that the ambition of governments, the ignorance of the masses and soldierly brutality cause, it would still be worth the effort. Princely honour, popular well-being and war's morality all have an equal stake in it.

CHAPTER III

On the Regulation of Weapons and
the Policing of Combat

Since war is action pursuant to the right of force, it is subject to rules and has its *conventions*. As such it has a genuine procedure, and its verdict, delivered in the circumstances and for the purpose required, is sound. Its execution, surrounded by the requisite formalities, are as just as they are efficacious. *Conventions* is a term that has as much currency in the language of military men as it does in that of the jurisconsults.

There is nothing arbitrary about these rules or *conventions* in the prosecution of war: they flow naturally from the very notion of warfare, from the nature and purpose of it. Contravention of them constitutes a crime liable to severe punishment in the event that one loses. Likewise, should one emerge the winner, contravention will diminish and sometimes cancel out the victory, or just taint the new order of things.

Adherence to the laws, rules or conventions of warfare is therefore a matter of the utmost importance. In order to get a fair grasp of this, let us review what occurs in a duel.[16]

Odious, and even absurd in most instances, and for that very reason rightly looked down upon, the duel is nevertheless deserving of our approval when we see a man of courage, having received some deadly slight, for which regular justice makes no provision, forgo revenge and generously offer to fight his

---

16. In November and December 1848, Proudhon was challenged to two duels. First, by Félix Pyat and then by Charles Delescluze. Two shots were fired in the first, but no one was hurt. Proudhon declined to duel Delescluze, suspecting, with Pyat having already failed, an attempt to assassinate him. Proudhon described the whole affair as a "ridiculous comedy", and it exacerbated bitter infighting on the left of the Constituent Assembly of 1848, to which he had been elected a deputy. A month later, the government put Proudhon on trial for denouncing Louis Napoleon III as a "traitor" of the revolution. In June 1849, after three months on the run, he was incarcerated for three years. Louis Napoleon III declared his *coup d'état* in December 1851. For more on this episode, see K. Steven Vincent, *Pierre-Joseph Proudhon and the Rise of French Republican Socialism* (Oxford: Oxford University Press, 1984), 182–90. [A.P.]

adversary. There are some slights that kill their target morally if they are allowed to go unpunished and yet which cannot be put right through the courts. If we accept that justice is one of man's greatest assets, and that as a result his dignity consists in this entitlement to justice, like the medieval *seigneur*, we have to grant that he is at least entitled to the right to challenge his offender and take him on in a fight. Mightier than the policy of kings and the wisdom of the jurists, universal conscience permits it, and it is because it is universal conscience that speaks, and which imposed rules upon duelling, the murder committed by the duellist is pardonable.

In a duel, the location, time and weapons are agreed; seconds are appointed; chances are equally divided; the combatants are prohibited from acts of treachery, ambush, cruelty and outrage. From the instant they are brought face to face, each merits the other's respect; insofar as possible, neither is afforded any advantage other than that deriving from his own natural vigour and appreciation of his rights. Once these conditions have been met, and, under the supervision of witnesses, the signal is given... Things proceed in good faith; the last word is spoken. The winner does not allow himself a callous thought, not a single word of invective; he will not lay his hands on the loser, be the latter dead or wounded; he will consider his person, his corpse, his memory, his weapons and everything belonging to him as sacred. He will not go on to marry his widow; he will not move into his house; he will not attend the funeral. It may well be that the deceased is the person slighted; he will at least retain his honour, his reputation as a man of courage, who preferred death to derision. In death, he will come to be missed by honourable men, but will die with the satisfaction that in the moment of danger he struck remorse into the heart of his enemy and left him with the odious burden of his death. This is what duelling does to the consciences of duellists. Yet the enormous abuses cannot be dissevered from the duel, and nothing spares duellists from being prosecuted and stigmatized under the law and, in most instances, receiving but a lukewarm reception from public opinion.

Now, considered in terms of its nature and purpose, warfare enjoys every advantage over the duel from the moral point of view. It rules out any notion of slight and hatred on the part of the belligerents, so much so that, should one of the two belligerent powers have slighted the other, the former owes the latter reparations in all military propriety, prior to their joining battle, which could not be the case with a duel, since once such reparation had been made the duel would be rendered impossible.

Warfare also has a positive and tangible purpose: either the amalgamation of two peoples and the formation of one, larger, State, or the separation of two races, two peoples hitherto united politically, but which religion or some other cause have irrevocably divided; or, finally, the demarcation and balancing of sovereignties. Meanwhile, the only possible outcome of the duel, the only satisfaction sought, albeit by implication, by the side that issues the challenge, is blood and death.

Finally, warfare conducted with propriety and leading to a sound victory delivers justice. It proves something, the superior force of the victor; as a result, it establishes his righteousness, whereas the duel's validity does not go any further than the matter at issue: of itself, it proves nothing; if it delivers justice, that is down to mere chance, since the outcome of the confrontation could as easily have gone the way of the caster of aspersions as of their recipient.

Measured alongside the duel, war strikes us as the very acme of human virtue, a godly judgment to which the conscience of nations appeals for the highest and most solemn verdict. The field of battle is the real assizes of the peoples, the communion and paradise of the brave. How then could that supreme court operate without rules? How could warfare, deliverer of justice, be devoid of conventions?

Let the reader pay especially close attention here, if he will, and, as he reads my words, set aside all prejudice. Humanity's errors are only as stubborn as they are deep-rooted, sanctified by custom and time, and the public mind has difficulty grasping this. It is not a bland paradox to assert the reality of the right of force; it is no more gross to argue that as war is a sort of judicial proceeding, that the means of constraint are not all equally suited to it, and that one way of fighting, which might result in victory going to the weaker side and nullifying the blessings of force, would constitute an affront to the rights of peoples and a veritable felony.

Let us recall, one last time, how the case for war arises between two nations, which is to say a dispute that can only be settled, as Cicero had it, by means of force.

We have families, tribes, born far apart from one another, living on an immense plateau, in vast forests, in a long valley, living and multiplying utterly independent of each other for some time. As they thrive, they form small States and soon these, in conformity with the law of their expansion, eventually brush up against one another. At first, a demarcation issue crops up, which is settled by means of ordinary law, or at any rate is susceptible to it. Such a situation could not last for long. The frictions between the tribes make it hard for them to shift; all manner of problems arise, regarding rights of way and easement, intermingling and alliances are agreed, not to mention food shortages. In short, it becomes necessary for these hordes, tribes, cities, clans to resolve into a small number of States, a republic or a kingdom, which, as far as most of these microscopic States are concerned, entails a loss of individuality and independence.

The quarrel, which seemed, initially, to be destined to be reduced to a matter of ownership or trade, turns into something quite different: the survival, not of persons, but of political community. Is there a basis for annexation, yes or no? These are the terms in which the issue is posed. If yes is the answer, then what part will superior force play? Which State is going to bestow its name, its laws, its language and its gods on the rest? Where will the core annexation take place? This is the question that hovers over every war and that scholarly jurisprudence ignores; a question that can quite evidently only be settled by force; the resolution of which therefore requires a struggle in which there will, of necessity, be bloodshed, the swallowing up of wealth, and one nationality sacrificed, but which, in the final analysis, viewed from the vantage point of international law and progress, is nothing more than juridical action.

We are too soft-hearted to embrace the notion of such a tragedy. Such blood-stained justice we find repugnant; deep down, however, it is the only rational one, the only honourable one, the only legitimate one. The upper hand belongs to the stronger people, the liveliest people, the people that, by dint of its labour, genius, the organization of its power, the exercise of its rights, is possessed of the greater measure of political capability. Because in a people, force is not gauged simply by the number of its men and the vigour of their brawn; it also includes faculties of spirit, courage, virtue, discipline, accumulated wealth and productivity. The formation of large States, inevitable at a given point in history; the honour of naming them, supplying the component parts thereof; all of these are the prerogatives of force. Granting ascendancy to the weaker side would be more than injustice, it would be folly. Now, how are we to distinguish the stronger from the weaker other than by combat, wherein both the contending parties will have to deploy whatever physical and moral energy, intelligence, civic virtue, patriotism, accumulated learning, industrial genius and even poetry they can command? For the force of nations is, let us reiterate, made up of all these things, and war is proof of that.

Therefore, and we cannot say this too often, in the gravest issue by which a man's soul can be quickened, that of discovering which, of two peoples doomed by necessity to amalgamate, is to wield the upper hand, the *right of force*, so decried since Aesop, IS positively THE BETTER. War is a judgment; as such, it has to proceed with the utmost circumspection, abiding by all of the conventions and with the assurance of justice. Logic wishes it so, and the instincts of nations declare it so. All the warriors and Statesmen, all the historians and jurisconsults are agreed upon it, when they unanimously acknowledge that war has to be preceded by a declaration of the aggressor's grievances and a denunciation. When they talk about war's *conventions* and *laws*; when they deliver up to infamy the barbarian who trespasses against them, they recognize war's conventions. The commander in the field is to the enemy commander what the plaintiff is when faced by his adversary in the courtroom; at that point, both represent the personification of their people; they represent its force, its honour and all its faculties.

This was why the Roman consul was at once general and magistrate, why he was the very embodiment of all authority, and why the Romans, who, inside the city, described themselves as *quirites* or spear-carriers (bourgeois), adopted the designation *milites* (troopers) in the field. The former, deriving from *quir*, meaning pike or javelin, the name of the God of war, distinguished the free man from the slave and the emancipated slave, who had no entitlement to bear arms. It was the badge of righteousness, the insignia of property. The latter was indicative of political solidarity, with the army *corps* as its image. Warfare, which brought into play all the resources of the nation, was therefore just a variety of justice, a variant of religion. It was described as pious, just, holy and sacred; and was attended by all manner of formalities, ablutions and ceremonies; so that the most religious and most legalistic of peoples was at the same time the most warlike.

All of this demonstrates that the conduct of war cannot be left to happenstance or be abandoned to the savagery of the soldier any more than to the whims of generals. Since every nation is entitled, whether attacking or for self-defence, to deploy its natural assets, and to capitalize upon its position and all favourable circumstances, it follows from this that war may vary in terms of its operations. It may culminate in a clash of armies in the open countryside, or involve a series of manoeuvres on land and sea, sieges, etc. For it is not just a matter of the side making demands needing to be the stronger; it also needs to be in a position to overwhelm the enemy at home, in his stronghold, in all the fullness of the resources at his command; which demands an effort far superior to that which a straightforward battle would require. In any case, and no matter the weapon of choice, once the terrain has been selected and the mode of combat chosen, it is strikingly obvious that a code of honour has to be enforced, in the absence of which the war would cease to be a juridical act; it would degenerate into banditry. The mounting of attacks by the two sides would no longer imply valour; it would be cowardice. Given those conditions, the war would be meaningless; it would boil down to an extermination. Slaughter would turn into the sole guarantor of dishonourable victory; the winner, doomed to the utter destruction of the loser, would have accomplished nothing except a feat of infamy and impotence.

Every trespass against war's procedural laws will be punished, either by a backlash from force or by the decline that sooner or later besets the guilty party. The Spaniards' destruction of the kingdoms of Peru and Mexico, like the expulsion of the Jews and the Moors, wholesale murders that were followed up by odious dispossession, hastened the Spanish people's corruption, and were assuredly the most active causes of their decline. Over the past three centuries, Spain, falling a notch with every reign, has been paying the price for her wars and the maverick nature of her conquests. Saint Batholomew's Day and the *dragonnades* nudged France on to the same downward slope and would have doomed her to the same fate, had she not been raised up again by philosophy at the end of the eighteenth century and by the revolution.[17] In the wake of the February Revolution [of 1848], war broke out between the bourgeoisie and waged labourers, the two main factions of the people, over work and wages. Force determined that the social question was not yet ripe and that the labouring class was still too brutish, in short, that deferring to the righteousness of socialism was not, for the time being, appropriate. But in June 1848 and December 1851, the reaction wanted to go further. They were intent on stifling a claim that could only be postponed, and to extract from victory more than it could deliver. Can you tell me now where that reactionary France is to be found, and whether it might not have been better advised to respect the rights of the vanquished than overstating its claims and trespassing against its own liberty?[18]

To cut a long story short, by being the measure of force, and sanctifying the coronation of the stronger and the subordination of the weaker, war's lawmaking is final. Everything that can guarantee that the contest is above board and honourable, and force's successes legitimate, is a duty of war; anything that might be a contravention, pervert the victory, give the defeated cause to protest, generate poisonous resentments, etc., is prohibited. That honour code of war is designed to regulate its detailed application.

In warfare, as in the Olympic Games or the tournaments of the Middle Ages, there are some things that honour and justice command the combatants to eschew. Someone who bites his opponent's arm in order to break free of a hold is hounded out of the arena; the duellist who attacks his opponent from behind before the latter is on guard, is held to be a murderer. The same goes for war. If war were only a hunting-down of evildoers and pirates, one could envision the gendarmes dispatched to deal with them resorting to anything – steel and fire, violence and trickery – to crush them. But this is a hard-working, peaceful populace subject to the courts that we are revolutionising; this

---

17. The Saint Bartholomew Day Massacre (24th August 1572) began as a Catholic-led series of political assassinations, that turned into mob violence and the massacre of thousands of Huguenots in Paris and across France. [A.P.]

18. For more on the revolution of 1789 and 1848, see Proudhon's *Confessions of a Revolutionary* (1849), excerpted in McKay, ed., *Property is Theft!*, 395–477. [A.P.]

is a political power that any other power may be equally entitled, in a specific instance, to subject to its rules, but which has a corresponding entitlement to resist such subjection and counter force with force. The argument, in such a dispute, that all means are permitted, as long as they succeed, is yet another instance of the natures of things being misconstrued and a lie uttered to the conscience of the human race.

Yes, war, like any prosecution or judicial action, is subject to rules; it has its conventions, outside of which anything that occurs between the combatants can be deemed non-binding; in short, there is a righteousness to it. The entire military practice of nations bears witness to this; there is no notion as familiar to us as that of *conventional warfare*, no expression more frequently invoked among publicists. So that the real issue is no longer whether warlike activity should or should not be governed by rules, but whether the widely accepted rules, which civilized peoples unanimously flatter themselves that they abide by, are what they ought to be, which is to say, if they speak to the principle of war and to its purpose.

Here I cannot help raising once again and with added energy the wrongheadedness of the authors. Since they deny the right of force as a matter of principle, and consequently regard all acts of war as judicially vacuous, how can they welcome its code? How can they subscribe to such laws? How can they offer them their support? Repudiating the ordeal or trial by combat,[19] Grotius wastes no time discussing its rules; the very same condemnation applicable to the act extends to its conventions as well. Why is this not the practice with regard to warfare? Having lamented war as by nature anti-juridical, what sort of connivance allows him to countenance, in the name of right, the so-called lawful procedures and practices that, in most cases, are the most odious things that blind rage and barbarism can devise?

According to Grotius, and all the writers on this subject, not only does warfare authorize wounding and killing, which is an inevitable consequence of combat, but *murder* as well; it countenances *poisoning*; countenances the *putting of entire populations to the sword*, regardless of age or sex; countenances their *transportation*; countenances *looting, arson and destruction*; countenances *rape*; countenances *enslavement*; countenances the *slaughter of captives*; countenances *pillage, ransom, dispossession and confiscation*; countenances grave-robbing. All of it done, they say, and we shall furnish proof of this, as part of the right of warfare. No army has ever been held to account for it; and to this day, as we shall see, this is what goes by the name of conventional warfare.

---

19. GROTIUS, *De Juri Belli ac Pacis*, Book III, ch. IV. [H.M.]

I know that the authors urge clemency upon the army commanders with all the force at their command, also that the progress in mores has to some extent softened these rigours of the alleged laws of warfare in practical terms, and that it has become military custom to refrain from all *needless* cruelty and devastation. But the case for UTILITY stands. In war, every person, from common soldier up to commander-in-chief, is the only interpreter of utility, within the parameters of his activity. One can but guess what utility amounts to in the eyes of an armed man, in the heat of battle, to whom the lives of his fellow-men have become trifles, and who can see danger on every side. No matter how safe he may feel, he is going to kill, burn and loot; and there will be utility, indeed, a necessity in all this.

Therefore, war is not, as Virgil had it, just an outbreak of rage and hatred, a contest involving devastation and plunder, and wherein everything that the ordinary courts hold damnable becomes permissible.

Tum certare odiis, tum res, rapuisse licebit.[20]

As I say, warfare, which until now has seemed to us the most grandiose manifestation of righteousness, turns into the monster described by the poets, the Fury of destruction and carnage.

Oh! Were war merely what it purports to be, what it has always aspired to become: the recourse to force in a contest of force. None would more readily pay it tribute than myself. If only the jurists, enabled by serene research to retain more composure than the heat of battle allows the soldiery, had drawn this clear distinction between use and abuse in this contest of powers. If only we had been able to look to some sort of reform in this formidable exercise of armed force, then I confess, that far from the bloodshed's striking terror into me, I would see this mystery of death and justice as the last word in human happiness and would worship warfare as the sublimest manifestation of conscience, and would bow before the cannon's roar like the people of Israel before the voice of Jehovah.

Unfortunately, this is not how things are. In its operation, warfare is not such as its principle and purpose suppose it to be. The theory says white, the practice implements black; whilst the inclination is towards righteousness, the reality looks no further than extermination. Between the deed and the idea, not only is there an utter contradiction, but it looks to be beyond remedy. And so, it will be a tricky question to answer why, with the principles being so patently

---

20. "Then it will be lawful to vie in hate, then to ravage". *Virgil Aeneid (Vol II): Books 7–12. Appendix Vergiliana*, Translated by H. Rushton Fairclough. Revised by G. P. Goold (Cambridge. MA.: Harvard University Press 2001), 172–73. [A.P.]

obvious, with the jurists' arguments, the honour code of the warriors, the conscience of the masses, the interests of the winners and losers alike, and with everyone finally being of the same mind, why it has not been possible to rid the
duelling between States of the horrors that besmirch it.

CHAPTER IV

The Critique of Military Operations and Tactics: An Examination of What Caused the Downfall of the First French Empire

The principles underpinning the following critique are:

1. War is the judgment of Force. – It only takes place between States for reasons with direct or indirect bearing on the political life of nations.

2. The manner in which this judgment is delivered consists of pitting forces or powers against one another. The verdict goes to the winner.

3. Force is not just physical, brawn; it is above all a moral thing. – As Napoleon used to say, in war, moral force is to physical force what 3 is to 1. Courage and all the spiritual faculties of citizens, as well as their bodily vigour, industry and wealth, are part and parcel of the State's force.

4. Therefore if there actually is a right of war, and surely no one could now query it, that right is primarily designed to regulate conflict, ensure that the fight is conducted fairly, and the victory legitimate, by bringing into play the full range of physical, intellectual and moral resources of the parties; by prohibiting treachery and fraud; by banning, on pain of steep punishments, all deeds that are an affront to ordinary morality. The man who marches off to do battle for the sake of his homeland has to rise above himself, not just in terms of his vim and bravery, but in terms of his virtue, and needs to well-nigh become a saint.

5. We should add, by way of an aside, that there is a tendency in every people to confine the contest to a sort of closed field, where force, courage and right also have their parts to play. In the case of the international disputes, which war is supposed to settle, there is almost always a battle, a day, such as at Jemmapes,

Zurich, Marengo, Austerlitz, Wagram, Leipzig or Waterloo,[21] that decides the fortunes of peoples, dynasties and governments. This is what might be described as the duel between nations. It is with an eye to ensuring success, whilst simultaneously curtailing the horrors, that populaces are of one mind in giving a wide berth to military operations: the duel is fought out between armies alone.

Having set out those principles, the first question that arises is this:

Is it a lawful war, such as the right of force intends, when it involves swordplay and scheming; attacking the enemy through recourse to ambush and ruse; splitting his forces by means of feinting manoeuvres, then swooping upon him unexpectedly and destroying him piecemeal; nullifying his resources by marauding through his territory, putting his homes and stores to the torch and capturing his vessels; finally, substituting, insofar as one can, cunning for force, expertise in arms for courage, group manoeuvres for numbers and mass support. We are right to be surprised by this, and it is not the least of the contradictions we will have to identify in military operations. War is the claim to and exercise of the right of force, and it appears, from the behaviour it entails, that its sole purpose is to frustrate force, thwart its triumph and undermine its reason.

Lest anyone accuse *me* of resorting to ambush, let me caution the reader that the discussion into which I mean to enter is designed to achieve nothing less than a complete renewal of strategy and tactics, by claiming on behalf of the right of force and for the sake of the honour of arms themselves, that a more precise distinction needs to be made between things that are legitimate in warfare and those that should be held to be illicit, and that, thereafter, operations should be determined by legislation. Such distinctions and determinations are not easily made, I will concede, but when were distinctions ever easy? Whoever draws a distinction sets out a definition. Logic dictates that every definition comes with a caveat, *omnis definitio periculosa*.[22] In which regard, war is no worse served than right, philosophy, natural history and all the sciences. Far from the warrior losing patience with these precautions, his self-respect should glory in them.

So, I return to my query: According to the law of war, what should the overall rule be where tactics are concerned? To what extent can guile be substituted for force, and ought one to countenance surprise attacks and ruses?

At first glance, it would seem that because war is the verdict of force, everything that strays from the pathways of sheer force ought to be discounted. But the question is more complex than it might seem. In a State, collective power

---

21. Jemmapes (1792), Zurich (1799), Marengo (1800), Austerlitz (1805), Wagram (1809), all French victories, Leipzig (1813), Waterloo (1815), the major defeats that led to the downfall of Napoleon I. [H.T.]

22. "Every definition is dangerous". [A.P.]

[*puissance*] and intelligence also count as a force; industry and art are forces too. Unless exempted from military service, the way churchmen, teachers and magistrates are, such forces ought to have their part to play in war. Removing the legitimate means of triumphing through use of the moral and intellectual faculties is not just impossible but would be a nonsense, whether the alacrity and the steadiness of glance, sangfroid, vigilance, mental agility, rapidity of movement, application of the processes of art and industry, the appliance of science. Anyone incapable of self-protection, mobilization, turning things to his advantage, gathering together his resources, or who, in an age of high civilization would like to revert to sling and club, such a person would be undeserving of victory, and all the more unworthy of it in that the purpose of victory is sovereignty and the verdict of force was not, it would appear, established so that brutes might be assured of power. Once battle ends, intelligence recoups its rights; force prevails but the spirit rules.

This is the sense in which we have to understand the argument that the ancients used to make for war-time ruses and stratagems. Subject to the almost exclusive imperium of force, as they were when the sciences and arts were in their infancy, they were all the more appreciative of the price of intelligence, and in war-time it was primarily by their wits that they lived. In their simplicity, they mistook for wits, science and high reasoning what was merely guile, nicety and deceit. It even looks as if the victories they counted most glorious were those scored by means of stratagem and with as little exertion as possible. But, in war as in peace, humanity has moved on; tactics and strategy, having become sciences, have abrogated these *old ploys of war*. Cleverness is no longer displayed in wild cunning, but rather in the gauging of strength, time, speed and man-power; through anticipation, the art of governing men, stirring them up, mobilizing them and extracting every last drop of energy from them. Today's army commander smiles at the ancient heroes' sleight of hand; if he knew that that was the best idea he could come up with, he would feel lost.

In accordance with such considerations, one wonders, therefore, to what extent and in what capacity guile can play its part in trials of force, and whether the skill and dexterity deployed in warfare might extend as far as those snares and traps readily deployed against miscreants and wild beasts, but shunned by the old codes of chivalry and which we are loath to see used against honest foes?

An important part of the art of warfare, according to the authors, consists of these two operations that are the very opposite of each other: surprising the enemy and evading him. In this regard, the manoeuvres of the army commander are merely a more or less permissible and well-understood extrapolation from the moves of swordsmanship. The teachers of the military arts say: "The most successful moves, the ones that secure the weightiest and most telling outcomes, are those the knowledge and mechanics of which have been withheld from the enemy". What Napoleon used to term *catching red-handed.*

Red-handed doing what? Halting, bivouacking, mounting a flanking movement or on parade, mustering or fanning out? Vigilance is, to be sure, vital in warfare; whilst a general can be forgiven for having got lost, his letting himself be caught napping is unforgivable. But do not over-rely on tactics, take care not to walk into an ambush, because, as we will have to point out on more than one occasion, thus fall the vainglorious. Under the duelling code and the notion of warfare, strictly speaking, right demands each stands *en garde.* With both sides on guard, they clash with all their might. I am not going to go that far: that would be lapsing into a different abuse out of undue politeness. Telling the enemy, as the French did at Fontenoy, *You English gentlemen may fire the opening shots,* would be bravado for which a general today would have to answer before a court martial.

But would the opposite be any less abnormal? Attacking without warning, from behind and under cover of darkness; cutting the enemy's throat while he sleeps, torching him in his camp, crushing him as he scatters, overwhelming him by superior force of arms. Since Homer, that has indeed been deemed sound warfare, the great secret behind victory. Being outdone in terms of man-power or materials, and perhaps even courage, and evading certain defeat, resorting to ruse or trickery to crush an enemy, who is on every count superior, will make the victory that much sweeter. But it turns on its head any notion of a contest of forces and consequently of deciding by force of arms.

I can just hear the outcry: war is not a tournament and treating it like a matter of honour would be over-stating its morality! It is an engagement between two States, in which each State is fighting for its territory, its independence or its supremacy, it might be that even its very existence is at stake. *Destroy me or I shall destroy you*; that is the warrior's watchword. In such a situation, the law of public safety prescribes that there can be no compromise with the enemy: *Dolus, an virtus, quis in hoste requirat?* as the poet has it.[23]

Let us not fall back on hackneyed, rambling disquisitions. Is war really just a matter of uncovering a gang of marauders, of fending off a pirate raid? Let the gendarmerie, the city guards and the whole populace do their best; there's no need to step outside of the provisions of the code of criminal prosecution. But is there an equivalence between an assault on individuals and their property and undeclared warfare between two sovereign powers, prompted by some political motive? Therein lies the crux of the matter.

If, on the one hand, warfare is anything more than an act of banditry, or, on

---

23. Virgil *Aeneid*, op. cit., Book 2. §390, "whether this is deceit or valour, who would ask in warfare?" [A.P.]

the other, the hunting-down of miscreants, there are laws to warfare and, after everything we have seen, there cannot be the slightest doubt about this.[24] This is a point that ought to have been established once and for all by now and it would be childish to revisit it. So, let us press on.

If there are laws to warfare, those laws, according to the nature and purpose of the war, exclude all actions typical either of banditry or the prosecution of guilty parties, not to mention the hunting down of wild animals. We ought to be as certain about this second point as we are about the first and should cling forcefully to it.

There is a third proposition demonstrated by reason and attested to by history: the laws of war permit no infringement. If the contraventions made are too trivial to tip the battle one way or the other, they counterbalance one another and the victory acquires the validity of a definitive verdict. If, on the other hand, victory has been secured by fraud or contrivance, by which I mean in defiance of the reason of force, it remains ineffective. Sooner or later, a counterfeit victory is rendered null and void.

In light of these considerations, we have nothing further to add and every objection crumbles. The only position we can take is to acknowledge in good faith that, if licentiousness, deceit and all manner of contrivance are to be ruthlessly excluded from anywhere, it is above all in military operations. So, under the rules of combat [*droit guerrier*], what are the rules governing the tactics of war? That is the question I pose.

In order to persuade the reader that, contrary to widespread opinion, it is primarily physical and moral force that should emerge victorious in war; that the skills of the tactician and strategist should be only secondary considerations, and then only as guide-lines for force; and more especially, that any sort of trickery and sophistry should be painstakingly kept out of it, lest it render the victory null and void, let me take the example of a captain rarely accused of irregularity in his operations, but who took strategy and tactics to such a high degree of precision as to invest them with such a character of intellectuality that, when faced by him, the enemy forces had their value halved and the enemy generals were beaten before they had so much as fired a single cannon-shot. That captain was Napoleon.

General Jomini, after having, with soldierly admiration, recounted the Italian campaign of 1796–1797, and been brought back down to earth by the context in which he was writing, lets this admission slip:

---

24. It should be clear that Proudhon is not referring to positive or scientific laws, but social ones. *Lois de la guerre* or *formes de la guerre* could also be translated as military *norms*. [A.P.]

GENERAL CAUSES decide the fates of empires and endow victories with their more or less important outcomes.[25]

General causes – did you get that? – dominate the science of strategy and endow its victories with their true outcome by confirming or rendering them null and void. And what are those general causes against which victory itself is powerless?

In addition to pointing out how the celebrated Austrian campaign was, from start to finish, a mockery of the law of force, due more to the enemy generals than to any skill on the part of General Bonaparte, the general-turned-historian discloses to us, first, how the Austrians, impelled by necessity or lack of foresight, split up into a host of small corps and were destroyed piecemeal in spite of their superior force, by a foe who was sprightlier and still marshalled together. He then demonstrates how, when the armies involved were of equal strength, the outcomes were, as we saw in Arcola, unremarkable. Where the Austrians had strength of numbers, the victory went to them, as it did in the battles of Salò and La Corona. He demonstrates how, in numerous circumstances, the fortunes of Bonaparte and his army were down to chance, to a mistake by the enemy, Austrian good-naturedness, to General Bonaparte's cunning, if I may use that word, and how, at Rivoli a ten-minute delay might have denied the latter the most splendid and most telling of victories. He shows us how these wonderful victories, in which the fighting man's skill and cunning played a greater part than actual force, brought only precarious conquest; how, from the very next year, 1796, the Italy we had conquered with an inferior force was slipping away from us, leading by 1800 to a brand-new Italian campaign and to another one on the Rhine; how, in order to consolidate a questionable dominance, Napoleon was dragged, by other

---

25. JOMINI, *Histoire critique et militaire des guerres de la Révolution,* édition de 1842, t III, 91 n. 2. On Jomini, a military author, see SAINTE-BEUVE, *Nouveaux lundis, vol.* XIII, 1–182 [H.M.]

HENRI JOMINI (1779–1869) A Swiss national who initially fought alongside the French before offering his services to the emperor of Russia after Berthier had denied him a general's rank. From 1804, he devoted himself to the study of the art of warfare. The book cited by Proudhon was published after the peace in 1815. [H.T.]

Jomini argued that the key to military success was focusing all of one's attack or fusillade on one precisely determinable geometric point. He drew this conclusion from his experiences of Napoleon's campaigns, the advances of utilitarian reason and Newtonian physics, and in anticipation of the perfectibility of artillery and of military manoeuvres. He was arguably the first military positivist. For an excellent collection of essays on most of the strategists discussed by Proudhon, see Peter Paret, Gordon A. Craig and Felix Gilbert, (eds.) *Makers of Modern Strategy: From Machiavelli to the Present* (Princeton: Princeton University Press, 1986). [A.P.]

conquests of the same sort, into further over-extending himself; how, in the end, this great captain, further misconstruing the true principles of warfare and the law of force, and having gathered half of Europe into his Empire by means of ill-advised annexations, succumbed under an avalanche of these counter forces, leaving France smaller after his downfall than she had been when he took over.

Certainly, Bonaparte had grounds for fighting the way he fought Beaulieu, Wurmser and Alvinzy,[26] since they left him open to it. Not that I am reproaching the French general for his victories. But I do say that, given the manner of his winning them, they could not have had the implications he credited them with.

I recognize all the wonderous heroism in Bonaparte's first campaign. I will go further and state that victory went to the righteous cause. God forbid that I should deny the righteousness of the revolution! I will even add, confining myself to pure considerations of war, that the Austrian generals, with their sluggishness, their presumption, and their pedestrian minds, did not deserve to win and that, like every reader who read the accounts of these battles, I have always felt the delight one feels at the sight of stupidity punished and pride humbled. But is it any less the case that in that first Italian campaign, the victory was not exactly to force, and so, as a result, the conquest was unsound? Consequently, might we venture that this brilliant debut by the Republic's youngest general cast a spell that later brought about the Emperor's downfall.

Antiquity furnishes us with an example which is comparable to that of Napoleon in many regards: the example of Hannibal.

Just ponder what Rome and Carthage were at the outset of the Second Punic War. Either I am gravely mistaken or it will be acknowledged that Rome had the greater force. In Carthage, there were major figures but no soldiers. The army with which Hannibal invaded Italy was made up of Numidians, Spaniards, Gauls, allies who had defected from the Roman side, but very few Carthaginians. Certainly not the hallmark of a great national power. The quality of these rag-bag soldiers also fell notably short in comparison to the calibre of the Roman soldier. Finally, Rome still enjoyed a numerical advantage. It seemed, for all intents and purposes, as if Hannibal entered Italy only in order to meet his end there. However, thanks to the dexterity of his tactics,

---

26. JEAN-PIERRE, BARON DE BEAULIEU (1725–1819), commander-in-chief of the Austrian army in Italy, defeated by Bonaparte in 1796. DAGOBERT-SIGISMOND WURMSER (1724–1797), a native of Strasbourg, he initially served in the French army (1745–1797) before becoming an Austrian general. He was beaten by Bonaparte in Mantua in 1797. JOSEPH, BARON D'ALVINZY (1735–1810), Austrian field-marshal beaten by Napoleon at Hondschoote (1793), Arcola (1796) and Rivoli (1797). He went on to become governor of Hungary in 1798. [H.T.]

his wonderful actions and thanks to the ineptitude of the Roman generals, Sempronius, Flaminius and Varro, he pulled off four huge victories in Ticino, in Trebbia, near Lake Trasimene and in Cannae, and for seventeen years, without fresh man-power or money, he held out in Italy. Rome was thereby punished for the incompetence of her leaders and the poor electoral choices of her plebs. But force was on Rome's side nevertheless. This was evident, first of all, in her containing Hannibal for a year, after the defeat at Trasimene, under the supervision of Fabius Cunctator; then, following the disaster at Cannae, when Hannibal did not even trouble to lay siege to the town; and later, with the whole world raised against her by Carthage, Rome still waged war in Spain, in Italy, in Sicily and everywhere, and ended by taking it to Africa. It was obvious then what real force meant, no matter how unintelligently it might have been handled. Hannibal, though in Italy and with those four mighty victories under his belt, had failed to bring Rome to her knees; a single battle, won by Scipio the Younger against Hannibal in Zama, broke Carthage and decided the fate of the whole of Africa. Outdone in that battle, Hannibal and his motley crew of foreigners could not forever withstand the onslaught of Rome's legions, unfortunately for his homeland.

These observations regarding the determinants of the contest between States, and the factors that brought about the downfall of the first empire, are of such importance that I cannot but dwell upon them a little longer.

We have just seen General Jomini vouchsafing to us, in just a few lines, the secret and philosophy of the imperial epic, albeit not realizing the import of his words. As if seeking to appeal the verdict of force ultimately brought against Napoleon, Monsieur Thiers, however, rejects Jomini's explanation. He points an accusing finger at the Emperor's bad policy, his overblown desires, the exorbitance of his genius, his misuse of the blessings of fortune: he invokes all the commonplaces of academic morality reinvigorated by the Greeks, whereas he has nothing but plaudits for his hero's strategic plans.

Strange as it may sound, whenever I read this otherwise so absorbing *Histoire du Consulat et de l'Empire,*[27] where everything is illogically lauded

---

27. ADOLPHE THIERS (1797–1877) published a ten-volume *Histoire de la Révolution* (1824–1827). In January 1830 he launched the newspaper *National*, which opposed Charles X's absolutism and leaned towards the Duc d'Orléans. He was, therefore, one of the leading lights of the regime once the Duc mounted the throne as Louis-Philippe following the July Revolution. In 1848 he became the leader of the Party of Order, opposed to socialism and was Proudhon's chief foe in the National Assembly. In 1870, he was against the war with Prussia that was to lead to the downfall of Napoleon III. In February 1871, he went on to head the executive of the French Republic, signed the terms of a peace agreement with Prussia and then crushed the Paris Commune in a bloodbath. His nineteen-volume *Histoire du Consulat et de l'Empire*, dates from 1855. [H.T.]

and blamed, I am tempted to plead the case for the first Napoleon. Given the war machine Bonaparte had inherited from his predecessors, and which it fell to him in turn to perfect, plus the Revolution as a general cause of war, the Emperor pursued his policy out of necessity. In that regard, I dare say that the statesman in Napoleon was less open to reproach than the general. Having become the sword of modernity, the promise of global imperium and, whenever he looked at his adversaries, quite possibly thinking himself invincible, Napoleon had to press ever onwards, even though he had no idea where he was headed. His policies ought to have followed his tactics, rather than his tactics being subordinated to his policies. There were two forces driving him on and which he was unable to resist: on the one hand, the thrust of revolution and, on the other, the superiority of his weaponry. This was what he understood with sovereign intelligence, and which he espoused for a time with unprecedented success. But his successes misled him. In the end, he was doomed, not that his reasoning was mistaken, but because his starting-point, war, conceived and prosecuted in a certain way, was wrong-headed and all the more so in that, by propagating the revolutionary idea so vigorously, he ought to have expected to deal with it himself one day.

Talk of the ambition of this man and the fire in his imagination is a Seneca-style criticism. In his policies, all Napoleon ever did was live up to the situation foisted upon him by war. He would have been unwavering had his conquests come somewhat more slowly, had he imposed different conditions on the vanquished or had he waged a different sort of war. This is what Monsieur Thiers could never see; he marvels at the unexpected turns of events, prostrates himself before these victories that leave historians, readers and soldiers breathless; he fails to understand that warfare, being a faculty of humanity, does not conjure anything up in the twinkling of an eye and, like vegetation and life itself, needs time to complete its handiwork.

So, let me say again: the real snare in which Napoleon was caught was the tactics in which he displayed such brilliance, in which he was so lucky. His genius routed, so to speak, the forces of the enemy, much more so than his might triumphed over them. His rivals barely had time to see themselves beaten and could not explain their defeat. But, not able or not daring to annex every one of the beaten States to the Empire, and obliged, as the victor to exploit his victory, lest he be seen to walk away from his own success, he tried curtailing the enemy's force by just bringing them to heel, which was the worst possible arrangement. There is no middle ground here: a State is either independent or it is not. Napoleon realized this in the end, when, returning from Russia, he watched as his supposed vassals defected one after another and turned against him. But this was no failing of his, whatever anyone says: the blame lay with a ' war that trapped him in this middle-of-the-road policy. Too much and too often, he substituted speed for man-power, inspiration for force and the intensity of his action for time. This was the delusion in his life, a delusion so strong that it seduced his contemporaries and all his comrades in arms and continues to seduce the historians to this very day. But it is a quite phantasmagorical thing. Do you want the full truth about Napoleon? The point is not to exaggerate the man nor to underplay the hero; just turn the evaluation of his historian and admirer, Monsieur Thiers, on its head.

When all is said and done, what was it that brought about the Emperor's downfall? It was, as General Jomini puts it, that he ran out of force when confronted by the growing power of his enemies. And how, having overcome all the powers in Europe, one after the other, and expanded his empire with their spoils, had he run out of force? That seems contradictory. The reason was this: on the one hand, the Emperor's victories were due much less to his superior forces than to his tactical superiority. As a consequence of Napoleon's conquests having been accomplished with such wonderful skill but (why not admit it?) in contravention of the right of force, those States withstood incorporation that much better. So that after having, as he reckoned it, defeated and conquered Europe, he found Europe raged against him. There lies the mystery, and all of Monsieur Thiers's temperate morality and middle-of-the-road political musings signify absolutely nothing.

Napoleon is wronged by talk of his talent as a tactician and strategist, when this gift can be used as the basis for belittling his policy and, we might add, his heroism. If ever a man was born to mobilize the masses of humanity, fill the soldiery with enthusiasm and lead them into contests of force, without looking to ruse and artifice, it was assuredly him. His selfless and authentic warrior soul pervades his proclamations. His times and his education made him something else; he was their victim. The art of warfare never brought forth such a virtuoso; and never was one so blessed with victory as humbled by force. Examined in this light, the career of Napoleon I assumes a different aspect; at the sight of the great captain misled by a false science, one feels greater sympathy for him. As to his policies, it could be no more: a feat of genius applied to a problem, the particulars of which made it insoluble.

Napoleon's masterpiece was the French campaign of 1814. In sixty-one days, between 29th January and 30th March, eighteen battles were fought by Napoleon in person, and by his generals, not to mention the fortuitous incidents thrown in the mix. According to the historians, Napoleon never displayed more genius, activity and blessed audacity; never had he earned so many and such bloody laurels in a shorter span of time. And yet that marvellous campaign ended with the fall of the capital, the downfall of the Emperor and his abdication! Turn your gaze on the allies; they had never been so frequently, so utterly beaten; the fortunes of their arms had never gone so badly against them; under attack from such weak forces, they had never lost so many men. And the result of all these defeats was to bring them to the foot of the [Vendôme] Column as victors, to make them arbiters of France's fate and allow them to change her dynasty and government and restore her boundaries to where they had been prior to the invasion of 1792.

The reason behind all these seemingly contradictory things is straightforward and accessible to every intelligence, and is a wonderful confirmation of our principles. It was not, as Monsieur Thiers would have us believe, following the tragic poets, a whim of fate. For a start, it takes a force far superior to that needed to overwhelm an army on the field of battle to crush a nation. And France was under attack on her home territory. Secondly, if that superior force exists, tactical resourcefulness is pointless and sooner or later the invaded nation is going to have to confront the invading hordes. Deploying overwhelming force will reverse any partial setbacks at a stroke. Up until the capture of Soissons, the allies resembled hounds attacking a tiger in the thicket, tentatively marching through hostile territory, arriving by a variety of routes because they were forced to split up. The Emperor had all the positional advantages: he was invisible and forever swooping unexpectedly on his separated foes, dealing out murderous blows left and right, from the front and from the rear. But once the allied armies finally joined up, the formidable commander did not dare come to grips with them again; he had to resign himself to taking a last stand, hoping to lure them back onto his terrifying chessboard and, in so doing, he delivered the capital to them. All his trophies were annihilated; it was hopeless, needless bloodshed.

Faced with this startling validation of the rational laws of warfare, and the powerlessness of the art of guile to compensate entirely for force, we might argue that if intelligence and the full spectrum of the moral faculties of a people have their parts to play in warfare, they can only be as directors of force and not at all as substitutes for it. As a result, we should not put our trust in quick victories, easy conquests or makeshift annexations. All violence that strays from the character of a generous struggle, and anything that substitutes the horrors of unresisted extermination and the carnage of ambush for a proper duel between the warring parties, deserves to be condemned.

Consequently, what are the definitions and rules that, at first glance need to be imposed upon warring people, especially their officers and tacticians? That is a task I surrender to the experience of military men, cautioning them here and now that if they do not come up with a way of reforming warfare, then this is the end of the noble profession of arms. As for myself, I reckon I am all the more entitled to deny any competence here since, as we shall see later, I conclude, not with a reformation of warfare, but with its transformation, which is a quite different matter.

CHAPTER V

The Critique of Military Operations: On the Destruction of the Enemy's Resources. On Marauding, Seizures, Levies and Hirelings

War has, to date, been conducted randomly because it lacks a theory built on sound principles and precise definitions. Like government, family and property, it has imposed itself as a necessity, regarding which one may argue the pros and cons, but the higher reason and purpose of which none could fathom. Anything good and just that it has produced, it has produced thanks to the energy of its nature; the evil it has done is the handiwork of men's ignorance. Those who have sought to draw up the laws have been rather crude in their reasoning, basing them on analogies and approximations, occasionally invoking civil law or penal law, sometimes citing the logic of public safety or the voluntary rights of peoples and frequently looking to charity for assistance. No one has succeeded in discovering a governing principle, something holding it all together. There is also the most extreme discrepancy prevailing over the solutions proposed, and if one wanted to cite an example of the jumble of ideas of which the human understanding is capable, one need only cite the authors who have written on the rights of war.

There is significant distance between thinking about warfare as lawful combat in which the contending forces should be confronting and defeating one another, rather than destroying one another, and the first and foremost theory of military men, which is to wage war for destruction. Even if they do not wage war solely for destruction's sake, it nevertheless seems to them that destruction is indeed the condition and method of warfare, and in their eyes the most frightful acts of devastation are permitted. Turenne was once reproached, in the presence of General Bonaparte, for razing the German Palatinate. The young warrior's response was: "Turenne was quite within his rights if he reckoned that action to be of service to the accomplishment of his plans".

Turenne had indeed been operating on the basis of the right of war as spelled out by the writers on this subject. What they excoriated was not devastation per se, but *useless* devastation. But how are we to identify the utility of such rigour? How far does utility stretch? About that, not a word. It will be up to the general to decide. So land is laid waste, crops burned, vines and fruit trees cut down, forests cleared, towns and villages put to the torch and no mercy is shown either to age or sex, even the livestock is slaughtered. A certain colonel in Africa[28] once smoked out six hundred Arab men, women, children and the elderly who had retreated into a cave with their livestock, with about as much thought as a pack of jackals. He was entitled to do so, you may say, if he reckoned that he needed to make an example of them and by reason of reprisal. As always, we have the same argument of "utility". Not that I am accusing that colonel who, I have no doubt, was acting conscientiously. But I wonder if that is the spirit of warfare.

Striking terror, Grotius said,[29] is war's entitlement; wiping out a population is a very sad thing, but it may be permissible if it seems vital for the security of the army. During his first expedition to Italy, Bonaparte resorted to the rigours of this ancient code on more than one occasion, and General Jomini, whose sense of humanity bridles at the sight of these shootings, nevertheless forgives them on the grounds that for a general his army's security is the over-arching law. But, without going back over what was said in the previous chapter (that Bonaparte with his 33,000-strong force was not there in strength and that his victories, gained primarily through tactics, could not be enforced on the Italians), let me retort here that the army's own security was no excuse for such excesses. Warfare, like duelling, is a contest between courage and strength, and leaving behind a trail of innocents has nothing to do with the struggle. On this score there is plainly something missing in the thinking of the jurist as well as of the warrior. Please, no more talk of the right of war; it amounts to nothing more than savage raging against savage; it has nothing to do with either politics, justice or force.

With two armies in the field about to join in battle, I can well understand how a few homes or a clump of trees might be torn down, a ditch filled in and impediments hampering the fight cleared away: the destruction here is carried out with an eye to battle. The justice of war directs it. But when the devastation is huge and has no purpose other than the enemy's ruination, I cannot countenance it, even if it were a reprisal. That is not war; it is savagery.

Here I seek, with some entitlement, a definition of useful and useless destruction in war. I have set down the principle, being the right of force; I now

28. In June 1815, Colonel Pélissier had cornered the Ouled-Ria in the Dahra caves where almost six hundred of them were asphyxiated. [H.M.]

29. GROTIUS: "Violence and terror are the very stock-in-trade of wars," *De Juri Belli ac Pacis*, Book III, chap. I, § 6. [H.M.]

await the rule. Note that we do so also with regard to those whose inconsistency of practice we criticize.

Because of the right of war and certain more or less formal arrangements between States, regular armies expect to engage with corps of regulars like themselves when they enter the enemy homeland. Anyone taking part in war without a uniform, without a superior officer, is shot as a brigand. I applaud that policy, the meaning of which is not in doubt and which represents a step along the road to the genuine right of war. But, then, let the armies themselves deploy as corps; let them show respect for homes, persons and property; let them fall back on their own resources in the meeting of their needs; stop referring to the principle that in war-time armies are entitled to subsist at the population's expense, and let there be no further tolerance of swarms of marauders roaming the countryside and foraging, looting and demanding ransom for their own gain and engaging in arbitrary requisitioning, following the example set by the generals.

In the war in Spain in 1808, the Spaniards, having grown rusty in the profession of arms, and incapable of standing in a line and carrying out manoeuvres, fell like sheep before the French armies. Unable to defend themselves *en masse* against the hoards, they resorted to forming guerrilla bands and set about ambush warfare in which 500,000 French lives were lost. The latter, ashamed of the role in which they had been cast, but obliged by their military oath to do their duty, were not slow to find such partisan warfare as ferocious as it was craven; any time they could get their hands on guerrillas, they strung them up. Anyone suspected was executed. The *right of reprisals*, the authors say. But, please, from whom did the initial trespass come? Was it not those who, surprising the Spanish nation in *flagrante delicto*, unarmed and trusting, betrayed its hospitality and then invited that outraged nation to join in unequal, derisory battles? In short, had it not come from the soldiers from Austerlitz and Friedland? On Saint Helena, Napoleon gave the Spaniards credit. "They wanted no part of me, and I have nothing more to say".[30] Not that that was enough. The political considerations that triggered the war in Spain might have been unanswerable, except that the manner in which that war was fought would still be odious. After his three campaigns, in 1805, 1806 and 1807, had Napoleon grown so weary of winning as to mount such an under-handed attack upon a friendly and unarmed nation?

When it comes to marauders, the military raise objections. They say: "*War should be self-sustaining*". That is a professional motto, an article from the old rights of peoples, which nobody queries. The Romans, scrupulous where

---

30. Mémorial de Sainte-Hélène, Monday, 6 May, 1816. [H.M.]

stratagems were at stake, were shameless in putting this maxim into effect. Its reciprocity banished any hint of irregularity.

Let me observe, first of all, that on this score, the military authors do not see eye to eye.

> Before the Revolutionary wars, we were so convinced of this truth (that marauding is a scourge upon discipline and a blight upon armies) that by common accord the practice had been for armies to be fed out of their own storehouses; that, as a result, their marches kept pace with the movements of the ovens, and any swift manoeuvre was prohibited because the bread supply could not keep pace. The French armies that survived on requisitions and which trusted for their subsistence to the fertility of the territories into which they were bringing warfare, scored startling successes against such methodical warriors. From which it was inferred that setting up storehouses was redundant and that, to borrow Napoleon's dictum, *war should be self-sustaining*.[31]

One of the consequences of this observation would have been to reduce the rewards of success. This was one of the main factors in the defeats sustained by Marshal Wurmser in 1797, and by Monsieur de Kray in 1800, etc.[32] These hapless generals' chances of victory were that much more curtailed by the fact that, as they were fighting on home ground, they had to manage their allied or subject countrymen, the spoliation of whom was becoming another weapon in the enemy's arsenal.

But the author whom I am quoting adds that this arrangement is subject to terrible difficulties.

> It cost the French armies twice as many men in the barren countryside of Spain as in formal battles, because in order to survive they were forced to disperse across vast areas, which prohibited their coming together when needed, and delivered them up, impotent, to enemy bands.

The observation is well made. In warfare, in the contest of forces, marauding is ultimately more of a nuisance than useful. Well and good. But we are interested in right, and the author I cite does not say that this well-founded consideration of interest has made the nations of Europe wash their hands of this odious

---

31. LAURILLARD-FALLOT, *Cours d'art militaire*, Vol. I, 33. [P-J.P.]

32. PAUL DE KRAY DE KARJOWA (1735–1804), the Hungarian general commanding the army in Germany in 1800. He was forced to retreat when faced with Moreau and was dismissed. [H.T.]

practice. It remains part of the current code that anything that has a contribution to make to the enemy's *ruination* is permissible. Nor has it been abandoned by the strategists who, whilst wary of it, reserve their right to have recourse to it on occasion. To quote their despicable maxim, it is not the purpose of warfare to assert the rights of the stronger for the least outlay, as the right of force would have it, but, where possible, to substitute the lesser force for the greater. Because it is imbued with this way of thinking, Napoleon boiled down the art of warfare to this laconic dictum: *Split up for survival and muster for battle.* It accounts for his successes and his setbacks.

Where is the law, the real law of war, here? That is what I ask the jurists, if the military cannot come up with an answer. In order to make things easier for the pedants, let us lay down a few ground-rules.

The material expression of war's purpose is conquest, meaning conquest of the defeated country or a portion thereof, which falls under the rule of the winner. In that purely political sense, it is true to say that the enemy's territory, his towns, fortresses, warehouses and everything that goes to make up its political and military force, is transferred to whichever power has achieved victory through force. Everything, therefore, is up for grabs; and, since the nation stands by its government, it could be argued that the winner has, following victory, an entitlement not only to seize the revenues of the invaded State, but to add on a surcharge, by way of recovery of outlay and compensation. Thus far, I cannot see anything not authorized by the right of force.

But the expropriation of private individuals, the looting of homes, the stripping of churches, museums, is all that fair warfare? I can understand the seizure of items serving the purposes of war: but does that involve the stealing and impounding of individuals' effects and livestock? I will confess to tolerating foraging for horse-feed; but is it to be taken to the lengths of sustaining men?

We see how the rehabilitation of the right of force and, I might even say, the restoration of the principle and dignity of war might bring a new aspect to our analysis. It is not pointless sensitivity that prompts me to make these criticisms, much less a lament for so much lost wealth. It is the loftiest feeling for military honour, the truest and weightiest idea of right.

To the military I say:

You may strip a nation of its independence, dismantle its collectivity, change its institutions, move its capital and declare its dynasty deposed. You can install a garrison in its squares, ensconce yourself in its ports, absorb its soldiers into your regiments, absorb its budget into your own country's budget, in short, assume all of the prerogatives of sovereignty. But you cannot strike out at a single one of its citizens – except in the case of common-law criminality or on the battlefield – for the duration of the battle. You may not live at the expense of those over whom you have made yourselves masters; you may not require the slightest service of them without payment. Such is the right of war. You are the magistrates of force; beware, for if you misuse that force, you are nothing but corrupt officials.

But such is the spirit in which armies have been imbued, since time immemorial, that I fear that nothing can long wrest them back from their nonsensical and dishonourable practices. There is no point saying that marauding and requisitioning arrangements endow warfare with a character of banditry that cannot be squared with civilization, politics or the very notion of war. Still less is it worth pointing out the travesty of turning the exercise of force into the pursuit of plunder, with the advantage going to the greatest cowards and scoundrels. The response comes: What you say is fair; but *war is as war does!* ... You note that armies have the greatest interest in refraining from practices that lead them to ruination through indiscipline. We can concede that, but would add that it all depends on the circumstances and above all on the purpose, which is victory.

Well, no, this is not how war should be waged as it is not the way to secure victories, by which I mean lasting victories that place an indestructible seal upon their gains. And if you need another reason, here is one that I have borrowed from the great captain and to which you will have no answer.

According to the combined rules of the right of force and the rights of peoples, the State that pursued either the annexation or the subordination of another neighbouring State ought not only to be the stronger, but sufficiently strong to force the opponent to submit. This suggests that the invader army, after having come all that way, should, for as long as the fighting lasts, survive on its own resources. Napoleon used to complain, and rightly so, about the English attempts to blockade ports by means of simple declaration. He argued that, according to the principles of warfare, for a blockade to be put in place, there had to be an army of occupation. The very same rule should hold true for a war of invasion. In its absence, there would be nothing to prevent a gang of adventurers swooping out of the blue upon a country, holding its towns and countryside to ransom and holding off from withdrawing until they can no longer hold their position.

It so happened in the most recent campaign in Italy, thanks to a very rare circumstance, that the warring powers had an equal interest in managing the occupied population: Austria, as their sovereign; France and Piedmont as liberators. Just suppose that the Lombards had behaved as Austria's loyal subjects: regardless of the fact that the allied army was by then deeply committed, would it be acceptable, under the right of war, for that army to have looted and oppressed a territory that it ought to have only annexed by force, which is to say, through recourse to its own resources and not by seizing the inhabitants' food stores? Endorsing would justify the depredations of Attila, Genghis Khan and all the barbarians who insolently styled themselves the *blacksmiths of nations*, the *scourge of God*, but whose short-lived conquests never actually put down roots; it would be tantamount to giving brigandry and piracy a letter of recommendation.

There is something even more condemnable than the devastating destruction of the enemy's material resources or the pillaging of his inhabitants, and that is the corruption of its officers and soldiers and the undermining of the constancy of its citizens. In 1809, as he set off for the Wagram campaign, Napoleon issued a proclamation to the Hungarians, urging them to switch sides and promising to reward them by re-establishing their national autonomy.[33] He was not in breach of the established law in so doing, and I would not dream of holding him up to reproach. Napoleon did the same thing in 1812 with the Poles, at the time of his Russian campaign.[34] The Hungarians did nothing and so at least could not whine about their recklessness nor the bad faith of their tempter. The Polish were not so reserved: they rose up *en masse* and it went off like a powder-keg. Then, whenever they asserted their claim to freedom, the conqueror's response was that he did not reckon them to be mature or well-organized enough to become a free people; in which he was certainly not mistaken. Six months after that, he himself was defeated.

This is all typical of underhanded warfare. Naturally, the loyalty of the populace to the government, like the soldiers to the flag, is numbered among the component parts of the force of States. It is only to be expected, therefore, for the one that displays less cohesiveness to surrender the upper hand to the other; but the populace must have their say; it is not for the aggressor to take the initiative in this.[35] Spreading treason through the subjects of the enemy State is

---

33. For the text of this proclamation, dated 15 May, 1809, see *Correspondance de Napoléon*, vol. XIX, 13. "Hungarian! The time has come to regain your independence ... I want nothing from you: I wish only that you find yourselves a free, independent nation. Your union with Austria has brought you misery ... Resume your existence as a nation". [H.M.]

34. Reply to the deputies from the Confederation of Poland. Vilna, July 1812. [H.M.]

35. It has been reported in the German press that out of every ten prisoners taken by the French-Sardinians in the latest war in Italy, nine were Hungarian, Bohemian, Croats and Italians. Out of hatred for the Austrian government, these soldiers, worked on by emissaries and not, it needs saying, from the allied army but from their own countries, surrendered to the enemy instead of marching against him. Only the Germans stood their ground and faced up to the assault from the French-Italian army. We know how slight, apparently at least, was the margin of success in the battles of Magenta and Solferino. And this was seized upon in order to query whether, with everybody on Franz-Joseph's side having done their duty, and the victory having gone to Austria, the outcome should still have been deemed conventional and just.

This deceptively simple query, which could be repeated *ad infinitum* with regard to every battle and is always raised by those who denounce the right of force, serves best to sustain the

the same thing as sending infernal machines[36] to a head of State. For lobbying of that sort to be countenanced, it would have to be open and above board so that, by dint of reciprocity, each power might have the opportunity to bring influence to bear on the views of the opposing people, which would at least be a permanent way of sounding peoples' views on the propriety of war and the legitimacy of conquests. But at the same time, it would again be calling into question what war is supposed to have determined once and for all, namely, the formation of States through the absorption of nationalities. It would, as I say, conjure up a contradiction within the rights of peoples and doom politics in perpetuity to taking as many backward steps as it might have taken forward.

---

error. Nothing, they say, could alter their fortune: so the vanquished turned into the victor; right, ascribed by victory to B, was handed back to A. *E sempre bene*! Is that unacceptable?

Those raising this objection cannot conceive that in any halfway serious battle, there is always a point at which the victory looks uncertain, not to mention moments when it goes awry, as in the famous battles of Poitiers, Crécy and Agincourt. But this generally has to do with war being governed by deep-seated, complex causes that makes it an unimpeachable arbitration. Moreover, in all matters of force, right lies with force, no matter the side it may be on. The right of force sees neither party, nor doctrine, nor race; it recognizes neither Frenchmen, nor Englishmen, nor Austrians, nor Lombards, nor Poles, nor Russians, nor Catholic, nor Protestant. It is on the side of force: and that is all there is to it. If force shifts, it displaces force; if it settles somewhere, it settles itself and overrides everything that falls within the sphere of its jurisdiction. Let us apply these principles to the Lombardy campaign.

Let us suppose that due to a freak of the terrain, some gaffe on the part of the generals or for some other reason, fortune had gone against the allies in Magenta; they would have sought revenge at Solferino, just as the Emperor Franz-Joseph did. One cannot have it both ways: either the allies would have emerged as the victors, which would have balanced the advantages and necessitated a third battle; or they would have been defeated and, in this instance, victory continuing to favour Austria, there would have been proof, not that Italy has no right to aspire to independence, but that she has not, even in concert with France, the force required to obtain it; that, as a result, the hour of her emancipation is not yet upon us; in short, that Victor Emmanuel and Napoleon III, his ally, were in the wrong since they were staking a claim by force of arms the prerogative of force, and this against a forty-five year possession and in defiance of the wording of the treaties, when force was not on their side.

Things took a different turn. Let me replicate the same argument: the allies were within their rights and the proof is that they had the force. Let the emperor Franz-Joseph blame his misfortune on the defections of his soldiers; the objection is puerile and backfired on him. How could Austria hope to dominate Italy when she could not even rely upon her own troops and cannot count on her own subjects?

In refuting this sovereign reason of victory, you may strive in vain with your *ifs* and *buts* to swerve right or left; as long as victory remains the index of force, it is infallible. Let us say that, tomorrow, the Italians desert Victor Emmanuel II and recall the emperor and the Pope; that, as a result, the Austrians return in strength and crush the Piedmontese, then the victory will only be announcing this dismal truth yet again: there is no Italy, because in Italy there is no genuine force. [P.-J.P.]

36. The infernal machine was a concealed explosive device, or other improvised weapon, designed to kill. [A.P.]

Napoleon in turn found this out when his allies, following his example, separated the Emperor's cause from that of the nation,[37] and sowed division in the deeply unity-minded French people and thereby made invasion easy on two counts. Everybody knows that French dignity was lost by this; it was a dismal reprisal for the shame we inflicted on so many peoples which, in defiance of reason and nationality, had hitched their star to our wagon out of selfishness or fear.

We conclude, therefore, that the call to insurrection, as a device of war, falls outside of the right of war: it is immoral.

---

37. See the *Frankfurt Declaration* of 1 December, 1813: "The allied powers are not waging war on France, but upon the undue sway that, to the misfortune of Europe and France, the Emperor Napoleon has been wielding beyond the boundaries of his Empire". See ANGE-BERG, *Le Congrès de Vienne,* 1 vol. in-8°, vol. I, 78. [H.M.]

CHAPTER VI

The Critique of Military Operations:
Weapons, Espionage and the Ruse

Our verdict on the morality of a clash between two States, on the usefulness of the victory, the soundness of the conquest, the valour of the combatants and the glory of the generals, depends upon what we decide with regard to war.

Is war simply, as some claim, *the art of destroying the enemy's forces*? So be it. History is awash with persons who have distinguished themselves in that ghastly art; and, had we the space to expound upon strategy, tactics, siege technology, ballistics, we would in fact discover that, according to its practitioners as well as its theories, warfare has thus far had no other purpose. In which case let there be no more talk about the right of war. The right of war, the principle behind all heroism, without which the renown of conquerors would vanish, is an atrocious fiction, with this one peculiarity: that it turns the representatives of force into so many hypocrites. Of all the varieties of hypocrisy, is not the most cowardly the hypocrisy of bravery resorting to trickery and treachery?

Or is war instead, as we maintain, and as the ancient seed of Romulus instinctively sensed, the verdict of force? In which case, warfare, just like trial by combat or the duel, has its code of honour; it is possessed of a righteousness that does not consist of pointless philanthropic gestures or underhand formalities, but which is a logical deduction from the very idea of warfare, subsisting despite the trespasses of the warriors and with the sanction of history, confirming those deeds of war accomplished in accordance with that right, or rendering them null and void and punishing them when they offend against it.

There is no third option: we have to choose.

On the one hand, we have open, moral, fruitful warfare, war that holds defeat in as high an honour as victory and requires that the winners and the losers live alongside one another like brothers; on the other, perfidious and pointless warfare that degenerates into savagery and banditry and renders one people's hatred for another beyond the reach of reconciliation.

To the facts set out in the preceding chapter we shall now add a few more, no less serious ones.

Implicit in the use of force in national struggles is the spilling of blood. One might even say that the danger of death is necessary in order to bring virtues to light: alongside physical force, moral force, courage and commitment. Now, depending on whether the destruction of the enemy is to be regarded as war's special purpose, or merely as a possible consequence, though not one directly sought by the struggle between the forces, it is conceivable that, as in the case of a duel, the choice of weapons is not a matter of indifference. It is something in need of regulation and definition.

All sorts of weaponry – sabre, rapier, foil, dagger, poignard, knife, rifle, carbine, pistol, pike, lance, staff, club, axe, flail, hammer, and compasses (in duels between journeymen), etc., have been pressed into use in duelling. These days the only weapons acceptable are the rapier, the sabre, the foil and the pistol. In the middle ages, the duel was conducted on foot or on horseback, in armour or in one's shirt. These days, the fighting is only ever done on foot and in shirt-sleeves. Delving into the origin of this simplification of the duel, we discover that it had two aims in mind: the discounting of anything that might demean or make it ghastly, whilst at the same time equipping it with every means of highlighting the courage of the combatants.

I therefore wonder whether it should not be the same with war? Is war, as opposed to the duel, allowed to resort to any sort of homicidal instrument? What about poisoning, which can be done in a variety of ways, either by poisoning the weapons, hurling asphyxiating gases or tainting drink and food? Grotius's response is ambiguous in every instance. He states:

> Certain nations are in the habit of poisoning their arrows and it could not
> be claimed that the law of nature is against this. The nations of Europe,
> however, have done away with that practice in dealings with one another,
> as not within the *ways of open force*.[38]

As for drink and food, Grotius is scathing about poisoning these, nevertheless conceding that it is permissible to render water sources undrinkable by tossing corpses or lime into them, as well as tainting foodstuffs by the same means.

On this point, Vattel is one with Grotius.[39]

The celebrated jurist's uncertainty of principle stands exposed here. Is it the direct purpose of warfare to destroy the enemy? In which case, scruples are

---

38. Proudhon is not quoting verbatim here but is paraphrasing Grotius, *Di Juri belli ac Pacis*, Book III, ch. IV, §§ XV et XVI, translation by Barbeyrac, vol. II, 257–58, and Pradier-Fodéré, 3 vol. in-8°, 1867, vol. III, 107. [H.M.]

39. VATTEL, *Le droit des gens*, Book III, ch. VIII, § 157, translation by Royer-Collard, 3 vol. in-8°, 1835–1838, vol. II, 189. [H.M.]

out of place: mines, infernal machines, oil of vitriol [sulphuric acid], boiling water, poison, lime, carrion, dysentery, blinding, famine, pestilence, barbed or poisoned arrows, anything that inflicts incurable injury or kills instantaneously, one must include them all and, as the saying has it, they are all grist to the mill.

But is war primarily, as the Latin name suggests and its definition implies, a duel in terms of force and courage, in which death appears as a risk rather than as an end? In that case, plainly, there are grounds for the regulation of arms, in the absence of which war is nothing but an ugly contest between an army of Castaings and another made up of Brinvilliers.[40] I have no liking for that general. In one sea battle he had a supply of vipers in bottles, and had his men toss them on to the enemy vessels, seeking thereby, by a sort of treachery, what he had given up hope of obtaining by force.[41] And I regard any soldier as an assassin who bites his bullet with the thought that that bite will poison the projectile and surely kill the enemy.[42]

Our military men, and I will say this much for them, are generally horrified by such ploys. Therefore, I am merely asking them to be true to themselves. They believe in a right in warfare and consequently in arms regulation when they quibble at the poisoning of the enemy. Let them stick with that thought and now answer my question: Are we to regard as permissible under the laws of war such precision weapons as blast at huge removes and without missing their targets; these projectiles of every variety, cone-headed, hollow-pointed, spring-loaded, which, after puncturing the adversary's body, leave behind dangerous wounds worse than those caused by Orsini-type bombs?[43]

"The French", a correspondent from the *Times* wrote at the time of the war in Lombardy, "have recently introduced into service a new bullet, hollow-bottomed and in the shape of a pyramid. This shape endows the

---

40. The poisoner Castaing was executed in Paris on 6 December, 1823. La Brinvilliers, notorious for his crimes, was tortured to death in Paris on 7 July, 1676. [H.M.]

41. Hannibal, commanding the fleet of Prussia, the king of Bithynia, with whom he had sought refuge, used it to defeat the fleet of Eumenes, king of Pergamon, an ally of the Romans. [H.M.]

42. Not only were firing rates notoriously low during the nineteenth century, but hitting one's target with standard muskets, prior to rifling, was unlikely. Death was more likely to come from disease, or in unsanitary hospitals, than on the battlefield. With the development of rifling, and accurate artillery, and then spring-loaded guns, all things Proudhon discusses below, death was more of a certainty, but delivered at a distance for the first time in history. Thanks to the endeavours of Florence Nightingale and Mary Seacole, during the Crimean War, fewer died in hospitals thereafter too. For more on this topic, see, for example, Gwynne Dyer, *War* (New edition) (Reading: Periscope, 2017). [A.P.]

43. Orsini's attack on Napoleon III took place on 14 January, 1858. Orsini's bombs injured 156 people, eight of them fatally. [H.M.]

bullet with this property, that once the tip of the bullet strikes bone, the base of the pyramid opens up at angles and inflicts a horrific injury that I was shown by a doctor at the hospital, and which he described as *sehr schoen* [very beautiful]".[44]

Is this fact as reported in the *Times* correct? I have my doubts. The English press is not well-disposed towards French honour. Today, the French infantry is regarded as the bravest in the world when it comes to bayonet charges; it has demonstrated as much in the Lombardy Campaign. What need has it of spring-loaded bullets? ... In any event, if the French can claim the dismal credit of having invented it, they will not take long to discover the drawbacks of its imitations. Which is why I in turn bring the fact to the notice of the decency of all military, who certainly never dreamt up the spring-loaded bullet and whose bravery can do very well without the hellish inventions of the armourers.[45]

44. This reporting from the front was conducted by telegram, meaning war reporting was daily and immediate for the first time in history. Protests against the war, like Tennyson's "The Charge of the Light Brigade", were immediate, as were concerted initiatives to ameliorate and regulate it by international law. In short, the horrors of the Crimean campaigns shaped world history, as much as they shaped Proudhon's theory of international relations. It is also for this reason that Roger Fenton's doctored photograph entitled "Valley of the Shadow of Death" was chosen for the front cover of this book. It is arguably among the first examples of pacifist photography and was, like Tennyson's poem, inspired by the tragedy of the Charge of the Light Brigade. [A.P.]

45. The French are not, it would appear, on their own in being guilty of such contraventions of the laws of warfare. In *Le Nord* of 3 February, 1860, we read: "As you will know, General Dieu was seriously wounded in the Italian campaign. The gravest of his wounds was caused by an *exploding bullet, which exploded in his side. Some fragments of bones shattered by the projectile have lodged in his intestines and are causing frequent abscesses which require lancing.* The suffering caused the ailing hero by these repeated procedures is unimaginable. He bears it with a resignation which is all the more admirable given that he is aware of just how serious his injuries are, etc.".

Bayard used to ask, regarding the arquebus, if it were not a shame that a man of courage could be left open to death as the result of a harlot's trick [*friquenelle*] against which he had no defence, and which placed the brave man and the coward on a par with each other? I in turn ask, how do such atrocious inventions serve war's purpose? Were lance and sword not enough for us? True, with lance and sword one has to come to close quarters, which seems to be less amenable to our modern idea of bravery. Note, however, that the very nations that manufacture exploding bullets would be red-faced, as if at an act of treachery, if these were poisoned. Such delicacy!

Tribute is owed to the French artillery: it does not favour destructive inventions and I have heard it chastised for this by some *industrialists* who certainly also consider themselves friends of progress and philanthropists. Apparently, our gunners reckon that they have more than enough shrapnel and it is more dignified for men of honour to engage one another in a knife fight than pound one another from distances of four and five kilometres. Really, they could not be any more backward-looking. [P-J.P.]

Whatever the truth of the anecdote reported by the *Times*, the certain fact is that every nation in Europe is now making use of the carbine and the rifled barrel, the cone-shaped bullet and ball, which are more of a danger than round projectiles as such. There is even talk of issuing all French army soldiers, cavalry and infantry alike, with six-shooter revolvers. Why this questing after perfection? Far from boosting force and courage, it abets weakness and cowardice; and which one might even describe as useless, since victory only requires that the soldier be taken out of combat? Is this not missing the whole point and purpose of war, which is to settle squabbles between nations through the use of force? The Emperor Napoleon III displayed great concern for the French and Austrian wounded in the recent campaigns [which culminated at Solferino].[46] I would praise him even more if I discovered that he had used his authority over the army and his standing in the eyes of the great powers to get them to give up on the use of cone-shaped and spring-loaded bullets. I cannot recall which king of France it was who guaranteed a pension to the inventor of an infernal machine, on condition that he would keep it a secret from everyone. He said: "We have enough means of self-destruction; I refuse to launch a competition in that field". The example is worth following; it bears witness to a genuine feeling for the right of war and the rights of peoples.

It is mainly since the invention of gunpowder that thinking about the nature and right of war has been warped, especially with regard to arms control. The claim has been made that the use of the cannon had democratized the soldierly trade and dealt a significant blow to the nobility by neutralizing cavalry and diminishing the advantages of personal courage. I will admit that I would rather that the third estate had learnt how to counter cavalry with cavalry, even at the risk of seeing feudalism last for another hundred years.

Others, so-called friends of humanity, congratulate themselves at the sight of weapons and machinery of war keeping abreast of the progress of industry and becoming more and more murderous. War, they say, will peter out on account of the excesses of its destructive capability. They fail to see that ending war that way leads to political and social disorganization. Once weapons have reached the point where numbers and discipline, as well as courage, no longer mean anything in warfare, it is farewell to majority rule, farewell to universal suffrage, farewell to the empire, farewell to the republic, farewell to government

---

46. Following Solferino, the French emperor proposed a ceasefire. The Austrians accepted on 8 July and this was followed by the Armistice of Villafranca three days later. The Swiss businessman and humanitarian Henry Dunant visited the field of Solferino soon after the battle ended, prompting him to write a moving account of the plight of the wounded. The impact of the book led to the founding of the International Committee of the Red Cross in February 1863. [G.H.]

of any form. It will be power to the most villainous. Can they not see that if the people of Paris were to take it into their heads to deploy the means of destruction that advances in industry and the sciences have made available, no force would be able to repress them? So why has the uprising been silenced today? Because the people, even at the point of insurrection, believe in the right of war. They shy away from attacking the enemy from behind, from destroying the enemy using poison, rapid muzzle loading rifles [*fusils à jet*], Fieschi devices,[47] and percussion bombs. Even at the risk of their own lives, like Barbès,[48] they would rather advance into the open boulevards and take their chances, face to face, man to man.

It has been said that since the invention of fire-arms, war had become less murderous. The biggest battles this century have not produced carnage on the same scale as the battle of Cannae, say, where Hannibal slaughtered fifty thousand Romans, whilst losing twenty thousand of his own men.

The point I will concede; but I do not chalk this up to artillery, which would be sheer nonsense.

There are three main moments in a battle. The first is the point of engagement, *congressus*, when the two armies come to grips right along the line; then comes the battle proper, where the effort, *pugna, conatus*, lasts until one of the two armies falters and its battalions are smashed; and lastly, the killing, the *caedes*, which starts, with the flight of the vanquished, once his battalions have been smashed. So it was in the battle of Cannae, out of the ninety-thousand-strong Roman army, some fifty thousand were killed.

Such slaughter, the final act of battle, regularly mentioned by the writers on the subject, no longer exists for us moderns, other than as an accident. The crestfallen enemy withdraws, if he can, or drops his weapons. Rather than slaughtering them, they are taken captive. The winner being all the more likely to do this according to the distance at which he has fought. Fighting in the form of manoeuvres and volleys, rather than hand-to-hand, he is less keen on carnage. This is also one of the effects of the sentiment of humanity which I have touched upon on a number of occasions, a sentiment that had curtailed war's destructiveness without, however, making any improvement in its mores, as is evidenced by the invention of and improvements to firearms. In the past,

---

47. The Corsican nationalist, Guiseppe Fieschi's infernal machine, used in an assassination attempt of King Louis-Philippe on the Boulevard du Temple on 28 July 1835, was made up of twenty rifle barrels. "Jet" from verb to throw "*jeter*". This is likely a reference to the La Hitte system (*Système La Hitte*), named after the French general Ducos, Count de La Hitte. It was an artillery system designed in March 1858 and was implemented as rifled, muzzle-loading guns in the French Army around the same time. [H.M./G.H.]

48. ARMAND BARBÈS (1809–1870), a contemporary of Proudhon's on the republican left. [A.P.]

the numbers of dead and wounded during those first two stages of battle were fewer; the slaughter only began with the final stage. These days, the striking down is done at some remove, in huge volume and the numbers are fairly much the same; the victor's advantage can be seen in the numbers of captives taken. This, I grant, is a success for humanity, but it comes at the end; and there is sacrifice at the outset. It balances out, military valour is the loser and warfare more depraved.

When he realized that he had been trapped by Robespierre's cunning, Danton sourly stated that victory belongs to the greater scoundrel! According to the current maxims, the same could be said of war, and the victory promised to the brave would go instead to the most murderous. Let us suppose one of the sovereigns in today's Europe had sole possession of the secret of the rifle and the rifled cannon, Congreve-style rockets, Paixhansmortar shells.[49] In the event of war breaking out, would he feel justified in making use of them? If we were to follow Grotius's teaching on the laws of war, still current today, then definitely. History is filled with battles won by superior weaponry, rather than by the courage and force of the soldiery.

In my view, trophies of that sort carry a burden of shame and prove nothing. Warfare, as the right of force intends it to be, as the human race conceives of it and as the poets celebrate it, is a contest involving energy, bravery, consistency, prudence, even industry, if you will. It has been turned into extermination, which might still pass muster if it entailed the destruction of brigands, marauders and slavers, to whom the nations owe no debt of thanks or mercy. But between citizens fighting, not for plunder, but for the liberty and supremacy of their homeland, the right of war so construed is repugnant.

One act of disloyalty leads on to the next. Is it permissible in war to trick – let us be blunt about it – to lie to the enemy? Certainly, Grotius answers,[50] and then he launches into a lengthy dissertation, the substance of which is that, outside of what has been agreed by peace treaty designed to reorder the situation, all trickery aimed at luring the enemy into a trap is sound warfare. On this occasion, he utters the dangerous dictum, repeated by Machiavelli and the Jesuits:

---

49. Proudhon is referring here to tests conducted on the robustness and range of rifles and rifled guns between 1851 and 1860. See Lt-Colonel DE LA ROCQUE, *Étude historique de résistance des canons rayés,* 1855. For CONGREVE rockets, see the inventor's own treatise, GENERAL CONGREVE, *A Treatise on the General Principles, Powers and Facilities of Application of the Congreve Rocket System,* London, 1827, translated into the French by Correard in 1841. When tried out by the English in 1806 and 1807, in Boulogne and Copenhagen, they triggered widespread expressions of outrage. For the Paixhans howitzer, see M. MEYER, *Manuel historique de la technologie des armes à feu,* translated by Rieffel from the German, Paris, 1837. [H.M.]

50. Grotius, *De Juri Belli ac Pacis*, Book III, chap. I, §§ VI et seq. [H.M.]

that, for the sake of reason of State and in the name of religion, lying is allowed. To which we, parodying Horace, say: *Dulce et decorum est pro patria mentiri.*[51]

Let us for a moment accept this singular piece of jurisprudence, that because deceit is part of the right of war, it qualifies neither as crime nor offence. Then why shoot spies instead of simply taking them prisoner? What! Here we have a sniper, stretched out on his belly lurking behind a bush like a jackal, shooting at a passing battalion that simply cannot see him. If they go after him and chase him down, he will likely be shot, *vitam pro vita*,[52] and I have no quarrel with that. But if he manages to get away and the very next day in some nondescript incident, is taken prisoner, in the event of his being recognized there is no longer any entitlement to kill him for the previous day's incident; he will merely have been plying his trade as a combatant. So that the entirety of his offence will have been in *flagrante delicto*. By contrast, the peasant who may have tipped the sniper off about the battalion's arrival will be hanged, should he be caught and convicted.

There is more. Suppose that same soldier, which the right of war protects today as a sniper, throws off his uniform, casts away his arms, and dons a disguise as Du Guesclin did when he wrested the fortresses from the English, and sneaks into the enemy camp to observe what is going on there. He instantly becomes a spy himself, and, if caught, and even though his crime was a half-hearted thing, he will be shot without mercy. During the siege of Sebastopol, a Russian army officer, captured in the trenches of the allied army, where he was doing heroic work as a spy, came within an inch of such a death. He owed his survival exclusively to the speediness of his legs. I reiterate my question: How, if falsehood and ambush are covered by the right of war and if all armies engage in espionage, how can espionage be treated as being on a par with treason and murder?

I am labouring this point to make it strikingly obvious how deeply the military are convinced, in the depths of their souls, of the reality of the right of war and how this subject is nevertheless shrouded in darkness. The very thing that is punishable in an enemy as infamous under the right of war, is permissible in oneself as legitimate and honourable under the very same entitlement. In *Cours d'art militaire* by Monsieur Laurillard-Fallot,[53] lecturer at the Military School in Brussels, I read:

> Intelligent, well-paid men are sent in, under cover of commerce, delivering grain or livestock and establish contact with the enemy army's suppliers and the leaders of the commoners by requisitioning.

---

51. "It is sweet and fitting to lie for the homeland". [A.P.]
52. "A life for a life". [A.P.]
53. LAURILLARD-FALLOT, *Cours d'art militaire*, 2nd edition, Brussels, 1851. [H.M.]

There you have espionage recommended, advocated as a tactical tool consonant with the right of war. One of the qualities of a great general is to have made good use of and been well briefed by his spies. But at the mere mention of the enemy's spies, the writer switches to a different language. A few lines further on, he adds:

> Whereas humanity prohibits the taking of a man's life on the basis of mere suspicion, there is nothing to prevent detaining him until his reports have ceased to present a danger. Concern for our own defences compels us, and responsibility for the lives of all the men entrusted to our care, imposes upon us a duty to be unrelenting in dealing with proven *treachery*.

The suspected spy is detained; on conviction, he is shot as a traitor. Military reason of State is really no joke. But why does the writer I quote from fail to see that what he is fine with punishing in one case cannot become legitimate in the other; and, conversely, that what he recommends with regard to the latter he has no right to prohibit with regard to the former? Espionage is an act of warfare, and logic alone requires that it be called such. Therefore, either revert to real principles, of which you accept only a half, and steer clear in both instances of all treachery and ambush; or else have the gumption to sanction your shared treachery and treat one another's spies the way you do your snipers, patrols and runners. There is no middle ground.

All the newspapers have reported the story of the Austrian officer who, during the recent Italian war, had an entire Piedmontese family shot on suspicion of espionage. Eleven people, including an old man in his sixties and a fourteen-year old child, were executed. Monsieur Cavour exposed the fact and Europe was outraged. Monsieur Cavour was right, if we assume that the nature and purpose of war should be restricted exclusively to the resources of force and cannot assume any other character without disgracing itself. But that is not the code currently in place. According to that code, and its endless contradictions, but is, as it stands, enough to fully vindicate the Austrian officer, it is permissible to execute citizens for spying on behalf of their country, as well as the defectors, deserters and traitors, with whom they clearly had nothing in common. If this is the case, then it is also permissible to deter them by means of *terror*, another universally countenanced means of warfare occasionally entailing the slaughter of entire families, regardless of age or sex, guilt or innocence. Not that the execution of eleven Piedmontese spared the Austrians from being defeated, of course: but that is another matter. But the likelihood is that terror will still their tongues anyway; and who can say whether the fuss kicked up by Monsieur Cavour has not served the very purpose that the Austrian had in mind?

Grotius goes even further. He is of the opinion that in war, if one's aim is to mislead the enemy, then one can, quite honourably, run up his flag, display his colours and, if possible, steal his watchword. Examples of this sort of thing abound. Here I reiterate my earlier comment: how can we not see that, thanks to these unworthy and immoral practices, we are trading rational, selfless, just and productive warfare between men for the hunting of predators from a hide?

Among the military there is a saying that *a general can be defeated but must never be caught napping.* I should hope so. There is surprise and surprise, however, and I cannot equate the watchfulness of the fighting man with the felony of the coward who tricks him. It is a disgrace to humanity that a general, who is a man of decency serving his country in a regular war, should have to trouble himself with such risks. Should not the policing of war lift that burden from him?

On this, Vattel and the rest are absolutely of the same mind as Grotius. Vattel establishes very well that conventions should be observed between enemies,[54] but when it comes to acts of warfare, he is perfectly happy to see ruse and deception, *falsiloquium*, added to right. He even goes so far as to discern civilization's progress beyond barbarism in this practice:

> Since humanity obliges us to opt for the gentler means in the pursuance of our rights, if, by some ruse of war, some feinting manoeuvre devoid of treachery, we can capture a stronghold, catch the enemy unawares and overpower him, it would be better and really is more praiseworthy to achieve success that way rather than by means of a murderous siege or bloody battle.

And in a note he adds:

> There was a time when those caught in the attempt to capture a place by surprise were condemned to torture. In 1597, Prince Maurice attempted to surprise Vanloo. He failed in the attempt and, some of his men having been captured, were sentenced to death. The assent of both sides had introduced this new exercise of rights in order to obviate dangers of that sort.

That practice was on the right road, but, Vattel says, with unambiguous satisfaction: "The practice has since changed ... *Stratagems are the glory of great captains*". He goes on to say, forgetting that the facts he cites give the lie to his theory:

---

54. Vattel, *Le Droit Des Gens*, Book. III, chap. X, § 178. [H.M.]

We have witnessed peoples, and, for a long time even the Romans themselves, professing to uphold any sort of surprise, ruse or stratagem in warfare; others, such as the ancient Gauls, went so far as to mark the time and
place where they proposed to do battle. *There was more generosity than
wisdom in such behaviour.*

Titus Livy (Book XLII, c. 47) also quotes the case of senators damning the less
than honest behaviour observed in the war against Persia.

The true nature, purpose and essence of war follows from these extracts,
but they have never been queried or contradicted, and neither Grotius, nor
Vattel nor any of their successors knew anything about them. They have failed
to grasp its laws and it is fair to impute to them most of the harm accompanying
that failure over the past two centuries. How can an accusing finger be pointed
at the military when the sages teach that sort of morality?

In Lonato in 1796, General Bonaparte, accompanied by his command and
with a retinue of just twelve hundred men, was surrounded by four thousand
Austrians who called on him to surrender. We know how Bonaparte extracted
himself from those straits. He had the mediator's blindfold removed, informed
him that he was the general officer commanding and that the Austrians themselves were encircled by the French army and that he was giving them three
minutes to surrender. Germanic bonhomie duped by Italian cunning and four
thousand men surrendered their weapons to twelve hundred.

I like this sang-froid in Bonaparte, that nothing could surprise him; but
it pains me to see this trait held up for posterity to admire. Is that warfare? Is
that its law? Is it not, rather, a descent into depravity? Here we find a warrior,
who, following a series of victories, racked up thanks more to dexterity than
to force, is ultimately crushed by force. Would Bonaparte have been better advised to surrender, one asks? Ah, no. Had he been possessed at that moment
of as much greatness of soul as aplomb, then after bamboozling the Austrians
who were asking for his sword, he would have sent them away with arms and
baggage. Regardless, this is a case that I leave to the consciences of the military
to decide; the issue, as far as I am concerned, is a loftier one. Let me say that it
is a trespass against right, in a people-to-people quarrel, where the bravery of
the armies is aided by the GENIUS of the generals, and should be the deciding factor in victory, to mount surprise attacks and resort to trickery. Genius
in warfare does not mean falsehood, any more than seizure of the enemy's assets means plundering the inhabitants, any more than homicide in open battle
means murder. There may be an issue as to whether the four thousand Austrians
who had lost their way were entitled to carry off the twelve hundred Frenchmen
who had blundered into their path; I am no fonder of such freak circumstances

in war than I am in literature and the fine arts and would like a proper definition here. But I deny that those twelve hundred French were within their rights,
in a proper war, to carry off as prisoners four thousand men who, caught cold by
a boldly articulated falsehood, had been so simple-minded as to assume themselves done for. Deciding whether to cite Lonato as either an exemplar of the
presence of mind of a general, or of the irregularities to which the bravest might
resort, in an age in which the right of war is only half-acknowledged, will be a
fool's errand! But do not go holding up General Bonaparte's behaviour in this
circumstance as an example to be imitated; that would be a corruption of the
morality of armies and an education in the art of eternalising abysmal war between nations.

CHAPTER VII

The Critique of Military Operations: Vandalism, Sieges, Blockades, Rape, Pillage, Murder, Single Combat, Prisoners of War

In seeking a definition of what is and what is not permissible in warfare, we cannot possibly avoid repeating ourselves sometimes. The entire performance of the warrior falls under two headings: people and things. I hope I will be forgiven the odd repetition if, therefore, my purpose is to throw into sharper focus the anomalies in the practice and the difficulties in the theory.

Since war is the verdict of force, force is manifested in the struggle and the victory. In order to fight and win, forces need to engage in often complicated and difficult manoeuvres that require, in addition to lots of man-power, lots of time and money. So, from the strictly economic point of view, we can see warfare as a sort of industry, as the military always have down through the ages. We speak of *warcraft*, the *art* of war, and the *profession* of arms.

War therefore entails manpower; it has its raw materials, in the form of munitions, often the highly developed products of industry; it has its workers, who are the soldiers; it has its product, being conquest, the capture of a town, province or nation, or its liberation. Along with the spilling of blood, war therefore implies the sacrifice of a certain sum of capital and goods. In short, it has its income and expenditure accounts, like any other industry.

Industrial exhibitions, what we might describe as peaceful jousts, are expensive. Even so, they are allowed in the interest of industry itself and the progress of the nations. War costs even more because it is an armed contest between nations, fighting either for their independence or for their ascendancy. We are resigned to it, though, and once the heroic proclamations are over, we can only think of waging it quickly, with vim and vigour, the worst wars being the long wars with indecisive outcomes.

It follows that because war is not waged for its own sake, and men and things are not sacrificed for the pleasure of destruction, but rather for the sake of victory, which is to say with an eye to conquest, or, and it amounts to the same thing, supremacy; war, as I say, has its own economy too. Like labour it is conservative and productive; while consuming, it conserves and reproduces. All destruction outside of these rules is abusive and a trespass against right. It is sheer barbarism, the warfare of the wild animal.

One consequence of this principle is that the State that embarks upon war, the nation that acquiesces in it, the general who steers it, must have their sights set constantly on matching their sacrifices to the interest they are out to safeguard and the benefit they are out to reap. It would be flying in the face of the right of war, as well as of vulgar common sense, to expend more upon warfare in terms of man-power and money than the actual object of that war is worth. Such stubbornness would be blameworthy and would degenerate into savagery.

With that in mind, let us now turn to practicalities.

The story goes that, not knowing how to deal with the brigands infesting the Papal States, the papal police resolved to clear the forests they were using as their hide-outs. That deforestation gave rise to a scourge worse than banditry, *malaria*. Wasn't that a well worked-out policy? And does it not show the sheer incompetence of ecclesiastical government and of a government prohibited from reaching for the sword, even against brigands, doubtless for fear of losing their souls?

But here comes a more serious example. Napoleon accused the governor Rostopchine[55] of vandalism, for having set the city of Moscow ablaze as the French drew near. He called for him to be outlawed by civilized nations. The question arises: what are we to think of this deed, which some people join with Napoleon in describing as barbaric, while others dub it heroic?

For a start, destroying one's own country, setting storehouses alight in order to leave the enemy with nothing, is self-harm. Nobody is under any obligation to feed his enemy and everyone gets to set the price on their independence and liberty.

Then again, it was not the torching of Moscow that brought the French army to disaster; the marches and engagements on the road to the River Niemen had whittled it down by more than three quarters, but even after torching the city there were still plenty of provisions and munitions. So, the sacrifice offered

---

55. FEDOR VASILJEVITCH ROSTOPCHINE (1763–1826). Tsar Paul I's Minister of Foreign Affairs, he was cast into disgrace by Alexander I for having voiced his objections to the alliance with France and vanished from court until 1810. He oversaw the defence of Moscow at the time of the French invasion. On the day after the French had ensconced themselves in Moscow, a ferocious fire consumed the greater part of the city (September 1812). Even though he defended himself against such accusations in *The Truth About the Moscow Fire* (1813), there is every likelihood that alcohol storehouses were set alight on his instructions. [H.T.] For a survey of the debate on Rostopchine's having ordered the firing of Moscow – of which there is now "little doubt" – see Adam Zamoyski, *1812: Napoleon's Fatal March on Moscow* (London: Harper Perennial, 2005), 576 n. 9. [A.P.]

up by Rostopchine was a complete waste. Moreover, whether Russia could have thought herself in peril, even after the loss of her capital, is a matter worth considering. Napoleon was within his rights to say, while citing his own campaigns, that the capture of Vienna and Berlin had certainly done less damage to Austria and Prussia than the destruction of those two cities would have inflicted.

So much for the pros and cons. What is our decision?

One trespass against the right of war leads to another: *abyssus abyssum invocat.*[56] Rostopchine's behaviour was a response to Napoleon's. Setting to one side the actual cause of the war in Russia, which I do not query, I can observe that on crossing the Niemen, Napoleon was counting on two things; first, that he would be living off the land; secondly, that the Russians would pick up the gauntlet in one or two set-piece battles, after which they would be beaten and as such have to abide by the law of the winner. Now, this reckoning implied a double infringement of the right of war, not with regard to how Napoleon and his adversaries practised it, but what that practice tells us about war, which is what we are trying to determine.

If she were to be conquered, Napoleon would have to beat the Russians on their own turf. In order to do so, two conditions had to be met. The first being the ability to occupy the entire country militarily, bearing in mind the vastness of her territory, her main natural defence. Napoleon should not have been crossing the Niemen with four hundred thousand men; he should have brought 1,200,000, failing which he was in contravention of his own maxims by trying to subjugate Russia with a force that was far too weak.

The second condition is that the French armies ought to have been in a position to survive on their own means without extorting anything from the population, regardless of whatever resources the invading army might find, or any military storehouses it might manage to capture. Because, according to the critique we have made, marauding is a breach of the right of war, and in certain cases renders the victory null and void.

What happened bore out this theory. The French army had not gone a hundred leagues from the far bank of the Niemen before the campaign was practically lost. The victories at Smolensk and Moskowa did nothing to put things back on an even keel; the freeze that later descended on the French army was merely another twist in a disaster that was three-quarters complete.

Napoleon's performance in this inexcusable campaign provided the spark and, to some extent, the pretext for what Rostopchine did. On the one hand, it was obvious that Napoleon could not bring the war into Russia, and to within six hundred leagues of its capital, without engaging in mass marauding; the

---

56. *Bible,* Psalm 42: 18. [H.M.] "Deep calleth unto deep". [P.S.]

failed supply effort he tried to organize from Danzig to the Niemen is evidence of that. But it is equally clear that a country of fifty million souls would not gamble its independence on the outcome of a battle against a 400,000-strong army. That would have been leaving too much advantage to Napoleon. The law of force was no longer being observed by anyone. From that point on, Napoleon could no longer be considered a real conqueror, the representative of civilization and progress, because while we can agree that he thought of himself as such, he lacked numbers and force. He was an usurper of sovereignties, the trouble-maker of Europe, an adventurer who needed to be destroyed at any price, by being starved out. Rostopchine must have felt that he was acting with that much more authority, Napoleon having set him an example. On the principle that the salvation of the army is the supreme law for generals, to slow down the enemy Napoleon issued the order that whatever could not be carried off was to be put to the torch, and Monsieur Thiers tells us that Davout carried out no other order more conscientiously than this one.[57]

In life, everything's connected: a contravention of the right of force turns into a breach of the rights of peoples and with one trespass compounded by the next, the best-established power fades away. No matter what grievances Napoleon had against Alexander I, once he proved unable to absorb Russia, let alone occupy her, he should have refrained from invasion. The manner in which the war in Crimea[58] has been fought could, if need be, provide further justification for this proposition. Here, France deployed a far less formidable force than the one led by Napoleon I in 1812, and it had no other purpose than forcing Russia to make peace by destroying the fortress in Sebastopol. That is surely the most striking criticism that could be made of the 1812 expedition.

Let's change the subject. Everybody is familiar with the story, or book of Judith and the siege of Bethulia. According to the Biblical account, the Jews, under threat from an invading army, retreated into their strongholds. Having come to Bethulia, built atop a rock, and unable to seize it by means of a raid, the enemy general blocked the channel supplying the town's water. Those under siege were dying of thirst and obliged to surrender.[59] In this legend, which has entered popular memory, we can discern, from the vantage point of the right

---

57. Davout's command of the rear guard was otherwise an embarrassing failure and Napoleon replaced him with Marshall Ney. [A.P.]

58. It being an ambition of Tsar Nicholas to capture Constantinople, in 1853, France and England, allied to the Turks, declared war on Russia with an eye to preserving the integrity of the Ottoman Empire. They captured Sebastopol and the huge Russian naval dockyards there in 1854. [H.T.]

59. *Bible,* Book of Judith, 7, et seq. Holofernes, Nebuchadnezzar's general, laid siege to Bethulia. Judith, inspired by God, seduced and then murdered him. The town was spared. [H.T.]

of war, the story of every blockade. I shall not enter into whether there were
adequate grounds for war between the Assyrians and the Hebrews; I will simply
assume that. I merely ask whether Holofernes's behaviour conformed with the
right of war, which, as Cicero argues, is a blatant means of using force to sort out
quarrels.

Without the shadow of a doubt, the military reply. Holofernes was within
his rights here. If the Jews had wanted to avoid the inconveniences of the blockade, they had only to climb down from their rock and join the battle. Any fixed
siege is designed to force a powerless enemy who, by the very act of withdrawing
confesses this, but who, thanks to the arts of fortification, sets about compensating for numerical inferiority by holding the higher ground. Defending oneself in one's homeland, by means of ramparts, moats, etc., falls well within the
parameters of the right of warfare, given that it is up to the aggressor to bring
force to bear on the defender and to do so on home ground; and finally, if a nation were to find itself quite inaccessible on account of the nature of its topog-
raphy, it would be beyond the law of absorption and would have to be declared
neutral. This is the basis on which European law was induced to countenance
the independence of the Swiss Confederation which is, so to speak, floating in
the air, safe from conquest and incapable of bothering the surrounding powers.[60] But this right of defence in a fortified location implies that the engineer
has made provision for everything, from water and food to weaponry. If he has
not, the siege turns into a means of constraint that is all the more legitimate
because the besieger is subject to the same inconveniences as the siege victim,
and that when an army is forced into lifting the siege, it is normally because of
disease or lack of food.

I have nothing with which to contradict this argument. Self-defence in
a fortified, inaccessible location is legitimate, even though it may be a way of
evading the law of force, which is the law of war. But attacking a place with
thirst and famine, even though such methods are not brute force, is also legitimate, since that attack is designed to force the enemy into fighting. At bottom,
this double exception is covered by the rules. I shall not rehearse the reasons
given. Rather, let me arm myself with those same arguments, and to my interlocutors I say:

---

60. The unvarying neutrality of the Swiss Confederation was recognized in the 1815 treaties, not because the character of the terrain enabled it to evade the law of incorporation
and conquest, but because the contracting powers all had an interest in keeping the strategic
crossroads clear. The neutrality act was based on a formal implementation of the principle of
stability: "By this present act, the powers wish it to be known, in an authentic way, that the
neutrality and inviolability of Switzerland, as well as her independence of all outside influence, is in accord with the true interests of European politics". [H.M.]

So, men of war, you look upon warfare as the exercise of the right of force, a positive right, one you cannot evade in regular warfare other than in certain foreseeable exceptions. This is the reason why places under siege do not ordinarily expect to be attacked prior to surrender; they know that, over the interval leading up to the assault, their resources are being used up, while the enemy's fervour is growing; that a defence sustained over any longer period would not be any more honourable and that the enemy might take umbrage at an unduly obstinate resistance and exact revenge as he might for a crime. Which is also the reason why it is often stated in cases of capitulation that, unless an army arrives within a given period of grace, ready to do battle, the town is to be handed over to the besieger again. The plain implication of all of this is that there is a positive right of force, underpinning the right of war, and of which military men are profoundly aware, although they cannot tease out its principles, because they are not jurists; and which the jurists in turn expound in the direst possible fashion, not being military men themselves.

None of this could work any better. But we have to follow the law through each of it's deductions, and, other than in exceptional circumstances and with the anticipated amendments, we must abide by force, which rules out perfidy, plunder, massacre and pillage; do nothing that falls outside of the legitimate purpose of warfare, which can generally be boiled down to a question of supremacy, absorption or liberation. Finally, off the battlefield we must refrain from any trespass against persons or property, other than in the punishment of committed crimes and enforceable indemnification. Now, is this the way things work in warfare? No, war is more or less equally brutal among the civilized as among the barbarians. It seems that the conditions required by the right of force are repugnant to soldiers; that no one would want anything to do with the profession if it demanded so much virtue. As the proverb has it,

Fighting would die out but for fighters.[61]

It is as if slaughter, pillage and rape may be needed to satisfy whatever destructive instinct keeps the soldier's hand in, encourages him and boosts his morale. In every battle, in every town stormed and captured, carnage, plays a more or less significant role beyond the bounds of utility and danger alike. It might even be said that the civilized man is incapable of fighting in the absence of wrath and hatred. In the battle of Ligny, the French troops, carried away by hatred and whipped up by General Roguet's words, took no prisoners. The Prussians had their revenge two days after that, at Mont-Saint-Jean; Blücher

---

61. Uncredited proverb, likely from Pierre Corneille's classic tragi-comedy *Le Cid* (1636), Act IV, Scene III. [A.P.]

was minded to have Napoleon pay a personal price for his contraventions of the right of war.[62] But let us skip past these killings, which the formal reports cover up as best they can. Besides, on the field of battle, does one have time to take prisoners? Is it practicable? Would one not need to guard them? Kill! Kill! The dead do not return ... Let us speak of less gruesome matters.

Rape, we are assured, is not as common in armies as it once was. This is a step forward in which our modern warriors like to glory and on which I whole-heartedly congratulate them, if the compliment applies to them. But away with hypocrisy. There is rape and there is rape. The military honour of our own day is much less savoury than in the old days. In his *Histoire de la Révolution*, Monsieur Thiers refers to Bonaparte's fortunate soldiers who gained the favours of the Italian beauties, and, naturally, rules out the idea of rape. But is this what really happened? The foreign historians, Italian and otherwise, do not see eye to eye with us on this.

Whatever the reservations of our military gentlemen, the question of right stands; in this regard, we should not delude ourselves. According to the received wisdom, rape is permissible under the right of war; like pillage, it falls within the prerogative of victory. The only thing Grotius was able to invoke against rape was the precept of Christian morality, which bans the Christian from fornication. But in the ancient practices, when fornication was not even held to constitute a venial sin, rape in war-time was entirely right; or rather, there was no such thing. Just as the person who buys himself a female slave in order to make her his concubine cannot be accused of rape, given that, to adopt the Biblical language, the woman bought-and-paid-for has become his property, *pecunia ejus est*,[63] so the soldier who, in enemy country, lays hands on a woman cannot be charged with a crime unless his orders have, for some particular reason, forbidden that and this is because the female enemy is the soldier's *conquest*. The word has been passed down to us as part of the vocabulary of the gallant.

After the defeat of the Teutons, and after the wives of these barbarians had asked the consul Marius to spare their lives and honour, Marius, invoking the right of war, declined to accede to the latter of those two requests. As a general and magistrate, he could not deny his soldiers an entitlement they had earned at the risk of their lives. Why was the restraint of Scipio the Younger so admired

---

62. On 16 June, 1815, Napoleon bested the Prussian Blücher on the plains of Ligny. 18 June, 1815 marked the final encounter in the Napoleonic epic in the valley between the Mont-Saint-Jean-Waterloo plateau, manned by the Anglo-Dutch forces, and the La Rossomme or Belle-Alliance cliffs where the French army was camped. [H.M.]

63. *Bible*, Book of Exodus, 21:21. [H.M.] In the King James version this reads "for he *is* his money". [P.S.]

by the Romans? It is because victory afforded him an entitlement to possession of a young princess, that in returning her to her betrothed, and by sacrificing his own carnal appetites, he was acting politically, with respect for human dignity, performing a genuinely outstanding act of virtue. We know the advice given to Absalom by Achitophel in his rebellion against David: that he should rape his father's wives in sight of the people.[64] Victory accorded him that entitlement and policy made it his duty. In the minds of the ancients, possessing the prince's wife and bringing shame upon his authority represented a consecration of the transmission of the crown. The murderer of Caudalus, king of Lydia, became his successor by marrying his wife.[65] Something of the sort took place between one nation and another: in ordering the extermination of all of the males of condemned nations, Moses made an exception for the females.[66] We know that the Romans were born of abduction.[67] Oddly enough, of all of the facts of war, the most disgusting by its very nature and in respect of which honour and decency are least forgiving of the soldier's depraved soul, may well be the one which is most deserving of indulgence. Here we have an instinct encompassing both amalgamation and supremacy and clearly reminiscent of the purpose of war and the right of force.

Rape appears to be fading from soldierly practice.[68] But this is mere appearance, more the outcome of our style of warfare than of a genuine change in military mores. If public opinion, which is these days more respectful of sex than in ancient times, appears to have gained an advantage on theory on this point, the right of war, as it has always been practised and as still taught, does not formally oppose it. And the fact is that, on occasion, soldiers and officers barely restrain themselves. Must a woman have a pistol at her throat before it qualifies as rape? There are a thousand ways of qualifying it as such. That said, it is not my intention to cause my military compatriots any slight when I say that no army ever displayed greater lack of self-restraint than the armies of France. The Frenchman adds winsome manners to the right that the soldier has always laid claim to the enemy's womanhood, and that completes the bedazzling of the

---

64. *Bible,* Samuel, 2:16, 21–22. And reads "in the sight of all Israel". [P.S.]

65. Legend has it that the shepherd Gyges owned a ring that made him invisible and which he used in order to seduce the queen who incited him to murder her husband; he was the founder of the Mermnades dynasty at the beginning of the 7th century BC. [H.M.]

66. *Bible,* Book of Numbers, 31: 14–18. [H.M.] "But all the women and children [...] keep alive for yourselves". [P.S.]

67. The abduction of the Sabine women, in 749 BC. [H.M.]

68. In this Paris edition of *War and Peace,* Proudhon has altogether removed his illustration of this claim, present in the Belgian one, that Arabs and Turks are today less prone to rape young boys and men than they were in the past. See, *La Guerre et la Paix* (Brussels: Hetzel, 1861), vol II, 76. This omission is the only major difference between the two editions and a welcome correction too. [A.P.]

hapless woman, and renders the offence less of a horror for her and, as far as he is concerned, ennobles it.

The right of rape is merely a derivative of the claimed entitlement to make tributaries or slaves of the vanquished. Bossuet finds this just in principle and he declares it without embarrassment, in agreement here with the Bible and the whole of antiquity. He says: "In principle, the person of the vanquished becomes the property of the victor, who secures the right of life and death over it".[69] Christianity, it is true to say, has made us less bloodthirsty; furthermore, it has abolished slavery. But let us not delude ourselves: the principle invoked by Bossuet lingers still. The victor is still at liberty to assert it and, if he solemnly renounces it, and refrains from the spilling of blood or from reducing the vanquished to servitude, it is merely under cover of a fig leaf of Christian morality, that swells his devoutness or his pride.

It's the same for male slaves and female slaves. In principle – I am following Bossuet here – the male captive, if not put to death, is bound to the service of the victor and the female to his pleasures. They can only be spared this by other considerations. Just as we have seen the modern right of war arriving at the condemnation of rape via the fictitious sin of a lack of self-control, it is through the fiction of religious fraternity, through baptism, that slavery has been abolished, and by yet another fiction, the fiction of chivalrous manners, that, generally speaking, captives are spared slaughter. Except for these easements, things remain as they were in the past. If captives are not reduced to slavery, they are held for ransom, which is the exact same thing, or else they are deployed on public works. If need be, they can be exchanged; if need be, and no matter how little security demands it, they are slaughtered. The philanthropist groans at such *extremes* but dares not condemn them. How are we to answer people who have their own *principles* and who plead public safety?

If we are to be done with these monstrosities, which have claimed the lives of millions a thorough rebuttal is needed.

The right of life and death over the vanquished, a right credited to the victor, seems to me theoretically to derive from two sources, quite apart from primitive barbarism, which is also a factor. The first of these sources is that war, inevitably brought about by the rivalry between two States and the necessity of annexation, implies the moral extinction of one of those States. By reason of the citizen's attachment to his homeland, an attachment that makes him prefer his own death to his country's demise, we have extended the death sentence

69. Here, Proudhon has boiled down a formula from a passage from the Book of Deuteronomy quoted by Bossuet in his *Politics Drawn from the Very Words of Holy Scripture*, Book IX, Article V, Proposition V, entitled: *Make war fairly*. The biblical evidence cited above has been drawn from the same source. [H.M.]

pronounced by war against the State to include the human being. I need hardly demonstrate the flaw in this reasoning; I have refuted it already by distinguishing as I do between public right and the rights of peoples.

The other derives from understanding war as the assertion of the right of force, a right acknowledged by the whole of the ancient world. Accordingly, a defeated nation protesting its servitude could stand accused of having borne arms against right, which, strictly speaking, is a capital offence. Here the flaw in the argument derives from the fact that war must demonstrate, not merely claim, which side has the right of force on its side. It cannot be argued that the beaten side was at fault on the basis of its defeat, only that it was weaker.

This is how the confusion has slipped in. There is no right of life and death. Learned men talk about, and warriors act, on a falsity, even if the latter do not boast about it. Alas, the rivers of blood humanity has had to witness for having forgotten its most essential principles. Restore the correct meaning to right of war and, even should hostilities persist, there will be a universal three-quarters' reduction in carnage. You can rely upon the consciences of the military on this one.

Earlier, I mentioned marauding: pillage is not the same thing. The purpose of the former is the subsistence of the soldier; it proceeds on the basis of the principle that war ought to feed war. The latter is ignoble and immoral in a quite different way; its purpose is to line the soldier's pockets. We are not talking here about a case of need, but rather of greed. Here we may say that the jurist's science and military honour have been wholly overshadowed.

Our casuists argue: if it is permissible to strike the enemy, even unarmed and asleep, and to deprive him of his life, then it is going to be that much more permissible to deprive him of his goods. In this regard, even the most recent authors display not the slightest scruple. They are comfortable with it. *Neque est contra naturam spoliare eum, si possis, quem honestum est necare,* as Cicero[70] has it, in keeping with Aristotle, Plato and all the classical wisdom. Grotius, Vattel and the bulk of the jurists have taken it in turn to give it the nod, and in their speeches, they go out of their way to argue in favour of the right of *plunder*. There is not even any exception made for holy things, and none of the enemies, goods and chattels can possibly be deemed sacrosanct as far as the victor is concerned: The *Digest* adds, *Quum loca capta sunt ab hostibus, omnia desinunt vel sacra esse.*[71]

---

70. *De Officiis,* Book III, chap. VI. "And it is not opposed to Nature to rob, if one can, a man whom it is morally right to kill". Cicero, *On Duties,* trans. Walter Miller, (Cambridge, MA: Harvard University Press, 1913), 299. [A.P.]

71. *Digest,* Book XI, Part VII, § 36. "When a place is captured by an enemy, it always ceases to be religious or sacred". *The Digest of Justinian* (vol I), translation edited by Alan Watson (Philadelphia: University of Pennsylvania Press, 1988), 354. [A.P.]

It is laughable to witness the pious, honest Grotius expressing a minor reservation regarding instances where the victors and the vanquished might subscribe to the same faith. Conscience has its part to play, he says. However, as these objects are in the public domain and there is nothing easier than de-sanctifying them, they can be seized without injury to the respect owed to holy items. The Church suffers the circumstances of its parishioners! Is that not pretty? In Italy and Spain, our generals did not wait for de-consecration: true, the revolution had made them infidels. What else is there to be said? By right of pillage, it is permissible to go as far as to desecrate a tomb. Provided that we do not disregard the respect due to corpses, the ponderous author of *De Jure Belli ac Pacis* remarks, that trespass is quite permissible, graves being, after all, the property of the living and not of the dead.[72]

In the next Book, I shall revisit the matter of spoils and plunder, regarded there as the cause and purpose of warfare, not an effect. For the time being, I shall make do with one simple observation. At the edge of a forest, an honest man comes under attack from an evil-doer and kills him. What is he to do next? He will inform the courts so that the corpse can be retrieved and the incident reported. He will steer clear of robbing the corpse; in the reasonable belief that that would be to disgrace himself. I am talking here about a duel, where the winner is required to display the most extreme propriety towards the deceased. We are not talking about the destruction of a gang of brigands, with regard to whom there are no half measures, nor even about the satisfying of honour, without any self-seeking consequences, rather, a debate over political sovereignty to be settled between two nations through recourse to force. And the outcome of such a contest, the reward accorded to the victor, would be pillage...!

The more one delves into this barely-touched-upon issue of warfare, the more one is stunned by the enormity of the sophistry, the contradictions and craven reasoning that abound in it. It is permissible, we are told, to sneak up on the enemy, slip inside a post or fort and slaughter the garrison without giving it time to be on its guard; to creep into his tent and strike down the enemy general. Here, Grotius invokes the examples of Mucius Scaevola,[73] Aod,[74] and a host of others. Under that principle, the young man who tried to assassinate Napoleon in Schoenbrunn was within his rights,[75] whereas Napoleon, who hauled him up in front of a court martial and had him shot, was in breach of

---

72. Op. cit., Book III, chap. VI, § 3. [H.M.]

73. In 507 BC, Mucius Scaevola attempted to poison Porsenna, King of Clusium in Etruria, who was besieging Rome. Having failed, he held his hand over a brazier by way of self-punishment for his failure. [H.M.]

74. Israel's second judge Aod, murdered Egon, the king of the Moabites, who had been waging war on the Jews. [H.M.]

75. In 1809. [H.M.]

his. So, are we to conclude that it will be legitimate to put a price on the head of whomever one considers the author or driver of the war, as the Spanish king Philip II did with regard to William the Silent, and have him murdered? Here, Grotius recoils; he says "No, *the common interest of princes precludes that*".[76] That is some argument. And what of the common interest of peoples?

Returning to true principles, we say, however, that, war being the trial of strength, all murder, especially the murder of generals, is a felony. Which is why we challenge the actions of the likes of Aod, Balthazar Gérard,[77] Poltrot de Méré,[78] Ornano[79] and all who resort to treachery and murder in warfare. No matter how he wronged Germany, Napoleon became unassailable off the battle-field. In the European shambles, especially given the uncertainty surrounding principles and the reciprocal grievances, the war he waged, even if flawed in its forms, was at all times held to be a trial of strength.

One much-invoked question is on what basis we might trust the outcome of single combat, or combat between a set number of chosen men from both sides, say three against three, thirty against thirty, a hundred against a hundred, in order to bring war to an end and spare the bloodshed? Grotius denies the possibility. He says, "All one's force has to be deployed".[80] I share Grotius's view, but I cannot embrace his reasoning. Such combat, in which the few act for the many, where success is deemed proof of the validity of one's cause and the badge of divine protection, is, he argues, repugnant to charity and religion. It appears, instead, that such devotion might be charity in its sublimest form; as for religion, it no more cares about charity than it does about the conscript lottery.

As for myself, always taking the definition of warfare as my starting-point and basis for my arguments, and knowing that it is, that it seeks to be, and must be the assertion of the right of the strongest, and consequently a de facto demonstration of force, my answer is: Yes, the belligerent sides do have to deploy all their resources, and field all their strength, for the very reason that victory is owed to the strongest, which might not be the case if the battle were restricted to two equal fractions of the contending powers. Indeed, it is plain that such a way of waging war would be entirely to the advantage of the weaker

76. Op. cit., vol. III, 112. [H.M.]

77. The murderer of William of Nassau (or William the Silent), Prince of Orange, on whose head Philip II, king of Spain, had placed a price on 10 July, 1584. [H.M.]

78. Murderer of Duke François de Guise, who was laying siege of Orléans (18 February, 1563). [H.M.]

79. Michel-Angelo d'Ornano, acting on behalf of the Republic of Genoa, murdered his own cousin, Sampierro d'Ornano, who had inspired Corsica to rise up against the Republic (15 January, 1567). [H.M.]

80. Op. cit., vol. III., 106. [H.M.]

party as the champions from each side are assumed to be of equal individual value.

Let us bring this chapter to a conclusion. As we probe further into this critique, there is one thing that should be becoming clearer in the mind of the reader, a consequence of understanding the very contradictions that cloud this entire subject:

The right of war is a positive right, and the reason of force is a positive rationality, applicable to a certain order of deeds and ideas, with the same certainty as the right of labour is applicable to matters of production and exchange, the right of talent in matters of the arts, the right of love in marriage, etc. The multitude is aware of, armies affirm, civilization hails and progress clamours for the codification of the right of war, the reason of force, so profoundly misconstrued by the jurists. There is no denying that there has been for three thousand years an improvement in the ways and customs of war, and it cannot be denied that the right of force has been overshadowed because of the proliferation of rights, of which it was the first in the series. Finally, the best way to ward off the calamities of war, assuming that it persists, is precisely to take cognizance of the right of force.

CHAPTER VIII

The Critique of Military Operations. The Battle

The battle is the supreme, heroic act of warfare. Armies line up, front *contra* front, each seeking to overwhelm the other. Everything is done with this battle in mind. It is the clash that decides the fate of empires and which, by wrapping victors and vanquished alike in the mantle of glory, ought to sweep them, mixed and mingled, towards a better future. Let us see if the *dénouement* of this tragedy lives up to the claim.

Let us rehearse the principles once more.

The notion of justice, or, rather, of judicature, is inherent in warfare. Its consistency is that at certain points in human development, hitherto peaceful nations are inclined, on account of the needs of their circumstances, and in pursuit of a higher purpose, to swallow one another up; that, as a result, they come into conflict, and, incorporation having become inevitable and the time having come, supremacy rightly belongs to the most powerful. Which is the reverse of what happens in civil matters. In the case of ordinary justice dispensed to citizens by the State, force is on the side of reason and must remain law, here it can be said that, conversely, reason, law, and right belong with and should remain with force.

From which it follows that the contention between the powers involved, in other words, war, does not have their mutual destruction as its direct purpose, although it cannot proceed without the spilling of blood and the expenditure of wealth. Its purpose is the subordination of forces, or their fusion, or their equilibrium.

From whence it follows that in this sort of judicial duel, the modus operandi has to be regulated so that not merely the material forces, but also the moral resources of each belligerent power play their part, and that victory ultimately goes to the strongest, which is to say, to the side that carries the day on the widest variety of counts, army size, physical strength, courage, genius, virtue, industry, etc., with the two sides suffering as little damage as possible.

Outside of those principles, there is no war, in the human and juridical sense of the term: merely a clash between wild animals and, worse than that, a massacre by brigands. I might go as far as to say, with De Maistre, that[81] in terms of the horror and profound nonsensicality of the thing, what we have is Providence going mysteriously about its work.[82]

Therefore, scrutinizing the tactics that govern modern battles, to mention only those, I find that there is no discernible indication of high morality, nor of conservation, let alone certainty, the only thing that can render war honourable and victory legitimate. I even find that, in that respect, we have been making backward strides over the past two centuries. Not that we are any the less brave, of course, but for reasons that I shall explain later, we fight less bravely; we inflict more harm on the enemy, thanks to the violence of our clashes and the superiority of our arms, but we inflict proportionally more harm on ourselves, making victory suspect. More people are killed without any greater success being achieved. The democratic spirit that had permeated our armies since the Revolution looked like it would work entirely to the advantage of the soldier, and yet we have never witnessed such contempt for human life. In short, the materialism of the battle has increased as civilization has grown, the very opposite of what should have happened.

Such reproaches, which we are entitled to direct at modern tactics, represent so many violations of the right of war. It will take me only a few words to get my point across.

First, let us examine the clash between massed troops. I refuse to get into an argument about deep ranks and thin ranks, much less argue that the proper way to fight is for soldiers from both armies to attack one another simultaneously, in hand-to-hand, man-to-man combat, *virum vir*, then count which side has sustained the largest number of dead and wounded in those hundred or two hundred thousand duels. I cannot deny that the bloodiest of all those battles are the ones in which each soldier picks out his own enemy. I agree therefore that the marshalling of forces, which is one of our economic powers, should also be numbered among the legitimate ways of winning. In such marshalling, in this battle-field confraternity, there is also a moral element reminiscent of civic fellowship, the unity of the homeland, and it is certainly a force. If the French soldier, due to his instinctive feel for concentration and unity, is better disposed than any other towards tactics of this sort, if he is to be found rallying, unsolicited, in the middle of the fray, forming up into his platoon, even without waiting for orders from his officers, we have to accept him as a product of the nature which has shaped men and animals differently, endowing the horse with

---

81. *St Petersburg Evenings*, VIth Conversation. [H.M.]

82. For a full discussion of Proudhon's distinction between the religious concept of providence and his understanding of immanence, see Prichard, *op. cit.*, chapter 3, and Proudhon, *De La Justice* (1858).

his hoof, the bull with his horns, the lion with his claws and teeth, the Anglo-Saxon with his brawn and individuality and the Frenchman with his unity in combat.

That concession made, I say that in the event of war every nation has some way of employing its faculties and resources, depending on whether the war effort is guided by some notion of right or by a destructive fury; just as there are rules governing single combat, depending on whether it involves a matter of honour or a case of legitimate self-defence against a murderer. So how does it come to pass that in battles this principle of common sense, decency and humanity is almost entirely misunderstood? As a result of taking destruction as war's proper purpose, all we now see in our armed units, from platoon through to division, are man-mincing machines, engines of devastation. In his *Histoire du Consulat et de l'Empire*,[83] Monsieur Thiers confesses, despite his admiration for the emperor, that misuse of man-power and artillery had, in under fifteen years, turned battles into *appalling butcheries*, in which military virtue no longer counts for anything, and outcomes being no greater, nor above all, any more durable.

The art of handling soldiers, whilst having them operate in teams, the art in which Turenne excelled, seems to be on the way out. Pitting the masses, infantry, cavalry, artillery against one another, making mince-meat of human flesh, snatching victory by braving slaughter, this, in his latter years, was the sum total of Napoleon's art. In terms of mobilizing armies, sending them by the shortest and surest route against the enemy, in as short a time as possible, then taking up position, his skills were extraordinary, and appear to have grown with age and experience. On arrival on the battlefield, he scorned tactics, marshalled his masses and hurled them against the enemy, the way the giants of fable used to throw themselves against the mountain gods. He worked out the pace: unless he was mistaken, the enemy should be caught *in flagrante delicto* and mercilessly crushed. At Waterloo, he used the very same approach and was defeated; when the Prussians showed up, the hammer shattered on the anvil. And that, of course, is why, in the estimation of several critics, Napoleon, who had no peer as a strategist, is ranked as only a second-rate tactician.

Sebastopol was finally taken by the very same method. General Canrobert,[84] whose nerves, they say, were not sufficiently steely, had brought in General Pélissier to assume this great task. In Magenta and Solferino, things seem to have taken a rather different turn, if we are to credit the dispatches; soldierly

---

83. See Vol. XIV, 315 et seq., for a description of the battle of Moskowa. [H.M.]

84. General Canrobert who had taken over from Marshal de Saint-Arnaud in command of the army of the Orient, set about laying siege to Sebastopol, but, having fallen out with the English, he was replaced by General Pélissier. [H.M.]

initiative and the bayonet supposedly secured the victory. God grant that this is a reversion to more heroic combat! The effect of these monstrous clashes is horrendous. The secret can be reduced to a mechanical formula: mass multiplied by speed. There, genius and valour do not enter into it; whoever fights dirtiest has the better chance of winning. The art of war, if such an art exists, is these days nothing more than mutual slaughter. It ought to consist primarily of the deployment of courage, the conservation of strength whilst committing it, and gaining the greatest advantage for the least outlay, and crippling the enemy without wiping him out, where matter is only one factor, and spirit intervenes only to give the signal. But alas, the horror of war is equalled by the commanders' contempt for the soldier's life.

Don't go asking me what new, more humane and above all more convincing tactics I would introduce into battles. I am no more obliged to instruct our marshals in warfare than our men of letters are to write better poetry or better plays. I avail of my rights when I argue against some of them that their manoeuvres fly in the face of the right of war and against the others that their output runs counter to the art. And my criticisms are that much better grounded because, if over time respect for human life has been the least of the concerns of the men of war, and the style of fighting has changed many times, then we can assume that there must be one method better suited than the rest to the purpose of war and its essential conditions.[85]

85. I hope that there will be no malign inclination to misrepresent my reservations in order to conclude that there is nothing that can be done here and that the wisest course is to abide by the status quo. The critic is not obliged to produce masterpieces and unearth the truth; he merely exercises his right and has done his duty once he has proved that such-and-such an opus is bad and such-and-such a view a mistake. In this circumstance I am all the more justified in refraining, since I have already declared a quite different intent and, rather than seeking a mere reform of the practices of war, I wish to see it transformed utterly.

However, lest it be said that in engaging in a critique of military tactics I am dooming armies to inaction, allow me here to offer a pointer.

War, as I see it, is the gauging of forces.

The mission of a general is, therefore, to deploy the nation's forces in the most effective manner and maximize their impact, in a context of honour, openness and probity determined by right.

It is immensely difficult to carry out such a mission with a 100,000-man army and to draw from those variously armed 100,000 men all the effort of which they are capable both as individuals and as a group. Everybody knows that 10,000 men, well used, can beat 20,000, 30,000 and 100,000, so that, in the fairest battle, victory can favour the weaker side. Whilst such defeats do not necessarily lead to the undoing of States, as I have pointed out with regard to the Hundred Years' War between France and England, or the Second Punic War, etc., they at least have the result of postponing solutions by chastising the clumsy and making the conquest cost three or four times more than it should. This is the real problem facing every army commander who is a man of action par excellence but also, and we shall never tire of saying so, a man of justice. Now this is an immense issue. What, then, is the reproach

It is primarily to the invention of gunpowder and the growing ascendancy of firearms over bladed weapons that what I describe as the growing depravity of battle must be traced. But, note this, the use of artillery, after having suggested the idea of crushing blows, seems nowadays, and thanks to the perfection of weaponry, to be tending to render mass confrontations impossible. It takes only a little additional range, speed and accuracy of fire to work a fresh revolution in tactics that will certainly do nothing to boost the soldier's honour.

Another drawback with artillery is that it has, as Ancillon observed,[86] made wars more costly without making them fewer. The material expenditure in war has risen continiously since the invention of fire-arms, with the costs in terms of courage continually on the wane; that is the result of the impact of modern industry on the art of the tacticians and trials of strength. Every cannon-ball fired costs fifteen francs; every bronze cannon mounted, six thousand francs; a rifled barrel, twenty-five francs. An infantry soldier with four years' service, complete with arms and equipment, represents, with the outlay made by family and State, interest upon that outlay and lost labour, an average sum of twenty-five thousand francs. Soon we will no longer be saying that victory belongs to the largest battalions; we will be saying, victory belongs to those with the largest machines and the deepest pockets.[87]

I address to Napoleon, following Monsieur Thiers? It was not that, in one instance, he failed to triumph over a lesser force by means of a superior one, since that would have been to deny the right of force per se. And, consequently, it was not that, when faced with inept adversaries enjoying superiority of numbers, he sought to divide them in order to pick off those whom he could not have defeated *en bloc*, even though the victory thus obtained in such an instance was dubious and uncertain: every chastisement inflicted upon presumptuous and unintelligent force is deserved and therefore consistent with the right of war. My reproach where Napoleon is concerned is that in applying the principle of collectivity of forces, he made an army corps tantamount to a mass of material and he sought to humble the enemy by means of an onslaught of battalions rather than through the coordinated actions of men. It is, in short, that he muddled up the force of collectivity with that of weight. I say that this sort of application of the '93 dictum *Swamp the enemy*, is no longer proper tactics, that it is, therefore, not the way that human force should operate and that such materialism cannot but result in war becoming depraved, the soldier brutalised and consequently the misshaping of civilization.

Let me go further here. The very easily grasped distinction that I draw between the collective force proper to a group of men and that proper to a heap of raw material, between coordinated action and action underpinned by gravitation ought to enlighten the military. It is for them, having first immersed themselves in the RIGHT of war, to set the tactics, lest they bring their profession into disrepute and raise the horror of humanity against themselves; and, sooner or later, that of their own soldiers. [P.-J.P.]

86. Ancillon, *Tableau des révolutions du système politique en Europe*, vol. I, 165. [H.M.]

87. Among the characteristic features of our age, we ought to point to the competition between the civilized nations in terms of military industrialism. The English have their

The Roman soldier cost the State next to nothing and only became a drain on the resources of his family the day he took to the field; barracks life had no impact on his working practices and civic virtues. His military training took place within the context of farm-work; it was family tradition as much as a provision made by the city. As for his weaponry, swords and spears, passing from father to son, only needed sharpening generation by generation and after every campaign. By contrast, with our long-range weaponry, victory and the soldier's survival are primarily dependent upon positional advantage, cannon numbers, the marksmanship of the artillerymen, the precision of battalion volleys, and the intensity of the firing line, while theirs were more reliant upon the courage of the legionaries. In every clash, the Roman closed with the enemy, fighting hand to hand, faced battle-hardened troops, and counted his triumphs by the numbers of his wounds.

Advances in modern weaponry, we have to grant, run counter to the courage of the ancients. One of the outcomes of the recent campaigns, thanks to the use of rifled cannons, has, they say, been to render cavalry and reserves utterly redundant. New projectiles were able to pick them out at such a distance that they were paralysed or wiped out on the spot before they could even join the line and mount a charge. One more step forward like that and the massed infantries will be mutually unapproachable. An attacking column, dispatched at flat-out pace, is liable to be destroyed by a handful of men in less time than it takes to cover the hundred to one hundred and fifty step intervening gap, and the soldiers of higher civilization would be reduced to exterminating one another at a distance without ever managing to come to grips with one another. We might one day see an intermediary moving between the two armies at intervals of a quarter of an hour, carrying dispatches from commanding general to commanding general reading: "My losses stand at such-and-such a number of men; yours? Let us add them up ... You, sir, have the advantage". Such civilization! Such progress! How can one still believe in the justice of war, in a right of force?

Armstrong gun, made up of steel components welded together; that item sells for 50,000 francs apiece. A workshop has been set up to manufacture such guns; the premises and tools cost 12 million francs. Between the Armstrong gun and the rifled gun there is the same difference as obtains between the latter and the ordinary gun. At a huge range, the Armstrong gun can penetrate an armour-plated boat. As far as the English government is concerned, it is secret. The word is, however, that in the recent war in China, those famous guns failed to produce the results expected of them.

For her part, Prussia has obtained from a foundry worker the secret to smelting cannon-sized steel components, a considerable step forward in the manufacture of rifled guns and also, we are assured, in their power. Everyone is familiar with the Minié carbines, pump-action rifles, revolver handguns, Paixhans guns, etc. [P.-J.P.]

There is another line of critique that bears upon enlistment, military organization, guarantees for the soldier, the accountability of officers, the morality of command.

According to the principles expounded in Book Two, war, being a contest between nations in the interest of the State, it follows, *a priori*, that all the State's subjects, all the members of the city, without exception, ought to play their part in it. All men capable of bearing arms, join the army; the elderly, children and women are employed in the workshops, warehouses, ambulances, on fortification and trench-digging duties. The loss of an eye, a leg, an arm; deafness, short-sightedness, lack of height, blemishes in the complexion, in certain functions, are not enough for one to be excused service. The Convention acted in the true meaning of the law of war when it ordered a *levée en masse* and declared that the homeland was under threat. And the Republic was victorious.[88] One does not win against a nation armed like France was then. Now we have recruitment by sortition, fitness boards, dragging all manner of exemptions and substitutions in their wake. The National Guard, occasionally organized on a grand scale, occasionally whittled down to its minimum expression, depending on the mentality and inclinations of governments, has been retained as an emblem of the nation under arms, but in every instance it is laughable in terms of its sluggishness and uselessness.

The results of this arrangement are known. Abandoned to the care of government, warfare, now of interest to the nation only indirectly and as a tax, has become a career, as far as the ranking military, sons of the bourgeoisie, are concerned; as for the rest, the workers and peasants, it signifies a loss of status. On the pretext of ensuring that the nation is defended by the force of the army, the handsomest, strongest and finest flower of working youth is plucked and turned into the raw material of an army, which is then studiously distanced from the people. With such repeated skimming, the race is left diminished in its standing and its vigour, and the nation is left stricken in its sovereignty.

This first contravention of the right of war, identical in this respect to political right, leads on to another in respect to the selection of officers and generals.

Even more so than in peace-time, in war-time the man in whom command is vested ought to be appointed by the citizenry. At the very least, the man who takes up arms in defence of his country should choose his captain;[89] the *fédérés*

---

88. The principle of the *nation under arms* is set out thus in the 1793 Constitution: "All the French are soldiers: they are all trained in the use of weapons" (Article 109). "There is no commander in chief" (Article 110). "No armed corps may deliberate" (Article 114). [H.M.]

89. The 1791 Constitution Part IV, art. 6, summed up the elective principle in the army thus: "Officers are elected for a set term and can only be re-elected after an interval of service as soldiers". [H.M.]

did so back in '92 and no one has argued that their officers, the products of election, were less brave or less capable and, above all, lesser friends of liberty than
the ones who later made up the common currency of the Emperor.

Some say that elections for army positions would be destructive of subordination, without which an army cannot survive and that since the right of the
citizen-soldier flies in the face of the very purpose of warfare, to wit, the deployment of force, there are grounds for bending that political right before military
discipline.

Such an objection might be true in a monarchy where, since the army is
distinct from the nation, and warfare left to the direction of the prince, there
might be a desire to retain republican practice in appointing officers. Plainly,
that would be a contradiction. The issue therefore should be to find out whether
the dynastic interest should count for more than the national interest, for more
than the interest of war itself, which, like industry, insists upon the widest possible freedom in the deployment of maximum strength. But in a republic, in a
universal suffrage-based empire, where the nation still has full and undiluted
command of its sovereignty, where war and peace are still, ultimately, matters
for the country to decide, the exception no longer applies. The election of officers by the rank and file, in addition to flowing from the nation's public right,
stands guarantor for the morality of command, for the army's public spiritedness and therefore for its force.

But let us step away from political considerations, albeit that they matter
here, and let us consider it solely from the military point of view.

In terms of its shared danger and common effort, an army constitutes an
authentic association. The enemy's presence places the officers and men on the
same level; those who have fought in a war know something of this. If discipline is respected, it is conditional upon there being mutual commitment and
the rank and file placing its absolute trust in its leaders. In which case we have
no more self-indulgence, no more special privileges, and no one is sacrificed. In
the face of the enemy, self-indulgence and special privileges are tantamount to
treason; the sacrificing of a man, a corps, other than when absolutely necessary
in battle, is murder. Do we believe that this brotherhood in arms, which in an
army of free citizens extends from general to private soldier, is also firmly guaranteed in the current constitution of armies?

Independent of his subordinates, who have become junior officers, the officer, and more so the general, displays none of the devoted solicitude of election
and civic equality in relation to the soldier. Rank having become the badge of
inequality, justice, the soul of warfare is supplanted by command and a different
mentality tends to pervade the army. This is the world of the imperative, where,
since the superior officer is answerable only to his own superior, which actually

means answerable to no one, the lower ranks are, inevitably, sacrificed. In the hands of his general, the soldier is no longer a soul, the upstanding peasant in his village; he is a long-range weapon, a killing machine, a thing, just like cannons and munitions, a product of military industry, utilized because he comes as cheap as his cartridges and his rifle.[90]

Hence those Judaic maxims liable to such monstrous enactment, that in war it is permissible to sacrifice the part in order to save the whole, as Caiaphas put it: *expedit unum hominem pro populo mori*;[91] to leave regiments and entire corps exposed to certain destruction in order to buy success for some scheme, to confuse the enemy and sometimes for the sake of showing-off; to abandon the wounded, the sick, stragglers and rear-guards during a retreat. Hence the ghastly principle peddled by certain writers and diametrically opposed to the law of war, that the soldier in dire straits should allow himself to be slaughtered rather than surrender and that, no matter how feeble his resistance, his death will always inflict a cost upon the enemy. Hence, finally, this system of training which, in the absence of patriotism, sustains the soldier's courage and makes him, not the defender of his country but the devotee of someone's ambition.

This is the spirit in which the republicans have, not without a measure of bitterness, accused Napoleon I of having moulded his officers and fashioned his armies. They say that at Austerlitz he let one entire wing of his army be crushed just to draw the allies towards his right flank and lure them into his trap, whilst he had forty thousand men available to him who took no part at all in the action; in Moscow, despite the clamour from his soldiers, he held back his guard, which made his victory all the bloodier and all the less profitable; in the crossing of the Beresina, he was forced to flee to save himself because the salvation of the Empire hinged upon his personal survival. He had previously been seen in the Marengo campaign more eager to seek his own glory than to fly to the aid of Masséna,[92] whose sacrificed troops long nursed a grudge as a result. And again, exercising the sovereign power that the nation had vested in its first magistrate, he chose to dispatch thirty-five thousand republican troops on the pointless, ill-advised Santo Domingo expedition, troops whose spirit was no longer in tune with the principles of the 18th Brumaire and so became a potentially irksome influence on the army.

---

90. Proudhon's younger brother, Jean-Etienne, died while serving in the military in 1832. He never discovered the true case of his brother's death, but blamed "troubles" with his captain. His death, he said, made him "an irreconcilable enemy of the present order". Cited in Vincent, *op.cit.*, 48, 248 n. 61. [A.P.]

91. *Bible,* John 11: 50. [H.M.] "That one man should die for the people". [P.S.]

92. Who was besieged in Genoa from 21 April to 4 June 1800. [H.M.]

I will grant that criticism, but I would just remark, in Napoleon's defence, that the reproach is much less directed at him than at the thinking that was current in his day.

If, in different circumstances, Napoleon had acted, as some assume he did, on the spur of some Machiavellian reckoning, I would not be citing actions of that only the conscience of the historian can judge. I would regard the founder of the dynasty of the Bonapartes as the major culprit and I would refrain from further comment. But this is not how abuses worm their way into government and thence into war-time operations and army discipline. Trace back the chain of causation, and, just when you think that you have arrayed before you the failings of merely one man, you will stumble upon a current of opinion, an upsurge in national vigour which, depending on the idea driving it onwards, sometimes leads to lionization of the head of State, who is also the head of the army, and sometimes claims him as its first casualty. Now, is there anyone who cannot see here that the First Consul and, later, Emperor was prompted by a conundrum he could not control? On the one hand, he faced a backlash against the principle of authority following a long period of revolutionary unrest; and, on the other, the mistaken understanding of war that was current and which had led to the notion that victory was all the more glorious if it had been won by smallest numbers over the mightiest coalition.

There is no point arguing with accepted wisdom that necessity wanted things that way; that there is no other way of waging war; that the chivalric courtesy we call for in the name of the right of war is all well and good for novels; that the first duty of the soldier is sacrifice; that, after all, the fight is not a quest for glory, but a pursuit of interests and that it is in the nature of interests, once they come into conflict, to ride rough-shod over all morality and every ideal.

To which my response will always be that this so-called necessity is not real; that the laws of war are no harder to abide by than those of duelling; and as for interests, we were endowed with reason and a sense of justice precisely in order to strike a balance between them, and the first prerequisite of such balance is the right of force. Oh, please, let us not drag utilitarianism into warfare, any more than into morality. All war has to go by is its conscience, its right, its good name; and you can see even now what it is tending to turn into under the impact of wrongheaded thinking. What will happen if you implant *interest* in the hearts of soldiers and generals, in place of this lauded sentiment of honour?

If, in spite of such irrefutable considerations and out of laziness of mind, lack of heart or perverse purpose, we mean to persevere with a shameful system, then I would say that we should drop all talk of the right of war, international law or political rights. Away with liberty; away with homeland; the greatest scoundrels shall inherit the earth.

As for honest folk, they would do better to accept anything that comes along: usurpation from within, no matter where it comes from and, from outside, insult and belittlement. Better that than having to engage in contests they cannot possibly win without losing their humanity. The enemy is coming: To arms, citizens, form your battalions to face the foreigner! – And you, Sire, should look to your own protection. As for us, whom you deign in these circumstances to call *citizens*, what have we to lose by changing master? And what worse fate could await us than being soldiers?

CHAPTER IX

Various Matters
1. Are the Rights of Peoples Devoid of Sanction?
2. Declarations of War. 3. To What Lengths Can Resistance Be Taken? 4. Regarding Interruptions to Trade. 5. Whether the Subjects of Enemy Powers are Enemies. 6. On Alliances

Our critique of military operations is not all we had to say about the forms of war. There are still a host of questions arising from the fact of war, which the jurisprudence of the writers on this subject has, if I may make so bold, shredded, and which must be resolved in accordance with the same principles and in the same manner. Let us devote a few pages to them.

"The right of peoples", writes one contemporary author, "is a quite modern invention".[93]

What we have said about war, in this Book as well as in the preceding one, shows the extent and the sense in which, that beneficial proposition is to be understood. In fact, the ancients had an understanding of the rights of peoples, by which we mean of the right of war, that far exceeded that of the moderns; and the reason for that, as we have stated, is that the ancients took the right of force seriously. But even though the ancients had a firmer grasp of the rights of peoples, they do not appear to have left any theory of it behind, and it is only over roughly the past two centuries that the moderns have attempted to make up for that silence. The dates and chief milestones in this theoretical constitution of the rights of peoples are as follows:

The publication of Grotius's book *De Jure belli ac pacis*, 1625
The publication of Hobbes's book *De Cive*, 1647
The Treaty of Westphalia, 1648
Pufendorf's *Jus naturae et gentium*, 1672

---

93. Charles VERGÉ, Introduction to Marten, *Précis du droit des gens* (Vol. I, foreword, 1). [P-J.P.]

Leibnitz's *Codex juris gentium diplomaticus*, 1693
The Treaty of Utrecht, 1713
Wolff's *Jus gentium*, 1749
Vattel's *Le Droit des gens*, 1758
Ancillon's *Tableau des révolutions du système politique en Europe*, 1803–1805
The Treaties of Vienna, 1814–1815
The Treaty of Paris, 1856

I shall pass over in silence the numerous texts listed by Martens's French publisher, and which it is utterly pointless consulting since all they all do is parrot the masters and from which, consequently, we have nothing to learn.

So, what positive truth has this 235-year tradition of scholarship brought forth?

None. Ever since breaching or abrogating the treaties of Vienna, which laid the recent groundwork for peace in Europe, was added to the agenda of governments and peoples, the uncertainties hovering over the rights of peoples, hitherto trapped inside books, have been revealed, and nations are today learning, to their cost, that any wrong-headed notion in the realm of morals or politics ends up being translated into the life of society as a calamity.

Now, the error of the publicists, the one from which all the rest spring and which makes their theory of the right of war and of the rights of peoples an issue of nonsense and contradictions, is that, in refusing to acknowledge the existence and legitimacy of a right of force, they are obliged to look upon the right of war as the product of a fiction and then go on in turn to deny the rights of peoples, which, by denying the right of war, finds itself devoid of santion.

This is what emerges from the formal testimony of all those writers and there is little point our rehearsing it all over again.

1. *Is the rights of peoples deviod of sanction?* May the reader forgive me a few re-statements here.

In principle, justice, like truth, cannot have any sanction other than itself; good results from its exercise and evil from its infringement. But from the political and governmental point of view, in the practical and administrative sense of the term, justice's sanction lies in the omnipotence of the sovereign, which is to say, in his force.

Thus, in civil law, there are numerous ways in which public force is made manifest in support for the courts; *injunctions* and *summonses, seizure, forcible expropriation, affixing of seals, marking of boundaries, physical constraint, garnishment, sale by auction*, etc. In penal law we have *subpoenas, arrest warrants, summonses and remand warrants; imprisonment, shackles, stocks, hard labour, banishment, transportation, the guillotine.*

Following this analogy, we might wonder what the practical sanction of the rights of peoples might be? And as nations acknowledge no sovereign and they look to no authority and no force, we are inclined to say that the rights governing their dealings, valid in the internal context, are devoid of all sanction in an external one. There is war, you may say. But the jurists reply: force on its own proves nothing; it has to be authorized and commanded by a higher power, which is itself the organ and representative of justice. Since no such higher authority exists, the rights of peoples have no guarantor other than the reason and morality of governments, which is to say, that, in reality, the rights of peoples rests on thin air.

What, then, is war, if not the sanction of the rights of peoples?

War, our authors reply, is a constraint exercised by a nation that claims to be the injured party vis à vis some other nation, which it accuses of trespass against its rights and its interests. But it must be plain that, by declaring war, the aggressor sets himself up as both judge and jury which, in proper procedure, cannot be countenanced, above all when it comes to recourse to force. From which it follows that war on its own proves absolutely nothing; that victory confers no right; but, as wars must come to an end and international disputes arrive at a good or bad solution, there is a tacit agreement, designed to halt the bloodshed and ward off greater misfortunes, to recognize the righteousness of the winner, no matter which side secures victory; this is what we term the *voluntary rights of peoples*. For war to be entirely moral and legitimate, it would have to be launched under the aegis of a verdict handed down by a higher authority before which international disputes would be heard and which would be empowered to sit in judgment of them and to enforce its determinations. But this could never happen and that, the jurists argue, is why the rights of peoples, like the right of war, boils down to a fiction.

In short, the theory of the modern publicists, based upon analogy, results in the hypothesis of a monarchy, republic or worldwide confederation, the very thing nations most strenuously resist and the pursuit of which has triggered the most horrific wars down through the ages. Outside of *omniarchy*, the rights of peoples, they contend, remains a *desideratum* of science, an empty word. In terms of one another, nations *live in a state of nature.*

> Whilst it is true that sovereigns and States, in their capacity as moral persons, can be judged by the same law that is used to determine relations between individuals, each of them has its own sphere of action which is bounded by that of the others; where the liberty of one ends, that of the

next begins and their respective assets are equally hallowed; it is not that there are two different rules of justice, one for private persons and the other for States ... That entitlement exists, but it lacks external constraint; there is no coactive power capable of compelling the different States not to deviate from the path of justice in their relations ... The sovereigns are still in a state of nature, since they have not yet devised this common guarantee of their lives and their rights and since each of them is sole judge and sole champion of that which is exclusively its own and which the others must respect.[94]

Earlier, I quoted Monsieur Oudot's conclusion, denied by Ancillon, that because of the *state of nature* affecting sovereign states, and because of the lack of sanction for the rights of peoples, that the centralisation of all powers on earth was inevitable. I refer the reader again to that quotation in Book Two, Chapter V.[95]

But such an exaggeration of the principle of authority would amount to the most impracticable of utopias and it is surprising that it was not enough to alert the honourable jurists that they were on the wrong track. The idea of a universal sovereignty, dreamt up in the Middle Ages and formulated in Charlemagne's pact, is the negation of States' independence and autonomy, a negation of all human liberty, something that States and nations will be eternally agreed in repudiating. Furthermore, it would amount to the paralysis of humanity, absolutely the same as despotism within the State, or communism in the tribe, and would trap that State and that tribe in stagnation. Civilization only advances through the influence that political groups wield upon one another, in the fullness of their sovereignty and their independence. Set a higher power over them all, to judge and constrain them and the great organization grinds to a halt. Life and thought are no more.

No. It is just not possible that the rights of peoples is devoid of sanction, despite what its supposed inventors, the modern jurisconsults, might say. The rights of peoples derive their natural, legitimate, effective sanction from war, waged in accordance with the rules that are logically deduced from the right of force. It is not true that war, or the application of force as an instrument of justice between nations, should be lumped, as those same jurisconsults do, with the means of constraint employed in civil and criminal proceedings and that, as a result, it needs a legitimation of its own, an *exequatur*,[96] from a different sov-

---

94. ANCILLON, *Tableau des révolutions du système politique*, Vol. I, 2. [P-J.P.]

95. "This division of men into different nations or societies is a matter of regret. If only we might some day see the people brought together again in unity". [H.T.]

96. *Exequatur*: Whereby a State gives its consent to a foreign trial being held on its territory; or the procedure by which a verdict delivered in a foreign country is made *binding*. [H.T.]

ereignty. Reducing it to those terms is tantamount to misconstruing the nature and purpose of warfare: it amounts to understanding nothing of the progress of the human spirit or the laws of civilization and history. War, as we have shown through the theory of the right of force and its enforcement, is a unique right demonstrated by a display of force. For that very reason, war is, out of all the courts, the one least liable to error and the one quickest to recover from its mistakes; and it is this which ensures that, just as the rights of peoples reigns over every sort of law, so war, that affirms and stands guarantor for it, is the most powerful sanction of all.

From the publicists, error, regarding the nature of war and the sanction of the rights of peoples, flows all the nonsense which infests their writings and, thereafter, all the calamities and crimes that war brings in its wake; every man of common sense willing to appreciate the thinking that guides armies and their operations will be persuaded of this.

The following questions, lifted at random from the books of the learned men, complete our critique.

2. *Declarations of war*. According to Vattel, justice requires that there be a declaration of war before any hostilities begin. – Pinheiro-Ferreira asks: Why so, if war is merely the use of force to stake a claim to what one is due; if, furthermore, the means of constraint have to be designed to destroy or paralyse the enemy's forces? It is enough that the aggrieved nation should have given notice of its claim: once it has been refused, it is free to act. Letting the enemy know, by means of a declaration of war, that he should now be on his guard, is a nonsense.

There is no answer to this observation of Pinheiro's, and Vattel himself, after raising the principle of a declaration of war, retreats from it in these terms.

> The rights of peoples impose no duty to declare war in order to afford the enemy time to prepare himself against a justified offensive. Therefore, it is permissible for that declaration to be made only once one has arrived at the border with an army and even after one has set foot on enemy territory.[97]

What Vattel is legitimizing, under his fictional voluntary rights of peoples, is ambush. And what happens then? Once upon a time, people used to dispatch heralds to deliver such declarations well ahead of time; in Vattel's day, they confined themselves to putting up posters in the capital; now the ambassadors are expelled the day before and sometimes on the day after hostilities begin. And

---

97. Vattel, *Du Droits des Gens*, vol. II, 117. [H.M.]

there is nothing here that needs repeating, if war is as the modern jurisconsults define it.

It is a different story if war is, as we have been arguing, a lawful assertion of the right of force; and if, in addition, and as we have just established, it is the sanction of the rights of peoples. In which case, it is self-evident that it should proceed exactly as if it had been ordered by a higher authority, which is to say, been declared in advance and for the very purpose of allowing the nation under attack to look to its defences; without which victory for the aggressor would be an ill omen; being the result of a surprise attack rather than a demonstration of force. This is how the general feeling among nations wants it, and how they have, up until recently, practised and abided by it.

3. *To what lengths can resistance be taken?* Vattel claims that resistance becomes punishable when it is manifestly pointless. He says: "In which case it is *pig-head-edness* and not valour".

But under Vattel's system, which only accepts that war can be just on both sides if we also accept the fiction of the voluntary rights of peoples, and denies that force is vested with any judgment, this proposition is an inconsistency.

It may be the case that the stronger party is an unjust aggressor. For example, how can we find fault with a man who, coming under attack from four brigands, defends himself to his final breath rather than hand over his daughter, or his wife, his fortune or his children's daily bread? Even in the most favourable case, a war of conquest or simple ascendancy, how can we fault a people that chooses death over domination? I fully appreciate that the pretext that defence was pointless will provoke the vengeance of the winner. The siege provides a good illustration. In resisting the onslaught, the inhabitants run the risk of being put to the sword. But the enemy's vengeance does not make that resistance unjust; Vattel should have understood this as he denies the right of force.

Because I affirm the reality of the right of war and take that right as sanctioning the rights of peoples, whilst at the same time not forgetting that the purpose of a war may well be the extermination of a nationality, my conclusion can only be conditional. If war is, as I say, the sanction of the rights of peoples, we should all acknowledge its law, which is that of force, particularly since there is no shame in yielding to force. But if it entails annexation or political emancipation, then it strikes me that the two belligerent powers are the sole judges of the price that they respectively place on their aggrandizement or their liberty, and, consequently, on the extent of their resistance. Because in some instances defending oneself to the death can be an act of heroism, commanding the respect even of the victor, it seems to me that circumstances alone should determine which resolution to take, thus each side remains its own master too.

4. *On interruptions to trade.* According to Pinheiro-Ferreira,[98] the state of war is not sufficient grounds for the interruption of commercial relations between two countries. It was of course the Continental System that prompted this highly philanthropic opinion from Pinheiro-Ferreira, and we have to admit that, with such a principle, Napoleon I might have been humbled early in the proceedings. More to the point, it has to be acknowledged that commercial dealings, if they had had to be honoured and sustained, would in most instances have rendered military operations unfeasible. Profoundly convinced of the absurdity of the right of force and of the immorality of warfare, Pinheiro-Ferreira, unlike the others, won't haggle with prejudice. He made it his business to constrain war with all the conditions that might shorten it, hamper it and make it impracticable and impossible. That is the overall tone of this philosopher's writings.

Unfortunately, things do not lend themselves that readily to the whims of opinion; or just because it pleases us to define things as it suits our purposes, they abide by their indomitable natures nonetheless. Between two nations, war is a trial of strength. And what is trade? An exchange of resources. Let war be as brief as possible, I am all for that; but, at the point of combat, which is to say for the duration of the hostilities, all commercial dealings, meaning all exchanging of resources between the belligerent powers, must cease. Without that, war would become a game; it would be a fencing match rather than a judgment or sanction.

5. *Whether the enemy powers' subjects are enemies.* Under the generally followed arrangement, this is an issue laden with contradictions and pretty much insoluble. Grotius and Vattel have determined that, by virtue of the fellowship that obtains between the nation and its government, the subjects of the two warring powers are enemies. As a result, Vattel says, children, women and the elderly are to be counted as enemies. They belong to the winner, not that this constitutes grounds for their being massacred, he says. Pinheiro-Ferreira cries out against this teaching and we have to admit that his opinion, though feebly grounded in principle, is the more attractive in practical terms.[99]

Of course, it could be quite logically argued, as he does, that the State's cause cannot be untangled from that of private individuals. But what! If war is, as is claimed, only an arbitrary or inevitable substitution of force for justice; if victory per se proves absolutely nothing; if it is unacceptable that any right of

---

98. Note to § 233 in Book III of Vattel, *Du Droits des Gens*, vol. III, 448. [H.M.]

99. GROTIUS, op. cit., Book III, Vattel, *Du Droits des Gens*, Book III, chap. V, § 70 (t. II, 124). PINHEIRO-FERREIRA. notes to same § in Vattel and notes on chapter VII of Book III. [H.M.]

war is positively the same on both sides; if that equality is simply a figment of the jurists' imagination; if, as a result, war most often comes down to an exercise in princely ambition, Machiavellianism or imbecility, must all the innocents be held to account for all the follies of their princes? Would it not be a more humane practice, would it not be a huge stride in the direction of a definitive peace, to declare, by common accord, that in war peoples are not to be held complicit in the policy of their governments?

I leave it up to the reader to pursue this controversy, which may give rise to magnificent oratorical flourishes but unlikely to arrive at any conclusion.

Speaking for myself, I regard the actions of States as historically necessary and war as a judgment, so let me just say that, in warfare, it would be dangerous, ill-advised and immoral to untangle governments from their subjects, that they share the same cause, and that, as a result, they share the same responsibility. But let me add, in the name of the same principles, and here I would go further than Pinheiro, that in reality this antagonism is only to be found between groups, which is to say, between two moral entities known as States; so that, even in an all-out war, the purpose of which is the wholesale annexation of one of the powers by the other, the subjects of those powers are not, ANY MORE THAN THE SOLDIERS THEMSELVES, to be deemed, individually, as enemies. During lulls in the bitterest of fighting of the Crimean war, the French and Russians mingled as friends, as hosts, swapping a pipeful of tobacco, a swallow of brandy. This furnishes the most beautiful commentary I could offer on my thinking and on how the right of force should find expression.

6. *On alliances.* On this score, everything that I have come across in the authors amounts to antechamber politics and is undeserving of the slightest mention. Let us leave such vulgarities behind.

The laws of force alone govern the outward lives of States.

Under these laws, every power is by nature hostile to every other and in a state of war with them. It loathes combination and subjection alike. Its internal organization drives it in the direction of invasion; the more prolific and frequent its dealings with its neighbours, the stronger the tendency in the direction of absolute independence and the more jealous it becomes of its autonomy.

For as long as a State can hold on to its potential for action, domestic and foreign, it is respected; the moment this begins to fade, it is thrown into disarray. Sometimes one province, sometimes another, revolts against the central authority and splits off from the trunk; other times, it is partitioned by neighbouring States which annex it.

From which it follows that alliances between States are by nature difficult, lacking in virtue, have the shortest lifespans and relate only to some special purpose. So, the alliance between Russia, Prussia and Austria over the partitioning of Poland lasted only as long as the partitioning took; it served no other purpose, and the secret of its success was the very decrepitude of the Polish State. The renowned Holy Alliance, dreamt up by Tsar Alexander to prevent the return of the conquerors, and to which all of the powers of Europe signed up, only ever existed on paper. Once Napoleon I had been broken and pinned to his rock in Saint Helena, each of the signatory States reverted to living its own life, which is to say, to spreading and conquering insofar as its force and its mores allowed. Likewise, the alliance between the very same Alexander and the Emperor Napoleon to divide Europe between them was only a dream; the august contracting parties soon spotted that it was easier to have fifty more or less balanced States living alongside one another than two huge empires, which, having divided the world between them, found themselves cheek by jowl.

The alliance between two or several States, when it comes to pass, is therefore designed either to seek the dismemberment and partitioning of another State, and, consequently, the forming of a brand-new State out of the resultant debris or to boost their own power; either to resist invasion, or to the dominance of a State which, on the basis of its force, stakes a claim to supremacy over the rest.

And so, the course of events prompts power A to annex power B, in whole or in part. This is what the Germanic Empire, currently Austria, did to Italy, which was at once imperial, pontifical and federal and, by that very fact, unviable. For a time, this Germanic conquest received a double endorsement from the majority of Italians and public right in Europe. But, with the passage of time and even under the impact of the treaties that had confirmed that annexation, opinion shifted; the annexed population changed its mind; more importantly, it was important to power C that power B recover its integrity and independence and other powers, D, E and F, etc., signatories to those treaties, stood idly by. As a result, there was an alliance between B and C against A. What is the meaning of that alliance? That the right to live, or, and this amounts to the same thing, the right of force, has swung back to B and has therefore deserted A, as the war was about to demonstrate.

Political alliances are the theatres of defections and thanklessness. Small wonder. Promise takes second place to reason which itself is merely the right of force. It may be that Austria, by distancing herself from Russia in the Crimean war, acted rashly; that rashness being the whole and all of her offence. But she was entitled to put a foot wrong; it would have been better for her to lose Hungary than become a vassal of the tsar.

On the other hand, it may be that Italy, on her guard against Austria, keeps faith with France, and we shall rejoice at the fact. But Italy is within her rights to repudiate our alliance, which is what she will do without fail on the day Austria recognizes her.

CHAPTER X

Various Matters
7. Neutrals. 8. Mercenaries. 9. Hostages.
10. Armistices. 11. Captives. 12. Privateering.
13. Whether the Expansion of a State Becomes
Grounds for War for the Rest. 14. Peace Treaties

7. *Neutrals.* One will find nothing but ramblings in the works of the writers on this issue, as on the last. The law governing the revolutions of States goes right over their heads as they get lost in lazy detail and quibbles. That law is simply the manifestation, expansion, amalgamation or balance struck between collective forces. Vattel and Pinheiro, for instance, make it their business to identify the neutrals, what their rights are, which acts breach neutrality, what a treaty of neutrality might be, and so on. Martens has nothing better to offer. Except that, having read all this blather, one is somewhat less taken aback by this policy of *non-intervention*, which boils down to unrelenting intervention, and in which England's statesmen glory. The scholars have nothing to teach us, there is no rule in the conscience of nations and no faith in governments.

As I see it, given that the stirrings of civilization are merely the evolution of political powers, and war the expression of the conflict between them; given, furthermore, that all those powers, though sovereign and independent, are nevertheless more or less related, let me open by positing as a principle that, when war breaks out between two nations, every other nation is more or less affected by it and that, as a result, there are not and could not be any genuine neutrals.

But given, on the one hand, that war is legitimate in its nature, since it boils down to finding out whether such-and-such a State is to come into existence or be thrust back into nothingness; whether some other State is to experience growth or shrinkage; whether this one is to be absorbed by that one; and given that, on the other hand, war must be, insofar as it can, circumscribed and confined to its purpose, the convention is that all States that declare themselves alien to or indifferent to the change can be counted as neutrals.

Thus, when Holland and Belgium went their separate ways, the powers that signed up to the 1815 Treaties of Vienna agreed, at the request of France and England, to stay neutral. They were of the view, wrongly maybe, that the break-up of the kingdom of the Low Countries, founded by the Congress, was incapable of upsetting the overall balance, the particular concern of the treaties, as long as there was a proviso that Belgium, the new-born State, could not, under any circumstances, re-join France or Austria, to which she had previously belonged. That caveat by the great powers is the foundation stone of Belgian neutrality. There was the same sort of abstention during the recent war in Italy. Whether the diplomats know it or not does not much matter: the principle behind that abstention, which was in any case imposed by the force of events, was that by setting herself up as a unitary State, Italy, far from upsetting the balance, underpinned it, since she would be forging a new great power between the Austrian Empire and the French Empire.

The issue of neutrality or non-intervention raises another: the issue of knowing whether it is permissible for a neutral power to supply weapons and munitions to one of the belligerent powers. The jurists' response here has been unbelievable. They say that continuation of trade is no breach of neutrality, but that it would be a different story if, rather than goods, the supposedly neutral power was sending arms and war materials.

I say that the very opposite of that should be the case. If war is, as the jurists think, but one means of restraining a defaulting debtor, it is clear that neutrals should refrain from furnishing him with weapons; should there be any doubts as to whether right is on the side of the aggressor or the defender, they should still stay out of it, otherwise they would be prejudicing the situation, setting themselves up as judges over the proceedings and stepping outside of their roles. At most, it is permissible for them to keep up the relations that cannot have any effect on the outcome of the war.

But if war is, as I maintain, a contest of strength, the purpose of which is to determine the creation, annexation or the striking of a balance between two States, if it is the sanction of the rights of peoples, it is self-evident that, just as such a contest requires a prior declaration, it presupposes the right to arm oneself and therefore implies, where neutrals are concerned, the right to supply war munitions and arms to whichever side is short of them. The only thing from which they should desist would be making deliveries for free or which were so long term that they might be regarded as free. Wealth is a component of force; as a result, war being a trial of strength, each belligerent power should rely upon its own resources and not on the resources of an outsider. Any supply of forces implies an alliance and the breakdown of neutrality: it is war.

8. *Mercenaries.* Pinhero-Ferreira considers the use of mercenaries as contrary to the rights of peoples. This jurist argues that the mercenary soldier is supposed to have told the government that pays him: "As long as you pay me money, I will obey you, regardless of the justice or otherwise of the use to which you put my cooperation. From this moment on, you have it without restriction".[100] As a result, Pinheiro would have mercenaries held liable to the penalty exacted upon pirates.

War is a trial of strength; of itself, it does not imply injustice on the part of any of the conflicting powers. Pinheiro-Ferreira's view would not be questionable if the mercenary was placing himself in the service of a pirate; or if, in a legitimate war, citizens of arms-bearing age could be regarded as the States' only resource. But wealth is also a component of force and, just as an entrepreneur is allowed to hire workers and salaried servants, I see no reason why a band of entrepreneurs, merchants, farmers, at war with a different band, would be prohibited from hiring soldiers as well. It is their capital, converted into an army, into shipping, into cannons, that does the fighting. The verdict of war is not going to be wrong. The equivalence drawn between the mercenary soldier and the contract worker strikes me as that much more plausible in that, among those who look askance at him are those who object to conscription. The profession of arms, they say, requires a particular calling, like any trade. If it is a trade, why would it not be acceptable to ply that trade? So, unless we want to make it a crime for the worker to defend his employer, I cannot see that mercenary soldiers are open to reproach.

9. *Captives.* Vattel says: "If need be, say, when one is dealing with a ferocious, perfidious, redoubtable nation; where one cannot take prisoners; when [etc.]..., then the putting of prisoners of war to death is allowed". But, this casuist goes on to say: "We have to be sure that our salvation requires such a sacrifice".[101] This is what happened after the battle of Agincourt and during the Egyptian expedition, under the command of General Bonaparte.

"And can prisoners of war be enslaved?" – Vattel's answer to that is: "Yes, but only because one is entitled to put them to death". Another commentator chips in: "Yes, but only by way of war reparations".[102]

Plainly, Vattel and those who came after him are talking randomly about things they know nothing about. Here, the jurists have run out of arguments; they have absolutely no use for the voluntary rights of peoples. If it were at least possible to contend, first, that war is always a crackdown on a crime,

---

100. Vattel, *Du Droits des Gens*, III, 374. [H.M.]
101. Vattel, *Du Droits des Gens*, III, 179. [H.M.]
102. Vattel, *Du Droits des Gens*, II, 181. [H.M.]

and, secondly, that the loser is always and of necessity truly blameworthy, as the ordeal or judgment of God suggested, that would be straightforward. The prisoner would be sentenced to death on the basis of his having lost and if the winner, under the lash of necessity, was not able to mark him down for servitude or exchange, the unfortunate would be in no position to complain. But such a hypothesis is far too nonsensical; the theory of the very same jurists who deny the validity of trials of force oppose it.

What principle shall we invoke, then, as governing the fate of captives? To cite the voluntary rights of peoples is to damn the voluntary rights of peoples. What sort of right is there that leads to the massacre of brave men, free of all criminality and who, in fighting, were acting upon a sacred duty?

It is wonderous, and I would bring it to the reader's attention with all the vigour I can muster, that the much-scorned right of force is more reasonable than all the learning of the jurisconsults and more humane than all their philanthropy. War is a trial of strength – whoever is wounded in combat or outnumbered, surrenders his weapons and is out of the reckoning as far as the war is concerned, is not, strictly speaking, a prisoner but, for as long as the war lasts, he is stricken from the list of his fellow citizens. Stripped of his military rights,[103] he is barred from service for the remainder of the war and it is in order to ensure that that he will abide by that obligation that the winner places him under guard. The soldier who surrenders on the battlefield is implicitly promising to take no further part in the fighting. If it can be established that his submissiveness is only a feinting movement, he would be killed as a traitor and assassin and

---

103. Among the Romans, a man unfortunate enough to fall into enemy hands was registered as legally deceased; stripped, by virtue of his being captive, of his right to bear arms, he was also stripped of his political rights. Which appears to be Horace's suggestion in this verse on Regulus, a captive of the Carthaginians, dispatched to Rome, on his word, to negotiate peace:

Fertur pudicae conjugis osculum
Parvosque natos, ut CAPTIS MINOR,
A[b] se removisse, et virilem
Torvus humi posuisse vultum
(Carmina, Book III Ode 5, §40–45)

Regulus did not want peace with Carthage. As a result, he didn't want to buy back the prisoners: all the more so since he had, as their general, witnessed them refusing to fight, allowing their hands to be bound behind their backs and opting to consign their homeland to servitude rather than face their own deaths. And, having offered that manly advice to the Senate, this final act of justice imposed upon faithless soldiers, Regulus, well aware of the fate that awaited him upon his return to Carthage, had no more to say to any of his friends: *he shied away from his wife's and children's embrace and stood, motionless and sombre, eyes fixed on the floor, like a man bereft of his family and civic rights.* [P-J.P.]

This final part of the sentence, above, is a translation and paraphrase of this (corrected) verse of the original Ode. [A.P.]

justly so. But once the war is over, and the dispute settled, prisoners on both sides are returned; each re-joins his loved ones; that is right, the whole and all of right and nothing but right. There is nothing more.

In the two recent wars in Crimea and Italy, the belligerent powers – France, Russia, Austria – vied with one another in terms of the gentleness with which they treated their prisoners: this being one of the features that best indicates how far the conscience of nations is superior to the scholarly theories, and the sort of improvements that might yet be possible in warfare, if the will was there. But butchered captives, captives sentenced to convict labour, packed into hulks, shipped off to faraway wastelands two thousand leagues from their homeland; that is something for which there is no excuse and it breaches every law and all right and brings equal shame upon the generals and statesmen who order it and upon the jurists whose nonsensical advice authorizes it.

10. *Hostages*. Once upon a time it was common practice to take and to give hostages by way of guaranteeing international agreements and adherence to the laws of war. I cannot fathom why this practice has been abandoned. They say that it was inhumane to hold innocents accountable for the bad faith of their fellow citizens, so that, as the counsel of humanity prevailed, the guarantee became null and void.

But this is to misconstrue both the obligation imposed on the hostage and the meaning of the laws of war. Regardless of whether it is pursued to the bitter end or confined to a specific purpose, war directly affects the sovereignty of the State, which is to say that which the citizen holds most dear, his liberty and his nationality. So, whenever there is a peace treaty, truce or armistice between two belligerent powers, that is guaranteed by hostages, it means that the powers have given a commitment, in the event of a breach on the part of their fellow citizens, to bring all of their influence to bear to get them back, if need be, and in the event of a refusal on their part to submit to the enemy and serve his cause, to face prosecution themselves as accomplices in the treachery. Which, let me say again, is still merely justice; it is for the hostages to ponder their position and for the power receiving the hostages to accept as guarantors only men of influence, capable of answering for their actions. The sanctioning character of war is startlingly obvious here, more than in any other connection.

11. *Armistices and truces*. Armistices are limited or unlimited. In the former instance, hostilities resume with full right once the armistice expires; in the latter, it would be appropriate to give a few days notice. Sometimes negotiations are opened during the armistice; therefore, even though there might be a fixed expiry date, notice can still be given, meaning that the negotiations have broken down.

25

That is the rule and there is no need to reiterate it. It is as correct as if the jurisprudence of force itself had framed it. Our criticism will not be pointed in that direction. But the authors wonder whether it is honourable warfare to propose an armistice, under the pretext of negotiation, when the sole intention is to use that armistice to build up one's forces and then carry on with the war, and, as they cannot see beyond their own spectacles, people who see no problem with the use of trickery in warfare deliver a negative opinion here.

Following the battles of Lützen and Bautzen, Napoleon agreed to a forty day armistice, seemingly for peace talks with the allied powers but, in actual fact, as his historian Monsieur Thiers states, with the intention of overhauling his armies and embarking upon a fresh campaign with better odds. When it comes to the historians, some hold the allies blameworthy for having let themselves be fooled like that and for having afforded the half-beaten conqueror a precious respite; Monsieur Thiers on the other hand, in his *Histoire du Consulat et de l'Empire*,[104] castigates Napoleon for having miscalculated, given that, even as Napoleon was adding a further 100,000 men to his armies, the allies were doubling their own.[105]

In all these criticisms, from narrators and diplomats, there is a contempt for good faith and an admiration for trickery and a love of brute force that pains me. What the undisclosed reasoning of the Emperor and his coalition was I do not know; what I can be sure of is that they both behaved in accordance with the principles of the strictest justice. As I will always argue, warfare is a trial of strength. Napoleon was fighting to hold on to French supremacy in Europe, a supremacy momentarily achieved through the overflow of the revolutionary idea; the coalition powers were fighting for their independence and their autonomy. The issue was this: Was nineteenth century civilization to carry on under France's protection or through the parallel development of balanced States? Force of arms alone could settle such an issue. Both sides therefore had to muster all their resources, without which any victory might still have been open to question. Now, the armistice of 3 June, 1813 served that purpose. My conclusion, therefore, is that, since war presupposes a declaration and a deferment, similarly, if it turned out that after hostilities had been opened, one side or the other was in need of an armistice, it had an entitlement to one. The entire issue was its duration.

12. *Privateering*. The powers that signed up to the peace of Paris in 1856 laid down the following four principles:

---

104. Volume XVI, 681. [H.M.]

105. In his *Memoirs*, Metternich recounts a discussion on the matter of manpower and notes "Napoleon's plentiful illusions regarding the significance of his adversaries' strength". Vol. I, 1150. [H.M.]

330 WAR AND PEACE

1. Privateering is abolished.
2. Neutral flags cover enemy goods.
3. With the exception of war contraband, neutral goods are not subject to seizure, even when displaying an enemy flag.
4. Blockades are only binding to the extent that they are effective.

Those four articles are beyond reproach. They are indicative of a lofty feeling for the right of war and international law within the powers that adopted them, and the diplomats who introduced them into the public morality of peoples deserve every praise. The only thing about which I have any regrets, is that the Congress failed to see the principle from which its declarations emanated, and that, as a result, it failed to follow that principle through to the end. In fact, the truth in these articles does not come, as several have thought, from the fact that they are derived from notions endorsed by the jurisconsults, but from the fact that they are the application of the right of force to international disputes.

The recourse to privateering, in war-time, derives from the sorely misunderstood and much misused principle that, in political contests, subjects are supportive of their governments and share in their fortunes. The conclusion from this has been that, whereas governments make war on one another, private persons are entitled to arm themselves against one another and, given that all plunder seized from the enemy is well taken, are entitled to indulge in piracy. In his *Traité des Droits et des Devoirs des nations neutres*,[106] Monsieur HAUTEFEUILLE has deployed all his eloquence to justify this practice.

It is tiresome, when rebutting one's adversaries, to find oneself having to rebut the same claim over and over again; but it is a lot more tiresome to see serious minds debating the same nonsense.

Politically constituted States are organisms, living forces whose rule is that they expand and grow indefinitely, absorbing or subsuming everything that falls within their sphere of activity. The moment that two powers run up against each other, antagonism breaks out between them, by reason of the force that they have built up. Sometimes there is conflict, at other times, such being the state of warfare in our age, they act simply as counterweights to each another and a balance is struck between them. From which it follows that war, or the struggle between political groups, has sovereignty as its principle and purpose, that it is by nature just on both sides and that its verdicts, made necessary by the general trend of things, are just and legitimate. Go through the list of the wars

---

106. *Des droits et des devoirs des nations neutres en temps de guerre maritime*, 2nd edition. Revised, corrected and amended in the light of the 1856 treaty, 3 vols. in-8°, Paris, 1858. [H.M.]

that humanity has been through over the past three thousand years and you will not find one in twenty that is an exception to this rule. Looking no further back than the sixteenth century, could we name a single exception? The wars of religion, triggered by the Reformation, the war between Christian Europe and the Turks, the war for ascendancy within the Holy Roman Empire, which by then was merely honorific; the war in the Low Countries, for the independence of Holland and the formation of French unity; the war of succession in Poland, the Seven Years' War for the formation of a Northern State, Prussia acting as a counterweight to Austria; the war of American independence, the revolutionary wars, the wars of the Empire, the war in Spain, the war in Greece, the war in Belgium, the war in Crimea, the war in Italy; all of them were centred on an issue of sovereignty, be it the sovereignty of a principle or sovereignty of a State; each was, therefore, fighting for its very survival.

Given these conditions, is it reasonable to invoke, in defence of privateering, the mutual pillaging of private persons, the principle of the fellowship of nations and governments? Not at all. War takes place between States over sovereignty and not over despoilment: consequently, it implies that the subjects of the defeated State should mirror the condition of that State, meaning that their political lives may alter but that they will retain their properties.

The jurists do not see things that way. There is no point ignoring the facts or refusing to acknowledge them. In their view, war is always waged, on one side or the other, on behalf of an unjust cause; in its actions, justice is one-sided; unfortunately, its decisions prove nothing by themselves and only have value in the light of the voluntary rights of peoples. So, what does this celebrated voluntary rights of peoples say? That all means of constraint, notably piracy, can be deployed against the ill-intentioned aggressor or defender; but, given that in a war both sides are to be assumed to be equally righteous, and that each of them is within its rights to do whatever the other one does, the right of piracy on the part of the side that has a just cause holds true for them both. It would seem, would it not, that where there is any uncertainty about its righteousness, piracy ought to be banned. Not at all, the authors assure us, the entitlement to one of the two requires a tolerance that works in the favour of the other! Monsieur Hautefeuille says,

> If the rights of one nation are ignored by another, if its independence is in jeopardy, its honour attacked and it cannot secure just satisfaction by amiable means, it is duty-bound to have recourse to arms and to make war on the unjust aggressor. For a nation could not let a trespass against its rights, its independence, its honour go unpunished, without thereby acknowledging the trespasser's superiority, without ceasing

to be his equal and thus, without discarding the essential qualities of nationhood.[107]

So says the partisan author. Relying on these considerations, and after concluding his tirade, Monsieur Hautefeuille pronounces piracy legitimate. I will not follow him in his oratorical flourish: like Phokion, it is enough for me to have kicked his feet out from under him.

And now to our own conclusions, relying upon those four articles. If privateering is done away with, if the authority once accorded to private individuals to arm themselves for war and hunt down the enemy's trading vessels has now been rescinded, we have to follow the principle of justice through to its end and declare all property at sea and on land sacrosanct; the warships of the belligerent powers are no more entitled than ships armed by private persons to seize one another's trading vessels. This is the observation tabled by the United States's ambassador in the Congress. That proposal was not carried. The Congress of Paris saw fit merely to restrict governments' right to pursue hostilities and it refused to deprive them of the potential benefits of seizure, in which it showed itself inconsistent and illogical, and the United States declined to append its signature.

13. *Whether the growth of one State becomes grounds for war for the rest.* In the heyday of the rights of peoples this issue was notorious. Grotius was the first to raise it, and most politicians have answered in the affirmative.[108] Vattel dithers, mulling it over and then, like an idiot not knowing what to say, aligns himself with the majority opinion.[109] Pinheiro-Ferreira rejects this doctrine but on insufficient grounds. Nobody makes the simple argument, suggested by history, that the State is an organized entity, a living force whose law is to grow constantly, unless stopped by an equal or superior force. There would be no point entering here into the details of that growth, whether they are honest or illicit, or to speak of ambition, etc. Such commonplaces are all empty chatter. Every State has this tendency towards growth; as it grows, it poses a threat to the

---

107. Op. cit., vol. I, 98. [H.M.]

108. By contrast, Grotius spoke out against this doctrine: "There must be no truck with what some authors teach, that, according to the rights of peoples, arms may be taken up in order to undermine a Prince or State whose power is increasing by the day, for fear that if allowed to rise too high, it may place us in a position to do ourselves a disservice sometime ... that one is entitled to attack someone simply because he is in a position to do us harm himself, flies in the face of all the rules of fairness". *De Jure Belli ac Pacis*, Book II, chap, I. §XV. [H.M.]

109. VATTEL, Book II, chap. III, § 42–46 and Pinheiro-Ferreira's notes, vol. III., 380. [H.M.]

sovereignty of its neighbours; that is the principle. Every State that feels under threat therefore has the right either to seek some compensation for itself or to resist that growth, if it can; it is a matter of foresight and timeliness, but, above all, a matter of force.

In fact, it was the extraordinary strides made by one power that led to the establishment of the policy of balancing between nations; thus, the pre-eminence of the house of Austria under Charles V, led to the peace of Westphalia; the supremacy of the house of Bourbon under Louis XIV to the League of Augsburg, and to the peace of Utrecht; the supremacy of the French Empire under Napoleon I, to the peace of Vienna in 1814 and 1815.

The very same factor was behind the countless amalgamations and annexations that have taken place in Europe over a number of centuries now. Thus, the states of the German Confederation have been whittled down, a step at a time, from more than three hundred to thirty-eight and show every sign of being whittled down further. Thus, we see Italy striding towards unity; Belgium and Holland, divided at one point, are drawing together into a fraternal alliance. Meanwhile, other States are forming on the Danube, in the Balkans, amid the debris of the Ottoman Empire, whose evolution seems finished. On every side, force, balancing itself out, looms as the organ and sanction of right.

14. *Peace treaties.*[110] In respect of peace, as well as of war, the authors on this subject are as removed from truth as they are from experience and their thinking is as befuddled as any ever seen. How could their thinking be right? According to them, there is no such thing as the right of force; it is a contradiction in terms. War can be just on one side only; it is the necessary outcome of some slight suffered; victory by itself is proof of nothing. The state of war is a state of subversion: as a result, and this is Vattel's conclusion, peace is the reversion of conflicting powers *to their normal status.*

There are as many errors in such talk as there are words. States are organized forces whose law commands them to develop at the expense of their surroundings, indefinitely. Once two States come into contact, they therefore are naturally inclined towards the annexation of the one by the other; hence, it is their natural state to strike a balance between themselves or to fight until the stronger gets the better of the weaker. That balance cannot last forever; the internal activity of States is constantly modifying their power and makes their development very unequal. What then is peace? A suspension of armed conflict

---

110. The link between the rise and fall of nations and constitutional settlements is developed at length in two later texts: *Contradictions Politiques. Théorie du mouvement constitutionnele au XIXe siècle* (Paris: Lacroix, 1870), and *Si les Traités de 1815 ont cessé d'éxister. Actes du future congres* (3e edition) (Paris: Dentu, 1864). [A.P.]

caused either by weariness in these powers or by the equivalence of their force and settled by a treaty. That is all: there is no other substance to this word peace; and just as the saying goes that the real guarantee of peace is to be ready for war at any moment, so expertise in peace resides entirely in the study of war.

What are peace treaties worth now? What do they mean, what is their reach?

Starting as ever from the principle that war has its origin in some insult and that victory is proof of nothing, Vattel states that the peace treaty cannot but be a *compromise*. That is a radical mistake. The peace treaty prompted by victory, which is to say, by the verdict of force delivered in a trial of strength, is a real solution, a re-definition of a State. And in the interests of peace and for the honour of the victors, would that this were so. Without that, peace, already so precarious, would only be a compact imposed by violence and would soon be torn asunder by treachery. Some jurisprudence that would be, relentlessly teaching the nations that any advantage secured by force is an iniquity and that their peace treaties are mere frauds or perjuries!

I shall halt my critical comments at this point. They should be enough to show that whereas, among the military, their knowledge of the right of war is mistaken, they at least retain some vague awareness of it, whereas among the jurists everything, idea and belief alike, has perished.

Conclusion

Let us sum up this Book and try to set out its substance clearly.

There is a real, positive, incontestible right of force.

That right is the one most anciently acknowledged in history and the one most keenly felt by the masses. If it were permissible to believe in an ongoing decline in the species, this right of force would be the last one to perish and the one that would make up the lowest tier of our morality.

War is the assertion and demonstration of that right. In that respect, it turns into the sanction of the rights of peoples. Whether favouring conquest or protecting independence; whether making States subordinate to one another or striking a balance between them, war is progressive and conservative and, rather than destroying powers, it disciplines them and readies them for an unknown future. Through the forms in which it wraps itself and the more or less plainly understood rules that it imposes, warfare thus asserts its right, which is at the same time its verdict. By means of its overall outcomes and despite all of the concomitant breaches and anomalies, it is the consecration of right. Anyone who studies the history of the formation, growth and dissolution of States with the slightest attention, will soon spot that, as a rule, and judging events only in the round, what has happened had to happen and, all in all, given society and its constituent and developmental laws, war has delivered justice.

Hence the warrior's zeal, the poetic epics of war, the religiosity of arms, the belief in heroism and that prodigious expression that banishes conscience and silences every scruple: the *right of war*. Hence, again, the lofty jurisdiction of armies acknowledged by every people and to which every will defers as if to an oracle; hence the respect for treaties that are the consecration, for one side of its defeat and, on the other, of its victory, as if defeat and victory were a contract and as if armies, by slaughtering each other, were merely rendering and enforcing verdicts.

This is what the theory says, what the human race believes and impartial history, in its overall outcomes, bears witness to in turn.

This magnificent theory evaporates in practice. Either because civilisation, that seemed to us so old, has made such little headway, or because savagery still

lurks in our being, or because of some other reason, war, observed in its operations, now strikes us as simply the extermination of people and things, by every
means of violence and trickery; a perfected, organized, large-scale man-hunt, a
variation on cannibalism and human sacrifice. War could be defined as a state in
which men, reduced to their bestial natures, recover their right to do to one another all the harm that peace is designed to forbid them to do. Furthermore, the
warrior, demoralized by the jurist's nonsensical teachings, is himself no longer a
believer in justice in war, which he denies, *Jura negat sibi nata, nihil non arrogat
armis*,[111] and in denying it, he unwittingly denies his own heroism. One might
say that he upbraids himself for the indignity of his calling, believing it to be
vicious and craven. He holds his warrior code in contempt, even as he invokes
it; such is the manner in which he has been schooled, that he regards it as a tis-
sue of hypocrisies, inconsistencies and contradictions. His strategy and tactics,
the purpose of which ought to be to ensure, through the decency and sincerity
of combat, the integrity of the judgment of force, is reduced to a means of utter destruction, a collection of homicidal recipes that sometimes remind one of
hunting with hounds, sometimes of hunting from a hide or a den, forever reliant
upon surprise, force majeure, deceiving the enemy and sometimes upon his stupidity. So that, whilst warfare can be regarded in the overall historical context
as a divine dispensation of justice, like some wise and valiant Pallas, its verdicts
come at the price of so much evil that we begin to have second thoughts, not
just about the right of war, but about any sort of right, and to think of justice as
an unnatural ideal and war as a Gorgon.[112]

Things are much worse if we move on from the military and the practitioners of war to those who are charged with teaching us philosophy and laws.
The latter have no doubt that war is a horrible scourge, sustained by the vil-
lainy of princes and the barbarism of nations; it is an unnatural state in which
everything that happens is justice turned on its head and its actions have no
more value than they can draw from the necessity of *faits accomplis*, from the
resignation of peoples and the reciprocal amnesties of governments. For as long
as this antagonism endures, they say, there will be no virtue and no rest as far as
humanity is concerned, and right is going to be an empty word. Because civil

---

111. This may have been taken from the prolegomena to Grotius's *De Juri Belli ac Pacis*
and is attributed to Horace. "He denies that laws were not made for him and claims everything by force of arms". From Jon R. Stone, *The Routledge Dictionary of Latin Quotations:
The Illiterati's Guide to Latin Maxims, Mottoes, Proverbs, and Sayings* (Abingdon: Routledge,
2013), 270. [A.P.]

112. Pallas (Athene – Minerva), the warrior goddess and symbol of considered bravery.
The goddess of Wisdom and Intelligence, who oversees the arts and inventions. Gorgon, a
monster most often depicted with tresses made up of writhing snakes. The best known was
Medusa, who could turn anyone to stone that gazed upon her. [H.T.]

right relies on political right and this, in turn, relies on the rights of peoples which, in the end, having no sanction other than war, is effectively non-existent. So say the lawmen, and we should not forget that if true this assertion leaves us with no hope.

So, having acknowledged, defined and analysed the MORAL element that permeates and pervades war; having woven a theory around that element and having teased out its laws, we have just acknowledged within that same war that there is an opposing, *brutish* element. Within war, there is more than just religion, right, poetry, heroism and enthusiasm; there is at least an equal measure of anger, hatred, perfidiousness, an insatiable craving for plunder and the most blatant shamelessness. War shows us its two faces: the face of an archangel and the face of a demon. Therein lies the secret of the horror it inspires, and that horror, it has to be admitted, is as legitimate as the admiration that its heroism had initially inspired in us.

Whereupon a question arises: Where does war get that duality from? Put more simply and in order to stick to purely practical considerations, what is it that brings about this strange dissonance between the idea of war and its application? How has this anomaly managed to survive, worsen even, over forty centuries of civilization? Might war be growing worse because of humanity's progress? Might it be radically beyond reform? Is it a freak phenomenon, whose law is that it cannot be realized in accordance with its idea – what am I saying! – an idea that is growing darker, as a reading of our authors suggests? Is war a creation, like us doomed from the outset, and consequently, always a travesty that nobody could improve upon? Then what could be behind this peerless anomaly? What might its meaning be? Ever since humanity came into existence, everything – religion, politics, philosophy, laws, mores, the sciences, the arts, industry, everything, except war – has improved. Only war, that primordial and supreme manifestation of justice, the sanction of all right, has progressively deteriorated, in terms of the darkening of its idea, the forward leaps in its powers of destruction, the hypocrisy in its pretexts and the pettiness of its outcomes. Among the moderns, it stands out only by a certain affectation of philanthropy and politeness, that makes it the more immoral and the more nonsensical. What power, therefore, what curse is stopping warfare from becoming in practice what theory would have it be and what justice requires it to be?

This is the question that we must now resolve, and that cries out for further investigation on our part.

BOOK FOUR

ON THE PRIMARY CAUSE OF WARFARE

Give us this day our daily bread.
—Lord's Prayer

SUMMARY

War presents itself to humanity as the heroic, divine deliverer of justice. The phenomenology of conscience, which, all in all, is nothing more than the phenomenology of war itself, testifies to that. That was the subject matter of Book One. Indeed, examined through the testimony of the human race, which scholarly jurisprudence opposes in vain, and through analysis of its features, war looms before us as the first sovereign manifestation of right; it is the vindication and demonstration by force of arms of the right of force, itself the principle behind the rights of peoples, political rights and every other sort of right. That much we established in Book Two. Coming then to a more scrupulous examination of warfare and its operations, we found that the form and the principle were mismatched; setting out their divergence was the purpose of our Book Three. Now it falls to us to inquire into the cause of this dissonance, which makes warfare as odious as it had once seemed sublime. This will be the subject matter of Book Four.

Moving on to a re-examination of the reasons that motivate war and the influences that shape it, and following back the chain of causation and trying to reduce it all to a single expression, what do we find? That, to borrow Grotius's dictum, war boils down to the defence or vindication of oneself or of one's own; which is to say, that if, in its executions, it takes care at all times to wrap itself in lofty considerations borrowed from politics and the rights of peoples, at bottom, and even though those considerations lose none of their value, it is initially triggered by a lack of resources, which is to say by a rupture in the economic equilibrium. Thus, quite apart from the important reasons of State it cites, war ought to have as its purpose the securing of compensation, by means of the dispossession of the loser, for the deficit that afflicts the winner.

It follows from this that war has two drivers, it is the effect of two sorts of causes: a primary cause, the same down through the ages, and common to all States, all races, a shameful but unrelenting cause that wears disguises and hides itself away; and secondary causes, the only honourable and acknowledged ones, these being the ones we have spoken about and which can be deduced from political needs.

The organic laws of sustenance, labour and POVERTY; the moral law of temperance; the economic law of distribution of services and goods. The nature and universality of pauperism, engendered by trespass against those laws and constituting the number one cause of discord. The evolution of war outlined in accordance with this new outlook. Hero and pirate originally synonymous; the poetry of brigandry. Examples taken from the Bible. In politics and war, the Greek mind never climbed past notions of plunder and tribute; the ignominies of the Peloponnesian war. Progress in war – looting elevated to the status of conquest. Greece was supplanted by the Macedonians; the latter by the Romans. The spread of the spirit of conquest in modern times; though weakening, how the ideas of plunder and tribute remain inseparable from it. The potential consequences of all-out war in our own day between two civilized nations, according to established right: the universal threat. – Conquest, war's only purpose, divorced from any notion of pillage and tribute, turns into a contradiction and war becomes pointless. A revolutionary situation.

CHAPTER I

On the Need to Probe Beyond Political Considerations When Determining the Precise Causes of Warfare

The dissonance that we pointed out in the previous Book between the operations of warfare and the theory of a verdict of arms, suggests that we are still blind to its causes and that the secret of this phenomenon still partly eludes our inquiries.

According to philosophical analysis and universal conscience, war is one thing: in the details of its operations, it is quite another. Here, brutal in its horror; there, a sublime notion, a godly ideal.

This contradiction between the act and the ideal of war is, moreover, not at all coincidental; it is not an exception that affects only specific instances. It is general and consistent, and we have seen it worsen down through the ages: it has all the hallmarks of an incurable, chronic vice. Where does that come from? This is the puzzle we have to solve.

At first glance, we will find nothing on the road we have travelled to explain away the savagery, perfidy and plunder that war has always displayed in contradiction to its idea. On the contrary, it looks as if everything about its principles, its motives, its conditions, and its purpose is such as to elevate the soul and introduce it to heroism rather than provide an outlet for brutish passions, cruelty, lust and brigandry.

So, we have registered the existence of a right and, consequently the need for a jurisdiction of force. What is there in this ideal of war that is so offensive or ignoble, that riding roughshod over human dignity, raises its hackles, incites it to seek revenge and to criminality? Absolutely nothing; the most sensitive self-regard could not find any excuse for irritation there. The most humiliating of dominions is assuredly the rule of blind force over mind and liberty. But this is not the case with war. War presupposes the existence of a right of force, cousin to the right of intelligence, the right of labour and any other sort of right, its main, solemn exercise being in State-to-State relations. An expression of the right of force, the purpose of war is therefore to determine, by means of a contest between rival forces, which of the two contending powers has the better claim to, what? The spectre of intelligence? No; industrial superiority? No; ascendancy in the arts? No, no; political ascendancy, meaning the directing of force. Here right and force become identical terms; where is the insult, shame and humiliation in that? The combatants are driven by just one enthusiasm, patriotism. Persuaded of the legality and lofty morality of combat, they wrap it up in all manner of legal and solemn formulas: by what aberration does this pious and holy combat degenerate into plunder, devastation and murder?

Should we be looking to war's motives for the reason behind its fall into depravity? We are conversant with those motives and cannot find anything therein to account for dishonesty in combat and tactlessness in victory.

War comes in two varieties. On the one hand, international warfare. This is when the issue is the amalgamation of two races, the annexation of one State into another, the setting of boundaries between them, their subordination or, equally, the liberation of a subjugated nation, asserting its sovereignty by force of arms. And, on the other, civil or social war, when there is some great religious, governmental or feudal interest at stake and where defeat entails revolution for country and State alike.

In each of these instances, and there are no more, war, far from motivating or triggering the excesses for which it is so rightly taken to task, the idea of war strictly prohibits them. In fact, such excesses, far from being licensed by the right of warfare, are formally condemned by it; far from serving a righteous cause, it disgraces it; far from repressing or intimidating the enemy, they incite him and drive him into reprisals; far from hastening a solution, they delay it by means of a counterfeit victory.

But then, what is the connection between the grave issues of public or international law, which must be settled through a trial of strength, and this system of surprise attacks, ambushes, requisitioning, plunder, rape, devastation and massacre: these murderous tactics, these rifled cannons, these explosive bullets, these desperate crackdowns, these incendiary columns, these infernal machines? It is as if a private individual, suing his neighbour over a debt or some boundary dispute, rather than replying to a summons, were to poison his opponent's livestock, beat his children and his servants, and set fire to his crops. Let the plaintiff but take his revenge after losing his case and, blameworthy though such behaviour may be, it is nevertheless understandable; but for him to enter his plea brandishing a firebrand in one hand and a blunderbuss in the other, would be an unprecedented, nonsensical sight. Such is war, however, despite the shows of justice in which it drapes itself and despite the discipline on which warmongers so pride themselves.

The strangest thing is that one could dismiss all this evil as a surrender to the passions, training for combat, soldierly indiscipline, the criminality of a few perverse individuals, which peace, that friend of order, forces to stay hidden, and that licence in the field draws out and encourages. We would do better to accuse the army commanders and heads of State instead. All of them, in a sort of an unspoken agreement, and with frightening honesty of intention use the most fearsome weapons of destruction against one another. For the front-line soldier, marauding is explicable in terms of hunger, rape in terms of prolonged sexual abstinence and, above all, of that over-excitement of the vital faculties that war induces. Massacre derives its principle from the heat of the action and the thirst for vengeance. But what are such excesses alongside the deliberate, systematic destruction of which the soldier is merely the blind and irresponsible agent? The excuse of the passions no longer works when we are talking about the generals and the members of the government; and there are good grounds for asking how superior minds that are forever talking about the right and the rules of war and who, though they do not make them, comment upon them and enforce them; men in the grip of no passion, not even the urge to fight; that, without any need, not even hunger, can cold-bloodedly issue the orders for slaughter, organize a war that is a mockery of its own basic principles, without its doing any service at all either to their own glory or to their cause.

Whether the reader has been struck as much as I have by this pile of anomalies, I cannot say; the fact remains that there is a mystery there that cries out for explanation. The fact is that nothing, either in the notion of war, or in its principle, or in its conditions, or in its motives, or in its purpose, justifies this host of abusive and illegal acts that make up the customary practice of war. The certainty is that nine-tenths of these calamities cannot in any case be ascribed to the soldier's being quick to anger. Intentions cannot be put in the dock here: the error runs a lot deeper than human maliciousness.

In philosophy, the rule is that when you cannot explain something by its immediate determinant, the chain of causation should be traced back and that one should not stop until one has come to a principle that offers an explanation of everything. Let us follow suit. The motives behind war, insofar as they are known to us, are entirely honourable on all sides; the rules, as deduced from them, and governing military operations are, for their part, wholly chivalrous. Finally, the passions that at any moment might ignite the clash of arms can only give rise to individual, exceptional, fleeting excesses, out of all proportion with those protracted, incalculable calamities engendered by war. Therefore, it should be plain that there is some secret and still undetected influence holding sway over actions and warping them. Where does that influence come from? In other words, what is the prime cause of war?

Grotius, of all the writers on this topic, is the one who seems to us to have been most alive to the importance of this topic of research. He traces all the causes of war to a single cause, which he regards as primordial and therefore capable of explaining away all phenomena; *defence of oneself and of one's OWN*.[1]

Those few words are a revelation. If, as Grotius argues, war, political motive and reason of State, which we have identified, can be boiled down to a cause that is both more all-encompassing and more commonplace, to the protection of individuals and their properties; if such breaches as are committed in war against individuals and properties, in spite of the right of war itself, in spite of the right of force and of the rights of peoples, such breaches are explicable, they represent a response to a provocation proportionate with that provocation. Any protective measure against an enemy who begrudges us our lives, or against the thief who covets your property, is, by its very nature, permissible and therefore pardonable. It remains to demonstrate the truth of Grotius's view, that there is a connection between war, a necessity in the formation and evolution of States, and the *defence of oneself and of one's own*.

Alas! Here, Grotius abides by the most profound silence. Having raised war's prime cause as a hypothesis, and digging no deeper, Grotius moves on to security measures. Persuaded that, in order to stem the scourge and limit its ravages, it is important above all else to determine the rights and duties of every citizen, city and State, precisely and in every circumstance, the wise jurisconsult launches into lengthy inquiries into personal and actual rights, into property, marriage, inheritance, punishments, demarcation of territories, trade, etc. As there are legal matters in dispute everywhere, he has no difficulty concluding on that basis that there is a danger of war everywhere too, that war is no more likely to be abolished than trials; and besides, that just as there are rules of right and formal court procedures for dealing with quarrels between private individuals, so it is possible to identify the mutual obligations of States, and, up to a point, the formalities to be observed in the settlement of such disputes.

This is Grotius's plan and the foundation of his entire doctrine. Now, given everything that we ourselves have argued in the first three Books of this work, it is not hard to see how much this plan leaves to be desired. Not only does Grotius, as we have just been saying, fail to bridge the gap between the civil law of persons and properties, and the political law relating to dealings between nations, but he fails to show us how an implacable, impassioned defence of oneself and of one's own gets caught up in a war between one State

1. Grotius, *De Juri Belli ac Pacis*, Book II chap. I. Grotius lists Sovereignty among the assets liable to be gained, defended and alienated, insofar as it is a legacy. See Book Two, chap. VI. – See also, chap. VIII: *Des acquisitions que l'on rapporte communément au droit des Gens.* [H.M.]

and another, a war necessary in terms of its immediate cause, legitimate in its purpose, chivalrous in its forms and unimpeachable in its sanction. Not only, as I say, does Grotius fail to demonstrate the connection and the link between all of these things, but he confuses and identifies the different kinds of rights, civil right, political right, the rights of peoples, and he knows nothing of the right of force, for better or for worse, and ends up countenancing as essential to war, and part of its right, all the horrors that he set himself the task of averting. An idea occured to Grotius; he noted it in passing; but he was not able to trace it to its source and plot its sequence. In short, he spotted the fact; but he has not supplied its philosophy. Let the judicious reader, if he will, take a minute to reflect on this; either I am grievously mistaken, or he will acknowledge that at first glance, it was scarcely feasible for anyone setting out to track down the principles behind the rights of peoples to have done better than Grotius has. Speaking for myself, and I make no bones about this, had the work of that celebrated Dutchman never existed, had his successors in turn not furnished me with counter-arguments, then it strikes me that, save for the erudition that I lack and the authority that I also do not possess, I might have written my own version of Grotius's book: given how much his facts speak for themselves; given how sorely the truth needs obstinate criticism and, like the proceedings in our courts, adversarial arguments.

Having paid that tribute to Grotius, let us now try to tease out his thinking clearly.

Let me point out, for a start, that identifying the DEFENCE of oneself and of one's own as the prime cause of warfare amounts to examining the issue in but one of its aspects and, in chronological terms not even the first. For me to defend myself, there has to be someone who has *attacked* me; and why would he be attacking me, other than because he claims, wrongly or rightly, that I belong to him, that I am beholden to him, that I owe him something, either my body or what is mine? War is double-edged, implying both claim and rebuttal, without prejudicially assuming that one side is more in the wrong than the other. Grotius's mistake, and the mistake made by all who have come after him, is thinking that war is always and of necessity unjust on one side at least, whereas, according to war's idea, and in the vast majority of cases, it is as just on one side as it is on the other. The decency of each of the belligerent powers is inseperable from the very hypothesis of war.

What lies at the root of all human disputes, between States and between individuals alike, is the claim and denial of property.[2] Here we are venturing

---

2. "In the multitude of hidden causes which agitate nations, there is none more powerful or constant, none less obscure, than the periodical explosions of the proletariat against property. Property, acting by exclusion and encroachment, while population was increasing,

beyond politics proper; we are stepping into another sphere of ideas, into the sphere of social economy. In short, the State, like the individual, has to live, meaning it must consume; the sovereignty that it arrogates to itself or to which it stakes claim has no purpose beyond guaranteeing its sustenance: that is the fact of the matter, stripped down to brass tacks.

In order to have the final word on war, we therefore have to go back further than Grotius has done. We must consider that, independent of the promptings of religion, homeland, State, constitution, dynasty, as previously alleged, there is the informal – God forbid that declarations of war should ever bring it up! – but very real consideration of livelihoods. From that vantage-point, every individual belonging to one or other of the warring nations feels that his property is in jeopardy and not only turns into a defender of himself and his own, as Grotius puts it, but stakes a claim upon the liberty and property of the foreigner. As a result, war, just on both sides, as it is deemed to be from a political point of view, becomes, in economic terms, equally immoral on both sides. Hitherto, it looked to us as if the purest patriotism, the loftiest sense of social dignity was the sole inspiration behind war; now we can see that a principle of selfishness, a principle of greed, plays a part in it, whence springs its corruption and its frenzies.

Now let us delve more deeply into this contention.[3]

---

has been the life-principle and definitive cause of all revolutions. Religious wars, and wars of conquest, when they have stopped short of the extermination of races, have been only accidental disturbances, soon repaired by the mathematical progression of the life of nations". (*What is Property?* 1840, Chapter V, § 3.) "Property is the most essential principle by the aid of which we can explain history's revolutions ... It positively governs history". (*Theory of Property*, posthumous). Proudhon returned to this theme several times over; taken, not from Laveleye whom he cites in his posthumous work, but from Germain Garnier *De la Propriété dans ses rapports avec le droit politique* (1792). [H.M.]

3. To account for the *contradiction* between war's phenomenality and its forms, between the idea and the fact, Proudhon falls back on the *philosophy of poverty*, which he posits as the chief cause of *an event that has just struck him as being as necessary*, constant and grandiose as labour, property, etc. This "proof" is effected by means of the method of the economic interpretation of history, of which Proudhon is one of the pioneers and of which he provides in Book Four of *War and Peace*, the most complete and suggestive example. This was one of the most clear-cut, original aspects of his thought and one of the leading characteristics of his oeuvre. [H.M.]

CHAPTER II

The Underlying Principles of Political Economy:
The Laws of Poverty and Equilibrium

The primary, universal and ever-constant cause of warfare, however it is ignited and by whatever it is prompted, is the same as drives nations to swarm, to establish faraway settlements, to quest after land and outlets for their surplus populations: *lack of livelihood* [*subsistances*]; in its extreme form, the RUPTURE OF THE ECONOMIC EQUILIBRIUM.

According to this new perspective, the purpose or object of warfare would therefore be, where the aggressor is concerned, to make good by plunder the penury by which he is tormented; and on the part of the injured party, to defend what he regards as his property, by whatever title it may hold it. In the final analysis, *pauperism*: there you have the root cause of all war.[4]

Here we have fallen from the bright heights of right into the maw of famine and envy! Sublime in terms of its professed mission as deliverer of justice, war's infamy derives from the secret cause that brings it about. Let it make whatever display it will of its trophies, the empires it has founded, the nations it has freed, the consciences it has liberated, the freedoms it has won; as the daughter of pauperism, it has greed for a godmother and crime for a brother. Can you guess now why war has failed to live up to its ideal?

The thesis I propose to set out here involves three questions:

1. Can the accused misfortunes of war be legitimately imputed to pauperism?
2. How does pauperism exercise its sway over the policies of government?
3. How does pauperism manifest in international relations?

I shall be sparing with economic considerations. Given that the real proof of my argument resides in facts, it falls under the remit of history.

---

4. "The mother of poverty, crime, insurrection, and war was inequality of conditions; which was the daughter of property, which was born of selfishness, which was engendered by private opinion, which descended in a direct line from the autocracy of reason". *What is Property?* 1840, Chapter V, 2nd part, § 1. [H.M.]

Let us not be deluded by the pride in our wealth and the fever of our sensual delights; pauperism is as much a blight upon civilized nations as on barbarian hordes. In any given society, well-being is not so much dependent on the stark sum of accumulated wealth, which is always less than one might imagine, as upon the relationship between production and consumption and especially the distribution of goods. Now, since, for a multiplicity of reasons that it would serve no purpose to enumerate here, the productive capacity of each people cannot keep up with the capacity for consumption, and as the distribution of goods is effected in a much more fitful manner than the production and consumption of them, it follows from all this is that there is a consistent universal unrest, that such-and-such a society, which thinks itself affluent is actually indigent. In short, everyone is affected by pauperism, the property-owner living off his rent as much as the proletarian who has nothing but his manual labour with which to support himself.

As this may seem like a paradoxical proposition, permit me to labour the point for a few moments.

Of all the requirements of our nature, the most imperious is our duty to feed ourselves. From what I have been told, there are a few varieties of butterfly that require no sustenance, but they eat their fill at the larval stage and their lives are ephemeral. Is it worth our while taking them as symbolic of an angelic life, freed from the burdens of the flesh? I shall leave it to the analogy-lovers to answer that. Be that as it may, man shares in the common condition of animality; he must eat, or, in economic jargon, consume.

There is our first economic law: it is a formidable law that pursues us like a fury if we fail to respond to it wisely, as it also does when we make ourselves its slaves and sacrifice every other duty to it. It is in our need to feed ourselves that we come closest to the beast; it is at its instigation that we become worse than brutes, when we sink into debauchery, or, ambushed by famine, do not shrink from recourse to fraud, violence and murder in order to appease our appetites.

However, the Creator who chose this mode of existence for us, followed his own counsel. The need for subsistence pushes us into *industry* and *labour*; this is our second law. Now what are industry and labour? The physical and intellectual exercise of a being made up of body and mind. Not only is labour necessary for the preservation of our bodies, but it is vital for the expansion of our minds. All that we possess, everything we know, is derived from labour; all science, all art and all wealth, are all due to it. Philosophy is just a way of generalizing and abstracting the results of our experience, which is to say, of our labours.[5]

---

5. The relationship between philosophy and labour is a recurring theme in Proudhon's political economy, from *What is Property?* right through to his posthumous works. One of the best statements of it is in *System of Economical Contradictions, or the Philosophy of Poverty* (trans. Tucker, 1846). [A.P.]

Just as it looked as if the law of consumption was the humbling of us, so the law of labour lifts us up. We cannot live by the life of the mind alone, as we are not pure mind; but, through labour, we spiritualize our existence more and more; and is that cause for complaint?

A question arises here, a most serious question, the solution of which determines both our current well-being and, if the ancient myths are to be credited, our future happiness.

What does man need to consume? How much, therefore, must he, how much can he, produce? How much must he labour?

The answer to that question will be our third law.

First off, let us note that man's capacity to consume is boundless, whereas his productive capacity is not. This has to do with the nature of things: consuming, devouring and destroying is a negative, chaotic, nebulous faculty; producing, creating, organizing, imparting being or form is a positive faculty, governed by numbers and measurement, which is to say, limitation.

If we look around us, we see that everything is bounded by created nature, by which I mean to say endowed with form. The globe on which we live has a circumference of nine thousand leagues; it takes it three-hundred-and-sixty-five-and-a-quarter days to complete its revolution around the sun. As it rotates and orbits it offers its poles to the central star. Its atmosphere is no deeper than twenty leagues; the ocean that covers four-fifths of its surface no deeper than three thousand metres, on average. A sufficiency of light, heat, wind and rain is doled out to us, of course, but also not excessively so and one might even say with a degree of parsimoniousness. The slightest variation, upwards or downwards, in this global economy, results in disorder. The very same law applies to the fauna and flora. The normal lifespan of a human being barely exceeds seventy years. It takes six years for an ox to reach maturity; a sheep, two years; the oyster three. A poplar thirty-five centimetres in diameter will be no less than twenty-five years old; an oak of the same thickness, a century. Wheat and most of the plants we grow as food are seasonal. Throughout the temperate zone, the best on earth, just one harvest is brought in; and look at how many parts of the surface of this planet are unworkable and uninhabited!

As for man, the manager and usufructuary of this domain, his muscle-power cannot, on average, match a tenth of one horse-power. He cannot, without being spent, deliver more than ten hours' effective toil per day, nor three hundred days per year. He cannot go a day without food and could not survive on half rations. In earliest times, back when the human species was scattered across the globe, nature had no problem supplying its needs. That was the golden age, the age of plenty and peace, over which the poets weep and since then, with mankind growing and multiplying, the need to work has made itself felt more and more, and scarcity has generated discord. Now, no matter what the climate, the population far exceeds nature's resources, and it can be stated quite truthfully that, in the age of civilization in which he has been living, from time immemorial, man has survived only on what he has wrested from the soil through dogged toil: *In sudore vultus tui vesceris pane tuo.*[6] This is what is known as production, wealth-creation, the items he consumes having no value in his eyes beyond their usefulness and the labour they cost him. So that, as the conditions of his welfare evolve, *abundance* and WEALTH appear as contradictory terms: as abundance may very well obtain where there is no wealth and wealth where there is no abundance, both terms therefore signifying the very opposite of what they appear to mean.

As a result, in his civilized condition, man secures through toil whatever he needs for the upkeep of body and the cultivation of his soul, *no more, no less.* The common, strict boundary line between our productivity and our consumption is what I term POVERTY, the third of the organic laws bestowed upon us by nature, and this is not to be conflated this with pauperism, of which more below.[7]

Here, there is no point in my disguising the fact that universal prejudice stands against me.

Nature, they say, is inexhaustible, and labour more and more industrious. We are a long way from having extracted from our old wet-nurse, the earth, everything that she has to offer us. A day will come when abundance, never having lost its price, may be able to describe itself as wealth, when, as a result, wealth will abound. When we shall be awash with all manner of bounty and live in peace and joy. Your law of poverty, therefore, is false.

Man has a fondness for bamboozling himself with word games. The hardest part of his philosophy will always be for him to understand his own tongue. Nature is inexhaustible in the sense that we will forever uncover fresh usefulness there, but conditional upon a relentless escalation in toil, which fits with the rule. The most industrious nations, the wealthiest ones, are the ones that work hardest. At the same time, for a reason that we shall shortly identify, those are the very ones where poverty wreaks the greatest havoc. Far from refuting it, the example of those nations confirms the rule. As for the advances of industry, they are primarily realized in relation to items that are not basic necessities, and for which we have least need to satisfy nature's dictum. But if that class of

---

6. *Bible,* Book of Genesis, 3:19, "In the sweat of thy face shalt thou eat bread". [P.S.]

7. "Therefore when economic theory, monitoring experience at some remove, came upon the word poverty, it took that word to signify the inner law of our development, the essence of our being, the form of our life. Rapid population growth, a slower growth in basic necessities, are the two faces of the same idea, of the same single phenomenon", *The Philosophy of Poverty,* vol. II, Chap. XIII. [H.M.]

item should, by however so little, exceed the limit set by securing subsistence, then, they instantly drop in value and the superfluous are reduced to nothing. Common sense, which just now seemed akin to the pursuit of wealth, then opposes output going beyond the bounds of poverty. Finally, we should add that, whilst overall wealth is boosted through labour, the population grows at an even faster rate.

From all this it follows that, given boundless potential for consumption and a forcibly restricted productive capacity, the most exact of economies is thrust upon us. Temperance, frugality, daily bread obtained by daily labour, wretchedness on hand to punish gluttony and sloth: whence the first of our moral laws.

Thus, the Creator, by making us subject to the need to *eat in order to live*, far from holding out to us the promise of a feast, as the gastrosophes and Epicureans would have us believe, sought to steer us, one step at a time towards the ascetic, spiritual life; it teaches us sobriety and order, and enamours us to them. Our destiny lies not in enjoyment, no matter what Aristippus[8] may have said: neither through industry nor art, nor from nature, have we secured ENJOYMENT for all, in the full sense in which the term is used by sensualist philosophy, which makes fleshly delights our sovereign good and our purpose. We have no other calling but the cultivation of our hearts and intellects and it is in order to help us, and, if need be, to force us into it, that Providence lays down a rule of poverty for us: *Beati pauperes spiritu*.[9] And also why, according to the ancients, *temperance* was the first of the four cardinal virtues; why, in Augustus's day, the new age poets and philosophers, Horace, Virgil, Seneca, used to lionize mediocrity and preach contempt for opulence; why Christ, in an even more touching fashion, teaches us to look to God for nothing more than our daily bread. They all realized that poverty is the principle behind social order and our only happiness here below.

One oft-cited fact, the true meaning of which seems, however, to have eluded us, is the average income, per month and per head, of a country like France, one of the most advantageously located countries in the world. About thirty years ago, that income was reckoned by some at 56 centimes and by others at 69. Quite recently, Monsieur Aug. Chevalier,[10] a member of the

---

8. Aristippus of Cyrene, a disciple of Socrates, used to teach that happiness and pleasure are the ultimate aim of man's destiny. [H.M.]

9. *Bible*, Matthew, 5:3. "Blessed are the poor in spirit". [P.S.]

10. AUGUSTE CHEVALIER, the deputy from L'Aveyron, was brother to the economist Michel Chevalier. [H.M.] MICHEL CHEVALIER (1806–1879) was imprisoned for his editorial role on the Saint-Simonian journal *Le Globe* in 1832, became professor of Political Economy at the College de France in 1841 and was subsequently a deputy and then senator in the French Assembly. [A.P.]

Legislative Body, in a budget speech, assessed the overall income of the nation at 13 billion, or 98 centimes per day per head. But some miscalculations in that assessment have been detected, so that the figure should be reduced by at least 1,500,000,000, bringing us to a figure of 87.5 centimes per day per head, or, for every family of four, 3.50 francs.

Let's go with that figure. A family of four can survive on a daily income of 3.50 francs. Obviously, of course, there will be no luxury there; the mother and daughters are not going to wear silk dresses; the father will not be frequenting the tavern; in the event of unemployment or sickness, or were accidents to befall him, he will soon run short and be facing indigence. Such is the law, the severe law from which nothing – other than in rare, exceptional cases – can rescue him, other than at the expense of others. The soldier's pay and sailor's pay and, broadly, every workman's pay are applications of this median, which ultimately has made us all that we are worth, all that we are. Poverty is the real providence of the human race.

It has been demonstrated by statistics that a nation such as ours, placed in the best circumstances, year in and year out, produces only to meet its own needs. The same can be said of every country; everywhere one will arrive at this conclusion, and we should take this on board, that man's condition here on earth is toil and poverty; his calling, science and justice; his primary virtue, temperance. Surviving on little whilst toiling a lot, and relentlessly learning, this is the rule which it befits the State to teach its citizens by example.

It will be said that this income of 87.5 centimes daily per head is not the last word in industry and that output can be doubled. My response to that is that if output is doubled, the population will not be long in doubling as well, cancelling out its impact. But let us look at the thing a little closer.

There is a logic to production, and it is prompted by need. Therefore, there is a natural link between the product to be created and the need by which the producer is driven. Should that need diminish, no matter by how little, labour too will diminish, and we will see a reduction in wealth: that is inevitable. Suppose demand falls and production stays the same, as the products are less in demand and would fall in value, it would be exactly as if a fraction of those items had never been produced.

There are two sorts of needs: need for basic necessities and need for luxury goods. Even though no exact demarcation line can be drawn between these two classes of needs, and even though their boundaries may not be the same for people of every sort, the difference between them is no less real: it can be identified if we compare their extremes. There is no one who, reflecting upon the ordinary run of his life, cannot say which are his essential needs and what luxury needs he may have.

Now, on scrutinizing the lives, habits, inclinations, and education of the vast majority of workers, it is easy to see that, as far as they are concerned, labour is at maximum intensity as long as it is needs-driven; it decreases quickly and soon peters out once the want of basic necessities has been filled and once labour's purpose has become luxury only. As a rule, man is disinclined to take up a burden other than when it strictly serves his purpose. In this respect, he can claim to be representing nature, which does not overdo anything. The *lazzarone*[11] who shies away from employment of any sort once he has a full belly, is one example of this. The black, whose liberation is being campaigned for, behaves the same way. Once his needs have been met, man tends to seek his ease, the first and most avidly sought of all the luxury gratifications. To extract a little additional work from him, one would have to double or triple his wages, paying him well above the value of his labour and that flies in the very face of the law of production itself. Here again practice bears out the theory. Production expands only where, due to a surge in population, there is a need for subsistence and thus an ongoing demand for labour. Whereupon wages tend to fall rather than rise and working hours to lengthen rather than shorten. Were the trend in the opposite direction, production would soon grind to a halt.

In order to increase wealth in a given society, with the population figures staying unchanged, three things are required: 1. endowing the toiling masses with fresh needs, which is achievable only through the cultivation of mind and taste, or, in other words, through a higher education, the effect of which is to draw them insensibly out of their proletarian condition; 2. husbanding them by means of an increasingly clever organization of work and industry, time, and, moreover, strength; 3. by ending parasitism, to the very same end. Those three preconditions for boosting wealth boil down to this formula: an increasingly equal distribution of knowledge, services and products. This is the law of balance, the greatest, and, one might even argue, the only rule of political economy, in that all the rest are just various expressions of it, the law of poverty itself being no more than its simple corollary.

Science states that there is nothing unfeasible about this plan; indeed, it is to the combined action (albeit rather feeble thus far) of these three factors, education of the people, improvement of industry and the eradication of parasitism, that we are indebted for what little progress has been achieved in humanity's economic circumstances over these past thirty centuries.

But who can fail to see that if, through education, the toiling masses are uplifted by one degree in civilization, in what I shall term the life of the mind; if its sensibilities are heightened, its imagination refined, its needs become more

---

11. *Lazzarone*: a sort of Neapolitan casual labourer living in a condition of idleness and poverty. [H.T.]

numerous, more delicate and lively, consumption must match these new demands and thus work increase in turn, and the position stays the same, meaning
that humanity, growing in terms of intelligence, virtue and grace, as the Gospel
has it, but still gaining only the daily bread of its body and soul, remains poor in
material terms?

What is going on in France right now is evidence of this. There is no question that production has soared over the past forty years; it may well stand today, proportionately, well above what it was in 1820. Yet the fact is that all who
lived under the Restoration find themselves, in whatever social class, in more
hardship than during the reign of Louis XVIII. Where is this coming from? The
fact is that, as I have been saying, mores in the middle and lower classes have
grown more refined and yet, for reasons that shall be explained in a moment,
the law of balance being increasingly misconstrued and infringed, the law of
temperance trampled underfoot, poverty has become more burdensome and
has turned into an affliction rather than the blessing that nature intended it to
be. We have exaggerated the superfluous and no longer have the necessary. Had
I to back this fact up with a few details, I would cite, with regard to the sixty
thousand patented inventions and improvements registered since the 1791 law,
the proliferation of steam-engines, the construction of railways, the expansion
in financial speculation, the doubling of the public debt, the increase in the
State budget from one billion to two billion, the fifty per cent or one hundred
per cent increase in rents and all consumer goods, all of it adding up to a state of
stagnation and unrelieved crisis.

So, at nature's behest, every nation, be it civilized or barbarous, and no
matter what its institutions and its government, is poor, and all the poorer for
departing from its primitive state of abundance, and has made greater strides,
through hard work, towards WEALTH. As the population of the United
States of America, the most blessed nation on today's earth, multiplies and takes
over the soil, and as the store of natural resources diminishes, the law of labour
becomes more insistent and, in an infallible sign of poverty, what could once
be had without effort or for virtually no effort acquires an ever rising price and
the original gratuity evaporates; the rule of VALUE gains the upper hand and
a proletariat is in the making... Something similar is going on in Spain. After
centuries of slumber, Spain is suddenly waking up to the call of labour and of
liberty. She has set about exploiting her territory; wealth springs from everywhere and for everyone. Wages are on the rise, which is entirely predictable,
in that it is the soil and the foreigner who are paying. But just wait until the
population catches up with this wealth, which may come to pass in less than
half a century, and we must hope that Spain will stand before you again in more

moral circumstances, just as she was between Isabella I and Isabella II,[12] in balance, which is to say, poor.

But, some devotee of Mammon, the goddess of money, will immediately tell me, there is no point to our going to all this effort. These national ventures, these mammoth undertakings, these wonderful machines, these fruitful inventions, this glorious industry, all they do is parade our impotence and we will be well advised to turn away from them. Engines of misery, outright deception! Because what is the point of all the sweating, all the racking of our brains, if all we can expect of our labours is what we need and nothing more? Wisdom resides in humble means, narrowness of mind, a frugal life-style and a humble household? To be sure, you perform a noble task, disheartening souls, making minds petty, dampening enthusiasms, stymying ingenuity; such is your civilization, your peace! Ah, so that is how you mean to rid us of war; we would a thousand times rather run the risk. Let us, if need be, lay out another billion for the budget and leave us with the prestige of our industry and our pipe-dream ventures.

My retort to anyone who might address me in such terms would be this: Cast aside the mask! We know you by your rhetoric to be an industrial quack, stock-market buccaneer, a financial plague, a foul parasite. Yes, step back, unburden labour from your odious presence, for your reign is coming to an end, and unless you can put your ten fingers to work, you run the risk of starving to death.

To the simpletons who are always seduced by the eloquence of the advertisement, let me say: How is it that you cannot understand that, even if there were a time when the farmer used to look to his spade for whatever he needed, later, when his numbers had grown, he was obliged to look to his plough and can you not see that it is by the effect of the same development that he has been prompted in our own day to demand machinery, steamships and locomotives? Have you worked it out that it takes wealth to sustain thirty-seven million souls in an area covering some twenty-eight thousand square leagues? So set to it, because, if you falter, you will slip into a shortfall and, instead of the plenty of which you dream, you won't even have your basic needs covered. To work! Add to and deploy your resources: devise machines, find fertilizers, introduce new livestock, grow new food crops, dig drainage ditches, replant forests, carry out clearances, irrigate and drain; restock your rivers and streams and lagoons, your ponds, with fish; open coalmines; refine your gold, silver and platinum; smelt iron, copper, steel, lead, pewter, zinc; spin, weave, stitch, make furniture, pottery, and especially paper and rebuild your houses; open up outlets, engage in

12. Isabella I of Castile (1454–1504); Isabella II (1830–1904). [H.T.]

trade and revolutionize your banks. All of this would be very well-advised on your part. Not that production is the whole story; as I recommended to you, we must see to it that services are extended to all on the basis of their individual faculties, and every worker's wage matched to his product.[13] Without that sort of balancing, you will be mired in misery and your industry turns into calamity. Now, once you have done your all, in terms both of your productive drive and the precision of your distribution, to make yourselves rich, you will be astounded to see that all you have actually done is earn your living and that you would not have enough to celebrate a fortnight's carnival.

You ask whether this industrial progress, still subject to the law of necessity, implies the betterment of the life of the individual, and meets the subsistence needs of a larger population? Of course, there is improvement in the life of the individual, but what does it consist of? In terms of the mind, of the spread of knowledge, justice and the ideal; in bodily terms, in a more discriminating consumption matched to the expansion of the mind.

The horse eats his hay, the ox his grass, the pig his acorn, the hen her chickenfeed. They do not switch food and are not at all discommoded by this. I have witnessed the farm-worker making a meal, day in and day out, of the same black bread, the same potatoes, the same *polenta*, seemingly untroubled by the fact. The only thing keeping him skinny is being over-worked. But the civilized worker, the one touched by the first rays of the enlightening Word, needs to vary his diet. He consumes wheat, rice, maize, vegetables, meat, fish, eggs, fruit and dairy produce; on occasion, he partakes of some wine, beer, cider, mead, tea, coffee; he salts his food, seasons it and prepares it in all sorts of ways. Rather than just clothing himself in a sun-dried sheepskin or bear pelt, he wears clothing woven from wool, hemp or cotton; he wears linen or flannel, dressing one way in summer and differently in winter. His body, which is no less thriving, albeit made of purer blood, reflecting the culture that his soul has received, requires attentions of which the savage condition knows nothing. Such is progress: not that it stops humanity from remaining

---

13. This is a reference to the product of labour, discussed at length in the sections that follow. Proudhon argues that the product of labour is always irreducible to any single labourer, the productive process being always collective and supply chains inherently complex. This is as much the case for intellectual work as manual. The surplus value of labour is the product of the efficiencies of this collective enterprise. But as the surplus is irreducible to any single person, rightfully it should remain the property of the collective, not of any one individual. Proudhon was also of the view that any product can be traded as specie. As he says in in his writing on his "The Bank of Exchange", "We must destroy the royalty of gold; we must republicanise specie, by making every product of labour ready money". See Pierre-Joseph Proudhon, "Organisation of Credit and Circulation" and "The Solution of the Social Problem" [trans. Swartz and Cohn] in McKay (ed.) *Property is Theft!*, 284. [A.P.]

poor, since it still only has what it needs and cannot waste a single day when hunger-pangs bite.

Can you see to it that man works, on average, upwards of ten to twelve hours' out of every twenty-four? Can you see to it that eighty do the work of one hundred, or that the family with a prebend[14] of 3.50 francs has 5 to spend? Well then, your shops, warehouses, your docks cannot hold more goods than are asked of them, or more than nine million families, with a total average income of eleven or twelve billion, earned through toil, can afford. Issue every man and woman who needs them with a half-dozen shirts, a cloth jacket, a change of dress, a pair of shoes and then see what you are left with. Let me know then whether you are living a life of plenty, if you are swimming in wealth.

This urban elegance, these colossal fortunes, these State splendours, this expenditure to pay the interest on public debt, for the army, for public works; these endowments, this civil list, this chatter about banks and stock exchanges and millions and billions; these intoxicating delights of which you sometimes hear, all of it leaves you dazzled and, by inspiring in you a belief in wealth, makes you down-hearted about your own poverty. But then just think: such magnificence is a levy upon the average paltry income of 3 francs 50 centimes a day per family of four, a levy upon what is produced by the toiler, before his wage is set. Revenue for the army is a levy on labour; revenue to pay the interest on public debt, a levy on labour; income from property, a levy on labour; the banker's, the entrepreneur's, the businessman's, the functionary's income, a levy on labour; expenditure on luxuries, therefore, is a levy on essentials. So, have no regrets. Face up manfully to the situation in which you find yourself and tell yourself, once and for all, that the happiest of men is the one that most readily embraces his poverty.

Ancient wisdom glimpsed these truths. Christianity was the first to formally posit the law of poverty whilst, however, tailoring it, as any mysticism would, to the meaning of its theology. A backlash against pagan sensuality, Christianity was unable to assess poverty in its true light; Christianity transformed poverty into suffering through abstinence and fasting, while sordid monks cast this heavenly damnation as atonement. Apart from that, the poverty in which the Gospel glories is the greatest truth that Christ preached to men.

Poverty is respectable: not for it, threadbare garments like the cynic's cloak; its household is clean, salubrious and enclosed; it changes its linen at least once

---

14. *Prebend*: A portion of property resulting from a partition. This term applied to the division of the *chapter house* operated by canons in the 12th century, when they ceased to live communally. [H.T.]

a week; it is neither wan nor famished. Like Daniel's companions,[15] it radiates
holiness while feeding on vegetables; it has its daily bread and it is happy.

Poverty is not *ease*; that, as far as the toiler is concerned, would spell corruption. It is not good for a man to take his ease: rather, he should always feel
the prick of need. Ease would be a step beyond corruption, it would be slavishness; and it is important for a man to be able to look beyond need on occasion,
and indeed to go without what he needs. But poverty nevertheless has its private delights, its innocent rejoicing, its family comforts, touching comforts that
throw the household's habitual frugality into relief.[16]

To dream of evading this poverty, a law of our nature and of our society, is
plainly out of place. Poverty is good and we ought to think of it as the principle
of our happiness. Reason commands us to accommodate our life to it by means
of a frugality in our mores, moderation in our pleasures, application to our labours and the utter subordination of our appetites to justice.

So why is that very same poverty, the purpose of which is to exercise our
inner virtue and ensure a universal balance, now pitting some of us against one
another and igniting war between nations? This is what we shall try to discover
in the next chapter.

15. The prophet Daniel was supposed to have lived in the 7th century BC. According
to the Bible he was brought to Babylon as a captive (c. 606) and raised with three of his
companions in the palace school so that they might later be employed in the service of King
Nebuchadnezzar. They refused to taint themselves with the dishes and wines brought to
them from the king's own table and would only accept vegetables and water. After ten days, it
was apparent that they looked better and seemed better fed than all the other youngsters. Enlightened by God, his visions are said to have resulted in his being made governor of all the
provinces of Babylonia. (*Bible*, Book of Daniel.) Even though the authenticity of the *Book of
Daniel* has been proclaimed by Jewish and Church tradition alike, it has been shown that the
text was not written until centuries later. [H.T.]

16. Proudhon is no doubt romanticising both his own peasant upbringing and his family's penury. But this makes it no the less compelling in our age of ecological collapse. [A.P.]

CHAPTER III

The Illusion of Wealth. The Origin and Universality of Pauperism

Man's destiny on earth is wholly spiritual and moral; the regime that this destiny imposes upon him is one of frugality. Compared with its capacity to consume, its infinite desires, and the splendours of its ideal, humanity's material resources are greatly restricted; humanity is poor and must be poor, for, short of that, it lapses back into animality thanks to sensory illusions and spiritual seduction, and is corrupted in body and soul and, in the throes of delight, loses the treasures of virtue and genius. Such is the law foisted upon us by our earthly condition and demonstrated also by political economy, statistics, history and morality. Nations that pursue material wealth and the pleasures it offers, as their ultimate blessing, are nations in decline. The progress and perfection of our species lies entirely in justice and philosophy. The increase in well-being does feature less as rewards and avenues to happiness than as expressions of our accumulated learning and a signal of our virtue. Faced with that reality of things, sensualist theory is guilty of being at odds with our social destiny, and is reduced to rubble.[17]

If we lived as the Gospel urges us to, in a spirit of joyous poverty, the most perfect order would reign on earth. There would be neither vice nor crime; by means of toil, by means of reason and virtue, men would constitute a society of sages; they would savour all the happiness their nature could accommodate.

---

17. On 16 September 1853, Proudhon wrote to one to his correspondents, a Monsieur Trouessart: "In order to persuade you of such a crucial point ... which, in my view, touches upon the loftiest issue that history has to show, the issue of the *decadence of nations*, I would need a formal dissertation ... You surely have every reason to argue that the advances made in terms of *utility* have not been enough to establish the morality of a people and preserve its honour, its life, its influence among nations ... Am I then, led to that *utilitarian*, I might even say almost immoral point? ... Like you, I regard material advantages as naught, unless they are *dictated* by the principles of honour and justice; like you, I protest at any split that might be pursued within society, and, consequently, against any trade-off between *well-being* and *virtue*... No progress in social economics without a parallel progress in public morals and vice versa; I challenge anyone to quote a contrary example from the entire history of the human race". [H.M.]

But that is unfeasible today and has never been witnessed at any time, due to the violation of our two great laws, the law of poverty and the law of temperance.

Right from the opening pages of this essay, I have stated that war was an internal, wholly psychological phenomenon; that if we wanted to familiarize ourselves with it, we had to study it in the conscience of humanity, in the accounts of the historians and the memoirs of the captains, and not on the battlefields. And I proved that assertion, first by showing that warfare is not merely one of the major categories of our practical reason, but, indeed, of our speculative reasoning; then, secondly, by bringing out its principle, the RIGHT *of force*: and, thirdly, by elaborating its eminently judicial character.

I am now going to demonstrate that all the excesses for which we have upbraided war derive from the same source: the soul, having initially strayed in pursuit of a false ideal, to wit, wealth, then misconstrued justice insofar as it is applied to matters pertaining to labour, industry and exchange, which is to say, to economic Right. Weaving our way through scenes of carnage, arson, despoilment and rape, we have not stepped outside of the realm of the mind; and everything we see, observe and judge good or bad, where war is concerned, is still a spiritual matter. As I have said, facts are merely characters translated by the mind's eye into conceptions of spirit.

Let's pursue this mysterious conjoining of pauperism and warfare, or, should I say depraved warfare, the two greatest scourges decimating the human race.

Leaving behind his initial plenty, compelled to work, learning through pain that there is a cost to his placing a value on things, man was gripped by a wealth-fever: from the very first step, this led him down the wrong path.

Man believes in what he terms *fortune*, the same way as he believes in sensual delights and all the illusions of the ideal. By virtue of the very fact that he must produce that which he consumes, he looks upon the amassing of wealth and the resultant pleasures as his purpose. And he pursues that purpose with gusto; the example of a few rich men has him believing that what has been permitted to a few is accessible to all; he would deem it a contradiction of his nature, a lie from Providence, if things were otherwise. Relying upon this mental induction, he imagines that there is no end to what he can add to his assets and that he can, availing of the law of values, rediscover his original abundance. He amasses, accumulates and hoards: his soul is sated, satisfied by that idea. The present century is imbued with this belief, crazier than any of the ones it purports to replace. The study of political economy, a quite modern science, which is as yet very poorly understood, impels minds to do so; the socialist schools vie with one another in this orgy of sensuality; governments do their best to foster the rise and cultivation of interests; religion itself, once so severe in its language, appears to be lending a helping hand. Generate wealth, make money, enrich yourself, surround yourself with luxuries; this has turned into a universal moral and governmental axiom. It has even been argued that the way to make men virtuous, to end vice and crime, was to spread *comfort* everywhere and triple or quadruple wealth: millions cost nothing to those who speculate on paper. Finally, by means of this brand-new ethic, an investigation has been conducted into how to inflame carnal appetites, the very reverse of what the one-time moralists used to say, that men had first to be temperate, chaste and modest and taught how to survive on little and be content with their lot, and only then would all fare well in society and in the State. It might be said that in this regard the public consciousness has been, so to speak, turned on its head: and today we can all see what the upshot of this singular revolution has been.

However, to anyone who can spare a few moments to reflect upon the laws of economic order, it is patently obvious that WEALTH, like WORTH, is not so much an indicator of a reality as of a relationship; the relationship of production to consumption, of supply to demand, of labour to capital, of product to pay, of need to deed, etc.;[18] a relationship generically and typically expressed by the worker's average WORKING DAY, examined from both sides, as *outlay* and as *product*. The working day: there we have it in two words, the balance sheet of public wealth, which may vary, from time to time but within narrower limits than the common man might think, as *assets*, thanks to the discoveries of industry, trade, extraction, agriculture, colonization and conquest; and, as *liabilities*, by epidemics, poor harvests, revolutions and wars.

It follows from this notion of the working day that collective output, as an expression of collective effort, should not, in any circumstance or by any appreciable amount, exceed the needs of the collective, what we have termed *its daily bread*. The notion of tripling or quadrupling a country's output, the way one might triple or quadruple one's order with a manufacturer of cloth or linen, that idea, as I say, is even more irrational than the squaring of the circle: it is a contradiction, a nonsense. Barring some matching increase in work, capital, population and outlets, and, above all, barring some parallel improvement in intelligence and mores, which is the most demanding and most expensive requirement, it is an illusion. But this is the very point that the masses refuse to understand, that the economists fail to highlight, and on which governments maintain a cautious silence. Produce, do business, enrich yourself: that is your only refuge, now that you no longer believe in God or in humanity.

---

18. See *The Philosophy of Poverty*, vol. I, Chap. II, "On Value"; vol. I, Chap. V, "Competition". And vol. I: "Summation and Conclusion"; – *What is Property?* Chap. III, §7, 2. – *On the Creation of Order in Humanity*, Chap. IV, §2. – *Solution of the Social Question. Organization of Credit*, §II: "Establishing Value". – *The General Idea of the Revolution*, VIth study §4; "Establishing value". – "On Justice", 3rd study, chap. VI, §19: Sellers and Buyers. [H.M.]

The effect of this illusion and of the bitter disappointment that is its ines-capable aftermath, is to whet appetites, and to make poor man and rich man, worker and parasite alike, intemperate and greedy; then insolvency arrives, to irritate him about his bad luck, nurture a hatred of society and, finally, push him into crime and warfare.

But what adds to the mess is the excessive inequality of the distribution of goods.

In the previous chapter we saw how France's gross per capita income does not, in all probability, exceed 87 francs 5 centimes a day. EIGHTY-SEVEN AND A HALF CENTIMES per day, per head: this is what we are allowed to regard as income these days, which is to say the average product and, thus, the average consumption in France, the expression of her just deserts.

Feeble as it may seem, if that income were guaranteed every citizen, mean-ing, if every French family, made up of father, mother and two children, en-joyed an income of 3 francs 50 centimes, at least, if the *minimum* and *maximum* for poor families, of which there are always many, never fell below 1 franc 75 centimes, or half of that 3 francs 50 centimes, or did not rise, in the case of the wealthy, above 15 or 20 francs; each family assumed to have produced whatever goods it might consume, there would be no unrest anywhere. The nation would enjoy unprecedented well-being; its wealth, ordered and distributed to perfec-tion, would be beyond compare and the government would be entitled to brag about the country's ever-increasing prosperity.

But the disparity between fortunes is also in need of moderating; as I say, the poorest families would have to be assured of an income of 1 franc 75 cen-times and the rich make do with ten times that figure. According to the recent reckoning of one learned and conscientious economist, the bulk of the Breton population has no more than 25 centimes to spend per day per capita; and, he goes on to say, that population is not regarded as being destitute.

Besides, we know that a large number of fortunes stand not just at 10 and 15 francs per family per day, but at 50, 100, 200, 500, 1,000 and we hear stories of some going as high as 10,000 francs. One point that needs to be made is that, since the exorbitant impetus given to enterprise, certain speculators, seemingly persuaded that all our fortunes are assured, and seeking payment in advance for their role, have started reckoning on the basis that individuals possess one, two, ten, twenty, thirty, fifty and eighty millions. Meaning that in anticipation of the nuptials of Gamache,[19] which they promise us will carry on forever, they levy somewhere between a hundred and as much as three thousand from the com-mon purse, which is temporarily doomed to go without sustenance. As for the

---

19. The reference is to Cervantes's *Don Quixote* and the Pantagruelian feast at which plenty degenerates into profusion. [H.T.]

country that tolerates such anticipatory charges without a word of objection, financial shambles, business stagnation, soaring debts show quite clearly what it ought to think of such dreams of Cockaigne.[20]

Now where does this shocking inequality stem from?

We could pin the blame on greed, which shrinks from no felony; on ignorance of the law of values; on the whims of business, etc. Those factors are assuredly not without influence, but there is nothing organic about them and they would not long survive widespread disapproval, were they not bound up with a more deep-seated, more respectable principle, the misdirected vigour of which is the source of the entire affliction.

That principle is the very same as the one that sets us to questing after wealth and luxury and gives us our enthusiasm for glory; the very same as gives rise to the right of force, and, later on, to the right of intelligence, and, finally, to the right of labour itself; it is our own sense of personal worth and dignity, from which springs our respect for our neighbours and for humanity as a whole, and which constitutes justice.

One consequence of that principle of human dignity, the starting-point for all justice, but one that will not genuinely become justice other than through a lengthy education of conscience and reason, is that, at first, not only do we give preference to ourselves over the rest in everything and for everything, but we extend that arbitrary preference to those who please us and whom we call our friends.

In the most fair-minded man, there is a tendency to hold his neighbour in esteem and to serve him, not according to that person's merits, but according to the sympathy his character inspires. It is that sympathy that brings forth friendship, so holy, which solicits favour, something as naturally free as trust and that is yet devoid of unfairness, but which soon develops into special favours, partiality, charlatanism, social distinctions and castes. On their own, advances in labour and the spread of social relationships could identify for us what is here by right and what is not; only experience of things could show whether, in our dealings with our fellows, a certain latitude is to be afforded the preferences of friendship, given that all personal considerations must evaporate in the face of economic justice; and that, if equality before the law is *de rigueur* everywhere, it is especially so when it comes to the remuneration of labour, in the distribution of goods and services.

Our exaggerated notion of ourselves, and the abuse of personal preferences, are things that push us into breaching the law of economic distribution and it is that breach that, combining inside us with the quest for pleasures, spawns

---

20. *Cockaigne*: An imaginary land where everything is abundant and readily to hand. [H.T.]

pauperism, a phenomenon as yet poorly defined but whose deleterious influence upon societies and States the economists are agreed in acknowledging.[21]

Let us attempt to take the measure of it.

Poverty is this law of our nature, which, compelling us to produce everything we need to consume, awards our labours nothing more than necessary. In a country such as ours, that need is, according to the most recent figures, 3 francs 50 centimes per family per day, the minimum being set, hypothetically, at 1 franc 75 centimes and the maximum at 15 francs. It being understood that, depending on location and circumstances, that minimum and maximum may vary.

Hence this proposition, at once true and paradoxical: in civilization, man's normal condition is poverty. On its own, poverty is no misfortune; we could, following the example of the ancients, describe it as mediocrity, if by mediocrity were not meant, in common parlance, such a fortune as, whilst not exactly opulence, nonetheless allows one to abstain from productive work.

Pauperism is abnormal poverty operating to subversive effect. No matter the particular deed that spurs it, it consists of a disparity between what a man produces and his income, between his outlay and his need, between the dream of his ambition and the power of his faculties and thus between the circumstances of citizens in relation to one another. Whether the fault originates with individuals or with institutions, with slavishness or prejudice, pauperism is a breach of the economic law that on the one hand requires man to labour in order to live and, on the other, matches his product to his need. For instance, the working man who in exchange for his labour receives the lower end of the average collective income, which is to say 1 franc 75 centimes a day for himself and his family, is mired in pauperism. He cannot be helped by that inadequate wage to recover his strength, maintain his household, raise his children, much less develop his reason. Imperceptibly, he slips into stagnation, demoralization and wretchedness. And let me say again that this violation is an essentially psychological factor; it is rooted, on the one hand, in the idealism of our desires and, on the other, in the overblown notion we have of our dignity and our small regard for that of other people. This is the smug, aristocratic spirit, still thriving in

---

21. "Pauperism derives from the imbalance between the product and the worker's wage, which is to say, from the revenue levied by the idle capitalist; that contention has been more than sufficiently demonstrated". *De la Création*, Chapter V, § 5, no. 529. – "Would you have pauperism, crime, warfare, upheavals and despotism be eternal features on earth? Then make the proletariat eternal". Id. no. 542. – In *La Célébration du Dimanche*, Proudhon spoke of the "canker of pauperism". In 1839, in which year that was written, the Academy of Moral Sciences ran a competition on the following topic: "Of what does poverty consist; how is its presence indicated in various countries; what are its causes?" Twenty-three submissions were received: the winner was Eugène Bret with *The Wretchedness of the Labouring Classes in France and in England*. [H.M.]

our self-styled democratic society, that makes the trading of goods and services fraudulent by introducing a personal factor, which, out of scorn for the law of values and outright contempt for the right of force, by its very universality, is unremittingly plotting to boost the fortunes of its chosen ones with countless pennies skimmed from everybody else's wages.

The manner in which that vicious distribution manifests itself in the over-all economy varies according to location and circumstances; but it always ends up with the inadequate pay of the labourer in relation to his needs. Let us cite only the most widespread of them:

a) The growth in parasitism, the proliferation in bureaucratic jobs and lux-ury goods industries. This is the state to which we are all inclined due to the power of our pride and our sensuality. Everybody wants to live off the common purse, hold a sinecure,[22] engage in no industry or sell his services for some re-ward out of kilter with its public usefulness, the sort of remuneration that only fantasy, some overblown regard for talent, etc. could offer. Such parasites, sine-curists and luxury workers are numbered in the hundreds of thousands.

b) Unproductive, inappropriate ventures making disproportionate de-mands on savings. What citizens are in their private lives, the State must inevitably be as well; the examples of ancient Greece, imperial Rome, post-Re-naissance Italy are proof of that. The main point to be made here is that expen-diture grows as receipts shrink, which sets the moralists railing against the arts, which they take for the cause of luxury whereas they ought to be seen merely as its instruments.

c) Excessive governmentalism[23] fostered by all these factors. In France the planned budget for 1862 stands at 1,919 million. Meaning that the nation, clue-less as to how to govern itself, pays out around one sixth of its income[24] to be governed. Since housing costs as much as government does, that leaves a mere

---

22. *Sinecure*: A salaried position entailing no actual work. [H.T.]

23. The concept of governmentalism is used by Proudhon to signify a mental change that comes about when people begin to administer others. It first appears in his writings around 1848, to signify the tendency of erstwhile revolutionaries to become socialised into the normal workings of the state, and thereby lose their revolutionary spirit. Proudhon uses the term in his Election Manifesto of 1848, where he states that "socialism is the contrary of governmentalism". Elsewhere, and more frequently, he associates governmentalism with communism. See, for example, Proudhon, "Election Manifesto" and "Theory of Property", in McKay (ed.), *Property if Theft!*, 378 and 780. Here and below it is also understood as a ratio-nality that emerges alongside the shift from conquest and plunder to the administration of appropriated goods and territories. The echoes we hear in Foucault's concept of governmen-tality are hard to ignore but have yet to be explored fully. [A.P.]

24. In 1998, taxes and levies accounted for upwards of eighty per cent of [French] G.D.P. [H.T.]

two-thirds to cover upkeep in terms of furniture, clothing, heating, education and subsistence.

d) The absorption of capital by the large towns, which, no matter how one looks at them, even as centres of production, but above all as producers of luxuries, never pays indigenous labour enough to cover what it levies from it, and caters solely for the amusement of idlers and the fortunes of a few bourgeois.

e) The exaggeration of capitalism, which reduces everything to finance and goes as far as to turn public services over to private ventures such as banks, railways, canals, etc. Let me add a comment here. One honourable member of the Legislature recently stated that our various lending firms had 500 million in disposable capital and that they were just waiting for peace to be assured before setting it into motion. Many people are tempted to conclude from that inexhaustible cash sum that the country's resources are similarly bottomless. But this is to ignore that, because of how the tax system works, the money in banks, railways, landed income, etc., does the rounds, merely passing through the hands of workers before always making its way back to its starting point, to wit, the coffers of the capitalist. France could have gobbled up ten times her assets and her reserves and that would still be the case. Where the manufacturer and the banker are concerned, cash may be referred to as capital, since it is the equivalent of a certain sum of subsistence goods and raw materials; in a society where cash is used only to facilitate exchange, or, at the most, as a down payment on banknotes and is not consumed, it amounts to fictitious capital; the only real capital being the products of labour.

f) Currency fluctuations derived either from the high price or depreciation of the coinage, or from the exportation of cash, or from changes to the currency. The result is massive speculation, to the detriment of producer and consumer. Thus, the discovery of the mines in California created an upheaval in the markets and brought silver currency to an end. Outside of such speculation, which the law was entitled to punish, the depreciation of gold caused by a glut in that metal would have been no more a cause of distress than depreciation in the price of sugar or cotton caused by a doubling of production of those commodities.

g) Finally, the rise in rental rates and in nearly all consumer goods. This means that, in the wake of the spread of parasitism and unproductive ventures, the expansion in State employment, the absorption of capital and of large towns, financial manoeuvres, the expansion in personal and State luxuries, only three-quarters, a third or a half of what he once consumed is left for the useful worker and that amounts to saying that his wages, even though the same in cash terms, has been reduced by fifty, sixty or eighty per cent.

The factors we have listed here impact one upon another, and the interaction between them makes matters even worse.

Thus, one of the drivers behind the recent enormous governmental works is the desire to come to the aid of the working classes. The intention is excellent: unfortunately, it could not succeed. Indeed, the upshot of the argument thus far is that by trying to use artificial means to combat pauperism, all the government has done is to make pauperism worse; it has no way out of this cycle. And then the capitalists put the finishing touch to the misery. When the country can no longer offer them a market, they emigrate; off they go, taking their industry with them and, along with it, wretchedness.

Once pauperism hits the working class due to imbalance in distribution, it does not take long to spread everywhere, percolating up from the lower to the higher levels and affecting even those who lead an affluent existence.

Among the unfortunates, pauperism is characterized by the *slow starvation* of which Fourier spoke,[25] an unremitting, year-round, life-long hunger; a hunger that does not kill in a day but that consists of all manner of privations and all sorts of regrets; that relentlessly undermines the body, befuddling the mind, stripping the conscience of all morality, degrading races, generating all sorts of malady and every vice, including drunkenness and envy, a distaste for work and savings, a depravity of the soul, an indelicacy of the conscience, an uncouthness of manners, laziness, beggary, prostitution and thievery. It is this slow starvation that underpins the working classes' quiet hatred of the comfortable classes, which, in times of revolution, shows itself in the sort of savagery that strikes enduring fear into the leisured classes, which incites tyranny and, in ordinary times, keeps the authorities constantly on their mettle.

With the parasite, there is a different impact: not famine this time, but an insatiable greed. We know from experience that the more the unproductive person consumes, the greater his eagerness to consume, due to the titillation of his appetites and the idleness of his limbs and brain. The fable of Eresichthon in *Metamorphoses* is emblematic of this truth.[26] Instead of the mythological Eresichthon, Ovid could as easily have picked the Roman nobles of his own day, munching their way through the income from an entire province in a single meal. As the rich man surrenders to the flame of delight that consumes him, pauperism hits him that much harder, rendering him at once prodigal,

---

25. In *De la Création*, Chap. III, §5, No 261, Proudhon quotes the passage from Fourier, which he references here: "In places where the civilized people does not perish of *urgent* hunger, it perishes of a *lingering* hunger due to privation; from the *speculative* hunger that forces it to feed on unwholesome things; from *imminent* hunger due to over-work, to indulging out of necessity in pernicious pursuits, excessive exhaustion leading to fevers and infirmities". [H.M.]

26. After he had cut down a few trees from a wood sacred to the goddess Demeter, she doomed Erisichton to the torments of a ravenous hunger; he ended up devouring himself. [H.T.]

avaricious and grasping. And what goes for gluttony holds true for all sorts of sensual delights; they grow more demanding as they are pandered to. Luxurious dining is but a fraction of the expenditure of the unproductive. Soon, as fantasy and vanity mingle together, no fortune is enough for him anymore; in the midst of his indulgences, he finds himself indigent. He has to replace his savings as they drain away; at which point pauperism takes complete hold of him. Pushing him into risky ventures and chancy speculation, into gambling and swindling until eventually, outraged, temperance, justice and nature have their vengeance in the shape of the most shameful ruination.

So much for the extremes of pauperism. But we should not imagine that, between those extremes and in that middling condition where labour and consumption are more fairly balanced, families are spared this scourge. The tone is set by the affluent class and everybody strives to follow suit. Souls are racked by the prejudice of fortune, the illusion conjured up by wealth. Tormented inside by artificial needs, the paterfamilias dreams, as he puts it, of *bettering his position*, which in most cases means adding to his wealth and expenditure. As a result of wallowing in that idea, he ends up trampling all over the future; then, as the price of goods and services rises and work dwindles and savings turn less stringent, the expenditure by the best-off soars without their noticing, the same as that of the bigwigs and the State and everywhere there is a deficit, revealed by the hobbling of business, financial and commercial crises, collapses and bankruptcies and soaring taxes and debts. Now do you understand how frugality, temperance and modesty in all things not only represent the virtues of supererogation,[27] but as far as we are concerned, they are imperative virtues?

Such is the spread of pauperism, endemic in humanity and covering every category in society. But in certain countries, such as Russia or Austria, where most families survive by working the land, producing nearly everything by themselves and for themselves and maintaining but few connections with the outside world, the affliction is less intense. Primarily, it is the government, without money and credit, or the upper classes supplied with a feeble income from the land and often paid in kind, that are destitute. As for the masses there, it can be stated that their livelihoods are secure and their needs assured, thanks to the country's mediocre levels of industry and trade.

In contrast, among those nations where labour is divided and interlocked, where agriculture itself is subject to industrial methods, where everybody's fortunes rely upon everybody else's, where the worker's wage is dependent upon a thousand factors over which he has no control, the slightest accident upsets these fragile connections and can destroy the subsistence needs of millions in

---

27. *Supererogation*: Going further than required; above and beyond the call of duty. [H.T.]

an instant. It is frightening to think of how little holds together the daily life of nations and what a multitude of factors there are that have a tendency to disorganize it. So we see that, while such splendid ordering held out the promise of delivering well-being for the masses, it can also, at the first misstep, bring them misery.

But, and note this, as it bears out the truth of this entire theory, in the serial miscalculations that drive nations into conflict, pauperism of the vulgar multitudes is not the most significant point. Indigence in the sovereigns occupies pride of place; followed by that of the great and wealthy. Here, as in everything, the plebs bring up the rear. Amid widespread distress, the poor man is not even afforded the honours due his poverty.

The rich, who consume on a large scale, are, if I may be permitted to make the comparison, like huge quadrupeds, at risk of starving to death on account of their very bulk and power, much more so than the rabbit, squirrel or mouse. Several species, the mammoth for one, have died out; others are on the road to extinction. The main reason for the extinction of these breeds is that they cannot find sustenance. The same goes for the aristocratic classes and families with great fortunes. Forever needy amidst the rabble sucking more out of them that is good for them, deep in debt, subject to claims and bankrupt, there is no question but that they are, if not the most interesting, then the most irritable of all the victims of pauperism.

Let us sum up this chapter.

In all its work of creation, Nature has taken as her maxim: Nothing excessive. *Ne quid timis.* As Fourier used to say, economy of means is one of Nature's chief laws.[28] Which is why, not content with condemning us to work, she affords us only that which we need, *quod sufficit*, and makes us subject to the law of poverty, thereby anticipating the precept of the Gospel and all the coenobitic institutions.[29] Should we chafe under that law and should the seductiveness of the ideal inspire in us a craving for luxury and pleasures, should some exaggerated notion of ourselves prompt us to ask more for our service than economic logic affords us, Nature, quick to chastise us, consigns us to wretchedness.

For as long as we all live, subjects and monarchs, individuals and peoples, families and trades, men of learning, artists, industrialists, public officials, rentiers and labourers, are therefore doomed to poverty. Our perfectibility, the very

28. See FOURIER, *Le nouveau monde industriel, ou invention du procédé d'industrie attrayante et combinée, distribuée en séries passionnées* (Paris, 1829). Proudhon, who was discernibly influenced by Fourierism in *De la création de l'ordre*, switched to being an opponent of that teaching in *The Philosophy of Poverty*. [H.M.]

29. *Coenobitism*: Matters relating to the religious living in communities back in the first few centuries of Christianity, under the direction of a superior and featuring group practice of the ascetic life. [H.T.]

law of our labours, wants it that way. Setting aside the inequalities of labour and capability, which can give rise to differential income, a differential barely perceptible in the masses, all we produce, ultimately, is just what we need in order to subsist. Whilst a few may receive more or less than that which the rule prescribes, the fault resides in all of us. So there is room for reform.

Analysed in terms of its psychological principle, pauperism derives from the same source as war, namely, the human being considered without regard to the intrinsic value of services and products. This innate worship of wealth and glory, this warped belief in inequality, may have deluded us at one point; they must evaporate before this analysis of experience, and man, condemned to daily toil, to rigorous frugality, should seek the dignity of his being and the gloriousness in his life elsewhere than in the pursuit of wealth and the vanities of command.

But, because we take exception to the precept of poverty and temperance, because we resist the law of sharing, which is nothing but Justice itself, pauperism assails us all and in the wake of pauperism comes discord and war.

CHAPTER IV

The Influence of Pauperism on the State and International Relations

After such a series of revolutions as those of 1789, 1799, 1814, 1830, 1848 and 1851, it might seem trivial to demonstrate that this malaise is all the more acutely felt the higher its reach, and that it may have a direct impact upon governments.[30] Ideas played their part there, of course: but what do those ideas signify? What do they represent? Interests. What prompted the convening of the Estates-General? The deficit. Why did the Constituent Assembly replace the absolute monarchy with a constitutional monarchy? Because the nation could not see its way to paying over to the prince any tax to which it had not given its consent, and because, in the final analysis, the constitutional system boils down to this: the protection of tax-payer income from the tax-collector, and taxation by consent. What was the civil constitution of the clergy? A dispossession. What was the reform of the 4th August but an expropriation?[31] Pauperism, therefore, is the primary cause of revolution.

From the Roman people's withdrawal to the Sacred Mount[32] and Napoleon III's letter to Fould,[33] his minister of State, regarding commercial freedom,[34] all

---

30. 1789, the start of the French Revolution; 1799, the coup d'état of 18th Brumaire bringing France under a single master in the person of First Consul Bonaparte; 1814, surrender of Napoleon I and the restoration of Louis XVIII; 1830, the so-called July Revolution, also known as the *Three Glorious Days*, when Charles X, the last symbol of absolute monarchy, was ousted and Louis-Philippe installed (he went on to establish a liberal constitutional monarchy); 1848, the revolution that ushered in the [Second] Republic; 1851, the coup d'état by Louis-Napoleon Bonaparte who re-established the [Second] Empire [in 1852]. [H.T.]

31. 4th August 1789 witnessed the abolition of feudal rights and the abolition of labour service obligations [*corvée*] and serfdom. [H.T.]

32. In 493 BC, burdened with debt, the people of Rome threatened to revolt. The consuls looked to the army. But the latter mutinied and withdrew to the Sacred Mount. Forty-five years later, the murder of a young plebeian was to furnish the pretext for a further withdrawal to the Sacred Mount, which ended with further concessions being made by the Senate. [H.T.]

33. ACHILLE FOULD (1800–1867), Louis-Napoleon Bonaparte's Finance minister when he was President and later after he became Emperor. [H.T.]

34. That letter, dated 5 January 1860, was published in *Le Moniteur* of 15 January:

political, economic and religious changes that have troubled nations can be reduced to this formula: the protection of the working masses from parasitical
exploitation, and guaranteeing a minimum income, be it for a quarter of an
hour, 1 franc 75 centimes per day per family, and the protection against fire, hail,
floods, epizootic outbreaks, sickness, unemployment, the oscillations of the
Stock Exchange, financial and business crises, navigational risks, etc., etc.

However, and even though the facts here leave no room for the slightest
doubt, let us take a closer look at the convulsions of that great period between
1789 and 1860.

In 1789, the revolution was made against the deficit caused by the expenditure of the court, against feudal rights, against the privileges of the guilds,
against clerical parasitism, against the unequal distribution of levies, which is
to say, against a state of affairs that was impoverishing in the extreme. The night
of 4th of August was that revolution's great victory; the culmination of all the
philosophy of the eighteenth century.

In the wake of the 4th of August, a reaction emerged in the name of religious ideas and the political institutions that were as sorely abused by the revolution as privileges had been, the names of the latter still commanding some
respect and their images still vivid. Since, in the estimation of the masses, those
institutions and ideas implied a reversion to the old abuses, a more radical revolution was mounted against them in '93, one enshrined in the republican calendar as the *sans-culottides* feast days.[35] This is how we see Catholic, pontifical Italy
denying the Pope's temporal authority and putting the very existence of the
Church and Catholicism in jeopardy, rather than endure further abuses. The
people sacrificed its religion and its gods for the sake of its daily bread.

Bread and the '93 constitution! was the cry that went up from the people
during the events of Germinal and Prairial.[36]

In 1796, Babeuf[37] attempted to end pauperism and pursued the revolution

---

"Napoleon III stated that there is but one overall system of sound political economy that,
by creating the wealth of the nation, has the capacity to foster affluence within the working
class". That system consisted of the abolition of tariffs. [H.M.]

35. The republican calendar had provision for five additional days and these days were set
aside for revolutionary celebrations: the feasts of Virtue, Genius, Labour, Reward and Opinion. They were dubbed the *sans-culottides*, redeeming the sneering *sans-culottes* label that the
aristocrats used to refer to the revolutionaries. [H.T.]

36. The constitution passed on 24 June, 1793 harked back to the principles enunciated
in the Declaration of the Rights of Man. That constitution, the most democratic that France
had ever known, was never implemented. Demonstrations by Parisians demanding bread and
the implementation of the constitution occurred between Germinal and Prairial (March–
May 1795) and were quickly broken up. [H.T.]

37. FRANÇOIS-ÉMILE BABEUF, known as GRACCHUS BABEUF (1760–1797)
championed communist ideas in the *Tribun du Peuple* newspaper. He orchestrated a plot to

in equality's name. He failed more because of the flawed nature of his system than the reaction from the propertied. The people were no more communist in 1796 than in 1848.

By 1799, pauperism had spread to the bourgeoisie. Everyone was pleading poverty. The Directory applied for bankruptcy; rent fell to eleven francs; paid in *assignats*, the rentiers were starving to death; not that the multitude seemed any richer; quite the opposite. Then came the revolution of 18th Brumaire.

In 1814, the setbacks encountered by our armies led to France being invaded. Napoleon was forced into abdicating. It was not the people that overthrew him: there was no over-population, thanks to the war; pauperism among the masses was barely discernible; and the collapse of the Empire did not seem a good idea as far as the people were concerned. But whilst there was a middling feeling of wretchedness among the multitude in France, the same was not true of the industrial and commercial bourgeoisie facing ruination as a result of the Continental System; nor was it true for the senators and all the high-ranking persons whose positions were compromised by the war; and, above all, it was not the same abroad, in Spain or Germany or Russia and all the countries through which our armies had marched. Hence the coalition of 1813 and the way it was hailed on the French side.

The Restoration fell apart in 1830: why? The bourgeoisie was jealous of the former nobles, accusing them of wanting to re-establish feudal rights, for which, it was thought, a billion had been paid out thus far to the émigrés. For its part, the Church was protesting against the predicament in which it had been placed and was calling for the return of its assets and tithes. Now, at that time and since 1825, the industrial regime has made pauperism more palpable; socialist newspapers and publications began to appear, denouncing wretchedness and talking about production, wealth and distribution and everything that might inflame appetites and ignite wrath. The memories, enthusiasms and interests of '89 were the soul behind the July revolution.

The 1848 revolution drew its inspiration from 1793 too. Business had slowed down; work languished in the doldrums and corruption was making the distress more unbearable; the bourgeoisie was unsettled and impatient. Worked up by Babeuf's ideas and by socialist propaganda, the masses were clamouring for political rights, that being the only way they had, they were told, of securing work and bread. There was wonder at the providential judgment that, after having lashed out at Charles X, was now hovering over Louis-Philippe. The very same hunger pangs that had toppled the Legitimist monarchy brought down the citizen monarch: therein lies the entire mystery.

---

overthrow the Directory and re-establish the 1793 constitution. Arrested and sentenced to death, Babeuf stabbed himself before climbing the gallows. [H.T.]

In 1851, the pendulum swung the opposite way. Reactionary greed backed the *coup d'état* against the social republic, which had been decimated over the previous three years by gunfire, transportation, prison and banishment. The *coup d'état* was all the more successful in that, whilst the conservatives welcomed it as a safeguard, the people embraced it as a protectorate.[38]

It is the same story with all the political, social and religious revolutions that comprise the history of nations. No matter the idea that served as their rallying-cry, they are all about interests. Now, in such circumstances, whoever says interest says distress, privilege, parasitism and famine.

When the sixteenth century Reformation against the Church erupted, the malaise was universal, and for over two centuries public outcry had blamed the Church. In addition to the income from its estates, the Church was in receipt of all manner of contributions, tithes, exemptions, annates, indulgences, etc., the vast bulk of which made their way to Rome. The people were living in straitened circumstances whilst the religious orders lived in opulence. The Papacy siphoned off all the cash for itself. The people, whose wretchedness had weakened their faith, were pressing for the clergy to revert to the frugal ways of the primitive Church: from as early as the first century Book of the Apocalypse, the refrain had been the same: denouncing the wealth of certain bishops, the successors to the apostles. Is the same charge not being levelled against the Pope to this very day? This outcry by wretchedness against the episcopate is so monotonous as to turn tedious. The *seigneurs* coveted the clergy's assets; the kings, eager to shrug off its temporal authority, asked nothing better than to stake their own claim to a portion of that wealth, as Philip the Fair did when he dispatched the Templars to the stake.

And marvel at how such royal, seigneurial, bourgeois and plebeian covetousness was able to dress itself up as the interest of religion and decency! The Templars were accused of immorality and atheism. Not that I am claiming that they were innocent; but no one would have questioned their virtue if they had only been somewhat less wealthy. After that the princes drew the distinction that suited them, between the temporal and the spiritual: as if the Church had known no more about it than them; as if the distinction did not imply the Pope's supremacy over kings, the precise opposite of the intended purpose! Let us not forget the earnest men, unwitting promotors and dupes of all these

---

38. In the presidential election of 19 December, 1848, Louis-Napoleon won by a landslide (securing over seventy per cent of the votes cast). Proudhon concluded that: "France has named Louis Napoleon President of the Republic because she is tired of parties". P.-J. Proudhon, *Les Confessions d'un révolutionnaire* (Paris: Marcel Rivière, 1929), 277. Cited in Roger Price, *The French Second Empire: An Anatomy of Political Power* (Cambridge: Cambridge University Press, 2008), 18. [G.H.]

revolutions and who, like the wise Gerson,[39] called for abuses to be rectified, but did not want to see customary practice tampered with. After them, along came the sectarians, Wycliffe, Jan Hus and Luther,[40] who, going one step further, determinedly attacked the religious doctrine. Finally, Münzer[41] and his peasants had their say on the matter: they directed their fire at worldly goods and were simultaneously the most logically minded and most practical of them all. The peasant wars on the Rhine and in Westphalia were as much the consequence of the reformationist advice of the pious, orthodox Gerson as they were of Luther's theories and the slap that Nogaret[42] gave to Boniface VIII.

There is no point in our labouring the point any further. The establishment of Churches and States has no purpose beyond the protection of interests, balancing them and arranging them in hierarchical order. Now, since interests are always at odds with one another, thanks to pauperism, and always unresolved, there is permanent agitation: revolutions are its crisis points. Reduced to its real meaning, every political, economic, religious or social quarrel amounts to a jacquerie.[43]

---

39. JEAN CHARLIER known as JEAN DE GERSON (1362–1428) attempted to heal the Great Schism by seeking to persuade the Avignon Pope Benedict XIII to step down and the Roman Pope Gregory XIII to do likewise. He did contrive to have a general council meet in Constance (1414), which healed the Schism and condemned Jan Hus. [H.T.]

40. JOHN WYCLIFFE ([1320s]–1384) championed the rights of the temporal authorities against the Roman Curia and envisaged secularization of the clerical assets diverted away from their legitimate use by a corrupt clergy. The Schism led to his imagining that the Church might well manage without a Pope and prompted him to affirm the Bible as the supreme authority. JAN HUS (1369–1415) argued in favour of Wycliffe's writings before the University of Prague in 1403. In 1410, the archbishop had those writings burnt and placed Hus and the city of Prague under an interdict. Excommunicated by Rome, Hus was compelled to appear before the Council of Constance. His own writings were consigned to the pyre and he himself was sent to the stake. MARTIN LUTHER (1483–1546) contrasted the practices of indulgences with the message of the apostle Paul in 1517. He then went on to deny the authority of the Pope, the hierarchy, priestly celibacy, monastic vows, the cult of the saints, Purgatory and the Mass. In 1520 he was excommunicated. [H.T.]

41. THOMAS MUNZER (late-fifteenth century–1525), founder of the Anabaptist sect who, in Mulhausen in Thuringia in 1524 proclaimed common ownership of assets and unleashed the Peasant Wars. Defeated and captured by the confederated princes, he was beheaded. [H.M.] For a rip-roaring novel on the anarchistic politics of the anabaptists, see the novel by the Italian collective known as Luther Blisset, Q, translated by Shaun Whiteside (London: Random House, 2003). [A.P.]

42. GUILLAUME DE NOGARET (mid-thirteenth century–1313) was one of the main leaders of Philip the Fair's struggle against the Templars and the Papacy. In 1303, he arrested arrested the Pope and – though he may not have slapped the Pope – he at least insulted him after invading his palace. The Pope only survived that by a few days. [H.T.]

43. A jacquerie was a peasant revolt against aristocratic luxury, common during the Hundred Years' War. [A.P.]

You may say that the influence of pauperism on the State is an established fact, and is the primary cause of revolutions. This is such a commonplace that we might almost look upon it as one of Monsieur de la Palice's *vérités*.[44] But to return to our subject. Is pauperism also the primary cause of wars? How is it that peoples, racked by misery, not content with turning on their governments, their nobles, their clergy, their dynasties, their bourgeois, end up blaming one another and wage a war as blind as it is pointless?

I could, as so many others do, fall back upon human folly, the flawed counsels of hunger, the Machiavellism of princes and nobles who, down through the ages, have seized opportunities to wage war as a way of diverting the people's impatience and safeguarding their own power. There is some truth to such considerations; that I do not deny; however, they are not entirely satisfactory, theoretically speaking. There is no way for a sound critic to attribute such flimsy causes to a phenomenon like war, which, let us not forget, encompasses the physiology and the psychology of humanity and governs a real right, the right of force.

Therefore, I believe I am on the right track in pointing out that the considerations of international law, upon which declarations of war are all but exclusively reliant, are as closely bound up as can be with considerations of an economic order; so that if political motives are to be regarded as the apparent trigger of war, economic needs are its secret and primary cause, and deep down, everyone knows this.

It is a fact acknowledged by statistics that attacks on property diminish when the well-being of the masses increases. As a general rule, somebody who has enough to live on does not concern himself much with his neighbour. It is the same with peoples. Just as no revolution would occur in a State if the needs of its citizens were being met, so there would also be no war between States if they were not driven to it by a force that dominates them. Guarantee a nation its freedom, security and livelihood and it will not be bothered about what bordering States are doing. It will talk neither of amalgamation, nor of annexation, nor of readjusting borders; it will even sell its own nationality cheaply, as did the peasants of Galicia, content to become Austrians just as long as they were delivered from their *seigneurs*; and as witnessed by the peasants of Lombardy, cursing their landlords and caring about the king as much as they do the emperor.

Alas! Nationality only comes into play, and the warrior spirit only possesses the prince and the people, once there is some threat hanging over their livelihoods and property or when there is a dearth of outlets or territory.

---

44. A truism so self-evident as to be the object of ridicule. [A.P.]

Whereupon the issues of pre-eminence, balance, colonies, etc., arise and these, as we have seen, only force can settle.

Why disguise it? The law of incorporation or dismemberment, which we have seen play such a huge part in politics and history, presents a quite different face when we come to seek its hidden motives by peeling back the causes, one after another. Just as the State, that organ of collective force, the embodiment of justice is, in the last analysis, merely an economic expression; just as international relations, wars and peace treaties, in spite of all the majesty with which force endows them, are also economic expressions and monuments to our penury. Land, hunger, the hope of tribute, the burning thirst for bounty from abroad, all lurk at the bottom of our diplomacy. All will shortly become increasingly obvious when, looking beyond broader considerations, we delve into the facts...

We have, therefore, every reason to make a distinction between the primary cause of war and its secondary motives or causes, the latter being of a purely political character and the former exclusively economic. It may even be the case that the political motives for war, more specious than real, lift the veil on the real cause: this pre-eminence of the cause of war over its motives is, as we shall see, one of the features of the current era. Is that any reason to go on pointing an accusing finger at the bad faith of princes, as the historians do? As if heads of State, acting in that capacity, were not the representatives of their peoples and afflicted by the very same pauperism as their subjects!

As a rule, the motives that declarations of war rely upon are serious and real; they speak to a political necessity. But the primary cause dominates them; and whilst it may still be permissible, where war is concerned, to query the legitimacy of such a cause, its presence, regrettably, is undeniable. There is nothing on earth more constant and more implacable than the wretchedness of the human race. *Ego sum pauper et dolens*:[45] that, had the warriors boasted as much philosophy as they do courage, would be the motto they would emblazon upon their banners.

So, the primary cause of every war is one and the same. It may vary in intensity and not be absolutely determined: but it is ever present, ever active and, to date, indestructible. It bursts with jealousies, rivalries, border issues, easements, questions relating to, if I may make so bold, dividing walls between properties. That is where the responsibility of nations lies. But for the influence of pauperism, but for the disorder that a rupture in the economic equilibrium introduces into States, war would be impossible; no secondary trigger could impel nations to arm themselves against one another. Therefore, it is up to nations to look to

---

45. *Bible*, Psalm 70:5: "I am poor and needy". [A.P.]

their domestic economy and to ensure, through toil, that temperate practices prevail, that interests are balanced, as a counter to pauperism, the only real risk of war.

But if, in the absence of the distress that convulses nations, war is impossible, like an effect with no cause, it cannot quite banish conscience and win acceptance other than through international law, legitimized by *raison d'état*. This is where the responsibility of political leaders comes in; only their initiative has the ability to shift war from possibility into deed. One initial and remarkable effect of the application of economic principles is that nations, having become stable, are no longer able to spontaneously turn on one another; mass invasions belong to the age of barbarism, as the last resort of a forest-dwelling, nomadic lifestyle. Just as peoples are becoming industrious and hard-working, so war is becoming a prerogative of governments. It is up to statesmen therefore to gauge the extent to which general discomfort has been aggravated further by the outsider; in which case, the stewardship of public safety allows one power to enforce the rigours of international law against another and to appeal to a judgement of force. In every instance, the statesman should remember that his responsibility is that much greater, in that, no matter what he may do, war still has its odious side, in that it is driven by pauperism and all its concomitant vices, greed, the craving for money, the thirst for sensual pleasures and all the corruptions and all the crimes engendered by sensuality grappling with scarcity.

This identification which we have just made of the primary cause of warfare takes us to fresh terrain, of which the ancients had little notion, that of political economy. There we will be making more than one discovery. Right now, it is easy to foresee, and this is something the jurists of the old school never suspected, that as regards the conduct of war, the rules of right, sublime in theory, will prove flimsy barriers for people out for personal gain while others defend their property. What might *the forms of war* look like between armies marching under the standard of hunger? We shall conclude that to do justice in war and in peace, a philosophical and subjective familiarity with right will not be enough. Practical familiarity with the laws of production and exchange will be needed too, without which the application of right remains arbitrary and war inextinguishable.

CHAPTER V

War and Plunder. Confusing War's Political Motives With Its Economic Cause

We have to establish, by numerous and solid examples, that the facts are in universal agreement with this superior view that identifies pauperism as war's primary cause. Everybody knows that the barbarian invasions between the fourth and tenth century of our era were caused by famine; that before Jesus Christ, the Romans' endless wars had been triggered by the exploitation of the patricians. But the dismal cause of war is not always so obvious: politics disguises it; it has to be extricated from the myriad pretexts that cover it, which sometimes does not seem easy. The common man is guided by the superficial; he is loath to delve into primary causes, first principles, initial phenomena, the search for core ideas and the breaking down of factors. In relation to causes, above all, he clings to the most immediate ones; which means that he understands next to nothing of the way the world works and of his own life. In particular, history is a closed book to him.

Let us show first that originally the primary cause of war and its political motives merged; that will afford us a better grasp of the reason why the latter can, in the long run, be distinguished, and what consequences are to be expected from this differentiation.

When the desert herdsmen swooped down on Egypt, which they made their farmstead for several centuries, they were spurred on by unremitting famine: the memory of that has been preserved in the book of Genesis. Around Sesostris's time,[46] the Egyptians, having driven these looters out, sought compensation by making the distant hordes tributaries. In this they were prompted by the same cause. Are we now to believe that neither famished factions had political motives? The Bedouins' ancestors might have said to the children of Osiris: "You have toiled; you have worked the soil, dug canals, built towns: wonderful. But who awarded you ownership? Where are your title deeds? How is it you get the fertile valley and we the desert? If you were to pay us a levy,

---

46. Named Sesostris by Herodotus, Senusret III ruled for two decades during the Twelfth Dynasty, 1897–1878 BC. [A.P.]

it would merely be fair compensation". What some demand, others refuse; ig-noring the traded insults on both sides of which we know nothing, there are no further grounds for fighting. Oddly enough, property, which is one of the mainstays of the civil law in every State, has never quite been acknowledged between the nations, and it cannot be. War, the daughter of famine, unleashes plunder; the heroes back in earliest times made no bones about that. Brigandry, dating back to before recorded history, is the unadulterated expression of the right of war and is given its due, confused as it is with the exercise of seigneurial rights, with the right of force.

The founders of the Egyptian, Assyrian, Mede and Persian empires, all behaved that way. Raids, demanding tribute under threat of arson and massa-cre, were their entire policy. To a sultan from Nineveh, Babylon, Persepolis or Ekbatana, tribute was his entitlement as sovereign. As far as their neighbours were concerned, the name of each people became synonymous with pirates, corsairs, brigands or buccaneers. Which is how the word for the Chaldaeans, *Kasdim*, is used in the Bible. No sooner has the right of force been asserted than it disgraces itself: its infamy shall never be expunged.

The same thing was done in turn by the Phoenicians and the Greeks, ad-ept at navigation, founders of colonies, their imports were largely the prod-uct of raids. Later, along came the Gauls, the Cimbri, the Teutons, the Goths, the Franks and the whole teeming Germanic horde; followed by the Huns, Alans, Avars, Arabs, Mongols, Turks, Bulgars, Hungarians, Normans, Gog and Magog,[47] all of them spewing forth at different times from the plains of Scythia, the depths of Asia, the slopes of the Urals, the Carpathians, the Caucasus and the Altai. A nation would rise up as one man, mount massive raids on better-off territories, demanding land or at least rights of passage and, while negotiating and passing through, exercising its right of war and claiming plunder. Wherever they might stop, if stop they did; wherever they managed to overpower the natives and claim tribute from them, and unless they were themselves extermi-nated, there they would found an empire, whereupon a whole rabble of orators, poets and historians would celebrate the glories of its founder.

Which proves, however, that the idea of right was not entirely missing from the minds of all these marauders; the fact is that they proceeded with a solemn gravitas and honestly held religiosity. The story of Jephthah has bequeathed us the most priceless evidence of that.

Jephthah was a bastard, driven from the household of his father by his

---

47. Strictly speaking, in the Bible, Gog is the name given by Ezekiel to the king of the Land of Magog, which is to say, the nation of northeastern Asia Minor, mainly the Scythi-ans. In figurative terms, that tandem of words (Gog-Magog) was the personification of the *enemies of God's people*, the *unbelievers*, as opposed to the *justified*. [H.T.]

legitimate brothers, and, in order to escape penury, forced to become a warrior, a *pugnator*, rising to become the leader of some brigands, in the manner of Romulus. *Congregati sunt ad eum viri inopes et latrocinantes, et quasi principem sequebantur.*[48] Like the medieval *condottieri*,[49] it occasionally happened that he embarked upon expeditions on behalf of peaceful populations that had been slighted by their neighbours. Commissioned by the inhabitants of Gilead to fight the Ammonites, with the promise of a judgeship over the whole of Israel if he were successful, Jephthah began by dispatching a deputation to the king of the *Beni-Ammon*. One needs to read that monument to heroic diplomacy for a thorough understanding of war, its righteousness and its wretchedness.

> And Jephthah sent messengers unto the king of the children of Ammon, saying, What hast thou to do with me, that thou art come against me to fight in my land?
>
> And the king of the children of Ammon answered unto the messengers of Jephthah, Because Israel took away my land, when they came up out of Egypt, from Arnon even unto Jabbok, and unto Jordan: now therefore restore those lands again peaceably.[50]

The facts cited by the children of Ammon were the truth: the disputed territories were a dependency of their State; they were pressing their claim, albeit rather belatedly. And what was Jephthah's answer to that?

> Israel took not away the land of Moab, nor the land of the children of Ammon.
>
> But when Israel came up from Egypt and walked through the wilderness unto the Red Sea and came to Kadesh;
>
> Then Israel sent messengers unto the king of Edom, saying: Let me, I pray thee, pass through thy land. But the king of Edom would not hearken thereto. And in like manner they sent unto the king of Moab: but he would not consent: and Israel abode in Kadesh.
>
> Then they went along through the wilderness and compassed the land of Edom, and the land of Moab, and pitched on the other side of Arnon, but came not within the border of Moab: for Arnon was the border of Moab.

---

48. *Bible*, Book of Judges, 11:3. "Then Jephthah fled from his brethren, and dwelt in the land of Tob: *and there were gathered vain men to Jephthah, and went out with him*". [A.P.]

49. *Condottieri*: Mercenaries who played crucial roles in medieval Italy. [H.T.]

50. *Bible*, Book of Judges, 11:12–13. [A.P.]

And Israel sent messengers unto Sihon, king of the Amorites, the king of Heshbon: and Israel said unto him: Let us pass, we pray thee, through thy land into my place.

But Sihon trusted not Israel to pass through his coast; but Sihon gathered all his people together and pitched in Jahaz and fought against Israel.

And the Lord God of Israel delivered Sihon and all his people into the hands of Israel, and they smote them: so Israel possessed all of the land of the Amorites, the inhabitants of that country.

And they possessed all of the coasts of the Amorites, from Arnon even unto Jabbok, and from the wilderness even unto Jordan.

So now the Lord God of Israel hath dispossessed the Amorites from before his people Israel, and shouldeth thou possess it? Wilt not thou possess that which Chemosh thy god giveth thee to possess? So whomsoever the Lord our God shall drive out from before us, them will we possess.

And now art thou anything better than Balak, the son of Ziphor, king of Moab? Did he ever strive against Israel, or did he ever fight against them?

While Israel dwelt in Heshbon and her towns, and in Aroer and her towns, and in all the cities that be along by the coasts of Arnon three hundred years, why, therefore did ye not recover them within that time?

Wherefore I have not sinned against thee, but thou dost me wrong to war against me: the Lord the Judge be judge this day between the children of Israel and the children of Ammon.[51]

You can guess what came next. The Ammonites suffered a huge defeat: Israel's sovereignty over the lands was confirmed under the same principle by which it had been established, war; and Jephthah, made a prince by that victory, was judge over Israel for six years.

Such was primitive law-giving: the right of force in its loftiest as well as its most abusive sense, but with a sincerity of religion and a quietness of conscience covering all excesses: – *I have given you the land of Canaan, Jehovah told the Hebrews, and I have wrested it from the natives. Kill them all: I, your God, Jehovah, order that of you.*[52] As I have stated elsewhere, the loss of nationhood

---

51. *Bible*, Book of Judges, 11:15–27. [P.S.]

52. The source of this quote is not clear. But the Book of Numbers, 13, §1–3 comes close. (KJV) It reads: "And the Lord spake unto Moses, saying, 'Send thou men, that they may search the land of Canaan, which I give unto the children of Israel: of every tribe of their fathers shall ye send a man, every one a ruler among them.' And Moses by the commandment of the Lord sent them from the wilderness of Paran: all those men were heads of the children of Israel". [A.P.]

entails expropriation and death. This was the law of hunger in the fullness of its horror. If I may borrow some Malthusian language, it is a feature common to all emigrants who, from Hebrews to Mormons, have so often placed civilization in jeopardy, that their industrial faculties did not match their faculties of proliferation, confronting them with the necessity of travelling far and wide in search of their fortune or starving to death. If the book of Genesis is to be credited, the Hebrews, some seventy of them having entered Egypt, made up a population of two million souls four hundred years later. Such was the proliferation of this race that the Egyptians had found themselves compelled to have new-borns cast into the Nile, the way one does with puppies. In those straits, they naturally pushed for plunder, for war; as for work, they had not reached the degree of indignity which characterizes our century, of fighting over it with arms in hand.

So much is rapine the very essence of warfare that it has served as an expression of its ideal. All warlike nations have conscripted beasts of prey – the eagle, the falcon, the owl, the lion, the wolf, the leopard – into their coats of arms. The poets and sacred scriptures of the ancient peoples understand and celebrate war primarily as a vehicle for plunder. Listen to the patriarch Jacob, on his deathbed, prophesying Judah's future glory:

> Judah is a lion's whelp. From the prey, my son, thou art gone up; he stooped down, he crouched as a lion, and as an old lion; who shall rouse him up? Judah, thou art he whom thy brethren shall praise... The sceptre shall not depart from Judah, nor a law-giver from between his feet, until Shiloh comes ...[53]

The Peace-Maker, he who sought no plunder, Solomon. Warfare and conquest were the marks of royalty. The monarch had only to stop fighting and he became unworthy; his subjects would call him to account; they will strip Judah of his sceptre: *Auferetur sceptrum de Juda*.[54] They will say: where is the man who led us to victory, who fattened upon the remains of the enemy and never let our swords go rusty? ... Furthermore, of his youngest son, Benjamin, Jacob said:

> Benjamin shall raving as a wolf; in the morning he shall devour the prey, and at night he shall divide the spoil.[55]

---

53. *Bible*, Genesis, 49:9. [P.S.]

54. *Bible*, Genesis, 49:10. "The sceptre shall not depart from Judah, nor a lawgiver from between his feet". [P.S.]

55. *Bible*, Genesis, 49:27. [P.S.]

What is important to highlight, for the sake of a perfect understanding of that age of bellicose initiative, is that war is, to an equal extent, both private and national; it is a pursuit accessible to all, with no privilege for prince, town or State. Up until the sixth or fifth century before Jesus Christ there was no real distinction between war and armed robbery, be it by surprise attack, ambush or pitched battle. The *mighty host* of which the Gospel speaks is a reference to those old practices. The synonym or correlation between warfare and brigandry is found in all the ancient tongues: great plunderer, great warrior. Nimrod, described in the Bible as a mighty hunter in the sight of Jehovah was, like Romulus, a gang leader. The Greek heroes were as much pirate entrepreneurs as they were leaders of States. A passage in *The Odyssey*, quoted by Grotius, testifies to these mythological personages seeing no shame at all in the craft of the brigand and the corsair; evidence that thinking had not altered by the time Homer was writing. Piracy was universally held in high regard and was the object of wide-ranging speculation; it was for its furtherance that navigation was invented and the earliest trading nations organized. For a long time, even after the cities had made their peace, war was prosecuted in the name of and on behalf of private individuals: Solon, Herodotus, Plutarch, Sallust, Caesar and the rabbis, etc. mention this. Peace treaties between States were not binding upon their citizenry; armed plundering of one another was looked upon by all the jurists as having its roots in natural law. That ancient custom had left some traces behind in Roman law; it survived the advent of Christianity. To it can be traced the authority issued in modern times to private persons to engage in armed piracy, on the strength of *letters of marque*. Besides, we know how popular the brigands are in the mountains of Crete, Spain and Calabria, even in our own day.

That way of life could not last. The historic contradiction, wherein two cities might be at peace with one another, even as their inhabitants were waging war on one another, was too violent. Then, with the land-owning nobility and the mercantile aristocracy enriching themselves, the former by means of slave labour and usury and the latter by means of commerce and speculation, they inevitably brought into disrepute an industry [pirating] whose very name was testimony to misery. State policy and emerging mores therefore did away with private warfare: proud princes, who had no desire to appear destitute, looked for honourable terms in which to cloak the cause and purposes of expeditions, and so the designations *brigand* and *pirate* gradually fell into disrepute. Cicero uses this insulting label for peoples making war for the sole purpose of plunder, arguing that in his view towns and kings ought not to take up arms other than on justice's behalf. That was a splendid lesson intended for the she-wolf's sucklings, but it fell on deaf ears. Only with difficulty were peoples and princes able to come up with the idea of purely political warfare. Justin recounts one of the misdeeds of Philip, king of Macedonia, that, not content with the conquests he achieved through his shrewd politics, he still sought the rewards of piracy,[56] in accordance with the old practices. Just imagine, if possible, the frightful disorder of a society wherein the mightiest head of State had a vested interest in the expeditions of freebooters whom he backs with his influence and, if need be, his force of arms! ... *You call me a rogue*, one pirate answered Alexander who had called upon him to end his exploits, *because I have but one ship: you would call me king, had I, like you, two hundred of them.*[57] Actually, the difference between conqueror and pirate in the fourth century before our era is indiscernible. The pirates of Cilicia were a considerable population, which the Romans never quite managed to destroy, despite the pledge made by Caesar, and I imagine that they only faded away under the avalanche of the Turks who were bigger plunderers than the Cilicians themselves.

The State's appropriation of war as its private preserve did not *ipso facto* strip warfare of its aspect of despoilment; by contrast, the fire behind brigandry springs from that precise difference between individual enthusiasm and the huge appetites of collectives. As the philosopher Antisthenes used to say,[58] *Let us wish the enemy lots of luck but little courage.* Hardly mealy-mouthed comment there. Prior to their conquering the world, the Romans could also not conceive of any other purpose to warfare. It has been remarked time and time again that right, which religion possessed in the highest measure, initially meant to them only a prerogative of the race and not a relationship of humankind. Right was an exclusively quiritarian[59] attribute: when the juridconsults, broadening the notion, declared that right was shared by all men, the game was up for the republic: Rome was subsumed into humanity.

That, however, was not the people's understanding of it. As far as they were concerned, the peace of the Caesars gave the signal for a share-out, something akin to a first course in a banquet. Rome had long since grasped the notion that the city made men equals, and the idea had brought it victory over the senate. But the idea that tribute should no longer be extorted out of the nations making up part of the empire, as the closure of the temple to Janus indicated, that idea, it just could not fathom. According to Suetonius, Nero, having learnt that there was some unrest among the Gauls, gave the order that it should be

---

56. JUSTIN, *Abrégé de l'histoire universelle de Trogue Pompée*, translated by Pierrot and Boitard (Paris: Garnier, 1862), Book VIII, chap. IV. [H.M.]

57. For more on this theme, see Noam Chomsky, *Pirates and Emperors, Old and New: International Terrorism in the Real World* (Boston: South End Press, 2003). [I.M.]

58. Disciple of Gorgias and Socrates and founder of the Cynic School. [H.M.]

59. Old Roman, and parochial. [A.P.]

allowed to run its course. His reckoning was that repression visited upon a larger number of towns would bring him in more substantial plunder: *Adeoque lente ac secure tulit ut gaudentis etiam suspicionem praeberet tamquam occasione nata spoliandarum iure belli opulentissimarum provinciarum.*[60] And so, finally, we have highlighted the shameful and still extant article in the alleged code of war that authorizes armies at war to *forage* on the lands of the enemy, to indulge in *marauding* and which allows the victor to indulge, *ad libitum*, in complete or partial spoliation of the vanquished. Need we go any further to demonstrate that what the well-meaning Grotius and all his successors have taken for a natural consequence of war is, rather, its primary cause and, in the secret reckonings of the belligerents, its purpose and end? Because ultimately, as Aristotle was right to note, one does not wage war for the pleasure of doing so. The right invoked is never anything more than the argument for some interest; warfare without an interested motive, waged on behalf of sheer right, a highly rational warfare, would be in practical terms, as we have been pointing out, nonsensical on the part of the State that might embark upon it. When France says that she is fighting for ideas, no one believes her and she is held up to ridicule.

Here, then, is what we have established:

Warfare, fostered by pauperism and undertaken with a view to plunder, initially orchestrated indifferently, sometimes by private persons, sometimes by towns, later turns into the preserve of the State. The right of war becomes the sovereign's prerogative. Piracy, the last expression of private warfare, is now held as infamous and deserving of the ultimate penalty. But that has done nothing to strip warfare of its aspect of plunder; civic arms are no more immaculate than heroic arms; far from it, plunder, the right of the victor, exercised on a broader scale, is displayed in all its ignominy.

And this carries on until, thanks to a set of circumstances that we shall highlight later, the plundering of populations and the devastation of territories raises widespread reproach, where conquest turns into straightforward political annexation and forces the conqueror to look to the exploitation of his subjects for the profits of his profession. The history of the Greeks, from the end of Dorian tyranny up until Alexander, presents us with the first and most interesting of these transitions in this regard. We need to see from every angle what Greek civilization was; so marvellous in so many respects, the historians

---

60. SUETONIUS, *The Lives of Caesars, 6, Nero*, XL, §4. "He was at Naples when he learned of the uprising of the Gallic provinces, on the anniversary of his mother's murder, and received the news with such calmness and indifference that he incurred the suspicion of actually rejoicing in it, because it gave him an excuse for pillaging those wealthy provinces according to the laws of war". *Suetonius. Volume II*, trans. and ed. J. C. Rolfe, (Cambridge: Harvard University Press, 1914), 156–57. [A.P.]

have established that it went into eclipse at the very point where, according to the ordinary laws of society, it ought to have taken a new development, if only the Greek race, with all its genius, had been able to come up with the idea of an authentic civilization.

CHAPTER VI

Warfare from Greeks to Alexander: The Transition from Piracy to Conquest

The Dorian system[61] was organized plunder, bearing some resemblance to our old feudal system. Holding the city-dweller to ransom, exploiting the peasant, robbing the traveller, capturing trading vessels, all of these were the stock in trade of the knights of ancient Hellas. That ghastly regime survived for ten centuries. It triggered many waves of emigration that filled the islands and the entire coastline of the Mediterranean, Asia, Africa, Italy, Gaul, Spain, all of which went on to thrive at a time when the mother country was still groaning in the darkness of her middle ages. In the end and with the exception of Sparta, the Dorian tyranny was routed everywhere; with democracy, a new era arrived. After the failure of the two expeditions of Darius and Xerxes, the peninsular and continental power of the Greeks underwent a sudden, extraordinary expansion. But the old Dorian spirit, the spirit of plunder, resurfaced in the civil strife in the country, all the bitterer in that it came from the lowest levels and, after the last revolution, was embodied, not by a handful of manorial nobles, but by the urban bourgeoisie and the plebs of the republics.

For a start, anyone who was of Greek extraction but had not belonged to the confederation against the Persians, was declared liable to pay tribute; this was the fate of the islands of Karystos, Naxos and Thasos, which had all been subjugated by the Athenians. There may well have been grounds for finding some fault in the wrong-headed patriotism of these islanders that had given the Great King's vast fleets and countless armies a scare. But to degrade them and make them tributaries rather than target them for an amalgamation that safeguarded every interest, was a step beyond the rights of peoples and made

---

61. The Dorians were one of the three main groups of peoples in ancient Greece (along with the Aeolians and the Ionians) who invaded the country from the north in the twelfth and tenth centuries BC. They initially settled in Sparta, in Argolis and Corinth and in the Peloponnese. They then invaded and overran Crete, the Dodecanese, southwest Asia Minor, Sicily and southern Italy. They destroyed the Mycenaean civilization in Sparta and Crete both and reduced their subjects to Helot status. On the other hand, there followed a progressive inter-mingling of conqueror and conquered. [H.T.]

prejudicial use of the right of force. We are reminded of the king of Saxony, condemned by the Congress of Vienna to forfeit half of his States for not having spoken out against Napoleon early enough.

Things in the Peloponnese were much worse: the Mycenaeans and Helots were placed under the yoke of the Spartans.[62] Up until the nineteenth century, the praise bestowed upon this latter community of rogue nobles is unfathomable, organized exclusively for brigandry, and living in a penury, due to their hatred of any useful occupation, which they had made into an article of their public law. War for plunder and plunder as a means of survival; there, in short, we have the whole institution of Lycurgus and Spartan virtue. It was the model that Plato borrowed for his utopian republic.

The quarrel between Sparta and Athens arose over the partition of tributary towns. To us civilized people of the nineteenth century, such a dispute looks outrageous and monstrous. Towns and whole populations of Greek

---

62. The inhabitants of Laconia were divided into Helots (semi-slaves) who carried out the agricultural work, the *perioikoi*, a class of free men without any political rights and who were comprised mainly of traders and merchants, and the *spartiates* (or equals), a ruling class of rulers and soldiers, descended from the Dorians.

The foundation of Sparta's greatness is credited to the laws of Lycurgus, a semi-legendary Spartiate lawmaker believed to have lived in the seventh century BC. From the fourth century BC onwards, the Spartiates looked upon themselves as merely a military garrison that dedicated all its pursuits to warfare. The individual belonged to the State. Boys started their military training at the age of seven and were enlisted at the age of twenty. Although permitted to marry, they had to live in barracks up until the age of thirty. Between the ages of twenty and sixty, all Spartiates were duty bound to serve as *hoplites* (foot-soldiers) and to take their meals in the *phidition* (mess-hall).

The first conflicts faced by Sparta (on the Taygetos mountain range in the southern Peloponnese) were with Messenia (in the southwest of the Peloponnese) and Argos (a city in the northwest). The war with Messenia ended c.668 BC with the defeat of the Messenian Dorians, most of whom were then reduced to helot status. At the time of their wars against the Achaeans and the Dorians of Argos, the Spartiates were very often the victors. Raised in an austere discipline, they became a race of fierce and ascetic warriors, quite capable of the ultimate sacrifice for patriotic reasons, but incapable of espousing a level-headed political and economic program. The Peloponnesian War which erupted in 404 BC saw the rivalry between Sparta and Athens reach its height. After Athens was defeated in 404 BC, Sparta dominated Greece. But her inflexibility triggered a fresh war, in the course of which the Thebans, under the command of Epaminondas, stripped her of her power (371 BC) and her territorial possessions, confining the State to its original boundaries. Sparta was effectively in permanent competition with Athens, and in the Greek world embodied a political ideal that stood in contrast to Athenian democracy: an aristocratic, warrior society that exalted masculine force and austere morals. She also embodied landed power, as opposed to the maritime imperialism of Athens. Later, Sparta became part of the Roman province of Achaea and appears to have known renewed prosperity during the early centuries of the Roman Empire. The city itself was destroyed by the Goths in 336 BC. [H.T.]

blood, religion and Hellenic language, were turned into vast metayages[63] by other towns, for the sole reason that during the war of independence they had clung to their neutrality: what an abuse of force! And how the heroism of those who fought at Marathon, Salamis and Thermopylae is diminished by the remembrance of it! But there is a beginning to everything. The imposition of tribute rather than political annexation was, initially, the crudest exercise of the right of force. War, or tribute: in those times, that dilemma was the whole and all of the rights of the peoples.

Just as, back then, every individual was a citizen or an enemy, a free man or a slave, and always assumed to be a slave unless he could produce his proof that he was born free, similarly every town unable to assert and uphold its sovereignty by force of arms was awarded tributary status. So, possession of those towns that were left outside of the federal compact, true money makers to those with federated status and in possession of force, was fought over. Then they fought for the empire of Greece herself, or, as we would put it these days, for unity; they struggled to seize hold of the strategic points like the isthmus of Corinth, the possession of which might have guaranteed the enslavement of the entire country. The battle of Tanagra, fought for that very reason, proved indecisive. From 459 [BCE] onwards, that being the year the great Midian war ended, Kimon,[64] in order to divert the Greeks away from these internal wars, held out the prospect of fresh prey: the whole of Persia was waiting to be plundered. But for that to happen, the towns would have to be rallied and their strength concentrated, and divided loyalties were at their height, so much so that tributaries, such as Mitylene, Euboea, Boeotia, Megara, Potidaea, Samos, etc., seized the opportunity to rebel against the payment of tribute and to win back their freedom.

The Peloponnesian war had a curious triggering. Corinth's colony, Kerkyra, had founded a colony of its own, Epidaurus. Seemingly under the principle that

---

63. A metayage is equivalent to sharecropping. The landlord grants the landless worker permission to farm a piece of land (but not to own it) in return for a share of the product. This was one of the primary means of keeping freed slaves tied to their former masters in both Rome and North America. [A.P.]

64. KIMON (c.510–450 BC), Athenian general and politician, the son of Militiades, winner in the battle of Marathon (490 BC). He fought in the battle of Salamis and later worked with the Greek general Aristides in commanding the allied Greek fleet dispatched to Asia Minor to liberate the Greek colonies there from Persian rule. In 466 BC, he faced a Persian fleet near Eurymedon (today's Köprü in Turkey) where he destroyed or captured nearly two hundred ships and thrashed the Persian land army the same day. Following a revolt by the helots in Sparta, against whom he sided with the Spartiate army, he lost the confidence of his allies and was stripped of his command. After that the democracy led by Pericles ostracized him. On his return in 451, Kimon secured a five-year armistice between the Spartiates and the Athenians and contributed funding towards the rebuilding of Athens. [H.T.]

the progeny of livestock belongs to the owner, the Corinthians laid claim to Epidaurus, which the Kerkyrans were determined to hold on to. The Athenians took the side of the Kerkyrans, meaning that they upheld the tributary's right to create tributaries of its own; the Thebans sided with the Corinthians. Plataea, allied with Athens, was attacked and war broke out (431 BC).

Here we see the Greek mind in all its glory. So essential to war was plunder that it was to all intents its motive, its reason and its purpose, and at first the belligerents paid much less attention to joining forces than to the quest for booty. They could have been mistaken for a gang of looters on the rampage.

Then, that same year, in 431 BC, the Lacedaemonians crossed into Attica, overland. For their part, the Athenians sailed down to lay waste to the Peloponnese. We have it from Justin that the Spartans, those swaggering belittlers of wealth, made a show of seeking battle rather than plunder. But the Athenians, on the advice of Pericles, reckoned that there was little point risking a battle when they could swoop on Laconia at no risk and carry off more plunder than they had lost.

In 430, Attica was invaded once more as retaliation and Potidaea was captured by the Athenians.

In 428, Attica was invaded for a third time – at the same time, the Athenians were obliged to race to Mitylene, one of their tributary cities, which had just risen in revolt. Luck was starting to turn against them. They lacked sufficient force to keep what they owned and, what is more, for what they had hopes of owning.

In 427 and 425 came the fourth and fifth invasions of Attica, followed by reprisals against the Peloponnese.

In 424, Athens seized hold of the island of Kuthera on the coast of Laconia. In retaliation, the Lacedaemonian general Brasidas laid siege to Amphipolis, an Athenian-owned town.

This carried on up to the Sicilian expedition, devised by the famous Alcibiades in the same spirit as the raids on the Peloponnese, which had brought Athens such misfortune. The armies looked ill-suited for battle; they made no attempt to engage; it was all about who was going to deny the enemy the greatest plunder. Meanwhile, they tried to sneak up on one another and set ambushes; and then woe betide the hapless! The battles of the ancients were not clashes but killings. It was during this time that all of Athens's allied towns deserted her. There was a massive uprising of the tributaries: history at least offers this consolation that, with the tigers ripping one another apart, the sheep were safe. After a mixture of successes and set-backs, the Athenian army was slaughtered at Aegos-Potamos, whilst spread out in search of plunder. This was a common occurrence in the old wars. Athens was finally captured by Lysander: the demise of Greek freedom can be dated from that point. No less given to looting than the Greeks, the Carthaginians seized the chance to swoop on Sicily and make tributaries of Selinunte, Himera, Agrigento, Gela and Kamarina. Tyranny ensconced itself in Syracuse. Such were the exploits by which Greece's finest age, the age of Pericles, was distinguished. From the manner of their waging war alone, we can see that the Greeks were scarcely born to make laws for the world; that honour goes to a people braver than them, to the Romans. *We are the offspring of heroes*, they used to say, their heads filled with Homer. In fact, the topic most frequently mentioned in *The Iliad* and *The Odyssey* is loot.

Supremacy in Greece then passed to Lacedaemonia:[65] the old Dorian principle was in the ascendant for a second time. Since Athens – which owed its power to its navy and to trade, and commanded respect for her arts – had fallen back on the old maxims during war-time, her defeat was inevitable; that was Justice. History does not put up with such contradictions. The bird of prey of Taygetos was getting ready to swoop down on Persia, which was split between two pretenders and had an army of Greek mercenaries in her employ. But the Lacedaemonians were the most grasping and ruthless of overlords and Greece could not but take a step backwards. Rather than follow them against the great king, the Greeks opted to sell their services. Sparta was thrust back into isolation and Athens regained her freedom. Agesilaus's victories in Asia were undone by Conon. Set-back followed set-back and Lycurgus's city, on the brink of succumbing, only averted that threat by betraying Greece in the so-called Peace of Antalkidas. At pretty much the same time, Rome fell to the Gauls. There is no need to say what brought the latter to Italy. Plunder was the keynote: *Woe to the conquered!*

Under the treaty of Antalkidas,[66] a product of the most profound Machiavellianism, all the Greek cities in Asia were surrendered to the Great King; in return, all of the ones in Greece proper, big and small, were proclaimed INDEPENDENT. This was Greece doubly done to death. Let's skip this transfer of the Asian Greek cities to Persia, something that Sparta had no entitlement to do; there cannot be anyone who does not appreciate how

65. Sparta by another name. [H.T.]
66. ANTALKIDAS (fourth century BC) Greek admiral and politician, born in Sparta. In 387 BC, he conducted successful negotiations with the king of Persia over aid to Sparta in her war with Athens. In return, Persia would secure recognition from Sparta of her ascendancy over the Greek cities in Asia Minor. Antalkidas commanded the Spartiate fleet in several battles in the Hellespont (today's Dardanelles), at the end of which the Athenians were driven out of the Aegean Sea. In 386 he forced the Athenians to the peace table in what became known as the Peace of Antalkidas. After Sparta's decline, Antalkidas became such a target of public contempt that he starved himself to death. [H.T.]

fateful it was. But, we hear, by declaring all the cities in Europe independent and setting the tributaries free, and proclaiming equality, Sparta was rendering service to democracy. Wrong: it was primarily there that her treason lay. Greece could now not survive without unity. In those times, federation was just a word: the only connection that might have made a great power of Greece was centralization and, by way of a temporary stratagem of centralization, tribute. Thus was Greece reduced to dust by means of that general liberation as well as the surrender of the Asian cities to the king of Persia: her power was smashed to the core. There was only one way of overhauling the league, the one indicated by Kimon: the conquest of Persia itself. But things were not yet ready for such an undertaking and widespread disintegration triggered by the peace of Antalkidas, left the Greeks incapable of it. It was written that the spoils of Asia, so fervently coveted, were not for them and that they would lose even all their former possessions. At that point, decline was making giant strides.

The moment that despicable treaty became known, cities such as Athens, which had their own tributaries, cried treachery and refused to give up; the good and bad motives behind this, we know. Did the Lacedaemonians, relentless in their handiwork, seize upon this as a pretext on which to bring relief to said tributaries? No, it provided them with an excuse for overrunning them. They mounted attacks on Mantinea, Phlius, Olunthos, the main city in Khalkidike, and they stormed the stronghold of Thebes. Then it was the turn of Boeotia to step in and take charge of the Greeks' retaliation. Pelopidas and Epaminondas routed the Spartans. That breed of brigand would have been banished from the scene, had Epaminondas not perished in his final victory (362 BC).

Here Justin passes this very grave comment:

> In the wake of the battle of Mantinea, the Athenians fell into torpor and dissolute ways. There developed among them the practice of sharing the State's income among the people of the city and of spending on feasts and spectacles what had previously been used for the upkeep of the fleet and the army.[67]

We can guess the source of the treasury that they saw fit to share. Of course, had it been the sum of contributions raised from the inhabitants, it might have been more straightforward just to cut taxes. But it was the tribute levied upon her satellite cities: tribute, booty, plunder, and still more plunder.

With the Greeks in decline, the fortunes of the Macedonians prospered.

67. JUSTIN, *Abrégé de l'histoire universelle de Trogue Pompée*, translated by Pierrot and Boitard (Paris: Garnier, 1862), Book VI, chap. IX. [H.M.]

Philip[68] carried on with Sparta's policy: under the treaty of Antalkidas, he backed the claims of the allied and tributary cities and, to be safe, seized them. To no avail, Demosthenes denounced the king of Macedonia's tactics: to the degenerate Athenians, that great orator's harangues were just more entertainment. For assistance against Philip, they looked to Persia, which had been acting as mediator in all inter-Greek disputes ever since that notorious treaty. Besides, the Greeks had only ever fought their wars pirate-style; their *syntagma* was not strong enough to stand up to a phalanx.[69] In the battle of Khaironeia, Philip easily had the better of a long-winded plebs, as bereft of moral sensibility as of political sense. Appointed the Greeks' supreme commander at the Corinth assembly, to the applause of all those who had, for the preceding century and a half, weathered both the savagery of the Spartans and the demagoguery of Athens, he left his son, Alexander, Europe as his inheritance and Asia for him to conquer.

Greek history affords us sight of war unadorned and in its development, driven by its primary cause: warfare between clan chiefs, and between nobles and plebeians during the long Dorian tyranny; warfare between city and city; finally, Greece under the command of Alexander and at war against the Persians.

---

68. PHILIP II (382–336 BC), king of Macedonia (359–336). Held hostage in Thebes as an adolescent, Philip observed the political and military practices of that city which at the time was the dominant power in Greece. On his return to Macedonia, he was appointed as regent and wasted no time in seizing the throne. He overhauled the Macedonian army after the model of the Theban phalanxes and, in under two years, had copper-fastened the safety of his kingdom and tightened his grip on the throne. After that, he set about implementing a policy of territorial expansion. In 357, he seized the Athenian colony of Amphipolis in Thrace, making himself master of the gold mines on Mount Paggaion, enabling him to fund the ensuing wars. In 356, he seized Potidaia in Khalkhidike and Pydna on the Gulf of Thermaikos and then, in 354, took Methone and closed on Thessaly. By 352, he had arrived at the pass of Thermopylae. He inspired the great Athenian orator Demosthenes to deliver his *Philippics*, a series of speeches denouncing the threat posed by Macedonia to the freedom of the Greeks; the first *Philippic* was delivered in 351. In 348, Philip had overrun Thrace and Khalkhidike. Two years after that, he made peace with Athens, which was at war with him at the time, for the sake of protecting his ally, the city of Olunthos in Khallhidike. At the request of the Thebans, Philip intervened in the third holy war (339) against the Locridans in Phokhaia, which region he sacked. Egged on by Demosthenes, the Athenians and the Thebans then joined forces against him, but their army was completely smashed in 338 at Khaironeia. Philip's victory left him the unchallenged overlord of Greece. In 337, all the other Greek cities, with the exception of Sparta, assembled in Corinth and recognized Macedonia's supremacy and concluded a pan-Hellenic alliance under his aegis. Two years later, just after he had been received full authority from the Corinthian League to lead the war on Persia and just as he was making ready his expedition, he was murdered. Regarded as the greatest statesman and general of his day, Philip of Macedonia laid the groundwork for the Macedonian military might that his son Alexander the Great used in order to conquer and Hellenize the Middle East. [H.T.]

69. *Syntagma*: Greek military corps. *Phalanx*: Macedonian military corps. [H.T.]

Those three phases might be defined thus: war for spoils, war for tribute, war for conquest; in short, a war of despoilment, everywhere and at all times. The prejudice that held that work was a slavish thing, relentlessly upset the balance between needs and resources, which industry elsewhere failed to make good and thus had to be made good by war abroad; there was no escaping this predicament. The common man always has an empty stomach: the aristocrat always seems fallen on hard times; the city, being the most substantial community, is forever operating at a loss. As for war's motives, or, if you prefer, its pretexts, there is no shortage of those. The history of the Kerkyrans and Corinthians provide us with an instance of that where Epidaurus is concerned. In the absence of local issues, wasn't it but the great problem of Greek unity?

Should there be any lingering doubts now that pauperism and, consequently, plunder was, quite apart from high political considerations that the philosopher historian may discern, the primary cause of Alexander's expedition, let me focus on just one fact. At his coronation, Alexander began by exempting his Macedonian subjects from taxes and levies of every description; all he asked of them was men for his armies. Now, at that point, Greece, which had the king of Macedonia as her supreme commander, had not been paying him any tribute; the upshot was that Alexander, on assuming power, and deliberately dismissing any of the resources of his own country, intended to support himself exclusively at the foreigner's expense. In relation to his army, he espoused the principle, resuscitated at the beginning of the century with varying effects, of sustaining war by means of war and, as to those staying home, he made them an advance payment of their part of the plunder by exempting them from taxation.

Unlike the Romans, the Greeks were not born to rule over the world. But what we have said about the Greeks and their martial practices in no way diminishes the qualities of their race, one of the best endowed in terms of physical beauty, sharpness of mind, poetry, language and a gift for the sciences and arts. But in the fourth century BC, juridical sensibilities were feeble and the rights of peoples had barely emerged, the right of force was cynically asserted in the most abusive manner, collective life was pretty much non-existent, and individualism was taken to extremes. As the cult of Homer's poems testifies, ancient Greek civilization had developed under the influence of the heroic ideal, that being nothing more than the ideal of the plundering warrior. And not the least extraordinary feature of that blessed breed was the fact that it had grown up and had been illumined in conditions that seemed incompatible with the rise of genius. It collapsed and faded away just as its freedom to plunder was stripped away from it; at the very moment when, under the baton of the king of Macedonia, it was now being denied licence to run loose.

Could it be true, therefore, that in certain races the most eminent faculties only grow in the shade of the most monstrous vices? Proof that the modern Greeks are indeed the offspring of the ancients is the fact that they have clung to the subtle, sophistic, indomitable Dorian spirit more grimly than to plunder. But what would you expect from a civilization that sets out to strike a balance in all things, where science leaves no more room for sophistry, where philosophy has lifted the veil on the mystery in every contradiction, where the entrepreneurial spirit has replaced the spirit of adventure, where advances in the rights of peoples are stripping warfare of its poetry and making the tragic and the epic impossibilities? In certain respects, the anarchic Greece of antiquity bears a lot of resemblance to medieval Italy; in other respects, she is reminiscent of those mountain dwellers of the Caucasus, handsome and heroic as the Greeks were, and broken with such difficulty by the czars, despite their immense force. What the future holds in store for those still rather backward tribesmen, we do not know: but we would not be surprised if, for many a long century to come, they fail to be distinguished by anything grand, given that their ingenuity depends essentially on their warrior idealism and that, since their submission, they have retained nothing that might lend thrust and fruitfulness to their intelligence.

CHAPTER VII

War and Conquest. The Distinction between War's Political Motives and Its Economic Cause

Alexander ushered in the authentic age of the conquerors; his name is rightly celebrated for that.

From this individual onwards, warfare seems to have taken on a fresh appearance. Its primary cause is still, as we shall see later, pauperism; but it is better disguised in terms of international policy, its haughtiness seemingly scornful of the notion of a biting poverty, but, deep down, those are simply its corollaries. Cities no longer fight one another over plunder as much; that is a side-line by which the soldier, or even the general, may still be tempted but with which the statesman is scarcely concerned these days. Wars are fought over provinces. This is the age of annexation and amalgamation. State formation has the wind in its sails; the days of the independence of cities, mirrored in Hellenic times by the plurality of gods, are numbered. Tributaries who have everything to gain by revolution, by acquiring the rights of citizenship offered to them, are in favour of it. On every score, nationalism is losing strength, both on account of the risks of war and the advantages offered by a powerful protectorate.

Resistance, indeed, merely speeds things up. After Alexander's death, there came the Achaean League, the Aitolian League, and a third one, the Lacedaemonian League. Leagues and alliances, which in one sense seem like a backward step and were bound up with laughable reform schemes, such as Agis's,[70] viewed from a different angle, replicated the inevitability of annexation before finally succumbing to their own contradictions. Brand-new feelings were at work in the multitudes, putting a strain on the old, staunch patriotism. The game was up, and unity was the order of the day. Everywhere, the local gods deserted the cities placed under their protection. One of Alexander's successors, Demetrios nick-named *Poliorketes*, taker of cities, was famed for his conquests. But, as if to prove that he, like Alexander, was merely an agent of the revolution,

---

70. AGIS IV, king of Sparta (245–241 BC) tried to restore Lycurgus's constitution, proposed the forgiveness of debts and a redistribution of lands and thereby provoked the hatred of the aristocracy and was condemned to death by strangulation. [H.T.]

he refused to set aside as a refuge for himself any of the many places he had co-
erced. Death overtook him in Asia, where he had fled to live as a mere private
individual (283 BC).

Let us not forget, though, that despite this growth in the political component in affairs of warfare, despite advances in international law, the main driver
of events was still pauperism, a state of widespread penury and hardship. Just as
there had been an original coming together to ward off individual distress, so
now there was a tendency to band together against craft and municipal misery:
greater gods and mightier princes were looked to for salvation. Along with the
appetites of great empires, the worries of smaller States lent themselves to a re-
drawing of the political map. Is there not something similar under way today?
Bring up talk of giving France a boundary on the Rhine: provided that you can
manage local freedoms and susceptibilities, there will be no shortage of individuals who will welcome their loss of nationality as a blessing, once they can see it
as, in one case, a wider range of outlets for goods and, in another, the prospect
of work or of a downpour of alms.

And so, States are formed along more generous lines and the cities incorporated into them enjoy the same benefits as the metropolis; this was a
distinguishing feature of the period in Greek and Asian history that followed
Alexander's death. Thus, it can be argued that the Greeks or Macedonians, it
makes no difference here, were shown the way by the Persians. And then war
broke out again over borders and relations between these impromptu States
and, finally, over supremacy, which is to say, as usual, over the largest budget,
the daily bread of governments. The historians' eloquence has painted all these
events in political colours. But the economist cannot be guided by such appearances: he wants to get to the bottom of things and what does he discover? That
it is need that prompts every move and lies behind all agitation and that where
nations fail to support themselves by means of economic organization, they
strive to get it by reworking States, and this is not something that can be done
unopposed, which is to say, without warfare.

Continuing to the wars of Alexander's successors, these were all the more
murderous in that, on taking over from that great conqueror, they continued
the huge despoilment and found nothing but wasteland and anarchy. As to the
wars of the Romans, their shameful motives we have mentioned already, but
they still managed to complete the task begun by Alexander. And let us skip
the whole of the Middle Ages, when there was ghastly poverty and when feudal brigandry served, as that of the Dorians before it, as a prelude to a new age
of conquest, and then to a further reshuffling of Europe. A proper appreciation of these huge developments in warfare would take us too long. Let us leap
straight to the modern age and in order to gain a proper understanding of war

of conquest, the great war, let us transport ourselves mentally to the heart of one of those great States, obliged by economic imbalance to unremittingly look abroad for the wherewithal to fill the yawning chasm within.

A State with a growing population under the crush of pauperism has to seek increased resources, territorial expansion, colonies, communications, possession or at any rate unfettered access to rivers, lakes and mountain passes, outlets to the sea, *windows on the world*, as Peter I, the founder of Petersburg used to say.

But all of this had to be won first.

Conquest over, it needs defending and the exploitation of it needs to be assured against both incursions from without and revolts from within; this requires an ongoing deployment of forces and simply perpetuates and keeps the war going. To speak truthfully, all of that falls short and is never enough. One has to encircle, man strategic positions, take over access points, erect barriers and, oddly enough, look to one's own defences not just against invading enemy armies but also against the equally formidable influx of goods from abroad. What are tariffs but warfare? And what lies beneath tariffs, what are they, other than fear of letting one's capital be undermined by speculation and fear of debt, in short, by the spectre of famine?

Which bears out our basic proposition: that the number one cause of agitation and war is pauperism, and it is endemic in societies. Nations and trades, private persons and governments, plebs and nobility, proletarian and prince, they are all prey to discomfort; the deficit does not leave us a minute's rest. Heads of State have merely to let go of the reins: peoples are going to gallop away. When it comes to destroying one another and further self-impoverishment, neither blood nor treasure come at a higher price. Which is why, when fire breaks out, the historian and the publicist need not really seek after what caused it: the only issue is finding out how the monster broke free of its fetters, or by what intrigue, freak of fate or clumsiness on the part of the nation's officers, had it burst upon the world?

In light of these considerations, the peaceful dispositions of governments can be gauged by the state of their finances, the agricultural-industrial position of their peoples, the total debt, the parallel growth in parasitism and the proletariat. Tranquillity abroad hinges upon order at home; that is as certain as any mathematical axiom. The people's sixth sense on this score is wonderful; wretchedness means that it can sense the approach of war at quite some remove, *procul odoratur bellum*,[71] the way the famished ogre used to catch the scent of fresh meat.

Pray tell, which State in Europe is not operating at a loss right now? We have shown how a nation only produces what it needs; with each day, humanity

---

71. *Bible*, Book of Job, 39:25. The text here refers to the war-horse. "He smelleth the battle afar off". [P.S.]

looks to God and toil for its daily bread. But outlay always overruns revenues quite substantially, precisely because humanity, a whole-hearted believer in wealth, conducts itself on that basis. The public and private debts of European nations may well be in excess of a hundred billion; and, remarkably, it is the countries that produce the most and best and which do most business that are the most heavily burdened. They are also the ones most inclined to warfare, meaning to invasion.

For the past four centuries, the discoveries of the navigators have furnished the European powers with plentiful sources of profit and vast outlets for their populations. The settlements founded in the two Americas, Africa, Asia, Australia and Oceania have played a considerable role in the peace of the world. But that situation could not last for long. Soon, every corner of the globe will have been explored; the land has been claimed everywhere; countries that until recently were wastelands fill up with European settlers, who promptly become the enemies of their mother-countries and quite ready to take up arms against them. Where is there left to conquer around the globe? The day that India, Australia, the islands of Oceania, Africa and all the lands currently subject to European exploitation, proclaim or recover their independence; when, with sovereign control over their own wealth, raising the prices of their produce and competing with our own goods, they deliver nothing except for a fair return, on that day all the nations around the globe will find themselves blockaded by one another and plunged into a pauperism of their own. So, unless a balance can be struck everywhere between output and consumption and if powers of fertility continue to outstrip industrial capabilities, political motives not being in short supply, strife is going to erupt, inexorably and universally.

At the moment, all the signs point to war. Of course, looking no further than the political side of things, no statesman has ever had to face such complications. These next questions arise all at the same time, scabrous, irksome and conceived in terms most likely to drive the diplomat to despair, and drive the masses on to the field of battle: the question of political reform and question of nationality; the question of stability in Europe and the question of natural borders; the question of centralization and the question of federation; the question of intervention or non-intervention and of protectorates; the question of the temporal and the spiritual; of serfdom and the issue of slavery; the free trade question and the compulsory trade question;[72] the question of the life and death of States and the issue of their succession; the question of their absolute independence and the matter of their deference to a supreme Diet.

Governments, to be fair to them, fear war and make the utmost effort to

---

72. It is likely that the reference here is to the debate around whether trades should be certified by the State or not, not to free trade between states. [A.P.]

evade it. But they are forced to anticipate it and make ready for it; nothing more is needed for it to break out.

However, is there merely one issue lurking behind these matters of high politics, that mass diplomacy is brazenly left to resolve to the satisfaction of all interested parties? One issue that accounts for the enormous imbroglio that has had peoples worrying for the past fifteen years as they await decimation by war?

As I have said and as anyone can readily appreciate, it is pauperism. Here, I am genuinely afraid of being taken to task for reiterating the same points too often. But the facts are so unmistakable, so persistent: they shine such a bright light upon the contemporary situation and the whole of previous history. This is a matter of such high interest for Europe, that I would reckon myself worthy of reproach by the reader if, due to some pointless literary delicacy, I were to overlook any hint of my conviction in the souls of others.

Let us admit as much, peoples of Europe, one and all, and our offering of a brotherly handshake to one another will not be long delayed.

The workers of the February Revolution, proclaiming universal [male] suffrage and the emancipation of the proletariat in one fell swoop, did what the Sans-Culottes of 1793 had done before them, what the Reformation's peasants did in the sixteenth century, the Hussites in the fifteenth, the Jacques in the fourteenth, the Bons-hommes in the thirteenth and the Albigensians in the twelfth. They put their finger on the open wound. The cause of warfare, as of any revolution, is a question of equilibrium, not political nor international equilibrium, but economic equilibrium. February's workers were defeated in June 1848 and December 1851; did that make the factor they denounced any less present and the sway of that factor over the government any less real? For the duration of the Presidency, things have been left hanging: a violent situation which everyone assured themselves the 1852 elections would deliver us from. The coup d'état of 2nd December merely anticipated the solution: let us take a look at what came next.

I have no desire to criticize the imperial government. From my vantage-point, I can state without weakness or flattery that the imperial government has done what any other would have done in its place; it has been the expression of the universal mind, and, as it was the product of universal suffrage, it cannot be taken to task for that. It is a case of my countering one doctrine with another or, if you prefer, of my highlighting a paradox regarding a prejudice. An appeal to public reason does not amount to an attack on the government.

The issue of work and pauperism having been raised, two ways of resolving it offered themselves: one consisted of promoting the spread of wealth, boosting output by increasing the number of businesses, credit, traffic routes, etc., etc. The other consisted of relentlessly drawing the extreme classes back towards those middling circumstances, that we have cited as the very expression of order, through improved application of right and a loftier understanding of the principles of 1789.

The first of these solutions was favoured not only by the bourgeoisie but also by the masses and not only by fashionable theories but by public opinion. We are not producing enough, was the cry that went up on every side; we are not getting from the land all that we potentially could; we are allowing our capital to snooze. It is not a matter of *cutting our clothes but of making our jackets last longer* ... That message prospered. At first glance, there was in that arrangement, something at once fraternal, entrepreneurial and of the conqueror, that must have delighted conservatives and democrats and engaged the government.

The other solution seemed more severe. It ruled out giving a fillip to industry, agriculture and lending, but, without appreciating what might have been expected of freedom rather than of power, it failed to look forward to wealth and comfort for the toiling masses. On the one hand, it was aware that total value was always in proportion with subsistence, and subsistence to needs; on the other, that if the system stayed the same, the increased production would only ever bring benefit to a tiny number, assuming that it brought anyone any benefit at all. It confined itself to promising the citizenry nothing other than liberty and equality as a reward for unremitting toil and unrelieved frugality! ... Besides, this theory was not even proposed. It underlaid republican thinking: but failed to break loose from the political formulas and concerns enveloping it. After a few allusions had been made to it, there was an outcry about plunder. The word was that, rather than enriching the poor, the republic was still out to impoverish the rich and thrust everyone into poverty, etc.

To satisfy both conservative demands and the proletariat's needs, the imperial government therefore did two things: it gave an impetus to big business, limited companies, and it embarked upon vast projects right across the empire. Which it still does. In so doing, the imperial government was, let me say again, merely acting in line with the prevailing prejudice. It did not believe, such thinking being forbidden, as certain innovators claimed, that the cure for pauperism lay in restoration of the balance between services and wages, in a more equitable distribution of products, in a phased lowering of interest rates and discounts, in forgiveness of debts, in the farmer's sharing in the land's economic rent or at least in its surplus value [*mieux-value*],[73] in workers' association for

---

73. "*Mieux-value*" was one of many terms coined by the French historian and economist, J. C. L. Simonde de Sismondi, and developed by both Proudhon and Marx. See Mark A. Lutz, *Economics for the Common Good: Two Centuries of Economic Thought in the Humanist Tradition* (Abingdon: Routledge, 2002), 55–57. [I.M.M]

the provision of public services at cost price, in eradication of parasitism and finally in a return to frugal living. Taking the empiricists at their word, it believed that the actual remedy lay in an increase in the wealth that was dependent on it to create and, it resolved, by means of its concessions, encouragements, orders and projects, to generate an overproduction that, according to it, must drive society and guarantee well-being, if not wealth, to all.

There is a view widely held among Parisian workers that when things are going well in the construction industry, everything is going well. The imperial government appears to have been guided not just by construction, but also by building railways, canals, mines, etc., and, above all banks, just as the workers were guided by the construction industry. Its engineers were screaming at it to build railways, canals, roads, and the means of transport will cry out for goods; open collieries and the coal will lead to the building of steam engines and machines will render goods; organise credit and the capital lent out will bring you riches: build, demolish, and the money spread around the labouring masses will fuel your trade. It does not seem to have occurred to anyone that whilst exaggerated development in one or in several industries always acts as a kind of impetus to others, such an artificial impulse is unsustainable; that in fact services are proportional to each another, but that as a whole they are proportional to NEEDS; that therefore one had to begin with those needs, initially through educating the people, which is an undertaking of high liberalism, and then by procuring their needs at the best price, rather than depriving them of what is necessary in order to create the superfluous.

The results of this we now know. There would be no point in our trying to apportion the blame for the abuses of speculation and the high jinks with which it has soiled its hands; these things are too serious for the entire responsibility to be pinned on fraud and ineptitude. There was actual over-production, meaning creation of *useless goods*, aggravating pauperism. And let it not be said that the goods created represent an exchange value, given that a goodly number of these items have only a nominal value, that others are priced beyond their [actual] value, that the best of them are merely substitutions, and that the losses and miseries caused by all this prodigious commotion should still have to be taken into account.[74]

The people of Paris will certainly be better housed once the works beautifying the city are finished. And God forbid that I should attack the probity and perfect regularity of the undertakings! I have not read the documentation and

---

74. See Proudhon, *La revolution démontrée par le coup d'état*, Chap. VII, §4: Acts of 2 December regarding economic reform. – *Manuel du spéculateur a la Bourse*: Final considerations, §1st, industrial feudalism: the process of the crisis. §2, the industrial empire: the crisis at its height. §3, industrial democracy; labour partnered with labour; crisis over. [H.M.]

am not part of the parliamentary opposition. This is a case of my countering one economic theory with another economic theory; what I am tracing back is the physiology of pauperism and its impact on governments, relative to a few attempts at betterment, all tried by government at the prompting of public opinion itself. But still, the people of Paris were housed before, not all that badly and not all that expensively. A century rather than a decade might have been spent on refurbishments and no one would have uttered a word of complaint; the whole thing could have been handled quietly without upsetting business, without any burden placed on the city and without any loss on the part of tenants and landlords. Instead of which what sort of a choice do we have before us? If rents fall, as the government is hoping, and revert to the levels they were at before, then the entire city will find itself in the same state as the Hôtel de Rivoli: it will be a venture that will be written off as a loss and there will still be some truth in the statement that, over a ten-, fifteen- or twenty-year period, the welfare of the Parisian population will have been diminished by whatever the expenditure has been on compulsory purchases orders, demolitions, rebuilding, relocations, rent rises, etc. If rents do not come down or fall only very slightly, the very fact of rising rental costs will have introduced an enduring factor making all tenants in Paris and across France all the poorer.

Do you want another example? Let me borrow from the trade treaty with England.[75] Nothing the imperial government has done has earned the emperor such high praise; further evidence that the emperor, for all the sham despotism, actually governs however opinion dictates. We now know from the official record that the implementation of that treaty has resulted in a 90 million fall in [State] revenues, necessitating the raising of certain taxes by the same sum; that, in addition, a sum upwards of 40 million in savings has been asked for so as to equip French industry to compete with the outside world. – One day, you may say, France will reap the benefits of this treaty. – To which my answer is: Those who live that long will see. Every day brings fresh grief. Meanwhile, a good number of industrial towns are in dire straits; the people, promised cheaper calico, cutlery, coal and other articles, are paying more for their wine and brandy, which are needs of a different type; meanwhile, we have added 40 million to our capital account, which is not quite the same as adding to our wealth. Then, when we are in a position to compete with the English, we will not be any the richer, since the value of new goods will still have to keep in line with subsistence costs, and, if subsistence costs fall, the population increases.

Sure, it is a good thing that nations drive one another on: but here, as

75. The trade treaty reached with England on 23 January 1863 did away with the old barriers and replaced them with a system of moderate tariffs. It was the target of lively controversies between protectionists and free traders. [H.M.]

before, there was a model to follow: above all, there was no reason to suppose that the implementation of free trade should bring us wealth like manna from heaven. Someday, the French people will learn from painful experience what it really means to focus on exports, and close its domestic market, which is what France is doing, through poor circulation of services and goods.

One notion professed by the imperial government and espoused by the Legislature is that *the automatic outcome of growth in public prosperity is a rise in the cost of life's basic necessities*. Why, then, this trade treaty, which was intended to lower the cost of things? But it would be too easy to play the critic here. I prefer to pick up on the imperial thinking and state, but in a loftier sense: Yes, since man must consume if he is to live, and produce through toil what he consumes, and perfect himself physically and morally, then, as a result, everyday toils more and better, it is true to say that the more he progresses in terms of civilization, the more work the essentials of life require, and the more costly they become, and, therefore, the more important it is for society that services and goods be shared equally. From which my conclusion is, therefore, that pauperism cannot be combatted by means of relocations; wealth cannot be generated through speculation; plenty assured by means of trade treaties; the word of the emperor is the true message of the Gospel. The way to combat pauperism is to instruct the people, to teach them, as did Jesus Christ and before him Pythagoras, of toil, temperance and righteous action.

So, pauperism, already so palpable in French society under Louis-Philippe's government, when five per cent stood at 116 francs, has grown in intensity as a result of the very means employed to combat it, the sole outcome of which has been to inflate everyone's outgoings out of all proportion to their income. Empiricism and a sham spirit of conservatism are at fault for having had a hand in trying to misrepresent these facts and denying the consequences to which they lead. That the nation should stick to the mistaken path or routine to which it was committed, with that sort of experience behind it, should be a cause of amazement, even though we are living in an age when nothing should astound us on account of its folly anymore.

Which brings me to the thorny issue. In France like everywhere else, pauperism is part of our make-up, and it is chronic; this may be taken as read. Over the past thirty years it has been exacerbated by the wrong-headed, sometimes political and sometimes economic measures to which our governments have committed themselves. Does that make it right to claim that it was the cause of the Crimean and Lombardy wars, or indeed the occupation of Ancona and the siege of Antwerp? Can we possibly admit that such a notion raised its head in the councils of the State, that Emperor Napoleon [III] had gone to war as a distraction from the national misery, and is ready to do so?

Anybody who would reduce the issues down to those sorts of terms has missed my point. I stated that war's primary cause was pauperism; that notions of high politics comprise its secondary or immediate cause. I then pointed out how, initially, the cause of war and its political motives blended into one; war itself was identified with plunder. That was the age of the heroes. Thereafter, *raison d'état* was distinguished from the economic cause and war was waged primarily with a view to conquest or annexation, but without it thereby ceasing to depend, in terms of its origins, upon that cause. Which brings us to where we are. Leaving the notion of power to one side, the point is to fathom what higher, conscious or unconscious influence prompts it. It is within those parameters alone that I was able to dare cite France and the actions of her government.

What I am not about to undertake is some unearthing of the private, political or dynastic reasons that prompted the emperor to undertake those two expeditions, especially as I have no real urge to discover them. State secrets are unfathomable to contemporaries: they are revealed, if they are revealed at all, only to posterity. The fact is that what prompted the Eastern war was not the salvation of Turkey, which has today been abandoned; nor was it a desire to tear up the 1815 treaties, since all that campaign achieved was to consolidate them. Nor was it the desire to be of service to the revolution, since revolutionary auxiliaries were shunned and the war kept solely political. Finally, it was not religious zeal either, since there is no end of preaching tolerance and, today, the Latin Church has been placed in check by the dropping of the Pope's temporal authority. As for the war in Italy, it is equally the fact that it has not exactly been fought for Italy's independence, nor to please the revolution, nor even with the aim of cutting Austria down to size, since it has stopped halfway: Lombardy having been overrun, there was no stomach for a conquest of Venetia; that one of the emperor's fears as he stepped into the ring was not just that he might run into a coalition there, but might have revolution on his heels; that in signing the peace of Villafranca,[76] the emperor, with military foresight, promoted confederation rather than unity and placed that confederation under the oversight, not of the emperor of Austria or of the king of Piedmont, but of the Pope, a prince who never brandishes the sword and whose only weaponry is the anathema.

Let me say it again: I do not know what the French emperor's purpose was and it is none of my business. I can see how a politician tasked with monitoring the deeds of the government might feel uneasy. Of course, had I had a seat in the Legislature during the sitting that is drawing to a close, before giving my endorsement to the imperial policy, I might have raised some respectful query

76. For more on the significance Proudhon attached to the treaty of Villafranca, which he hailed as "the good news", see Prichard, "Deepening Anarchism" (2010). [A.P.]

about the matter. I would not have believed that the event, such as it was, would satisfy a democrat as a justification for the undertaking. After so many declarations and disclosures, I would have asked the ministers for an oral explanation of what His Majesty thought he was doing in Italy. Coming from the lips of a representative of the people or from a journal of revolution, that question might have been perfectly justified. Here, in a book of doctrine, on the philosophy of war and peace, the answer, whatever it might have been, would be of little account. For the reasons we have outlined, war is something that is always in the background, which the princes do not govern according to their whim and can chose little more than the pretext and the timing of its emergence.

Therefore, independently of the Emperor Napoleon III's secret motives, he was, in my view, compelled to embark upon those two campaigns, by his very origin, his name and his title, and the very circumstances of his existence, much more so than Louis-Philippe's government and the republic itself had been. I say that the real author of the Crimean and Lombardy campaigns was not the emperor, but the situation, the nation, and that, whilst the masses were not consulted, they did applaud. If they applauded, it was because they thought they could see in those two campaigns a war on counter-revolution, on the European aristocracy and the coalition of despots and everything that it had learnt to despise since 1789. So deeply did it hold this belief that the imperial government is today taking advantage of this popular opinion in order to portray its policy as revolutionary, liberating, democratic and I might go so far as to say a social policy, whilst the reactionaries from the Senate and the Legislature strive to drag him back to the reactionary sentiments that seemed to animate him in 1852, 1855 and 1859.

Now what does this word Revolution mean in the mind of the French people? The destruction of feudal privileges and, by necessary extension, of all land-owning, industrial, capitalist and mercantile privileges; the right to work, to a fair distribution of earnings, the end of exploitation and of parasitism. The French people became sympathetic to the liberty of other peoples by means of this chain of ideas: do you think that if it had had the slightest suspicion that the Polish national question was a matter for the Polish aristocracy alone, it would have the slightest interest in the resurrection of Poland and the emancipation of the Poles? No, no: what the French people seek in the reconstitution of nations is the guarantee of their own revolution, the complement of that revolution. Which is why it is currently supportive of Italian unity, at its own risk and despite imperial prudence. French democracy,[77] currently represented

---

77. French democracy, or *La démocratie française*, refers to a political campaign and movement, less to French democracy *per se*. The latter had been limited to male suffrage since 1852, and to plebiscites to validate Napoleon III's regime. [A.P.]

by two or three newspapers and five or six deputies, makes this commitment to
Italian democracy in defiance of the country's military interests. It is primarily
out to drive the Papacy, the [Austrian] empire and its feudatories, the king of
Naples and the Duke of Tuscany, out of the peninsula. French democracy regards all of these as representatives of divine right. It would rather deal with
another first-class power and run the risk of huge ingratitude, than let Italian
federation leave the door open to the return of the old system. It is true to say
that the French democracy has demonstrated magnanimity here. It may well be
wrong in its reckonings, which are sweeping, unremarkable, and a superficial
view of things: fervour is a bad counsellor. But as to intentions, there is nothing
there to take issue with. The revolution, at home and aboard, annexing if necessary, is the extinction of pauperism, whether the French democracy knows it or
not. Subsistence is at stake: there is a case for war.

CHAPTER VIII

More on the Same Subject

Pauperism has made England its capital: of all nations, England is also the one that has mounted the most invasions: as Monsieur de Ficquelmont has it:

> The English aristocracy has delivered the world to the whims of the English people. If England does not owe her wealth to plunder, she owes it to exploitation. England is out to serve the entire globe, as long as she can be sole supplier ... Her free trade theory is nothing except the forcible exclusion of all who are her inferiors in terms of capital, industry and means of transport. England needs a monopoly on the world if she is to retain her position.[78]

Which is why the English have established strongholds in all the seas: Gibraltar, Malta, Corfu, Perim, the Cape, Saint Helena, in addition to their trading-posts. Cannon warfare is just an auxiliary to the war of capital as far as she is concerned. One day, though, her gigantic appetite will be answered by a no less colossal ambition. If England were to blockade the world with her fleet, could the world not blockade England by closing her ports? The *Continental System*, pending a raid that had been put off until better days, was Napoleon's great idea. In breaking the Treaty of Amiens,[79] England thought she was preventing Europe from being conquered, but merely hastened that conquest. After having absorbed Italy, Belgium and Holland into his empire, Napoleon was prompted to go on and absorb Portugal, Spain, Westphalia, Hanover, the Hanseatic cities and the whole of the German Confederation. Had he but had the time, he would not have failed to get his hands on Constantinople, the future capital of the world, as he used to say. He never worked out how to starve England.

Now the continent, restored to itself, no longer closes its ports to the English: it makes do with slapping tariffs on them and competing with them.

---

78. Ficquelmont, *Pensées et réflexions morales et politiques* (1859) (in summary). [H.M.]

79. The short-lived Treaty of Amiens brought the Revolutionary Wars to a close in 1802. [A.P.]

To which the English respond with their orchestrated free trade propaganda, in which they are aided and abetted of course by those who, enjoying natural monopolies or manufacturing on their own account at very low cost, ask nothing better than to pay the lowest market prices both for their raw materials and everything they themselves cannot provide, even should it spell the doom of their fortunes and the independence of their own country. If only Napoleon III, who has seen fit to give free trade a go, had taken it into his head to ask England, which is at present wholeheartedly behind independence for the Italians, to grant the very same independence also to the Irish and the Hindus, etc., as well as evacuating and demolishing her strongholds, all by way of precondition for and guarantee of unadulterated freedom of trade. I would love to know what Messrs Bright and Cobden's answer might be to that categorical challenge.[80]

The Anglo-Saxon race has a large appetite: this is one of its distinguishing features. Like the leopard[81] included in its coats of arms, it is armed for conquest, *sicut leo rapiens et rugiens*.[82] Here physiology gives us the secret of politics and the explanation of history. For all its industrial development, the English people remains the most aristocratic of all peoples and the most famished; the former explains the latter and vice versa. It is in England that one finds the largest fortunes and the most fearful misery; there that we find the most energetic producers and the most intrepid consumers. The English people have laboured tremendously; but still they go hungry. Utilitarianism was born in England, it might even be argued that it is in the blood of the English. All the philosophers, moralists, theologians, novelists and statesmen in Great Britain are imbued with it. It will be said that it was in France that political economy was spawned: Adam Smith learnt from Quesnay. But how France has let herself be outstripped by her rival! True, this English, Malthusian political economy sits uncomfortably alongside the Declaration of the Rights of Man; by temperament, we seek to equalize wealth rather than consuming or producing. And, whilst the tricolour rosette lets its conquests slip through its fingers, to the delight of the British leopard, which clings tightly to them; *to us the glory, to her the profit* ... England's finest triumph has been to infuse us with her maxims: we

---

80. JOHN BRIGHT (1811–1889) and RICHARD COBDEN (1804–1865) were two of the most prominent leaders of the English free trade movement, which overcame the reluctance of the prime minister Robert Peel after eight years of struggle (1838–1846). Cobden was the negotiator of the Cobden-Chevalier free treaty in 1860. "Bright and Cobden, the apostles of free trade, the most iniquitous bamboozlement ever visited upon the French people". (*Correspondence*, 12 October 1861.) [H.M.]

81. According to historic heraldry, the animals on the English coat of arms are leopards, not lions. [I.M.]

82. *Bible*, Psalm 12:13. "They gaped at Me with their mouths, as a ravening and a roaring lion". [A.P.]

shall not better her on the terrain of consumption and production: instead, we shall moor our ships at Brest ten times more readily than at Plymouth.

England only intervenes in the affairs of other countries in order to extract trade treaties, and promises her support to those who buy her goods. She dreams of taking over China the way she has India; she anticipates social warfare right across Europe and even in her own ranks, and having devoured the Irish plebs and Scottish plebs, she cannot feed her own: England is fortifying her shores, casting cannons, building up her navy, exercising her volunteers, inflates her budget, raising her discount (no doubt on the strength of her free trade theory) and equipping herself to deploy steel and fire against any who might talk of touching her trade, her conquests, her monopolies. The general misery and wretchedness in Great Britain this winter has been horrifying, yet the British nation's output has never stood so high. Subsistence is at stake: there is a case for war.

After France and England, is it worth the bother of mentioning the rest? RUSSIA with, indeed because of her territorial vastness, feels ill at ease. In Asia, she brings weight to bear on China, India and Persia, where she will sooner or later run up against the English. She controls the Caucasus and part of Armenia: her settlers are inching along the Asian coastline as far as Constantinople. She has turned the Black Sea into a Russian lake and is out to open up a route to the Persian Gulf via the Euphrates and the Tigris. In Europe her ambition reaches as far as Constantinople. For Russia, Constantinople could be, like Petersburg, a gateway, a warehouse, a market, a stronghold. The Ottoman Empire is dead, cries the *l'Invalide Russe*:[83] the time is right to send the Turks packing, back to the steppes of Turkestan. The twenty million serfs emancipated by the emperor need an outlet. The Russian boyars,[84] who will shortly be finding themselves serf-less, need trade, speculation and purpose. The eternal borrower State that cannot keep its cash at home needs money. Subsistence is at stake: there is a case for war.

AUSTRIA is in roughly the same situation. Her port of Trieste is not enough for her: she would gladly add the mouth of the Danube and Salonika to it. But how is she to reach agreement with Russia, with Russia asking for Constantinople? Dispossessed of Lombardy which, year in and year out, used to bring her in thirty million net, according to the reckoning of one Italian economist, she would like to have it back and, if the opportunity were to come along, have it back she will. The peasants of Lombardy might be used as her auxiliaries: she would only have to offer them a morsel of land, as she has the Galicians. The curious point here is that, by making this move, Austria could flatter herself that

83. A Parisian journal for Russian patriots, published between 1813 and 1917. [A.P.]
84. The second highest rank of the Russian or east European nobility. [A.P.]

she is doing the revolution a better service than any that we ourselves have done it by handing Lombardy over to Victor Emmanuel. Subsistence is at stake: there is a case for war.

Why, over the last few years, have the nations of Europe seemed so prone to feelings inimical to France? In Spain, following a silly rumour that Napoleon III had his eye on Catalonia, memories of 1808[85] were warmed up; likewise, in Germany, Switzerland and Belgium, memories from 1813 were resuscitated in connection with the annexation of Savoy. What am I saying? Europe seems to want to be more liberal, more revolutionary than us, just to hamper us. Spain is half progressive and half republican; Italy mocks our advice even as she pleads for our intervention and wraps herself up in her unity;[86] Germany closes her federal ranks and offers the imperial crown to the king of Prussia who says neither yea nor nay; Belgium has had her say; Switzerland bears us a deep grudge; England is laying the groundwork for electoral reform; Austria, as Monsieur Billault[87] has said, is saving herself by granting her peoples all the constitutions they are asking for; Russia has emancipated her serfs. What the coalition of sovereigns back in 1813 were promising to grant their peoples once the campaign

---

85. Napoleon I managed, through chicanery, to draw the Spanish king Carlos IV and his son Ferdinand VII down to Bayonne and took them prisoner. He forced them to step down from the throne and, in June 1808, handed it over to his own brother, Joseph, who was then the ruler of the kingdom of Naples, who was then replaced by Murat. The Spanish people organized ferocious resistance to the French invader. Proudhon revisits the war in Spain in Book Five, Chapter II. [H.T.]

86. It is noteworthy that in the discussions arising out of the decree of 24 November, both within the Legislature and the Senate, and in the newspapers, the conservatives' patriotism has proved much more susceptible than the democrats' where Italian unity has been concerned. In 1815, the saying was *more royalist than the king*. Today the saying is, and it is the democrats that have given rise to this proverb, *more pro-unity than the emperor*. As far as Monsieur Cavour's Italy is concerned, French democracy is implicitly trusting; it makes great play of national pre-eminence. What are we to make of such disinterested politics? Can it be that a youthful democracy is abjuring any idea of warfare and conquest and that, for added safety, it reckons that, through the creation of an Italy that is one and indivisible, to cage the imperial eagle, so to speak? The democrats across the Rhine would be forever in the debt of their brethren in France. In any event, the latter's efforts are a wonderful boost to the efforts of the Italians. Some days ago I asked a traveller freshly arrived from Italy if, in the event of war between France and Europe, the Italians would march alongside us. – Yes, he replied, as long as England herself marches alongside France; otherwise, no. Because, as far as Italians are concerned, and even though she has not done a thing on behalf of their independence, England represents freedom, whereas France ... represents protection. [P-J.P.]

87. AUGUSTE BILLAUT (1805–1863), served as deputy under the July Monarchy and was under-secretary of State in 1840, a member of the Constituent Assembly from 1848 to 1858. In 1860 he was appointed minister without portfolio and tasked with introducing the government's draft laws into the Chamber. He was one of the most ardent champions of Napoleon III's policies. [H.T.]

was over, they are now offering them today PRIOR to the battle. The French nation, they are telling them, was not made for freedom; they can only deliver you slavery ...

What can the reason be for such fears and calumnies? It is always the same: war is conquest; and conquest is not only annexation, but also requisitioning, war taxes, despoilment, levying of men, plunder and all the soldierly affronts. Starting from that, alas, all too true principle, France stands accused of wanting to devour Europe again; her budget, her swelling debts and her extravagant spending are cited as evidence of that. But let us not lose sight of the fact that those who claim to be so afraid of being gobbled up by us would gladly gobble us up themselves. Let both camps admit the fact. He who unremittingly points an accusing finger at French ambition is tormented by the same goad. Prussia, who back in 1804 could not decide whether to accept or reject Hanover, and lusts after Holstein and has the ambition of swapping its name of the kingdom of Prussia for the more grandiose designation of German Empire, Prussia, which was drawn across the Rhine by the treaties of 1815, which boasts French-speaking subjects in Luxembourg, would need no encouragement to cross the Meuse and press on to the Marne. What nation in Europe, driven by hatred of the First Empire, would not be delighted to strike the path to 1815 once again, and make do with a scrap of that great body known as France? Liberalism, constitutionalism, philosophy, shared principles and tendencies, play no part in this: conquer or be conquered, that is the law. Subsistence is at stake: there is a case for war.

The people today do not wait for overtures from their princes. When it is not a case of governments attacking one another, we have populations turning on their governments, demanding reforms, and, if those reforms are not forthcoming, making revolutions. The proletarian blames the bourgeois who, in turn, blames the nobility, the Church, the court, the army. The two emperors, Napoleon III and Franz Joseph, were scarcely back from Villafranca than they were mobbed by their peoples who were clamouring for freedoms. *Bread and the '93 Constitution*, cried the rebels in Prairial. *Bread or lead*, cried those in 1848. How could we deny these well-beloved people full freedom? One of them passed his decree of 24th November and the other his ordinance of 27th February.[88] And still their subjects are not content! Thus, following the

---

88. Under a decree of 24 November 1860, Napoleon III afforded the Chamber the right to frame a response to the speech from the throne and allowed the proceedings to be published at length in *Le Moniteur*. By means of the *Patent* or Constitution of 26 February 1861, Franz-Joseph turned the Council of State into a genuine parliament, made up of two houses, the House of Lords and the House of Representatives. Austria thereby became a constitutional monarchy under the terms of the charters granted. [H.M.]

war in Crimea, the Muscovite peasants clamoured for their emancipation; the Romanians, Montenegrins, Serbs and Maronites and all Turkey's Christians lobby the sultan for access to political rights, which is parliamentary talk meaning that they are not prepared to pay any longer. Victor or vanquished, the head of State is certain to hear famine knocking at his door.

What was the Italian bourgeoisie after? Were its dreams ever of Italian unity? Does it even understand the workings of the constitution? Has it a religion or any belief? It was rather weak, with little landed wealth and no influence and no place in government. Did it want, like the bourgeoisie of 1830 or that of 1789 to be, or rather, to have something, get into business, claim its share of the budget, turn a profit out of the sell-off of national assets, grow fat? In short: could any bourgeoisie want anything else? It had an entitlement to it, to be sure: far be it from me to upbraid it for that. *What is the Third Estate?* Nothing. *What does it want?* Everything. Take the measure of that message of Sieyès: it represents the motto of any bourgeoisie preparing to replace the higher castes, the clergy, the court and the nobility. But in order to enjoy the gains made by the revolution with some degree of security, the Italian bourgeoisie understands that a constitutional monarchy offers it greater guarantees than a republic. This was the bourgeois thinking in '89 and 1830; it was the thinking of the reaction in 1848 and 1852. Look at the unity with which these bourgeois rally around Monsieur Cavour against the Mazzinians and the Garibaldians! ... The shrewd ones among them also think that gratitude in politics is a burdensome virtue and, just as they united around the emperor of the French in order to expel the German emperor, so they reunite around Victor-Emmanuel by way of repaying a debt to the French Emperor. Nothing is too much for them. As for the multitude, that brute force, flesh and blood that can only bleat its support, it will be left with nothing: my mistake, with conscription. Apply this, *mutatis mutandis*, to all of Europe's aristocracies, bourgeoisies and democracies and come to this conclusion: subsistence is at stake and there is a case for war.

To be sure, modern nations have managed to conjure up resources to which ancient societies had no access; the comparative population figures for different periods in history testify to that. The power of credit, the cash supply, the feats of industry, the art of agriculture, the significance of trade, the servicing of budgets and huge debts, all of these are such as to boggle minds and banish the ignoble thinkers of wretchedness and envy far from the councils of high policy. Seeing the ease with which loans are covered in France, who would not swear that the country is a land of plenty and a ruddy faced nation?

But all that is just prestige. Once there is a breakdown in the balance between needs and resources, and God only knows how long it will take us to restore that balance, and above all, once the disparity between the minimum and the maximum has become so exorbitant, then, it can be stated with certainty, we have pauperism. Deficit is the rule and well-being the exception. Politics can re-adjust its gears all it likes, and the sovereigns make a show of being guided by the most liberal intention, but it will make not one bit of difference. There is a dour envy smouldering in every stratum of society from top to bottom, and, in the absence of an economic order founded upon truth and right, war is an inescapable inevitability. War, I say, in all its guises and all its forms: war of plunder and war of conquest, border warfare, war over outlets, colonial war, wars of religion and wars of principle, dynastic wars, race wars and caste wars, wars of succession and partitionist wars, wars over influence and wars over stability, wars of independence, civil war and social war. In all these guises, the underlying cause of war remains the same: but that is what bothers peoples and governments the least. The struggle to survive, the poor man's lack of basic necessities, inadequate income in the case of the rich man, the burgeoning debts and the hole in the State budget, in short, starvation. The god of hosts and the god of wretchedness are one and the same god: this no more brings one of them honour than it does the other, but it is the truth.[89]

The Emperor Aurelian used to tell the Roman people that they were the kindliest, most jovial, easily governed people, as long as they were well fed, well dressed and well entertained. One day, in the course of a riot, he had his praetorians slaughter eight thousand of them. After which he refrained from setting foot in Rome. Aurelian's message encapsulates the whole policy of the Caesars, as well as that of the Senate, and lifted the veil on the principle of

---

89. To forecasts of world-wide warfare we are indebted to two publications recently produced by republican pens, one by Monsieur Jean Reynaud, the other from Monsieur Villiaumé, author of a *Popular History of the Revolution*.

The first of these publications, I have not read; I have merely heard tell that the writer has set out to disclose the true thinking of the French Revolution and French republicans on this sparkling subject of warfare and conquest. It goes without saying that Monsieur Jean Reynaud takes exception to the resurrection of militarism.

L'Esprit de la guerre (Paris, 1861) by Monsieur Villiaumé is intended to serve the same purpose. The writer primarily has in mind the means whereby a definitive peace can be achieved; those means are supposedly such that, if this honourable publicist is to be credited, with their aid, nine-tenths of wars could be averted. Besides, Monsieur Villiaumé was a lot less concerned with writing a doctrinal book than an anthology of practical precepts. Given that the French people's mission is not yet over, and deeming warfare inevitable and operating with the utmost urgency, he has collated within his book everything useful that the authors who have dealt with these matters have supplied us with and afforded greater space to matters of *military policy, strategy, tactics and civil war*. My hope, nevertheless, is that the French people will have no need, as Monsieur Villiaumé assumes, of his forceful instruction. There are lots of incitements to war; but there is no less resistance to it. It was with a view to strengthening the latter that I have embarked upon this work; in respect of which my thinking certainly does not differ from that of Messrs. J. Reynaud and Villiaumé. [P-J.P.]

warfare and its ambiguous morality. These days everybody thinks along the same lines as Aurelian. There is little credence placed in the political causes of war and, besides, everybody knows that since 1848 the real issue on the agenda is the issue of the proletariat. Also, whilst some call for war with an eye to conquest, others want it as a way to reduce the numbers of consumers, the very same way as useless mouths are driven out in times of siege. We have even seen republicans making this arrangement the foundation of their politics. According to them, the provisional government ought to have driven the people out on to the fields of battle: Monsieur de Lamartine, with his peace policy, had betrayed the revolution. For its part, the people embraced all these considerations: "There are", it said, "too many people in the world: we must venture outside the country. If that brings no plunder, well, it will still have ensured a break in the clouds". Oddly enough, the conquerors who are normally regarded as the authors and instigators of every war, are still the ones who show the greatest concern for human lives and, where there is a shred of humanity remaining in these great struggles, we owe it to them. – *When is he going to start his war?* One peasant who had voted for Louis-Napoleon asked on 2 December. *Under that other fellow, we paid not one penny: the enemy covered all the costs...* The brothers and sisters, nephews and nieces of the soldiers who perished in Dobrudja, in Crimea, at Magenta and at Solferino have shed a tear in their memory. Then they console themselves with the thought that France will in the end secure some morsel of land and that will bring in a little money that they will one day inherit.

Conquer, conquer and keep on conquering; since the dawn of society this has always been the inclination of States, prompted by endemic pauperism. To live, surrounded by growing discomfort, despite conquest or indeed because of conquest, such is their condition. Out of all the powers, England is the one that has conquered the most and she exploits one hundred and twenty million Indians, commands an entire continent, and has half of Africa under her control, and England is also the greediest for new possessions and touchiest about the annexations of her neighbours. The smaller States such as Switzerland, Belgium, the Grand Duchy of Baden, too weak to expand at the expense of their neighbours, have given this up in favour of hurling groups of their emigrants to all corners of the globe; once upon a time Ireland, Scotland and Switzerland were the most likely to hire out their militias to the foreigner. Expatriation and mercenary soldiering are safety valves for second- or third-rate sovereigns, who are barred from exercising their right of war.

All praise to the potentates; to them alone is the world indebted for what little ease it enjoys: their greatness stands guarantor for our security. And the sceptre will not be wrested from their hands until the day the world has found its economic constitution, which is merely the constitution of peace itself, the ultimate goal of all revolutions. In Jacob's testament, it is written of them: "*Non auferetur sceptrum ... donec veniat pax, et ipsa est expectatio gentium*".[90]

---

90. *Bible*, Book of Genesis, 49:10. Proudhon has tinkered with the text in order to make it fit; it actually reads: "*Non auferetur sceptrum de Juda, et dux de femore ejius, donec veniat qui nittendus est, et ipse erit expectatio gentium*". [H.M.] In the King James English: "The sceptre shall not depart from Judah, nor a lawgiver from between his feet, until Shiloh come; and unto him shall the gathering of the people be". [P.S.]

CHAPTER IX

That Conquest, Which Should Have Ended Plunder, Has Preserved It

I think I have demonstrated more than amply that all conquest is triggered by pauperism on the part of the conqueror. But, by virtue of the political considerations, which have determined it, conquest remains no less legitimate; the entirety of our Book Two was spent demonstrating that contention. Indeed, conquest is merely the political annexation called for by international relations and effected by means of the right of force.

Given that legitimacy, conquest, one would have thought, should have banished any sort of plunder and pillage from warfare and made up for the vice of its inception through a boost in the virtue of its operations; so why is the very opposite happening?

I put this question to the jurists, the statesmen and the military men.

But I won't wait for their response.

It is believed that the last word has been said whenever an accusing finger has been pointed at the human heart and the violence of its passions; it is, rather, the connectedness of ideas as well as the contradictions between them that we should be denouncing. The mind is conscience's chief tempter and the initial instigator of sin. Genesis represented it in the form of the serpent that spoke to Eve, man's spouse, which is to say, his conscience.

To whom do riches naturally belong? To the mighty, the man endowed with strength and thereby entitled to command honour and glory. Is the paterfamilias not the owner of everything his child has: is the master not also the owner of what is produced by his servant or his slave? Does the *seigneur* not have a claim upon the industry of his vassal and the landowner upon his tenant's harvest? In every instance, implicit in force is the right of ownership; might the same not be true, all the truer, in warfare, where this right of force prevails unadulterated, encapsulating within itself all these various rights – the rights of father over child, master over servant, sovereign over subject; where the despoilment of the vanquished is compensation for the risk of war?

Therefore, according to the extant right of war, the ownership of the conquered country, public property and private property, moveable property and real estate, belongs to the victor. The law of war, as defined by the pedants and by prejudice, makes no distinctions. It might even be argued that, if the ancient world is to be believed, it is only with the aid of this confusion that war is explicable, that it has any meaning or purpose and, so to speak, any morality. The opinions of the ancients on this score were, as we have seen, unanimous. As for the moderns, it can readily be seen from the twists and turns of the authors that the warrior's moderation with regard to private property in the enemy country counsels prudence, or, at best, Christian charity. Strictly speaking, he could help himself to it all since he can always invoke compensation or the necessity of his feeding himself and depriving the enemy of his resources. Leaving the wealth of the vanquished untouched would amount to a failure to profit from victory, an essential point in the art of winning; it would amount to adding the defeat of the victor to that of the vanquished and that would be a nonsense. Despoilment is the endorsement of defeat: an army that triumphs and comes away empty-handed is committing suicide.

This is the message of tradition, and we must admit that while that tradition is wholly mistaken from the viewpoint of the genuine right of war and the genuine rights of peoples, since war has no purpose other than bringing States together or forcing them apart, from the vantage-point of the primary cause that leads to war, to wit, pauperism, from the vantage-point of the right of force per se, being the sole right acknowledged at the outset and, for a very long time, the only one war saw fit to acknowledge, it is hard to deny that its logic is correct. The mistake lies in new rights sprouting on the primitive trunk of the right of force over the course of events and by the fact of war itself, and that the warrior, who assumes that in every battle everything is called into question, does not concern himself with these rights: he pays no heed to the passage of time. Of him it can be said, not only that he is out of step with his times, but also that he is out of step with war itself. Plunder therefore remains a concomitant of conquest: a few more words on the matter will open our eyes to the extent to which these two things, mutually exclusive to any enlightened conscience, are bound closely together.

If war were a duel between diplomats and generals, then of course we might reform it in line with the argument presented here. But it is a struggle between the masses and there is nothing chivalrous about the masses. Honour is the essence of chivalry, and plunder that of war, that is what is primarily responsible for its popularity. In the absence of that bait, it is doubtful that it would have as many supporters and, especially, as much brawn to wage it. The king conquers: that is his calling; the multitude plunders. Does the hound that retrieves the game not have an entitlement to its share of the quarry?

As we have seen, the ancients made full use of the right of plunder. Feted by the historians as conquerors, Ninus, Sesostris, Nebuchadnezzar, Cyrus and Cambyses and others were marauders, as were Attila, Genghis Khan, Tamburlaine and Mohammed II. Ancient Greece, as we have seen, was no exception to that tradition. Philip and Alexander ushered in the age of annexation. As far as the princes were concerned, conquest became the chief purpose of war, but plunder remained the prerogative of armies. Soldiers and generals looked to it for their pensions; this is what the Roman example shows.

After having defeated the enemy armies, Rome seized from the city temples whatever treasures the pious confidence of private persons had deposited there – statues, paintings, [sacrificial] tripods, tapestries, urns, etc. She then went on to strip the inhabitants of their furniture, clothing, jewels, goods, savings, livestock and slaves, without precluding the confiscation of their lands, or, rather, of rental income payable in money or in kind. Then she requisitioned the corn that was distributed free to the people from the rulers of Egypt, Sicily, and right along the African coast. And, in this, Rome was purely and simply exercising the right of war. She had been fighting, not just on behalf of the empire, but also for the wealth of nations. It never occurred to anyone to upbraid her for this. She had won: that word said it all. Conqueror of territory and of men, she seemed all the more to have conquered other values; the making of any distinction would have been, how shall I put this?, thievery from the army. Rich spoils stripped from the body of the enemy were the finest adornment of its triumphs, the acme of its glory. What was she going to glory in without that? She did not fight for ideas: ideas back then were something that Providence kept close to its chest: there were no journalists around who could extricate them. She did not think she was rich enough to be able to afford her *glory*: in those days, the word glory was synonymous with plenty and wealth: it was nothing to brag about, unless the enemy paid the price. Under the emperors, three-fourths of the pay of the highest-ranking officers was made up of chattels and comestibles gifted by the emperor; plunder, unmistakable even from a mile away.

Roman conquest ought to have triggered an international legal separation of conquest from pillage, but it seems that the former was conceived of as a means of consolidating the latter instead. Indeed, the permanent confiscation of a country's entire net product, the despoilment of its wealthy and well-off families, is still the most effective step at the disposal of a conquering State when countering the still vibrant nationality of the defeated people. As a rule, one need not fear of rebellion emanating from the plebs; it comes rather, from the nobility, the bourgeoisie, the clergy, all who own, who wield influence, who participate in government. As societies currently stand, the ruination of the upper class in a country by means of confiscation of landed revenues, of business, financial and industrial profits, would, despite the superiority of the modern plebs over the ancient plebs, curtail that country's life, activity, thought and progress. In high antiquity, however, that was the unvarying policy of the conquerors. In accordance with Tarquin's precept, the aristocracy[91] was wiped out; it was banished, impoverished, sold off, unless, in some rare act of generosity, the option was exercised to make it a share-cropping, emphyteusis-bound[92] tenant on its own properties. If need be, the lower classes were drawn into the dispossession of their betters and that was that. The country fell quiet. Political life petered out. This was how the tsars dealt with some of the Polish nobility. It was due to Austria not knowing how, or because of failure to apply this principle to the empire's restless populations, that it ended up on the wrong side of the Lombards and the Hungarians. Take a look at what the Turks did to the nations they subjugated. What sort of political life survived in Egypt and right across Africa, in Syria, in Asia Minor, in Thrace, Macedonia and Greece itself? Despoilment, more so than slaughter, wiped it all out. Had the civilizing genius of the Arabs been added to their military energy, the Turks would have absorbed the invaded races and founded a power centred on the Mediterranean but straddling Asia, Africa and Europe, that would have finally triumphed over a divided Christianity. But Turkish force was mere brute force. Unlike the Arabs they had only a flimsy grasp of conquest. The Ottoman warriors only ever understood the base aspects of war: slaughter, plunder, devastation and rape. They were the ones who, by the savagery of their apostolate, brought Islam, so glorious under the Caliphs, into disgrace and killed it off; they ended up killing themselves off through the corruption of their despotism, They remain numerous and strong, but stifled by the Christian populations re-emerging everywhere from the ashes.

It was up to Christianity, whose name might be construed as *conquest*, to conquer all the nations of the earth for Christ' spiritual kingdom. It was up to Christianity, that religion of unity and detachment, to reform warfare, untangling conquest from the pagan, self-seeking custom of plunder. It failed to do

---

91. Sextus, the son of Tarquin, having captured Gabies, sought his father's advice. The only response from the latter was to lop the head off the tallest poppies in his garden. Sextus understood and put the rich and the nobles from the conquered city to death. On the policy of extermination of aristocrats, see CAESAR, III, 16: *Omni senatu necato*; VI, 12: *omni nobiliate interfecto*, and so on. – MACHIAVELLI, *The Prince*, chap. V and VIII. MONTESQUIEU, *Thoughts on the Universal Monarchy*, 26, states, regarding the Tartars: "There was no ruse they could not devise in order to be rid of the princes and nobility of the country they were bent on subjugating". [H.M.]

92. *Emphyteusis*. A lease granted on a plot of land for a very lengthy period, possibly even in perpetuity, in return for the obligation to pay a fee and leaving the tenant duty-bound to make the land profitable and to work it. [H.T.]

so, and the idea never so much as occurred to it. Christianity's triumph was that part of the Middle Ages stretching from Charles Martel to Saint Louis, an age of anarchy and wretchedness that has been compared to the tyranny of the Dorians and that could be characterized as reciprocity between brigands. Even the bishops asserted their seigneurial rights and were not the least ruthless. Now, what did such seigneurial rights amount to, partially preserved up until the revolution? The right of plunder, exercised as an extension of the right of conquest, and pronounced Divine Right by a Church that had become as barbarous as it had initially seemed reforming and democratic. Reduced to ruin in spite of their banditry and forced into selling off their lands, the nobles joined the crusades, doubtless to wrest the Holy Land, Christ's legacy, back from the infidels and thereby secure forgiveness for their sins, but also and primarily in the hope of rebuilding their fortunes; not that the religion of Christ forbade its knights to do so, any more than Mohammed's did its sheikhs, and a fair few of them achieved it.

In the fourteenth century, war became a freemasonry of plunderers. The *grandes compagnies*[93] held France to ransom. Duguesclin only succeeded in ridding the kingdom of them by placing himself at their head and leading them, first, on to the lands of the Avignon papacy, upon which he imposed a levy, and then into Spain where he set about deposing the legitimate king, Don Pedro, known as Pedro the Cruel, for the benefit of his half-brother, Henri de Trastamara. The *condottieri* revolutionized Italy, driving out the lords who were no longer able to pay them, auctioning off cities, which goes to show how little store they placed by conquest and how much plunder was their preference; only when buyers failed to step forward did they decide to make themselves sovereigns. This curious institution of armies lacking homelands, lacking leaders and bereft of any considerations of nationality is one of the strangest phenomena to come out of the muddle to which barbarism and Christianity had reduced the world, wedded to each other and battering the empire. Only with the Thirty Years' War and after the extermination of Tilly's and Wallenstein's hosts by Gustavus-Adolphus did it disappear from the scene.

---

93. Bands of mercenaries raised by the princes during the Hundred Years' War period. During the thirteenth and fourteenth centuries, these became increasingly common as units vital for the purposes of feudal conflicts previously led by knights alone. Peace left these soldiers penniless and they regularly plundered whatever countryside they halted in. One alternative to looting was ransom, which even the Pope had to pay to avert the taking of Avignon. In the latter half of the fifteenth century, the raising of a standing army by Charles VII provided the monarchy with the wherewithal to effectively pursue those who had turned into *extortionists*. They represented the transitional phase between the feudal army, recruited on the basis of service owed to the feudal lord, and the king's army made up of regular regiments. [H.T.]

From Francis I onwards, carried away by its appetite for wealth, the nobility became increasingly needy: under Louis XIV, it only survived by the largesse of the monarch. Its servility, its turpitude matched its avarice. This breed of swordsmen shaped the pugnacious character that has, since the seventeenth century, become one of the distinguishing features of the French people. As the king could not go on giving, war represented a supplementary income. The competition between Louvois and his brother Le Tellier, and Colbert and his son Seignelay,[94] a rivalry that so well encapsulated the frictions between the hubristic, famished nobility and a bourgeoisie made rich through hard work, was, according to the Abbé de Saint-Pierre,[95] the cause of the Dutch War of 1671–1678 and the bombardment of Genoa, two acts that did most to make Louis XIV's power despicable in the eyes of Europe. Whilst the king waged war in order to add to his States, the nobles did so to enrich themselves at the enemy's expense. Villars, the hero of Denain, essentially a good man, naively confided to Louis XIV, in his letters, about the portion he awarded himself of the war levies he slapped on the cities, not that that stopped him from repeatedly seeking further rewards from the king.[96]

Not until the French revolution was there any indication of the beginnings of a change in military mores. The French people, in which vanity is a larger factor than avarice, is, as we know, less inclined to devour the enemy than to remake him in its own image: that was the spirit of assimilation that has made France so perfectly one. At the cost, however, of disentangling the lofty notion of conquest from the ignoble idea of plunder!

Bonaparte, the most disinterested of our generals, the most indifferent to wealth and most unashamed suitor of conquest, was the first to adopt this rare

---

94. FRANÇOIS-MICHEL LE TELLIER, MARQUIS DE LOUVOIS (1641–1691) Secretary of State for War during the reign of Louis XIV and responsible for reforming the army and inventing the *dragonnades,* which terrorised the Huguenots in Paris. His younger brother was CHARLES MAURICE LE TELLIER (1642–1710), Archbishop of Reims. JEAN BAPTISTE COLBERT (1619–1683) First Minister of State under Louis XIV. His son was the MARQUIS DE SEIGNELAY (1651–1969), who became Secretary of the Navy in 1683 and finalised the Black Code governing slavery and religion in the French colonies in 1685. [A.P.]

95. *Annales. Politiques* (1658–1740), published by Drouet, 1912, 131–32. [H.M.]

96. Between 1707 and 1714, the investments made by Marshal de VILLARS (1653–1734) amounted to 993,000 *livres.* The 1707 campaign alone brought him in 400,000 *livres.* In spite of the practices of the day, on this score his contemporaries were scathing in their criticisms of the hero of Denain. Saint-Simon spoke of his harpy-like avarice. Marlborough, Villars's famous partner, abided by such practices too. He had a quarter-master overseeing looting and he received an annual revenue of £6,000 sterling from the Jewish speculator Medina in return for a commitment to brief Medina promptly on whatever he recouped from his victories. [H.M.]

example which has rightly been lauded: *to take nothing for oneself*. Any contributions he levied went into the treasuries of the army or to the national museums, as did the spoils from churches, monasteries and palaces that he had his commissioners seize and which he forwarded to Paris as his most glorious trophies. The right of war – need I rehearse this again? – countenances no despoilment, not even under such a high-minded pretext: and no matter the pride we felt as we gazed upon the halls of the Louvre, upon the masterpieces from some nation we defeated by force of arms, we must generously concede that we had no entitlement to lay hands upon them. But even as justice makes progress, we must, at the same time, admit that General Bonaparte's conduct was one of the things that brought the Republic most honour.

Later, by which time he was emperor, he used to tell his generals: *Thou shalt not plunder, I shall give you more than you would have seized*. I am well aware that, here too, it was the enemy who bore the cost of his awards. But wasn't he merely ending plunder and wastefulness and reducing the right to *plunder* to a straightforward war tax? Here, it pleases me to recognize the fact that, because the empire has provided me with plenty of opportunities for criticism, Napoleon approached *right* the way he approached his conquests. An economist has roughly gauged the foreign receipts amassed by Napoleon between 1806 and 1810: the figure for those seven years stands at around one billion seven hundred million. Meaning that foreigners were fully entitled to complain: 1814 and 1815 were their compensation. As the saying goes, *easy come, easy go*. Bear that in mind and have nothing more to do with plunder. But what of the city that opts to make a hefty contribution rather than endure three days of looting?

Monsieur Thiers tells us, apropos of the siege of Tarragona: "Succumbing to a feeling widespread among all troops, our soldiers regarded Tarragona as their property and have stormed the city".[97]

This was nature caught in the act. *War is looting*, thinks the soldier, in his heart of hearts. What is the point of your talking to him about politics and the rights of peoples? Given the position in which battle has placed him, he has no way of understanding you. To no avail the bravest and best-obeyed leader shouts to him: *Thou shalt not plunder, I will give you more than you would have seized!* No, sire, plunder! ... There is something in that word that sits better with the warrior's pride and holds his imagination in thrall: what can I say? Something that seems to be more in tune with his conscience. The warrior does not bargain his life away for gold; he wagers it bravely against the enemy's life: plunder is merely the marker of his victory, a trophy. *Two hours of looting*! Therein lies the real triumph and the least a general can offer his men following an attack.

---

97. *History of the Consulate and Empire*, vol. XIII, 299. [H.M.]

And where are we now? Has there been any progress since Napoleon? In 1830, we conquered Algeria. Rubbing shoulders with the Arabs was bad training for our officers. The history of the *boudjous* [silver coins] of General Bugeaud,[98] a general with no interests of his own, like Bonaparte, looms large in everyone's memory. The Doineau trial has come along in more recent years to afflict opinion even further. Is it going to be said that the first lesson in civilization delivered by French conquest to the Bedouins, Tuaregs and Sudanese Blacks, was a lesson in plunder?

Crimea, a wasteland, and Lombardy, friendly territory, have schooled our soldiers in temperance, thank the heavens. But who would flatter himself that at the first opportunity they will not seek recompense when we saw an eminent jurisconcult like Monsieur Hautefeuille, barrister at the Court of Cassation and on the Council of State, arguing in 1860 that letters of marque and the right of seizure are essential components of the right of war? *Thou shalt not plunder*, Napoleon used to say; whereas Monsieur Hautefeuille counters: Play the pirate, go for plunder; it is your right and, both as soldiers representing your country's interests and as plain private individuals, it represents your own interests.

According to the principles currently governing armed piracy, once two nations go to war, piracy between them resumes, organized by private persons and authorized by governments, the way it once was between Athens and Sparta. This is the most lucrative branch of the trade, the one that suits seamen above all. Piracy, the jurists say, is one of the quickest ways of bringing the enemy to his knees. Naturally: but one could say the same of the seizure of properties by land forces. So why is it that what is permissible in the case of a naval serviceman and of the ship owner is not for the land solider and the irregular? Why is warfare is all profit for some and all sacrifice for others?

Monsieur Hautefeuille's book, the *Journal des Débats*, states:

War is war. It must be taken for what it is. We will never stop it harming private fortunes any more than of the State's. *It would not even be a good thing for matters to be otherwise*, because, the day the State's interests differ from those of individuals, the nation will be teetering on the edge of ruination.

---

98. THOMAS ROBERT BUGEAUD (1784–1849), enlisted in 1804 and served in the campaigns of the Empire. He was dispatched to Algeria in 1836, beating Abd-el-Khader in 1837 and signed the heavily criticized Treaty of La Tafna with him. Appointed governor-general in 1840, he proved to be an outstanding administrator. Made a marshal in 1843, he won the battle of Isly in 1844 and embarked upon a colonization drive. He died of cholera in 1849. He was one of the most popular men of his day. [H.M.]

As slickly argued as it is written. In that glib style and even glibber morality, we recognize the academic, conservative mind of the *Débats*. Reshaping warfare, what an undertaking! Accept us for what we are: we will be no better nor worse off for it and are certain that we will wander no further astray than our fathers did. So, warfare, according to Monsieur Hautefeuille and according to the *Journal des Débats*, is not merely conquest, as Napoleon was inclined to believe, but plunder as well. And when the powers gathered in congress to propose that trading vessels and their cargoes were not safe in hostilities, by way of easing the costs of war, their plenipotentiaries provoked a hue and cry for going too far when they suggested to preserve the pursuit of such vessels for warships and do away with letters of marque. But there are kindly bourgeois lawyers and journalists to protest at that exorbitant State privilege and to plead the pirates' case in the name of political morality.

The Political and Social Revolutions that Would Follow War Between France and England

Neither reason, nor a loftier justice, nor the honour of nations, is enough to overturn age-old abuses, entrenched by custom and given legal standing. The scourge of interests, which sometimes spawns the greatest cowardice, can only bring about certain conversions. To those who might not be persuaded by our arguments, I offer the following hypotheses by way of a possible application of the existing law and beg them to make known their feelings on the matter.

After having rumbled for a long time, imagine that war erupts between France and England. There will be motives and pretexts aplenty for it. One factor will be the resentment of previous struggles and old insults, plus, of course, the need for annexation: what the Channel has ripped asunder, politics will never reunite, but ascendancy over Europe and the globe might. Also, for the moment, let us ignore the other great powers; let us suppose we are back in the days of Austerlitz and Friedland. The continent has succumbed to France; a single champion holds out against her, England. On both sides the newspapers are preaching war to the death and the need to have done with it. Hearts soar with the semi-legendary accounts of the Hundred Years' War; each of the two nations reminisces about her victories, her conquests and her high deeds. The English celebrate the events at Écluse, Crécy, Poitiers and Agincourt; they remember having had possession of Dunkirk, Calais, Boulogne, Le Havre and Bordeaux. Once upon a time, their kings were kings of France and the lands of *oc* and of *oïl* came within an inch of becoming the lands of *yes*. British soil has remained virgin territory, untouched by the French, never even frequented by their tourists. The English people brag that, in their wars with France, they always came out on top; only on one occasion did France have the better of them, but she was fighting England alongside a body of troops of English stock in the American war. It was England that shattered the great king's pride in the war of the Spanish Succession; it was England that felled the great emperor. What matter the fleeting set-back at Fontenoy alongside so many victories, the upshot of which was that Europe was saved from French insolence twice over and Great Britain guaranteed her dominion of the seas.

These diatribes, as reported on this side of the Channel, exasperated the French people. If there is anything in France likely to bring common cause to her divided factions, war with England is it. The Legitimists bear a grudge against the English government for having plotted the overthrow of the Bourbons; the Orléanists, for having laid the groundwork for the downfall of Louis-Philippe; the Republicans for having backed the coup d'état on 2 December. Socialism is the enemy of England because it sees her as the heartland and stronghold of an exploitative, Malthusian capitalism, which it has pledged to destroy. The clergy despises her for her Pritchard-style missions.[99] The twenty-four years she made war on the republic and the Empire is etched into the hearts of the entire nation: the sieges at Toulon and Dunkirk; the defeats at Aboukir, Trafalgar, Waterloo, the loss of its colonies, the Perim and Suez incidents, access rights, Morocco and, latterly, the belated English intervention in the Italian revolution. Never has there been such a mountain of combustible materials between two countries, and it would take only a spark to ignite it. Should war be declared, it will end only with definitive defeat for one or other of the two great powers.

And now let us take a cursory look at the faculties of the two countries.

Population: Since the annexation of Savoy and Nice, France now has some thirty-seven million inhabitants; Great Britain, twenty-eight million.

Territory: France's is more extensive and of better quality.

Industry, trade, agriculture, shipping and colonies: England leads on every one of these counts.

War: The French army is the mightiest destructive machine in existence, superior even to what it was during the First Empire.[100] But that advantage is countered by the superiority of the English navy and the superior range of its activity. Whilst land forces move slowly and are poorly marshalled in this country, England's navy encircles the globe.

Government: England's is a constitutional bourgeoisie, France a military

99. The English missionary George Pritchard (1796–1883) settled in Tahiti where he engaged in trade, was appointed Consul in 1837, only to be expelled in 1844 by Admiral Dupetit-Thouars. The Pritchard Affair triggered a lively incident between France and England. [H.M.]

100. While Napoleon III was aware of Prussia's growing strength, most on the British and French sides were slow to realise that the Prussians had by this time moved ahead in the industrialized arms race. By 1870, Prussian numerical superiority allowed General Helmuth von Moltke to encircle and destroy the French at Sedan in 1870, which led to Bismarck's march on Paris and the formation of the Paris commune in 1871. Compare, William H. McNeill, *The Pursuit of Power: Technology, Armed Force and Society Since AD 1000* (Chicago: University of Chicago Press, 1982), chapter 7, with Roger Price, *The French Second Empire: An Anatomy of Political Power* (Cambridge: Cambridge University Press, 2008), 420–21. [A.P./G.H.]

monarchy. The former has the advantage in peace-time; the latter, we are assured, is to be preferred in time of war.

Public debt, budget: France's debt stands at around ten billion, and English debt at twenty. France has the advantage. But that advantage turns into a disadvantage if we compare the capital amassed in both countries, gross product, profits and the budget. In which regard, the advantage switches to England.

Social conditions: In France there is less inequality in fortunes; by contrast, the entrepreneurial spirit is more developed in England. The Englishman works harder and consumes less. The talent for invention is at the same level in both countries, but England extracts more from her discoveries than France, which pays hers only mediocre attention.

All in all, it can be said that the strengths of the two States are pretty much on a par. Many an English patriot will deny that, and many a French patriot will also ignore it, but the physical, intellectual and moral qualities of the two races are about the same.

Where the outside world is concerned, what England owes to the influence of her protective force, her invasive commerce, her vast capital resources, her liberal institutions, France obtains by virtue of her continental location, her centralization, her revolutionary propaganda and her armies. As to their own nationals, a case can be made for British pride and French vanity being equally unbearable everywhere.

We can tally the implications and risks of an all-out war of supremacy between these countries from these factors. Since England has the advantage in terms of her aristocracy and bourgeoisie, her trade, her wealth, and her colonies, then plainly, according to the current rights which make all means valid in breaking the enemy, as well as according to the counsels of the most commonplace prudence, should France emerge the victor she would need to focus on English wealth, her navy, her colonies, her capital, Great Britain's manufacturing and her bourgeois and titled aristocracy. By the same reasoning, England would strike out at French centralization and France's military organization, should England win this supremely decisive battle.

Let us take a closer look at those two alternatives, one at a time.

Let us assume, first, that after a smooth crossing and an initial defeat of the English navy, one hundred thousand Frenchmen come ashore on the coast of England, followed in short order by another hundred thousand and, if need be, a further two hundred thousand. It is reasonable to think that faced with regulars in such numbers, the English volunteers, no matter how brave, would not long hold their ground. With England invaded and defeated, and London, Birmingham, Manchester and Liverpool occupied, with England's naval resources forced into surrender by the invasion of the country, in accordance with the established right of war, France could, in pursuit of her interest in future supremacy and the definitive subjugation of her rival:

Disarm the entire nation;

Expropriate, despoil, the whole of the aristocracy and bourgeoisie and reduce them to proletarian status;

Declare the public debt, mortgaged debt and company debt null and void;

In the wake of this immense relief, lease the land in small four- to ten-hectare lots and see to it that the rent is slashed by more than fifty per cent its current rate;

That the same treatment is meted out to the mines, textile industries, construction and the entirety of English industry, and these are then handed over to the workers for an average of two per cent of the capital;

All of the Royal Navy, shipyards and arsenals are declared impounded; India and the colonies would be transferred to France; as for commercial shipping, it would be partly directed to French ports and the remainder handed over to the dockers, organized along the same lines as the farmers, miners and all the other workers.

Finally, a four billion levy in cash, paintings, statues, jewellery, crockery, furniture and bedlinen, goods and commodities would be imposed upon the upper classes and split between the State and France's seven million least well-to-do families.

In the name of and on behalf of the French people, tax-collectors in every parish in England and in Scotland would be responsible for levying, in twelfths, the taxes set down for agriculture, industry, mining, commerce, fisheries, etc.

That done, to the common satisfaction of the English plebians, freed and enriched through the ruination of its nobles and bourgeois, and with the French popular classes gorging on the spoils taken from the enemy, there would be no more rivalry between the opposite sides of the Channel, no more English aristocracy, no more English exploitation, no more English hubris. England would have even cast aside her bishops and her government. An occupying army and high-level policing, these are all a conqueror would need to underpin his pleasures and maintain order. France would then rule alone: the revenues she would extract from the other side of the Channel would cover the expenses of the empire; the French people, having nothing to pay, would revert to being the most light-hearted in the world; obedience would be a trifling matter to them; and Albion's merry men, rid of its exploiters and content with its lot, would reach out a brotherly hand to her.

With *raison d'état* wedded to economic reason, and public order considerations to humanitarian considerations, the legality of this great act of dispossession and de-nationalization would not be found wanting.

In terms of the jurisprudence of war, to which all the jurists from Grotius through to Monsieur Hautefeuille subscribe, and which is more or less intelligently applied by all conquerors, from Nimrod to Napoleon, by all the aristocracies raging from the Biblical patriarchs to the boyars of Muscovy and the lords of England, by all bourgeoisies, from Tyre and Carthage through to Venice, Amsterdam and London, according to these rules, this is what a victorious France would be entitled to foist upon her rival following a war for supremacy in Europe. Indeed, the only way of containing a defeated nation, where annexation is not feasible, is to resort to spoliation of its entire wealthy class and to turn the country into one vast metayage, by dividing the population against itself and making the largest, poorest class a partner in the despoilment of the wealthy class.

Let us turn now to a different outcome. Backed by a European coalition, England destroys the French fleet in a second Aboukir; the imperial armies are wiped out at a second Leipzig, followed by a second Waterloo; France is invaded, and Paris is captive. What will the conquerors think? Baron Stein, the most liberal mind in the whole of Germany, but no lover of France, as Blücher and the *Tugendbund* recounted forty-six years ago, and, with my own ears, I have heard it reiterated by his successors; after having worked on the economic make-up of the country, in a manner akin to the one we proposed in the case of England, the English will put an end to French unity, the number one cause of French militarism and Europe's worries. Here there is no aristocracy to be uprooted: the point is to affect a dismemberment of the country by pushing the equality principle, so beloved of the people, as far as it will stretch.

With the nation thus disarmed, her fortresses and ports destroyed, her arsenals emptied, her warships impounded, all her debts forgiven, be they public debt, mortgage debt, company debt, unsecured debt, a war tax of a few hundred million will be levied upon the bourgeoisie, the land would be handed over to the peasants in inalienable freehold parcels by means of a charge amounting to more or less fifty per cent of the land's income; transportation, manufacturing, banking, mining, shipping, having been turned into public services and the working class made beneficiaries of ventures rather than the rentier bourgeoisie and shareholders.[101] For additional reassurance, the country's larger industries would be

---

101. Proudhon repeatedly called for worker ownership of companies. See for example, "What is really needed would be to make of the railroads a new kind of property, to perfect the law of 1810 relating to mines, and make it applicable to railroads, granting the privilege of running them, under fixed conditions, to responsible companies, not of capitalists, but of workmen", *General Idea of the Revolution* (1852), trans. J. B. Robinson (New York: Haskel House, 1969), 151. And from *The Federative Principle* (1863): "Workers' association will remain a utopia as long as government does not understand that it must not perform public services itself or convert them into corporations but entrust them by term lease at a fixed rate

abolished, with the exception of the production of luxury and fashion goods, in which English positivism cannot compete with French refinement. That's why, in place of her ancient art schools and trades bodies, Italy has marble and paint suppliers run exports from that country. A portion of the profits brought in by agriculture, commerce and industry would be set aside to cover the costs of new States, a portion being paid over to the enemy by way of tribute.[102]

With these broad measures in place, the dividing of the French Empire into twelve independent regencies, each with its own law-making powers and executive authority appointed by the people, proceeding to its universities, judicial organization, central bank, stock exchange, etc. The nations absorbed by the French Empire would be brought back into existence: Normandy, Flanders, Lorraine, Alsace, Burgundy, the Auvergne, the Touraine, Dauphiné, Provence, Languedoc, etc., with Rouen, Lille, Metz, Strasbourg, Dijon, Clermont, Orléans, Lyon, Marseilles, Toulouse, Bordeaux and Nantes as their capitals.[103]

To consolidate these efforts, it would remain to destroy Paris. To destroy Paris does not mean razing her homes; Paris is more than material things; she is an idea and it is the idea that needs attending to. Once the Empire has been decentralized, it would take only the demolition of the city's 150 main monuments, its churches, palaces, theatres, ministries, town halls, museums, barracks, prisons, hospitals, schools, academies, conservatories, courts, market-places, warehouses, triumphal arches, columns, the Stock Exchange, the Bank of France, the Town Hall, the bridges and the railway stations. All the moveable goods belonging to the State, to the city and to public establishments can be removed and relocated to the twelve brand-new capitals. Given the availability of a massive population such as that of Paris, it would be easy to dispatch back to the departments, and give them a stake in the success of the operation. Eight days would be enough for this ultimate act of vandalism to be carried out.

---

to companies of united and responsible workers", in McKay, ed., *Property is Theft!*, 718. [I.M.]

102. In a fit of pessimistic prophecy, Proudhon wrote to Gouvernet on 26 August 1860: "Italy is in the throes of revolution; Hungary; Poland; the whole of Germany are just waiting for their chance to get involved; Russia would capitalize upon this mess and strike the Orient; England is braced against us. On every side I see national wars, not incipient political wars". [H.M.]

103. Before finishing off and "reducing war to a nonsense", Proudhon, in keeping with his theory of the right of force and the role of warfare in the composition, organization, growth and decline of States, here posits fragmentation of the unitary state as a hypothetical consequence of defeat. He was to revisit this notion on several occasions, and it carries within it the seeds of his *Du Principe fédératif, qua* the foundation of peace. "Therefore," he says in *De la Capacité politique des classes ouvrières*, "it would be up to me to show how history in its entirety is merely serial composition and de-composition; that pluralities or federations are unfailingly succeeded by agglomerations and those agglomerations by break-ups", second part, chap. XV. [H.M.]

Within six weeks, nineteen out of every twenty inhabitants of the Seine department, would be dispatched back to the provinces. Paris now would be nothing but a heap of materials and, over the centuries, she could keep the whole of France supplied. People would come there to buy ready-made houses that could be shipped over long distances and used in the construction of a brand-new France. The twelve regencies, each of them with between two and four million inhabitants, would form a confederation of mini-States, which, once conjured into existence by the foreigner and founded upon plunder and bankruptcy, would constitute the greatest foes of unity. Nationality is a fickle sentiment in the multitudes, and so easily mistaken for parochialism, that the urban and rural plebians, having grown rich thanks to the political ruination of the nation, would take to this with alacrity and, just as the bourgeoisie did back in 1814, would offer the foreigner a vote of thanks. In every time of crisis, gangs of motley figures appear spontaneously to harness the public sentiment and inspire fear, pity or disgust before going on to disappear without trace. 1789 had its *brigands*, 1793 its *sans-culottes*, 1796 its *jeunesse dorée* and 1815 its *verdets*.[104] We, in turn, would have the partisans of dismemberment shouting encouraging cries of: *Down with France!* A number of military men, scholars and artists, anyone with any feeling for life and French dignity, seeing their homeland guillotined, would blow their brains out or lose their minds: three years on and that would be an end of it. A great State, a great nation would have disappeared. But the vines would still blossom, and the countryside blanketed in crops; the wine would flow, the money would circulate and there would be drinking and singing and laughter and love-making like there was the day after the Flood; *Nubebant et bibebant, plantabant et aedificabant.*[105] Thus decapitated, its leaders gone, the people might be even happier than their masters: O vainglory of war and politics!

All men love their country. Those for whom States are merely vain abstractions and who do not believe that the life or well-being of individuals can be salvaged, that anything can be salvaged, should ponder that. In everything that I have just been saying, there is not one iota of exaggeration. Of course, war

---

104. This was the name given to the volunteers of Trestaillon and Truphemy, the leaders of the *white terror* in the Midi; they were named after the green ribbons they wore on their arms. [H.M.]

105. Here Proudhon is condensing two verses from the Gospel of Saint Luke, 17: 26–29, which read: "And as it was in the days of Noah, so shall it be also in the days of the Son of man. They did eat, they drank, they married wives, they were given in marriage, until the day that Noah entered into the ark, and the flood came, and destroyed them all. Likewise also as it was in the days of Lot; they did eat, they drank, they bought, they sold, they planted, they builded. But the same day that Lot went out of Sodom it rained fire and brimstone from heaven, and destroyed them all". [A.P.]

no longer has plunder as its openly avowed, direct purpose. Surely, conquest, pursued by Louis XIV, Frederick II and Napoleon, was designed for purposes other than extracting tribute in the Turkish way. But given where nations stand economically at present, it may be that the ruination and decomposition of a society and the expropriation of an entire nation might seem like the only way of bringing the bloodletting to an end. To this end, we have quoted directly from the authors: in order to break a stubborn and regenerating enemy, any means that holds out the prospect of victory is permissible, including the dissolution of the State, the partitioning of its territory, the seizure of its colonies, the expropriation of its citizens. This is how the third estate harnessed the State during the revolution, when dealing with the clergy and nobility: so why would a nation not do likewise vis à vis another nation? And finally, O deeply wise *Journal des Débats*, if ever war were to flare up again between the bourgeoisie and the proletariat and if the latter were to emerge as the master, why would the proletarian not also press home his victory where the bourgeois is concerned? *Patere legem quam ipse docuisti*,[106] he might tell you. To which you will reply, whilst lowering your head: The choice was yours, Dandin.[107] *Meritò hæc patimur.*[108]

What I have left to say of conquest and of the character it has tended to assume in modern times will lend such apprehensions even greater plausibility.

---

106. "Obey the law that you yourself have forged". [A.P.]

107. A wealthy social climbing peasant: *George Dandin ou le mari confondu* is a French Comédie-ballet in three acts by Molière. [M.M.B]

108. A Gregorian Chant, and from Genesis 42:21 (Latin Vulgate) *"We are verily guilty"*. [A.P.]

CHAPTER XI

What Conquest has a Tendency to Become: The Reduction of War to the Absurd

Men rarely have the courage of their convictions. Such laziness is the source of much inconsequence; it is also a safeguard against wrath. For all the verbiage of the jurists, the rhetoric of the historians and the bragging of the military men, doubt has wormed its way into our minds. We have not asked ourselves, as precisely as I have, what the right of war is, *per se*; what its principle is; what the conditions for its exercise are; the extent to which it is permissible to ransack and slaughter; and whether, therefore, the despoilment of the defeated has anything to do with war's laws and political purpose, whether it authorizes the destruction of a nationality and the expropriation of an entire people, as was my hypothesis in the previous chapter. These questions and many another are suggested by the laughably misconstrued notion of a right of force and lurk hidden in the conscience of peoples.

For want of a scholarly critique – if I may be so bold – the overall influence of civilization, the softening of manners, the muddled sense of a superior constitution towards which humanity is being driven, have begun to dilute the ferocity of the warrior. The man who is permitted everything is gripped by a secret shame: he feels that notions of devotion, honour, liberty, notions of which he is the representative and the hero, are not compatible with the practices of brigandry, and the notion of plunder fills him with an insuperable disgust. The age of conquest may be gone, but he knows nothing of that; he tells himself that war, whatever its underlying cause, is intended, not to settle some economic problem, but to resolve a political issue; that war is therefore fated to be waged between States rather than peoples; that in no circumstances could conquest have the effect of conjuring up entire populations of settlers and serfs by means of despoilment and degradation: that the annexation of a city or province in no way implies the despoilment of private persons; that, the right of conquest, such as the rights of the people imagine it to be, being exercisable only by the State, is subject to the rules governing the expansion and borders of States and rules out any notion of confiscation and enslavement.

Today, every civilized nation subscribes to sentiments such as these, which is why they are even seeping into the military. Just as there is an unspoken agreement, as Grotius has said, that a price is not to be placed on the heads of princes, even though there are grounds for thinking that war is entirely of their making, there is an unspoken agreement to spare the proletarian class in the event of conquest, as their death would be tantamount to endorsing the decapitation of peoples. What European sovereign would rule over a nation made up exclusively of outcasts? England does not, with regard to the Hindus, whose rajahs and brahmins it manipulates. To date, nations have lived and grown through their aristocrats; which is the reason why Poland is not going to be thought of as subjugated and annexed once and for all as long as it retains a nobility to represent it and raise objections; and it is why universal conscience takes a dim view of executions and confiscations carried out against that nobility by conquerors incapable either of weakening it or replacing it.

But, if this is a trend in modern mores, and whilst it has been agreed by civilization that the absorption of one country into another entails the annexed inhabitants' having full entitlement to, not merely equality of rights under law but also respect for their possessions, what further benefit can conquest offer and why does war not end itself, for want of being able to serve any useful purpose? Why should Piedmont care about securing Lombardy, or Austria about having lost her, if, in the final analysis, that province's inhabitants were to enjoy the same benefits and bear the same burdens as those of the State into which they find themselves absorbed; if, under the rules of good governance, the tax paid by each locality must be spent only on servicing that locality? What do Piedmont, France or Switzerland stand to lose or gain from the annexation of Savoy under those conditions? What benefit would a border on the Rhine bring us French? And, conversely, what difference does it make to Lombardy whether she is described as Piedmontese rather than Austrian: or to Savoy, on becoming republican by uniting with the Swiss, or imperial by going over to the French; or to Belgium by holding on to her independence or being drawn into our orbit? With equal rights before the law, something that no conqueror State withholds any more; with a budget reduced to its fairest expression; with free trade gaining favour everywhere; with access to political freedoms, the nationality question is, from the vantage-point of interests, utterly without significance. Finally, what becomes of the question of territory, borders, colonies, shipping, or customs, if, on the one hand, plunder, tribute, confiscation, land, colonies, and trading privileges, the purpose for which the war is supposedly being fought, for which it has always been fought, even though care was always taken not to say a word about it, what if that war aim was no longer there; if moreover, there was the same freedom everywhere, if rights were all the same, if the differences between institutions were only nominal, if, finally, solidarity between cities and between individuals alike, whilst not ruling out independence, offered the same guarantees and the same reservations all round?

Plainly, war, shorn of the secret, shameful motive that defines it, through the abolition of plunder, piracy, war taxes and all manner of requisitioning, and then enveloped by all the civil, political and international rights that it has, itself, generated, is going to find itself purposeless; it will not occur to anyone to have recourse to it, since neither wealth nor the honour of the homeland have any further interest in it; international problems, reduced to issues of simple rights, can be resolved through diplomacy or arbitration; finally, the justice of force and its entire apparatus and everything that relies upon it, everything that assumes it, implies it, upholds it, that whole jurisdiction and entire jurisprudence, have to be done away with, there being nothing left on which to sit in judgment.

This is a most grave conclusion, given that we are faced here with something very different from straightforward disarmament and the end of butchery. This observation has implications for the entire political system, which is wholly based upon warfare and which has hitherto seemed irreplaceable. The question has been posed right from the opening pages of this study: what is society under the State? And what is the State itself in the absence of what Rousseau terms the PRINCE, be he monarch or magistrate, hereditary or elected, which is to say, in the absence of warfare incarnate as man and sword-bearer?[109]

The situation is pressing, and we wonder how war is going to escape it, and what society is going to become without it, should warfare fail the test.

If I may be allowed to use this wholly military metaphor, it is here that we are going to see warfare driven back into its last entrenchment, detonating its contradiction and standing exposed in all its ugliness.

The same goes for ideas and institutions as for cities and States: they will fight to the death. War, and I speak of it as I would a living person, defending its threatened existence, war is not about to go away; it is unwilling to die. It has long since anticipated the challenge that it will have to face; as a far-sighted tactician, it has made arrangement for its retreat, via a secret passage down which we shall all follow it.

As we have stated, the primary cause of war is pauperism or, to put it another way, the rupture of economic equilibrium. Its unspoken but actual

109. *The Social Contract*, Book III, chap. I: "What then is government? An intermediate body set up between the subjects and the Sovereign, to secure their mutual correspondence, charged with the execution of the laws and the maintenance of liberty, both civil and political. The members of the body are called *magistrates* or *kings*, that is to say, governors, and the whole body bears the name *prince*". [H.M.]

purpose is to make good the budget shortfall by means of conquest. Once, and less harmoniously, this was done by means of confiscation, tribute and plunder. Do away with war's primary cause and it no longer exists. Deny it the purpose that that cause assigns to it and it loses its *raison d'être*. Now, as it currently appears to be impossible to stamp out pauperism, and war has not been entrusted with that task; and, consequently, as antagonism seems to be inherent in humanity, war cannot be eradicated and, given that it exists, it has to consume. So, what is it going to do, if, on the one hand, it is compelled by its own law to treat its conquest as its very own State and manage it like a good housewife, and, on the other, it makes it a point of honour to shun plunder?

War cannot lie to its cause. Being the daughter of famine, and after having sought sustenance abroad, but forced by the advances of civilization to renounce aboard, it is going to fall back upon its fellow-nationals; like Saturn, it will devour its own offspring and it is in order to add to the number of its victims and ward off its own suicide that it continues to seek conquests.

In other words, war has a tendency to side-step the LIBERALISM that pursues it by seeking refuge in *governmentalism*, in other words a system of exploitation, administration, trade, manufacturing, education, etc., by the State. So, no more plunder, as that lacks nobility; no more imposition of war taxes, no more property confiscations, no more piracy, each city to be left with its own monuments and masterpieces, and there will even be help available, in the form of the supply of capital, and subsidies will be afforded the annexed provinces. But there will be militaristic governance, exploitation and administration; the whole secret lies there.

A State can be compared to a general partnership or limited company in which there are huge capital assets to be managed, great affairs to be conducted and huge profits to be made; as a result, the founders, directors, administrators and inspectors and all the officials have rewards to look forward to and more magnificent salaries. As a result, its services are organized and prioritised accordingly, in order of the merits and service records of the personnel. The more the State expands, the greater the assets needing management; but the more money passes through its hand, the more there is left, of course, for its staff and all its operatives.

Pauperism, the primary cause of warfare, is still active and indeed operates even more intensely at the top than lower down, so there is always militarism at home and a proclivity to conquest abroad; except that war, instead of plundering and bringing pressure to bear on the conquered people, realises its benefits in a different form. Just as in the days of Alexander and Caesar, heroic plunder has changed into conquest so conquest itself tends to turn into *governmentalism*.

Prefectures, commissionerships, endowments, bribes, sinecures, salaries, pensions have taken the place of pro-consular exactions, dispossessions, *latifundia*, slave auctions, confiscations, tributes and the supply of cereals, pelts, wood, etc. It is primarily at the point of take-over that the big moves are made. All those services to be created, all those jobs to distribute! All those promotions! All that bureaucracy! And for businessmen, all that speculation! Such is war in its highest phase, war with equality before the law, in the absence of expropriation and plunder.

One effect of this arrangement is a surge in the expenditure of the State, which ought to be called by its true name, *war fees*, as hierarchy is consolidated and, as it spreads, or, and it amounts to the same thing, as *governmentalism* grows, it deepens. Under the Empire of Napoleon I, who was still making war in the old style, the spread of the central authority and its meddling were, despite the severity of the administration, a far cry from what they later became. The budget was under a billion. Under the Restoration, the July monarchy, the 1848 Republic and the Second Empire, political hierarchy expanded, the central administration was boosted by everything that had been lost from local life, and the 1860 budget was reckoned at ONE BILLION, NINE HUNDRED AND TWENTY NINE MILLION. The upshot is that the expansion in government, associated with huge public works, is what strikes the greatest fear into smaller States. Like small animals in the presence of large predators, they are afraid of being gobbled up, unless, like poor Savoy, they hope to extract more from their overlords than the latter could ever extract from them. In which case, it could be said it is a case of rats devouring elephants: for in this world of extermination, there always has to be something feeding on something else.

And so war turns on the wheel. Having absorbed everything within its reach, everything unable to defend itself, each State is induced to take up arms against itself and to treat itself like a conquered country. This odd conclusion, which the nineteenth century should have highlighted more than in any other age, given its political and industrial progress, is one of the gravest dangers menacing peoples and governments.

In 1823, the Legitimist monarchy felt the need to win the army over and present it in a way that made it feared abroad, whilst at the same time revive its title and breathe new life into its tradition at home. On the advice on Monsieur de Chateaubriand[110] and with Russia's, Austria's and Prussia's endorsement, it launched the war in Spain. This was legitimism triumphant; the Duke of Angoulême became a hero and the *emigrés* were elated. What reward could

---

110. Royalist, diplomat, historian and a seminal literature figure in nineteenth-century France, François-René de Chateaubriand's name is now more commonly associated with a somewhat excessive method of cooking sirloin steak. [A.P.]

they expect from Spain after having rescued her from her revolution? None: the Spanish war was the disinterested action of a policy of order. But, for France, there was to be a price to pay: in 1825, a billion in reparations were voted through by way of compensation for the favours rendered for the victory scored over the Cortes. Of course, that vote was not prompted by the right of war; other considerations lay behind it and made it less hateful to the bourgeoisie and the peoples. But enforcing that compensation would not have been thought feasible, but for the support of the victors of Trocadero.[111]

Five years later, in 1830, that very same Legitimist monarchy seized Algiers. There several unexpected millions were seized; then a gamble was taken to use the July ordinances to further milk the revolution, which, on this occasion, refused to pay up.[112]

Need I speak of Louis-Philippe's government, nick-named the *peace-at-any-price* government? What good did its African campaigns, the seizure of Antwerp and the occupation of Ancona do it? Arguably, none, other than to add, for better or worse, through plots and insurrections, to the growing contempt and grumbling poverty. All that we can say is that, more than eighteen years of war, which we have waged against no one, relieved us of the sum of at least six billions at the point of a bayonet.

And where are we now? Since 1852, our armies have been blessed with glory again; but that is not the issue. France maintains an army of six hundred thousand men: the other powers follow suit, depending on their means. Whether we do or do not have war, whether we are the victors or the vanquished, the upshot is this: by virtue of equality before the law, no longer denied any annexed country, and of the political freedoms that have become the common inheritance of

---

111. In January1823, Louis XVIII, caving in to the far right, declared war on Spain in order to place a Bourbon on the Spanish throne. In September, the Duke of Angoulême and twenty-four thousand men rescued Ferdinand VII who was an out-and-out prisoner of the Cortes. He determined immediately upon a policy of ferocious repression and *apostolic terror*. A disheartened Angoulême declined the title of Prince of Trocadero that Ferdinand wanted to bestow upon him. He made his way back to France to a hero's welcome.

 A first plan to compensate emigres – who had fled France during the revolution and returned during the restoration of Louis XVIII – was rejected by the House of Peers in 1824. In January 1825, a new bill was tabled to put an end to their complaints and allay quarrels between old and new proprietors. The vote of the *billion emigres* gave rise to a great debate which laid bare all the political and financial *considerations* for and against. This second project, allocating balance sheet indemnity to the emigres of thirty million annuities with a capital of one billion to be created in five years, was passed on 27 April, 1825. [H.T.]

 112. Algiers fell on 5 July, 1830. 25th July saw the signing of the ordinances restricting freedom of the press and amending the voting laws in favour of property owners and ordering the dissolution of the Chamber of Deputies; on 27 July, day one of the *Three Days of Glory* [of the 1830 Revolution], Charles X fled. [H.T.]

nations, affording no benefit, the fact remains that armies that, under the terms of the right of war, should be living on warfare and enriching their respective homelands, are feeding on its own people. Out of a budget of one billion, nine hundred and twenty-nine million, the Department of War absorbs six hundred million. This is what is known as an *armed peace*. At the time of the Crimean expedition, the government borrowed, in addition to its budget, another one billion, five hundred million; the war in Lombardy required an additional five hundred million, making a total of two billion over a five year period. Add on the pensions, endowments, army fund and the never-ending war tithe that Napoleon I, for all his gift for fuelling war through warfare, was forced to introduce and which we have been paying for upwards of fifty years, and which, unless there is a change in the system, we are going to be paying for century after century, and that brings us to the singular outcome that, in the final analysis, war is reduced to turning the citizenry into fodder for their soldiers.

Now, in the light of these facts and the aftermath that they trail in their wake and the countless ideas they bring forth, I return to the hypothesis spelled out in the preceding chapter regarding war between France and England.

War can be regarded as indestructible, because its cause is economic anarchy, or what we call freedom of trade and industry, which all the civilized nations are at one in acknowledging as a scientific truth. The proof is that Europe, which has been living in the era of armed peace, is progressively arming itself with every passing day, rather than striving for disarmed peace.

Given the contemporary conditions surrounding it, conquest brings the conqueror no benefit; far from it, it serves only to make the State's expenditure swell at a quicker rate than its revenues. Add that the motives for war, having been constantly confined to the realms of politics, have a tendency, thanks to the impact of political scepticism and widespread disillusionment, to be perceived as economic motives and therefore to become identical to the primary cause.

Accepting the hypothesis of an all-out war between France and England, and given, on the one hand, that any such war could not be ended by annexation, given that the nature of things is contrary to that; and, on the other, that the professed purpose of it would be, on this side, to capture the ascendancy which industry, commerce and wealth have guaranteed England; and, in order to destroy France's influence on the continent in terms of the power of centralization and armies, then, plainly, if one wanted to be done with it for good, the victorious nation would, shunning all sham generosity and all phoney shame, declare the political dissolution and mass expropriation of the defeated nation, on pain of the risk of some day falling victim to terrifying reprisals, in order to end this bitter rivalry and devise some other solution.

Note, moreover, that such a dreadful outcome would be authorized under the right of war as implemented down through the ages and as the jurists teach it. Nor would the rights of the peoples be contradicted, since, if those same authorities are to be believed, the rights of peoples mean nothing other than the right of war; finally, political rights and civil rights, just like economic rights, would not conflict with it, since, in the case of the private individual, those rights would defer to the right of war, the supreme law of which is public safety.

To be sure, if the case for war was put to both the French and the British nations in those terms, the prospect of such an eventuality would give them pause for thought.

A majority on both sides being on the look-out for some accommodation, war could never be declared; the issue of perpetual peace between the two peoples would be, in effect, resolved.

But are we to believe on the other hand that, if the decision were to be brought before the court of opinion only after the war itself had already been declared, the winning nation would let itself be assuaged; that, between the certainty of dominance guaranteed forever, the lure of enormous plunder and a budget covered by foreign tribute, and the possibility of its succumbing to further battles and being treated in accordance with the rigours of victory, it would show any hesitation? I say that the latter nation would be out of its mind if, having right and power on its side, it was to show the slightest scruple. It would be undeserving of its victory and would not deserve to live. A government heeding the counsels of moderation in such circumstances would be a traitor to its own homeland.

This, however, is where we stand, given the traditional, classic international right that prevails across Europe. There is no nation that is not facing this dilemma today – I mean the dilemma of choosing, on the one hand, between the loss of its political independence and sovereignty, of finding itself stripped of all its wealth, real estate and belongings, and made eternally subject to tribute; and feeding on itself, should it not be able to find other prey, on the other.

Conclusion

After acknowledging the juridical nature of war and its humanitarian vocation, we delved into whether its verdicts and enforcements were, in practical terms, consistent with what theory expected of it. But we made a painful discovery. Viewed at some remove, and in the round, the verdicts of war are valid and just; they are self-sanctioning. It might be said of them what the psalmist has to say of the judgments of the Eternal One: *Judicia Domini recta, justificata in semetipsa.*[113] Scrutinized in such detail, they are no longer merely some ghastly caricature of the proceedings of justice. What is described as *war according to the rules*, if looked at properly, is brigandry made law.

Regarding which, and wondering where this frightening contradiction might be coming from, and delving deeper than we had previously done into the causes of war and its motives, stepping outside of political considerations in order to plunge into the realm of economics, we have come to the belief that the prime, universal and always immediate cause of war is pauperism, meaning a rupture in the economic equilibrium.

As we have stated, humanity has been placed under a range of organic laws from which it cannot escape without becoming corrupted and made wretched.

The first such law is the law of nourishment, or rather, of consumption, quintessential to the physiology of our being.

The second is the law of labour, whereby man consumes only what he procures for himself, or, in economic jargon, what he produces.

The third is the law of poverty, whereby man, by working, produces only a sufficiency. The purpose of this law is to keep man forever elevated above animality, render him more and more free, master of his senses, appetites and passions, by spiritualizing his existence.

From that law of poverty, imposed by nature's foresight, we derive a fourth, which is the law of frugality and temperance, whereby man directs the running of his household to his social destination.

---

113. *Bible*, Psalm 19:9, "The judgments of the Lord are true and righteous altogether". [P.S.]

Finally, the fifth law is designed to distribute services and products around the members of the community, in accordance with the preceding points, and in such a way as to level out conditions and fortunes as soon as possible, without overlooking anyone's rights: this being the law of justice.

Now what do we find? As a result of popular ignorance, the importuning of the senses, the illusions of the ideal and overblown personal entitlement, all of these laws are misconstrued and breached. The law of consumption is breached when, rather than its being regarded as a means, it is mistaken for an end; the law of labour is breached when work is looked upon as a misfortune and a punishment and when everyone seeks to offload onto his neighbour, which leads to slavery and the proletariat; the law of poverty is breached due to the fascination with wealth; the law of temperance is breached by the craving for luxury and questing after sensual delights; finally, the law of justice is breached through personal considerations, which spawn parasitism, unequal education, an imbalance in functions and the erroneous distribution of products.

But nature, reason and justice are unforgiving when outraged. They find their punitive sanction in pauperism, which, swooping down on society and attacking every class, deepens the deficit, engenders tyranny in the State, sows discord between nations, pushing them into war, the essence of which it then goes on to corrupt and deprave.

So, the mystery of iniquity now stands before us, unveiled. We have understood how war, caused by famine, leads to plunder and how that shameful reality has become the ideal of heroes. We have seen war, from the dawn of societies, blurring its political motives with its economic cause and becoming synonymous with brigandry; all the epics celebrate the glory of such renowned pirates, and religion itself has been generous in bestowing its blessings upon them. As we have seen, such hypocritical warfare, initially free and private, has spread and gradually turned into an exclusively public undertaking, a State prerogative, whilst at all times clinging to its piratical character. We then witnessed the birth of *conquest*, whereby warfare displays its political, revolutionary and providential side, in accordance with the right of force; and we have seen these two things, plunder and conquest, the first a response to the pauperism that causes war, the second to the *raison d'état* that motivates it, clearly distinguish themselves from one another, in theory, but without ever ceasing to march in step and working together in practice.

With civilization carrying on with its victorious march, in spite of warfare and, often, by means of warfare, we have arrived at this curious situation in which nineteenth-century Europe finds itself. Even though the heads of State and the enlightened elements within nations may have had their fill of it, the state of war persists; armies and the means of destruction are more formidable

BOOK FOUR · CONCLUSION

than ever; at the same time, even though contempt for plunder seems to be getting the upper hand and conquest resolved into a pure political annexation; as far as the conquering State is concerned, the benefits of conquest are reduced to the exploitation of its very own subjects. For things to be different, we would have to revert to the system of the ancient warriors, of the Spartans *vis-à-vis* the Helots, the Romans *vis-à-vis* their subject nations, the Turks *vis-à-vis* the Christians. That is, once the battle has been won, to proceed by means of an extravagant extrapolation of political motives, with the dismantling of the beaten State, expropriating the nation *en masse*, make it a tenant in its homeland, and force the subjugated country into a small-holding for the profit and greater glory of the victor.

Either it exploits its own nationals, or it enforces servitude abroad; this is the dilemma with which war confronts the conqueror today.

With that dilemma in mind – and it is quite impossible for heads of State to escape it – we shall rehearse the question considered at the end of Book Three, and adjourned pending further information regarding the causation of war: Are there grounds on which to imagine a reform of the code of war and to steer its operations back in the direction of a better practice?

This question is important, because, while on the one hand it can be argued that politics has had its day and that the reign of *raison d'état* is over, that war has consequently achieved its purpose and that there is no more detachment nor attachment to be effected between nations, in short, whether an extension of the regimen of war is a likely prospect given the present circumstances of society; on the other, none seem able to admit that the conquerors should strive for the advancement of civilization at their own expense, and, like contestants at the Olympic Games, settle for a simple laurel wreath as the price of their victories.

So, once again, is the reform of war possible? And should no such reform be feasible, then what is to become of humanity's progress and what becomes of civilization?

BOOK FIVE

THE TRANSFORMATION OF WAR[1]

Pacis imponere morem[2]
—Virgil

SUMMARY

THESIS: War, its supporters say, is a form of primitive justice, rooted in nature and in conscience, and susceptible to reform. The abuses that besmirch it are not an argument against it, any more than the aberrations of love, fatherhood and inheritance constitute a legitimate prejudice against family and marriage. The jurisdiction of force is beyond destruction; it is necessary, it should be ameliorated rather than abolished, which would be an affront to humanity, a negation of public right and the rights of peoples; a nonsense. Such a reform of war is all the more plausible in that the very factor that caused it to become

---

1. Proudhon here is applying to war the dialectical approach by means of which he had demonstrated "the transformation of syllogism" (*De la création*, Chap. II, § 4), "the transformation of labour" (Id., chap. IV, §§ II and III), etc. Transformation being synonymous, not with reform but with Progress which "in the purest sense of the term ... is the movement of the idea, *processus*; innate, spontaneous, essential, irrepressible and indestructible ... From which it follows that as the essence of the mind being movement, truth, which is to say reality, in nature and in civilization alike, is essentially *historical*, subject to advances, conversions, evolutions and metamorphoses", *Philosophy of Progress*. [H.M.]

2. Virgil, *Aeneid*, Book IV, §850. "Crown peace with justice". The full verse reads: "Roman, be sure to rule the world (be these your arts), to crown peace with justice, to spare the vanquished and to crush the proud". From *Virgil Vol 1: Eclogues. Georgics. Aeneid: Books 1–6*, trans. H. Rushton Fairclough and revised G. P. Goold (Cambridge: Harvard University Press, 1999), 592–93. [A.P.]

depraved, to wit, pauperism, can, without plunging into some economic utopia, substitute fair compensation for the arbitrary extortion of the victor, as is fully permissible under the right of war in its loftiest interpretation and which cannot inspire recrimination nor hatred. That, in substance, is the affirmative view when it comes to the matter of war's susceptibility to reform.

Response: The response from the adversaries of militarism is, first, that any such proposed reform does nothing to destroy the primary cause of war, which leaves an odious suspicion hovering over its motives. Secondly, that even accepting that war will be waged in the future for purely political reasons, with no admixture of shameful avarice, and that, as a result, it may be reformed in respect to all that concerns tactics, the mutual fidelity of combatants, respect for persons and property, etc., that would still leave this delicate question: namely, the settlement of expenses and indemnities. Now, in terms of entitlement, no compensation is due for the actual outlay on war, being due only for breaches of the laws of war. In fact, if the compensation sought were to represent the winner's full outlay, it would be exorbitant and would end in wholesale plunder. War therefore is still fraught with this contradiction, not to say with an indelible ignominy, and it is the charge of greed and bad faith that the warring sides are forever invoking. Far from countenancing any chance that war will be reformed, it has a tendency to become more depraved, rendering it, come what may, mutually iniquitous. Look to the evidence of history, and the hypocrisy of official motives.

To escape from this difficulty, allow us to observe: 1. That the issue raised by war is complex and needs to be broken down. 2. That the economic question has to be dealt with ahead of the political question. 3. That, in terms of economics, war's jurisdiction does not apply. Which leaves just one option, to wit, to suspend hostilities and, appealing to public reason, to organize the great human antagonism along new lines. Only in that new sense is peace an active, competitive peace, where the forces locked in combat are reproduced rather than destroyed, and where the right of force is fully and wholly satisfied. This peace is the logical conclusion of humanity's military evolution. It is up to the rights of peoples, to political economy and the diplomatic history the nations to say if, and how, we should be acting, henceforth, to implement the findings of our analysis and set a course for universal pacification.

FIRST CHAPTER

That in Every War, and on Both Sides, the Immorality of the Cause and Iniquity of the Ends Entails the Dishonesty of Means

No matter the extent and ascendancy of interests, in the final analysis, and in accordance with the genealogy of right, the economic order is placed under the protection of the political order; it finds its guarantee in political power; politics is inseparable from society. Thus, politics is warfare in its essence, in its institutions, and in law. Is warfare susceptible to reform, then? That question has never been put; yet there is no question more pressing.

At first glance, there does not seem to be anything unfeasible about a reformation of military mores. The history of civilization could just as well be defined as a series of reforms: reforms in religion, reforms in the State, reforms in marriage and the family, reforms in ownership, in inheritance, in exchange, in industry, reforms in justice. It is through an uninterrupted series of improvements that society rises to its purest state, and that man realises, within and around himself, the ideal conceived by his conscience.[3]

Why might war, the greatest act of social existence, the one that philosophical analysis has led us to regard as the holiest and most solemn, and which history and poetry are at one in holding up to us as the most fruitful and most glorious, why would warfare, prey to abuse like everything human, not be reformed?

Why might we not manage to impose stricter rules on feats of arms, the way we once did on trial by ordeal, and as we are still doing with duelling?

The matter is certainly worth examining. Among humans, there is nothing of greater concern than this. The subject demands we confront it. The principle behind any reform, the element of right, is to be found in this: war is a trial of

---

3. Proudhon states in *The Philosophy of Progress* (1853): "That which dominates all my studies, its principle and aim, its summit and base, in a word, its reason; that which gives the key to all my controversies, all my disquisitions, all my lapses; that which constitutes, finally, my originality as a thinker, if I may claim such, is that I affirm, resolutely and irrevocably, in all and everywhere, *Progress*, and that I deny, no less resolutely, the *Absolute*". [I.M.]

strength. A number of symptoms also appear to suggest a reformist tendency within warfare: the softening of the customs of war, the horror inspired by massacre, the shame of plunder, the presumed equality before the law of conquered countries. All these considerations are such as to hold out the prospect, over time, of improved discipline; but can we really expect a modicum of progress from that quarter?

Prior to our scrutiny of war's primary cause in the preceding Book, such a question might have been premature. Guided by the thrust of political events and the rigour of right that prevails over them, we might have failed to answer. But yes, war is susceptible to reform, because it is the expression of right, the manifestation of national dignity, the sovereign act of patriotism, liberty's protestation against fatality. War, just and glorious, but dishonoured by passion, greed and prejudice, can be reformed; it must be.

But our response could not possibly be the same. No, we should say, war cannot be reformed, because its primary cause is tainted; because the legitimacy of its political motives cannot undo the ignominy of its economic rationale; thanks to the actions of one or other of the belligerent powers and, most often, thanks to the actions of both of them, there is a principle of iniquity still mixed in with war, that corrupts its very essence and banishes all decency without hope of its ever returning.

We know all about that original vice; it is wretchedness, its spur poisoning consciences, nurturing envy, ambition, avarice, wrath, hatred and pride; it leads to bad faith, treachery, violence, thievery and murder and paralyses every moral sentiment in the combatants. Is a perversion of nature susceptible to correction by means of skill or discipline, and is regulation of practice enough to reform a power misshapen in the very act of gestation? No, Christian theology answers us here; what is born bad can only be altered through the intervention of the creator; this is the principle upon which the Christian religion is founded. By which sacrament can war be regenerated? That, as Monsieur de Maistre would say, is for you to find out.

Our view is that because interests have been warped by our half anarchic, half absolutist world, nations and individuals alike are insuperably suspicious of one another; that no matter how the activities of diplomacy may strive to disguise it, that suspicion undermines the honourability of the powers; thereafter, matters cannot operate as the notion of honest combat requires between enemies who misconstrue each other; finally, and this is what makes the ailment incurable, that iniquity is all around, although it is not always and everywhere the same. Thought of as the verdict of force, war is sublime; it occupies the midpoint between justice, of which it is one form, and the poetry and the enthusiasm of religion. But there is no iniquity with which it is not tainted to its roots:

it may have a face like an archangel and have the name of God inscribed on its shield; but it has a dragon's feet and tail.

They say that a reform, even if it might not eradicate that odious cause, would at least makes its influence disappear, which would be enough for force to be regularly deployed; that it is up to nations to come to agreement on banning any arbitrary extortion, all marauding, all plundering; to confine their possible rights of conquest to political annexation and the payment of fair indemnities. What could be so hard about that?

Indemnity! The very word gives away the innate indignity of war and the fatal contradiction to which it leads.

In terms of the rights of war, as we have deduced them from their principle, to wit, the right of force, and from its purpose, which is the evolution of States; even as depicted for us by the authors who, all in line with Vattel, teach that war should not be deemed just on both sides: the loser is due no indemnity. It was entitled to defend itself; besides, only through victory could the right of the stronger be established; as a result, each side must cover its own costs and, on that score, the defeated is due nothing.

The analogy with everyday justice shows as much. What do the legal costs in civil, commercial or criminal cases consist of? The judges' salary, hearing costs and the fees of the lawyers. At the outset, each side pays for its own counsel; the losing side is liable only for the magistrate's fees and the cost of the proceedings. Why so? Because no one is allowed to ignore the law and the losing party's plea is held to have challenged the law; as a result, since he should not have brought his action, he ought now to be held liable to pay.

But in warfare there is no judge but force, no tribute other than the battlefield; the costs of war fall into the same category as that which litigants lay out for their own defence: consultations with lawyers, memoranda, expert opinions, bailiff services, excerpts from minutes, etc. Besides, victory alone indicates which is the stronger party; up until fully and resoundingly defeated, the vanquished party is within its rights; in combat he does not violate the right of war, he obeys it. On that score, therefore, as far as the winning side is concerned, it has no entitlement to look for compensation: its indemnity comes in the form of conquest. For there to be any basis for compensating both belligerent powers, one of them would have to have contravened the laws of war; but in that case the indemnities might well be due from the victor himself which, as we have seen, changes the question entirely.

In fact, if the victor's claim to be reimbursed for his outlay on the war were admissible, plunder would simply have changed its name and would be going under the name of indemnity. The sum would stand so high that he would have to forego any payment or take the course indicated in Chapter X of the previous Book, that is, expropriate the enemy country of all its real estate and belongings and reduce its population to servitude.[4] As is clear from his correspondence with his brother, Joseph, Napoleon I, who was clever enough to fuel war by means of war, and who, over a five year period, we are assured, wrested from the enemy upwards of one billion, seven hundred million, was always short of money and forced to increase his budget. Yet of those seventeen hundred million, not a centime was payable to the families, who, whilst paying their taxes and the war levy, still had cause to weep over their offspring. During the Crimean War, the ordinary as well as the extra-ordinary expenditure of France, England, Turkey and Piedmont on materials alone was at least five billion. Add to that two hundred thousand men at twenty thousand francs per head and there you have a total of nine billion francs. Where was Russia going to find such a sum? Wars have been seen to last twelve, twenty, thirty, eighty or even a hundred years: what indemnity could cover such outlay? Now, the further on we go, the more burdensome war becomes and, as for the exorbitance of its outlay, that goes beyond recoupment.

So, whichever way we look at it, war, brought about by a deficit, forces the nation embarking upon it to choose between the total plundering of the enemy or the using up of its own capital. There is no half way: it must either feed upon the enemy or its enemy will feed upon it. Do you think that it will show any hesitation? Above all, do you believe that confronted with that inevitable choice, that implacable dilemma, the two parties will have any illusions as to their intentions towards each other?

Examples will serve us better than arguments here. Let me begin with the most straightforward cases; we shall then tackle the most complicated and most modern ones.

Pirates. A pirate gang sets itself up in inaccessible reaches at the end of narrow inlets strewn with treacherous reefs unfathomable to all outside navigators. The pirates of Cilicia were like that: Caesar, having fallen into their clutches, swore to see them hanged. Those pirates captured trading vessels, plundering their cargoes and holding the crews to ransom. Not content with that, they forced towns and villages to pay them tribute, unless they wished to see themselves ransacked and put to the torch. What must the populace have felt at such

---

4. This entire passage, in which Proudhon contrasts the right of indemnity, which he queries, with the right of conquest, a derivative of the right of war, which he regards as the righteous political incorporation of people and territories (See below, Book Five, Chapter III), is crucial to any explanation of the stance he adopted on the 1815 treaties. Furthermore, he draws a clear-cut distinction between the former rights of peoples, in respect of which our author is rigorously logical, and the new right, based on debt payable and on which his forecasts as an economist display in a prophetic light today. See *Si les Traités de 1815 ont Cessé d'Exister* (1863). [H.M.]

insolent blackmail? They must have wanted the leader executed without trial and then to swoop on the corsairs' nest and exterminate every last one of them; the sort of thing the likes of Hercules and Theseus did to their brigand counterparts. All means are fair when faced with malefactors such as these, and any bandying of words would have been an acknowledgment that they had some sort of entitlement and a recognition of their authority. It cannot have occurred to anyone that a hard-working, peaceful population scratching out a living from the land and the water ought to have challenged them to a duel or paid them tribute. Dealing with such plunderers in accordance with the laws of war would have been tantamount to guaranteeing them impunity for all their misdeeds. Cartouche and Lacenaire and their gangs would simply have needed to say that they were at war with society and, in the event of their being defeated, they would at least have saved their skins! In which circumstances, there would have been every advantage to a life of brigandry: it was decent folk who would have been worse off. Execution, rather than warfare, therefore looks wholly deserved here. The man who steps outside of the laws of the human race cannot then invoke its guarantees; he is a beast with a human face, a monster.

Note, though, that the brigands in need of chastisement do not accept the position they are placed in. They argue that society as a whole is awash with inequality, privilege, injustice, usury and fraud and that land is unfairly distributed; that some have been given the good land whereas others get nothing but the sea, the deserts and the rocks. They reach for the example of castes living on the backs of slavish exploitation, of kings in receipt of tribute payments, of State-wrecking conquerors; they take stock of the universal state of war and the rule of force. Such arguments are not, of course, unanswerable, and I think my readers will readily spare me the need to refute them. But they are enough to satisfy the conscience of the pirate, who, for his own part, and knowing what treatment civilized people have in mind for him, pays them no heed. In his eyes, his murders, rapes and arson attacks are merely reprisals. With antagonists like these can war be waged according to the rules of honour and righteousness? It would be like suggesting to an officer of the French army, decorated with the Legion of Honour, that he trade sabre blows with a convict. Let us move on.

The Sabines. Grotius accepts[5] that a war waged by a population made up entirely of males, and fought with a view to seizing women, like the Romans did when they started abducting the daughters of the Sabines, would not be an unjust war.

---

5. Grotius, *De Juri Belli ac Pacis*, Book II, § XXI. Grotius bases his view upon a text from Saint Augustine who stated that "had the Romans taken up arms against their neighbours over the latter's unjust refusal to provide them with women, they would then have been entitled to seize them under the right of war". [H.M.]

Indeed, what is at play here is the principle of the perpetuation of families, through the miscegenation of races; in spite of the most pig-headed prejudice, down through the ages, the deduction from that principle has been that marriages between Jews and Gentiles, Greeks and barbarians, Catholics and Protestants, nobles and commoners, whites and coloureds, have legitimacy. Under which article of the rights of peoples were the Sabines intent upon removing Romulus and his companions from the list of political societies by refusing marriage alliances with them?

By contrast, what is there more sacred than the right of the paterfamilias, of the woman, to withhold, in the one case, his child and, in the other, her very person and wed only a husband of her own choosing? Note that the Romans were refugees, something akin to bandits. Family honour as well as individual freedom was affected. Therein lies the crux of the tragedy; on this side, the inviolable family and therefore, on the Roman side, an unjust and odious war; this was rape by force of arms. Then again, Rome was not compelled to perish and Sabine insolence degenerated into a conspiracy against the rights of people, into outright national murder. The Romans could have said: "Had we been more numerous, richer, nobler, in short, stronger, you would have found us to be quite honest people. Well, we shall show you how strong we are ..." What would have happened had love all of a sudden passed judgment instead of force; if the rape victims, out of self-respect, had not thrown themselves, children in their arms, between their husbands and fathers? With the matter referred to the court of force, the war grew venomous; fury acknowledged no more laws. This was a war of family versus abduction, of modesty versus violence, of decency versus crime, of the whole of society versus some tainted persons ejected from its midst. All means were permitted when it came to driving them out of Italy, and God knows what the Romans, driven to despair, and insulted in their reproductive ambitions, would have done to their persecutors!

Barbarians. If the family sanctuary could be violated, would land be inviolable? The land has been given to the collectivity of nations and the same solidarity envelopes them. Looked upon as the exploiters and usufructuaries of the world, we have obligations of a higher order to the privileges of habitation and of the indigenous. In light of that order, we are all accountable and, regrettably, all in *debit*.[6] Within this anarchy of interests barely covered by the veneer of arbitrary politics, who are we to regard as sovereign? Who can argue that he is a legitimate proprietor? Who is in a position to plead good faith and possession dating back to times immemorial? As we well know, all ownership implies

---

6. Debit: The sum for which a public accountant is found liable by the Court of Accounts, either because he had a duty to recover it or because he has embezzled it. [H.T.]

reciprocity, in addition it imposes upon the owner an obligation to exploit his property. Failing this, it is open to challenge.

Driven out of their forests by famine, the Barbarians were asking for land. Whilst the civilized peoples, Greek and Roman, reckoned themselves the strongest, their reply was the Malthusian response: "No place for you at the banquet of property". In less harsh terms, this meant: "That if the globe has been given in ownership to humanity, each nation has received the usufruct of the territory it inhabits; it is for it to exploit it, meet its consumption needs from it, strike a balance between population and produce, turning to unoccupied lands if need be, that the demand made by the hordes was out of order and violated all established rights. Next to the family, what is there more deserving of respect than the ancestral home, more sacred than the soil of the motherland? *Barbarus has segetes!*[7] This was the outraged cry that has been echoing uninterruptedly in Italy, from Julius Caesar down to Victor Emmanuel. Every threat of invasion has been answered down through the age, and for all time to come, by the one so light heartedly delivered by Paul-Louis Courier[8] to the ministers of the Holy Alliance:

> If you have come here to plunder us in the name of the most holy and indivisible Trinity, then we, speaking on behalf of our families, our fields, our flocks will greet you with rifle fire. Stop relying upon the genius of the emperor and the heroic valour of his invincible guard to defend us; we will look to our own defences, with an irksome determination, as you very well know, that throws tactics into disarray, thwarts the waging of war *by way of example*, and is enough to undo the most astutely worked out plans of attack and defence. Therefore, if you are wise, bear in mind the advice I am about to offer you. Whenever you march into Lorraine or into Alsace, give the hedges a wide berth; steer clear of the ditches: keep clear of the bushes, trees, thickets, and watch out for the tall grass; do not go too close to the farms and skirt around the villages with care. Because the hedges, ditches, trees and bushes will open fire on you from all sides, not individual shots nor in platoon strength, but a gunfire whose aim is true and murderous; and, no matter where you go, you will not find a hut nor a henhouse not garrisoned against you. Send no spokesmen, for they will be taken captive; – no detachments, for they will be destroyed; no representatives, because... Bring your provisions; bring sheep, cows, pigs and do not forget to escort them as well as your wagons. Bread, meat, fodder and

---

7. Virgil, *Eclogues*, 30–31. "Is a godless soldier to hold these well-tilled fallows? a barbarian these crops?" [A.P.]

8. PAUL-LOUIS COURIER (1772–1825), classicist and anti-monarchist. [A.P.]

the rest, make provision for them all; for you will find nothing wherever
you go, if you go; and you will bed down in the open, when you do bed
down; because if we cannot keep you out of our homes we know that it
is better to rebuild them than ransom them; we would prefer the former,
as it costs less ... There is little pleasure in conquering people who do not
want to be conquered.[9]

However, during the Empire and at the opening of the fifth century of our era,
there were unused lands. Corruption and Roman exploitation had left them
empty. Might it not have been fair for them to abandon these lands that the
conquerors left untilled? Then how were the Romans able to justify their ownership? But Rome could not surrender her conquests; besides, the owner does
not reason with the man who has nothing. He would be ashamed to.

We know what became of this great contest between civilization and barbarism. Right was not entirely on the side of the civilized, nor wrong entirely on
the barbarians' side. In this uncertainty as regards right, in this division of the
gods, who had to prevail, I will not say naturally, but legally? Who but the stronger? Which is what happened, and people welcomed it. When Greco-Roman
society sank into corruption, drained of its energy as well as of its virtue; when,
on the other hand, the barbarians, proliferating and learning from their defeats
and embracing Christianity, gained the upper hand, the conquest was carried
through and humanity was regenerated. It was the righteous triumph of force,
but that did not alter the fact that, confronted by an enemy with a grudge over
property and precisely because of that grudge over property, war forgot all its
rules – what am I saying? – felt entitled to forget them.

The Greeks and Persians. When, after having subjugated the Greeks in Asia,
the great king came to command those in Europe to also pay him tribute, or
else to come down on to the plains and come to grips with his thirty thousand
troops; should the Greeks have submitted, on the pretext that the Persians were
at the time more advanced than them in terms of civilization and politics, having, since Cyrus, the founder of their monarchy, supplanted the Assyrians and
the Medes, inheriting their power, their wisdom and their glory and had an empire already that stretched from the banks of the Indus to the Mediterranean,
from the Black Sea, Caucasus and Caspian Sea, as far as the Ocean and the Red
Sea? Did the disciplining of nations, the policing of seas, the oneness and peace

---

9. *Pamphlètes: Xe letter au redacteur du Censeur.* The text by Courier (1772–1825) has
been tampered with by Proudhon here, the latter being in the habit of paraphrasing or rejig-
ging his quotations. The passage ought to read: "If you come to plunder ... them, on behalf of
their families ... they will greet you with rifle fire. No longer reliant upon the Emperor's wits
to defend them, they will stand up for themselves", etc. [H.M.]

of the world, require that Greece, as well as her islands and then Italy, Africa, Spain and Gaul, should in turn join that great incorporation? The tribute being asked did not even cover a tenth of the losses that nations were ultimately having to pay for their internal divisions and wars on one another, which, at best could be deemed a token of reassurance. In any case, a portion of it would go back to Greece, which was in need of policing. So, as a result, should they lay down their arms, receive the great king's satraps and defer to his suzerainty? Should the Greeks have submitted or should they have agreed to the duel they were being offered?

There would certainly have been some truth in the conqueror's demand; this was demonstrated later since, no sooner had they been rescued from fear of the Asians than the Greeks set about slaughtering one another; they ended up, one hundred and fifty years later, under the dominium of the Macedonian who introduced the great monarchy foreseen by the Persians, with the support of the Greeks themselves. And yet, despite such fine considerations, the correctness of which history had to confirm one day, who would dare to say that the Greeks were bound by the right of war and of peoples to take seriously the alternative that was put to them?

The Greeks would, I imagine, have replied: "That they are not familiar with the king of the Persians; that they had nothing to do with him; that they were in the habit of governing themselves and that they simply could not see that the world needed, for the sake of the happiness of all and the glory of just one man, to be constituted as a universal monarchy; that, instead, they were bound to cling to their independence; that they asked nothing better than to live alongside him in true friendship and understanding, and to contribute to the peace of the world, but that there was no way that they could agree to becoming his subjects; that if he persisted with his pretensions, they could only attribute his schemes to the promptings of ambition and greed, to a spirit of plunder and pride; that rumours of his splendours had reached even them, and that they had reason to think that his need for fresh tribute counted for a lot more in his schemes than any enthusiasm for civilization; that, that being the case, they beseeched him, if he had no other proposition to put to them, to stay home and leave them in peace, given that, if he were to venture with his three million men into their passes and creeks, they had their minds made up to give him a bandit's welcome and greet his Persians like dogs".

And they were as good as their word: whilst we might have our reservations here regarding the countless breaches that were the accompaniment to that war, we cannot but applaud the determination of the Greeks. What would have become of them, what might have become of western civilization if, deferring without a fight to the law of force, they had readily submitted, or let themselves be crushed in open country as the Persians were inviting them to do? Greece's salvation was simultaneously the patriotism of her children and the style of warfare in which they engaged in defending themselves, as if in a fortress, in country impassable to such a strong army. Their victory was legitimate from the point of view of the rights of peoples as well as that of the right of force. The time had not yet come when nations had to form themselves into one great empire; the king of Persia therefore had no grounds to threaten the Greeks' independence. As for the ensuing fight, we have pointed out, when dealing with the laws of war, that the plaintiff has to be in a position to compel the defendant, not merely on the field of battle but in his homeland. The outcome of the war was therefore, here, as in the barbarian invasions of which we recently spoke, what it had to be; not that that is any obstacle to our disapproving of the infringements that must have been committed in it, with the Persians being, in Greek eyes, fearsome brigands and the Greeks, in the minds of the Persians, abominable seditionists, with each of them treating the other accordingly.

Let us close, therefore, with this novel and memorable example, that where warfare is concerned, blatant or assumed iniquitousness of intent entails out-and-out disloyalty, which, however, does not necessarily nullify the victory. This is an affliction for which there is no cure and which no reform could render any more palatable.

CHAPTER II

More on the Same Subject.
The Question It Raises

The war in Spain. Napoleon's 1808 invasion of Spain is, in respect of the matter under consideration, so analogous with that of Greece by the Persians in 490 BC, that I cannot resist making the comparison.

I do not know a single historian, even one friendly with the Emperor, who has not found fault with this poisonous campaign, even in its principle and its motives. Monsieur Thiers himself, endlessly pleading extenuating circumstances on behalf of his hero, has nothing of any import to say on the subject. After regaling us with the Bayonne intrigues,[10] he ends up leaving us as contemptuous of Napoleon the conqueror as of the statesman. For all the historian's oratorical precautions, we begin to query whether the Emperor was anything but an adventurer and a charlatan. Napoleon made it all too obvious that his ambition, his personal glory, concerned him much more than the success of the revolution. The same thing happened to him here as happened to Louis XIV with regard to the Flanders campaign; his policy, its manifestations and all his arguments scandalized people and he incurred the shame of failure more than Louis XIV had.

But the philosopher-historian cannot stop at such *ad hominem* judgments; he has to delve deeper into things and, if need be, compensate for the feebleness of the arguments advanced by the authors of the events he recounts with his analysis.

If vowing loftily by the French revolution and calling upon Europe to witness his oath, Napoleon, had said to the Spaniards:

"The requirements of the war I am waging against Great Britain in the interest of freedom of the seas, of trade and of the security of nations; the welfare of my Empire; observance of the treaties I have concluded with most of the powers and which are fair recompense for my victories; finally, the triumph of the revolution, whose sword I hold in one hand and in the other her shield,

---

10. Battle of the Bayonne, 14th April, 1814. [I.M.]

necessitate that Spain in turn should join my system. To those ends, Spaniards, I need to replace your dynasty and revolutionize your society. Furthermore, I have no quarrel with your nationality; I am not demanding any contribution from you in terms of man-power or money and have no intention of staking my claim to one single square kilometre of your territory. You yourselves will choose your new sovereign. All that I ask is that you gravitate into my orbit, that you abide by my policy and adopt our principles; otherwise, prepare yourselves to do battle in the open countryside and in your strongholds, against our invincible troops ..."

To that declaration, as blunt as it is emphatic, Napoleon might have been able to add these prophetic words:

"You cling to your independence, your dynasty, your religion; the revolution scares you and you look upon us right now as heretics and atheists. Well, had you been unlucky enough to get the better of my military, Spaniards, before another ten years were up, you would see a redoubling of the tyranny by which you are burdened and would have to blush at scandals even greater than the Godoy and Marie Louise scandals;[11] the Frenchmen who portray themselves to you right now as liberators, you would be inviting back as the auxiliaries of despotism, the clergy that flatters and agitates you, would then swiftly become the focus of your hatred; you would sell off their assets and you would have your turn at playing the heretic, the atheist, the revolutionary, the republican ..."

If, as I say, Napoleon had addressed the Spaniards in that vein, would his cause have appeared, would it appear today, to be so bad? Did he step outside of the right of war and the right of people? Is it not obvious that all he had done was steal a march on Providence and that in more than one respect his conquest would have been more conservative than the patriotism of the Spaniards?

What leads statesmen astray and sets the historians waffling, is that they never have a sufficiently lofty grasp of events as a whole, that they are over-inclined to look for the reason behind events to the intrigues of politics, rather than looking to the circumstances of peoples and that they do not have a firm grasp of the right of force and its implementation. The higher causes that triggered the 1808 war in Spain were every bit as legitimate as the ones that had been behind the Marengo campaign; despite the incident and the unseemliness in Bayonne, they are equally justifiable in the court of history. In fact, every continental State trading with the English turned on the Emperor, and this was even more remarkable in that the institutions of that State were less consonant with the principles of revolution. European interconnectedness is a principle that overrides even the balance of power in Europe; after all this was the principle

---

11. Manuel de Godoy was the guard and lover of Maria Louisa Teresa of Parma (1751–1819), Queen of Spain. [A.P.]

invoked by Napoleon, albeit from the viewpoint of the new right. Victory then marked the ascendancy of the thought and politics of 1789, of which he was supposedly the representative; so, one had to be with him or against him; there was no middle ground. He was all the more alive to this in that his experience of national struggles had brought him nearer to spotting the dangers of resistance, however minimal, and the need for it to be crushed. The idea of a regenerated Spain was not undetected either; it was after the meeting of the Cortes, caused by the entry of the French army, that Spain embarked upon a modern existence. As for the Spanish dynasty, changing it was crucial; the life she has been leading between 1793 and the present day proves that Napoleon had not been maligning her.

Does it follow from all that that the Spaniards had only to submit? Definitely not. My intention was to highlight yet again the nature of the right of war and rights of peoples, both of them rooted in the right of force; I wanted to show that where there is a case for war according to the rules of politics, war is just on both sides and that, no matter what may have been said, this was the case with the war in Spain, among others. I indicated the motives by which Napoleon was prompted, even though he himself may not have had a clear and comprehensive sense of them. Those motives still stand, but they do not undo the ones by which the Spaniards were prompted.

Indeed, in terms of nationality, what could have been more exorbitant that the emperor's intentions? Such arrogance! Timidly, the Spaniards explained to Napoleon: "That they considered him the greatest man of the age; that his armies were second to none and that they had no intention to oppose them; that they would be pleased and proud to be welcomed into his alliance and into his family, but that the circulation of products had to remain as free as the sea herself; that there was a contradiction between fighting for freedom of transportation and the interception of goods; that if France was in a position to substitute her own produce for the imports they sourced in England, then they would gladly give their preference to the French, but, if not, concern for their subsistence precluded them from turning away British goods; that if the continental system, the brainchild of the emperor, could not be reconciled with this plain common sense, then some thought had to be given to reforming that system; that it was up to Napoleon to see how he might humble the English without affecting neutral nations' lives; that, Spain not being at all involved in this war, it would be unfair to oblige her to bear the costs; that, furthermore, they thought it a mischievous way of regenerating a nation to deprive her of her independence and, changing her dynasty and stripping her, so to speak, of the insignia of her sovereignty: that they were therefore vehement in their desire to remain masters in their own household; that their well-being would suffer less that way; and finally that if he, Napoleon, Emperor of the French, was committing trespass against their nationality by occupying their country by force, they, for their part, would look to defend themselves and were holding him answerable for events from that point onwards; as to his predictions, it was a maxim of theirs that people of heart must above all else do their duty and trust to God for whatever might ensue".

What ensued, we know. Napoleon, openly or potentially at war with Europe, soon had good reason to believe that matters could not be handled so quickly nor all at once, and that skill and speed are no substitutes for force in warfare. He was not able to conquer Spain. At first, the French generally emerged as the winners from pitched battles; all of the cities, bar one, Cadiz, were occupied; all the strongholds fell. But there was a mass uprising by the Spaniards; a series of setbacks drained and decimated the imperial legions and, more than anything else, so did the guerrilla warfare in which four or five hundred thousand French were murdered one after another, at every crossroads, pass and tavern in Spain. Not that they perished unavenged; a million Spaniards of every age and sex were slaughtered in retaliation.[12]

That's war for you: politics would like it one way; alas! the all too well-founded suspicion of greed and bad faith make something else of it. What is the point of one side serving notice of its demands, backing them up with the strongest arguments, suggesting a duel, formal warfare, if the other side rejects the case for war, declines to fight, asserting its independence and accusing the enemy of being out for nothing more than plunder? Politics, revolution or civilization: those are the only viable options. A nation forced into war, attacked in its homes, its independence in jeopardy, will always make war in the Spanish manner and in accordance with the arrangement so picturesquely described by Paul-Louis Courier. There would be no point in the powers' deciding at twenty future congresses that they will refrain from warfare and all illicit practices; at the earliest opportunity, that splendid commitment would be forgotten about. There would be talk of evil intent, secret ambition, bad faith and, after much mutual accusations and recriminations, there would be a lapse back into the old ways. Anyone who might argue purity of motives, and that he was merely responding to necessity, would meet with this sarcastic query: Do you wage war for the glory?

---

12. The insults heaped on the royal family, hatred of the foreign occupier and a very lively religious sentiment in the Spaniards were to make them opponents of the persecutor of the Pope. The resistance was orchestrated by councils [*juntas*]. Men who had once been soldiers of the revolution now found themselves having to fight, not against kings but against a people fighting for its freedom, stalking the invader around every bend in the road and furiously slaughtering him. [H.T.]

The Peloponnesian War. Let us take a leap backwards. In Chapter IV of the preceding Book we saw how the Greeks who were so welcoming of the stranger wage war on one another. A few thoughts on the subject are, naturally, called for at this point.

Once the great war against the Medes had ended, the question of unity was raised as far as Greece was concerned. It was impossible that such a tiny country, surrounded by mighty enemies, should stay divided into a multiplicity of microscopic States. The largest of which, such as Sparta or Athens, by arming all of their able-bodied citizens, just about managed to field twenty-five thousand men. A choice had to be made between a federal republic or a unitary republic, monarchy being repugnant to them all. For each city with any aspiration to the status of capital city, inflating its ambitions and repudiating the rights of the others, it was now or never if the situation were to be resolved by force. The war of extermination waged against the Persians might have seemed excusable; among the Greeks, fighting for their federal constitution, the war must have been holy. What would the conditions be? Let us review them in a few words.

As in the Middle Ages, in trial by combat, the champions had to swear to the purity of their cause, prepare themselves for combat by praying and receiving the sacrament. Likewise, nations in conflict, after having exchanged their papers, and acknowledged the reality of their dispute, the urgency of a resolution and the impossibility of arriving at one other than by force of arms, having settled the conditions of battle and the aftermath, having stipulated the rights of the victor and the obligations upon the vanquished, were required, before coming to blows, to hand one another a certificate of honourability and sign a peace treaty. Such was the ideal of warfare, as revealed in the Nordic religions and the chivalric novels; finally, this was how the self-esteem of the warriors and the conscience of nations wanted it to be. The Greeks were very well able to understand this; they had merely to develop their own heroic tradition to that end. But the opposite occurred.

The war that broke out between the Greeks over national unity, otherwise known as the Peloponnesian War, was one hundred times gorier and uglier than any they had fought against the Persians. Never had plunder, ambition and hatred engendered such infamy. The issue of federation was never even mooted: as far as Athens and Sparta were concerned, the avowed purpose of the war was to reduce every Greek city to the status of a tributary, to make sovereign disposition of the nation's resources and use them, as the Romans did later with the forces of Italy, in order to conquer, plunder and devour the world. Oddly enough! the kinship which looked like it should have been blunting the edge of the war was the very thing that rendered it doubly horrific. Hatred between brothers is a cordial hatred; wars over political expansion between people who share the same blood and the same language are the worst wars of all. And it is always the same cause that poisons the contest – ignominy in the motivation, and between rivals there is no mistaking it.

The wars of religion. If there is one instance in which war ought to have been free of all thoughts of avarice and refrained from all outrage, this is most certainly the one. Anyone fighting in God's name ought not to indulge in anything of which God and justice disapprove. Well now, let us take a look.

A man translates the holy scriptures into the vulgar tongue and argues that every one of the faithful is entitled not just to read them, but also to interpret them according to his own ideas. This is the principle of freedom of scrutiny which, in a theological formulation, slips into religion. There is no shortage of arguments and authorities in support of this novelty. But the unitary, sovereign Church contends that such democratism, introduced into the realm of religion, spells its ruination. Faith is personal and, as such, an act of conscience; as dogma, it relies on authority. Who is to decide between Luther and the Pope? Over the course of the debate, freedom of scrutiny makes inroads so rapid that after a few years it can no longer be curtailed by the usual methods of the Inquisition. War alone can decide – quite apart from the fact that matters of dogma do not fall within its remit – whether the heretics are to be permitted to pursue their form of worship within a society that has, up until recently, been wholly orthodox. More than ever, religion, in accordance with justice and warfare, ordains that the two camps avoid anything that might invest their struggle with the appearances of sin in their encounters with each other. Common sense even suggests that whichever army proves the more magnanimous, or less in the grip of a susceptibility to wrath and greed, is going to be able to consider itself the representative of truth.

Now, look at the historical record: is that the way the wars of religion were fought? No: and the reason is easily guessed. The spiritual is indissolubly bound up with the temporal, which it translates in its own way. The religious institution has a corresponding political and social institution; the greater the rule authority plays in the former, the more it will impinge upon the latter. That said, we can readily see why a population is drawn into changing its religion. Rightly or wrongly, it concludes that the old faith is too favourably disposed or insufficiently ill-disposed towards equality; because it accuses the Church of complicity in the exploitation of peoples. The vested interest that heresy conjures up will in turn be repellent to the orthodox conservatives, threatened in their privileges and material interests. There is no point in our invoking the Albigensian war or the war in Vaud or the Hussite war, the Anabaptist war and so on; the sale of the assets of the clergy, the plundering of churches and monasteries, the confiscations visited upon the new religionists, etc., by way of reprisals. To the scandal of ungodliness is added the infamy of avarice; war turns diabolical; how dare the victors, whoever they may be, sing the *Te Deum*?

A word about the crusades. Islam, properly considered, had a claim on the sympathy of Christians. It was the religion of Moses that Mohammed had finally substituted for the backward desert hordes' worship of idols. At the time of writing, Mohammedanism, which Europe's philosophy and superior morality shun, is gaining ground among the peoples of the Sudan, thereby paving the way for the civilization trotting along behind it. The Papacy and the Caliphate could have come to an agreement. Nowhere does the Koran teach intolerance; it acknowledges the mission of Moses and of Jesus Christ; it says that God has given each people the laws that suits it, but that he sent Mohammed to the Arabs. What could be more conciliatory? Let Mohammed and his successors complete the rout of the worship of idols; honour the prophet in the eyes of the peoples who heeded him and even aid him in his endeavours; that is what a philosopher Statesman might have suggested when this new faith emerged. Twelve hundred years before Dupuis,[13] Volney and the German exegetes, Mohammed was arguing that, in the eyes of God and reason, all religions are one. He asked: how can they excommunicate and wage war on one another?

But it is on this very score that Mohammed has shown, assuming that he was sincere, the shallowness of the human heart. Soon, it was not enough for the Muslims to secure themselves a place in the sun through their religion: not content with using the irresistible argument of the scimitar in order to convert the desert tribes, they in turn conceived the ambition of laying the foundations for a catholicity of faiths; they too engaged in messianic endeavour; they too realized that the temporal is ruled by the spiritual; at which point, clashing with Christianity, they became intolerant and set about waging war simultaneously upon ideas, individuals and assets. Faced with an all-conquering Islam that had already made itself master of Sicily, Italy, Spain and France, the crusades became a necessity; how can politicians like Ancillon misconstrue that? Conquest has to be countered by conquest; stopping the enemy was not enough, he needed to be driven back into his lair. After that the religious motivation was submerged beneath the self-serving motive; any decency in warfare was no longer possible. The crusade thus conformed with Mohammedan propaganda; on setting off for

---

13. CHARLES-FRANÇOIS DUPUIS (1742–1809), lecturer in Latin at the Collège de France (1787), served in the National Convention as a deputy before becoming a member of the Council of Five Hundred and was actively involved in the organizing of central schools. He was the author of *Origine de tous les cultes ou Réligion universelle* (1795), in which he argued that all forms of worship, not excluding Christianity, could essentially be traced back to the worship of the sun and stars. [H.T.]

the Holy Land it was off in search of absolution and wealth, as heavily burdened with debts as it was with crime.

Let us not lose sight of this principle; in religious nations, religion is the very essence of interests. The greater the faith, the more ferocious the interests become; which is why wars of religion are by far the bloodiest, the ones worst stained with devastation, arson and rape. Hatred between peoples is directly related to how zealously they feel God's cause. You would keep war in check, foist laws upon it and dampen its fury. Please, make no appeal to piety, for that would be throwing oil on the flames.

Revolutionary wars. These I am quoting from memory only. Earlier, I acknowledged the economic driver that had caused the French Revolution; I recalled how the plebs were under pressure, the bourgeoisie jealous, the clergy, nobility and court more and more grasping, the entire nation racked by a pauperism that was becoming less and less bearable with each passing day.[14] To be sure, our forefathers had understandable reason for the indignation that overwhelmed them from 1789 to 1800. The principles they steered to success were fair principles, the purest and loftiest expressions of righteousness. Is it any less the case that, by the very nature of things and under pressure from circumstances, starveling revolutionary France was as much the agent of plunder as she was of justice? The Revolution, and here I use the term in the sense of the war against the ancien regime, though sublime in its motivation, was tainted in its actions and then compromised in its ends: truth requires that this be said.

Object, if you will, that the interests of the ancien regime were the first to set an example of selfishness; that the new maxims, stripping the nobility of what was left of their privileges, the clergy of their enormous assets, their exemptions and their tithes, and the crown of its *veto*, and all of these refused to acknowledge this new justice and declared a war of avarice and pride upon the nation. The indignity of some is no excuse for that of others. The blues' greed being seized upon as an excuse for the disloyalty of the whites,[15] revolution and counter-revolution were soon nothing more than exchanged insults. The ensuing war could therefore not help being a war of revenge and mutual extermination. Koblenz, the Vendée, Quiberon are etched in our memories. Could it have been otherwise? I will admit that I do not see it. It is not my intention there to query the judgment of the Revolution; grievances being the same on both sides, then, cancelling one another out, victory should have paid them no heed and it has brought in a fair judgment by awarding the final verdict to those who had the force.

14. See above, Book Four, Chapter IV and Chapter VIII. [H.M.]
15. *Les bleus* were the Revolutionary Guards of 1793, *les blancs* the royalists. [A.P.]

On the basis of these examples and so many more, which I shall refrain from citing, let us now attempt to arrive at some useful comment.

Whether the subject be the Church or the State, the principles of philosophy or those of religion, the independence of a country or the freedom of its citizens, the rights of the *seigneur* or those of the worker, there is always, deep within war, a yours-and-mine issue raised by that bad advisor, Famine. Anyone delving into the secret heart of things always stumbles upon that intimate cause of war, pauperism, alongside perfectly admissible religious or political promptings. Hence the depravation in military mores and all the licentiousness that follows from it. Formal warfare would be understandable between Greek and Roman, Jew and Gentile, heretic and orthodox, republican and aristocrat, if there were a way of reducing it to pure issues of nationality, religion and government. But what righteous tie, what regard for humanity could there still be between the plunderer and the plundered, the farmer and the pirate, the master and the slave, the property-owner and the *redistributionists*? Here the motive behind the war is shameful and its purpose, criminal. In the light of which, what is the point of formalities? Everyone dubs his adversary the *enemy*, which is tantamount to saying *brigand*. Just as a man afflicted with a disease from birth could not be entirely regenerated in this life, war, being corrupt at the root, is beyond reform.

Now, in order to fix our ideas, let us try to reduce this array of facts down to one simple proposition.

What engenders the anomalies of which warfare offers us a painful display is the presence and connections between two sorts of causes and thus two types of purposes; a political cause and purpose and an economic cause and purpose. Out of this dualism comes all the disruptions of war and the inextricable promiscuity of justice and iniquity, the good and the evil, which shape its character.

Now, philosophy teaches us that in all things, in the governance of society as well as in the sciences, the way to get to the truth and to right is to draw a careful distinction between ideas and viewpoints, separating the causes, identifying the components, examining everything in isolation, and never making any pronouncement about a broad issue before being confident about the particular issues that make it up.

In short, the issue of war and peace is complex: if it is to be resolved, it needs breaking down.

For a start, is that breakdown acceptable? And if so, what is the outcome for war going to be? This is what we shall examine in the next chapter.

CHAPTER III

A Prior Consideration: Politics Subordinated to Economics; the Incompetence of Trial by Strength; the Suspension of Hostilities

Let us look back on the road we have travelled, and, in what amounts to the same thing as far as we are concerned, at the situation in which modern Europe has been placed by the trends in warfare that we have exposed.

Having restored the right of force to its ancient dignity and defined its just limits; having, secondly, acknowledged the legitimacy of the judgment of war, registered the abuses mixed in with such lofty jurisdiction, and set the opinions of the jurists to rights on a host of points, we queried whether a reform of warfare, in terms of its forms and practices, ought not to be our number one priority? Because, following the way we rehabilitated it, there was no sign of its being purely and simply abrogated; the political make-up of States, the laws that govern their preservation and their evolutions would not allow us, and the confusion prevailing in international relations was scarcely calculated to offer us any encouragement to do so.

A reform of warfare, we said, would have its counterparts in all the reforms that, down through the ages, have refreshed and sustained humanity's institutions. Advances in mores and enlightenment carry us in that direction, the conscience of the warrior disposes him to it, and the honour of civilization cries out for it. Is such a reform possible?

In order to shed some light on this subject, we delved into what was the supreme, universal cause of war, a cause of which all political, religious and other pleas successively advanced by the belligerent sides, cannot have been anything more than variations in expression, depending on times, places and mores. And we found that in fact all of war's motives or pretexts reduce themselves to a question of interests, raised by this blight, heretofore deemed ineradicable, pauperism. The whole of our Book Four was devoted to demonstrating this contention.

At first glance, this discovery, as dismal as it is serious, nevertheless had nothing in it to make us despair of a reform. After all, the interests of which

States are merely the protectors and representatives are one thing, and war, the purpose of which is to decide which of all the competing groupings gets to centralize, protect and govern those same interests, is quite another. Consequently, war's austere and immaculate right is one thing, and the spirit of plunder mingling with it quite another. Political economy is no more the realm of fraud and bad faith than politics; so why would war, dealing from on high and from below with the political formulas of economic issues be, of necessity, depraved?

Stripped down to its true principles, the right of war even came to our rescue. As the purpose of the right of war is to settle international disputes by forceful means, one of the basic consequences flowing from it is the distinction that must be drawn between the public domain, the one and only object of conquest, and the private property placed beyond its reach. Hence all these prescriptions of the laws of war: *plunder* is prohibited; *marauding* condemned; *tribute* declared an abusive, mis-application of the law of conquest; no *indemnity* is owed by the vanquished to the victor, other than for infringements of the laws of war; CONQUEST is acceptable only in the sense of purely political annexation; as for the system of *exploitation* at gunpoint, which would tend to become the chief purpose of States and war's ultimate purpose, that would be a caricature of conquest and war reduced to a nonsense. The jurisdiction of force resulting in every country being treated like a tributary by its own government would be the most monstrous of contradictions.

In short, given the care it has always taken in disguising its original cause, and the discretion with which it surrounds itself in economic matters, etc., and the distaste it is beginning to show for extortion and plunder, war has amply demonstrated how plunder runs counter to it and how favourably it would look upon a reform.

Unfortunately, war cannot be dissevered from its cause, since it has no *raison d'être* without that cause. And, since war cannot be untangled from its cause, that is, pauperism, it also cannot be purged of the suspicion of despoilment, because, without despoilment, however disguised, war turns into a nonsense and victory into an enormous deception. War is therefore fatally contaminated and its depravation irresistible; this we have proven logically and with facts, in the first two chapters of our Book Five.

How are we to get out of this predicament now? International disputes only grow and proliferate and we know how unsuccessful diplomacy has been in defusing them. Besides, war is not amenable to reform.

Here we make a proposition as parliamentary as it is philosophical and juridical, a proposition, moreover, that does not at all conflict with the right of force:

Self-evidently, we said, rather than a single problem needing resolution, we have two of them: a political issue relating to the formation, demarcation and dissolution of States, an issue that warfare is supposed to solve; and an economic issue bearing upon the organization of productive assets and the distribution of services and goods, an issue that neither war, nor the State, nor, indeed, religion, have hitherto concerned themselves.

So that, according to our exposition of the cause of warfare, the economic issue predates and outweighs the other and dominates it, it is absolutely necessary that, before entering into a debate on matters of international politics, in which the final decision is the prerogative of warfare, we began by enlightening ourselves on economic relations. Without that, all we would be doing by fighting is going in circles; we will never know our rights in all their fullness; we will remain suspect to one another; we will never even know why we take up arms, why some of us describe ourselves as Catholics, others as Protestants or free-thinkers; why we make up one nationality on this side of the Rhine and a different one on the other side; why, included among our number, there are royalists and why republicans; or whether democracy is freedom or despotism.

This investigation is all the more indispensable in advance of any declaration of war, given that, because of the onward march of revolutions, interests have taken precedence over matters of State. Indeed, what governs the modern world is neither a dogma, nor a faith nor a tradition; not the Gospel nor the Koran, nor Aristotle nor Voltaire; nor is the 1852 constitution, or the 1793 one; it is the BOOK OF RECKONING[16] every page of which is inscribed in large letters with just these two words: on the back, DEBIT; and on the front, CREDIT.

But who is to act as the judge in this preliminary matter? Who will speak with authority in this new science? Where are we to look for solutions, definitions and verdicts? Can the verdict of force, sovereign in matters of State, legislate for economic matters?

Here it seems clear that we must shift to a different jurisdiction. Political economy no more falls under the remit of warfare than religion does. As a science, it is beholden directly to observation and reason; as the purpose or stuff of right, it falls within political or civil right, or, to put that better, it gives rise to a brand new, special right, which we have to acknowledge and establish, just as we have recognized and established the right of force; I refer to *economic right*.[17]

Once economic right has secured recognition, had its purpose defined, its

---

16. *Book of Reckoning*: In accountancy, the old name for the *great ledger* in which the shopkeeper would record all his transactions under the headings *Debit* and *Credit*. [H.T.]

17. See, *De la Capacité politique des classes ouvrières*, part two, "The Development of the labour idea; Creation of economic rights". [H.M.]

parameters outlined, its formulas devised and its relationship with civil rights, political rights and the rights of peoples established, only then will we be able to re-join the political debate cognizant of cause and utility; consequently, we will again then be in a position to defer, if need be, to trial by combat and look to the logic of force. Until then we would be wilfully blind madmen, reprobates in the eyes of nature and Providence, if, once such an incident has been raised, we were to try to disregard it and refer our disputes to the court of arms like we used to.

Given the problem facing every nation, given the universal ignorance looming like the darkness of chaos over ideas of that sort, the conclusion is that all such hostilities must be suspended and an armistice of indefinite duration signed between the powers. It is for public reason, for jeopardized interests, to see to it that this resolution prevails. If they have but the will for it, they have the power to do so.

"Just as the thirsty doe bellows after springs of living water", so humanity yearns for peace. Is it going to secure that oft-promised, and after so many centuries, as yet intangible peace? On more than one occasion the world thought it had it within reach, and every time it has slipped through its fingers. Are we to know a happier outcome now?

I shall refrain from offering any categorical response to such a specific question. The notion of perpetual peace has become a utopia. Besides, years cost civilization nothing and the more we study history, the more we find that, in everything, in rights as well as in science, humanity likes to proceed with caution. Peace has it under its spell; it chases after happiness. But tell humanity that making peace, living happily means that we must first make no more war and you will see hesitation; it has such a horror of negation and is so loath to surrender a single one of its prejudices and be separated from the smallest part of itself.

God forfend that I should preach the sweet virtues and felicities of peace to my fellow men! I too am human and what I like best about man is the bellicose humour that hoists him above all authority, and all love as well as all fatalism, and whereby he stands revealed on earth as its legitimate sovereign, THE ONE who can fathom the logic of things and who is free. I would merely observe that, in these times in which we live, war, in terms of its inner workings, can no longer be embarked upon without some odious suspicion being projected on to the aggressor; in terms of form, it is no longer feasible.

Let me say, first off, that the authentic cause underlying warfare can no longer be disguised and that all the political considerations in which it might try to wrap itself look more and more like *logomachy*.[18] This is also true of the mul-

---

18. *Logomachy*: quibbling over words. [H.T.]

titudes and governments. Would England, say, wage war on behalf of a principle, on behalf of an idea? Well, no! All England cares about is exploitation, as Monsieur de Ficquelmont says, unless a raid upon her shores is involved. Now, every nation has pretty much embraced the English sentiment; they all do their best to ape England's exploitative policy. 1814–1815, a time that ushered in the era of constitutional governments in Europe, was also, for the very same reason, the time when the preponderance of interests came into existence. And the masses fall in line with the thinking of their governments. Like the bourgeois, the proletarian only has any regard for freedom, suffrage and all that flows from it, to the extent that he hopes to benefit from them; this being a point that the 1848 demonstrations and the mores of 1852 should have placed beyond doubt.

The spirit of greed and plunder is the true characteristic of the present day. The poor man exploits the rich one, the worker his employer, the tenant and the farmer their landlord, the entrepreneur his share-holders, exactly the same as the investor exploits and brings pressures to bear on the industrialist, the landlord the farmer and the manufacturer the wage-earner. There is something else that, in the event of another war, offers a good reflection of this antagonism: I refer to taxation, which the poor man would gladly see fall exclusively upon the rich, by means of taxes on luxury goods, progressive taxation, taxes on inheritance, capital, rental income, etc.: and which the rich man strives to visit upon the poor by means of consumer levies, proportional, personal and industrial taxation, etc., etc.

Such a regime cannot last, it amounts to selfishness, dishonesty, contempt for man and for principles turned into maxims and deified. Criticism has long done justice to these idols and we know the costs of worshipping them. At least we have the certainty that politics has now been exposed to daylight and that war, should it spread, reveals its true cause and would only be a lapse back into the ghastliest cannibalism. We glimpsed a sample of this in the manner in which the June 1848 uprising was put down.

In two words, or in a hundred, war is a social war, even between the most honourable nations, and whatever the officially professed motives. It is henceforth nothing but a war for exploitation and property. Suffice to say that until such time as economic right is secured, both between nations and between individuals, war has no other earthly role. Once politics is under the dominion of economics, the jurisdiction of force is temporarily abrogated.

Not that we should misconstrue that jurisdiction, any more than the righteousness of which it is an emanation; quite the contrary. The modern mind, alien to theology, weary of metaphysics, eager for positive ideas and in love with things that can be priced and counted, is all for the glorification of force. Isn't force everything that the materialist world worships – wealth, power, credit, life and beauty? Isn't it labour? War used to be aimed only at the melding or balancing of political forces; now it is a matter of the organization of economic forces. Now, when it comes to solving this new problem, what use would warfare and its bloody court be?

To any intellect heedful of the meanings of history, warfare held its most recent session between 1792 and 1815, in the campaigns of the Republic and Empire. Its precedents date from Valmy, Jemmapes, Neerwinden, Fleurus, Toulon, Montenotte, Rivoli, Aboukir, the Pyramids, Saint-Jean-d'Acre, Novi, Zurich, Marengo, Hohenlinden, Austerlitz, Trafalgar, Jena, Friedland, Bailen, Wagram, Torres-Vedras, Saragossa, Los Arapiles, Vitoria, Borodino, the Beresina, Leipzig, Paris and Waterloo. Its findings were taken on board by Louis XVIII in Saint-Ouen.[19] The constitutional arrangement, an expression of the politics of interests and corollary of the celebrated treaty of 1815, granted it a recess. To be truthful, what it has done since then has not been an act of war but police work. If an effort were made to revive it, war would, as far as the people is concerned, be bereft of ideals and represent a hideous reality. No matter how its soldiery might strive, there are no more haloes for them. Woe, therefore, woe betide him who, mistaking the spirit of the times, would push civilization into further strife! Woe betide the nation that forgets itself and would look to force of arms for what only science, labour and liberty can give it!

Like any magistracy, war has known its abuses of power and its iniquities. Its judgements are teeming with irregularities and appalling violence. But the base remains, though we may forget it in favour of established rights, flawed proceedings, cruelty in its handiwork and the ignominy of plunder. Who today would contend that the verdicts brought in four hundred years ago, in civil or in criminal matters, were unfair and nullified just because the judge was in receipt of sweeteners, because the hearings were secret, the guilty parties subjected to torture and their assets impounded? The same goes for war: whatever it has done for the advancement of civilization stands forever; all the rest is worthless.

Which brings us to the present, and we shall applaud its high deeds; we shall re-read its poems and lionize its heroes. Our task is no longer to set forces in contention against one another but to strike a balance between them. But, at bottom, is that not what war was seeking? No matter how we may look at it, war reached its conclusion in peace; it would be to misconstrue it and insult it if we were to believe it eternal. War and peace are sisters in the dispensation of justice; what battle draws forth from the one, the opposite creates in the

19. Under the Declaration of Saint-Ouen (2 May, 1814), Louis XVIII undertook to introduce a liberal constitution, representative government in the form of two chambers, to guarantee freedom of the press and of worship, a public debt and freely accepted taxation and to regard the sell-off of national assets as final and irrevocable. [H.M.]

other; the basis and the proceedings are the same. War, tasked with measuring powers against one another and with regulating their rights, is an indispensable preliminary joust. All the civilized nations have shown what they are made of; we know what the rest are worth; their weakness spares them from judgment. The test has now been conducted and the experiment is at an end. Political balance is affirmed: it is up to economic science and the arts of peace to come to a conclusion.

CHAPTER IV

The Final Objections of Militarism

Now at last we know what to think of war; we can flatter ourselves that our knowledge of it is extensive. The theory and the practice, the noumenon and the phenomenon, the principle and the purpose, the cause and the pretexts, the rule and the abuse, the good and the evil, the grandeur and the misery, creation and destruction, progress and decline, contradiction and logic; we have said it all. We know that war has proved necessary, needed for the sake of justice and the education of the human race; principles and deeds have come together to teach us that. We know too, with as much theoretical certainty, backed by the inklings of a realization, that we are dealing with a time in history when war, having run out of steam, should leave the stage, lest humanity suffer a disastrous degradation. The final outcome therefore being in favour of right, we can, after so much conflict and so many ills, pride ourselves upon our past and assert ourselves as the embodiment of divine justice, which manifests itself equally through the verdicts of warfare and the creations of peace.

However, since the hypothesis of a perpetual peace always relies, as has been said, solely upon a theoretical "given"; as we can never state, in fact, that the state of peace has been finally attained, doubt continues to loom over our minds, all the more speciously, in that it avails itself of a tradition of some seven or eight millennia and in that the considerations upon which it is based are not lacking a certain truth.

"1. The sceptics tell us that the notion of everlasting peace springs from the inconveniences of every sort that are entailed in war, and which have resulted in its having been regarded down through the ages as the most horrific scourge. Stretching back to the beginning of the world, poets, theologians, philosophers and economists and, above all, women, have been of one mind in cursing war and seeing it as one of the testimonials to human malice and a sign of heavenly vengefulness. But that argument, built upon feminine dread,[20] and fulsomely

---

20. The seeming emasculation of French society was a permanent preoccupation for Proudhon. Saint-Simonianism romantic pantheism was a symptom of this "feminisation" of society. In the final months of his life his ramblings on this subject became increasingly

expanded by a false morality, has no influence today. Warfare, as articulated in its authentic idea, could not be held to be an evil. It is a form of justice, the sovereign act of the conscience of peoples and, as far as the warrior is concerned, the instant of supreme happiness.

"Without doubt, warfare is teeming with abuses: just like the ordinary courts, there are flaws in its proceedings, what we might describe as the invalidations of victory; it gives rise to a host of prevarications. But, as you yourself have conceded, it has that in common with all of mankind's institutions, and with every one of nature's creations. Like the natural world, the social world is flawed in its achievements, a blend of good and bad, beauty and ugliness, of virtue and vice, order and disorder; does it follow from that that we should have condemned society, family, State, marriage, property, justice and man himself as evil? Is life evil because it is often afflicted with diseases and ends in death?

"2. War is taken to task for its inglorious origins, the pauperism endemic in humanity, or, in less scathing terms, the absence of economic equilibrium. We grant those origins, there being no way of denying them without blatantly lying. What anti-war implications might this have? That in the initial stages all things are laboured, clumsy, often ignoble and sometimes blameworthy. The same could be said of any legislation, any institution, all justice, be it civil or criminal. Marriage started out originally as thuggish fornication, not to say rape. Is marriage regarded as any the less unblemished for all that? As to the hypothesis, tacitly embraced by the adversaries of the regime of war, that an economic constitution of humanity, which would balance forces, would extinguish pauperism and, by suppressing the cause of war, abolish the thing itself: that is a utopia that every civilization, and every period in history has passed down to the next, the same way as they pass down dreams of brotherhood and equality and there is no need for us even to refute this.

"3. A more serious reason, if there were any basis to it, would be the one that grows out of the subordination of the political idea to the economic idea. There is no doubt about it that the importance of economic interests has become, over these last three centuries, colossal; and there is no denying that the participation in government of the masses, bourgeois and plebs alike, has been the consequence of this everywhere. The steering of States has become more complicated and harder; more than ever before, politics has drifted away from the old *raison d'état* maxims; it has had to devise other rules for itself and to rely more on the laws of the useful and the prescriptions of right. Does it follow from that that politics is in actual fact subordinated to the economy? Not at all.

derranged, suspecting De Herricourt's writings were a front for a Saint-Simonian conspiracy against him. See Pierre-Joseph Proudhon, *La Pornocratie, ou les femmes dane les temps modernes* (Paris: Lacroix, 1875). [A.P.]

As the preferences of the people have been consulted more, initiative coming from the top has strengthened to the same extent. Among other evidence, we might cite the trend towards centralization, a feature common to all the States in Europe. The principle of division, which is the principle of economics, is countered by the principle of concentration, which is the principle of politics. The one summons up the other; which amounts to saying that, if labour is the condition of a nations' existence, warfare is the form and condition of States and as a result it retains its predominance and is never-ending.

"4. The argument based on progress no longer holds true. Never-ending war! The cry goes up. The slave has gained his freedom, the man and the citizen have asserted their rights, the nations have exercised their sovereignty. The tax-payer votes on taxation; the mercenary can become master; woman is almost man's equal; so why would nations not move on from the state of war to a state of definitive peace? As if progress consisted of developing beings along lines that run counter to their nature, rather than abiding by their nature! In the preceding examples, the transition derives from the very nature of being and its laws; it is what philosophy, jurisprudence and war itself – through the verdicts that it has been called upon to deliver – have established. But where is the proof that humanity, having warred for seven or eight thousand years, and being increasingly warlike, has to undergo a sudden alteration of its nature and, in under one generation, just because it has equipped itself with railways, lending institutions, electrical telegraphy, must move on, without further ado, from that chronic state of war to a hitherto unknown and wholly indefinable state of peace?

"5. Such progress is allegedly a necessity, on the basis that conquest is useless from the point of view of profits. We are told that pillage, bearing the mark of infamy and, with tribute no longer justifiably extracted from conquered populations, war's material aim, the only one that has a bearing on its cause, vanishes, and war becomes purposeless. A moment's consideration and governments will unanimously proclaim everlasting peace.

" – But why should we not look upon this fiscal nonsense of conquest as a step forward in the morality of war instead? War is misrepresented when credited with knowingly and necessarily acquisitive tendencies. Plunder, enslavement, tribute, exploitation itself can disappear without war thereby ceasing to be a condition of human existence. Is its role as a deliverer of justice over? Has it run out of issues to be referred to its court? Nationalities, the amalgamation of peoples, miscegenation, natural or agreed borders, federations, centralizations, the creation of new States, religious transformations, the economic agitation that pits all the classes in society against one another; the balancing of the continents, their exploitation and their policing; is there not enough there to sustain war for forty centuries? Parliamentary rule is still only in the trial stages; on its own, it has enough to keep armies busy for fifty years. And when we consider that, where such ideas are concerned, questions generate further questions and so on into infinity, but none of them soluble by ordinary arbitration procedures, since nations, mindful of their sovereignty and their independence, reject that: oh, to be sure, there are no grounds for thinking that war will find itself redundant. No matter how delicate one's nerves and feeble one's mind the risk is going to be, rather, that we will faint at the sight of the rivers of blood and mountains of corpses the future promises.

"6. Time and again it is said: One question overrides all the others and that is the economic question. We must finally get to grips with it; it is all the more inescapable in that, once this issue has been broached, all the rest are reduced to mere pretexts and bad faith pretexts at that. Now, this is a matter that plainly does not fall within war's remit. Therefore, war must first be postponed until the issue raised has been resolved; then, in the event that a solution can be arrived at, and the cause generating war effectively done away with, war needs to offer its resignation.

"This is the sophistry of the prosecuting counsel. Accepting that objection would reverse the order of justice; we shall prove as much by using an analogy borrowed from political economy itself.

"Agriculture certainly falls under the remit of political economy. As an industry it is not covered by civil law. However, if the soil is to be cultivated, it must first belong to someone. No ownership, no cultivation; the starting-point for subsistence. All the economists are agreed on this. Now, who decides where ownership lies in this dispute? The civil courts. Is the judge about to look into whether economic right outweighs civil right here? No: he will ascribe the land to the rightful owner and tell him to cultivate his fields howsoever he pleases, in accordance with science or as his pleasure dictates.

"The same goes for matters of sovereignty. They require resolution independently of the wider economic issues connected to it, or, indeed, which brings them into being. As a result, economic relations between nations are governed by amiably concluded trade treaties. But, just as the cultivation of the soil presupposes ownership, treaties presuppose sovereignty, which, if brought into play, promptly becomes subject to war's judgment.

"7. Do those who, after the manner of the Abbé de Saint-Pierre, peddle the idea of perpetual peace and hold innocent congresses in its honour, take it on board that the notion of peace is a negative one, inorganic in its nature and synonymous with inertia and nothingness? As societies currently stand, in a state that you yourselves acknowledge has already lasted for six to eight thousand years and which the average human being takes for granted, what is peace?

An arbitrary or fortuitous *interlude* in warlike activity; nothing more. It cannot be thought of otherwise, on the basis of the facts. Bestowed or won, or indeed imposed upon the belligerents by necessity and the exhaustion of their forces, peace is, to tell the truth, merely war's silent affirmation. In terms of ontology and phenomenally speaking, it has no other value. In short, peace is war at rest; is that not something to be shouted from the rooftops?

"You speak of the *balance of forces* as peace's special handiwork. This is a conception of your mind upon which we can offer you our compliments. By balancing forces, peace would become something halfway between being and non-being; it might not be death, but it would not yet be life either. For if the forces are balanced, if they are no longer being expended, absorbed, assimilated, joined, transformed, then in actual fact, they no longer act; war having ground to a halt, humanity dies and the world ends. You have described war as a ghastly prejudice, the daughter of pauperism, mother of theft and murder. True, your peace may claim to be immaculate: it is a mummified corpse.

"8. Finally, as the pacifists have it, war may well be the law of the animal world; that it should become the law of the moral world is repugnant. We can conceive of its marking the transition, the painful transition, from the first of those worlds into the second and accept that argument; as an organic, definitive state, war implies contradiction.

"That difficulty is resolved in advance by what you yourselves have stated, that war is a form of justice and thus deals in morality. Weaklings [*femmelettes*] ask how beings blessed with reason can even think that they are doing themselves honour by engaging in such terrifying combat. Instead, they should be asking how, if the world is made up of forces, how those forces, interacting with one another, are consequently in contention with one another. Because the interplay of forces bears no resemblance to the dancing of the muses who, in their harmonious chorus, pass one another, link up with one another, retreat, join up again, without their deft, rapid movements generating any strains or collisions. Forces do nothing for show; of necessity, their actions bring about an outcome; for this is happen, they must collide with each other, break each other, devour each other. Only in those circumstances are they productive.

"War is the natural state of the human race; war is life. Peace, a true peace, universal and perpetual, would spell death. All peoples were organized for warfare early on; we know of none organized for peace. On this point, the practical reason of the nations is in tune with their instinct: As the famous Roman adage goes: if you want peace, prepare for war: *Si vis pacem, para bellum*. Indeed, there is no peace but for the strong and only as long as he stays strong; he finds rest in victorious force. But force is used in rest and in action alike; it needs gymnastics if it is to recuperate. The history of nations is little more than the narrative of their battles; peace is featured there only in the form of brief truces. What peace was ever more widely hailed, even by the vanquished, than the peace of 1814? And for the past few years, not just the French, but the Germans, Italians, Swiss, Hungarians, the Russians, and all the nations signatory to the treaties have been competing with one another in damning the proceedings of the Vienna Congress, monuments to the greatest, most glorious peace ever made between men. Is it not a fact that, ultimately, peace is never anything more than a dream: *Dicebant: Pax, pax et non erat pax?*[21] As soon as peace becomes drawn out, populations grow restless as if about to perish, as if civilization was defaulting upon its destiny, that is, moving on from discovery to discovery, from battle to battle.

"Hence these queer notions whereby mysticism and empiricism join hands, but which testify to a reason superior to that of the philosophers, to wit:

"That war is part of God's plans and part of the order of Providence;

"That through peace, societies are corrupted and that they are regenerated by blood;

"That perpetual peace, like the supreme good, is an absolute, an other-worldly thing;

"That man's earthly destiny is to make war on his neighbour, given that he can never, by science, be delivered from all doubt and all dispute or, by wealth, all discomfort;

"That the contrary would suppose a metamorphosis of ideas, passions, characters and mores, which there is no reason to anticipate happening;

"That it is therefore not wrong to see the profession of arms as the noblest one, since it best expresses the godliness of our nature;

"As a result, that the hypothesis of an everlasting, unwavering peace is a dangerous error that runs counter to religion, morality, all traditions, and is subversive of all hierarchy as well as of all discipline and has already, under the designation of *quietism*, been condemned by the Church of Jesus Christ.

"Let us therefore boldly play our part: and, without philosophizing so much, which is unwholesome in a being whose destiny is to act, let us show that we are men, come what may.

"When the secret power steering all creatures, God or demon, towards an unknown end, has decided that we must fight, no reason, morality or charity can stand against it: war is inevitable. The immorality then would reside in the desire to escape it. Let us, then, wage that war generously, swiftly and well, and let us seek only to discover honour in defeat and victory alike. The evil does not reside in the infliction or suffering of death; it lies in living in craven abjection.

---

21. *Bible*, Jeremiah, 8:11. Saying: "Peace, peace, when *there is* no peace". [P.S.]

"On the other hand, should that very same power determine that there has been enough bloodshed, be it satisfied or sated, peace in turn becomes a forced conclusion. No more conquerors, no more heroes: everything conspires to have arms laid aside. Prides turn flabby, hatreds soften, courage can be stilled and hitherto inexorable interests slacken; the previously incompatible ideas for which we fought turn conciliatory. As if by magic, contradiction has disappeared. Therefore, let us make peace and let us savour it without woolliness or illusion".

CHAPTER V

Objections Answered: By its Very Evolution, it is War that Resolves Itself in Peace. The Transformation of the Antagonism

I believe I have now, conscientiously and with a sincerity of expression which they would doubtless not receive elsewhere, set out all the objections that might be raised today against the hypothesis of an unlimited truce, I refuse to say definitive pacification, for we have no way of knowing the setbacks to which civilization is susceptible, which is enough to satisfy theory and interests alike.

Straight off, the reader will note that these objections derive their strength exclusively from the thoroughgoing study we have made of war. Indeed, up until such a critique came about, war was as likely to trigger lamentation as to inspire panegyrics; but it could not find room for an authentic debate. No one was in a position to attack it, any more than they could defend it, in philosophical terms. It was, as I have said, a mystical, godly thing. It was endured and it disappointed; or, in the intoxication of triumph and making a virtue of necessity, we gloried in it. But, as a result, it never occurred to anyone to look upon it as permanent, or as transitory. War was beyond the appreciations of men.

Now that the mystery has been penetrated, or nearly so, and now that events appear to be tilting in the direction of peace, then, understandably, reasoned objections in favour of the perpetuity of war are coming forward. Those objections rely upon the very same facts as made us believers in peace; on the previously denied right of force, which we have re-established; on the justice-delivering quality that we have acknowledged in warfare; on the non-accidental but positive role that it has played in our civilization; they are primarily driven by this consideration, that as peace cannot be established permanently, other than by means of the abolition of the very cause of war, that is, pauperism, such a revolution is beyond human wisdom and ought to be regarded as a utopia.

In order to answer that line of argument, which is certainly not easily done, since society is always in a state of war and since war has a six-thousand-year foothold, whereas peace is still at the project stage, a prospect, then, as I see it, rather than wearing ourselves out with the objections, we should attack the enemy in his stronghold and march directly upon his capital which, once it falls, will deliver up all the rest to us. Now, that capital, the fundament of all of militarism's arguments, is nothing but the law of antagonism, which we ourselves have acknowledged (see Book One, Chapter VI) as a universal law of nature and humanity, a corollary of the law of justice or of balance. With the law of antagonism explained, everything is explained: the warfare thesis becomes the peace thesis.

Like the world of nature, the world of society is built upon forces.

These forces are of themselves expansive, invasive and thus opposing and antagonistic; they live and develop at one another's expense and are productive only insofar as they use one another up. Such is the great law of creation, which is at the same time the law of the preservation and reproduction of beings.

Believers in the everlasting character of war therefore reach for this overall theory of forces, the antagonisms between them and their mutual absorption. They say: "Humanity, like nature, is always in the making, always being renewed: it is through war that it renews itself. Talk of peace is the affirmation of decadence and death".

But, before making such affirmative pronouncements about humanity's warrior future, we would be well-advised to be sure of two things: 1. The sort of creativity sought by warfare; 2. Whether the antagonism of forces, which we have gauged to be beyond reform in its present condition, may not be liable to some sort of alteration, which would merely be the actual end towards which war strives.

Because, and our adversaries are of this opinion, antagonism only has value in relation to the creativity of which it is the agent, every time war breaks out between two powers, it is with a view to a new state of affairs, which, in the providential order, is to replace the previous one, whether it involves the formation of a new State to replace the others, or whether the war is simply designed to determine their boundaries and their relationships. But what, broadly speaking, is war's purpose? Over the past three thousand years we have seen it shift from formation to formation, from reorganization to reorganization, from revolution to revolution. States and countless nationalities have been swallowed up by this struggle. Does war therefore not have some loftier purpose, or are we to believe that it is caught up in a never-ending cycle, destroying and replacing for the sheer pleasure of replacing and destroying?

Besides, if war is truly creative and fruitful, none of what it destroys, or rather, transforms needs go to waste. The same applies to war's creations as to chemical compositions or decompositions; everything should revert to a balance; not a single atom can go astray. In that regard, and independently of the objections we have raised regarding breaches of the laws of war, we have to ask ourselves whether war does what it does well; whether there is no wastefulness in its handiwork, and, thus, whether its modus operandi is, in that respect, beyond reproach, and whether we might not need to amend it?

We are entitled to pose these questions to our adversaries since they arise out of their own principles and could not be omitted without confusion or bad faith. Now, due to the fact that we are posing such questions, it is plain that we have reverted to the hypothesis of pacification, being, if not absolute, then at least unlimited; which we need to demonstrate with a depiction of war's evolution.

Therefore, I say that war's goal, or to put it another way, the purpose of the antagonism within humanity, is to bring about and ensure the absolute triumph of justice, in short, of civilization; but I would add that, in order to bring this higher creation to fruition, antagonism in its current form – war – is powerless; it mishandles what it sets out to do and it has now become vital, not just to subject it to reform, but to bring about a thoroughgoing transformation of it.

And I put this proposition to the test by noting that war, from the point of view of every aspect of its development, ends in a self-transformation which I describe as peace.

From the vantage point of *Right*, of which it is the most solemn and incorruptible representative, War takes us through this range of rights: Right of force, right of war, rights of people, political rights, civil rights, ECONOMIC RIGHT, etc. (see Book Two, Chapter XI). Now, as these days economic rights raise an issue that needs settling ahead of any fresh clash between the powers, and with war having declared itself not competent to resolve such an issue, it is clear that an agreed armistice, of indefinite duration, should first be signed by all States, lest they lie their way into war, trespass against its law and drag it backwards.

The vantage point of *Revolutions*. – Humanity, guided and judged through war, has passed through a series of several stages, and it is important to grasp their overarching tendency: the rule of castes or of slavery; the system of a universal empire, of which the Jews dreamt and of which the Romans made a reality; the theocratic or feudal system; the system of divine right monarchies, for which that of the constitutional monarchies was substituted. Currently, we have the working plebs supplanting the capitalist, landowning and patentee bourgeoisie and who makes its appearance by these two mottos: *Right to work* and *Universal Suffrage*. As to the latter movement, we are still only in the early stages. But who cannot see even now the profound incompatibility between the state of affairs currently in the making and the system of warfare that characterizes divine right monarchy and feudalism? Is it not patently obvious that, as we saw just now, with war drifting further and further away from the rights of force, and through the acknowledgment of new rights, curtailing its own imperium, that, likewise, we are seeing it narrowing even further by steering civilization away from caste rule towards the rule of freedom and economic equality?

As far as nineteenth century Europe is concerned, what is the over-arching issue? No longer is it religion and tolerance, the unity of the Church and its alliance with Empire; nor is it the monarchy, aristocracy or democracy; nor is it centralization, nor political decentralization, nor European equilibrium, nor the principle of nationality or natural borders. All these issues have their place in the debate, but only as secondary or ancillary issues. Among the contested institutions, there are some – such as the temporal power of the Popes – that are on the brink of disappearing for good; others that seem to be on the rise again, even though there may have been reason, a few years ago, to think that they were coming to an end; examples might be constitutional monarchy and unitary government. Universal suffrage itself, this suffrage that everybody respects, but in which no one has faith, is even now beginning to lose its sheen.[22] The key question, the major concern that takes precedence over all the rest but about which there is a reluctance to say a word, is the economic question. It is on this basis that Napoleon III reigns, whether he is holding back the impatient plebs or shying away from the retrograde logic of bourgeois or clerical self-preservation.

From the vantage point of *International Law*, how can anyone still deny that war has, more or less, finished its handiwork? It is war that has brought us to this international system, that all attacks merely consolidate further and further, and that is customarily referred to by the eminently economic expression, *European balance*. Universal monarchy is unwanted; a hierarchy of States is unwanted; the idea of a confederation or of a European Diet is repugnant; everybody asserts his independence, his nationality, his autonomy. Should Russia be humiliated in Crimea, a new State, detached from Turkey, immediately takes shape on the lower Danube and helps to flank the system from there. Should Austria suffer a loss on the Italian side, an Italian State takes shape, which, if it can survive, will provide fresh assurance of stability. All the old causes of squabbling melt away in the face of mutuality of interests. The July Revolution thought it was working wonders by separating Holland and Belgium, which had

---

22. Throughout his life, Proudhon was an ardent critic of universal suffrage within the parameters of the nation state. His defence of universal suffrage in the infinite overlapping associations of social, political and economic associations of public life, what he called "natural groups", was equally as consistent. For a full discussion of this aspect of his thought, see Anne Sophie Chambost, *Proudhon: L'Enfant Terrrible du Socialisme* (Paris: Armand Collin, 2009).

been united by the 1815 treaties; lo and behold, without the slightest thought of their absorbing each other, they are drawing together and embracing each other. The same is happening with the two Scandinavian States, Sweden and Denmark. Whilst France and England engage in an arms race, mistrusting each other, they go together to visit China and sign a free trade treaty. Trade treaties and customs unions are tending to replace annexations and alliances; between France and Belgium, there is a trade treaty; between the German States, politically separate, a trade alliance. Politics, nowadays means political economy; what would you have war do in that context?

The vantage point of *Conquest*. – Here too war has had its last say. At first it was waged for plunder; then it was waged for tribute and then for annexation. Now what does it have left? Exploitation: that is suicide. It is necessary to disarm, on pain of contradiction, of retrogression. To work!, war tells us; you have done enough fighting. Produce, exchange, learn how to see one another as people and act fairly in your dealings; banish your ignorance, become philosophers, artists even, if you can; I do not get involved in such things. Your business, like your arts and your science, falls outside of my remit.

From the vantage point of *Military Means* – The arms trade is demonstrably an upside-down or subversive industry. Strictly speaking, regardless of the genius deployed in it, there is no art, no craft in warfare. It is for the public to be curious and to study this matter. I wanted to educate myself about this heroic profession for the sake of which every nation maintains nurseries of apprentices and high schools at huge expense; all I could see on every side was industry and still more industry. Our sapper and artillery captains train in the same schools as our bridge- and road-building engineers; there are surveyors, architects, physicians and chemists. Where is the difference between our naval officers and merchant captains? Napoleon I used to brag that he had learnt every trade, from cartwright to book-keeping to transport; he was in need of such polytechnic learning in order to carry out his great works as well as to overcome opposition. In warfare, in fact, there are two things that need to be overcome: man and his industry.

Originally, the weapons of war were merely work tools and hunting gear; the hunter's bow and his pike, the butcher's knife, the harvester's scythe, the blacksmith's hammer, the shepherd's crook. Modern science has added its explosive mixtures, its iron hulls and the full range of its metal-working tools, transformed into bullets and shells against which nothing can stand. The June 1848 insurrection ensured that even the blind could see that a man of industry can, in an instant, turn into a gunner, engineer, tactician or strategist. Over the four days that the fighting lasted, the rebels had learnt how to dig trenches, throw up ramparts, manufacture powder, cast balls, cannons and bullets. In this respect, it can be said that the army only makes progress thanks to industry and that the working classes, should their thoughts turn to revolt, would always have the edge on the gunners and sappers and would trounce every army. In short, war is becoming increasingly industrialized: how could it fail to rely on industry, when it is barely distinguishable from it?

To anyone paying any attention to the overall development of war, it should be plain that the tendency within humanity is not in the direction of the suppression but rather to a transformation of antagonism into, what has, ever since the beginnings of society, been conventionally referred to as PEACE. That prediction is going to become a certainty, if, after having briefly retraced these trends in warfare, we ask war itself to interpret them for us. Here, the historian's reason no longer applies and it is up to the right of war itself to have its say.

The purpose of war is to determine which of two contending powers enjoys the prerogative of force. It is forces in contention, not their destruction; the struggle between men and not their extermination. Outside of combat and the ensuing political annexation, it should refrain from any damage against persons or properties. We need not go on demonstrating these things; the critique we have made of war's forms and its original cause has turned the brightest of lights upon all these points; even our adversaries are coming around to these principles.

From which it follows that antagonism, which we recognize as a law of humanity and nature, does not amount, where man is concerned, to a fistfight or wrestling. It could as easily be a struggle of industry and progress; when all is said and done, in the spirit of war and for the purposes of high civilization that it pursues, it amounts to the very same message: "To the victor the spoils", says War. Or, responds Labour, Industry, Economics; what constitutes the valour of a man, of a nation? Is it not his genius, his virtue, his character, his acquired knowledge, his industry, his work, his wealth, his frugality, his liberty and his patriotic devotion? Didn't the great commander say that in warfare moral force is to physical force what 3 is to 1? Do the laws of war, chivalric honour not teach us in turn that in fighting we should look to our honour and refrain from all insult, treachery, plunder and pillage? So, let us struggle: we do not need to charge with bayonets and fire rifles at each other for that. Just as, through the effect of war, right, exclusively private to begin with has turned into a social right [*droit reel*], so war in its turn must cease to be a private matter and become entirely social [*réelle*]. In these new battles, we will also be required to demonstrate determination, commitment and a contempt for death and the pleasures of the flesh; we will have just as many wounded and bruised; and anybody who is cowardly, weak, uncouth, bereft of courage of the heart or mind, should not expect any less subjection, disapproval and misery. Wage-labour, pauperism and vagrancy, the ultimate shame, await the vanquished.

Therefore, the transformation of antagonism derives from its definition, its operation, its law; and is a product of its purpose. Indeed, antagonism does not aim at destruction pure and simple, unproductive expenditure, extermination for the sake of extermination; its purpose is ever-better production, endless improvement. In which respect, we must acknowledge that labour offers antagonism the prospect of a theatre of operations more vast and fruitful than war.

For one thing, let us point out that in the industrial arena the contending forces are every bit as fervent as on the fields of slaughter; there too we see mutual destruction and absorption. I will even go so far as to say that, in labour as in warfare, the raw material of the battle, its chief outlay, is still human blood. In a non-metaphorical sense, we live off our own substance and, through the exchange of our products, the substance of our brethren. But with this huge difference, that in the struggles of industry the only real vanquished are those who have put up no fight or fought cravenly; which has the consequence that labour provides its armies, and often more than them, with everything that they use up, something that war does not and never could. In labour, production follows upon destruction; forces used up are resurrected again out of their dissolution, with renewed vigour. The purpose of antagonism, which we want to take advantage of, demands that. If things were otherwise, the world would revert to chaos; a day would come when, as at the dawn of creation, there would be nothing left but emptiness and atoms: *Terra autem erat inanis et vacua.*[23]

Napoleon I had glimpsed this truth when he claimed, citing the Romans, that war has to be self-supporting: he stated, "With soldiers, I earn millions; with millions, I raise more soldiers". The great *condottiere* sensed that warfare, if it is to have a meaning, a value, a morality, has to replace its forces as it uses them up. But the way in which he flattered himself that he was resolving the problem was as fantastic as his victories; on the one hand, it was dismissive of the vanquished; as for the supposedly victorious nation, setting aside the reversal in its fortunes that brought it back to the *statu quo ante bellum*, statistics have taught us what twenty-five years squandered on war did to the health and vigour of the French people.

After these general reflections on the law of antagonism, a few words should be enough to refute the objections raised:

a) War, we are told, is justified by its very morality. – Yes, in terms of its idea, which is the right of force; yes, in terms of the purpose implicit in the exercise of that right and which represents the forward movement of civilization. But not in terms of war's cause and its practice; the former pointing an accusing finger at a disorder, which it is beyond the competency of war to set straight;

---

23. *Bible,* Genesis, 1:2. "The earth was without form and void". [P.S.]

the latter being entirely at odds with the law of antagonism per se, which requires that, on being destroyed, forces be replaced. Go ahead and support the idea of never-ending warfare, you are free to think what you like; but stop short of lying about it.

b) And also: War consigned to extinction is a utopia, given that the eradication of pauperism, meaning humanity constituted on economic lines, is itself a utopia. It is like someone arguing that an individual should never die, since he has no known heir. I will concede that we can only come up with an as-yet indefinite notion of the economic arrangement that, I contend, should take over from the reign of politics or war, both of these being expressions, as I see it, of the same thing. In that respect and to that extent, doubt is warranted. But in order to deny movement and the future, we should not make too much of the disfavour into which some socialist theories have fallen. One thing at any rate has come to light, that the religion of war is on its way out, like those of royalty and nobility; and the logic of economic interests is increasingly outweighing *raison d'état*; labour, once regarded as a curse, is now glorified to the same extent as virtue. Labour, once slavish toil, now prevails under the designation universal suffrage; and, some day, it will govern. It has already begun to assume power in the guise of representative government; and is half-way there. I say again that we do not know what is going to happen once universal disarmament has come to pass; but we can rest assured that war has found itself a successor.

c) The importance of political issues, it is observed, grows with that of economic issues; so, it is impossible for economic interests to overshadow government. – Mistake: we have to concede that the growing influence labour wields operates at the expense of *raison d'état*; that influence is moving quicker than the governmental idea, upon which labour inflicts decisive defeats by means of the hindrances it puts in war's way. The 1814–1860 period of history demonstrates that. Now, without war, what is politics reduced to?

d) To insist: Such a profound and sudden alteration in human mores is unprecedented and defies understanding; a tradition so many centuries long does not come to a sudden halt. But who is claiming that it has to happen that way? The peace revolution has been twenty-five centuries in the making. It started with Daniel's famous monarchies, and has not relented in working its way through Alexander's conquests, the Roman Empire and Catholic Christianity. The treaties of Westphalia and Vienna are its two most recent landmarks. War and peace are interlocking; but the travails of the former blind us to the advances of the latter. To put that a better way, war and peace are two different forms of one and the same trend, of one and the same law: antagonism.

e) There is the argument that there are a host of issues that war, the verdict of force, may yet have to settle. – Those issues, once labour has established its preponderance and the laws of economic solidarity have been made known, conquest pronounced pointless, plunder outlawed, become secondary; they are the responsibility of congresses; public reason is sufficient to resolve of them. As for the forces themselves, as we have said, they were fighting on a different battlefield.

f) We have treated war's plea of ignorance of economic issues as an act of bad faith or chicanery. We have been told that it's not war's place to be settling matters of credit, earnings, association, exchange, etc.; but that still leaves one political issue – one might even describe it as an international yearning – to be sorted out, and on it rests the entire edifice of the economy. And that issue falls under war's exclusive remit. Borrowing the very same style, my answer to that is that the *pétitoire*, the one who claims a right to something, is being incessantly reframed and transformed by the *possessoire*, the one in possession. Just as ownership has evolved from Roman *quiritary* rights, war is bound to undergo an even profounder alteration and to fall directly under the jurisdiction of commerce, and the State, transformed by the abolition of the feudal principle and divine right, will tend to assume a purely administrative character and to confine itself to the management of the budget; just the same as international relations are tending to boil down to purely economic relations, finally ruling out any presumption of a jurisdiction of force.[24]

g) Finally, the law of antagonism is invoked once more. The notion of peace, we are told, is negative. Society has been shaped by war, so how could it fall under the law of nothingness? But it follows from everything that we have said that peace does not spell the end of antagonism, which would effectively mean the end of the world. Rather peace is an end to slaughter, an end to unproductive expenditure of manpower and wealth. As much as and more than war, peace, the essence of which had not been well understood thus far, must become positive, real [*réelle*] and formalised. Endowing the law of antagonism with its true formula and its lofty reach, peace offers us a foretaste of what its organic power is going to be. Finally, peace, which clumsy language has thus far made the contrary of war, is to war as philosophy is to myth: the latter is retained for the amusement of children and for the embellishment of literature; it is reason's province alone to direct man's conscience and action.

In short, the hypothesis of a universal and definitive peace is legitimate. It derives from the law of antagonism, the whole phenomenality of warfare, the contradiction between the juridical notion of war and its economic cause, the

---

24. This discussion is first articulated, in the same terms, in *What is Property?* See Pierre-Joseph Proudhon, *What is Property? Or An Inquiry into the Principle of Right and of Government*, trans. Donald Kelley and Bonnie Smith (Cambridge: Cambridge University Press, 1994), 37. [A.P.]

increasingly established preponderance of labour in the direction of societies, and lastly by advances in RIGHT, the right of force, international law, political rights, civil rights, economic rights. War has been the symbol and peace the realization. The establishment of right in humanity is the very abolition of war; it is the organisation of peace. All peoples have welcomed that promise; they have all dreamt of turning their swords into ploughshares and their spears into sickles. So far, the world has known many a temporary peace; in the past two centuries alone, there have been the peace of Westphalia, the peace of Nijmegen, the peace of Utrecht, the peace of Aix-la-Chapelle, the peace of Amiens, the peace of Tilsit, the peace of Vienna. We need PEACE today; the world no longer understands nor wants anything else.

On which conditions are we going to secure that organized peace, the articles of which are not for any power to dictate and the guarantee of which, being reliant on the regulated clash of forces, is superior to all the armies in the world?

Peace cannot gain traction and stand above all infringements by resorting to subscriptions and meetings, with federations, amphictyons,[25] and congresses, as the Abbé de Saint-Pierre used to believe. Statesmen are as impotent as philosophers; the Holy Alliance has failed; no philanthropic propaganda is going to get anywhere. Peace signed at the point of sword is never anything better than a truce; peace devised at a symposium of economists and Quakers would be laughable, like the notorious 'Lamourette kiss'.[26] Only working humanity is capable of putting an end to war, by creating economic balance, which presupposes a radical revolution in ideas and mores.

For the reign of peace to be ushered in, *pacique imponere morem*, we must, to borrow from our evangelical forefather, start with a change of mind, Μέτανοιτε.[27] Step one in this conversion is the cleansing of war of all thought of plunder, by applying to it the ordinance of the Ten Commandments: *Non furaberis*[28]; secondly by understanding our earthly destiny, so well signalled by the stoic maxim: *Sustine et abstine*;[29] and, finally, by abiding by the over-arching condition of democratic and social equality: the laws of production and distribution.

---

25. *Amphictyons*: Name given in ancient Greece to political as well as religious coalitions of states, centring on some sanctuary. [H.T.]

26. ADRIEN LAMOURETTTE (1742–1794), a Constitutional bishop, swore an oath to the Civil Constitution of the Clergy prior to being elected to the Legislative Assembly. In the wake of the events of 20 June 1792, he called for reconciliation between all sides and persuaded his colleagues to embrace one another. The expression "*Lamourette kiss*" has survived as a euphemism for reconciliations lacking sincerity. [H.T.]

27. 'To repent'. [A.P.]

28. 'Thou shalt not steal'.

29. 'To bear and forebear'. [A.P.]

Is that revolution possible? Is it imminent?

My response to that categorical challenge is this:

Neither the metaphysics of the philosophers, nor the compilations of the jurists, nor the expertise of the industrialists, or indeed the protocols of the diplomats and the constitutions granted by the potentates are going to supply us with the means to make a reality of this high hope. The wisdom of individuals, schools, Churches, councils of State is of no avail here. Political and socialist speculation has had its day. War, like religion, and the same as justice and labour, poetry and art, has been a manifestation of the universal conscience: peace will be a manifestation of universal conscience too.

GENERAL CONCLUSIONS

A New Right: A New Mission

THE PHENOMENALITY OF WAR: War is the most profound and most sublime phenomenon of our moral life. Nothing else can be compared to it, neither the imposing celebrations of worship, nor the acts of sovereign power, nor industry's mammoth creations. In the harmonies of nature and humanity, it is war that sounds the mightiest note; it hits the soul like a thunderclap, like the hurricane's roar. A blend of genius and audacity, poetry and passion, supreme justice and tragic heroism, even after the analysis that we have made and the censure we have hurled at it, its majesty leaves us stunned and the more we muse upon and ponder it, the more the heart swells with enthusiasm for it. War, which a false philosophy and an even more false philanthropy, had nothing to show us except a frightening scourge, the explosion of our innate mischief and the manifestation of heavenly wrath; war is the most incorruptible expression of our conscience, the act which, ultimately and in spite of the tainted influences mingling with it, brings us the greatest honour in the eyes of Creation and of the Eternal One.

THE IDEA OF WAR: The idea of war is the same as its phenomenality. It is one of those ideas that, from the moment it appears, swamps the understanding and, so to speak, infiltrates every intuition, every sentiment, and logic designates these ideas as *categories* on account of their universality. War is, indeed, one and trinity, like God, the mingling in a single nature of these three roots: *force*, being the principle of movement and of life and which we can find in the ideas of cause, soul, will, liberty and mind; *antagonism*, action-reaction, the universal law of the world and, like force, one of Kant's dozen *categories*; and justice, the soul's sovereign faculty, the principle of our practical reason, manifested in nature as a *balance*.

THE PURPOSE OF WAR: If we move on from the phenomenality and the idea of war to its purpose, it will lose none of our admiration. The aim of war, its role in humanity, is to set all human faculties in motion, in order to conjure up *right* above and beyond those faculties, to universalize it and, with the aid of that universalization of right, to define and initiate society.

But what is right?

It is here that war, sublime in its manifestations, universal in terms of its idea, juridical and thus providential in its mission, sets us marvelling even more on account of the certitude and, forgive me for saying so, the positivism of its teaching.

THE DEFINITION AND REALITY OF JUSTICE, ACCORDING TO WAR:[30] If we look to the theologians and the philosophers, justice, supposedly, has no positive, actual or organic form within us; it is not a fact. It is the mind's conception of a conventional relationship between persons and interests, but a relationship that only becomes binding upon the will in the light of a higher motive determining it. That motive or prompt, where the believer is concerned, is fear of God; for the unbeliever, economic interest, of course. I shall leave to one side the intermediary, halfway-house systems of utilitarianism and religion.

Plainly, in the eyes of the theologian and likewise those of the rationalist, justice per se means nothing to man; we are masters when it comes to paying it some or no heed, without the essential outcome being either merit or demerit for ourselves. What is more, if interest, the higher motive invoked by Hobbes, sees fit to contravene justice; if serving God, the supreme motive of the Christian, requires the sacrifice of every other human obligation, justice is going to have to be abandoned without hesitation; it would be an act of impiety for someone to prefer his duty over his God, and deceitful for him to prefer that over his interest.

War offers us a quite different notion of justice.

According to our analysis of the right of force, justice is respect for human dignity, in the most widely accepted sense, considered in the round and successively in each of its manifestations. That respect is innate within us; of all our feelings, it is the one farthest removed from animality; of all our affections, it is the most consistent and its operation, which in the long run outweighs any other motive, determines the character and operation of society. As for myself, respect for human dignity makes up what I call my right; where my fellows are concerned, it constitutes my duty.

---

30. Here, Proudhon is summarising some of the theses he had explored in *De la Justice* (1858) and adapting these to his theory of war, on which topic he had touched several times in this major work. "What is there that is more inhuman than war? And yet, it is susceptible to being invested with many of the applications of the principle *Do unto others*, etc., applications which altogether make up the RIGHT OF WAR, two words that howl when yoked together ... The rule of force can never be the rule of right". (VIIIth Study, chap. III, § XVI). "The Right of War is a NEGATIVE JUSTICE, consisting of a sort of an unspoken agreement to be guided by force". (XIIth Study, chap. III, §4, *in fine*). See also *Justice poursuive par l'église*, second part, §3, in fine. [H.M.]

Therefore, justice is not simply a notion of relationship, a metaphysical notion, an abstraction: it is, in addition, a fact of the conscience, and therefore an organic, positive faculty, a reality, like love, ambition, friendship, a taste for the beautiful and luxury, etc.

The consequences of such a realization of justice within humanity are immense.

ACCORDING TO THE DEFINITION OF IT PROVIDED BY WAR, JUSTICE IS SOCIETY'S PRINCIPLE AND PURPOSE: If, as needs saying, justice is more than an abstraction, if it is a power and if war's mission has been to ensure that this power prevails and relentlessly grows between peoples, it follows first of all that justice is simultaneously the principle underlying the law governing our actions, the reason of our lives, and the expression of our happiness.

Hobbes's theory is wrong: our over-riding motive is not selfishness; it is not the preservation of our body and limbs, it is not our interest, be it well or wrongly construed. If we take it as an established fact, that is because justice is, for us, completely different from interest; we are indebted to war for having demonstrated as much.

The theory of the idealists and mystics is as false as that of the utilitarians. Our supreme prompt is not an ideal, unless that ideal be the very ideal of righteousness. We have seen idealism seduce souls, sometimes through the illusion of wealth, sometimes using the lure of carnal pleasures; we have seen it drive society into pauperism, and, through pauperism, tip it into war, only to corrupt that too. That prompt is not love, which is subordinated to justice once and for all through the establishment of the family, the basis of which is paternal authority, the right of force, no less; nor is it religion, since religion which may vary in its forms, always invokes justice, whereas justice itself stands on its own, imposing itself on every sect and remaining immutable; finally, it is not freedom, which is always ardently invoked in times of decadence and despotism, but which cannot exist in the absence of justice, which derives its rule from justice, whereas justice per se is a law unto itself and may even dispense with freedom.

Justice is a driving force and final cause of humanity; this is because it is, as we have explained, not merely an idea, but a power; every power seeks to expand at the expense of its surroundings; justice, being the first of our powers, sweeps the rest before it and subordinates them. And if we seek material proof of that truth, war will supply it. We have seen the evolution of war result, through the consecration of the right of force, in Roman domination, meaning the proclamation of universal right; we then saw the Middle Ages attempting to bring about an initial, half-realist, half-mystical establishment of that right, by means of an alliance between the Papacy and the Empire; we know today that right is not going to be established, once and for all, universalized and accomplished, except by means of the elimination of the religious factor and the acknowledgment of economic right, by which I mean, through the Revolution. Justice, in the context of humanity, is immanent and real; this is the great lesson that war has to offer.

AGAIN, ACCORDING TO THE SAME EVIDENCE, JUSTICE IS THE BASE AND FULCRUM OF ALL BELIEF: If justice is civilization's motivation and end, if it outweighs all force, all dogma, all ideals, it follows that justice is the basis of all belief, just as the right of force is the trunk on which every other right buds and grows, one after another. It is no longer speculative reasoning, natural or revealed theology, a philosophy of nature or of mind that sets the criteria and law for speculative reason, as used to be the case. The nineteenth century discovered its principle and, I would make so bold as to say, its religion, thanks to that enormous, radical shift.

Here War tells us: "Morality, the expression of freedom and human dignity, is free-standing; it is not reliant on any principle; it overshadows all doctrine and all theory. In man, conscience is the higher power, the others serving as its instruments and acolytes. Just as it is not religion that makes man, nor the political system that makes the citizen, but much more man who makes his religion and the citizen who makes his government; moreover, the rules by which you live and your sociability should not be deduced from some idealist metaphysics or theodicy; instead, your understanding should be ruled by your conscience and it is to that conscience that you must look in search of the surety of your ideas and even the proof of your certitude. Justice sits in judgment of dogma the same way as it judges interests. Mortals, follow the example I set for you: just as I render unto force what is force's due, heedless of religions or races, you in turn should render unto genius whatever is genius's due, to labour that which is labour's due, to beauty that which is beauty's due, to virtue, virtue's due. Your rights are not vain concepts reliant on fanciful abstractions: they are real prerogatives linked to real faculties. Justice within you is reality and sovereign thought at once. Which is why, in the future, you will have no religion other than justice: I, War, your first teacher and the greatest of your gods, tell you this ..."

THE RIGHTS OF PEOPLES, ACCORDING TO WAR: Unbending in its logic, in its performance war is not found wanting by its own maxims. In Book Two of this study, we saw how, from the right of force to the right of war, and from the higher principle that justice is immanent within humanity, the expression of its freedom and courage, we can deduce *the rights of peoples*. War deals with nations, not according to the arbitrary categories of some fictitious legislation, but in accordance with their positive or empirical merits; it acknowledges right only where there is a jurisdictional power and quality. Neither nationality, nor legitimacy nor antiquity, nor orthodoxy itself can override it; nationality, legitimacy and orthodoxy are mere words in war's court of justice.

It is to no avail that France has galvanized Italy; to no avail that, under that powerful sponsorship, the remnants of the old people-king relationship were gathered together again into a single State; if the New Italy cannot boast the energy of temperament, the liveliness of conscience that every nation needs in order to establish its sovereignty; if her politics are still the politics of Machiavelli; if, in order to keep her governors in check, she has no recourse other than the dagger; if her superstitious and undisciplined populations shy away from armed service, then Italy has no right to exist, politically. As has been said, Italian nationhood is only a geographical expression; sooner or later, unless a more radical revolution comes to her rescue, she will fall back under the domination of the foreigner. France herself, obliged to step in a second time, would be prompted to partition her in the same manner and in accordance with the same entitlement as Poland was partitioned last century... God forfend that I should hold Italy's cause hopeless by this point! But, in terms of the present hypothesis, who, having wept over this second demise of Italy, could accuse the co-partitioning powers of iniquity? It needs saying and repeating that a nation has no entitlement to be recognized as a power and to enjoy autonomy, the only reason for its existence: it has to command both force and virtue. The iniquity would be to leave a race too innocent, lacking independence, or overly corrupted to sustain political life, to fend for itself, leaving it to await some comprehensive overturning of things: the iniquity would be to affirm that which the right of force would have condemned.

POLITICAL RIGHT, ACCORDING TO WAR: Just as there is no right of nationhood, by virtue of which a nation, merely on the basis that it exists, can stake its claim to sovereignty unless it also possesses force and all the features that go to make up a sovereign nation; so there are no rights of man and the citizen either, by virtue of which the individual members of a country's population can, on the simple grounds of their being men and citizens, demand of their government that it respect all their freedoms. Unless they also possess the qualities that afford the citizen and man force, courage, an understanding of rights, domestic virtues, frugal mores, love of labour and, above all, a staunch resolve to sacrifice life and limb rather than suffer any violation of their dignity, there are no rights. In which respect, political rights merely replicate the maxim of the rights of peoples, albeit on a smaller scale.

Thus, it is no good proclaiming the unity of the human race and expecting to proclaim the abolition of slavery and equality for all before the law on the basis of that semi-physiological, semi-mystical premise. If your serf or slave is by nature incapable of raising himself up to the level of his master; if he cannot struggle with the latter in terms of warlike valour, industry, philosophy and the arts; if, decidedly and despite all instruction, the caste in need of emancipation constitutes, as they say of the black, an inferior variety of men, you will have done nothing for it in awarding it its freedom. Left to its own devices, it will fall into a worse state than before. Civic equality and human brotherhood no more rely upon a metaphysics of right than they do on the sharing of the same sacraments; they rely upon an equivalence of faculties, services and products. What your slaves are clamouring for is not liberation pure and simple; it is tutelage.

Let us follow this reasoning through. There is no point in a newly freed nation, fallen into despotism due to a series of missteps and unfortunate circumstances, bemoaning the harm done it by its sovereign, alleging this sovereign is its agent, elected by its votes; or that he has pledged to respect acquired rights and is only there to watch over public freedoms. If that nation, otherwise brave when faced by the enemy, shows no pride in the face of the master with which it has endowed itself, if selfishness and cowardice have banished public spiritedness from their hearts; if licentiousness and softness have made headway into its families; if wealth, the only ambition, is prized more highly in the eyes of the masses than respect for the constitution and the laws, a nation thus degraded has forfeited its right to be free; the authority that holds it in bondage is being neither ungrateful, nor traitor, but is enacting justice.

In handing down a broad ruling, the *Civil law* could have ensured that all the offspring of the same father receive equal shares to his legacy on the presupposition of an equality that is not found in nature, but which we have a duty to bring about. What it could not do is make the prodigal, the idler, the insane, as deserving in the eyes of public opinion as the thrifty, the hard working and the clever child; that, as a result of their nature they have the same entitlement to right. It is under this light that the code acknowledges the paterfamilias's ability to alter, by means of a will, any abnormality the generality of the law might introduce in practical terms; so true is this that the law is built, not upon abstractions but upon realities, the most senior of which is force.

As political law has a more direct connection than civil law with the right of force, it is also more rigorous. No constitution, no omnipotence could guarantee unworthy citizens a freedom that they have demeaned by their dissolute ways. As power cannot be anything other than the expression of society, and if society is deficient in right, the authorities have to govern by whim. Despotism thereby becomes both the representative and the executioner of public immorality and it will persist until society is converted or sinks into corruption.

WAR'S LEGISLATIVE AUTHORITY AND JURISDICTION:
Following this general review of the essence, reality and advancement of justice
within us; on the initially undetected but now manifest role that it plays as a
principle, prompt and purpose of civilization; on the exclusively justice-delivering character of the new moral order which, overpowering all thought and
knowledge, and indeed posing as a broad philosophy, tends to supplant the old
belief: look how many previously obscure things the study of war has made intelligible! The torch whose sole purpose seemed to be to set things ablaze has
become the lighthouse piercing our darkness from afar.

War is part of the human constitution, but it may no longer be doomed
to be eternal. It is the primary form assumed by antagonism in us, antagonism
being a law of humanity as well as of nature and indispensable to social movement. Thus, we can see war in two different lights: one political and legislative,
the other economic.

Under the first of these lights, war operates as the organ and mandatory
of the most primordial of all rights, the *right of force*. The universal conscience
testifies to that right; without it, the whole edifice of justice crumbles and the
constitution of society, the onward march of civilization and the meaning of religious myths defy explanation. On the other hand, with this right, everything
becomes rational and lucid; we see civilization develop, step by step, by means
of war; the law poses its formulas and all the varieties of right disentangle themselves from one another and define themselves in accordance with the principle
and on the model of the right of the strongest: the right of war, the right of peoples, political rights, civil rights, economic rights, philosophical rights, rights
of intelligence, right to freedom, the right of love and family, and the right of
work.

Moreover, as the special organ of the right of force, war does not extend
its competence beyond issues of force. Which is why, having created the State
as its substitute in the regulation of disputes between private persons, war reserves only the resolution of disputes between States for itself. A terrifying jurisdiction, with no councils, no witnesses, no jury, no magistrate and no hearing;
where the parties are at once their own judges, their own guarantors, their own
advocates. But the judgments of war are no less certain, effective and incorruptible for that. Woe betide any who try to evade it! Woe betide those who
decline to fight, or who, having agreed, try to bend its laws! Victory will do
him no good and, sooner or later, force, aggrieved and scorned, will turn on
him. I shall not rehearse here the causes of the downfall of the first Napoleonic
Empire, overthrown by force, because force had had less to do in its establishment than guile; nor that decisive argument against the Papacy which, holding
spiritual power, and able to command the world of belief and morality, soon

declined and found itself doomed to lead a wretched existence, because it did not know how to, could not or would not wage war and which, in the name of belief, scorned the jurisdiction of force. Let us make do with remembering that war is the best form of judgment there is and that it is not for any other authority, whatever it may be, to confirm or query its verdicts. The annexation of Savoy and Nice to France, of Tuscany and The Marches to Piedmont, were, in the wake of the victories at Magenta and Solferino, able to dispense with the formality of universal suffrage.[31] What does citizens dropping their ballot papers into a box matter when set alongside that of soldiery shedding their blood!

By creating right in humanity and making the study of such right a positive, objective science, war has spoken louder than all revelation and its authority surpasses even that of the Gospel itself. The law of love has produced nothing comparable to the creations that have grown out of the right of force. It is thanks to war that at last we know, contrary to the messianic idea and contrary to the suggestions coming from the evangelical fraternity and Papal feudalism, that the human race's political constitution cannot be a monarchy, nor a catholicity of nations; nor a federation or community of States gathered together under the authority of a Diet; nor a hierarchy of principalities and kingdoms such as was devised in the Middle Ages following the compact between the Papacy and the Empire. A universal monarchy would be the fusion of all forces and thus the negation of antagonism, utter stagnation; a universal federation would result in those same forces being reduced to inertia by their submission to a common authority; the federative system is only feasible between small States combining for the sake of mutual defence against attacks from larger ones; finally, a universal hierarchy would result in a universal compression, which would always imply the cessation of antagonism and consequently death. The political system for humanity is a general balance struck between mutually solicited and constrained States, wherein freedom and life are constantly produced by their interaction with one another, I might even say the threat they pose to one another. That balance is PEACE, initially negative, which we shall see consolidating and flourishing once we have acknowledged the other side to war.

POLITICAL ECONOMY ACCORDING TO WAR: For the upkeep of his body and the expansion of his mind, man is compelled to feed both;

---

31. The plebiscite was one implementation of the Napoleonic principle of the people's sovereignty. In its proclamation to the inhabitants of the "ceded" territories, the French government posed the question in these terms: The circumstances in which this redrawing of the border comes about are so extraordinary that they do no injury to any principle and establish no dangerous precedent. It is being done "neither by conquest nor by insurrection ... but rather by the freely given consent of the legitimate sovereign, supported by popular acclaim". (Quoted by Seignobos: *Histoire de la France contemporaine*, published under the supervision of Lavisse, vol. VII, 119–20). [H.M.]

consumption, material and moral, can be considered his primary purpose. Now, man can only consume whatever he can obtain by means of daily endeavour; so *labour* is his second purpose. But on average such labour only secures him his bare necessities; *poverty*, there is our third purpose. Labour, sobriety and prudence; liberation from the senses and the ideal; that is our law. More than a warrior, man is, in accordance with the predictions of nature, an ascetic. It is so that we can properly sustain ourselves that we have been gifted with the conditions of labour and of poverty, that conscience in its turn, the very same conscience that affirms the right of force, imposes a fresh law upon us, that we share services and products on as equal a basis as possible, without trespass against the dignity and rights of any. So that justice appears as our fourth and final purpose. As to the manner in which economic justice comes to pass, in other words the fair distribution of services and products, war has pointed the way for us. There will still be a struggle or competition between forces: not a bloody, armed struggle, but rather a struggle involving labour and industry, in accordance with the principle that, just as the hero proves himself in the fray, so the worker can be judged by his handiwork.

Thus, human life, set by war on the path of justice, subjected to the laws of labour, sacrifice, frugality, equity, can be described as an ascent from nature to the spirit, an ascent that is nothing but the evolution of freedom itself.

But, swept along by his senses, seduced by earthly pleasures, deceived by the illusion of wealth, slave to his idealism, intoxicated by his opinion of himself, man misunderstands his law and fails in his purpose. He holds labour in contempt; he cannot moderate his appetites, nor curb his imagination, nor respect his own dignity in that of his fellow men; he enters life's arena with outlandish inclinations, as Spinoza might say, with inadequate ideas. From that point forwards, war is depraved; it becomes suspect to everybody and irredeemably disloyal. Under the spur of pauperism, war switches from being the bearer of justice to being theft and murder; depending on how civilized it is, its purpose now is plunder, tribute, dispossession and eventually the exploitation of man, victor and vanquished alike. Reduced to absurdity by this unseemly misrepresentation of *conquest*, war loses all its prestige and becomes impossible. A brand-new problem arises outside of the parameters of war's jurisdiction; the economic problem, the resolution of which, by transforming antagonism, gives birth to and makes a reality of peace.

Thus, despite the pauperism that perverts it and, indeed, driven by that pauperism, war, at all times leading to a just conclusion, leads us to disarmament. It led us there recently by means of the balance between nations; now it is leading us there again by this inescapable position of the economic problem, regarding which war itself is at pains to declare that it has no competence.

THE PARTY OF DEMOCRACY AND ITS APPROACH TO WAR:
For any man of good faith that has followed war's progress through the various
parts of this study, it must be apparent that the trend of events leads in the direction of peace. I will even go so far as to say that the advent of this decisive
pacification cannot be far off; in all likelihood, peace will be the handiwork of
the nineteenth century. But it is no less true that, at the time of writing, peoples
and governments seem to be bent on war more than ever; you would think that,
before heading back to Hell, the relentless Bellona has demanded one last sacrifice. Blood must be spilled...

To whom is this thirst for carnage, in contradiction with war's most authentic tendencies and conclusions, to be credited? I shall leave it up to my
readers to assess the policy of the powers and I shall refrain from saying anything here that might shock governments. But allow me to deplore the fact that
one faction of the French democracy, pushing the government into war out of
some misconstrued enthusiasm for revolution, is letting down its idea, France's
true mission.

All outstanding issues can be boiled down to just one: the Peace of Vienna.

Certain more or less official mouthpieces of the democratic movement
have felt it their duty to THANK the imperial government for having *torn up
the 1815 treaties*, as if this were an act of heroism, necessary for the French people's security and glory. Through that declaration alone the aforesaid mouthpieces of the democracy have proved that words meant everything to them and
ideas nothing. They have given the government they adulated reason for laughter if not embarrassment.

It is fashionable in France, a sort of commonplace for which the most distinguished minds and the best pens reach, to claim that the 1815 treaties no
longer apply. As for myself, I will admit that I see the very opposite. The 1815
treaties strike me as sturdier than ever; and denying their existence and authority seems to me to be almost as laughable as denying the existence and authority
of the revolution.

A distinction needs to be made between two things in the 1815 treaties as in
any treaty coming at the end of a long war: 1. The basic, generic and nevertheless
indestructible idea produced by events, and which make up the substance, explicit or implicit, of those treaties; 2. The more or less arbitrary enforcement of
that notion, which is therefore always open to revision.

The idea behind the 1815 treaties is, first of all, the balance between powers,
ensuring that all political supremacy, all protectorates and consequently all wars
of ambition or conquest are rendered impossible; secondly, by way of a guarantee of that balance, the establishment of constitutional rule in every State.
In spite of all the accusations and all the reticence, this is what underlies the

1815 treaties; what the coalition of peoples who rose up against Napoleon in 1813, on the one hand, and the tradition of '89 on the other, insisted had to happen. Considered in terms of their underlying intent, the 1815 treaties merely carried on and expanded upon the thinking of '89; they did civilization greater service than the imperial suzerainty at which Napoleon aimed. Thanks to those treaties, the France of '89 can boast of having achieved victory once and for all. – As to the enforcement, the fact is that it left something to be desired, not just where France was concerned, insulting pre-emptive measures having been taken against her, but also the continental nations, several of which offended by the partition and most of which were slow to come into possession of the rights and freedoms promised to them.[32]

It is up to us to examine, from the dual angle of principle and enforcement, whether the 1815 treaties can or should be TORN UP as the Jacobins are clamouring for; or whether the right course, instead, would be to ask that certain details of them be amended, meaning that they should be reinforced.[33]

Does the party of democracy reject the principle of balance, or of *countervailing forces* demonstrated by Ancillon fifteen years ahead of the Vienna Congress, and which became the basis for public law in Europe? Joke, if you like, about that stability that must not be mistaken for stagnation; the fact is that no power would dare challenge it. That would be tantamount to suggesting that it was out to overrun the continent: which it would not dare do.

Does the party of democracy repudiate the principle of representative government, the chief creation of '89? That would be to deny the revolution. For all its worship of authority and strong power, it does not go that far.

Therefore, the party of democracy affirms the thinking behind the treaties; it does not want to see them torn up; instead, it asks that they be respected. The treaties of 1815 are there, as are the 1648 treaties; the thinking behind them has made inroads into the conscience of the peoples; they have been embraced by history and civilization. To talk about tearing them up is to step back two centuries in time.

Let us move on to enforcement and see what has been done over the past forty-five years.

As far as France is concerned: After 1814, France continued with the social renewal that was interrupted by the great emperor's victories and conquests, and thanks to a special provision in the 1815 treaties, was the first to enjoy a representative system. That arrangement continued up until 1852 when, for

32. For an exploration of this matter see, *De la Justice dans la Révolution et dans l'Église*, by P-J. Proudhon, fourth book of the Belgian edition. [P-J.P.]

33. For a fuller discussion see Proudhon, *Si les Traités de 1815 ont cessé d'exister* (1863). [A.P.]

reasons that we need not go into, it was suddenly restricted to the institutions and freedoms of 1804. In this respect, we might state that the 1815 treaties had been torn up. Is that what the democracy party thought it was giving thanks to Napoleon III for? As to the surveillance visited upon us by the Congress of Vienna, that was ended back in 1830 and 1831, first of all because of the conquest of Algeria and then on account of the creation of the kingdom of Belgium and the demolition of the fortresses erected along that border – Courtrai, Menin, Philippeville, etc. The credit for having made these amendments to the treaties belongs to the Restoration and the July government. The imperial government made another one by annexing Nice and Savoy; we are entitled to state that that was not such a happy move if the compensation for that annexation, as far as foreigners were concerned, was Italian unity.

As far as other countries are concerned, we can see that the treaties are being strengthened on a daily basis, first of all, through the spread of parliamentary rule and then by State-formation, by means of amalgamations and alliances which increasingly assure the balance. Thus, just a few years ago, we had the Danubian provinces established; then, the better to contain both Austria and France, there was a move in the direction of establishing a united Italy; the various States belonging to the German Confederation tend to group together into a German Empire; and Belgium and Holland, harking back to the thinking of 1815 but each retaining its individuality, are drawing as close to each other as they can. Belgium had torn down her border posts; now here she is fortifying Antwerp. Whose fault was that? In my view, it would be a serious mistake to imagine that Austria is on the verge of break-up, because her component peoples are, on the one hand, asserting their national rights and reminding the emperor of the empire's federative principle and, moreover, calling for reforms: in each instance all the population is doing is referring back to the spirit of the treaties. They should be pitied if they thought otherwise. Peace is being organized right across Europe under the aegis of the right of war, and the handiwork of 1815 is being completed and consolidated, pending the definition of economic rights. It may be that in this drive towards a balanced peace more than a reorganisation in the constitution and demarcation of powers takes place, that such-and-such a dynasty pays the price for its pig-headed opposition to progress with its decline; what does that do to the treaties? Imagining that all this is being done for the greater glory of the Bourbons or to humiliate Bonaparte would be a petty interpretation and do small honour to the nations represented in Vienna.

As a result, the 1815 treaties have created a new, indestructible European order of things, that time and experience may learn to improve, and infringing it can only be to the detriment of peoples and of civilization.

Amid this swirl of regeneration, is France now to agree that war's bugle call

should be heard? Right now, what does she have to offer the world? Is it freedom? But that can be found everywhere and, here, only to a lesser extent. Is
it representative government? But we have, of our own free will, given up on
that, partly at any rate. Is it philosophy? Germany knows more about that than
we do. Free trade? We take our English rivals as our models. Is that what the
rights of man mean? Tsar Alexander did not wait for us before emancipating his
twenty million serfs. Since the emancipation decree, there has been a formidable order in place in Russia ... Finally, is it nationality?

Much ado is made about this alleged principle, which is recognized neither
under the right of war nor under the rights of people; it would have brought
civilization to a standstill, had it been recognized; and even today has no reason to seek recognition, as nationality is, more than ever, indefinable; and in
any event, could only ever achieve any semblance of enforcement if larger States
were first dismantled, military rule done away with and political rights subordinated to economic rights.

For one thing, what is nationhood, faced with such popular abdications,
such amalgamations, such federation, such fusions, balanced by such constitutions, such distribution of power, such laws of balance, such decentralizations
and such emancipations? What is nationhood set beside these tariff reforms,
such comingling of peoples, such reunion, this miscegenation, this similarity,
not to say increasing commonality, of laws, rights, mores, guarantees, industry,
weights and measures, and currencies? Is it not obvious that if politics places
this old question of nationhood back on the agenda, which has always been denied by the law of progress as much as by the right of force, and momentarily
abolished by the Roman Empire and Christianity, it is only because politics really has nothing more to say; because nationalities, ground into the dirt by war
for four thousand years, are now just one big compound; in short, that war has
finished its work and it is now time for political economy, for peace to have
their say.

If certain politicians were to be believed, the imperial government should
declare war on Europe in order to secure recognition of nationalities. Why can
they not see, instead, that war, if it were to become widespread, could not have
any outcome other than to further reduce the number of independent nationalities by generating a sort of a Europe-wide *duum-* or *quadrum-virate*,[34] made up,
say, of Russia and France or, indeed, of Russia, France, Germany and England,
with all the second- or third-rate powers orbiting around them like satellites, assuming that they have not actually been wholly absorbed? That was the unspoken reasoning behind Tilsit,[35] which neither France nor Russia has forgotten, of

---

34. Rule or dominium by two or four. [I.M.]
35. The Treaty of Tilsit, signed on 7 July 1807, between Napoleon I and Tsar Alexander I

course. Whereupon freedom would vanish into these vast amalgamations along with nationality: and that would be the end of the Revolution.

Three names, three shadows, share the privilege of stirring up opinion with the aid of that word *nationality*, dragged back from beyond the grave: namely, Italy, Hungary and Poland.

Nothing could be fairer than the population of Italy clamouring for constitutional freedoms and guarantees. That was the thinking in 1815 and 1789 and the wish of Europe as a whole. In this respect, Napoleon III and Victor-Emmanuel, in taking up arms against Austria, were merely reflecting the opinion of the times and the spirit of the treaties that Austria was effectively trampling over with its backward-looking policy and intrusive tendencies. But there is a huge gulf between claiming that the various States on the peninsula, seizing upon nationality as the pretext, should meld into a single State; that, in order to expedite that outcome, France should rearm at Piedmont's behest and recall her troops from Rome; or, to put it a better way, it would be a frightful nonsense.

To my mind, Italian unity is a war machine momentarily trained on Austrian rule, the French protectorate and the Papacy. I cannot help seeing it as an odious mystification, if nationality and above all freedom are at stake. There are enough of the five great powers in Europe to maintain the balance; the creation of a sixth is a redundant effort with which people can very well do without. So, right now, which of us cannot see that, behind this pointless pretext of unity, Italy has already lapsed back into a servitude worse than the previous version; that, pushed into monarchist centralization she is compromising her very nationality, partly by the French aspiring to make Italy a vassal, partly by English Machiavellianism out to use the peninsula as a weapon against France,

---

of Russia gave the Tsar a free hand in Sweden. In return, Russia agreed to join the Continental System against Great Britain. There was also a clause providing for the dismemberment of Turkey's European possessions and for these to be split between Russia and France. That treaty was followed on 9th July by the signing of a second treaty at the expense of Prussia, which found itself stripped of half of its territory with the creation of the kingdom of Westphalia and the Duchy of Warsaw, based on the territories conquered by Prussia between 1793 and 1795, with Danzig (Gdansk) becoming a free city. Under that treaty, Prussia had to join the Continental System and found her army reduced to forty-two thousand men. The sovereign status of Napoleon's three brothers – Joseph Bonaparte, Louis Bonaparte and Jerome Bonaparte – respectively kings of Naples, Holland and Westphalia, was acknowledged. This alliance was not fated to last. On 31 December, 1810, French intransigence obliged the Tsar to open Russian ports to US ships whilst simultaneously imposing stiff tariffs on French goods, which were imported overland. British goods were soon pouring into (French-dominated) central Europe from Russia. This effectively destroyed the Continental System. See, Adam Zamoyski, *1812: Napoleon's Fatal March on Moscow* (London: Harper Perennial, 2005), 69–70. [H.T./G.H.]

rather than marshalling her forces? Is this not the start of a European quadrum-
virate? As to the French army evacuating Rome, I shall return to that shortly.

The conduct of the Hungarian magnates[36] is very different. They do not
talk about breaking off from the imperial coalition, which Hungary joined of
her own volition back in the sixteenth century. They realize that their safeguard,
with the Germans to the north, Russians to the north-east and Latin races to
the south and west, resides within that mighty alliance. What they are asking
for, in addition to respect for their national prerogatives, is federative constitutional guarantees, in accordance with the spirit of 1815. True, thanks to this
middle-of-the-road nationalist policy, Hungary's magnates have made themselves suspect in the eyes of the party that preaches unity in Italy and separation
in Austria, all in the name of nationality. But where would that lead us? What is
this two-faced policy? Who are they fooling here?

The same ramblings with regards to Poland, the same unjustifiable manoeuvres. What they demand on behalf of the populations of the former Poland, as
well as for those of Hungary, Italy and Bohemia is the enjoyment of the same
rights and freedoms promised by the coalition powers in 1813, and which have
become part of Europe's patrimony; high time too. This thesis is its own defence; it is unnecessary to invoke nationality. But, as to the resurrection of a State
condemned by its own kings, enforced under the right of force and in accordance with the forms of war, I would be as keen on that as I would talk of re-establishing Witikind's Saxony, the kingdom of Austrasia or that of the Visigoths.

Poland, unless she is a plaything handed over to fantasist politicking by
the kindliness of the powers, must include, along with the Duchy of Warsaw,
Poznan, Lithuania, Podolia, Galicia, Krakow, Dantzig itself and Koenigsberg.
By what right would one or other of these provinces be left out of the resurrection? And how are the Poles to get access to the Baltic? Staking such a
claim means dismembering Prussia, Austria and Russia, by warfare, treaties and
long-established possession: can they be serious? Does anyone think that the
great powers, the quadrumvirate to come, rather than dying for the emancipation of their respective [Polish] subjects, will not opt to reach some accommodation in gaining new possessions? ... Then again, what would be the purpose
of thereby annulling the verdict of warfare, this denial of an eight-hundred year
history? What is it meant to make good? What idea is it intended to resurrect?
What was lost to the world by allowing Poland to perish? Is there such a thing
as a Polish idea? Poland still has nothing to offer the world but her Catholicism

---

36. *Magnates*: In Poland and Hungary, statesmen of great note. In Hungary, the title was
initially used only for the higher barons in the kingdom. Over the centuries the definition
widened in order to include the heads of noble families. Having long been Hungary's only
political representatives, they were now only the upper Chamber. [H.T.]

and her nobility. Later, no doubt, Poland would enter her revolutionary phase; she, like 1789 France, would proclaim the rights of Man and the Citizen; like the France of 1848, she would recognize the right to work. Well then, let Poland, by vigorously picking up the pace, and starting right now, keep up with progress. Nations work on behalf of one another; there would be absolutely no point, as far as the advancement of humanity and the happiness of the Poles are concerned, in Poland replicating the handiwork of 1793, the campaigns of the Republic and the Empire, the parliamentary endeavours of 1814–1851. May the Polish nobles support the idea of February, the end of militarism and the constitution of economic right, and, by serving general civilisation, they will serve their country better than by a futile display of nationality.

In short, are political rights and freedoms the issue? Let us follow the unrest of 1814–1815, as interpreted by 1830: it was that which made liberal Spain, liberal Italy, liberal Belgium, liberal Germany and liberal Austria. We have no need to depart from that course. Is a more radical revolution called for? Is there a need for a more radical revolution? This is the thought of 1848: but nationality serves no more purpose than war. Nationalities have to be increasingly pushed into the background by the economic constitution, the decentralization of states, the mixing of races and the permeability of continents.

Rather than chasing after obsolete utopias and reigniting spent passions, let the French democracy, instead of clinging to old formulas, old ideas and old paradoxes, march in step with the times; study the spirit and matters of the age; take note of its direction of travel, and it will be persuaded that there is no longer the slightest reason to wage war; provoked by prejudices, by retrospective quibbles, there would be nothing organic, civilizing or liberal about it; it could only be a war of fantasy until such time as it turns into a war of chaos, the war of the have-nots against the haves.

SPIRITUAL POWER AND WAR: Outside of matters of political freedom and international balance, which have descended into banality and even become secondary, the French democracy has one initiative to take, which no power will contest: the creation of a new spiritual order through the constitution of economic rights.[37]

It is worth observing that the ending of the age of war coincides with the ending of the Christian mission. Indeed, theological symbolism is an emanation

---

37. After Joseph de Maistre, to whom France's *mission* was so clear and so great, and along with Comte, Saint-Simon, Pierre Leroux and a host of 1848 ideologues, Proudhon referred to his role in the *creation of a new spiritual order*. As a pessimistic moralist, he touched on this subject in many passages in his writings and in his *Correspondence*. The *Appendix* to *Les Confessions d'un révolutionnaire* (1849) offers us a gripping rehearsal of this. Written in Sainte-Pélagie in [October] 1851, it appears only in editions published after that date. [H.M.]

from warlike thinking and that the very same revolution that did away with divine right should repeal force's jurisdiction.

It fell to the organs of that revolution to sum up the issue of papal government and say to France that: just as within the individual, the soul commands the body, in society and in the State the spiritual commands the temporal; that it has been the same in every ancient society where the two powers were still united, right up until the arrival of Christianity; that, by making a distinction between the two powers, Christianity did not sever, nor alter nor reverse the order of their relationship; that ever since the days of the apostles, the bishops, guardians of the faith, leaders of the spiritual community, were also the judges and ministers of its interests; that following the abolition of primitive communism, they proved to be equally the regulators of mores and thereby indirect judges of all social transactions; that they settled differences, received donations, distributed alms, administering Church assets and hospices and taught the young; that, after Constantine's victory over Maxentius,[38] the power of the episcopate simply grew and grew; that after the fall of the Empire, the bishop of Rome became the real sovereign in Italy and the director of policy against the Greeks and the Barbarians; that Charlemagne's pact put the finishing touches to this arrangement by appointing the emperor a bishop from without, just as the Pope was a bishop from within and bringing the former under the oversight of the latter through the duty of orthodoxy, and that Pepin's gift, by awarding the pontifical sovereign a domain of his own, was merely a forfeit paid to the Holy See, the seat of Christian conscience, a counter to potential breaches of faith by princes and kings.

As I say, it fell to men with some grasp of the new righteousness to show that the restrictions introduced thereafter by princes to papal supremacy were the effect, not of the organic separation of the two powers, but of a revolution carried out in the spiritual realm itself, all unbeknownst to the peoples; that the spiritual, incapable of delivering peace to humanity, as its founder had undertaken to do, and a stranger to the right of war and the rights of peoples and thus not qualified for the governance of States, had been recognized as false by the heads of the nations who confined it as theology and reduced it to the administration of the sacraments; it was subsequently abrogated once and for all by the French Revolution and thus the Gospel had been supplanted by the RIGHTS OF MAN and grace by the reign of liberty; that, as a result, a new spiritual

---

38. CONSTANTINE I (*The Great*) (274–337), converted to Christianity in 312 AD, on the eve of a battle that was won against Maxentius, his Italian rival. The senate welcomed the winner as the saviour of the Roman people. Constantine unified the Empire, overhauled the Roman State and laid the groundwork for Christianity's victory by the end of the fourth century. [H.T.]

order had been ushered in, according to which justice was the principle and the foundation of all wisdom, just the same as, in previous times, revealed dogma had tried to act as the principle and standard for all justice and all philosophy; but, unlike Christianity, wherein the spiritual is represented by the priestly hierarchy, the Revolution has made the public conscience the sole interpreter of right, the sole judge of matters temporal and the sole sovereign, which constitutes true democracy and marks the end of priesthood and militarism.

And the Revolution's spokesman would have concluded: the Papacy having, through the force of events, and not at all as the result of any defection on the part of peoples or treachery on the part of princes, been dispossessed and placed in the care of those who were once, in accordance with the spirit of Christianity, merely vicars, and having no place to freely lay its head, the world was about to find itself, due to the decomposition of Christian society, spiritually bereft and without any moral and juridical basis; that all haste needed to be made in ending that danger-laden interregnum by means of a determined reversion to the institutions and principles of '89 and affirming the Rights of Man, justice's embodiment in the ranks of humanity; that that was the only way of ending the rifts, restoring modesty in mores and serenity to souls, organizing an actual, fruitful peace; that, to this end, the duty of the government was, not to tear up the 1815 treaties, the policy having been followed over the previous ten years having merely nurtured and affirmed this higher thinking, but to rescind the concordat, wrest the education of the people out of the hands of the clergy and provide for a reform in mores through the discipline of interests. On those conditions, France can back off from her guardianship of the Holy See and leave the protectorate of Catholicism to whomsoever may want it.

The official and unofficial party of democracy has preferred to dwell in equivocation, by protesting its respect for the Christian religion and its veneration for the person of the sovereign pontiff. It has argued that the Papacy would be mightier once it had cut its ties to the earth and that the glory days of the Church would return once the Church looked as if it were preoccupied by heavenly matters alone; it dared to state that the Revolution itself was merely Christianity in terms of its imperishable morality and hopes; by that affectation of religiosity, it betrayed the Revolution and held the Christian faith up to ridicule. Whose fault is it, then, if minds are now focused on war? Our leaders' politics are like their conscience; unprincipled. Their words sow the wind and we reap the whirlwind.

Humanity is like one huge brain with all these ideas churning around, but where truth eventually triumphs over error. France holds peace and war in her hands. No power thinks to attack her; on the contrary, they fear her and are wary of her; not that that is anything she should pride herself upon. Whatever

France decides will happen. Evolution-through-warfare is at an end: that much research has shown. Do we want that evolution to start over? According to the principles that we have established, one after the other, the analysis we have made of its motives and causes, the situation at which Europe has arrived, there is not, at present, one single rational case for war. The policy of warfare has spent itself and we know where we stand on the economic question. But anything can be seized upon as a pretext: what shall we choose? The unrest of 1814–1815, continuing the unrest of 1789 and leading to that of 1830-1848, has brought about all that we see: the wars waged over the past ten years have not added anything fundamental, nor indeed useful. Everything of value to civilization, to the balance in Europe, to the advancement of right, the Crimean and Lombardy campaigns could have been obtained without cost. Are we to resume 1848 or continue 1859?[39] That question I pose both to the February republicans and to those conservatives who had initially rallied around the Republic. Whenever France, all-powerful due to her thought and example, can no longer extract any profit from her victories, are we to give up on thinking and have recourse to arms?

Besides, whatever men decide, we need not fret about events. Men are petty. Up to a certain point they are able to disturb the course of things, but by doing so, they can only hurt themselves. Humanity alone is great, is infallible. Now, I believe I may say in its name: HUMANITY RENOUNCES WAR.

---

39. The choice here is between the 1848 revolution for a social and democratic republic, or to continue waging the Second Italian War of Independence of 1859. [A.P.]

Index

armistice, 328–9, 484
arms trade, 486
Armstrong gun, 308n86
army commanders, 117
Aron, Raymond, **23, 32**; *Paix et guerre entre
les nations*, **32**
Arria, 232, 232n3
asceticism, **28, 29**, 351, 369n29, 389n62, 501
assassination, 300–1
assimilation. *See* amalgamation/assimila-
tion
Association, **20, 23**, 76n29, 117, 132, 156,
179, 402–3, 431n101
Astraea, 99, 99n66
astrology, 183n87
atheism, 148–9
Athens, Athenians, 172, 175–7
Attica, 391
Augustus, 100
Aurelian, 415–16
Aurelius, Titus and Marcus, 218
Austerlitz, Battle of, 258, 258n21, 271, 311,
427, 473
Austria, 179–80, 185, 191n96, 202–6,
204n113, 239, 239n8, 241–2, 242n11,
262, 263, 274, 275–6n35, 286, 322–3,
328, 411–12
Authority, 215–218, 229–230, 316–317
average incomes, 351–3, 362, 364. *See also*
working day
axiom of war, 64

Babeuf, François-Émile, 44, 44n3, 372–3
Bacon, Francis, 148–9
balance: of power, 479; international,
181–5, 214–15, 242, 371–8, 400; law
of, 181–2, 349–50, 353, 354; and right
of force, 168, 181–5; of world, 349–50.
See also economic equilibrium
Balkan Wars, 200n107
bankruptcy, 85n40
barbarism, 30, 235, 237, 454–5
Barbeyrac, Jean, 114, 114n3, 187
basic necessities, 352–3. *See also* asceticism
battle of Actium, 100, 100n68
battles, 283–4, 303–13, 306–7n85
Bayard, 281n45
Beaulieu, Baron de, 263, 263n26
beauty, 82
Belgium, 43n1, 325

Bellona, 81, 81n35
Benedict XIII (pope), 375n39
Benso, Camillio (Count De Cavour),
73n18
Bentham, Jeremy, 153
Beresina, 311
Bergmann, Frédéric-Guillaume, 67, 67n8
Bethulia, 293–4
Billaut, Auguste, 412, 412n86
Black people, **25, 25n80**, 206–7, 208–9,
209n120, 353. *See also* African Ameri-
cans
blockades, 273, 280, 293–4, 330
bombs, 280, 280n43
Bonaparte, Louis-Napoléon. *See* Napoleon
III
Bonaparte, Napoleon. *See* Napoleon I
Boniface VIII (pope), 375, 375n42
book overview, **2–3, 5–9, 36**
book one overview, 223–5
book two overview, 223–5
book three overview, 335–7
book four overview, 443–5
book translation, **37–8**
Bossuet, Jacques-Bénigne, 106, 106n78, 298
Bouglé, Celestin, **31–2**
boundaries, 436–7
Bourbon Dynasty, **10**, 245n15
Bourbon Restoration, 373, 439
Bourgeois, Nicolas, **4**
bourgeoisie, 373, 413–14, 434
bravery, 304. *See also* heroism; warriors
Bret, Eugène, 364n21; *The Wretchedness of
the Labouring Classes in France and in
England*, 364n21
Breton Club, 44n2
Bright, John, 410, 410n80
budgets, 439, 441, 452
Bugeaud, Thomas Robert, 425, 425n98
Bull, Hedley, **32n104**, 135n34
bullets, 280–2, 281n45
Buonarotti, Filippo-Michele, 44, 44n3; *His-
tory of the Babeuf Conspiracy*, 44n3
Burlamaqui, Jean-Jacques, 114, 114n6

cannons, 282
canon law, 170
Canrobert, François Marcellin Certain de,
305, 305n84
capitalism, 76, 171, 366, 409

parasitism, 353, 365, 367, 372

pardons, 70–1

Paris, 403–4, 432–3

Paris Commune, 264n27

Party of democracy, 502–8

Party of Order, 264n27

passions, 343

patriarch, father, 70, 144–5, 153, 166, 168, 171, 383, 418, 431

patriarchy, 4, 166–7, 171, 222

patriotism, 145

pauperism: overview, 7; abolishment of, 476; and capitalism, 409; as cause of revolution, 371, 372–3; combatting, 367; and conquest, 416; defined, 364, 364n21; and economic distribution, 363–4; and militarism, 438; origin and universality, 359–70; as psychological, 364–5; and rich people, 367–9, 373; as root cause of all war, 347, 376–8; as same source as war, 370; the State and international relations, 371–8; and useless goods, 403; and violence, 6–7; war as distraction, 405–6. See also poverty

peace: overview, 99; and animosity, 108; and antagonism, 489–90; armed peace, 441; balance of forces, 479; and colonialism, 400; competitive, 447; by contract, 154, 155; defined, 153, 153–4n58, 479; devotees as hypocrites, 85–6; and free trade, 77n30; and jurists, 333–4; man vs. beasts, 121; as manifestation of universal conscience, 492; as needed, 491; as nothingness, 58; and opulence, 88; perpetual, 140–1, 475, 478, 479–80; as ridiculed, 73; right of force as peaceful, 172; and self-interest, 156; and strength, 479; universal, 490–1; and war, 99–110, 489, 490–1; war transformed to, 484, 487, 491; and war's end, 471; without illusion, 481

Peace Congresses, 77n30, 102

Peace of Antalkidas, 392–4, 392n66

Peace of Westphalia, 77–8, 77–8n33

Peasant Wars, 375, 375n41, 375n43

peasants, 10, 13, 150, 183, 191n96, 205, 221, 285, 309, 311, 358n16, 375, 376, 388, 401, 411, 414, 431, 434n107

Peloponnesian Wars, 389–90, 463–4

penal law, 132, 315–16

the people (masses): beliefs vs. learned men ideas, 113–22, 126–8; and conquerors, 127, 127n31; as enemies, 320–1, the people and force, 251

Pepin the Short, 73, 73n20

Pericles, 390n64, 391, 392

perpetual peace, 140–1, 475, 478, 479–80

perpetual war, 211n122, 482–3

Persia, 393, 456–8

phenomenology, defined, 59n2

Philip I (King of Castile), 196, 196n103

Philip II (King of Macedonia), 394–5

philosophical rights, 222

Philocles, 176–7

philosophy of history, summary, 3–4, 14–23, 63n3

philosophy of property, 346n3. See also property

philosophy of right, 2n6, 8, 139

philosophy of war, 14, 14n30

phrenology, 24

Piccolomini, Aeneas Silvius, 101, 101n69

Piedmont, 45, 45n4, 240–3, 240n10, 241–2, 245, 245n15, 276n35, 286. See also Crimean War

pillage. See pillage/plunder

Pinheiro-Ferreira, Silvestre, 114, 114n5, 122, 318, 320, 326, 332

pirates, 22, 53, 253, 340, 380, 384–5, 394, 425, 444, 452–3. See also plunder/pillage

pistols, 12

Pius II, Pope (Aeneas Silvius Piccolomini), 101, 101n69

Pius IX, Pope, 46n5

Pius VII, Pope, 185

Pius XI, Pope, 242–4

Plato, 97, 104, 299, 389

plebs, 75, 84n40, 108, 126, 183, 203, 215, 218, 264, 369, 371n32, 388, 394, 399, 411, 420, 421, 430, 433, 466, 476, 484, 485

plunder/pillage: Ancient Greece, 391–6, 463; and conquest, 418–26; end of and war, 477; England's wealth, 409; Holy Alliance, 455; and jurists, 299–300; and Napoleon I, 423–4; nations forced to, 452; political vs. economic